THE LEGAL REGIME OF NUCLEAR ENERGY: A COMPREHENSIVE GUIDE TO INTERNATIONAL AND EUROPEAN UNION LAW

FABRIZIO NOCERA

intersentia
Antwerpen – Oxford

Distribution for the UK:
Hart Publishing
Salter's Boat Yard
Folly Bridge
Abingdon Road
Oxford OX1 4LB
UK
Tel: + 44 1865 24 55 33
Fax: + 44 1865 79 48 82

Distribution for North America:
Gaunt Inc.
Gaunt Building
3011 Gulf Drive
Holmes Beach
Florida 34217-2199
USA
Tel: + 1 941 778 5211
Fax: + 1 941 778 5252

Distribution for Switzerland and Germany:
Schulthess Verlag
Zwingliplatz 2
CH-8022 Zürich
Switzerland
Tel: + 41 1 251 93 36
Fax: + 41 1 261 63 94

Distribution for other countries:
Intersentia Publishers
Groenstraat 31
BE-2640 Mortsel
Belgium
Tel: + 32 3 680 15 50
Fax: + 32 3 658 71 21

The Legal Regime of Nuclear Energy: A Comprehensive Guide to International and European Union Law
Fabrizio Nocera

ISBN 90-5095-490-1
D/2005/7849/62
NUR 828

ACKNOWLEDGEMENTS

The preparation of this publication was started some time ago and it has become increasingly engaging, due to the steady growth of nuclear international and EU legislation especially since after the Chernobyl event, and in general to the intensive action carried out by the competent international organizations, in order to improve and enrich the law of nuclear energy. Beyond its inevitable limits and imperfections, my work on this project has always been inspired by the genuine intent to provide an as comprehensive and updated text as possible, for use by the many categories of people interested in nuclear law professionally and for other purposes. In this respect, I feel indebted to all those people, since their interest was to me a decisive incentive to pursuing my work.

In other respects, of course, I must express my deep gratitude to some colleagues, with whom I have developed an excellent friendship, thanks to the work performed together for very many years in different fora. My first thought goes to Martha ROGGENKAMP, of outstanding expertise in energy law, whose encouragement was paramount since the very start of my work on the volume. Her assistance was also invaluable in establishing links with the publishers and fostering their interest in the publication. Secondly, my profound appreciation is directed to Patrick REYNERS, former Head of Legal Affairs at the Nuclear Energy Agency of OECD, whose availability to present the volume only adds prestige to it. Thirdly, I am most grateful to Intersentia's organizing mind Hans KLUWER, for his patience and understanding when confronted with certain delays, although they were beyond my control, for his useful suggestions and for his trust in the final result.

PREFACE

The publication of this new volume, addressing the international instruments and the European Community legislation in the domain of nuclear energy, must be surely welcomed. Such ambitious work actually reflects a revival of interest in this legal discipline, which could already be detected in the creation, a few years ago, of the International School of Nuclear Law in Montpellier (France), as well as in the fostering of activities carried out in the subject area especially by the Nuclear Energy Agency of OECD and by the International Atomic Energy Agency.

It is indeed equally appropriate to congratulate F. Nocera on having accomplished this engaging task, the result of which will certainly be precious both for those who are involved in nuclear law and for researchers in the academic world. The volume, which collects in an articulated and consistent structure the vast number of instruments and acts governing the use of nuclear energy up to the end of 2004, is certainly bound to remain a valid working tool for many years to come.

It is true that the Author is uniquely qualified to carry out the work, given his deep knowledge of texts in the elaboration of which he has very often been personally involved, both as a lawyer within the European Commission and on the basis of his past and present capacity of national expert.

Patrick REYNERS

FOREWORD

This volume is intended as a presentation of current international and European Union legislation in the field of nuclear energy. Although such legislation does not evolve at the same rate as it does at national levels, it has nevertheless developed substantially over the past fifteen years or so. In many cases, new legislation was adopted in response to the Chernobyl accident; in other cases, developments consisted in important amendments or additions to existing legislation. Moreover and apart from legislation geared exclusively to nuclear energy, there exists a set of instruments and acts which includes nuclear energy to the extent to which it is pertinent to related aspects, such as environmental protection, waste disposal and so on. It is recalled that, for the purposes of this volume, by "legislation" are intended in a broader sense also non-binding norms like recommendations, guides, resolutions etc

The volume aims at bringing these many texts together, thus providing all those concerned with nuclear law (specialists, scholars, researchers, administrators, judges, teachers, etc.) with an indispensable tool both for daily practice and for consultation purposes. It offers up-to-date, comprehensive and systematically arranged texts accompanied by the relevant background information, to serve as a ready source of direct reference. The book, which is structured in two parts, includes also an outline of the origin, development and contents of nuclear energy law, as well as an appendix dealing with case law. The two parts may be summarised as follows:

1. *PART I* deals with the *provisions governing the safe use* of nuclear energy. Specifically, it is concerned with (a) the statutes of international organisations and references to non-exclusively nuclear international bodies and NGOs; (b) international instruments and acts on nuclear safety and radiation protection (including early notification and mutual assistance in the case of a nuclear accident, and certain related matters such as environmental impact), i.e. conventions, regulations, directives, recommendations and decisions; (c) international conventions on nuclear third party liability and compensation following a nuclear accident; (d) agreements between governments or between these and international organisations on technical-scientific, industrial and commercial co-operation in the field of nuclear energy.

2. *PART II* addresses *provisions aimed at preventing non-peaceful use* of nuclear energy, as well as *the pollution of the environment at large* by radioactive substances.

Specifically, it is concerned mainly with treaties, conventions, and other agreements on the prevention of (a) diversion to non-peaceful purposes and (b) proliferation of nuclear weapons; (c) the Iaea and Euratom regimes of safeguards and security; (d) the physical protection of nuclear material and facilities; (e) the de-nuclearization of certain areas of the globe; (f) the prevention of radioactive pollution of the environment (including pollution in a trans-frontier context).

Every instrument or act is preceded by introductory material providing information on its origin and development, focusing on content, legal standing and scope. Cross-references are used in such material whenever useful to ensure an overall outlook and a better understanding of the links existing between many of the instruments and acts considered. For the main instrument under revision during the preparation of the volume, such indication is provided in the relevant introductory material. Texts within each separate chapter are as a rule presented in chronological order, except where a different criterion is deemed more appropriate. It will be understood that, given the extremely vast number of texts at hand (in any case published *in extenso* by the organization of origin) which would have resulted in a far oversized volume, a selective approach had to be adopted. This applies especially to texts not exclusively geared to nuclear energy, as well as to the very many annexes (often of a merely technical nature), to protocols supplementing the main legal text, and the like. It is hoped that this will not impact on the appreciation of the copious instruments and acts included in the volume.

3. The *Outline,* which takes account of the grouping into the two Parts, is intended to help readers realize beforehand the vastness and variety of areas covered by the legislation considered, the constant efforts made to improve it and to adjust it to the needs arising from changing reality, the distinctive features attached to it both in comparison to other similar legislation and in the general context of international legislation, and its validity despite the many and growing difficulties encountered by nuclear energy during the last two decades or so.

4. The *Appendix* presents some important case law based on European Court of Justice's rulings adopted between the end of 1978 and the end of 2002. This case law is all the more important since it has had a significant impact on nuclear legislation in the European Union.

5. Both the explanatory material and the actual texts are reproduced entirely in English, firstly because of its "universal" nature and secondly, because English is one of the official languages adopted for all the instruments and acts concerned. Besides, English nuclear terminology is by far the most developed and indeed has been so from the very beginning of the nuclear era. For understandable reasons,

the collection of those instruments and acts appearing in the volume had to be closed at a certain date, which is December 31, 2004. Developments under way at that date or expected to be finalized within a not long time-span after it are referred to in the concerned parts of the volume

Finally, it is noted that, although the volume is obviously in-keeping with its nature of a legal publication, the language used for the background and introductory material has been conceived bearing in mind also potential readers such as for example non-specialists in nuclear law, non-lawyers or scholars whose legal training is still in progress, and so on.

TABLE OF CONTENTS

AN OUTLINE OF NUCLEAR ENERGY LAW: ITS ORIGIN, DEVELOPMENT AND CONTENTS

INTRODUCTORY REMARKS

The initial stage of the law of nuclear energy dates back to the late 1950s. Since then nuclear law has steadily developed in connection and in parallel with the remarkable impetus given to the manifold applications of nuclear energy and ionising radiation in very many countries of the world. This has resulted in nuclear law becoming and indeed remaining for a long period an independent branch of law. In more recent times, along with the developing of disciplines and needs related to industrial activities (broadly intended), nuclear law has gradually become an integral part of law in general, given especially its interconnections with the legal regime of the environment, safety at work, public health, land management and so on and so forth.

It should be remarked, on the other hand, that to this day nuclear law preserves a specific feature which is not comparable to many other areas of law: it is the very close relation between international and national law, to be put down to the particularly copious range of instruments and acts adopted by the competent international organizations, largely reflected in national legislation, not to speak of the extremely numerous technical standards issued by those organizations, which in general provide a common basis to the relevant national provisions of a technical nature. It should be also recalled the important role played in the nuclear energy area by "resolutions", although they are not among legally binding instruments as they rather entail a "political" commitment by the governments participating in them. This publication includes only the text of a European Union Council resolution addressing a particular area, while it simply refers to various other ones at the root of certain instruments or acts specifically dealt with in the volume.

Despite the difficult times through which nuclear energy has struggled especially since after the Chernobyl accident (1986), the role of nuclear law is still widely recognized not only in respect of peaceful applications in industry, research, medicine, agriculture etc., but also as an indispensable tool to prevent non-peaceful uses, as well as the pollution of certain areas of the globe, the undue and illicit movement of nuclear materials etc. All the above is confirmed by the constant developing and expanding of international nuclear law, which ensures even more effectiveness to an already most advanced legal regime. The distinction between the law governing the safe use in peaceful applications and that aimed at preventing any non-peaceful use (as well as the impressive number of related instruments and acts) is clearly reflected in the grouping adopted in this volume. The whole provides full evidence of the constant efforts made to improve nuclear law and to adjust it to any need which might arise from changes in the political, economic and social reality of our times.

The general outline of nuclear energy law to be found hereunder follows as closely as possible the grouping in two parts and the order of issues adopted for the volume. More detailed explanations and information are obviously a matter for the introductory material to instruments and acts.

THE PROVISIONS GOVERNING THE SAFE USE OF NUCLEAR ENERGY AND IONISING RADIATION

The creation of **international organisations** to act in the field of nuclear energy was certainly the first step necessary and indeed the main source of the vast set of instruments and acts governing its safe use. The action carried out by those organisations is to be regarded within their statutory framework encompassing various tasks including laying down legislation proper and technical standards, which have a distinctive impact on national legal regimes. This impact varies depending on the binding nature, or otherwise, of the instruments and acts involved.

Three are the main international (inter-governmental) organisations acting eminently in the nuclear energy field: the International Atomic Energy Agency (IAEA) in Vienna, the Nuclear Energy Agency (NEA, former ENEA) in Paris, and the European Atomic Energy Community (EAEC, alias Euratom) in Brussels. It is noted that this qualification is consistent with the original instruments by which they were set up, the subsequent institutional developments being addressed in the introductory material in Chapter I of this volume. In relative terms, it may be said that the Vienna and Paris agencies' normative output of a binding nature (mainly conventions adopted under their sponsorship) covers a limited percentage of the extremely vast set of norms (mostly technical recommendations) issued by them; the Brussels Community's action rests chiefly on a large number of (binding) regulations and directives (although also various recommendations are the result of that action), which is due to the powers conferred on the EAEC to this effect by the treaty establishing it.

It is worth recalling the dual importance of Community legislation, taking into account that the three European Communities have been quite distinctive as geo-economic entities, although the institutional developments under way will entail new instruments (see again Chapter I, in particular the Introductory Material to Euratom), and that the enlargement of the European Union results in a considerable increase in the number of countries having to comply with EU legislation. On the other hand and more in general, it should be stressed that, despite the non-binding nature of the many standards, recommendations, guides etc. adopted by the above mentioned organisations, their technical and scientific value is such that they often provide a common background for the international and national relevant legislation.

Non-exclusively nuclear intergovernmental organisations, active nevertheless in certain nuclear energy-related areas (radiation protection) are especially the International Labour Office (ILO) and the World Health Organisation (WHO), both based in Geneva. The result of their action in the domain of radiation protection of workers and of the public appears in Chapter II of the volume.

As to non-governmental organisations, mention must be made above all of the International Commission on Radiological Protection (ICRP), whose innumerable recommendations adopted since the late 1950's are the basis for international and national standards addressing radiological protection in all activities involving ionising radiation.

Nuclear safety and radiation protection are no doubt among the areas mostly rich in instruments and acts governing the many different practices and circumstances to which they are related. It is worth pointing out that, on the whole, legislation proper is importantly more copious at European Union level (in terms of regulations and directives), while on a world-wide scale the reference principles and standards for a great number of countries are the above mentioned ICRP Recommendations. These are also the basis not only for the EU Directives but equally for the extremely vast body of IAEA and NEA recommendations in the matter of radiation protection. Besides, the IAEA Conventions on early notification of a nuclear accident and on mutual assistance in case of an emergency, although not falling in the category of instruments specific to radiation protection, are relevant notably as pertaining to the manifold set of measures adopted following Chernobyl.

On the other hand, two more IAEA Conventions mark a significant step forward in the area of nuclear safety and of the safe management of radioactive waste. Nuclear safety (closely linked to relevant technology and to the intrinsic safety of an installation, machine, apparatus etc.) traditionally has been (and still is) regarded by individual States as falling within their own exclusive competence and responsibility. The

Convention on Nuclear Safety adopted under the IAEA's sponsorship is in fact the first one of its kind, although in actual fact it basically lays down general obligations and objectives. The other IAEA Convention on waste and spent fuel is equally the first instrument of a binding nature addressing this issue, which is of great importance and concern to many parts of the world.

The Vienna Agency and, to a much lesser extent but with an emphasis on certain specific operations and issues, the Paris Agency have been and are very active laying down recommendations: these range from the safety at nuclear installations to the protection requirements in the use of plutonium-fuelled pace-makers, to give an idea of the both general and the very particular nature of such recommendations. It is noted that the two Agencies have also issued basic standards on radiation protection, which are taken into account, for reasons of technical and scientific consistency, when laying down the similar Euratom basic standards (and vice versa). It is also noted that, as far as radiation protection of workers and of the public is concerned, the corresponding recommendations issued by the ILO and the WHO respectively (within their more general competence) are important institutionally and historically, but in practice their bearing is limited given the existence of detailed recommendations (and, at the EU level, of binding standards via directives or regulations) adopted by the nuclear organizations specifically and exclusively competent in the matter. It might be added that, consequently and logically, national legislation implementing such detailed and binding standards goes well beyond the requirements of other acts of a more general nature (e.g. the ILO Convention on radiation protection of workers).

Also Euratom is engaged in issuing recommendations which address radiation protection, mostly in application of given provisions under the Treaty establishing it and concerning issues such as environmental radioactivity, classification of radioactive waste etc.. However, as pointed out earlier on, the most substantial regulatory work performed by Euratom is reflected in regulations and directives: the former cover radioactivity and contamination following a nuclear accident and date back to relatively recent times (in direct or indirect connection with Chernobyl), while the latter cover both basic standards (which appeared for the first time in 1959) and specific areas or activities, often supplementing the basic standards. As far as regulations are concerned, it is important to recall that those adopted immediately after and as a direct consequence of Chernobyl are based on the Treaty establishing the Economic European Community (EEC) and not on the Euratom Treaty. The Directives other than basic standards address various issues, ranging from information to the public in case of an emergency, to protection of itinerant workers, to shipment of radioactive substances, protection in medical exposure to radiation etc.

The EEC Directive on the Environmental Impact Assessment of certain public or private projects (which covers also most nuclear installations and activities) is worth a special mention here, since it may be regarded as a significant step (as of 1985, when the Directive was first adopted) towards an increased consideration for environmental problems at the international level, with a decisive impact on national legislation.

The international regime of **nuclear third party liability and compensation** occupies a special place within the law of nuclear energy, because since its first establishment in the very early 1960s was based on the fundamental principles of (the operator's) strict and absolute liability, associated with compulsory financial security. Such feature, specific to this regime, not only has it been preserved for several decades now also throughout the revised conventions in the field, but is also a fundamental trait of new conventions adopted in 1997. The establishment of the regime in point originates from the need to avoid an unlimited (in money and time) liability, to ensure compensation to possible victims of a nuclear accident independently of fault, and to create the best possible conditions for a steady development of nuclear energy for peaceful purposes.

Traditionally, the two basic Conventions adopted over forty years ago and supplemented over time by other instruments are referred to as the pillars supporting the "Paris system" and the "Vienna system" respectively. While their origin, structure and contents are addressed in the introductory material, here it is worth stressing that, apart from creating the new special regime on a "regional" and on a "world-wide" scale, the merit in the set of provisions under consideration is also in their having evolved so as to fill certain fundamental lacunae, as it may be understood by looking to the 1988 Joint Protocol bridging the Paris and Vienna Convention, or indeed to the massive revision occurred between 1997 and 2004 concerning the international regime as a whole. It must be added that, whatever the attitude might be to nuclear energy and its peaceful use, the installations in operation in the world falling under the nuclear third party liability regime are several hundreds and, although for different reasons, the interest in a coverage (ensured by the participation in that regime) for the eventuality of an accident is obviously shared by both operators and potential victims.

The international legal regime of nuclear energy includes a series of **multilateral and bilateral instruments** like conventions, agreements etc., concluded between States and international organizations in order to start ***technical and scientific co-operation***, as well as ***co-operation in nuclear industry and trade,*** which would facilitate the development of nuclear energy and its numerous peaceful applications. Such co-operation consists in the exchange of know-how and experience, the realization of joint projects, the free movement of experts and materials etc. It is noted that the vicissitudes affecting nuclear energy especially since after Chernobyl have not had a significant impact on the conclusion of the instruments in point because, apart from the role played by international organizations on the strength of their statutory tasks, peaceful applications of nuclear energy in industry, research, medicine etc are extremely important for many countries in the world. It should be added that in various cases, these instruments are intended also to contribute, albeit indirectly, to non-proliferation. Agreements have been concluded since the 1950s and some have been terminated either because no longer important or because the intended purposes had been achieved. Examples of agreements (multilateral) are CERN, Halden, Eurodif, and (bilateral) between Euratom and various countries like the USA, Canada, Australia, Japan or organisations like the ILO and the IAEA.

THE PROVISIONS GOVERNING THE PEACEFUL USE OF NUCLEAR ENERGY, ETC.

The number of instruments and acts pertaining to this domain is equally very large and includes several heads of issues. It is noted that the relevant developments consist not only in the revision of certain instruments occurred over time, but also in the adoption of new ones not governing exclusively nuclear energy but addressing it among other issues: this applies especially to those instruments concerned with the prevention of pollution of the environment at large.

The most copious amount of specific instruments and acts under consideration is concerned with **treaties, conventions and other agreements aimed at preventing the diversion of nuclear energy to non-peaceful purposes and the proliferation of nuclear weapons.** The IAEA and Euratom have always played a major role in this respect, the former on the strength of its statute and in connection with the Non Proliferation Treaty as of its adoption (1968), the latter based on the relevant provisions of the Euratom Treaty and derived regulations. These two systems (whose ultimate common aim is in fact to ensure the peaceful use of nuclear energy) are co-ordinated by way of specific agreements and joint action. In addition, the Vienna Agency is active issuing rules (however non-binding as such) on the export of nuclear material, equipment and technology, as well as by means of a Convention in the domain of physical protection of nuclear materials and facilities, intended to prevent the theft or the unauthorized diversion of these materials or sabotage to facilities).

Various treaties have moreover been stipulated for the so-called "**de-nuclearization** of certain areas of the globe, i.e. to keep them free from nuclear weapons. The first example is the Antarctic Treaty dating back to the late 1950's, and the most recent one is the Comprehensive Nuclear Test Ban Treaty (1996), but other treaties addressing for example Latin America, ocean-beds and the outer space are equally important.

Finally, many conventions, protocols etc. have been adopted for the **protection of the environment and prevention of pollution** from various sources, including nuclear energy and ionising radiation. Again, the first convention addressing (however very briefly) also discharge of radioactive substances into the sea dates back to 1958, but a very large number of such conventions followed over time addressing sea-dumping of waste, the protection of certain seas (Mediterranean, North-East Atlantic, Baltic. etc.) or areas of the globe (e.g. South Pacific) and pollution in a trans-boundary context. Among the actions taken in the latest years, it is worth recalling, given its high political importance, the well known Kyoto Protocol adopted in1997, which addresses *inter alia* nuclear energy, to the effect of incorporating conditions that specifically exclude it as an option for implementation (under the "flexibility mechanism" allowed by the Protocol) by developed countries or by those in economic transition. A more detailed examination of the relevant material in the section concerned shows the extent of the on-going international action geared to improve the regime of pollution prevention in general, and that reference to nuclear energy and materials is usually made on the basis of specific parameters already set out by the competent nuclear organizations.

PART ONE
PROVISIONS GOVERNING THE SAFE USE

Unlike for Part Two of the volume (the presentation of which is intended to explain the main reasons for so grouping and addressing the instruments and acts included therein) a presentation however brief of the structure of this Part One was believed to be redundant, since the relevant elements are addressed fairly extensively in the Outline to be read in the preceding pages.

CHAPTER ONE
INTERNATIONAL NUCLEAR ORGANISATIONS

International nuclear organisations were set up in the second half of the 1950s, with a view to achieving wide-ranging and intensive co-operation between the different States in promoting the peaceful use of nuclear energy, after the tragedy of nuclear warfare perpetrated during World War II. These organisations have been active (and indeed still are very much so) in framing a vast set of rules for countries involved in development and regulation of the peaceful and safe use of nuclear energy in the scientific, industrial, medical and other fields. This chapter addresses the instruments establishing these nuclear organisations, including such amendments to them as have been introduced over the years.

It must be noted that, in the European context, a number of other instruments (Single European Act of 1986, Maastricht Treaty of 1992, Amsterdam Treaty of 1997 and Nice Treaty of 2001) have been adopted throughout the years, and have introduced extensive amendments to the previous treaties by which three separate Communities (coal and steel, economic and atomic) had been established during the fifties. These amendments have had an impact also on the Treaty establishing the European Atomic Energy Community (Euratom), but only as to institutional arrangements such as the voting rights of member States. On the other hand, in very recent times the European Union countries started a project for the establishment of a "constitution" for the European Union and this project was finalised when this volume was being prepared. As a consequence of the "constitution" (to be incorporated in a treaty), all the instruments above mentioned will have to be regarded as superseded (the European Coal and Steel Community having already been discontinued several years ago). As to the Euratom Treaty in particular, it is envisaged to adapt it to this institutional development by way of a Protocol to the constitution treaty, but preserving its independent features.

THE INTERNATIONAL ATOMIC ENERGY AGENCY (IAEA)

(New York, 26 October 1956)

The International Atomic Energy Agency (IAEA), which has its headquarters in Vienna, was established at the New York Conference of September 1956, with the aim of accelerating and promoting the contribution of atomic energy to peace, health and prosperity in the world at large. The Agency is part of the United Nations grid through a co-operation agreement signed in 1957, which gives it virtually exclusive world-wide competence to deal with issues connected with the peaceful use of nuclear energy. The Agency enjoys complete autonomy in carrying out its tasks.

The Agency's tasks are several. It plays a ***normative*** *role and has sponsored a vast body of technical standards and recommendations on safety and protection regarding the use and transport of radioactive substances (see Chapter II). These standards and recommendations make up the common technical matrix on which the different countries draw in framing their own national regulations (often assisted by the Agency itself). In certain cases, such standards and recommendations are adopted jointly by the Agency and other international (not specifically "nuclear") organisations like WHO, ILO and FAO (see Chapter II). Under the IAEA's aegis also various international conventions have been adopted in the domains of, nuclear safety, safe management of spent fuel and radioactive waste, early notification of nuclear accidents, mutual assistance in case of a radiological emergency, and nuclear third party liability (see Chapters II and III). Besides, the Agency provides assistance to Member States (in particular developing countries) in laying down their nuclear legislation, organizes (at IAEA or in various countries) training courses on regulatory and technical aspects of nuclear energy, and so on. Even more important is the Agency's role in* ***guaranteeing the peaceful use*** *of nuclear energy through an appropriate system of multilateral and bilateral agreements, as well as in ensuring, by means of suitable international instruments, the non-proliferation of nuclear weapons (see Sections I, II and III in PART TWO).*

Several amendments have been made to the Agency's Statute, the most important ones being those concerned with Article VI (Board of Governors and membership of States on the Board) and the amendment adopted in 1999 (to the effect of increasing the number of the Agency' members) considered to be the most far-reaching . The current Members of the Agency are 138.

STATUTE OF THE IAEA

Article I:
Establishment of the Agency

The Parties hereto establish an International Atomic Energy Agency (hereinafter referred to as "the Agency") upon the terms and conditions hereinafter set forth.

Article II:
Objectives

The Agency shall seek to accelerate and enlarge the contribution of atomic energy to peace, health and prosperity throughout the world. It shall ensure, so far as it is able, that assistance provided by it or at its request or under its supervision or control is not used in such a way as to further any military purpose.

Article III:
Functions

A. The Agency is authorized:
1. To encourage and assist research on, and development and practical application of, atomic energy for peaceful uses throughout the world; and, if requested to do so, to act as an intermediary for the purposes of securing the performance of services or the supplying of materials, equipment, or facilities by one member of the Agency for another; and to perform any operation or service useful in research on, or development or practical application of, atomic energy for peaceful purposes;
2. To make provision, in accordance with this Statute, for materials, services, equipment, and facilities to meet the needs of research on, and development and practical application of, atomic energy for peaceful purposes, including the production of electric power, with due consideration for the needs of the under-developed areas of the world;
3. To foster the exchange of scientific and technical information on peaceful uses of atomic energy;
4. To encourage the exchange of training of scientists and experts in the field of peaceful uses of atomic energy;
5. To establish and administer safeguards designed to ensure that special fissionable and other materials, services, equipment, facilities, and information made available by the Agency or at its request or under its supervision or control are not used in such a way as to further any military purpose; and to apply safeguards, at the request of the parties, to any bilateral or multilateral arrangement, or at the request of a State, to any of that State's activities in the field of atomic energy;

6. To establish or adopt, in consultation and, where appropriate, in collaboration with the competent organs of the United Nations and with the specialized agencies concerned, standards of safety for protection of health and minimization of danger to life and property (including such standards for labour conditions), and to provide for the application of these standards to its own operation as well as to the operations making use of materials, services, equipment, facilities, and information made available by the Agency or at its request or under its control or supervision; and to provide for the application of these standards, at the request of the parties, to operations under any bilateral oe multilateral arrangements, or, at the request of a State, to any of that State's activities in the field of atomic energy;
7. To acquire or establish any facilities, plant and equipment useful in carrying out its authorized functions, whenever the facilities, plant, and equipment otherwise available to it in the area concerned are inadequate or available only on terms it deems unsatisfactory.

B. In carrying out its functions, the Agency shall:
1. Conduct its activities in accordance with the purposes and principles of the United Nations to promote peace and international co-operation, and in conformity with policies of the United Nations furthering the establishment of safeguarded worldwide disarmament and in conformity with any international agreements entered into pursuant to such policies;
2. Establish control over the use of special fissionable materials received by the Agency, in order to ensure that these materials are used only for peaceful purposes;
3. Allocate its resources in such a manner as to secure efficient utilization and the greatest possible general benefit in all areas of the world, bearing in mind the special needs of the under-developed areas of the world;
4. Submit reports on its activities annually to the General Assembly of the United Nations and, when appropriate, to the Security Council: if in connection with the activities of the Agency there should arise questions that are within the competence of the Security Council, the Agency shall notify the Security Council, as the organ bearing the main responsibility for the maintenance of international peace and security, and may also take the measures open to it under this Statute, including those provided in paragraph C of Article XII;
5. Submit reports to the Economic and Social Council and other organs of the United Nations on matters within the competence of these organs.

C. In carrying out its functions, the Agency shall not make assistance to members subject to any political, economic, military, or other conditions incompatible with the provisions of this Statute.

D. Subject to the provisions of this Statute and to the terms of agreements concluded between a State or a group of States and the Agency which shall be in accordance with the provisions of the Statute, the activities of the Agency shall be carried out with due observance of the sovereign rights of States.

Article IV: Membership

A. The initial members of the Agency shall be those States Members of the United Nations or of any of the specialized agencies which shall have signed this Statute within ninety days after it is opened for signature and shall have deposited an instrument of ratification.

B. Other members of the Agency shall be those States, whether or not Members of the United Nations or of any of the specialized agencies, which deposit an instrument of acceptance of this Statute after their membership has been approved by the General Conference upon the recommendation of the Board of Governors. In recommending and approving a State for membership, the Board of Governors and the General Conference shall determine that the State is able and willing to carry out the obligations of membership in the Agency, giving due consideration to its ability and willingness to act in accordance with the purposes and principles of the Charter of the United Nations.

C. The Agency is based on the principle of the sovereign equality of all its members, and all members, in order to ensure to all of them the rights and benefits resulting from membership, shall fulfill in good faith the obligation assumed by them in accordance with this Statute.

Article V: General Conference

A. A General Conference consisting of representatives of all members shall meet in regular annual session and in such special sessions as shall be convened by the Director General at the request of the Board of Governors or of a majority of members. The sessions shall take place at the headquarters of the Agency unless otherwise determined by the General Conference.

B. At such sessions, each member shall be represented by one delegate who may be accompanied by alternates and by advisers. The cost of attendance of any delegation shall be borne by the member concerned.

C. The General Conference shall elect a President and such other officers as may be required at the beginning of each session. They shall hold office for the duration of the session. The General Conference, subject to the provisions of this Statute, shall adopt its own rules of procedure. Each member shall have one vote. Decisions pursuant to paragraph H of article XIV, paragraph C of article XVIII and paragraph B of article XIX shall be made by a two-thirds majority of the members present and voting. Decisions on other questions, including the determination of additional questions or categories of questions to be decided by a two-thirds majority, shall be made by a majority of the members present and voting. A majority of members shall constitute a quorum.

D. The General Conference may discuss any questions or any matters within the scope of this Statute or relating to the powers and functions of any organs provided for in this Statute, and may make recommendations to the membership of the Agency or to the Board of Governors or to both on any such questions or matters.

E. The General Conference shall:
1. Elect members of the Board of Governors in accordance with article VI;
2. Approve States for membership in accordance with article IV;
3. Suspend a member from the privileges and rights of membership in accordance with article XIX;
4. Consider the annual report of the Board;
5. In accordance with article XIV, approve the budget of the Agency recommended by the Board or return it with recommendations as to its entirety or parts to the Board. for resubmission to the General Conference;
6. Approve reports to be submitted to the United Nations as required by the relationship agreement between the Agency and the United Nations, except reports referred to in paragraph C of article XII, or return them to the Board with its recommendations;
7. Approve any agreement or agreements between the Agency and the United Nations and other organizations as provided in article XVI or return such agreements with its recommendations to the Board, for resubmission to the General Conference;
8. Approve rules and limitations regarding the exercise of borrowing powers by the Board, in accordance with paragraph G of article XIV; approve rules regarding the acceptance of voluntary contributions to the Agency; and approve, in accordance with paragraph F of article XIV, the manner in which the general fund referred to in that paragraph may be used;
9. Approve amendments to this Statute in accordance with paragraph C of article XVIII;

10. Approve the appointment of the Director General in accordance with paragraph A of article VII.

F. The General Conference shall have the authority:
1. To take decisions on any matter specifically referred to the General Conference for this purpose by the Board;
2. To propose matters for consideration by the Board and request from the Board reports on any matter relating to the functions of the Agency.

Article VI:
Board of Governors

A. The Board of Governors shall be composed as follows:

1. The outgoing Board of Governors shall designate for membership on the Board the ten members most advanced in the technology of atomic energy including the production of source materials, and the member most advanced in the technology of atomic energy including the production of source materials in each of the following areas in which none of the aforesaid ten is located:
1. North America
2. Latin America
3. Western Europe
4. Eastern Europe
5. Africa
6. Middle East and South Asia
7. South East Asia and the Pacific
8. Far East.

2. The General Conference shall elect to membership of the Board of Governors:
(a) Twenty members, with due regard to equitable representation on the Board as a whole of the members in the areas listed in sub-paragraph A. 1 of this article, so that the Board shall at all times include in this category five representatives of the area of Latin America, four representatives of the area of Western Europe, three representatives of the area of Eastern Europe, four representatives of the area of Africa, two representatives of the area of the Middle East and South Asia, one representative of the area of South East Asia and the Pacific, and one representative of the area of the Far East. No member in this category in any one term of office will be eligible for re-election in the same category for the following term of office; and
(b) One further member from among the members in the following areas: Middle East and South Asia, South East Asia and the Pacific, Far East;

(c) One further member from among the members in the following areas: Africa, Middle East and South Asia, South East Asia and the Pacific.

B. The designations provided for in sub-paragraph A-1 of this article shall take place not less than sixty days before each regular annual session of the General Conference. The elections provided for in sub-paragraph A-2 of this article shall take place at regular annual sessions of the General Conference.

C. Members represented on the Board of Governors in accordance with sub-paragraph A-1 of this article shall hold office from the end of the next regular annual session of the General Conference after their designation until the end of the following regular annual session of the General Conference .

D. Members represented on the Board of Governors in accordance with sub-paragraph A-2 of this article shall hold office from the end of the regular annual session of the General Conference at which they are elected until the end of the second regular annual session of the General Conference thereafter.

E. Each member of the Board of Governors shall have one vote. Decisions on the amount of the Agency's budget shall be made by a two-thirds majority of those present and voting, as provided in paragraph H of article XIV. Decisions on other questions, including the determination of additional questions or categories of questions to be decided by a two thirds majority, shall be made by a majority of those present and voting. Two-thirds of all members of the Board shall constitute a quorum.

F. The Board of Governors shall have authority to carry out the functions of the Agency in accordance with this Statute, subject to its responsibilities to the General Conference as provided in this Statute.

G. The Board of Governors shall meet at such times as it may determine. The meetings shall take place at the headquarters of the Agency unless otherwise determined by the Board.

H. The Board of Governors shall elect a Chairman and other officers from among its members and, subject to the provisions of this Statute, shall adopt its own rules of procedure.

I. The Board of Governors may establish such committees as it deems advisable. The Board may appoint persons to represent it in its relations with other organizations.

J. The Board of Governors shall prepare an annual report to the General Conference concerning the affairs of the Agency and any projects approved by the Agency. The Board shall also prepare for submission to the General Conference such reports as the Agency is or may be required to make to the United Nations or to any other organization the work of which is related to that of the Agency. These reports, along with the annual reports, shall be submitted to members of the Agency at least one month before the regular annual session of the General Conference.

Article VII:
Staff

A. The staff of the Agency shall be headed by a Director General. The Director General shall be appointed by the Board of Governors with the approval of the General Conference for a term of four years. He shall be the chief administrative officer of the Agency.

B. The Director General shall be responsible for the appointment, organization, and functioning of the staff and shall be under the authority of and subject to the control of the Board of Governors. He shall perform his duties in accordance with regulations adopted by the Board.

C. The staff shall include such qualified scientific and technical and other personnel as may be required to fulfill the objectives and functions of the Agency. The Agency shall be guided by the principle that its permanent staff shall be kept to a minimum.

D. The paramount consideration in the recruitment and employment of the staff and in the determination of the conditions of service shall be to secure employees of the highest standards of efficiency, technical competence, and integrity. Subject to this consideration, due regard shall be paid to the contributions of members to the Agency and to the importance of recruiting the staff on as wide a geographical basis as possible.

E. The terms and conditions on which the staff shall be appointed, remunerated, and dismissed shall be in accordance with regulations made by the Board of Governors, subject to the provisions of this Statute and to general rules approved by the General Conference on the recommendation of the Board.

F. In the performance of their duties, the Director General and the staff shall not seek or receive instructions from any source external to the Agency. They shall refrain from any action which might reflect on their position as officials of the Agency; subject to their responsibilities to the Agency, they shall not disclose any industrial secret or other confidential information coming to their knowledge by reason of their official duties for the Agency. Each member undertakes to respect the international character of the responsibilities of the Director General and the staff and shall not seek to influence them in the discharge of their duties.

G. In this article the term "staff" includes guards.

Article VIII:
Exchange of information

A. Each member should make available such information as would, in the judgement of the member, be helpful to the Agency.

B. Each member shall make available to the Agency all scientific information developed as a result of assistance extended by the Agency pursuant to article XI.

C. The Agency shall assemble and make available in an accessible form the information made available to it under paragraphs A and B of this article. It shall take positive steps to encourage the exchange among its members of information relating to the nature and peaceful uses of atomic energy and shall serve as an intermediary among its members for this purpose.

Article IX:
Supplying of materials

A. Members may make available to the Agency such quantities of special fissionable materials as they deem advisable and on such terms as shall be agreed with the Agency. The materials made available to the Agency may, at the discretion of the member making them available, be stored either by the member concerned or, with the agreement of the Agency, in the Agency's depots.

B. Members may also make available to the Agency source materials as defined in article XX and other materials. The Board of Governors shall determine the quantities of such materials which the Agency will accept under agreements provided for in article XIII.

C. Each member shall notify the Agency of the quantities, form, and composition of special fissionable materials, source materials, and other materials which that member is prepared, in conformity with its laws, to make available immediately or during a period specified by the Board of Governors.

D. On request of the Agency a member shall, from the materials which it has made available, without delay deliver to another member or group of members such quantities of such materials as the Agency may specify, and shall without delay deliver to the Agency itself such quantities of such materials as are really necessary for operations and scientific research in the facilities of the Agency.

E. The quantities, form and composition of materials made available by any member may be changed at any time by the member with the approval of the Board of Governors.

F. An initial notification in accordance with paragraph C of this article shall be made within three months of the entry into force of this Statute with respect to the member concerned. In the absence of a contrary decision of the Board of Governors, the materials initially made available shall be for the period of the calendar year succeeding the year when this Statute takes effect with respect to the member concerned. Subsequent notifications shall likewise, in the absence of a contrary action by the Board, relate to the period of the calendar year following the notification and shall be made no later than the first day of November of each year.

G. The Agency shall specify the place and method of delivery and, where appropriate, the form and composition, of materials which it has requested a member to deliver from the amounts which that member has notified the Agency it is prepared to make available. The Agency shall also verify the quantities of materials delivered and shall report those quantities periodically to the members.

H. The Agency shall be responsible for storing and protecting materials in its possession. The Agency shall ensure that these materials shall be safeguarded against

1. hazards of the weather,
2. unauthorized removal or diversion,
3. damage or destruction, including sabotage, and
4. forcible seizure. In storing special fissionable materials in its possession, the Agency shall ensure the geographical distribution of these materials in such a way as not to allow concentration of large amounts of such materials in any one country or region of the world.

I. The Agency shall as soon as practicable establish or acquire such of the following as may be necessary:

1. Plant, equipment, and facilities for the receipt, storage, and issue of materials;
2. Physical safeguards;
3. Adequate health and safety measures;

4. Control laboratories for the analysis and verification of materials received;
5. Housing and administrative facilities for any staff required for the foregoing.

J. The materials made available pursuant to this article shall be used as determined by the Board of Governors in accordance with the provisions of this Statute. No member shall have the right to require that the materials it makes available to the Agency be kept separately by the Agency or to designate the specific project in which they must be used.

Article X:
Services, equipment, and facilities

Members may make available to the Agency services, equipment, and facilities which may be of assistance in fulfilling the Agency's objectives and functions.

Article XI:
Agency projects

A. Any member or group of members of the Agency desiring to set up any project for research on, or development or practical application of, atomic energy for peaceful purposes may request the assistance of the Agency in securing special fissionable and other materials, services, equipment, and facilities necessary for this purpose. Any such request shall be accompanied by an explanation of the purpose and extent of the project and shall be considered by the Board of Governors .

B. Upon request, the Agency may also assist any member or group of members to make arrangements to secure necessary financing from outside sources to carry out such projects. In extending this assistance, the Agency will not be required to provide any guarantees or to assume any financial responsibility for the project.

C. The Agency may arrange for the supplying of any materials, services, equipment, and facilities necessary for the project by one or more members or may itself undertake to provide any or all of these directly, taking into consideration the wishes of the member or members making the request.

D. For the purpose of considering the request, the Agency may send into the territory of the member or group of members making the request a person or persons qualified to examine the project. For this purpose the Agency may, with the approval of the member or group of members making the request, use members of its own staff or employ suitably qualified nationals of any member.

E. Before approving a project under this article, the Board of Governors shall give due consideration to:

1. The usefulness of the project, including its scientific and technical feasibility;
2. The adequacy of plans, funds, and technical personnel to assure the effective execution of the project;
3. The adequacy of proposed health and safety standards for handling and storing materials and for operating facilities;
4. The inability of the member or group of members making the request to secure the necessary finances, materials, facilities, equipment, and services;
5. The equitable distribution of materials and other resources available to the Agency;
6. The special needs of the under-developed areas of the world; and
7. Such other matters as may be relevant.

F. Upon approving a project, the Agency shall enter into an agreement with the member or group of members submitting the project, which agreement shall:

1. Provide for allocation to the project of any required special fissionable or other materials;
2. Provide for transfer of special fissionable materials from their then place of custody, whether the materials be in the custody of the Agency or of the member making them available for use in Agency projects, to the member or group of members submitting the project, under conditions which ensure the safety of any shipment required and meet applicable health and safety standards;
3. Set forth the terms and conditions, including charges, on which any materials, services, equipment, and facilities are to be provided by the Agency itself, and, if any such materials, services, equipment, and facilities are to be provided by a member, the terms and conditions as arranged for by the member or group of members submitting the project and the supplying member;
4. Include undertakings by the member or group of members submitting the project: (a) that the assistance provided shall not be used in such a way as to further any military purpose; and (b) that the project shall be subject to the safeguards provided for in article XII, the relevant safeguards being specified in the agreement;
5. Make appropriate provision regarding the rights and interests of the Agency and the member or members concerned in any inventions or discoveries, or any patents therein, arising from the project;
6. Make appropriate provision regarding settlement of disputes;
7. Include such other provisions as may be appropriate.

G. The provisions of this article shall also apply where appropriate to a request for materials, services, facilities, or equipment in connection with an existing project.

Article XII:
Agency safeguards

A. With respect to any Agency project, or other arrangement where the Agency is requested by the parties concerned to apply safeguards, the Agency shall have the following rights and responsibilities to the extent relevant to the project or arrangement:

1. To examine the design of specialized equipment and facilities, including nuclear reactors, and to approve it only from the view-point of assuring that it will not further any military purpose, that it complies with applicable health and safety standards, and that it will permit effective application of the safeguards provided for in this article;
2. To require the observance of any health and safety measures prescribed by the Agency;
3. To require the maintenance and production of operating records to assist in ensuring accountability for source and special fissionable materials used or produced in the project or arrangement;
4. To call for and receive progress reports;
5. To approve the means to be used for the chemical processing of irradiated materials solely to ensure that this chemical processing will not lend itself to diversion of materials for military purposes and will comply with applicable health and safety standards; to require that special fissionable materials recovered or produced as a by-product be used for peaceful purposes under continuing Agency safeguards for research or in reactors, existing or under construction, specified by the member or members concerned; and to require deposit with the Agency of any excess of any special fissionable materials recovered or produced as a by-product over what is needed for the above-stated uses in order to prevent stockpiling of these materials, provided that thereafter at the request of the member or members concerned special fissionable materials so deposited with the Agency shall be returned promptly to the member or members concerned for use under the same provisions as stated above.
6. To send into the territory of the recipient State or States inspectors, designated by the Agency after consultation with the State or States concerned, who shall have access at all times to all places and data and to any person who by reason of his occupation deals with materials, equipment, or facilities which are required by this Statute to be safeguarded, as necessary to account for source and special fissionable materials supplied and fissionable products and to determine whether there is compliance with the undertaking against use in furtherance of any military purpose referred to in sub-paragraph F-4 of article Xl, with the health and safety measures referred to in sub-paragraph A-2 of this article, and with any other conditions prescribed in the agreement between the Agency and the State or States concerned.

Inspectors designated by the Agency shall be accompanied by representatives of the authorities of the State concerned, if that State so requests, provided that the inspectors shall not thereby be delayed or otherwise impeded in the exercise of their functions;
7. In the event of non-compliance and failure by the recipient State or States to take requested corrective steps within a reasonable time, to suspend or terminate assistance and withdraw any materials and equipment made available by the Agency or a member in furtherance of the project.

B. The Agency shall, as necessary, establish a staff of inspectors. The Staff of inspectors shall have the responsibility of examining all operations conducted by the Agency itself to determine whether the Agency is complying with the health and safety measures prescribed by it for application to projects subject to its approval, supervision or control, and whether the Agency is taking adequate measures to prevent the source and special fissionable materials in its custody or used or produced in its own operations from being used in furtherance of any military purpose. The Agency shall take remedial action forthwith to correct any non-compliance or failure to take adequate measures.

C. The staff of inspectors shall also have the responsibility of obtaining and verifying the accounting referred to in sub paragraph A-6 of this article and of determining whether there is compliance with the undertaking referred to in sub paragraph F-4 of article XI, with the measures referred to in sub-paragraph A-2 of this article, and with all other conditions of the project prescribed in the agreement between the Agency and the State or States concerned. The inspectors shall report any non-compliance to the Director General who shall thereupon transmit the report to the Board of Governors. The Board shall call upon the recipient State or States to remedy forthwith any non-compliance which it finds to have occurred. The Board shall report the non-compliance to all members and to the Security Council and General Assembly of the United Nations. In the event of failure of the recipient State or States to take fully corrective action within a reasonable time, the Board may take one or both of the following measures: direct curtailment or suspension of assistance being provided by the Agency or by a member, and call for the return of materials and equipment made available to the recipient member or group of members. The Agency may also, in accordance with article XIX, suspend any non-complying member from the exercise of the privileges and rights of membership.

Article XIII:
Reimbursement of members

Unless otherwise agreed upon between the Board of Governors and the member furnishing to the Agency materials, services, equipment, or facilities, the Board shall enter into an agreement with such member providing for reimbursement for the items furnished.

Article XIV:
Finance

A. The Board of Governors shall submit to the General Conference the annual budget estimates for the expenses of the Agency. To facilitate the work of the Board in this regard, the Director General shall initially prepare the budget estimates. If the General Conference does not approve the estimates, it shall return them together with its recommendations to the Board. The Board shall then submit further estimates to the General Conference for its approval.

B. Expenditures of the Agency shall be classified under the following categories:
1. Administrative expenses: these shall include:
(a) Costs of the staff of the Agency other than the staff employed in connection with materials, services, equipment, and facilities referred to in sub paragraph B-2 below; costs of meetings; and expenditures required for the preparation of Agency projects and for the distribution of information;
(b) Costs of implementing the safeguards referred to in article XII in relation to Agency projects or, under sub-paragraph A-5 of article III, in relation to any bilateral or multilateral arrangement, together with the costs of handling and storage of special fissionable material by the Agency other than the storage and handling charges referred to in paragraph E below;
2. Expenses, other than those included in sub-paragraph 1 of this paragraph, in connection with any materials, facilities, plant, and equipment acquired or established by the Agency in carrying out its authorized functions, and the costs of materials, services, equipment, and facilities provided by it under agreements with one or more members.

C. In fixing the expenditures under sub-paragraph B-l (b) above, the Board of Governors shall deduct such amounts as are recoverable under agreements regarding the application of safeguards between the Agency and parties to bilateral or multilateral arrangements.

D. The Board of Governors shall apportion the expenses referred to in sub-paragraph B-1 above, among members in accordance with a scale to be fixed by the General Conference. In fixing the scale the General Conference shall be guided by the principles adopted by the United Nations in assessing contributions of Member States to the regular budget of the United Nations.

E. The Board of Governors shall establish periodically a scale of charges, including reasonable uniform storage and handling charges, for materials, services, equipment, and facilities furnished to members by the Agency. The scale shall be designed to produce revenues for the Agency adequate to meet the expenses and costs referred to in sub paragraph B-2 above, less any voluntary contributions which the Board of Governors may, in accordance with paragraph F, apply for this purpose. The proceeds of such charges shall be placed in a separate fund which shall be used to pay members for any materials, services, equipment, or facilities furnished by them and to meet other expenses referred to in sub-paragraph B-2 above which may be incurred by the Agency itself

F. Any excess of revenues referred to in paragraph E over the expenses and costs there referred to, and any voluntary contributions to the Agency, shall be placed in a general fund which may be used as the Board of Governors, with the approval of the General Conference, may determine.

G. Subject to rules and limitations approved by the General Conference, the Board of Governors shall have the authority to exercise borrowing powers on behalf of the Agency without, however, imposing on members of the Agency any liability in respect of loans entered into pursuant to this authority, and to accept voluntary contributions made to the Agency.

H. Decisions of the General Conference on financial questions and of the Board of Governors on the amount of the Agency's budget shall require a two-thirds majority of those present and voting.

Article XV:
Privileges and immunities

A. The Agency shall enjoy in the territory of each member such legal capacity and such privileges and immunities as are necessary for the exercise of its functions.

B. Delegates of members together with their alternates and advisers, Governors appointed to the Board together with their alternates and advisers, and the Director

General and the staff of the Agency, shall enjoy such privileges and immunities as are necessary in the independent exercise of their functions in connection with the Agency.

C. The legal capacity, privileges, and immunities referred to in this article shall be defined in a separate agreement or agreements between the Agency, represented for this purpose by the Director General acting under instructions of the Board of Governors. and the members.

Article XVI:
Relationship with other organizations

A. The Board of Governors, with the approval of the General Conference, is authorized to enter into an agreement or agreements establishing an appropriate relationship between the Agency and the United Nations and any other organi zations the work of which is related to that of the Agency.

B. The agreement or agreements establishing the relationship of the Agency and the United Nations shall provide for:
1. Submission by the Agency of reports as provided for in sub-paragraphs B-4 and B-5 of article III;
2. Consideration by the Agency of resolutions relating to it adopted by the General Assembly or any of the Councils of the United Nations and the submission of reports, when requested, to the appropriate organ of the United Nations on the action taken by the Agency or by its members in accordance with this Statute as a result of such consideration.

Article XVII:
Settlement of disputes

A. Any question or dispute concerning the interpretation or application of this Statute which is not settled by negotiation shall be referred to the International Court of Justice in conformity with the Statute of the Court, unless the parties concerned agree on another mode of settlement.

B. The General Conference and the Board of Governors are separately empowered, subject to authorization from the General Assembly of the United Nations, to request the International Court of Justice to give an advisory opinion on any legal question arising within the scope of the Agency's activities.

Article XVIII:
Amendments and withdrawals

A. Amendments to this Statute may be proposed by any member. Certified copies of the text of any amendment proposed shall be prepared by the Director General and communicated by him to all members at least ninety days in advance of its consideration by the General Conference.

B. At the fifth annual session of the General Conference following the coming into force of this Statute, the question of a general review of the provisions of this Statute shall be placed on the agenda of that session. On approval by a majority of the members present and voting, the review will take place at the following General Conference. Thereafter, proposals on the question of a general review of this Statute may be submitted for decision by the General Conference under the same procedure.

C. Amendments shall come into force for all members when:
(i) Approved by the General Conference by a two-thirds majority of those present and voting after consideration of observations submitted by the Board of Governors on each proposed amendment, and
(ii) Accepted by two-thirds of all the members in accordance with their respective constitutional processes. Acceptance by a member shall be effected by the deposit of an instrument of acceptance with the depositary Government referred to in paragraph C of article XXI.

D. At any time after five years from the date when this Statute shall take effect in accordance with paragraph E of article XXI or whenever a member is unwilling to accept an amendment to this Statute, it may withdraw from the Agency by notice in writing to that effect given to the depositary Government referred to in paragraph C of article XXI, which shall promptly inform the Board of Governors and all members.

E. Withdrawal by a member from the Agency shall not affect its contractual obligations entered into pursuant to article XI or its budgetary obligations for the year in which it withdraws.

Article XIX:
Suspension of privileges

A. A member of the Agency which is in arrears in the payment of its financial contributions to the Agency shall have no vote in the Agency if the amount of its arrears equals or exceeds the amount of the contributions due from it for the preceding two years. The General Conference may, nevertheless, permit such a member to vote if it is satisfied that the failure to pay is due to conditions beyond the control of the member.

B. A member which has persistently violated the provisions of this Statute or of any agreement entered into by it pursuant to this Statute may be suspended from the exercise of the privileges and rights of membership by the General Conference acting by a two-thirds majority of the members present and voting upon recommendation by the Board of Governors.

Article XX:
Definitions

As used in this Statute:
1. The term "special fissionable material" means plutonium-239; uranium-233; uranium enriched in the isotopes 235 or 233; any material containing one or more of the foregoing; and such other fissionable material as the Board of Governors shall from time to time deter mine; but the term "special fissionable material" does not include source material.
2. The term "uranium enriched in the isotopes 235 or 233" means uranium containing the isotopes 235 or 233 or both in an amount such that the abundance ratio of the sum of these isotopes to the isotope 238 is greater than the ratio of the isotope 235 to the isotope 238 occurring in nature .
3. The term "source material" means uranium containing the mixture of isotopes occurring in nature; uranium depleted in the isotope 235; thorium; any of the foregoing in the form of metal, alloy, chemical compound, or concentrate; any other material containing one or more of the foregoing in such concentration as the Board of Governors shall from time to time determine; and such other material as the Board of Governors shall from time to time determine.

Article XXI:
Signature, acceptance, and entry into force

A. This Statute shall be open for signature on 26 October 1956 by all States Members of the United Nations or of any of the specialized agencies and shall remain open for signature by those States for a period of ninety days.

B. The signatory States shall become parties to this Statute by deposit of an instrument of ratification.

C. Instruments of ratification by signatory States and instruments of acceptance by States whose membership has been approved under paragraph B of article IV of this

Statute shall be deposited with the Government of the United States of America, hereby designated as depositary Government.

D. Ratification or acceptance of this Statute shall be effected by States in accordance with their respective constitutional processes.

E. This Statute, apart from the Annex, shall come into force when eighteen States have deposited instruments of ratification in accordance with paragraph B of this article, provided that such eighteen States shall include at least three of the following States: Canada, France, the Union of Soviet Socialist Republics, the United Kingdom of Great Britain and Northern Ireland, and the United States of America. Instruments of ratification and instruments of acceptance deposited thereafter shall take effect on the date of their receipt.

F. The depositary Government shall promptly inform all States signatory to this Statute of the date of each deposit of ratification and the date of entry into force of the Statute. The depositary Government shall promptly inform all signatories and members of the dates on which States subsequently become parties thereto.

G. The Annex to this Statute shall come into force on the first day this Statute is open for signature.

Article XXII:
Registration with the United Nations

A. This Statute shall be registered by the depositary Government pursuant to Article 102 of the Charter of the United Nations.

B. Agreements between the Agency and any member or members, agreements between the Agency and any other organization or organizations, and agreements between members subject to approval of the Agency, shall be registered with the Agency. Such agreements shall be registered by the Agency with the United Nations if registration is required under Article 102 of the Charter of the United Nations.

Article XXIII:
Authentic texts and certified copies

This Statute, done in the Chinese, English, French, Russian and Spanish languages, each being equally authentic, shall be deposited in the archives of the depositary Government. Duly certified copies of this Statute shall be transmitted by the depositary

Government to the Governments of the other signatory States and to the Governments of States admitted to membership under paragraph B of article IV.
In witness whereof the undersigned, duly authorized, have signed this Statute.

DONE at the Headquarters of the United Nations, this twenty-sixth day of October, one thousand nine hundred and fifty-six.

THE NUCLEAR ENERGY AGENCY (NEA)

(Paris, 20 December 1957)

The (formerly: European) Nuclear Energy Agency is one of the specialised agencies of the Organisation for Economic Co-operation and Development (OECD). It was set up following a "decision" adopted by the Council of the Organisation in September 1957 and entered into force on 1st February 1958. Following accession by Japan as the first non-European full Member State, the Agency changed its name to Nuclear Energy Agency (NEA) with effect from 20 April 1972. Also the Commission of the European Union participates in the Agency's work.

The Agency's aim is to promote co-operation among countries of Western Europe with regard to the peaceful use of nuclear energy through joint ventures, scientific and technical co-operation, exchange of information and of technical data, the harmonisation of relevant and related legislation, and the evaluation of national nuclear programmes helping governments to work out their nuclear policies in a safe and environment-friendly manner, also by adopting appropriate legislation. Similarly to IAEA, under NEA's aegis certain international conventions on nuclear third party liability are adopted (see Chapter III).

The instruments at the Agency's disposal in carrying out its normative role in the areas defined by its Statute include "decisions" and "recommendations". The latter have been extensively used in the field of health protection against ionising radiation, in addition to those handed down by IAEA and the European Atomic Energy Community. In certain cases, these recommendations are adopted jointly with other international (not specifically "nuclear") organisations like WHO, ILO, FAO, and with ICRP (a non-governmental international commission). For these recommendations, see Chapter II).

The Agency collaborates with the other competent international organisations, often through special co-operation agreements.

The latest change to the Agency's Statute dates back to 1995 and concerns the procedure (article 17) to be followed in order to become a member of NEA.

The current members of the Agency (which are Members of OECD) are 27.

STATUTE OF THE OECD NUCLEAR ENERGY AGENCY

PART I

Article 1

a. There is hereby established within the framework of the Organisation an OECD Nuclear Energy Agency (hereinafter referred to as the "Agency").
b. Taking due account of the public interest and mindful of the need to prevent the proliferation of nuclear explosive devices, the purpose of the Agency shall be to further the development of the production and uses of nuclear energy, including applications of ionizing radiations, for peaceful purposes by the participating countries, through co-operation between those countries and a harmonization of measures taken at the national level.

Article 2

The tasks assigned to the Agency shall be carried out, under the authority of the Council, by the Steering Committee for Nuclear Energy (hereinafter referred to as the "Steering Committee"), by the bodies which the latter has established in conformity with the provisions set forth below to assist it in its work or perform tasks of common interest to a group of countries, and by the Secretariat of the Agency which shall form part of the Secretariat of the Organisation.

Article 3

The Steering Committee shall be competent to deal with any question relevant to the purpose of the Agency under conditions resulting from the provisions set forth below and from other applicable decisions of the Council.

Article 4

a. The Agency shall promote technical and economic studies and undertake consultations on the programme and projects of participating countries relating to the development of research and industry in the field of the production and uses of nuclear energy for peaceful purposes, in collaboration with other bodies of the Organisation in matters falling within their competence.
b. To this end, the programmes and projects shall be examined by the Steering Committee according to a procedure to be laid down by it.

Article 5

a. The Agency shall, where appropriate, promote the formation of joint undertakings for the production and uses of nuclear energy for peaceful purposes, endeavouring to secure the participation of the greatest possible number of countries.
b. If a group of participating countries declares its intention to set up a joint undertaking, the countries concerned may agree to undertake the necessary work for this purpose among themselves within the Organisation at their own cost, whatever the position adopted by other participating countries. The Working Parties or Study Groups set up in accordance with this paragraph shall keep the Steering Committee informed of their progress and report to it on their conclusions.
c. When joint undertakings have been established on the initiative or with the assistance of the Agency.
   i. The Steering Committee – or a Restricted Group of the Steering Committee composed of representatives of the countries which take part in the undertaking – shall exercise the functions assigned to it by the agreements concluded for the establishment of the undertakings concerned;
   ii. The joint undertakings shall report each year to the Steering Committee and, where appropriate, to a Restricted Group of the Steering Committee on the state of their affairs and their development;
   iii. The Steering Committee shall consider such problems of general interest as may be raised by the operation of joint undertakings, with a view to proposing any necessary measures to the Governments;
   iv. The agreements concluded for the creation of joint undertakings should contain provisions under which participating countries or groups of participating countries not taking part in joint under-takings might subsequently accede to them or benefit from the results of their activities.

Article 6

a. Given the need to prevent the proliferation of nuclear explosive devices, a security control shall be established with a view to ensuring that the operation of joint undertakings and the materials, equipment and services made available by the Agency or under its supervision shall be used solely for peaceful purposes.
b. The security control may be applied, at the request of the parties, to any bilateral or multilateral agreement, or, at the request of a participating country, to any of that country's activities in the field of nuclear energy.
c. The organisation of this control and the functions of the Agency relating to its exercise shall be the subject of a special Convention on security control.

Article 7

a. The Agency shall encourage the development of research into the production and uses of nuclear energy for peaceful purposes in participating countries.
b. To this end, it shall, where appropriate, promote the conclusion of agreements for the joint use of research installations built by participating countries and, in accordance with the conditions set forth in Article 5 above, the creation of joint research establishments.
c. The Agency shall encourage the exchange of scientific and technical information related to its purposes between participating countries.

Article 8

a. The Agency shall:
   i. contribute to the promotion, by the responsible national authorities, of the protection of workers and the public against the hazards of ionizing radiations and of the preservation of the environment;
   ii. contribute to the promotion of the safety of nuclear installations and materials by the responsible national authorities;
   iii. contribute to the promotion of a system for third party liability and insurance with respect to nuclear damage;
   iv. encourage measures to ensure the most efficient use of patented inventions in the field of nuclear energy;
   v. so far as may be consistent with Article 1(b) above, contribute to the elimination of obstacles to international trade or to development of the nuclear industry;
   vi. contribute to the dissemination of information which may be freely distributed on the peaceful uses of nuclear energy, in particular on the safety and regulation of nuclear activities as well as on the physical protection of nuclear installations and materials.
b. For the purpose of the above-mentioned objectives, the Steering Committee shall:
   i. submit to the participating countries recommendations or common rules to serve as a basis for harmonizing national laws and regulations;
   ii. encourage the establishment between participating countries of joint services necessary, in particular, for the protection of public health and the prevention of accidents in the nuclear industry.
c. The Agency shall undertake its activities referred to in paragraphs (a) and (b) above, as far as possible in collaboration with the International Atomic Energy Agency an the Commission of the European Communities.

PART II

Article 9

The Steering Committee shall be composed of representatives of all Governments which participate in the present Decision.

Article 10

a. The Steering Committee shall designate each year a Chairman and Vice-Chairmen from among its members. It shall adopt its own Rules of Procedure.
b. The Steering Committee may give its advice, in particular, in the form of recommendations, to participating countries on any question within its competence.
c. Whenever it is necessary to take decisions which are binding on Governments and which exceed the powers specially conferred on the Steering Committee, the latter shall submit proposals to the Council to this end.
d. The Steering Committee shall report each year to the Council on the execution of its duties and on the situation and prospects of the nuclear industry in participating countries.

Article 11

a. The reports and proposals prepared by the Steering Committee shall, when appropriate, call attention to the different attitudes adopted by the members.
b. The decisions, opinions or recommendations of the Steering Committee shall be adopted by mutual agreement of those of its members present and voting.
c. However, decisions of the Steering Committee which relate to the adoption of the agenda, the undertaking of studies, the establishment of Working Parties and the submission of questionnaires to participating countries, shall be adopted by a majority of the members of the Steering Committee present.
d. Decisions which are binding on Governments and which are taken by the Steering Committee within the powers conferred upon it shall commit only those countries which have accepted them.

Article 12

a. The Steering Committee may establish such Commissions and Working Parties as it may consider necessary to assist it in the performance of its duties and entrust them with the execution of any task relevant to the purpose of the Agency.
b. Restricted bodies may be established to study questions or execute functions of interest to a group of participating countries, in accordance with the conditions

set forth in Article 5 above or in a decision of the Council. Special expenditure assignable to the work of these bodies, such as the cost of studies or the remuneration of experts, shall be chargeable to the countries concerned.

Article 13

a. The Steering Committee shall perform its duties in collaboration with the competent bodies of the Organisation.
b. The Steering Committee shall consult these bodies on questions which come within their competence. These bodies shall consult the Steering Committee on all questions relating to the production and uses of nuclear energy for peaceful purposes.

Article 14

a. The Steering Committee and its subsidiary bodies shall be assisted by the Secretariat of the Agency.
b. Expenditures relating to the working of the Agency shall be covered by the Budget of the Organisation. To this end, the Steering Committee shall prepare annual estimates of expenditure, which shall be submitted to the Council for approval.
c. Expenditure of the Agency which is subject to special financial rules shall be covered by separate budgetary provisions and countries which make no financial contributions to such expenses shall abstain when the relevant item in the Budget is approved.

Article 15

a. In the performance of its duties, the Steering Committee shall take account of the work done by other international Organisations concerned and may, subject to paragraphs (b) and (c) below, co-operate with them.
b. The Steering Committee shall, in agreement with the Council, establish relations with international governmental Organisations concerned with nuclear energy questions.
c. The Steering Committee may establish contact with international non-governmental Organisations concerned, within the framework of decisions or arrangements approved by the Council.

Article 16

a. The provisions of the present Decision do not affect rights and obligations resulting from treaties previously entered into by Governments participating in the present Decision.

b. Since the present Decision does not affect the exercise of competences granted to the European Atomic Energy Community (EURATOM) by the Treaty entered into at Rome on 25 March 1957, the Agency shall establish with the said Community a close collaboration, details of which shall be determined by common agreement.

Article 17

a. Participating countries shall be countries the Governments of which participate in the present Decision.
b. Any Member country of the Organisation, the Government of which does not participate in the present Decision, may notify the Secretary- General of its wish to do so and shall become a participant in the Decision upon approval of the Council on the recommendation of the Steering Committee.
c. Any other Government invited by the Organisation to participate in the present Decision may do so by addressing to the Secretary-General an acceptance of that invitation. The Organisation may suspend or terminate that participation by giving one month's written notice of suspension or twelve months' written notice of termination to that Government.
d. Any Government participating in the present decision may terminate the application thereof to itself by giving twelve months' notice to that effect to the Secretary-General.

Article 18

The provisions of Supplementary Protocol No. 1 to the Convention on the Organisation for Economic Co-operation and Development shall apply to the representation of the European Atomic Energy Community (EURATOM) in the Agency and in its Steering Committee as well as to the participation of the Commission of the European Communities in the work of the Agency and of its Steering Committee.

Article 19

The present Decision shall enter into force on 1 February 1958.

THE EUROPEAN ATOMIC ENERGY COMMUNITY (EAEC, alias EURATOM)

(Rome, 25 March 1957)

The European Atomic Energy Community (also named Euratom) was set up by the Treaty of Rome of 25 March 1957. The six founder States of the European Coal and Steel Community (ECSC, Treaty of 18 April 1951) decided, in addition to establishing a European Economic Community (EEC), to pool their activities in developing the energy source of the future. Euratom was therefore created with the aim of establishing the conditions needed to promote the rapid development on nuclear activities for peaceful purposes in the member States of the Community by means of studies, research and the spread of technical know-how, in conjunction with the harmonisation of safety standards in the area in point. The Community also took upon itself to guarantee, through appropriate controls, the peaceful use of nuclear materials, to further the development of nuclear industry by ensuring the equitable supply to users of such materials, to establish a common nuclear market and, finally, to forge the necessary links to promote progress in the nuclear arena.

The European nuclear organisation is therefore part and parcel of Europe's economic, scientific and political development, which aims to steer nuclear energy into civil uses, a similar task being tackled at the international level by the International Atomic Energy Agency (IAEA).

The Euratom Treaty stipulates very important provisions covering health and safety, supplies of nuclear materials, safeguards for the peaceful use of nuclear energy, the nuclear common market within the Community etc. The instruments provided for under the Treaty (Article 161) to implement Community law include "regulations" (binding in their entirety, directly and immediately applicable in member States), "directives", "recommendations", "decisions" and "opinions". It is recalled in particular that directives are binding on member States only as to the result to be achieved, with the choice of form and methods being left up to member States.

Various "regulations" have been adopted by Euratom addressing issues such as e.g. nuclear safeguards or maximum contamination levels of foodstuffs after a nuclear incident, but also certain requirements concerning investments in nuclear activities, or certain basic definitions of nuclear materials. On the other hand, Euratom opted for the "directive" in order to lay down the so-called "basic standards" on radiation protection and many other standards in specific areas like radiation protection in nuclear medicine and radiology, in the shipment of radioactive substances etc. Some "decisions" have been adopted in specific areas, such as the exchange of information in the case of a radiological emergency, or nuclear safety. The "recommendation" (not binding) is instead favoured in other specific areas such as guidelines for the application of certain Euratom Treaty provisions, radioactive waste classification and disposal etc. For these regulations, directives, decisions and recommendations, see Chapter Two in this PART ONE and Chapter One in PART TWO.

It should be moreover recalled that the European Commission adopted in the past (1965-66) two recommendations concerning nuclear third party liability, which is specifically governed by international conventions (Paris, Brussels, Vienna etc., see Chapter THREE). These recommendations (not published here) are important merely historically, since under the Treaty, Euratom competences in the matter are limited to article 98, which simply puts on member States the obligation to facilitate the conclusion of insurance contracts covering nuclear risks. The recommendations aimed to harmonize the main provisions adopted nationally to implement the Paris and Brussels Conventions.

Mention should also be made of a Directive and a Decision adopted towards the end of 2003. The Euratom (Council) Directive is concerned with the control of high activity radioactive sources, while the (Council) Decision amends the previous one of 1998 (approving the accession of the European Atomic Energy Community to the IAEA 1994 Convention on Nuclear Safety) on the basis of the European Court of Justice's ruling of December 2002 (see relevant case law in the Appendix to the volume).

It is noted that the Regulations on definitions (under article 197) and on investments (under article 41) mentioned above are added to Chapter Two of PART ONE, although not strictly relating to safety and protection as such.

The text of the Euratom Treaty is here included (while annexes and protocols are omitted on practical grounds) in its full text, as amended over time (see Introductory material to the Chapter, also as to recent institutional developments affecting the Treaty).

The executive organs of Euratom were merged with those of the ECSC and the EEC by the Treaty of 8 April 1965, establishing a single Council and a single Commission of the European Communities. The original number (six, i.e. Belgium, France, Germany/Fed. Rep., Holland, Italy, Luxembourg) of member States of the European Communities including Euratom has increased in time This is made possible by Article 205 of the Euratom Treaty, which entitles European States to become members of this Community; the request for accession is normally accepted by a Council "decision". The enlargement started with the accession of Denmark, Ireland and the United Kingdom during the first half of the 1970s, and subsequently of Greece (1979), Spain and Portugal (1985). Further enlargement took place in the course of 1994/95, with the accession of Austria, Finland and Sweden. It is added that applications have been submitted during these last years by various countries especially from Central and Eastern Europe to accede to the European Union. As of May 2004, ten new countries have in fact become full members of the Union (the total number of members being currently 25).

TREATY ESTABLISHING THE EUROPEAN ATOMIC ENERGY COMMUNITY

Note: The Protocol on the privileges and immunities of the European Atomic Energy Community has been repealed by the second paragraph of Article 28 of the Merger Treaty; see Protocol on the privileges and immunities of the European Communities.

HIS MAJESTY THE KING OF THE BELGIANS, THE PRESIDENT OF THE FEDERAL REPUBLIC OF GERMANY, THE PRESIDENT OF THE FRENCH REPUBLIC, THE PRESIDENT OF THE ITALIAN REPUBLIC, HER ROYAL HIGHNESS THE GRAND DUCHESS OF LUXEMBOURG, HER MAJESTY THE QUEEN OF THE NETHERLANDS,

RECOGNIZING that nuclear energy represents an essential resource for the development and invigoration of industry and will permit the advancement of the cause of peace,
CONVINCED that only a joint effort undertaken without delay can offer the prospect of achievements commensurate with the creative capacities of their countries,
RESOLVED to create the conditions necessary for the development of a powerful nuclear industry which will provide extensive energy resources, lead to the modernization of technical processes and contribute, through its many other applications, to the prosperity of their peoples,
ANXIOUS to create the conditions of safety necessary to eliminate hazards to the life and health of the public,
DESIRING to associate other countries with their work and to cooperate with international organizations concerned with the peaceful development of atomic energy,
HAVE DECIDED to create a EUROPEAN ATOMIC ENERGY COMMUNITY (EURATOM) and to this end have designated as their Plenipotentiaries:
HIS MAJESTY THE KING OF THE BELGIANS:
Mr Paul Henri SPAAK, Minister for Foreign Affairs,
Baron J. Ch. SNOY ET D'OPPUERS, Secretary General of the Ministry of Economic Affairs, Head of the Belgian Delegation to the Intergovernmental Conference;
THE PRESIDENT OF THE FEDERAL REPUBLIC OF GERMANY:

Dr Konrad ADENAUER, Federal Chancellor,
Professor Dr Walter HALLSTEIN, State Secretary of the Federal Foreign Office;
THE PRESIDENT OF THE FRENCH REPUBLIC:
Mr Christian PINEAU, Minister for Foreign Affairs,
Mr Maurice FAURE, Under Secretary of State for Foreign Affairs;
THE PRESIDENT OF THE ITALIAN REPUBLIC:
Mr Antonio SEGNI, President of the Council of Ministers,
Professor Gaetano MARTINO, Minister for Foreign Affairs;
HER ROYAL HIGHNESS THE GRAND DUCHESS OF LUXEMBOURG:
Mr Joseph BECH, President of the Government, Minister for Foreign Affairs,
Mr Lambert SCHAUS, Ambassador, Head of the Luxembourg Delegation to the Intergovernmental Conference;
HER MAJESTY THE QUEEN OF THE NETHERLANDS:
Mr Joseph LUNS, Minister for Foreign Affairs,
Mr J. LINTHORST HOMAN, Head of the Netherlands Delegation to the Intergovernmental Conference;

WHO, having exchanged their full powers, found in good and due form, have agreed as follows.

(*) EDITORIAL NOTE: The reader will find below a complete amended version of the Treaty establishing the European Community as it results from Title IV of the TEU: Provisions amending the Treaty establishing the European Atomic Energy Community [Article I(1) to (29)].

TITLE I
THE TASKS OF THE COMMUNITY

Article 1

By this Treaty the HIGH CONTRACTING PARTIES establish among themselves a EUROPEAN ATOMIC ENERGY COMMUNITY (EURATOM).
It shall be the task of the Community to contribute to the raising of the standard of living in the Member States and to the development of relations with the other countries by creating the conditions necessary for the speedy establishment and growth of nuclear industries.

Article 2

In order to perform its task, the Community shall, as provided in this Treaty:
a. promote research and ensure the dissemination of technical information;

b. establish uniform safety standards to protect the health of workers and of the general public and ensure that they are applied;
c. facilitate investment and ensure, particularly by encouraging ventures on the part of undertakings, the establishment of the basic installations necessary for the development of nuclear energy in the Community;
d. ensure that all users in the Community receive a regular and equitable supply of ores and nuclear fuels;
e. make certain, by appropriate supervision, that nuclear materials are not diverted to purposes other than those for which they are intended;
f. exercise the right of ownership conferred upon it with respect to special fissile materials;
g. ensure wide commercial outlets and access to the best technical facilities by the creation of a common market in specialized materials and equipment, by the free movement of capital for investment in the field of nuclear energy and by freedom of employment for specialists within the Community;
h. establish with other countries and international organizations such relations as will foster progress in the peaceful uses of nuclear energy.

Article 3 (*)

(*) As amended by Article I(1) TEU.

1. The tasks entrusted to the Community shall be carried out by the following institutions:
- a EUROPEAN PARLIAMENT,
- a COUNCIL,
- a COMMISSION,
- a COURT OF JUSTICE,
- a COURT OF AUDITORS.

Each institution shall act within the limits of the powers conferred upon it by this Treaty.

2. The Council and the Commission shall be assisted by an Economic and Social Committee acting in an advisory capacity.

TITLE II
PROVISIONS FOR THE ENCOURAGEMENT OF PROGRESS IN THE FIELD OF NUCLEAR ENERGY

Chapter 1
PROMOTION OF RESEARCH

Article 4

1. The Commission shall be responsible for promoting and facilitating nuclear research in the Member States and for complementing it by carrying out a Community research and training programme.
2. The activity of the Commission in this respect shall be carried out within the fields listed in Annex I to this Treaty.
This list may be amended by the Council, acting by a qualified majority on a proposal from the Commission. The latter shall consult the Scientific and Technical Committee established under Article 134.

Article 5

For purposes of coordinating and complementing research undertaken in Member States, the Commission shall, either by a specific request addressed to a given recipient and conveyed to the government concerned, or by a general published request, call upon Member States, persons or undertakings to communicate to it their programmes relating to the research which it specifies in the request.
After giving those concerned full opportunity to comment, the Commission may deliver a reasoned opinion on each of the programmes communicated to it. The Commission shall deliver such an opinion if the State, person or undertaking which has communicated the programme so requests.
By such opinions the Commission shall discourage unnecessary duplication and shall direct research towards sectors which are insufficiently explored. The Commission may not publish these programmes without the consent of the State, person or undertaking which has communicated them.
The Commission shall publish at regular intervals a list of those sectors of nuclear research which it considers to be insufficiently explored.
The Commission may bring together representatives of public and private research centers as well as any experts engaged in research in the same or related fields for mutual consultation and exchanges of information.

Article 6

To encourage the carrying out of research programmes communicated to it the Commission may:

a. provide financial assistance within the framework of research contracts, without, however, offering subsidies;
b. supply, either free of charge or against payment, for carrying out such programmes, any source materials or special fissile materials which it has available;
c. place installations, equipment or expert assistance at the disposal of Member States, persons or undertakings, either free of charge or against payment;
d. promote joint financing by the Member States, persons or undertakings concerned.

Article 7

Community research and training programmes shall be determined by the Council, acting unanimously on a proposal from the Commission, which shall consult the Scientific and Technical Committee.

These programmes shall be drawn up for a period of not more than five years.

The funds required for carrying out these programmes shall be included each year in the research and investment budget of the Community.

The Commission shall ensure that these programmes are carried out and shall submit an annual report thereon to the Council.

The Commission shall keep the Economic and Social Committee informed of the broad outlines of Community research and training programmes.

Article 8

1. After consulting the Scientific and Technical Committee, the Commission shall establish a Joint Nuclear Research Centre.

This Centre shall ensure that the research programmes and other tasks assigned to it by the Commission are carried out.

It shall also ensure that a uniform nuclear terminology and a standard system of measurements are established.

It shall set up a central bureau for nuclear measurements.

2. The activities of the Centre may, for geographical or functional reasons, be carried out in separate establishments.

Article 9

1. After obtaining the opinion of the Economic and Social Committee the Commission may, within the framework of the Joint Nuclear Research Centre, set up schools

for the training of specialists, particularly in the fields of prospecting for minerals, the production of high purity nuclear materials, the processing of irradiated fuels, nuclear engineering, health and safety and the production and use of radioisotopes.
The Commission shall determine the details of such training.
2. An institution of university status shall be established; the way in which it will function shall be determined by the Council, acting by a qualified majority on a proposal from the Commission.

Article 10

The Commission may, by contract, entrust the carrying out of certain parts of the Community research programme to Member States, persons or undertakings, or to third countries, international organizations or nationals of third countries.

Article 11

The Commission shall publish the research programmes referred to in Articles 7, 8 and 10, and also regular progress reports on their implementation.

Chapter 2
DISSEMINATION OF INFORMATION

Section 1
Information over which the Community has power of disposal

Article 12

Member States, persons or undertakings shall have the right, on application to the Commission, to obtain non exclusive licenses under patents, provisionally protected patent rights, utility models or patent applications owned by the Community, where they are able to make effective use of the inventions covered thereby.
Under the same conditions, the Commission shall grant sublicenses under patents, provisionally protected patent rights, utility models or patent applications, where the Community holds contractual licenses conferring power to do so.
The Commission shall grant such licenses or sublicenses on terms to be agreed with the licensees and shall furnish all the information required for their use. These terms shall relate in particular to suitable remuneration and, where appropriate, to the right of the licensee to grant sublicenses to third parties and to the obligation to treat the information as a trade secret.
Failing agreement on the terms referred to in the third paragraph, the licensees may bring the matter before the Court of Justice so that appropriate terms may be fixed.

Article 13

The Commission shall communicate to Member States, persons and undertakings information acquired by the Community which is not covered by the provisions of Article 12, whether such information is derived from its own research programme or communicated to the Commission with authority to make free use of it.
The Commission may, however, make the disclosure of such information conditional on its being treated as confidential and not passed on to third parties.
The Commission may not disclose information which has been acquired subject to restrictions on its use or dissemination such as information known as classified information unless it ensures compliance with these restrictions.

Section 2
Other information

(a) Dissemination by amicable agreement

Article 14

The Commission shall endeavour, by amicable agreement, to secure both the communication of information which is of use to the Community in the attainment of its objectives and the granting of licenses under patents, provisionally protected patent rights, utility models or patent applications covering such information.

Article 15

The Commission shall establish a procedure by which Member States, persons and undertakings may use it as an intermediary for exchanging provisional or final results of their research, in so far as these results have not been acquired by the Community under research contracts awarded by the Commission.
This procedure must be such as to ensure the confidential nature of the exchange. The results communicated may, however, be transmitted by the Commission to the Joint Nuclear Research Center for documentation purposes; this shall not entail any right of use to which the communicating party has not agreed.

(b) Compulsory communication to the Commission

Article 16

1. As soon as an application for a patent or a utility model relating to a specifically nuclear subject is filed with a Member State, that State shall ask the applicant to agree that the contents of the application be communicated to the Commission forthwith.

If the applicant agrees, this communication shall be made within three months of the date of filing the application. If the applicant does not agree, the Member State shall, within the same period, notify the Commission of the existence of the application.
The Commission may require a Member State to communicate the contents of an application of whose existence it has been notified.
The Commission shall make any such request within two months of the date of notification. Any extension of this period shall entail a corresponding extension of the period referred to in the sixth subparagraph of this paragraph.
On receiving such a request from the Commission, the Member State shall again ask the applicant to agree to communication of the contents of the application. If the applicant agrees, communication shall be made forthwith.
If the applicant does not agree, the Member State shall nevertheless be required to make this communication to the Commission within 18 months of the date on which the application was filed.
2. Member States shall inform the Commission, within 18 months of the filing date, of the existence of any as yet unpublished application for a patent or utility model which seems to them, prima facie, to deal with a subject which, although not specifically nuclear, is directly connected with and essential to the development of nuclear energy in the Community.
If the Commission so requests, the contents of the application shall be communicated to it within two months.
3. In order that publication may take place as soon as possible, Member States shall reduce to a minimum the time taken to process applications for patents or utility models relating to subjects referred to in paragraphs 1 and 2 concerning which a request has been made by the Commission.
4. The Commission shall treat the above mentioned communications as confidential. They may only be made for documentation purposes. The Commission may, however, make use of the inventions communicated to it, either with the consent of the applicant or in accordance with Articles 17 to 23.
5. The provisions of this Article shall not apply when an agreement concluded with a third State or an international organization precludes communication.

(c) Grant of licenses by arbitration or under compulsory powers

Article 17

1. Failing amicable agreement, non exclusive licenses may be granted either by arbitration or under compulsory powers in accordance with Articles 18 to 23:
a. to the Community or to Joint Undertakings accorded this right under Article 48 in respect of patents, provisionally protected patent rights or utility models relating to inventions directly connected with nuclear research, where the granting of such

licenses is necessary for the continuance of their own research or indispensable to the operation of their installations.
If the Commission so requests, such licenses shall include the right to authorize third parties to make use of the invention, where they are carrying out work for or orders placed by the Community or Joint Undertakings;
b. to persons or undertakings which have applied to the Commission for them in respect of patents, provisionally protected patent rights or utility models relating to inventions directly connected with and essential to the development of nuclear energy in the Community, provided that all the following conditions are fulfilled:
i. at least four years have elapsed since the filing of the patent application, save in the case of an invention relating to a specifically nuclear subject;
ii. the requirements arising out of the development of nuclear energy, in the Commission's conception of such development, in the territory of a Member State where an invention is protected, are not being met with regard to that invention;
iii. the proprietor, having been called upon to meet such requirements either himself or through his licensees, has not complied with this request;
iv. the persons or undertakings applying for licenses are in a position to meet such requirements effectively by making use of the invention.
Member States may not, in order to meet such requirements, take any coercive measures provided for in their national legislation which will limit the protection accorded to the invention, save at the prior request of the Commission.
2. A non exclusive license may not be granted as provided for in paragraph 1 where the proprietor can establish the existence of legitimate reasons, in particular that he has not had sufficient time at his disposal.
3. The granting of a license pursuant to paragraph 1 shall confer a right to full compensation, the amount of which shall be agreed between the proprietor of the patent, provisionally protected patent right or utility model and the licensee.
4. The provisions of this Article shall not affect those of the Paris Convention for the Protection of Industrial Property.

Article 18

An Arbitration Committee is hereby established for the purposes provided for in this Section. The Council shall appoint the members and lay down the Rules of Procedure of this Committee, acting on a proposal from the Court of Justice.
An appeal, having suspensory effect, may be brought by the parties before the Court of Justice against a decision of the Arbitration Committee within one month of notification thereof. The Court of Justice shall confine its examination to the formal validity of the decision and to the interpretation of the provisions of this Treaty by the Arbitration Committee.

The final decisions of the Arbitration Committee shall have the force of res judicata between the parties concerned. They shall be enforceable as provided in Article 164.

Article 19

Where, failing amicable agreement, the Commission intends to secure the granting of licenses in one of the cases provided for in Article 17, it shall give notice of its intention to the proprietor of the patent, provisionally protected patent right, utility model or patent application, and shall specify in such notice the name of the applicant for and the scope of the license.

Article 20

The proprietor may, within one month of receipt of the notice referred to in Article 19, propose to the Commission and, where appropriate, to the applicant that they conclude a special agreement to refer the matter to the Arbitration Committee.
Should the Commission or the applicant refuse to enter into such an agreement, the Commission shall not require the Member State or its appropriate authorities to grant the license or cause it to be granted.
If, when the matter is referred to it under a special agreement, the Arbitration Committee finds that the request from the Commission complies with the provisions of Article 17, it shall give a reasoned decision containing a grant of the license to the applicant and laying down the terms of the license and the remuneration therefor, to the extent that the parties have not reached agreement on these points.

Article 21

If the proprietor does not propose that the matter be referred to the Arbitration Committee, the Commission may call upon the Member State concerned or its appropriate authorities to grant the license or cause it to be granted.
If, having heard the proprietor's case, the Member State, or its appropriate authorities, considers that the conditions of Article 17 have not been complied with, it shall notify the Commission of its refusal to grant the license or to cause it to be granted.
If it refuses to grant the license or to cause it to be granted, or if, within four months of the date of the request, no information is forthcoming with regard to the granting of the license, the Commission shall have two months in which to bring the matter before the Court of Justice.
The proprietor must be heard in the proceedings before the Court of Justice.
If the judgment of the Court of Justice establishes that the conditions of Article 17 have been complied with, the Member State concerned, or its appropriate authorities, shall take such measures as enforcement of that judgment may require.

Article 22

1. If the proprietor of the patent, provisionally protected patent right or utility model and the licensee fail to agree on the amount of compensation, the parties concerned may conclude a special agreement to refer the matter to the Arbitration Committee. By doing so, the parties waive the right to institute any proceedings other than those provided for in Article 18.
2. If the licensee refuses to conclude a special agreement, the license he has been granted shall be deemed void.
If the proprietor refuses to conclude a special agreement, the compensation referred to in this Article shall be determined by the appropriate national authorities.

Article 23

After the lapse of one year, the decisions of the Arbitration Committee or the appropriate national authorities may, if there are new facts to justify it, be revised with respect to the terms of the license.
Such revision shall be a matter for the body which gave the decision.

Section 3
Security provisions

Article 24

Information which the Community acquires as a result of carrying out its research programme, and the disclosure of which is liable to harm the defense interests of one or more Member States, shall be subject to a security system in accordance with the following provisions.
1. The Council shall, acting on a proposal from the Commission, adopt security regulations which, account being taken of the provisions of this Article, lay down the various security gradings to be applied and the security measures appropriate to each grading.
2. Where the Commission considers that the disclosure of certain information is liable to harm the defense interests of one or more Member States, it shall provisionally apply to that information the security grading required in that case by the security regulations.
It shall communicate such information forthwith to the Member States, which shall provisionally ensure its security in the same manner.
Member States shall inform the Commission within three months whether they wish to maintain the grading provisionally applied, substitute another or declassify the information.

Upon the expiry of this period, the highest grading of those requested shall be applied. The Commission shall notify the Member States accordingly.

At the request of the Commission or of a Member State, the Council may, acting unanimously, at any time apply another grading or declassify the information. The Council shall obtain the opinion of the Commission before taking any action on a request from a Member State.

3. The provisions of Articles 12 and 13 shall not apply to information subject to a security grading.

Nevertheless, provided that the appropriate security measures are observed,

a. the information referred to in Articles 12 and 13 may be communicated by the Commission:

i. to a Joint Undertaking;

ii. to a person or undertaking other than a Joint Undertaking, through the Member State in whose territory that person or undertaking operates;

b. the information referred to in Article 13 may be communicated by a Member State to a person or to an undertaking other than a Joint Undertaking, operating in the territory of that State, provided that the Commission is notified of this communication;

c. each Member State has, however, the right to require the Commission to grant a license under Article 12 to meet the needs of that State or those of a person or undertaking operating in its territory.

Article 25

1. A Member State notifying the existence or communicating the contents of an application for a patent or utility model relating to a subject specified in Article 16(1) or (2) shall, where appropriate, draw attention to the need to apply a given security grading for defense reasons, at the same time stating the probable duration of such grading.

The Commission shall pass on to the other Member States all communications received in accordance with the preceding subparagraph. The Commission and the Member States shall take those measures which, under the security regulations, correspond to the grading required by the State of origin.

2. The Commission may also pass on these communications to Joint Undertakings or, through a Member State, to a person or to an undertaking other than a Joint Undertaking operating in the territory of that State.

Inventions which are the subject of applications referred to in paragraph 1 may be used only with the consent of the applicant or in accordance with Articles 17 to 23.

The communications and, where appropriate, the use referred to in this paragraph shall be subject to the measures which, under the security regulations, correspond to the security grading required by the State of origin.

The communications shall in all cases be subject to the consent of the State of origin. Consent to communication and use may be withheld only for defense reasons.
3. At the request of the Commission or of a Member State, the Council may, acting unanimously, at any time apply another grading or declassify the information. The Council shall obtain the opinion of the Commission before taking any action on a request from a Member State.

Article 26

1. Where information covered by patents, patent applications, provisionally protected patent rights, utility models or applications for utility models has been classified in accordance with Articles 24 and 25, the States which have applied for such classification may not refuse to allow corresponding applications to be filed in the other Member States.
Each Member State shall take the necessary measures to maintain the security of such rights and applications in accordance with the procedure laid down in its own laws and regulations.
2. No applications relating to information classified in accordance with Article 24 may be filed outside the Member States except with the unanimous consent of the latter. Should Member States fail to make known their attitude, their consent shall be deemed to have been obtained on the expiry of six months from the date on which the information was communicated to the Member States by the Commission.

Article 27

Compensation for any damage suffered by the applicant as a result of classification for defense reasons shall be governed by the provisions of the national laws of the Member States and shall be the responsibility of the State which applied for such classification or which either obtained the upgrading or extension of the classification or caused the filing of applications outside the Community to be prohibited.
Where several Member States have either obtained the upgrading or extension of the classification or caused the filing of applications outside the Community to be prohibited, they shall be jointly responsible for making good any damage arising out of their action.
The Community may not claim any compensation under this Article.

Section 4
Special provisions

Article 28

Where, as a result of their communication to the Commission, unpublished applications for patents or utility models, or patents or utility models classified for defense reasons, are improperly used or come to the knowledge of an unauthorized person, the Community shall make good the damage suffered by the party concerned.
Without prejudice to its own rights against the person responsible for the damage, the Community shall, to the extent that it has made good such damage, acquire any rights of action enjoyed by those concerned against third parties. This shall not affect the right of the Community to take action against the person responsible for the damage in accordance with the general provisions in force.

Article 29

Where an agreement or contract for the exchange of scientific or industrial information in the nuclear field between a Member State, a person or an undertaking on the one hand, and a third State, an international organization or a national of a third State on the other, requires, on either part, the signature of a State acting in its sovereign capacity, it shall be concluded by the Commission.
Subject to the provisions of Articles 103 and 104, the Commission may, however, on such conditions as it considers appropriate, authorize a Member State, a person or an undertaking to conclude such agreements.

Chapter 3
HEALTH AND SAFETY

Article 30

Basic standards shall be laid down within the Community for the protection of the health of workers and the general public against the dangers arising from ionising radiations.
The expression basic standards' means:
a. maximum permissible doses compatible with adequate safety;
b. maximum permissible levels of exposure and contamination;
c. the fundamental principles governing the health surveillance of workers.

Article 31

The basic standards shall be worked out by the Commission after it has obtained the opinion of a group of persons appointed by the Scientific and Technical Committee from among scientific experts, and in particular public health experts, in the Member States. The Commission shall obtain the opinion of the Economic and Social Committee on these basic standards.
After consulting the European Parliament the Council shall, on a proposal from the Commission, which shall forward to it the opinions obtained from these Committees, establish the basic standards; the Council shall act by a qualified majority.

Article 32

At the request of the Commission or of a Member State, the basic standards may be revised or supplemented in accordance with the procedure laid down in Article 31. The Commission shall examine any request made by a Member State.

Article 33

Each Member State shall lay down the appropriate provisions, whether by legislation, regulation or administrative action, to ensure compliance with the basic standards which have been established and shall take the necessary measures with regard to teaching, education and vocational training.
The Commission shall make appropriate recommendations for harmonizing the provisions applicable in this field in the Member States.
To this end, the Member States shall communicate to the Commission the provisions applicable at the date of entry into force of this Treaty and any subsequent draft provisions of the same kind.
Any recommendations the Commission may wish to issue with regard to such draft provisions shall be made within three months of the date on which such draft provisions are communicated.

Article 34

Any Member State in whose territories particularly dangerous experiments are to take place shall take additional health and safety measures, on which it shall first obtain the opinion of the Commission.
The assent of the Commission shall be required where the effects of such experiments are liable to affect the territories of other Member States.

Article 35

Each Member State shall establish the facilities necessary to carry out continuous monitoring of the level of radioactivity in the air, water and soil and to ensure compliance with the basic standards.
The Commission shall have the right of access to such facilities; it may verify their operation and efficiency.

Article 36

The appropriate authorities shall periodically communicate information on the checks referred to in Article 35 to the Commission so that it is kept informed of the level of radioactivity to which the public is exposed.

Article 37

Each Member State shall provide the Commission with such general data relating to any plan for the disposal of radioactive waste in whatever form as will make it possible to determine whether the implementation of such plan is liable to result in the radioactive contamination of the water, soil or airspace of another Member State.
The Commission shall deliver its opinion within six months, after consulting the group of experts referred to in Article 31.

Article 38

The Commission shall make recommendations to the Member States with regard to the level of radioactivity in the air, water and soil.
In cases of urgency, the Commission shall issue a directive requiring the Member State concerned to take, within a period laid down by the Commission, all necessary measures to prevent infringement of the basic standards and to ensure compliance with regulations.
Should the State in question fail to comply with the Commission directive within the period laid down, the Commission or any Member State concerned may forthwith, by way of derogation from Articles 141 and 142, bring the matter before the Court of Justice.

Article 39

The Commission shall set up within the framework of the Joint Nuclear Research Center, as soon as the latter has been established, a health and safety documentation and study section.

This section shall in particular have the task of collecting the documentation and information referred to in Articles 33, 36 and 37 and of assisting the Commission in carrying out the tasks assigned to it by this Chapter.

Chapter 4
INVESTMENT

Article 40

In order to stimulate action by persons and undertakings and to facilitate coordinated development of their investment in the nuclear field, the Commission shall periodically publish illustrative programmes indicating in particular nuclear energy production targets and all the types of investment required for their attainment.
The Commission shall obtain the opinion of the Economic and Social Committee on such programmes before their publication.

Article 41

Persons and undertakings engaged in the industrial activities listed in Annex II to this Treaty shall communicate to the Commission investment projects relating to new installations and also to replacements or conversions which fulfil the criteria as to type and size laid down by the Council on a proposal from the Commission.
The list of industrial activities referred to above may be altered by the Council, acting by a qualified majority on a proposal from the Commission, which shall first obtain the opinion of the Economic and Social Committee.

Article 42

The projects referred to in Article 41 shall be communicated to the Commission and, for information purposes, to the Member State concerned not later than three months before the first contracts are concluded with the suppliers or, if the work is to be carried out by the undertaking with its own resources, three months before the work begins.
The Council may, acting on a proposal from the Commission, alter this time limit.

Article 43

The Commission shall discuss with the persons or undertakings all aspects of investment projects which relate to the objectives of this Treaty.
It shall communicate its views to the Member State concerned.

Article 44

The Commission may, with the consent of the Member States, persons and undertakings concerned, publish any investment projects communicated to it.

Chapter 5
JOINT UNDERTAKINGS

Article 45

Undertakings which are of fundamental importance to the development of the nuclear industry in the Community may be established as Joint Undertakings within the meaning of this Treaty, in accordance with the following Articles.

Article 46

1. Every project for establishing a Joint Undertaking, whether originating from the Commission, a Member State or any other quarter, shall be the subject of an inquiry by the Commission.
For this purpose, the Commission shall obtain the views of Member States and of any public or private body which in its opinion can usefully advise it.
2. The Commission shall forward to the Council any project for establishing a Joint Undertaking, together with its reasoned opinion.
If the Commission delivers a favourable opinion on the need for the proposed Joint Undertaking, it shall submit proposals to the Council concerning:
a. location;
b. statutes;
c. the scale of and timetable for financing;
d. possible participation by the Community in the financing of the Joint Undertaking;
e. possible participation by a third State, an international organization or a national of a third State in the financing or management of the Joint Undertaking;
f. the conferring of any or all of the advantages listed in Annex III to this Treaty. The Commission shall attach a detailed report on the project as a whole.

Article 47

The Council may, when the matter has been submitted to it by the Commission, request the latter to supply such further information or to undertake such further inquiries as the Council may consider necessary.
If the Council, acting by a qualified majority, considers that a project forwarded by the Commission with an unfavourable opinion should nevertheless be carried out,

the Commission shall submit to the Council the proposals and the detailed report referred to in Article 46.
Where the opinion of the Commission is favourable or in the case referred to in the preceding paragraph, the Council shall act by a qualified majority on each of the proposals from the Commission.
The Council shall, however, act unanimously in respect of:
a. participation by the Community in the financing of the Joint Undertaking;
b. participation by a third State, an international organization or a national of a third State in the financing or management of the Joint Undertaking.

Article 48

The Council may, acting unanimously on a proposal from the Commission, make applicable to each Joint Undertaking any or all of the advantages listed in Annex III to this Treaty; each Member State shall for its part ensure that these advantages are conferred.
The Council may, in accordance with the same procedure, lay down the conditions governing the conferment of these advantages.

Article 49

Joint Undertakings shall be established by Council decision.
Each Joint Undertaking shall have legal personality.
In each of the Member States, it shall enjoy the most extensive legal capacity accorded to legal persons under their respective national laws; it may, in particular, acquire or dispose of movable and immovable property and may be a party to legal proceedings.
Save as otherwise provided in this Treaty or in its own statutes, each Joint Undertaking shall be governed by the rules applying to industrial or commercial undertakings; its statutes may make subsidiary reference to the national laws of the Member States.
Save where jurisdiction is conferred upon the Court of Justice by this Treaty, disputes in which Joint Undertakings are concerned shall be determined by the appropriate national courts or tribunals.

Article 50

The statutes of Joint Undertakings shall be amended, where necessary, in accordance with the special provisions which they contain for this purpose.
Such amendments shall not, however, enter into force until they have been approved by the Council, acting in accordance with the procedure laid down in Article 47 on a proposal from the Commission.

Article 51

The Commission shall be responsible for carrying out all decisions of the Council relating to the establishment of Joint Undertakings until the bodies responsible for the operation of such undertakings have been set up.

Chapter 6
SUPPLIES

Article 52

1. The supply of ores, source materials and special fissile materials shall be ensured, in accordance with the provisions of this Chapter, by means of a common supply policy on the principle of equal access to sources of supply.
2. For this purpose and under the conditions laid down in this Chapter:
a. all practices designed to secure a privileged position for certain users shall be prohibited;
b. an Agency is hereby established; it shall have a right of option on ores, source materials and special fissile materials produced in the territories of Member States and an exclusive right to conclude contracts relating to the supply of ores, source materials and special fissile materials coming from inside the Community or from outside.

The Agency may not discriminate in any way between users on grounds of the use which they intend to make of the supplies requested unless such use is unlawful or is found to be contrary to the conditions imposed by suppliers outside the Community on the consignment in question.

Section 1
The Agency

Article 53

The Agency shall be under the supervision of the Commission, which shall issue directives to it, possess a right of veto over its decisions and appoint its Director General and Deputy Director General.

Any act, whether implied or expressed, performed by the Agency in the exercise of its right of option or of its exclusive right to conclude supply contracts, may be referred by the parties concerned to the Commission, which shall give a decision thereon within one month.

Article 54

The Agency shall have legal personality and financial autonomy.
The Council shall lay down the statutes of the Agency, acting by a qualified majority on a proposal from the Commission.
The statutes may be amended in accordance with the same procedure.
The statutes shall determine the Agency's capital and the terms upon which it is to be subscribed. The major part of the capital shall always belong to the Community and to the Member States. The contributions to the capital shall be determined by common accord of the Member States.
The rules for the commercial management of the activities of the Agency shall be laid down in the statutes. The latter may provide for a charge on transactions to defray the operating expenses of the Agency.

Article 55

The Member States shall communicate or cause to be communicated to the Agency all the information necessary to enable it to exercise its right of option and its exclusive right to conclude supply contracts.

Article 56

The Member States shall be responsible for ensuring that the Agency may operate freely in their territories.
They may establish one or more bodies having authority to represent, in relations with the Agency, producers and users in the non European territories under their jurisdiction.

Section 2
Ores, source materials and special fissile materials coming from inside the Community

Article 57

1. The right of option of the Agency shall cover:
a. the acquisition of rights to use and consume materials owned by the Community under the provisions of Chapter 8;
b. the acquisition of the right of ownership in all other cases.
2. The Agency shall exercise its right of option by concluding contracts with producers of ores, source materials and special fissile materials.

Subject to Articles 58, 62 and 63, every producer shall offer to the Agency the ores, source materials or special fissile materials which he produces within the territories of Member States before they are used, transferred or stored.

Article 58

Where a producer carries out several stages of production from extraction of the ore up to and including production of the metal, he may offer the product to the Agency at whichever stage of production he chooses.
The same shall apply to two or more connected undertakings, where the connection has been duly communicated to the Commission and discussed with it in accordance with the procedures laid down in Articles 43 and 44.

Article 59

If the Agency does not exercise its right of option on the whole or any part of the output of a producer, the latter:

a. may, either by using his own resources or under contract, process or cause to be processed the ores, source materials or special fissile materials, provided that he offers to the Agency the product of such processing;
b. shall be authorized by a decision of the Commission to dispose of his available production outside the Community, provided that the terms he offers are not more favourable than those previously offered to the Agency. However, special fissile materials may be exported only through the Agency and in accordance with the provisions of Article 62.

The Commission may not grant such authorization if the recipients of the supplies fail to satisfy it that the general interests of the Community will be safeguarded or if the terms and conditions of such contracts are contrary to the objectives of this Treaty.

Article 60

Potential users shall periodically inform the Agency of the supplies they require, specifying the quantities, the physical and chemical nature, the place of origin, the intended use, delivery dates and price terms, which are to form the terms and conditions of the supply contract which they wish to conclude.
Similarly, producers shall inform the Agency of offers which they are able to make, stating all the specifications, and in particular the duration of contracts, required to enable their production programmes to be drawn up. Such contracts shall be of not more than 10 years duration save with the agreement of the Commission.

The Agency shall inform all potential users of the offers and of the volume of applications which it has received and shall call upon them to place their orders by a specified time limit.
When the Agency has received all such orders, it shall make known the terms on which it can meet them.
If the Agency cannot meet in their entirety all the orders received, it shall, subject to the provisions of Articles 68 and 69, share out the supplies proportionately among the orders relating to each offer.
Agency rules, which shall require approval by the Commission, shall determine the manner in which demand is to be balanced against supply.

Article 61

The Agency shall meet all orders unless prevented from so doing by legal or material obstacles.
When concluding a contract, the Agency may, while complying with the provisions of Article 52, require users to make appropriate advance payments either as security or to assist in meeting the Agency's own long term commitments to producers where these are essential to carrying out the order.

Article 62

1. The Agency shall exercise its right of option on special fissile materials produced in the territories of Member States in order:
a. to meet demand from users within the Community in accordance with Article 60; or
b. to store such materials itself; or
c. to export such materials with the authorization of the Commission which shall comply with the second subparagraph of Article 59(b).
2. Nevertheless, while continuing to be subject to the provisions of Chapter 7, such materials and any fertile wastes shall be left in the possession of the producer, so that he may:
a. store them with the authorization of the Agency; or
b. use them within the limits of his own requirements; or
c. make them available to undertakings in the Community, within the limits of their requirements, where for carrying out a programme duly communicated to the Commission, these undertakings have with the producer a direct connection which has neither the aim nor the effect of limiting production, technical development or investment or of improperly creating inequalities between users in the Community.

3. The provisions of Article 89(1)(a) shall apply to special fissile materials which are produced in the territories of Member States and on which the Agency has not exercised its right of option.

Article 63

Ores, source materials and special fissile materials produced by Joint Undertakings shall be allotted to users in accordance with the rules laid down in the statutes or agreements of such undertakings.

Section 3
Ores, source materials and special fissile materials coming from outside the Community

Article 64

The Agency, acting where appropriate within the framework of agreements concluded between the Community and a third State or an international organization, shall, subject to the exceptions provided for in this Treaty, have the exclusive right to enter into agreements or contracts whose principal aim is the supply of ores, source materials or special fissile materials coming from outside the Community.

Article 65

Article 60 shall apply applications from users and to contracts between users and the Agency relating to the supply of ores, source materials or special fissile materials coming from outside the Community.

The Agency may, however, decide on the geographical origin of supplies provided that conditions which are at least as favourable as those specified in the order are thereby secured for the user.

Article 66

Should the Commission find, on application by the users concerned, that the Agency is not in a position to deliver within a reasonable period of time all or part of the supplies ordered, or that it can only do so at excessively high prices, the users shall have the right to conclude directly contracts relating to supplies from outside the Community, provided that such contracts meet in essential respects the requirements specified in their orders.

This right shall be granted for a period of one year; it may be extended if the situation which justified its granting continues.

Users who avail themselves of the right provided for in this Article shall communicate to the Commission the direct contracts which they propose to conclude. The Commission may, within one month, object to the conclusion of such contracts if they are contrary to the objectives of this Treaty.

Section 4
Prices

Article 67

Save where exceptions are provided for in this Treaty, prices shall be determined as a result of balancing supply against demand as provided in Article 60; the national regulations of the Member States shall not contravene such provisions.

Article 68

Pricing practices designed to secure a privileged position for certain users in violation of the principle of equal access laid down in the provisions of this Chapter shall be prohibited.
If the Agency finds that any such practices are being employed it shall report them to the Commission.
The Commission may, if it accepts the findings, set the prices of the offers in issue at a level compatible with the principle of equal access.

Article 69

The Council may fix prices, acting unanimously on a proposal from the Commission.
When the Agency lays down, in pursuance of Article 60, the terms on which orders can be met, it may propose to the users who have placed orders that prices be equalized.

Section 5
Provisions relating to supply policy

Article 70

Within the limits set by the budget of the Community, the Commission may, on such conditions as it shall determine, give financial support to prospecting programmes in the territories of Member States.
The Commission may make recommendations to the Member States with a view to the development of prospecting for and exploitation of mineral deposits.

The Member States shall submit annually to the Commission a report on the development of prospecting and production, on probable reserves and on investment in mining which has been made or is planned in their territories. The reports shall be submitted to the Council, together with an opinion from the Commission which shall state in particular what action has been taken by Member States on recommendations made to them under the preceding paragraph.
If, when the matter has been submitted to it by the Commission, the Council finds by a qualified majority that, although the prospects for extraction appear economically justified on a long term basis, prospecting activities and the expansion of mining operations continue to be markedly inadequate, the Member State concerned shall, for as long as it has failed to remedy this situation, be deemed to have waived, both for itself and for its nationals, the right of equal access to other sources of supply within the Community.

Article 71

The Commission shall make all appropriate recommendations to Member States with regard to revenue or mining regulations.

Article 72

The Agency may, from material available inside or outside the Community, build up the necessary commercial stocks to facilitate supplies to or normal deliveries by the Community.
The Commission may, where necessary, decide to build up emergency stocks. The method of financing such stocks shall be approved by the Council, acting by a qualified majority on a proposal from the Commission.

Section 6
Special provisions

Article 73

Where an agreement or contract between a Member State, a person or an undertaking on the one hand, and a third State, an international organization or a national of a third State on the other, provides inter alia for delivery of products which come within the province of the Agency, the prior consent of the Commission shall be required for the conclusion or renewal of that agreement or contract, as far as delivery of the products is concerned.

Article 74

The Commission may exempt from the provisions of this Chapter the transfer, import or export of small quantities of ores, source materials or special fissile materials such as are normally used in research.
The Agency shall be notified of every transfer, import or export operation effected by virtue of this provision.

Article 75

The provisions of this Chapter shall not apply to commitments relating to the processing, conversion or shaping of ores, source materials or special fissile materials and entered into:

a. by several persons or undertakings, where the material is to return to the original person or undertaking after being processed, converted or shaped; or
b. by a person or undertaking and an international organization or a national of a third State, where the material is processed, converted or shaped outside the Community and then returned to the original person or undertaking; or
c. by a person or undertaking and an international organization or a national of a third State, where the material is processed, converted or shaped inside the Community and is then returned either to the original organization or national or to any other consignee likewise outside the Community designated by such organization or national.

The persons and undertakings concerned shall, however, notify the Agency of the existence of such commitments and, as soon as the contracts are signed, of the quantities of material involved in the movements. The Commission may prevent the commitments referred to in subparagraph (b) from being undertaken if it considers that the conversion or shaping cannot be carried out efficiently and safely and without the loss of material to the detriment of the Community.
The materials to which such commitments relate shall be subject in the territories of the Member States to the safeguards laid down in Chapter 7. The provisions of Chapter 8 shall not, however, be applicable to special fissile materials covered by the commitments referred to in subparagraph (c).

Article 76

On the initiative of a Member State or of the Commission, and particularly if unforeseen circumstances create a situation of general shortage, the Council may, acting unanimously on a proposal from the Commission and after consulting the European Parliament, amend the provisions of this Chapter. The Commission shall inquire into any request made by a Member State.

Seven years after the entry into force of this Treaty, the Council may confirm these provisions in their entirety. Failing confirmation, new provisions relating to the subject matter of this Chapter shall be adopted in accordance with the procedure laid down in the preceding paragraph.

Chapter 7
SAFEGUARDS

Article 77

In accordance with the provisions of this Chapter, the Commission shall satisfy itself that, in the territories of Member States:

a. ores, source materials and special fissile materials are not diverted from their intended uses as declared by the users;
b. the provisions relating to supply and any particular safeguarding obligations assumed by the Community under an agreement concluded with a third State or an international organization are complied with.

Article 78

Anyone setting up or operating an installation for the production, separation or other use of source materials or special fissile materials or for the processing of irradiated nuclear fuels shall declare to the Commission the basic technical characteristics of the installations, to the extent that knowledge of these characteristics is necessary for the attainment of the objectives set out in Article 77.

The Commission must approve the techniques to be used for the chemical processing of irradiated materials, to the extent necessary to attain the objectives set out in Article 77.

Article 79

The Commission shall require that operating records be kept and produced in order to permit accounting for ores, source materials and special fissile materials used or produced. The same requirement shall apply in the case of the transport of source materials and special fissile materials.

Those subject to such requirements shall notify the authorities of the Member State concerned of any communications they make to the Commission pursuant to Article 78 and to the first paragraph of this Article.

The nature and the extent of the requirements referred to in the first paragraph of this Article shall be defined in a regulation made by the Commission and approved by the Council.

Article 80

The Commission may require that any excess special fissile materials recovered or obtained as by products and not actually being used or ready for use shall be deposited with the Agency or in other stores which are or can be supervised by the Commission. Special fissile materials deposited in this way must be returned forthwith to those concerned at their request.

Article 81

The Commission may send inspectors into the territories of Member States. Before sending an inspector on his first assignment in the territory of a Member State, the Commission shall consult the State concerned; such consultation shall suffice to cover all future assignments of this inspector.
On presentation of a document establishing their authority, inspectors shall at all times have access to all places and data and to all persons who, by reason of their occupation, deal with materials, equipment or installations subject to the safeguards provided for in this Chapter, to the extent necessary in order to apply such safeguards to ores, source materials and special fissile materials and to ensure compliance with the provisions of Article 77. Should the State concerned so request, inspectors appointed by the Commission shall be accompanied by representatives of the authorities of that State; however, the inspectors shall not thereby be delayed or otherwise impeded in the performance of their duties.
If the carrying out of an inspection is opposed, the Commission shall apply to the President of the Court of Justice for an order to ensure that the inspection be carried out compulsorily. The President of the Court of Justice shall give a decision within three days.
If there is danger in delay, the Commission may itself issue a written order, in the form of a decision, to proceed with the inspection. This order shall be submitted without delay to the President of the Court of Justice for subsequent approval.
After the order or decision has been issued, the authorities of the State concerned shall ensure that the inspectors have access to the places specified in the order or decision.

Article 82

Inspectors shall be recruited by the Commission.
They shall be responsible for obtaining and verifying the records referred to in Article 79. They shall report any infringement to the Commission.
The Commission may issue a directive calling upon the Member State concerned to take, by a time limit set by the Commission, all measures necessary to bring such infringement to an end; it shall inform the Council thereof.

If the Member State does not comply with the Commission directive by the time limit set, the Commission or any Member State concerned may, in derogation from Articles 141 and 142, refer the matter to the Court of Justice direct.

Article 83

1. In the event of an infringement on the part of persons or undertakings of the obligations imposed on them by this Chapter, the Commission may impose sanctions on such persons or undertakings.
These sanctions shall be in order of severity:
a. a warning;
b. the withdrawal of special benefits such as financial or technical assistance;
c. the placing of the undertaking for a period not exceeding four months under the administration of a person or board appointed by common accord of the Commission and the State having jurisdiction over the undertaking;
d. total or partial withdrawal of source materials or special fissile materials.
2. Decisions taken by the Commission in implementation of paragraph 1 and requiring the surrender of materials shall be enforceable. They may be enforced in the territories of Member States in accordance with Article 164.
By way of derogation from Article 157, appeals brought before the Court of Justice against decisions of the Commission which impose any of the sanctions provided for in paragraph 1 shall have suspensory effect. The Court of Justice may, however, on application by the Commission or by any Member State concerned, order that the decision be enforced forthwith.
There shall be an appropriate legal procedure to ensure the protection of interests that have been prejudiced.
3. The Commission may make any recommendations to Member States concerning laws or regulations which are designed to ensure compliance in their territories with the obligations arising under this Chapter.
4. Member States shall ensure that sanctions are enforced and, where necessary, that the infringements are remedied by those committing them.

Article 84

In the application of the safeguards, no discrimination shall be made on grounds of the use for which ores, source materials and special fissile materials are intended.
The scope of and procedure for the safeguards and the powers of the bodies responsible for their application shall be confined to the attainment of the objectives set out in this Chapter.
The safeguards may not extend to materials intended to meet defense requirements which are in the course of being specially processed for this purpose or which, after

being so processed, are, in accordance with an operational plan, placed or stored in a military establishment.

Article 85

Where new circumstances so require, the procedures for applying the safeguards laid down in this Chapter may, at the request of a Member State or of the Commission, be adapted by the Council, acting unanimously on a proposal from the Commission and after consulting the European Parliament. The Commission shall examine any such request made by a Member State.

Chapter 8
PROPERTY OWNERSHIP

Article 86

Special fissile materials shall be the property of the Community.
The Community's right of ownership shall extend to all special fissile materials which are produced or imported by a Member State, a person or an undertaking and are subject to the safeguards provided for in Chapter 7.

Article 87

Member States, persons or undertakings shall have the unlimited right of use and consumption of special fissile materials which have properly come into their possession, subject to the obligations imposed on them by this Treaty, in particular those relating to safeguards, the right of option conferred on the Agency and health and safety.

Article 88

The Agency shall keep a special account in the name of the Community, called Special Fissile Materials Financial Account'.

Article 89

1. In the Special Fissile Materials Financial Account:
a. the value of special fissile materials left in the possession of or put at the disposal of a Member State, person or undertaking shall be credited to the Community and debited to that Member State, person or undertaking;

b. the value of special fissile materials which are produced or imported by a Member State, person or undertaking and become the property of the Community shall be debited to the Community and credited to that Member State, person or undertaking. A similar entry shall be made when a Member State, person or undertaking restores to the Community special fissile materials previously left in the possession of or put at the disposal of that State, person or undertaking.

2. Variations in value affecting the quantities of special fissile material shall be expressed for accounting purposes in such a way as not to give rise to any loss or gain to the Community. Any loss or gain shall be borne by or accrue to the holder.

3. Balances arising from the transactions referred to above shall become payable forthwith upon the request of the creditor.

4. Where the Agency undertakes transactions for its own account, it shall, for the purposes of this Chapter, be deemed to be an undertaking.

Article 90

Where new circumstances so require, the provisions of this Chapter relating to the Community's right of ownership may, at the request of a Member State or of the Commission, be adjusted by the Council, acting unanimously on a proposal from the Commission and after consulting the European Parliament. The Commission shall examine any such request made by a Member State.

Article 91

The system of ownership applicable to all objects, materials and assets which are not vested in the Community under this Chapter shall be determined by the law of each Member State.

Chapter 9
THE NUCLEAR COMMON MARKET

Article 92

The provisions of this Chapter shall apply to the goods and products specified in the lists forming Annex IV to this Treaty.

These lists may, at the request of the Commission or of a Member State, be amended by the Council, acting on a proposal from the Commission.

Article 93

Member States shall abolish between themselves, one year after the entry into force of this Treaty, all customs duties on imports and exports or charges having equivalent effect, and all quantitative restrictions on imports and exports, in respect of:

a. products in List A1 and A2;
b. products in List B if subject to a Common Customs Tariff and accompanied by a certificate issued by the Commission stating that they are intended to be used for nuclear purposes.

Non European territories under the jurisdiction of a Member State may, however, continue to levy import and export duties or charges having equivalent effect where they are of an exclusively fiscal nature. The rates of such duties and charges and the system governing them shall not give rise to any discrimination between that State and the other Member States.

Article 94

The Member States shall set up a Common Customs Tariff in accordance with the following provisions:

a. with regard to products specified in List A1 , the Common Customs Tariff shall be fixed at the level of the lowest tariff in force in any Member State on 1 January 1957;
b. with regard to products specified in List A2, the Commission shall take all appropriate measures to ensure that negotiations between Member States shall begin within three months of the entry into force of this Treaty. If, on some of these products, no agreement can be reached within one year of the entry into force of this Treaty, the Council shall, acting by a qualified majority on a proposal from the Commission, determine the applicable duties in the Common Customs Tariff;
c. the Common Customs Tariff on the products specified in Lists A1 and A2 shall be applied from the end of the first year following the entry into force of this Treaty.

Article 95

The Council may, acting unanimously on a proposal from the Commission, decide on the earlier application of the duties in the Common Customs Tariff on products in List B where such a measure would tend to contribute to the development of nuclear energy in the Community.

Article 96

The Member States shall abolish all restrictions based on nationality affecting the right of nationals of any Member State to take skilled employment in the field of nuclear energy, subject to the limitations resulting from the basic requirements of public policy, public security or public health.
After consulting the European Parliament, the Council may, acting by a qualified majority on a proposal from the Commission, which shall first request the opinion of the Economic and Social Committee, issue directives for the application of this Article.

Article 97

No restrictions based on nationality may be applied to natural or legal persons, whether public or private, under the jurisdiction of a Member State, where they desire to participate in the construction of nuclear installations of a scientific or industrial nature in the Community.

Article 98

Member States shall take all measures necessary to facilitate the conclusion of insurance contracts covering nuclear risks.
Within two years of the entry into force of this Treaty, the Council, acting by a qualified majority on a proposal from the Commission, which shall first request the opinion of the Economic and Social Committee, shall, after consulting the European Parliament, issue directives for the application of this Article.

Article 99

The Commission may make any recommendations for facilitating movements of capital intended to finance the industrial activities listed in Annex II to this Treaty.

Article 100

Each Member State undertakes to authorize, in the currency of the Member State in which the creditor or the beneficiary resides, any payments connected with the movement of goods, services or capital, and any transfers of capital and earnings, to the extent that the movement of goods, services, capital and persons between Member States has been liberalized pursuant to this Treaty.

Chapter 10
EXTERNAL RELATIONS

Article 101

The Community may, within the limits of its powers and jurisdiction, enter into obligations by concluding agreements or contracts with a third State, an international organization or a national of a third State.
Such agreements or contracts shall be negotiated by the Commission in accordance with the directives of the Council: they shall be concluded by the Commission with the approval of the Council, which shall act by a qualified majority.
Agreements or contracts whose implementation does not require action by the Council and can be effected within the limits of the relevant budget shall, however, be negotiated and concluded solely by the Commission; the Commission shall keep the Council informed.

Article 102

Agreements or contracts concluded with a third State, an international organization or a national of a third State to which, in addition to the Community, one or more Member States are parties, shall not enter into force until the Commission has been notified by all the Member States concerned that those agreements or contracts have become applicable in accordance with the provisions of their respective national laws.

Article 103

Member States shall communicate to the Commission draft agreements or contracts with a third State, an international organization or a national of a third State to the extent that such agreements or contracts concern matters within the purview of this Treaty.
If a draft agreement or contract contains clauses which impede the application of this Treaty, the Commission shall, within one month of receipt of such communication, make its comments known to the State concerned.
The State shall not conclude the proposed agreement or contract until it has satisfied the objections of the Commission or complied with a ruling by the Court of Justice, adjudicating urgently upon an application from the State, on the compatibility of the proposed clauses with the provisions of this Treaty. An application may be made to the Court of Justice at any time after the State has received the comments of the Commission.

Article 104

No person or undertaking concluding or renewing an agreement or contract with a third State, an international organization or a national of a third State after the entry into force of this Treaty may invoke that agreement or contract in order to evade the obligations imposed by this Treaty.

Each Member State shall take such measures as it considers necessary in order to communicate to the Commission, at the request of the latter, all information relating to agreements or contracts concluded after the entry into force of this Treaty, within the purview thereof, by a person or undertaking with a third State, an international organization or a national of a third State. The Commission may require such communication only for the purpose of verifying that such agreements or contracts do not contain clauses impeding the implementation of this Treaty.

On application by the Commission, the Court of Justice shall give a ruling on the compatibility of such agreements or contracts with the provisions of this Treaty.

Article 105

The provisions of this Treaty shall not be invoked so as to prevent the implementation of agreements or contracts concluded before its entry into force by a Member State, a person or an undertaking with a third State, an international organization or a national of a third State where such agreements or contracts have been communicated to the Commission not later than 30 days after the entry into force of this Treaty.

Agreements or contracts concluded between the signature and the entry into force of this Treaty by a person or an undertaking with a third State, an international organization or a national of a third State shall not, however, be invoked as grounds for failure to implement this Treaty if, in the opinion of the Court of Justice, ruling on an application from the Commission, one of the decisive reasons on the part of either of the parties in concluding the agreement or contract was an intention to evade the provisions of this Treaty.

Article 106

Member States which, before the entry into force of this Treaty, have concluded agreements with third States providing for cooperation in the field of nuclear energy shall be required to undertake jointly with the Commission the necessary negotiations with these third States in order to ensure that the rights and obligations arising out of such agreements shall as far as possible be assumed by the Community.

Any new agreement ensuing from such negotiations shall require the consent of the Member State or States signatory to the agreements referred to above and the approval of the Council, which shall act by a qualified majority.

TITLE III
PROVISIONS GOVERNING THE INSTITUTIONS

Chapter 1
THE INSTITUTIONS OF THE COMMUNITY

Section 1
The European Parliament

Article 107

The European Parliament, which shall consist of representatives of the peoples of the States brought together in the Community, shall exercise the advisory and supervisory powers which are conferred upon it by this Treaty.

Article 107a (*)

(*) As inserted by Article I(2) TEU.

The European Parliament may, acting by a majority of its Members, request the Commission to submit any appropriate proposal on matters on which it considers that a Community act is required for the purpose of implementing this Treaty.

Article 107b (*)

(*) As inserted by Article I(2) TEU.

In the course of its duties, the European Parliament may, at the request of a quarter of its Members, set up a temporary Committee of Inquiry to investigate, without prejudice to the powers conferred by this Treaty on other institutions or bodies, alleged contraventions or maladministration in the implementation of Community law, except where the alleged facts are being examined before a court and while the case is still subject to legal proceedings.
The temporary Committee of Inquiry shall cease to exist on the submission of its report.
The detailed provisions governing the exercise of the right of inquiry shall be determined by common accord of the European Parliament, the Council and the Commission.

Article 107c (*)

(*) As inserted by Article I(2) TEU.

Any citizen of the Union, and any natural or legal person residing or having its registered office in a Member State, shall have the right to address, individually or in association with other citizens or persons, a petition to the European Parliament on a matter which comes within the Community's fields of activity and which affects him, her or it directly.

Article 107d (*)

(*) As inserted by Article I(2) TEU.

1. The European Parliament shall appoint an Ombudsman empowered to receive complaints from any citizen of the Union or any natural or legal person residing or having its registered office in a Member State concerning instances of maladministration in the activities of the Community institutions or bodies, with the exception of the Court of Justice and the Court of First Instance acting in their judicial role.
In accordance with his duties, the Ombudsman shall conduct inquiries for which he finds grounds, either on his own initiative or on the basis of complaints submitted to him direct or through a Member of the European Parliament, except where the alleged facts are or have been the subject of legal proceedings. Where the Ombudsman establishes an instance of maladministration, he shall refer the matter to the institution concerned, which shall have a period of three months in which to inform of its views. The Ombudsman shall then forward a report to the European Parliament and the institution concerned. The person lodging the complaint shall be informed of the outcome of such inquiries.
The Ombudsman shall submit an annual report to the European Parliament on the outcome of his inquiries.
2. The Ombudsman shall be appointed after each election of the European Parliament for the duration of its term of office. The Ombudsman shall be eligible for reappointment.
The Ombudsman may be dismissed by the Court of Justice at the request of the European Parliament if he no longer fulfils the conditions required for the performance of his duties or if he is guilty of serious misconduct.
3. The Ombudsman shall be completely independent in the performance of his duties. In the performance of those duties he shall neither seek nor take instructions from any body. The Ombudsman may not, during his term of office, engage in any other occupation, whether gainful or not.

4. The European Parliament shall, after seeking an opinion from the Commission and with the approval of the Council acting by a qualified majority, lay down the regulations and general conditions governing the performance of the Ombudsman's duties.

Article 108

(Paragraphs 1 and 2 lapsed on 17 July 1979 in accordance with Article 14 of the Act [See Article 1 of that Act which reads as follows:
1. The representatives in the European Parliament of the peoples of the States brought together in the Community shall be elected by direct universal suffrage.]
[See *Article 2 of that Act which reads as follows:*

2. The number of representatives elected in each Member State is as follows:

Belgium	25
Denmark	16
Germany	99
Greece	25
Spain	64
France	87
Ireland	15
Italy	87
Luxembourg	6
Netherlands	31
Austria	21
Portugal	25
Finland	16
Sweden	22
United Kingdom	87] (*)

(*) Number of representatives as laid down by Article 11AA A/FIN/SWE in the version resulting from Article 5 AD AA A/FIN/SWE.
3. The European Parliament shall draw up proposals for elections by direct universal suffrage in accordance with a uniform procedure in all Member States. (*)
(*) On this point, see also Article 7(1) and (2) of the Act concerning the election of the representatives of the European Parliament.
The Council shall, acting unanimously after obtaining the assent of the European Parliament, which shall act by a majority of its component Members, lay down the appropriate provisions, which it shall recommend to Member States for adoption in accordance with their respective constitutional requirements. (**)
(**) Paragraph 3 as amended by Article I(3) TEU.

Article 109

The European Parliament shall hold an annual session. It shall meet, without requiring to be convened, on the second Tuesday in March. (***) (****)
(***) First paragraph as amended by Article 27(1) of the Merger Treaty.
(****) For the second sentence of this paragraph, see also Article 10(3) of the Act concerning the election of the representatives of the European Parliament.
The European Parliament may meet in extraordinary session at the request of a majority of its Members or at the request of the Council or of the Commission.

Article 110

The European Parliament shall elect its President and its officers from among its Members.
Members of the Commission may attend all meetings and shall, at their request, be heard on behalf of the Commission.
The Commission shall reply orally or in writing to questions put to it by the European Parliament or by its Members.
The Council shall be heard by the European Parliament in accordance with the conditions laid down by the Council in its Rules of Procedure.

Article 111

Save as otherwise provided in this Treaty, the European Parliament shall act by an absolute majority of the votes cast.
The Rules of Procedure shall determine the quorum.

Article 112

The European Parliament shall adopt its Rules of Procedure, acting by a majority of its Members.
The proceedings of the European Parliament shall be published in the manner laid down in its Rules of Procedure.

Article 113

The European Parliament shall discuss in open session the annual general report submitted to it by the Commission.

Article 114 (*)

(*) As amended by Article I(4) TEU.

If a motion of censure on the activities of the Commission is tabled before it, the European Parliament shall not vote thereon until at least three days after the motion has been tabled and only by open vote.
If the motion of censure is carried by a two thirds majority of the votes cast, representing a majority of the Members of the European Parliament, the Members of the Commission shall resign as a body. They shall continue to deal with current business until they are replaced in accordance with Article 127. In this case, the term of office of the Members of the Commission appointed to replace them shall expire on the date on which the term of office of the Members of the Commission obliged to resign as a body would have expired.

Section 2
The Council

Article 115

The Council shall carry out its duties and exercise its powers of decision in accordance with the provisions of this Treaty.
It shall take all measures within its powers to coordinate the actions of the Member States and of the Community.

Article 116 (*)

(*) As inserted by Article I(5) TEU.

The Council shall consist of a representative of each Member State at ministerial level, authorized to commit the government of that Member State.
The office of President shall be held in turn by each Member State in the Council for a term of six months in the order decided by the Council acting unanimously.
*** Second subparagraph as amended by Article 12 AA A/FIN/SWE. See also Council Decision of 1 January 1995 determining the order in which the office of President of the Council shall be held (see Volume I, p. 865).*

Article 117 (*)

(*) As inserted by Article I(5) TEU.

The Council shall meet when convened by its President on his own initiative or at the request of one of its Members or of the Commission.

Article 118

1. Save as otherwise provided in this Treaty, the Council shall act by a majority of its Members.

2. Where the Council is required to act by a qualified majority, the votes of its Members shall be weighted as follows:

Belgium	5
Denmark	3
Germany	10
Greece	5
Spain	8
France	10
Ireland	3
Italy	10
Luxembourg	2
Netherlands	5
Austria	4
Portugal	5
Finland	3
Sweden	4
United Kingdom	10

For their adoption, acts of the Council shall require at least:

- 62 votes in favour where this Treaty requires them to be adopted on a proposal from the Commission,
- 62 votes in favour, cast by at least 10 Members, in other cases. (*)

(*) Paragraph 2 as amended by Article 15 AA A/FIN/SWE in the version resulting from Article 8 AD AA A/FIN/SWE.

3. Abstentions by Members present in person or represented shall not prevent the adoption by the Council of acts which require unanimity.

Article 119

Where, in pursuance of this Treaty, the Council acts on a proposal from the Commission, unanimity shall be required for an act constituting an amendment to that proposal.
As long as the Council has not acted, the Commission may alter its original proposal, in particular where the European Parliament has been consulted on that proposal.

Article 120

Where a vote is taken, any Member of the Council may also act on behalf of not more than one other Member.

Article 121 (*)

(*) As inserted by Article I(6) TEU.

1. A committee consisting of the Permanent Representatives of the Member States shall be responsible for preparing the work of the Council and for carrying out the tasks assigned to it by the Council.
2. The Council shall be assisted by a General Secretariat, under the direction of a Secretary General. The Secretary General shall be appointed by the Council acting unanimously.
The Council shall decide on the organization of the General Secretariat.
3. The Council shall adopt its Rules of Procedure.

Article 122

The Council may request the Commission to undertake any studies which the Council considers desirable for the attainment of the common objectives and to submit to it any appropriate proposals.

Article 123 (**)

(**) As inserted by Article I(7) TEU.

The Council shall, acting by a qualified majority, determine the salaries, allowances and pensions of the President and Members of the Commission, and of the President, Judges, Advocates General and Registrar of the Court of Justice. It shall also, again by a qualified majority, determine any payment to be made instead of remuneration.

Section 3
The Commission

Article 124

In order to ensure the development of nuclear energy within the Community, the Commission shall:

- ensure that the provisions of this Treaty and the measures taken by the institutions pursuant thereto are applied;
- formulate recommendations or deliver opinions in the fields covered by this Treaty, if the Treaty expressly so provides or if the Commission considers it necessary;
- have its own power of decision and participate in the shaping of measures taken by the Council and by the European Parliament in the manner provided for in this Treaty;
- exercise the powers conferred on it by the Council for the implementation of the rules laid down by the latter.

Article 125 (*)

(*) As inserted by Article I(8) TEU.

The Commission shall publish annually, not later than one month before the opening of the session of the European Parliament, a general report on the activities of the Community.

Article 126 (*)

(*) As inserted by Article I(8) TEU.

1. The Commission shall consist of 20 Members, who shall be chosen on the grounds of their general competence and whose independence is beyond doubt. (**)
(**) First subparagraph of paragraph 1 as amended by Article 16 AA A/FIN/SWE in the version resulting from Article 9 AD AA A/FIN/SWE.
The number of Members of the Commission may be altered by the Council, acting unanimously. Only nationals of the Member States may be Members of the Commission.
The Commission must include at least one national of each of the Member States, but may not include more than two Members having the nationality of the same State.
2. The Members of the Commission shall, in the general interest of the Community, be completely independent in the performance of their duties.

In the performance of these duties, they shall neither seek nor take instructions from any government or from any other body. They shall refrain from any action incompatible with their duties. Each Member State undertakes to respect this principle and not to seek to influence the Members of the Commission in the performance of their tasks.
The Members of the Commission may not, during their term of office, engage in any other occupation, whether gainful or not. When entering upon their duties they shall give a solemn undertaking that, both during and after their term of office, they will respect the obligations arising therefrom and in particular their duty to behave with integrity and discretion as regards the acceptance, after they have ceased to hold office, of certain appointments or benefits. In the event of any breach of these obligations, the Court of Justice may, on application by the Council or the Commission, rule that the Member concerned be, according to the circumstances, either compulsorily retired in accordance with Article 129 or deprived of his right to a pension or other benefits in its stead.

Article 127 (*)

(*) As inserted by Article I(8) TEU.

1. The Members of the Commission shall be appointed, in accordance with the procedure referred to in paragraph 2, for a period of five years, subject, if need be, to Article 114.
Their term of office shall be renewable.
2. The governments of the Member States shall nominate by common accord, after consulting the European Parliament, the person they intend to appoint as President of the Commission.
The governments of the Member States shall, in consultation with the nominee for President, nominate the other persons whom they intend to appoint as Members of the Commission.
The President and the other Members of the Commission thus nominated shall be subject as a body to a vote of approval by the European Parliament. After approval by the European Parliament, the President and the other Members of the Commission shall be appointed by common accord of the governments of the Member States.
3. Paragraphs 1 and 2 shall be applied for the first time to the President and the other Members of the Commission whose term of office begins on 7 January 1995.
The President and the other Members of the Commission whose term of office begins on 7 January 1993 shall be appointed by common accord of the governments of the Member States. Their term of office shall expire on 6 January 1995.

Article 128 (*)

(*) As inserted by Article I(8) TEU.

Apart from normal replacement, or death, the duties of a Member of the Commission shall end when he resigns or is compulsorily retired.
The vacancy thus caused shall be filled for the remainder of the Member's term of office by a new Member appointed by common accord of the governments of the Member States. The Council may, acting unanimously, decide that such a vacancy need not be filled.
In the event of resignation, compulsory retirement or death, the President shall be replaced for the remainder of his term of office. The procedure laid down in Article 127(2) shall be applicable for the replacement of the President.
Save in the case of compulsory retirement under Article 129, Members of the Commission shall remain in office until they have been replaced.

Article 129 (*)

(*) As inserted by Article I(8) TEU.

If any Member of the Commission no longer fulfils the conditions required for the performance of his duties or if he has been guilty of serious misconduct, the Court of Justice may, on application by the Council or the Commission, compulsorily retire him.

Article 130 (*)

(*) As inserted by Article I(8) TEU.

The Commission may appoint a Vice President or two Vice Presidents from among its Members.

Article 131 (*)

(*) As inserted by Article I(8) TEU.

The Council and the Commission shall consult each other and shall settle by common accord their methods of cooperation.
The Commission shall adopt its Rules of Procedure so as to ensure that both it and its departments operate in accordance with the provisions of this Treaty. It shall ensure that these rules are published.

Article 132 (*)

(*) As inserted by Article I(8) TEU.

The Commission shall act by a majority of the number of Members provided for in Article 126.
A meeting of the Commission shall be valid only if the number of Members laid down in its Rules of Procedure is present.

Article 133

(Repealed)

Article 134

1. A Scientific and Technical Committee is hereby set up; it shall be attached to the Commission and shall have advisory status.
The Committee must be consulted where this Treaty so provides. The Committee may be consulted in all cases in which the Commission considers this appropriate.
2. The Committee shall consist of 38 Members, appointed by the Council after consultation with the Commission. (*)
(*) First subparagraph of paragraph 2 as amended by Article 26 AA A/FIN/SWE in the version resulting from Article 17 AD AA A/FIN/SWE.
The Members of the Committee shall be appointed in their personal capacity for five years. Their appointment shall be renewable. They shall not be bound by any mandatory instructions.
The Scientific and Technical Committee shall each year elect its chairman and officers from among its Members.

Article 135

The Commission may undertake any consultations and establish any study groups necessary to the performance of its tasks.

Section 4
The Court of Justice

Article 136

The Court of Justice shall ensure that in the interpretation and application of this Treaty the law is observed.

Article 137 (**)

(**) As amended by Article I(10) TEU.

The Court of Justice shall consist of 15 Judges. (***)
(***) First paragraph as amended by Article 17 AA A/FIN/SWE in the version resulting from Article 10 AD AA A/FIN/SWE.
The Court of Justice shall sit in plenary session. It may, however, form chambers, each consisting of three, five or seven Judges, either to undertake certain preparatory inquiries or to adjudicate on particular categories of cases in accordance with the rules laid down for these purposes. (*)
(*) Second paragraph as amended by Article 18 AA A/FIN/SWE.
The Court of Justice shall sit in plenary session when a Member State or a Community institution that is a party to the proceedings so requests.
Should the Court of Justice so request, the Council may, acting unanimously, increase the number of Judges and make the necessary adjustments to the second and third paragraphs of this Article and to the second paragraph of Article 139.

Article 138

The Court of Justice shall be assisted by eight Advocates General. However, a ninth Advocate General shall be appointed as from the date of accession until 6 October 2000. (**)
(**) First paragraph as amended by Article 20 AA A/FIN/SWE in the version resulting from Article 11 AD AA A/FIN/SWE.
It shall be the duty of the Advocate General, acting with complete impartiality and independence, to make, in open court, reasoned submissions on cases brought before the Court of Justice, in order to assist the Court in the performance of the task assigned to it in Article 136.
Should the Court of Justice so request, the Council may, acting unanimously, increase the number of Advocates General and make the necessary adjustments to the third paragraph of Article 139.

Article 139

The Judges and Advocates General shall be chosen from persons whose independence is beyond doubt and who possess the qualifications required for appointment to the highest judicial offices in their respective countries or who are jurisconsults of recognized competence; they shall be appointed by common accord of the governments of the Member States for a term of six years.

Every three years there shall be a partial replacement of the Judges. Eight and seven Judges shall be replaced alternately. (*)
(*) Second and third paragraphs as amended by Article 21AA A/FIN/SWE in the version resulting from Article 12 AD AA A/FIN/SWE.
Every three years there shall be a partial replacement of the Advocates General. Four Advocates General shall be replaced on each occasion. (*)
(*) Second and third paragraphs as amended by Article 21 AA A/FIN/SWE in the version resulting from Article 12 AD AA A/FIN/SWE.
Retiring Judges and Advocates General shall be eligible for reappointment.
The Judges shall elect the President of the Court of Justice from among their number for a term of three years. He may be re elected.

Article 140

The Court of Justice shall appoint its Registrar and lay down the rules governing his service.

Article 140a (**)

(**) As amended by Article I(11) TEU.

1. A Court of First Instance shall be attached to the Court of Justice with jurisdiction to hear and determine at first instance, subject to a right of appeal to the Court of Justice on points of law only and in accordance with the conditions laid down by the Statute, certain classes of action or proceeding defined in accordance with the conditions laid down in paragraph 2. The Court of First Instance shall not be competent to hear and determine questions referred for a preliminary ruling under Article 150.
2. At the request of the Court of Justice and after consulting the European Parliament and the Commission, the Council, acting unanimously, shall determine the classes of action or proceeding referred to in paragraph 1 and the composition of the Court of First Instance and shall adopt the necessary adjustments and additional provisions to the Statute of the Court of Justice. Unless the Council decides otherwise, the provisions of this Treaty relating to the Court of Justice, in particular the provisions of the Protocol on the Statute of the Court of Justice, shall apply to the Court of First Instance.
3. The Members of the Court of First Instance shall be chosen from persons whose independence is beyond doubt and who possess the ability required for appointment to judicial office; they shall be appointed by common accord of the governments of the Member States for a term of six years. The membership shall be partially renewed every three years. Retiring Members shall be eligible for re appointment.

4. The Court of First Instance shall establish its Rules of Procedure in agreement with the Court of Justice. Those rules shall require the unanimous approval of the Council.

Article 141

If the Commission considers that a Member State has failed to fulfil an obligation under this Treaty, it shall deliver a reasoned opinion on the matter after giving the State concerned the opportunity to submit its observations.
If the State concerned does not comply with the opinion within the period laid down by the Commission, the latter may bring the matter before the Court of Justice.

Article 142

A Member State which considers that another Member State has failed to fulfil an obligation under this Treaty may bring the matter before the Court of Justice.
Before a Member State brings an action against another Member State for an alleged infringement of an obligation under this Treaty, it shall bring the matter before the Commission.
The Commission shall deliver a reasoned opinion after each of the States concerned has been given the opportunity to submit its own case and its observations on the other party's case both orally and in writing.
If the Commission has not delivered an opinion within three months of the date on which the matter was brought before it, the absence of such opinion shall not prevent the matter from being brought before the Court of Justice.

Article 143 (*)

(*) As amended by Article I(12) TEU.

1. If the Court of Justice finds that a Member State has failed to fulfil an obligation under this Treaty, the State shall be required to take the necessary measures to comply with the judgment of the Court of Justice.
2. If the Commission considers that the Member State concerned has not taken such measures it shall, after giving that State the opportunity to submit its observations, issue a reasoned opinion specifying the points on which the Member State concerned has not complied with the judgment of the Court of Justice.
If the Member State concerned fails to take the necessary measures to comply with the Court's judgment within the time limit laid down by the Commission, the latter may bring the case before the Court of Justice. In so doing it shall specify the amount of the lump sum or penalty payment to be paid by the Member State concerned which it considers appropriate in the circumstances.

If the Court of Justice finds that the Member State concerned has not complied with its judgment it may impose a lump sum or penalty payment on it.
This procedure shall be without prejudice to Article 142.

Article 144

The Court of Justice shall have unlimited jurisdiction in:

a. proceedings instituted under Article 12 to have the appropriate terms fixed for the granting by the Commission of licenses or sub licenses;
b. proceedings instituted by persons or undertakings against sanctions imposed on them by the Commission under Article 83.

Article 145

If the Commission considers that a person or undertaking has committed an infringement of this Treaty to which the provisions of Article 83 do not apply, it shall call upon the Member State having jurisdiction over that person or undertaking to cause sanctions to be imposed in respect of the infringement in accordance with its national law.
If the State concerned does not comply with such a request within the period laid down by the Commission, the latter may bring an action before the Court of Justice to have the infringement of which the person or undertaking is accused established.

Article 146 (*)

(*) As amended by Article I(13) TEU.

The Court of Justice shall review the legality of acts of the Council and of the Commission, other than recommendations and opinions, and of acts of the European Parliament intended to produce legal effects vis à vis third parties.
It shall for this purpose have jurisdiction in actions brought by a Member State, the Council or the Commission on grounds of lack of competence, infringement of an essential procedural requirement, infringement of this Treaty or of any rule of law relating to its application, or misuse of powers.
The Court shall have jurisdiction under the same conditions in actions brought by the European Parliament for the purpose of protecting its prerogatives.
Any natural or legal person may, under the same conditions, institute proceedings against a decision addressed to that person or against a decision which, although in the form of a regulation or a decision addressed to another person, is of direct and individual concern to the former.

The proceedings provided for in this Article shall be instituted within two months of the publication of the measure, or of its notification to the plaintiff, or, in the absence thereof, of the day on which it came to the knowledge of the latter, as the case may be.

Article 147

If the action is well founded, the Court of Justice shall declare the act concerned to be void.
In the case of a regulation, however, the Court of Justice shall, if it considers this necessary, state which of the effects of the regulation which it has declared void shall be considered as definitive.

Article 148

Should the Council or the Commission, in infringement of this Treaty, fail to act, the Member States and the other institutions of the Community may bring an action before the Court of Justice to have the infringement established.
The action shall be admissible only if the institution concerned has first been called upon to act. If, within two months of being so called upon, the institution concerned has not defined its position, the action may be brought within a further period of two months.
Any natural or legal person may, under the conditions laid down in the preceding paragraphs, complain to the Court of Justice that an institution of the Community has failed to address to that person any act other than a recommendation or an opinion.

Article 149

The institution whose act has been declared void or whose failure to act has been declared contrary to this Treaty shall be required to take the necessary measures to comply with the judgment of the Court of Justice.
This obligation shall not affect any obligation which may result from the application of the second paragraph of Article 188.

Article 150

The Court of Justice shall have jurisdiction to give preliminary rulings concerning:
a. the interpretation of this Treaty;
b. the validity and interpretation of acts of the institutions of the Community;

c. the interpretation of the statutes of bodies established by an act of the Council, save where those statutes provide otherwise.

Where such a question is raised before any court or tribunal of a Member State, that court or tribunal may, if it considers that a decision on the question is necessary to enable it to give judgment, request the Court of Justice to give a ruling thereon.

Where any such question is raised in a case pending before a court or tribunal of a Member State, against whose decisions there is no judicial remedy under national law, that court or tribunal shall bring the matter before the Court of Justice.

Article 151

The Court of Justice shall have jurisdiction in disputes relating to the compensation for damage provided for in the second paragraph of Article 188.

Article 152

The Court of Justice shall have jurisdiction in any dispute between the Community and its servants within the limits and under the conditions laid down in the Staff Regulations or the Conditions of Employment.

Article 153

The Court of Justice shall have jurisdiction to give judgment pursuant to any arbitration clause contained in a contract concluded by or on behalf of the Community, whether that contract be governed by public or private law.

Article 154

The Court of Justice shall have jurisdiction in any dispute between Member States which relates to the subject matter of this Treaty if the dispute is submitted to it under a special agreement between the parties.

Article 155

Save where jurisdiction is conferred on the Court of Justice by this Treaty, disputes to which the Community is a party shall not on that ground be excluded from the jurisdiction of the courts or tribunals of the Member States.

Article 156

Notwithstanding the expiry of the period laid down in the third paragraph of Article 146, any party may, in proceedings in which a regulation of the Council or of the

Commission is in issue, plead the grounds specified in the first paragraph of Article 146, in order to invoke before the Court of Justice the inapplicability of that regulation.

Article 157

Save as otherwise provided in this Treaty, actions brought before the Court of Justice shall not have suspensory effect. The Court of Justice may, however, if it considers that circumstances so require, order that application of the contested act be suspended.

Article 158

The Court of Justice may in any cases before it prescribe any necessary interim measures.

Article 159

The judgments of the Court of Justice shall be enforceable under the conditions laid down in Article 164.

Article 160

The Statute of the Court of Justice is laid down in a separate Protocol.
The Council may, acting unanimously at the request of the Court of Justice and after consulting the Commission and the European Parliament, amend the provisions of Title III of the Statute. (*)
(*) Second paragraph inserted by Article 27 of the SEA.
The Court of Justice shall adopt its Rules of Procedure. These shall require the unanimous approval of the Council.

Section 5 (**)
The Court of Auditors

(**) Section 5 (Articles 160a to 160c, formerly Articles 180 and 180a) as inserted by Article I(14) TEU.

Article 160a

The audit shall be carried out by the Court of Auditors.

Article 160b

1. The Court of Auditors shall consist of 15 Members. (***)
(***) Paragraph 1 as amended by Article 22 AA A/FIN/SWE in the version resulting from Article 13 AD AA A/FIN/SWE.
2. The Members of the Court of Auditors shall be chosen from among persons who belong or have belonged in their respective countries to external audit bodies or who are especially qualified for this office. Their independence must be beyond doubt.
3. The Members of the Court of Auditors shall be appointed for a term of six years by the Council, acting unanimously after consulting the European Parliament.
However, when the first appointments are made, four Members of the Court of Auditors, chosen by lot, shall be appointed for a term of office of four years only.
The Members of the Court of Auditors shall be eligible for reappointment.
They shall elect the President of the Court of Auditors from among their number for a term of three years. The President may be re elected.
4. The Members of the Court of Auditors shall, in the general interest of the Community, be completely independent in the performance of their duties.
In the performance of these duties, they shall neither seek nor take instructions from any government or from any other body. They shall refrain from any action incompatible with their duties.
5. The Members of the Court of Auditors may not, during their term of office, engage in any other occupation, whether gainful or not. When entering upon their duties they shall give a solemn undertaking that, both during and after their term of office, they will respect the obligations arising therefrom and in particular their duty to behave with integrity and discretion as regards the acceptance, after they have ceased to hold office, of certain appointments or benefits.
6. Apart from normal replacement, or death, the duties of a Member of the Court of Auditors shall end when he resigns, or is compulsorily retired by a ruling of the Court of Justice pursuant to paragraph 7.
The vacancy thus caused shall be filled for the remainder of the Member's term of office.
Save in the case of compulsory retirement, Members of the Court of Auditors shall remain in office until they have been replaced.
7. A Member of the Court of Auditors may be deprived of his office or of his right to a pension or other benefits in its stead only if the Court of Justice, at the request of the Court of Auditors, finds that he no longer fulfils the requisite conditions or meets the obligations arising from his office.
8. The Council, acting by a qualified majority, shall determine the conditions of employment of the President and the Members of the Court of Auditors and in particular their salaries, allowances and pensions. It shall also, by the same majority, determine any payment to be made instead of remuneration.

9. The provisions of the Protocol on the privileges and immunities of the European Communities applicable to the Judges of the Court of Justice shall also apply to the Members of the Court of Auditors.

Article 160c

1. The Court of Auditors shall examine the accounts of all revenue and expenditure of the Community. It shall also examine the accounts of all revenue and expenditure of all bodies set up by the Community in so far as the relevant constituent instrument does not preclude such examination.
The Court of Auditors shall provide the European Parliament and the Council with a statement of assurance as to the reliability of the accounts and the legality and regularity of the underlying transactions.
2. The Court of Auditors shall examine whether all revenue has been received and all expenditure incurred in a lawful and regular manner and whether the financial management has been sound.
The audit of revenue shall be carried out on the basis of the amounts established as due and the amounts actually paid to the Community.
The audit of expenditure shall be carried out on the basis both of commitments undertaken and payments made.
These audits may be carried out before the closure of accounts for the financial year in question.
3. The audit shall be based on records and, if necessary, performed on the spot in the other institutions of the Community and in the Member States. In the Member States the audit shall be carried out in liaison with the national audit bodies or, if these do not have the necessary powers, with the competent national departments. These bodies or departments shall inform the Court of Auditors whether they intend to take part in the audit.
The other institutions of the Community and the national audit bodies or, if these do not have the necessary powers, the competent national department, shall forward to the Court of Auditors, at its request, any document or information necessary to carry out its task.
4. The Court of Auditors shall draw up an annual report after the close of each financial year. It shall be forwarded to the other institutions of the Community and shall be published, together with the replies of these institutions to the observations of the Court of Auditors, in the Official Journal of the European Communities.
The Court of Auditors may also, at any time, submit observations, particularly in the form of special reports, on specific questions and deliver opinions at the request of one of the other institutions of the Community.
It shall adopt its annual reports, special reports or opinions by a majority of its Members.

It shall assist the European Parliament and the Council in exercising their powers of control over the implementation of the budget.

Chapter 2
PROVISIONS COMMON TO SEVERAL INSTITUTIONS

Article 161

In order to carry out their task the Council and the Commission shall, in accordance with the provisions of this Treaty, make regulations, issue directives, take decisions, make recommendations or deliver opinions.
A regulation shall have general application. It shall be binding in its entirety and directly applicable in all Member States.
A directive shall be binding, as to the result to be achieved, upon each Member State to which it is addressed, but shall leave to the national authorities the choice of form and methods.
A decision shall be binding in its entirety upon those to whom it is addressed. Recommendations and opinions shall have no binding force.

Article 162

Regulations, directives and decisions of the Council and of the Commission shall state the reasons on which they are based and shall refer to any proposals or opinions which were required to be obtained pursuant to this Treaty.

Article 163

Regulations shall be published in the Official Journal of the European Communities. They shall enter into force on the date specified in them or, in the absence thereof, on the twentieth day following their publication.
Directives and decisions shall be notified to those to whom they are addressed and shall take effect upon such notification.

Article 164

Enforcement shall be governed by the rules of civil procedure in force in the State in the territory of which it is carried out. The order for its enforcement shall be appended to the decision, without other formality than verification of the authenticity of the decision, by the national authority which the government of each Member State shall designate for this purpose and shall make known to the Commission, to the Court of Justice and to the Arbitration Committee set up by Article 18.

When these formalities have been completed on application by the party concerned, the latter may proceed to enforcement in accordance with the national law, by bringing the matter directly before the competent authority.
Enforcement may be suspended only by a decision of the Court of Justice. However, the courts of the country concerned shall have jurisdiction over complaints that enforcement is being carried out in an irregular manner.

Chapter 3
THE ECONOMIC AND SOCIAL COMMITTEE

Article 165

An Economic and Social Committee is hereby established. It shall have advisory status. The Committee shall consist of representatives of the various categories of economic and social activity.

Article 166 (*)

(*) As amended by Article I(15) TEU.

The number of members of the Economic and Social Committee shall be as follows:

Belgium	12
Denmark	9
Germany	24
Greece	12
Spain	21
France	24
Ireland	9
Italy	24
Luxembourg	6
Netherlands	12
Austria	12
Portugal	12
Finland	9
Sweden	12
United Kingdom	24 (**)

(**) First paragraph as amended by Article 23 AA A/FIN/SWE in the version resulting from Article 14 AD AA A/FIN/SWE.

The members of the Committee shall be appointed by the Council, acting unanimously, for four years. Their appointments shall be renewable.
The members of the Committee may not be bound by any mandatory instructions. They shall be completely independent in the performance of their duties, in the general interest of the Community.
The Council, acting by a qualified majority, shall determine the allowances of members of the Committee.

Article 167

1. For the appointment of the members of the Committee, each Member State shall provide the Council with a list containing twice as many candidates as there are seats allotted to its nationals.
The composition of the Committee shall take account of the need to ensure adequate representation of the various categories of economic and social activity.
2. The Council shall consult the Commission. It may obtain the opinion of European bodies which are representative of the various economic and social sectors to which the activities of the Community are of concern.

Article 168 (*)

(*) As amended by Article I(16) TEU.

The Committee shall elect its chairman and officers from among its members for a term of two years.
It shall adopt its Rules of Procedure.
The Committee shall be convened by its chairman at the request of the Council or of the Commission. It may also meet on its own initiative.

Article 169

The Committee may be divided into specialized sections.
These specialized sections shall operate within the general terms of reference of the Committee. They may not be consulted independently of the Committee.
Subcommittees may also be established within the Committee to prepare, on specific questions or in specific fields, draft opinions to be submitted to the Committee for its consideration.
The Rules of Procedure shall lay down the methods of composition and the terms of reference of the specialized sections and of the subcommittees.

Article 170 (*)

(*) As amended by Article I(17) TEU.

The Committee must be consulted by the Council or by the Commission where this Treaty so provides. The Committee may be consulted by these institutions in all cases in which they consider it appropriate. It may issue an opinion on its own initiative in cases in which it considers such action appropriate.
The Council or the Commission shall, if it considers it necessary, set the Committee, for the submission of its opinion, a time limit which may not be less than one month from the date on which the chairman receives notification to this effect. Upon expiry of the time limit, the absence of an opinion shall not prevent further action.
The opinion of the Committee and that of the specialized section, together with a record of the proceedings, shall be forwarded to the Council and to the Commission.

TITLE IV
FINANCIAL PROVISIONS

Article 171

1. Estimates shall be drawn up for each financial year of all revenue and expenditure of the Community, other than those of the Agency and the Joint Undertakings, and such revenue and expenditure shall be shown either in the operating budget or in the research and investment budget.
The revenue and expenditure shown in each budget shall be in balance.
2. The revenue and expenditure of the Agency, which shall operate in accordance with commercial principles, shall be budgeted for in a special account.
The manner of estimating, implementing and auditing such revenue and expenditure shall be laid down, with due regard to the statutes of the Agency, in financial regulations made pursuant to Article 183.
3. The estimates of revenue and expenditure, together with the operating accounts and the balance sheets of the Joint Undertakings for each financial year, shall be placed before the Commission, the Council and the European Parliament in accordance with the statutes of those undertakings.

Article 172

(Paragraphs 1, 2 and 3 repealed)

4. Loans for the financing of research or investment shall be raised on terms fixed by the Council in the manner provided for in Article 177(5).
The Community may borrow on the capital market of a Member State, either in accordance with the legal provisions applying to internal issues, or, if there are no such provisions in a Member State, after the Member State concerned and the Commission have conferred together and have reached agreement upon the proposed loan.
The competent authorities of the Member State concerned may refuse to give their assent only if there is reason to fear serious disturbances on the capital market of that State.

Article 173 (*)

(*) As amended by Article I(19) TEU.

Without prejudice to other revenue, the budget shall be financed wholly from own resources.
The Council, acting unanimously on a proposal from the Commission and after consulting the European Parliament, shall lay down provisions relating to the system of own resources of the Community, which it shall recommend to the Member States for adoption in accordance with their respective constitutional requirements.

Article 173a (**)

(**) As inserted by Article I(20) TEU.

With a view to maintaining budgetary discipline, the Commission shall not make any proposal for a Community act, or alter its proposals, or adopt any implementing measure which is likely to have appreciable implications for the budget without providing the assurance that that proposal or that measure is capable of being financed within the limit of the Community's own resources arising under provisions laid down by the Council pursuant to Article 173.

Article 174

1. The expenditure shown in the operating budget shall include in particular:
a. administrative expenditure;
b. expenditure relating to safeguards and to health and safety.
2. The expenditure shown in the research and investment budget shall include in particular:
a. expenditure relating to the implementation of the Community research programme;

b. any participation in the capital of the Agency and in its investment expenditure;
c. expenditure relating to the equipment of training establishments;
d. any participation in Joint Undertakings or in certain joint operations.

Article 175

The expenditure shown in the operating budget shall be authorized for one financial year, unless the regulations made pursuant to Article 183 provide otherwise.
In accordance with conditions to be laid down pursuant to Article 183, any appropriations, other than those relating to staff expenditure, that are unexpended at the end of the financial year may be carried forward to the next financial year only.
Appropriations to cover expenditure shall be classified under different chapters grouping items of expenditure according to their nature or purpose and subdivided, as far as may be necessary, in accordance with the regulations made pursuant to Article 183.
The expenditure of the European Parliament, the Council, the Commission and the Court of Justice shall be set out in separate parts of the budget, without prejudice to special arrangements for certain common items of expenditure.

Article 176

1. Subject to the limits resulting from programmes or decisions involving expenditure which, in pursuance of this Treaty, require the unanimous approval of the Council, allocations for research and investment expenditure shall include:
a. commitment appropriations, covering a series of items which constitute a separate unit and form a coherent whole;
b. payment appropriations which represent the maximum amount payable each year in respect of the commitments entered into under subparagraph (a).
2. The schedule of due dates for commitments and payments shall be annexed to the corresponding draft budget proposed by the Commission.
3. Appropriations for research and investment shall be classified under different chapters grouping items of expenditure according to their nature or purpose and subdivided, as far as may be necessary, in accordance with the regulations made pursuant to Article 183.
4. Unused payment authorizations shall be carried forward to the next financial year by decision of the Commission, unless the Council decides otherwise.

Article 177 (*)

(*) As amended by Article 20 of the Treaty amending Certain Financial Provisions.

1. The financial year shall run from 1 January to 31 December.
Within the meaning of this Article, budget[1] shall include the operating budget and the research and investment budget.
2. Each institution of the Community shall, before 1 July, draw up estimates of its expenditure. The Commission shall consolidate these estimates in a preliminary draft budget. It shall attach thereto an opinion which may contain different estimates.
The preliminary draft budget shall include an estimate of revenue and an estimate of expenditure.
3. The Commission shall place the preliminary draft budget before the Council not later than 1 September of the year preceding that in which the budget is to be implemented.
The Council shall consult the Commission and, where appropriate, the other institutions concerned whenever it intends to depart from the preliminary draft budget.
The Council shall, acting by a qualified majority, establish the draft budget and forward it to the European Parliament.
4. The draft budget shall be placed before the European Parliament not later than 5 October of the year preceding that in which the budget is to be implemented.
The European Parliament shall have the right to amend the draft budget acting by a majority of its Members, and to propose to the Council, acting by an absolute majority of the votes cast, modifications to the draft budget relating to expenditure necessarily resulting from this Treaty or from acts adopted in accordance therewith.
If, within 45 days of the draft budget being placed before it, the European Parliament has given its approval, the budget shall stand as finally adopted. If within this period the European Parliament has not amended the draft budget or proposed any modifications thereto, the budget shall be deemed to be finally adopted.
If within this period the European Parliament has adopted amendments or proposed modifications, the draft budget together with the amendments or proposed modifications shall be forwarded to the Council.
5. After discussing the draft budget with the Commission and, where appropriate, with the other institutions concerned, the Council shall act under the following conditions:

a. the Council may, acting by a qualified majority, modify any of the amendments adopted by the European Parliament;
b. with regard to the proposed modifications:

- where a modification proposed by the European Parliament does not have the effect of increasing the total amount of the expenditure of an institution, owing in particular to the fact that the increase in expenditure which it would involve would be expressly compensated by one or more proposed modifications correspondingly reducing expenditure, the Council may, acting by a qualified majority, reject the proposed modification. In the absence of a decision to reject it, the proposed modification shall stand as accepted;

- where a modification proposed by the European Parliament has the effect of increasing the total amount of the expenditure of an institution, the Council may, acting by a qualified majority, accept this proposed modification. In the absence of a decision to accept it, the proposed modification shall stand as rejected;
- where, in pursuance of the two preceding subparagraphs, the Council has rejected a proposed modification, it may, acting by a qualified majority, either retain the amount shown in the draft budget or fix another amount.

The draft shall be modified on the basis of the proposed modifications accepted by the Council.

If, within 15 days of the draft budget being placed before it, the Council has not modified any of the amendments adopted by the European Parliament and if the modifications proposed by the latter have been accepted, the budget shall be deemed to be finally adopted. The Council shall inform the European Parliament that it has not modified any of the amendments and that the proposed modifications have been accepted.

If within this period the Council has modified one or more of the amendments adopted by the European Parliament or if the modifications proposed by the latter have been rejected or modified, the modified draft budget shall again be forwarded to the European Parliament. The Council shall inform the European Parliament of the results of its deliberations.

6. Within 15 days of the draft budget being placed before it, the European Parliament, which shall have been notified of the action taken on its proposed modifications may, acting by a majority of its Members and three fifths of the votes cast, amend or reject the modifications to its amendments made by the Council and shall adopt the budget accordingly. If within this period the European Parliament has not acted, the budget shall be deemed to be finally adopted.

7. When the procedure provided for in this Article has been completed, the President of the European Parliament shall declare that the budget has been finally adopted.

8. However, the European Parliament, acting by a majority of its Members and two thirds of the votes cast may, if there are important reasons, reject the draft budget and ask for a new draft to be submitted to it.

9. A maximum rate of increase in relation to the expenditure of the same type to be incurred during the current year shall be fixed annually for the total expenditure other than that necessarily resulting from this Treaty or from acts adopted in accordance therewith.

The Commission shall, after consulting the Economic Policy Committee, declare what this maximum rate is, as it results from:

- the trend, in terms of volume, of the gross national product within the Community;
- the average variation in the budgets of the Member States;

and

- the trend of the cost of living during the preceding financial year.

The maximum rate shall be communicated, before 1 May, to all the institutions of the Community. The latter shall be required to conform to this during the budgetary procedure, subject to the provisions of the fourth and fifth subparagraphs of this paragraph.

If, in respect of expenditure other than that necessarily resulting from this Treaty or from acts adopted in accordance therewith, the actual rate of increase in the draft budget established by the Council is over half the maximum rate, the European Parliament may, exercising its right of amendment, further increase the total amount of that expenditure to a limit not exceeding half the maximum rate.

Where the European Parliament, the Council or the Commission considers that the activities of the Communities require that the rate determined according to the procedure laid down in this paragraph should be exceeded, another rate may be fixed by agreement between the Council, acting by a qualified majority, and the European Parliament, acting by a majority of its members and three fifths of the votes cast.

10. Each institution shall exercise the powers conferred upon it by this Article, with due regard for the provisions of the Treaty and for acts adopted in accordance therewith, in particular those relating to the Communities' own resources and to the balance between revenue and expenditure.

Article 178 (*)

(*) As amended by Article 21 of the Treaty amending Certain Financial Provisions.

If, at the beginning of a financial year, the budget has not yet been voted, a sum equivalent to not more than one twelfth of the budget appropriations for the preceding financial year may be spent each month in respect of any chapter or other subdivision of the budget in accordance with the provisions of the Regulations made pursuant to Article 183; this arrangement shall not, however, have the effect of placing at the disposal of the Commission appropriations in excess of one twelfth of those provided for in the draft budget in the course of preparation.

The Council may, acting by a qualified majority, provided that the other conditions laid down in the first subparagraph are observed, authorize expenditure in excess of one twelfth.

If the decision relates to expenditure which does not necessarily result from this Treaty or from acts adopted in accordance therewith, the Council shall forward it immediately to the European Parliament; within 30 days the European Parliament, acting by a majority of its Members and three fifths of the votes cast, may adopt a different decision on the expenditure in exess of the one twelfth referred to in the first subparagraph. This part of the decision of the Council shall be suspended until the

European Parliament has taken its decision. If, within this period, the European Parliament has not taken a decision which differs from the decision of the Council, the latter shall be deemed to be finally adopted.
The decisions referred to in the second and third subparagraphs shall lay down the necessary measures relating to resources to ensure application of this Article.

Article 179 (*)

(*) As amended by Article I(21) TEU.

The Commission shall implement the budgets, in accordance with the provisions of the regulations made pursuant to Article 183, on its own responsibility and within the limits of the appropriations.
The regulations shall lay down detailed rules for each institution concerning its part in effecting its own expenditure.
Within the budgets, the Commission may, subject to the limits and conditions laid down in the regulations made pursuant to Article 183, transfer appropriations from one chapter to another or from one subdivision to another.

Article 179a (*)

(*) As added by Article 22 of the Treaty amending Certain Financial Provisions.

The Commission shall submit annually to the Council and to the European Parliament the accounts of the preceding financial year relating to the implementation of the budget. The Commission shall also forward to them a financial statement of the assets and liabilities of the Community.

Article 180

(Repealed)

Article 180a

(Repealed)

Article 180b (**)

(**) As amended by Article I(23) TEU.

1. The European Parliament, acting on a recommendation from the Council which shall act by a qualified majority, shall give a discharge to the Commission in respect

of the implementation of the budget. To this end, the Council and the European Parliament in turn shall examine the accounts and the financial statement referred to in Article 179a, the annual report by the Court of Auditors together with the replies of the institutions under audit to the observations of the Court of Auditors, and any relevant special reports by the Court of Auditors.
2. Before giving a discharge to the Commission, or for any other purpose in connection with the exercise of its powers over the implementation of the budget, the European Parliament may ask to hear the Commission give evidence with regard to the execution of expenditure or the operation of financial control systems. The Commission shall submit any necessary information to the European Parliament at the latter's request.
3. The Commission shall take all appropriate steps to act on the observations in the decisions giving discharge and on other observations by the European Parliament relating to the execution of expenditure, as well as on comments accompanying the recommendations on discharge adopted by the Council.
At the request of the European Parliament or the Council, the Commission shall report on the measures taken in the light of these observations and comments and in particular on the instructions given to the departments which are responsible for the implementation of the budgets. These reports shall also be forwarded to the Court of Auditors.

Article 181

The budgets and the account provided for in Article 171(1) and (2) shall be drawn up in the unit of account determined in accordance with the provisions of the financial regulations made pursuant to Article 183.
The financial contributions provided for in Article 172 shall be placed at the disposal of the Community by the Member States in their national currencies.
The available balances of these contributions shall be deposited with the Treasuries of Member States or with bodies designated by them. While on deposit, such funds shall retain the value corresponding to the parity, at the date of deposit, in relation to the unit of account referred to in the first paragraph.
The balances may be invested on terms to be agreed between the Commission and the Member State concerned.

Article 182

1. The Commission may, provided it notifies the competent authorities of the Member States concerned, transfer into the currency of one of the Member States its holdings of currency of another Member State, to the ex tent necessary to enable them to be used for purposes which come within the scope of this Treaty. The Commission

shall as far as possible avoid making such transfers if it possesses cash or liquid assets in the currencies which it needs.

2. The Commission shall deal with each Member State through the authority designated by the State concerned. In carrying out financial operations the Commission shall employ the services of the bank of issue of the Member State concerned or any other financial institutions approved by that State.

3. As regards expenditure which the Community has to incur in the currencies of third countries, the Commission shall, before the budgets are finally adopted, submit to the Council a programme indicating anticipated revenue and expenditure in the different currencies.

This programme shall be approved by the Council, acting by a qualified majority. It may be modified in the course of the financial year in accordance with the same procedure.

4. Member States shall provide the Commission with the currency of third countries needed for the expenditure shown in the programme provided for in paragraph 3 according to the scales laid down in Article 172. Amounts collected by the Commission in the currency of third countries shall be transferred to Member States in accordance with the same scales.

5. The Commission may freely make use of any amounts in the currency of third countries derived from loans it has raised in such countries.

6. The Council may, acting unanimously on a proposal from the Commission apply, in whole or in part, to the Agency and to Joint Undertakings the exchange arrangements provided for in the preceding paragraphs, and, where appropriate, adapt these arrangements to their operational requirements.

Article 183 (*)

(*) As amended by Article I(24) TEU.

The Council, acting unanimously on a proposal from the Commission and after consulting the European Parliament and obtaining the opinion of the Court of Auditors, shall:

a. make Financial Regulations specifying in particular the procedure to be adopted for establishing and implementing the budget and for presenting and auditing accounts;
b. determine the methods and procedure whereby the budget revenue provided under the arrangements relating to the Community's own resources shall be made available to the Commission, and determine the measures to be applied, if need be, to meet cash requirements;

c. lay down rules concerning the responsibility of financial controllers, authorizing officers and accounting officers, and concerning appropriate arrangements for inspection.

Article 183a (**)

(**) As inserted by Article I(25) TEU.

Member States shall take the same measures to counter fraud affecting the financial interests of the Community as they take to counter fraud affecting their own financial interests.
Without prejudice to other provisions of this Treaty, Member States shall coordinate their actions aimed at protecting the financial interests of the Community against fraud. To this end they shall organize, with the help of the Commission, close and regular cooperation between the competent departments of their administrations.

TITLE V
GENERAL PROVISIONS

Article 184

The Community shall have legal personality.

Article 185

In each of the Member States, the Community shall enjoy the most extensive legal capacity accorded to legal persons under their laws; it may, in particular, acquire or dispose of movable and immovable property and may be a party to legal proceedings. To this end, the Community shall be represented by the Commission.

Article 186

(Article repealed by Article 24(2) of the Merger Treaty)
[See Article 24(1) of the Merger Treaty which reads as follows:

1. The officials and other servants of the European Coal and Steel Community, the European Economic Community and the European Atomic Energy Community shall, at the date of entry into force of this Treaty, become officials and other servants of the European Communities and form part of the single administration of these Communities.

The Council shall, acting by a qualified majority on a proposal from the Commission and after consulting the other institutions concerned, lay down the Staff Regulations of officials of the European Communities and the Conditions of Employment of other servants of these Communities.]

Article 187

The Commission may, within the limits and under the conditions laid down by the Council in accordance with the provisions of this Treaty, collect any information and carry out any checks required for the performance of the tasks entrusted to it.

Article 188

The contractual liability of the Community shall be governed by the law applicable to the contract in question.

In the case of non contractual liability, the Community shall, in accordance with the general principles common to the laws of the Member States, make good any damage caused by its institutions or by its servants in the performance of their duties.

The personal liability of its servants towards the Community shall be governed by the provisions laid down in the Staff Regulations or in the Conditions of Employment applicable to them.

Article 189

The seat of the institutions of the Community shall be determined by common accord of the governments of the Member States.

Article 190

The rules governing the languages of the institutions of the Community shall, without prejudice to the provisions contained in the Rules of Procedure of the Court of Justice, be determined by the Council, acting unanimously.

Article 191

(Article repealed by the second paragraph of Article 28 of the Merger Treaty)
[See the first paragraph of Article 28 of the Merger Treaty which reads as follows:

The European Communities shall enjoy in the territories of the Member States such privileges and immunities as are necessary for the performance of their tasks, under the conditions laid down in the Protocol annexed to this Treaty. The same shall apply to the European Investment Bank.]

Article 192

Member States shall take all appropriate measures, whether general or particular, to ensure fulfillment of the obligations arising out of this Treaty or resulting from action taken by the institutions of the Community. They shall facilitate the achievement of the Community's tasks.
They shall abstain from any measure which could jeopardize the attainment of the objectives of this Treaty.

Article 193

Member States undertake not to submit a dispute concerning the interpretation or application of this Treaty to any method of settlement other than those provided for therein.

Article 194

1. The members of the institutions of the Community, the members of committees, the officials and other servants of the Community and any other persons who by reason of their duties or their public or private relations with the institutions or installations of the Community or with Joint Undertakings are called upon to acquire or obtain cognisance of any facts, information, knowledge, documents or objects which are subject to a security system in accordance with provisions laid down by a Member State or by an institution of the Community, shall be required, even after such duties or relations have ceased, to keep them secret from any unauthorized person and from the general public.
Each Member State shall treat any infringement of this obligation as an act prejudicial to its rules on secrecy and as one falling, both as to merits and jurisdiction, within the scope of its laws relating to acts prejudicial to the security of the State or to disclosure of professional secrets. Such Member State shall, at the request of any Member State concerned or of the Commission, prosecute anyone within its jurisdiction who commits such an infringement.
2. Each Member State shall communicate to the Commission all provisions regulating within its territories the classification and secrecy of information, knowledge, documents or objects covered by this Treaty.
The Commission shall ensure that these provisions are communicated to the other Member States.

Each Member State shall take all appropriate measures to facilitate the gradual establishment of as uniform and comprehensive a security system as possible. The Commission may, after consulting the Member States concerned, make recommendations for this purpose.
3. The institutions of the Community, their installations and also the Joint Undertakings shall be required to apply the rules of the security system in force in the territory in which each of them is situated.
4. Any authorization granted either by an institution of the Community or by a Member State to a person carrying out his activities within the field covered by this Treaty to have access to facts, information, documents or objects covered by this Treaty which are subject to a security system, shall be recognized by every other institution and every other Member State.
5. The provisions of this Article shall not prevent application of special provisions resulting from agreements concluded between a Member State and a third State or an international organization.

Article 195

The institutions of the Community, the Agency and the Joint Undertakings shall, in applying this Treaty, comply with the conditions of access to ores, source materials and special fissile materials laid down in national rules and regulations made for reasons of public policy or public health.

Article 196

For the purposes of this Treaty, save as otherwise provided therein:
a. person[1] means any natural person who pursues all or any of his activities in the territories of Member States within the field specified in the relevant chapter of this Treaty;
b. undertaking[1] means any undertaking or institution which pursues all or any of its activities in the territories of Member States within the field specified in the relevant Chapter of this Treaty, whatever its public or private legal status.

Article 197

For the purposes of this Treaty:
1. Special fissile materials' means plutonium 239; uranium 233; uranium enriched in uranium 235 or uranium 233; and any substance containing one or more of the foregoing isotopes and such other fissile materials as may be specified by the Council, acting by a qualified majority on a proposal from the Commission; the expression special fissile materials' does not, however, include source materials.

2. Uranium enriched in uranium 235 or uranium 233" means uranium containing uranium 235 or uranium 233 or both in an amount such that the abundance ratio of the sum of these isotopes to isotope 238 is greater than the ratio of isotope 235 to isotope 238 occurring in nature.
3. Source materials' means uranium containing the mixture of isotopes occurring in nature; uranium whose content in uranium 235 is less than the normal; thorium; any of the foregoing in the form of metal, alloy, chemical compound or concentrate; any other substance containing one or more of the foregoing in such a concentration as shall be specified by the Council, acting by a qualified majority on a proposal from the Commission.
4. Ores' means any ore containing, in such average concentration as shall be specified by the Council acting by a qualified majority on a proposal from the Commission, substances from which the source materials defined above may be obtained by the appropriate chemical and physical processing.

Article 198

Save as otherwise provided, this Treaty shall apply to the European territories of Member States and to non European territories under their jurisdiction.
It shall also apply to the European territories for whose external relations a Member State is responsible.
Notwithstanding the previous paragraphs:
a. This Treaty shall not apply to the Faeroe Islands. (*)
(*) As amended by Article I(26) TEU.
b. This Treaty shall not apply to the Sovereign Base Areas of the United Kingdom of Great Britain and Northern Ireland in Cyprus.
c. This Treaty shall not apply to those overseas countries and territories having special relations with the United Kingdom of Great Britain and Northern Ireland which are not listed in Annex IV to the Treaty establishing the European Community.
d. This Treaty shall apply to the Channel Islands and the Isle of Man only to the extent necessary to ensure the implementation of the arrangements for those islands set out in the Treaty concerning the accession of new Member States to the European Economic Community and to the European Atomic Energy Community signed on 22 January 1972. (***)
(***)Third paragraph added by Article 27 AA DK/IRL/UK modified by Article 16 AD AA DK/IRL/UK.
e. This Treaty shall not apply to the?land Islands. The Government of Finland may, however, give notice, by a declaration deposited when ratifying this Treaty with the Government of the Italian Republic, that the Treaty shall apply to the?land Islands in accordance with the provisions set out in Protocol No 2 to the Act concerning the conditions of accession of the Republic of Austria, the Republic of Finland and the

Kingdom of Sweden and the adjustments to the Treaties on which the European Union is founded. The Government of the Italian Republic shall transmit a certified copy of any such declaration to the Member States.
(*) Point (e) added by Article 28 AA A/FIN/SWE in the version resulting from Article 19AD AA A/FIN/SWE.

Article 199

It shall be for the Commission to ensure the maintenance of all appropriate relations with the organs of the United Nations, of its specialized agencies and of the General Agreement on Tariffs and Trade.
The Commission shall also maintain such relations as are appropriate with all international organizations.

Article 200

The Community shall establish all appropriate forms of cooperation with the Council of Europe.

Article 201 (**)

(**) As amended by Article I(27) TEU.

The Community shall establish close cooperation with the Organization for Economic Cooperation and Development, the details of which shall be determined by common accord.

Article 202

The provisions of this Treaty shall not preclude the existence or completion of regional unions between Belgium and Luxembourg, or between Belgium, Luxembourg and the Netherlands, to the extent that the objectives of these regional unions are not attained by application of this Treaty.

Article 203

If action by the Community should prove necessary to attain one of the objectives of the Community and this Treaty has not provided the necessary powers, the Council shall, acting unanimously on a proposal from the Commission and after consulting the European Parliament, take the appropriate measures.

Article 204

(Repealed)

Article 205

(Repealed)

Article 206 (*)

(*) As amended by Article I(29) TEU.

The Community may conclude with one or more States or international organizations agreements establishing an association involving reciprocal rights and obligations, common action and special procedures.
These agreements shall be concluded by the Council, acting unanimously after consulting the European Parliament.
Where such agreements call for amendments to this Treaty, these amendments shall first be adopted in accordance with the procedure laid down in Article N of the Treaty on European Union.

Article 207

The Protocols annexed to this Treaty by common accord of the Member States shall form an integral part thereof.

Article 208

This Treaty is concluded for an unlimited period.

TITLE VI
PROVISIONS RELATING TO THE INITIAL PERIOD

Section 1
Setting up of the institutions

Article 209

The Council shall meet within one month of the entry into force of this Treaty.

Article 210

The Council shall, within three months of its first meeting, take all appropriate measures to constitute the Economic and Social Committee.

Article 211

The Assembly (*) shall meet within two months of the first meeting of the Council, having been convened by the President of the Council, in order to elect its officers and draw up its Rules of Procedure. Pending the election of its officers, the oldest member shall take the chair.
(*) EDITORIAL NOTE: Notwithstanding the provisions of Article 3 of the SEA, and for historical reasons, the term 'Assembly' has not been replaced by the terms 'European Parliament'.

Article 212

The Court of Justice shall take up its duties as soon as its members have been appointed. Its first President shall be appointed for three years in the same manner as its members.
The Court of Justice shall adopt its Rules of Procedure within three months of taking up its duties.
No matter may be brought before the Court of Justice until its Rules of Procedure have been published. The time within which an action must be brought shall run only from the date of this publication.
Upon his appointment, the President of the Court of Justice shall exercise the powers conferred upon him by this Treaty.

Article 213

The Commission shall take up its duties and assume the responsibilities conferred upon it by this Treaty as soon as its Members have been appointed.
Upon taking up its duties, the Commission shall undertake the studies and arrange the contacts with Member States, undertakings, workers and consumers needed for making an overall survey of the situation of nuclear industries in the Community. The Commission shall submit a report on this subject to the European Parliament within six months.

Article 214

1. The first financial year shall run from the date when this Treaty enters into force until 31 December following. Should this Treaty, however, enter into force during the

second half of the year, the first financial year shall run until 31 December of the following year.

2. Until the budgets for the first financial year have been established, Member States shall make the Community interest free advances which shall be deducted from their financial contributions to the implementation of these budgets.

3. Until the Staff Regulations of officials and the Conditions of Employment of other servants of the Community provided for in Article 186 have been laid down, each institution shall recruit the staff it needs and to this end conclude contracts of limited duration.

Each institution shall examine together with the Council any question concerning the number, remuneration and distribution of posts.

Section 2
Provisions for the initial application of this Treaty

Article 215

1. An initial research and training programme, which is set out in Annex V to this Treaty and the cost of which shall not, unless the Council unanimously decides otherwise, exceed 215 million EPU units of account, shall be carried out within five years of the entry into force of this Treaty.

2. A breakdown of the expenditure necessary for the implementation of this programme is set out by way of illustration under main subdivisions in Annex V.

The Council may, acting by a qualified majority on a proposal from the Commission, modify this programme.

Article 216

The Commission proposals on the way in which the institution of university status referred to in Article 9 is to function shall be submitted to the Council within one year of the entry into force of this Treaty.

Article 217

The security regulations provided for in Article 24 concerning the security gradings applicable to the dissemination of information shall be adopted by the Council within six months of the entry into force of this Treaty.

Article 218

The basic standards shall be determined in accordance with the provisions of Article 31 within one year of the entry into force of this Treaty.

Article 219

Provisions laid down by law, regulation or administrative action to ensure the protection of the health of the general public and of workers in the territories of Member States against the dangers arising from ionizing radiations shall, in accordance with Article 33, be communicated to the Commission by these States within three months of the entry into force of this Treaty.

Article 220

The Commission proposals relating to the statutes of the Agency which are provided for in Article 54 shall be submitted to the Council within three months of the entry into force of this Treaty.

Section 3
Transitional provisions

Article 221

The provisions of Articles 14 to 23 and of Articles 25 to 28 shall apply to patents, provisionally protected patent rights and utility models, and also to patent and utility model applications in existence before the entry into force of this Treaty, under the following conditions.

1. When assessing the period of time referred to in Article 17(2), allowance shall be made, in favour of the owner, for the new situation created by the entry into force of this Treaty.
2. With regard to the communication of an invention which is not secret, where either or both of the periods of three and eighteen months referred to in Article 16 have expired at the date on which this Treaty enters into force, a further period of six months shall run from that date.
If either or both of those periods remain unexpired at that date, they shall be extended by six months from the date of their normal expiry.
3. The same provisions shall apply to the communication of a secret invention in accordance with Article 16 and Article 25(1); in such case, however, the date of entry into force of the security regulations referred to in Article 24 shall be the date taken as the starting point for the new period or for the extension of a current period.

Article 222

During the period between the date of entry into force of this Treaty and the date fixed by the Commission on which the Agency takes up its duties, agreements and contracts

for the supply of ores, source materials or special fissile materials shall be concluded or renewed only with the prior approval of the Commission.
The Commission shall refuse to approve the conclusion or renewal of any agreements and contracts which it considers would prejudice the implementation of this Treaty. It may in particular make its approval dependent upon the insertion in agreements and contracts of clauses permitting the Agency to take part in carrying them out.

Article 223

By way of derogation from the provisions of Article 60, reactors installed in the territories of a Member State which may go critical before the expiry of a period of seven years from the date of entry into force of this Treaty shall, during a period of not more than 10 years from that date, in order to take account of work and studies already initiated, be granted priority which may be exercised in respect both of supplies of ores or source materials coming from the territories of that State and also of supplies of source materials or special fissile materials which are the subject of a bilateral agreement concluded before the entry into force of this Treaty and communicated to the Commission in accordance with Article 105.
The same priority shall be granted during the same period of 10 years in respect of supplies for any isotope separation plant, whether or not it constitutes a Joint Undertaking, which comes into operation in the territory of a Member State before the expiry of a period of seven years from the date of entry into force of this Treaty. The Agency shall conclude the appropriate contracts, after the Commission has ascertained that the conditions for the exercise of the right of priority have been fulfilled.

FINAL PROVISIONS

Article 224

This Treaty shall be ratified by the High Contracting Parties in accordance with their respective constitutional requirements. The instruments of ratification shall be deposited with the Government of the Italian Republic.
This Treaty shall enter into force on the first day of the month following the deposit of the instrument of ratification by the last signatory State to take this step. If, however, such deposit is made less than 15 days before the beginning of the following month, this Treaty shall not enter into force until the first day of the second month after the date of such deposit.

Article 225

This Treaty, drawn up in a single original in the Dutch, French, German and Italian languages, all four texts being equally authentic, shall be deposited in the archives of the Government of the Italian Republic, which shall transmit a certified copy to each of the governments of the other signatory States.

IN WITNESS WHEREOF, the undersigned Plenipotentiaries have signed this Treaty. Done at Rome this twenty fifth day of March in the year one thousand nine hundred and fifty seven.

P. H. SPAAK	J. Ch. SNOY ET D'OPPUERS
ADENAUER	HALLSTEIN
PINEAU	M. FAURE
Antonio SEGNI	Gaetano MARTINO
BECH	SCHAUS
LUNS	J. LINTHORST HOMAN

CHAPTER TWO
NUCLEAR SAFETY AND RADIATION PROTECTION

This Chapter is devoted to the many international instruments and acts (conventions, regulations, directives, recommendations etc.) adopted in the vast areas of nuclear safety and radiation protection. While recalling the different legal standing of such instruments and acts and in fact despite this difference, it is worth stressing that also the non-binding texts have a considerable impact on national regimes, since various countries take them into account given their high technical-scientific value.

As pointed out in the previous Chapter as regards IAEA, NEA and Euratom, the texts published or referred to under Chapter Two show that certain standards and recommendation are adopted as a result of joint work between those organisations and other non specifically nuclear organisations, whose competence is of a more general nature covering areas like public health (WHO) or protection of workers (ILO). The Chapter covers also some EEC (European Economic Community, as opposed to Euratom, see Chapter One) regulations, which address the import/export of contaminated items as a consequence of the Chernobyl incident; the differences between EEC and Euratom regulations in this domain is explained in the relevant Introductory Material. It should be also noted that two more Euratom Regulations appear in the chapter, although not directly linked to radiation protection but important for the application of the Treaty. Besides, attention is drawn here to some resolutions, relevant for the area under consideration, adopted by the European Council, such as those of 1975 and 1992 on the technological problems of nuclear safety, and two more one of 1992 on the Action Plan on radioactive waste and the other of 1994 on the management of radioactive waste.

The particular importance of ICRP (International Commission on Radiological Protection) must be noted, especially as far as the guiding principles of radiation protection worldwide are concerned and the remarkably high number of subjects covered by ICRP recommendations.

Finally, though outside the strict domain of the Euratom Treaty, two Directives adopted jointly by the European Parliament and the Council of the EU in 1999 should be mentioned. These directives (1999/2/CE and 1999/3/CE) are aimed at attenuating differences among national legislation (in EU member States) on irradiated foodstuffs, by laying down conditions to which authorization of their treatment by ionising radiation is subject, the objectives the irradiation must pursue and a list of items which may be irradiated.

Given the extremely vast number of instruments and acts considered, it became necessary in various cases to simply mention them, especially since their importance and bearing are widely acknowledged. This applies especially to IAEA (and in part to NEA and ICRP) standards, recommendations, guides, codes of practice, manuals, reports etc.

THE IAEA CONVENTION ON EARLY NOTIFICATION OF A NUCLEAR ACCIDENT

(Vienna, 26 September, 1986)

This Convention (similarly to the Convention on mutual assistance following in the volume) is among the numerous and different actions taken by the competent international organisations in response to the nuclear incident (April 1986) at the Chernobyl (Ukraine, former part of the Soviet Union) nuclear power plant. Strictly speaking, the Convention in point is not concerned with safety and protection, in that it does not lay down specific rules in this area, but it is rather intended to regulate possible future nuclear accidents as regards the information to be given to all countries likely to be affected by their consequences, allowing them to take any necessary measure to minimize such consequences. As a matter of fact, international nuclear law existing at the time of the accident, although already considerably copious, did not put any specific obligation on States to notify an accident occurred on their own territory. The size of this "lacuna" became dramatically evident on the occasion of the Chernobyl event, and led the IAEA to promote the elaboration of a Convention to cover the "void".

The negotiations for this new (and the first one ever) Convention were particularly difficult and intensive, and they were condensed in three weeks of extremely hard work at the Agency, with the participation of experts from all interested countries in the world. The draft text prepared by the Agency itself was the object of further elaboration and very many amendments, in order to accommodate the various countries' needs and to sort out certain "sensitive" issues (such as, e.g., including or not in the scope accidents from nuclear weapons and tests).

It must be pointed out that during negotiations an agreement was easily found among the delegations about the conditions for the entry into force of the Convention, the basic idea being that every effort should be made to facilitate it as much as possible, thus making the instrument practically applicable in the short term. This is the reason why it was stipulated that entry into force would take place thirty days after consent to be bound had been expressed by only three States. The Convention entered in fact into force on October 27, 1986, and has now 91 contracting Parties. It is noted that also FAO, WHO and WMO (World Meteorological Organization) have acceded to the Convention, and that the European Community will do the same in a near future.

Lastly, attention is drawn to the fact that at least at the European Communities level, the 1980 Euratom Basic Standards on radiological protection had already provided for an obligation on each Member State to notify neighbouring Member States and to the Commission of any incident involving exposure of the population. Later on, the 1996 Basic Standards included a number of provisions referring to co-operation among (also non-Member) States in relation to possible radiological emergencies, so facilitating organisation of protection. On the other hand, the Council of the European Communities in 1987 had adopted a "decision" (no.87/600, addressed further on in this Chapter) on Community arrangements for early exchange of information in a radiological emergency (the so called ECURIE system).

THE STATES PARTIES TO THIS CONVENTION,

AWARE that nuclear activities are being carried out in a number of States,
NOTING that comprehensive measures have been and are being take to ensure a high level of safety in nuclear activities, aimed at preventing nuclear accidents and minimizing the consequences of any such accident, should it occur,
DESIRING to strengthen further international co-operation in the safe development and use of nuclear energy,
CONVINCED of the need for States to provide relevant information about nuclear accidents as early as possible in order that trans-boundary radiological consequences can be minimized,
NOTING the usefulness of bilateral and multilateral arrangements on information exchange in this area,

HAVE AGREED as follows:

Article 1
Scope of application

1. This Convention shall apply in the event of any accident involving facilities or activities of a State Party or of persons or legal entities under its jurisdiction or control, referred to in paragraph 2 below, from which a release of radioactive material occurs or is likely to occur and which has resulted or may result in an international trans-boundary release that could be of radiological safety significance for another State.
2. The facilities and activities referred to in paragraph 1 are the following:
   a. any nuclear reactor wherever located;
   b. any nuclear fuel cycle facility;
   c. any radioactive waste management facility;
   d. the transport and storage of nuclear fuels or radioactive wastes;

e. the manufacture, use, storage, disposal and transport of radioisotopes for agricultural, industrial, medical and related scientific and research purposes; and
f. the use of radioisotopes for power generation in space objects.

Article 2
Notification and information

In the event of an accident specified in article 1 (hereinafter referred to as a "nuclear accident"), the State Party referred to in that article shall:
a. forthwith notify, directly or though the International Atomic Energy Agency (hereinafter referred to as the "Agency"), those States which are or may be physically affected as specified in article 1 and the Agency of the nuclear accident, its nature, the time of its occurrence and its exact location where appropriate; and
b. promptly provide the States referred to in sub-paragraph (a), directly or through the Agency, and the Agency with such available information relevant to minimizing the radiological consequences in those States, as specified in article 5.

Article 3
Other Nuclear Accidents

With a view to minimizing the radiological consequences, States Parties may notify in the event of nuclear accidents other than those specified in article 1.

Article 4
Functions of the Agency

The Agency shall:
a. forthwith inform States Parties, Member States, other States which are or may be physically affected as specified in article 1 and relevant international intergovernmental organizations (hereinafter referred to as "international organizations") of a notification received pursuant to sub-paragraph (a) of article 2; and
b. promptly provide any State Party, Member State or relevant international organization, upon request, with the information received pursuant to sub-paragraph (b) of article 2.

Article 5
Information to be provided

1. The information to be provided pursuant to sub-paragraph (b) of article 2 shall comprise the following data as then available to the notifying State Party:
   a. the time, exact location where appropriate, and the nature of the nuclear accident;
   b. the facility or activity involved;
   c. the assumed or established cause and the foreseeable development of the nuclear accident relevant to the trans-boundary release of the radioactive materials;
   d. the general characteristics of the radioactive release, including, as far as is practicable and appropriate, the nature, probable physical and chemical form and the quantity, composition and effective height of the radioactive release;
   e. information on current and forecast meteorological and hydrological conditions, necessary for forecasting the trans-boundary release of the radioactive materials;
   f. the results of environmental monitoring relevant to the trans-boundary release of the radioactive materials;
   g. the off-site protective measures taken or planned;
   h. the predicted behaviour over time of the radioactive release.
2. Such information shall be supplemented at appropriate intervals by further relevant information on the development of the emergency situation, including its foreseeable or actual termination.
3. Information received pursuant to subparagraph (b) of article 2 may used without restriction, except when such information is provided in confidence by the notifying State Party.

Article 6
Consultations

A State Party providing information pursuant to sub-paragraph (b) of article 2 shall, as far as is reasonably practicable, respond promptly to a request for further information or consultations sought by an affected State Party with a view to minimizing the radiological consequences in that State.

Article 7
Competent authorities and points of contact

1. Each State Party shall make known to the Agency and to other States Parties, directly or through the Agency, its competent authorities and point of contact

responsible for issuing and receiving the notification and information referred to in article 2. Such points of contact and a focal point within the Agency shall be available continuously.
2. Each State Party shall promptly inform the Agency of any changes that may occur in the information referred to in paragraph 1.
3. The Agency shall maintain an up-to-date list of such national authorities and points of contact as well as points of contact of relevant international organizations and shall provide it to States Parties and Member States and to relevant international organizations.

Article 8
Assistance to States Parties

The Agency shall, in accordance with its Statute and upon a request of a State Party which does not have nuclear activities itself and borders on a State having an active nuclear programme but not Party, conduct investigations into the feasibility and establishment of an appropriate radiation monitoring system in order to facilitate the achievement of the objectives of this Convention.

Article 9
Bilateral and multilateral arrangements

In furtherance of their mutual interests, States Parties may consider, where deemed appropriate, the conclusion of bilateral or multilateral arrangements relating to the subject matter of this Convention.

Article 10
Relationship to other international agreements

This Convention shall not affect the reciprocal rights and obligations of State Parties under existing international agreements which relate to the matters covered by this Convention, or under future international agreements concluded in accordance with the object and purpose of this Convention.

Article 11
Settlement of disputes

1. In the event of a dispute between States Parties, or between a State Party and the Agency, concerning the interpretation or application of this Convention, the parties

to the dispute shall consult with a view to the settlement of the dispute by negotiation or by any other peaceful means of settling disputes acceptable to them.
2. If a dispute of this character between States Parties cannot be settled within one year from the request for consultation pursuant to paragraph 1, it shall, at the request of any party to such a dispute, be submitted to arbitration or referred to the International Court of Justice for decision. Where a dispute is submitted to arbitration, if, within six months from the date of the request, the parties to the dispute are unable to agree on the organization of the arbitration, a party may request the President of the International Court of Justice or the Secretary- General of the United Nations to appoint one or more arbitrators. In cases of conflicting requests by the parties to the dispute, the request to the Secretary-General of the United Nations shall have priority.
3. When signing, ratifying, accepting, approving or acceding to this Convention, a State may declare that it does not consider itself bound by either or both of the dispute settlement procedures provided for in paragraph 2. The other States Parties shall not be bound by a dispute settlement procedure provided for in paragraph 2 with respect to a State Party for which such a declaration is in force.
4. A State Party which has made a declaration in accordance with paragraph 3 may at any time withdraw it by notification to the depositary.

Article 12
Entry into force

1. This Convention shall be open for signature by all States and Namibia, represented by the United Nations Council for Namibia, at the Headquarters of the International Atomic Energy Agency in Vienna and at the Headquarters of the United Nations in New York, from 26 September 1986 and 6 October 1986 respectively, until its entry into force or for twelve months, whichever period is longer.
2. A State and Namibia, represented by the United Nations Council for Namibia, may express its consent to be bound by this Convention either by signature, or be deposit of an instrument of ratification, acceptance or approval following signature made subject to ratification, acceptance or approval, or by deposit of an instrument of accession. The instruments of ratification, acceptance, approval or accession shall be deposited with the depositary.
3. This Convention shall enter into force thirty days after consent to be bound has been expressed by three States.
4. For each State expressing consent to be bound by this Convention after its entry into force, this Convention shall enter into force for that State thirty days after the date of expression of consent.
5. a. This Convention shall be open for accession, as provided for in this article, by international organizations and regional integration organizations constituted by sovereign States, which have competence in respect of the negotia-

tion, conclusion and application of international agreements in matters covered by this Convention.

b. In matters within their competence such organizations shall, on their own behalf, exercise the rights and fulfil the obligations which this Convention attributes to States Parties.

c. When depositing its instrument of accession, such an organization shall communicate to the depositary a declaration indicating the extent of its competence in respect of matters covered by this Convention.

d. Such an organization shall not hold any vote additional to those of its Member States.

Article 13
Provisional application

A State may, upon signature or at any later date before this Convention enters into force for it, declare that it will apply this Convention provisionally.

Article 14
Amendments

1. A State Party may propose amendments to this Convention. The proposed amendment shall be submitted to the depositary who shall circulate it immediately to all other States Parties.
2. If a majority of the States Parties request the depositary to convene a conference to consider the proposed amendments, the depositary shall invite all States Parties to attend such a conference to begin not sooner than thirty days after the invitations are issued. Any amendment adopted at the conference by a two-thirds majority of all States Parties shall be laid down in a protocol which is open to signature in Vienna and New York by all States Parties.
3. The protocol shall enter into force thirty days after consent to be bound has been expressed by three States. For each State expressing consent to be bound by the protocol after its entry into force, the protocol shall enter into force for the State thirty days after the date of expression of consent.

Article 15
Denunciation

1. A State Party may denounce this Convention by written notification to the depositary.
2. Denunciation shall take effect on year following the date on which the notification is received by the depositary.

Article 16
Depositary

1. The Director General of the Agency shall be the depositary of this Convention.
2. The Director General of the Agency shall promptly notify States Parties and all other States of:
   a. each signature of this Convention or any protocol of amendment;
   b. each deposit of an instrument of ratification, acceptance, approval or accession concerning this Convention of any protocol of amendment;
   c. any declaration or withdrawal thereof in accordance with article 11;
   d. any declaration of provisional application of this Convention in accordance with article 13;
   e. the entry into force of this Convention and of any amendment thereto; and
   f. any denunciation made under article 15.

Article 17
Authentic texts and certified copies

The original of this Convention, of which the Arabic, Chinese, English, French, Russian and Spanish texts are equally authentic, shall be deposited with the Director General of the International Atomic Energy Agency who shall send certified copies to States Parties and all other States.

IN WITNESS WHEREOF the undersigned, being duly authorized, have signed this Convention, open for signature as provided for in paragraph 1 of article 12.

ADOPTED by the General Conference of the International Atomic Energy Agency meeting in special session at Vienna on the twenty-sixth day of September one thousand nine hundred and eighty-six.

THE IAEA CONVENTION ON ASSISTANCE IN THE CASE OF A NUCLEAR ACCIDENT OR RADIOLOGICAL EMERGENCY

(Vienna, 26 September 1986)

This Convention was adopted on the same date and in the same context as the Convention on Early Notification, as a consequence of the Chernobyl incident, in order to cope with similar events and situations where certain countries might need assistance. The Convention is intended to provide an international framework which facilitates the prompt and mutual provision of such assistance as the case may be, in order to mitigate the consequences of an incident or a radiological emergency. To this end, States are required to co-operate both between themselves and with the IAEA, which will provide its good offices to promote, facilitate and support such co-operation.

Like for early notification, also this Convention is the first one ever of its kind and it was similarly adopted at the end of long and stressing negotiations, after several and extensive amendments were made to the original proposal laid down by IAEA. Both the Agency and delegations, as for the Early Notification Convention, worked under enormous pressure especially vis-à-vis public opinion, which was very keen to see concrete results of an action taken to fill the very serious gaps in the specific international regime revealed by Chernobyl.

Under the new instrument adopted, the direction and control of assistance is the responsibility of the State requesting it, whereas the assisting State is entitled to any necessary facilitation, on the part of the assisted State, while carrying out its intervention. It must be added that, similarly to the Convention on Early Notification, the Convention on assistance provides for national authorities and contact points to be instituted, and that the conditions for entry into force (again, thirty days after consent to be bound expressed by only three countries) are intended to meet the same need, i.e. ensuring practical application in a very short delay. The Convention in fact entered into force on February 26, 1987, and it has 90 contracting Parties. It is noted that also FAO, WHO and WMO (World Meteorological Organization) have acceded to the Convention, and that the European Community will do the same in a near future.

As regards certain aspects associated to information in an emergency at the European Communities level, see introductory material to the Early Notification Convention.

THE STATES PARTIES TO THIS CONVENTION,

AWARE that nuclear activities are being carried out in a number of States,

NOTING that comprehensive measures have been and are being taken to ensure a high level of safety in nuclear activities, aimed at preventing nuclear accidents and minimizing the consequences of any such accident, should it occur,

DESIRING to strengthen further international co-operation in the safe development and use of nuclear energy,

CONVINCED of the need for an international framework which will facilitate the prompt provision of assistance in the event of a nuclear accident or radiological emergency to mitigate its consequences,

NOTING the usefulness of bilateral and multilateral arrangements on mutual assistance in this area,

NOTING the activities of the International Atomic Energy Agency in developing guidelines for mutual emergency assistance arrangements in connection with a nuclear accident or radiological emergency,

HAVE AGREED as follows:

Article 1
General provisions

1. The States Parties shall cooperate between themselves and with the International Atomic Energy Agency (hereinafter referred to as the "Agency") in accordance with the provisions of this Convention to facilitate prompt assistance in the event of a nuclear accident or radiological emergency to minimize its consequences and to protect life, property and the environment from the effects of radioactive releases.
2. To facilitate such cooperation States Parties may agree on bilateral or multilateral arrangements or, where appropriate, a combination of these, for preventing or minimizing injury and damage which may result in the event of a nuclear accident or radiological emergency.
3. The States Parties request the Agency, acting within the framework of its Statute, to use its best endeavours in accordance with the provisions of this Convention to promote, facilitate and support the cooperation between States Parties provided for in this Convention.

Article 2
Provision of assistance

1. If a State Party needs assistance in the event of a nuclear accident or radiological emergency, whether or not such accident or emergency originates within its territory, jurisdiction or control, it may call for such assistance from any other State Party, directly or through the Agency, and from the Agency, or, where appropriate, from other international intergovernmental organizations (hereinafter referred to as "international organizations").
2. A State Party requesting assistance shall specify the scope and type of assistance required and, where practicable, provide the assisting party with such information as may be necessary for that party to determine the extent to which it is able to meet the request. In the event that it is not practicable for the requesting State Party to specify the scope and type of assistance required, the requesting State Party and the assisting party shall, in consultation, decide upon the scope and type of assistance required.
3. Each State Party to which a request for such assistance is directed shall promptly decide and notify the requesting Slate Party, directly or through the Agency, whether it is in a position to render the assistance requested, and the scope and terms of the assistance that might be rendered.
4. States Parties shall, within the limits of their capabilities, identify and notify the Agency of experts, equipment and materials which could be made available for the provision of assistance to other States Parties in the event of a nuclear accident or radiological emergency as well as the terms, especially financial, under which such assistance could be provided.
5. Any State Party may request assistance relating to medical treatment or temporary relocation into the territory of another State Party of people involved in a nuclear accident or radiological emergency.
6. The Agency shall respond, in accordance with its Statute and as provided for in this Convention, to a requesting State Party's or a Member State's request for assistance in the event of a nuclear accident or radiological emergency by:
   a. making available appropriate resources allocated for this purpose;
   b. transmitting promptly the request to other States and international organizations which, according to the Agency's information, may possess the necessary resources; and
   c. if so requested by the requesting State, co-ordinating the assistance at the international level which may thus become available.

Article 3
Direction and control of assistance

Unless otherwise agreed:
a. the overall direction, control, co-ordination and supervision of the assistance shall be the responsibility within its territory of the requesting State. The assisting party should, where the assistance involves personnel, designate in consultation with the requesting State, the person who should be in charge of and retain immediate operational supervision over the personnel and the equipment provided by it. The designated person should exercise such supervision in cooperation with the appropriate authorities of the requesting State;
b. the requesting State shall provide, to the extent of its capabilities, local facilities and services for the proper and effective administration of the assistance. It shall also ensure the protection of personnel, equipment and materials brought into its territory by or on behalf of the assisting party for such purpose;
c. ownership of equipment and materials provided by either party during the periods of assistance shall be unaffected, and their return shall be ensured;
d. a State Party providing assistance in response to a request under paragraph 5 of article 2 shall co-ordinate that assistance within its territory.

Article 4
Competent authorities and points of contact

1. Each State Party shall make known to the Agency and to other States Parties, directly or through the Agency, its competent authorities and point of contact authorized to make and receive requests for and to accept offers of assistance. Such points of contact and a focal point within the Agency shall be available continuously.
2. Each State Party shall promptly inform the Agency of any changes that may occur in the information referred to in paragraph 1.
3. The Agency shall regularly and expeditiously provide to States Parties, Member States and relevant international organizations the information referred to in paragraphs 1 and 2.

Article 5
Functions of the Agency

The States Parties request the Agency, in accordance with paragraph 3 of article 1 and without prejudice to other provisions of this Convention, to:
a. collect and disseminate to States Parties and Member States information concerning:

   i. experts, equipment and materials which could be made available in the event of nuclear accidents or radiological emergencies;
   ii. methodologies, techniques and available results of research relating to response to nuclear accidents or radiological emergencies;
b. assist a State Party or a Member State when requested in any of the following or other appropriate matters:
   i. preparing both emergency plans in the case of nuclear accidents and radiological emergencies and the appropriate legislation;
   ii. developing appropriate training programmes for personnel to deal with nuclear accidents and radiological emergencies;
   iii. transmitting requests for assistance and relevant information in the event of a nuclear accident or radiological emergency;
   iv. developing appropriate radiation monitoring programmes, procedures and standards;
   v. conducting investigations into the feasibility of establishing appropriate radiation monitoring systems;
c. make available to a State Party or a Member State requesting assistance in the event of a nuclear accident or radiological emergency appropriate resources allocated for the purpose of conducting an initial assessment of the accident or emergency;
d. offer its good offices to the States Parties and Member States in the event of a nuclear accident or radiological emergency;
e. establish and maintain liaison with relevant international organizations for the purposes of obtaining and exchanging relevant information and data, and make a list of such organizations available to States Parties, Member States and the aforementioned organizations.

Article 6
Confidentiality and public statements

1. The requesting State and the assisting party shall protect the confidentiality of any confidential information that becomes available to either of them in connection with the assistance in the event of a nuclear accident or radiological emergency. Such information shall be used exclusively for the purpose of the assistance agreed upon.
2. The assisting party shall make every effort to coordinate with the requesting State before releasing information to the public on the assistance provided in connection with a nuclear accident or radiological emergency.

Article 7
Reimbursement of costs

1. An assisting party may offer assistance without costs to the requesting Slate. When considering whether to offer assistance on such a basis, the assisting party shall take into account:

a. the nature of the nuclear accident or radiological emergency;
b. the place of origin of the nuclear accident or radiological emergency;
c. the needs of developing countries;
d. the particular needs of countries without nuclear facilities; and
e. any other relevant factors.

2. When assistance is provided wholly or partly on a reimbursement basis, the requesting State shall reimburse the assisting party for the costs incurred for the services rendered by persons or organizations acting on its behalf, and for all expenses in connection with the assistance to the extent that such expenses are not directly defrayed by the requesting State. Unless otherwise agreed, reimbursement shall be provided promptly after the assisting party has presented its request for reimbursement to the requesting State, and in respect of costs other than local costs, shall be freely transferrable.

3. Notwithstanding paragraph 2, the assisting party may at any time waive, or agree to the postponement of, the reimbursement in whole or in part. In considering such waiver or postponement, assisting parties shall give due consideration to the needs of developing countries.

Article 8
Privileges, immunities and facilities

1. The requesting State shall afford to personnel of the assisting party and personnel acting on its behalf the necessary privileges, immunities and facilities for the performance of their assistance functions.

2. The requesting State shall afford the following privileges and immunities to personnel of the assisting party or personnel acting on its behalf who have been duly notified to and accepted by the requesting State:
   a. immunity from arrest, detention and legal process, including criminal, civil and administrative jurisdiction, of the requesting State, in respect of acts or omissions in the performance of their duties; and
   b. exemption from taxation, duties or other charges, except those which are normally incorporated in the price of goods or paid for services rendered, in respect of the performance of their assistance functions.

3. The requesting State shall:
   a. afford the assisting party exemption from taxation, duties or other charges on the equipment and property brought into the territory of the requesting State by the assisting party for the purpose of the assistance; and
   b. provide immunity from seizure, attachment or requisition of such equipment and property.

4. The requesting State shall ensure the return of such equipment and property. If requested by the assisting party, the requesting State shall arrange, to the extent it is

able to do so, for the necessary decontamination of recoverable equipment involved in the assistance before its return.
5. The requesting State shall facilitate the entry into, stay in and departure from its national territory of personnel notified pursuant to paragraph 2 and of equipment and property involved in the assistance.
6. Nothing in this article shall require the requesting State to provide its nationals or permanent residents with the privileges and immunities provided for in the foregoing paragraphs.
7. Without prejudice to the privileges and immunities, all beneficiaries enjoying such privileges and immunities under this article have a duty to respect the laws and regulations of the requesting State. They shall also have the duty not to interfere in the domestic affairs of the requesting State.
8. Nothing in this article shall prejudice rights and obligations with respect to privileges and immunities afforded pursuant to other international agreements or the rules of customary international law.
9. When signing, ratifying, accepting, approving or acceding to this Convention, a State may declare that it does not consider itself bound in whole or in part by paragraphs 2 and 3.
10. A State Party which has made a declaration in accordance with paragraph 9 may at any time withdraw it by notification to the depositary.

Article 9
Transit of personnel, equipment and property

Each State Party shall, at the request of the requesting State or the assisting party, seek to facilitate the transit through its territory of duly notified personnel, equipment and property involved in the assistance to and from the requesting State.

Article 10
Claims and compensation

1. The States Parties shall closely cooperate in order to facilitate the settlement of legal proceedings and claims under this article.
2. Unless otherwise agreed, a requesting State shall in respect of death or of injury to persons, damage to or loss of property, or damage to the environment caused within its territory or other area under its jurisdiction or control in the course of providing the assistance requested:
   a. not bring any legal proceedings against the assisting party or persons or other legal entities acting on its behalf;

b. assume responsibility for dealing with legal proceedings and claims brought by third parties against the assisting party or against persons or other legal entities acting on its behalf;
c. hold the assisting party or persons or other legal entities acting on its behalf harmless in respect of legal proceedings and claims referred to in sub-paragraph (b); and
d. compensate the assisting party or persons or other legal entities acting on its behalf for:
   i. death of or injury to personnel of the assisting party or persons acting on its behalf;
   ii. loss of or damage to non-consumable equipment or materials related to the assistance;

   except in cases of wilful misconduct by the individuals who caused the death, injury, loss or damage.

3. This article shall not prevent compensation or indemnity available under any applicable international agreement or national law of any State.
4. Nothing in this article shall require the requesting State to apply paragraph 2 in whole or in part to its nationals or permanent residents.
5. When signing, ratifying, accepting, approving or acceding to this Convention, a State may declare:
   a. that it does not consider itself bound in whole or in part by paragraph 2;
   b. that it will not apply paragraph 2 in whole or in part in cases of gross negligence by the individuals who caused the death, injury, loss or damage.
6. A State Party which has made a declaration in accordance with paragraph 5 may at any time withdraw it by notification to the depositary.

Article 11
Termination of assistance

The requesting State or the assisting party may at any time, after appropriate consultations and by notification in writing, request the termination of assistance received or provided under this Convention. Once such a request has been made, the parties involved shall consult with each other to make arrangements for the proper conclusion of the assistance.

Article 12
Relationship to other international agreements

This Convention shall not affect the reciprocal rights and obligations of States Parties under existing international agreements which relate to the matters covered by this Convention, or under future international agreements concluded in accordance with the object and purpose of this Convention.

Article 13
Settlement of disputes

1. In the event of a dispute between States Parties, or between a State Party and the Agency, concerning the interpretation or application of this Convention, the parties to the dispute shall consult with a view to the settlement of the dispute by negotiation or by any other peaceful means of settling disputes acceptable to them.
2. If a dispute of this character between States Parties cannot be settled within one year from the request for consultation pursuant to paragraph 1, it shall, at the request of any party to such dispute, be submitted to arbitration or referred to the International Court of Justice for decision. Where a dispute is submitted to arbitration, if, within six months from the date of the request, the parties to the dispute are unable to agree on the organization of the arbitration, a party may request the President of The International Court of Justice or the Secretary-General of the United Nations to appoint one or more arbitrators. In cases of conflicting requests by the parties to the dispute, the request to the Secretary-General of the United Nations shall have priority.
3. When signing, ratifying, accepting, approving or acceding to this Convention, a State may declare that it does not consider itself bound by either or both of the dispute settlement procedures provided for in paragraph 2. The other States Parties shall not be bound by a dispute settlement procedure provided for in paragraph 2 with respect to a State Party for which such a declaration is in force.
4. A State Party which has made a declaration in accordance with paragraph 3 may at any time withdraw it by notification to the depositary.

Article 14
Entry into force

1. This Convention shall be open for signature by all States and Namibia, represented by the United Nations Council for Namibia, at the Headquarters of the International Atomic Energy Agency in Vienna and at the Headquarters of the United Nations in New York, from 26 September 1986 and 6 October 1986 respectively, until its entry into force or for twelve months, whichever period is longer.
2. A State and Namibia, represented by the United Nations Council for Namibia, may express its consent to be bound by this Convention either by signature, or by deposit of an instrument of ratification, acceptance or approval following signature made subject to ratification, acceptance or approval, or by deposit of an instrument of accession. The instruments of ratification, acceptance, approval or accession shall be deposited with the depositary.
3. This Convention shall enter into force thirty days after consent to be bound has been expressed by three States.

4. For each State expressing consent to be bound by this Convention after its entry into force, this Convention shall enter into force for that State thirty days after the date of expression of consent.

5.
   a. This Convention shall be open for accession, as provided for in this article, by international organizations and regional integration organizations constituted by sovereign States, which have competence in respect of the negotiation, conclusion and application of international agreements in matters covered by this Convention.
   b. In matters within their competence such organizations shall, on their own behalf, exercise the rights and fulfil the obligations which this Convention attributes to States Parties.
   c. When depositing its instrument of accession, such an organization shall communicate to the depositary a declaration indicating the extent of its competence in respect of matters covered by this Convention.
   d. Such an organization shall not hold any vote additional to those of its Member States.

Article 15
Provisional application

A State may, upon signature or at any later date before this Convention enters into force for it, declare that it will apply this Convention provisionally.

Article 16
Amendments

1. A State Party may propose amendments to this Convention. The proposed amendment shall be submitted to the depositary who shall circulate it immediately to all other States Parties.
2. If a majority of the States Parties request the depositary to convene a conference to consider the proposed amendments, the depositary shall invite all States Parties to attend such a conference to begin not sooner than thirty days after the invitations are issued. Any amendment adopted at the conference by a two-thirds majority of all States Parties shall be laid down in a protocol which is open to signature in Vienna and New York by all States Parties.
3. The protocol shall enter into force thirty days after consent to be bound has been expressed by three States. For each State expressing consent to be bound by the protocol after its entry into force, the protocol shall enter into force for that State thirty days after the date of expression of consent.

Article 17
Denunciation

1. A State Party may denounce this Convention by written notification to the depositary.
2. Denunciation shall take effect one year following the date on which the notification is received by the depositary.

Article 18
Depositary

1. The Director General of the Agency shall be the depositary of this Convention.
2. The Director General of the Agency shall promptly notify States Parties and all other States of:
   a. each signature of this Convention or any protocol of amendment;
   b. each deposit of an instrument of ratification, acceptance, approval or accession concerning this Convention or any protocol of amendment;
   c. any declaration or withdrawal thereof in accordance with articles 8, 10 and 13;
   d. any declaration of provisional application of this Convention in accordance with article 15;
   e. the entry into force of this Convention and of any amendment thereto; and
   f. any denunciation made under article 17.

Article 19
Authentic texts and certified copies

The original of this Convention, of which the Arabic, Chinese, English, French, Russian and Spanish texts are equally authentic, shall be deposited with the Director General of the International Atomic Energy Agency who shall send certified copies to States Parties and all other States.

IN WITNESS WHEREOF the undersigned, being duly authorized, have signed this Convention, open for signature as provided for in paragraph 1 of article 14.

ADOPTED by the General Conference of the International Atomic Energy Agency meeting in special session at Vienna on the twenty-sixth day of September one thousand nine hundred and eighty-six.

THE IAEA CONVENTION ON NUCLEAR SAFETY

(Vienna, 17 June 1994)

This instrument was adopted under the aegis of the International Atomic Energy Agency, at a Diplomatic Conference convened in Vienna from 14-17 June 1994. It should be pointed out preliminarily that the Convention is the first one ever of its kind. The main reason for this lies in the approach to the issue traditionally adopted by States that nuclear safety is their exclusive competence, and therefore should be enforced primarily at national levels. Besides, it should be recalled that nuclear safety has relevant technological implications, in the sense that the development of nuclear technology is perceived as an ongoing process to be preserved within those States directly involved, and consequently is to be kept as independent as possible from "supranational" interference, although general non-binding principles and standards are accepted.

As a background to the Convention, another aspect is worth stressing, which is that, unlike other conventions to be found in this Chapter, it has its "political" origins and motivation in the intention to prevent rather than to cure. Already in 1991 the IAEA had convened a Conference on the "Safety of Nuclear Power: Strategy for the Future", where the need was declared "to consider an integrated approach to all aspects of nuclear safety.....which would be adopted by all Governments". Besides, the IAEA governing bodies were requested to organise "the preparation of a proposal on the necessary elements" of such integrated approach, on the basis of the "guidance and mechanisms already established in the IAEA". Later on, the Agency's General Conference of the same year supported the idea, notably recognizing its potentiality to lead to a framework convention as a pillar of an international nuclear safety regime, and invited the IAEA's Director General to prepare "an outline of the possible elements of a nuclear safety convention". The document was then examined and discussed by a group of experts from many countries convened at IAEA, who finalized it to be submitted to the Diplomatic Conference for adoption.

The large number of countries that were involved in the elaboration of the convention and in the Conference reflects both the high international interest and the willingness to improve nuclear safety, independently of national nuclear power programmes. On the other hand, since the Convention was the first international instrument on nuclear safety as such, its text did have to take into account a number of "desiderata" expressed by certain countries. In particular, the main concern was that the new convention would not hinder promotion and progress of nuclear power, not only in those countries where this had already reached a high degree of development, but also in other countries potentially ready to use nuclear power for peaceful purposes. All this, of course, without any prejudice of safety, but rather with the intent to provide an incentive to such use, which is in fact one of the main features of the new Convention.

More specifically, another important and in itself new feature of the Convention is the provision for the so called "peer review" mechanism, consisting essentially in periodical meetings of the contracting Parties to review the level of nuclear safety, on the basis of detailed reports submitted by individual countries on the measures they have taken to implement the obligations stipulated by the Convention.

Concerning its entry into force, it should be recalled that unlike the relevant conditions stipulated for other conventions in this Chapter (e.g. on Early Notification), the number of States required is quite high. Besides, the additional requirement that among the minimum 22 ratifying Sates 17 of them must each have at least one operating nuclear plant, gave rise originally to some pessimism as to the entering into effect of the new instrument. However, time has proved that States as a whole were and are sincerely keen to accept it as a particularly important step forward in the creation of an international nuclear safety regime. The Convention indeed entered into force in a fairly short time (October 24, 1996), and it has 53 contracting parties.

It is also important to note that the European (Euratom) Community became a party to the Convention by virtue of a Decision (approving accession) adopted by the Council in 1998. An amendment to this Decision was adopted towards the end of 2003, in order to make it consistent with the European Court of Justice's ruling of December 10, 2002. For this case law, its connection with the new Decision and the reasons for the amendment, see Appendix to the volume. The text of the amended Decision is published in the following pages, among the other Euratom instruments and acts. It is recalled that the Commission adopted its own Decisions in connection with the accession, the latest being of April 29, 2004, especially to take into account the enlargement of the European Union as of May 1, 2004.

PREAMBLE

THE CONTRACTING PARTIES

i. Aware of the importance to the international community of ensuring that the use of nuclear energy is safe, well regulated and environmentally sound;
ii. Reaffirming the necessity of continuing to promote a high level of nuclear safety worldwide;
iii. Reaffirming that responsibility for nuclear safety rests with the State having jurisdiction over a nuclear installation;
iv. Desiring to promote an effective nuclear safety culture;

v. Aware that accidents at nuclear installations have the potential for transboundary impacts;
vi. Keeping in mind the Convention on the Physical Protection of Nuclear Material (1979), the Convention on Early Notification of a Nuclear Accident (1986), and the Convention on Assistance in the Case of a Nuclear Accident or Radiological Emergency (1986);
vii. Affirming the importance of international co-operation for the enhancement of nuclear safety through existing bilateral and multilateral mechanisms and the establishment of this incentive Convention;
viii. Recognizing that this Convention entails a commitment to the application of fundamental safety principles for nuclear installations rather than of detailed safety standards and that there are internationally formulated safety guidelines which are updated from time to time and so can provide guidance on contemporary means of achieving a high level of safety;
ix. Affirming the need to begin promptly the development of an international convention on the safety of radioactive waste management as soon as the ongoing process to develop waste management safety fundamentals has resulted in broad international agreement;
x. Recognizing the usefulness of further technical work in connection with the safety of other parts of the nuclear fuel cycle, and that this work may, in time, facilitate the development of current or future international instruments;

HAVE AGREED as follows:

Chapter 1.
OBJECTIVES, DEFINITIONS AND SCOPE OF APPLICATION

Article 1.
Objectives

The objectives of this Convention are:
i. to achieve and maintain a high level of nuclear safety worldwide through the enhancement of national measures and international co-operation including, where appropriate, safety-related technical co-operation;
ii. to establish and maintain effective defences in nuclear installations against potential radiological hazards in order to protect individuals, society and the environment from harmful effects of ionising radiation from such installations;
iii. to prevent accidents with radiological consequences and to mitigate such consequences should they occur.

Article 2.
Definitions

For the purpose of this Convention:

i. "nuclear installation" means for each Contracting Party any land-based civil nuclear power plant under its jurisdiction including such storage, handling and treatment facilities for radioactive materials as are on the same site and are directly related to the operation of the nuclear power plant. Such a plant ceases to be a nuclear installation when all nuclear fuel elements have been removed permanently from the reactor core and have been stored safely in accordance with approved procedures, and a decommissioning programme has been agreed to by the regulatory body.

ii. "regulatory body" means for each Contracting Party any body or bodies given the legal authority by that Contracting Party to grant licences and to regulate the siting, design, construction, commissioning, operation or decommissioning of nuclear installations.

iii. "licence" means any authorization granted by the regulatory body to the applicant to have the responsibility for the siting, design, construction, commissioning, operation or decommissioning of a nuclear installation.

Article 3.
Scope of application

This Convention shall apply to the safety of nuclear installations.

Chapter 2.
OBLIGATIONS

General Provisions

Article 4.
Implementing measures

Each Contracting Party shall take, within the framework of its national law, the legislative, regulatory and administrative measures and other steps necessary for implementing its obligations under this Convention.

Article 5.
Reporting

Each Contracting Party shall submit for review, prior to each meeting referred to in Article 20, a report on the measures it has taken to implement each of the obligations of this Convention

Article 6.
Existing nuclear installations

Each Contracting Party shall take the appropriate steps to ensure that the safety of nuclear installations existing at the time the Convention enters into force for that Contracting Party is reviewed as soon as possible. When necessary in the context of this Convention, the Contracting Party shall ensure that all reasonably practicable improvements are made as a matter of urgency to upgrade the safety of the nuclear installation. If such upgrading cannot be achieved, plans should be implemented to shut down the nuclear installation as soon as practically possible. The timing of the shut-down may take into account the whole energy context and possible alternatives as well as the social, environmental and economic impact.

Legislation and regulation

Article 7.
Legislative and regulatory framework

1. Each Contracting Party shall establish and maintain a legislative and regulatory framework to govern the safety of nuclear installations.
2. The legislative and regulatory framework shall provide for:
   i. the establishment of applicable national safety requirements and regulations;
   ii. a system of licensing with regard to nuclear installations and the prohibition of the operation of a nuclear installation without a licence:
   iii. a system of regulatory inspection and assessment of nuclear installations to ascertain compliance with applicable regulations and the terms of licences;
   iv. the enforcement of applicable regulations and of the terms of licences, including suspension, modification or revocation.

Article 8.
Regulatory body

1. Each Contracting Party shall establish or designate a regulatory body entrusted with the implementation of the legislative and regulatory framework referred to

in Article 7, and provided with adequate authority, competence and financial and human resources to fulfil its assigned responsibilities.

2. Each Contracting Party shall take the appropriate steps to ensure an effective separation between the functions of the regulatory body and those of any other body or organization concerned with the promotion or utilization of nuclear energy.

Article 9.
Responsibility of the licence holder

Each Contracting Party shall ensure that prime responsibility for the safety of a nuclear installation rests with the holder of the relevant licence and shall take the appropriate steps to ensure that each such licence holder meets its responsibility.

General Safety Considerations

Article 10.
Priority to safety

Each Contracting Party shall take the appropriate steps to ensure that all organizations engaged in activities directly related to nuclear installations shall establish policies that give due priority to nuclear safety.

Article 11.
Financial and human resources

1. Each Contracting Party shall take the appropriate steps to ensure that adequate financial resources are available to support the safety of each nuclear installation throughout its life.
2. Each Contracting Party shall take the appropriate steps to ensure that sufficient numbers of qualified staff with appropriate education, training and retraining are available for all safety-related activities in or for each nuclear installation, throughout its life.

Article 12.
Human factors

Each Contracting Party shall take the appropriate steps to ensure that the capabilities and limitations of human performance are taken into account throughout the life of a nuclear installation.

Article 13.
Quality assurance

Each Contracting Party shall take the appropriate steps to ensure that quality assurance programmes are established and implemented with a view to providing confidence that specified requirements for all activities important to nuclear safety are satisfied throughout the life of a nuclear installation.

Article 14.
Assessment and verification of safety

Each Contracting Party shall take the appropriate steps to ensure that:

i. comprehensive and systematic safety assessments are carried out before the construction and commissioning of a nuclear installation and throughout its life. Such assessments shall be well documented, subsequently updated in the light of operating experience and significant new safety information, and reviewed under the authority of the regulatory body;
ii. verification by analysis, surveillance, testing and inspection is carried out to ensure that the physical state and the operation of a nuclear installation continue to be in accordance with its design, applicable national safety requirements, and operational limits and conditions.

Article 15.
Radiation protection

Each Contracting Party shall take the appropriate steps to ensure that in all operational states the radiation exposure to the workers and the public caused by a nuclear installation shall be kept as low as reasonably achievable and that no individual shall be exposed to radiation doses which exceed prescribed national dose limits.

Article 16.
Emergency preparedness

1. Each Contracting Party shall take the appropriate steps to ensure that there are on-site and off-site emergency plans that are routinely tested for nuclear installations and cover the activities to be carried out in the event of an emergency. For any new nuclear installation, such plans shall be prepared and tested before it commences operation above a low power level agreed by the regulatory body.

2. Each Contracting Party shall take the appropriate steps to ensure that, insofar as they are likely to be affected by a radiological emergency, its own population and the competent authorities of the States in the vicinity of the nuclear installation are provided with appropriate information for emergency planning and response.
3. Contracting Parties which do not have a nuclear installation on their territory, insofar as they are likely to be affected in the event of a radiological emergency at a nuclear installation in the vicinity, shall take the appropriate steps for the preparation and testing of emergency plans for their territory that cover the activities to be carried out in the event of such an emergency.

Safety of Installations

Article 17.
Siting

Each Contracting Party shall take the appropriate steps to ensure that appropriate procedures are established and implemented:
i. for evaluating all relevant site-related factors likely to affect the safety of a nuclear installation for its projected lifetime;
ii. for evaluating the likely safety impact of a proposed nuclear installation on individuals, society and the environment;
iii. for re-evaluating as necessary all relevant factors referred to in sub-paragraphs (i) and (ii) so as to ensure the continued safety acceptability of the nuclear installation;
iv. for consulting Contracting Parties in the vicinity of a proposed nuclear installation, insofar as they are likely to be affected by that installation and, upon request providing the necessary information to such Contracting Parties, in order to enable them to evaluate and make their own assessment of the likely safety impact on their own territory of the nuclear installation.

Article 18.
Design and construction

Each Contracting Party shall take the appropriate steps to ensure that:
i. the design and construction of a nuclear installation provides for several reliable levels and methods of protection (defense in depth) against the release of radioactive materials, with a view to preventing the occurrence of accidents and to mitigating their radiological consequences should they occur;
ii. the technologies incorporated in the design and construction of a nuclear installation are proven by experience or qualified by testing or analysis;

iii. the design of a nuclear installation allows for reliable, stable and easily manageable operation, with specific consideration of human factors and the man-machine interface.

Article 19.
Operation

Each Contracting Party shall take the appropriate steps to ensure that:

i. the initial authorization to operate a nuclear installation is based upon an appropriate safety analysis and a commissioning programme demonstrating that the installation, as constructed, is consistent with design and safety requirements;
ii. operational limits and conditions derived from the safety analysis, tests and operational experience are defined and revised as necessary for identifying safe boundaries for operation;
iii. operation, maintenance, inspection and testing of a nuclear installation are conducted in accordance with approved procedures;
iv. procedures are established for responding to anticipated operational occurrences and to accidents;
v. necessary engineering and technical support in all safety-related fields is available throughout the lifetime of a nuclear installation;
vi. incidents significant to safety are reported in a timely manner by the holder of the relevant licence to the regulatory body;
vii. programmes to collect and analyse operating experience are established, the results obtained and the conclusions drawn are acted upon and that existing mechanisms are used to share important experience with international bodies and with other operating organizations and regulatory bodies;
viii. the generation of radioactive waste resulting from the operation of a nuclear installation is kept to the minimum practicable for the process concerned, both in activity and in volume, and any necessary treatment and storage of spent fuel and waste directly related to the operation and on the same site as that of the nuclear installation take into consideration conditioning and disposal.

Chapter 3.
MEETINGS OF THE CONTRACTING PARTIES

Article 20.
Review meetings

1. The Contracting Parties shall hold meetings (hereinafter referred to as "review meetings") for the purpose of reviewing the reports submitted pursuant to Article 5 in accordance with the procedures adopted under Article 22.

2. Subject to the provisions of Article 24 sub-groups comprised of representatives of Contracting Parties may be established and may function during the review meetings as deemed necessary for the purpose of reviewing specific subjects contained in the reports.
3. Each Contracting Party shall have a reasonable opportunity to discuss the reports submitted by other Contracting Parties and to seek clarification of such reports.

Article 21.
Timetable

1. A preparatory meeting of the Contracting Parties shall be held not later than six months after the date of entry into force of this Convention.
2. At this preparatory meeting, the Contracting Parties shall determine the date for the first review meeting. This review meeting shall be held as soon as possible, but not later than thirty months after the date of entry into force of this Convention.
3. At each review meeting, the Contracting Parties shall determine the date for the next such meeting. The interval between review meetings shall not exceed three years.

Article 22.
Procedural Arrangements

1. At the preparatory meeting held pursuant to Article 21 the Contracting Parties shall prepare and adopt by consensus Rules of Procedure and Financial Rules. The Contracting Parties shall establish in particular and in accordance with the Rules of Procedure:
   i. guidelines regarding the form and structure of the reports to be submitted pursuant to Article 5;
   ii. a date for the submission of such reports;
   iii. the process for reviewing such reports.
2. At review meetings the Contracting Parties may, if necessary, review the arrangements established pursuant to sub-paragraphs (i)-(iii) above, and adopt revisions by consensus unless otherwise provided for in the Rules of Procedure. They may also amend the Rules of Procedure and the Financial Rules, by consensus.

Article 23.
Extraordinary meetings

An extraordinary meeting of the Contracting Parties shall be held:
i. if so agreed by a majority of the Contracting Parties present and voting at a meeting, abstentions being considered as voting; or

ii. at the written request of a Contracting Party, within six months of this request having been communicated to the Contracting Parties and notification having been received by the secretariat referred to in Article 28, that the request has been supported by a majority of the Contracting Parties.

Article 24.
Attendance

1. Each Contracting Party shall attend meetings of the Contracting Parties and be represented at such meetings by one delegate, and by such alternates, experts and advisers as it deems necessary.
2. The Contracting Parties may invite, by consensus, any intergovernmental organization which is competent in respect of matters governed by this Convention to attend, as an observer, any meeting, or specific sessions thereof. Observers shall be required to accept in writing, and in advance, the provisions of Article 27.

Article 25.
Summary Reports

The Contracting Parties shall adopt, by consensus, and make available to the public a document addressing issues discussed and conclusions reached during a meeting.

Article 26.
Languages

1. The languages of meetings of the Contracting Parties shall be Arabic, Chinese, English, French, Russian and Spanish unless otherwise provided in the Rules of Procedure.
2. Reports submitted pursuant to Article 5 shall be prepared in the national language of the submitting Contracting Party or in a single designated language to be agreed in the Rules of Procedure. Should the report be submitted in a national language other than the designated language, a translation of the report into the designated language shall be provided by the Contracting Party.
3. Notwithstanding the provisions of paragraph 2, if compensated, the secretariat will assume the translation into the designated language of reports submitted in any other language of the meeting.

Article 27.
Confidentiality

1. The provisions of this Convention shall not affect the rights and obligations of the Contracting Parties under their law to protect information from disclosure. For the purposes of this Article, "information" includes, inter alia, (i) personal data; (ii) information protected by intellectual property rights or by industrial or commercial confidentiality; and (iii) information relating to national security or to the physical protection of nuclear materials or nuclear installations.
2. When, in the context of this Convention, a Contracting Party provides information identified by it as protected as described in paragraph 1, such information shall be used only for the purposes for which it has been provided and its confidentiality shall be respected.
3. The content of the debates during the reviewing of the reports by the Contracting Parties at each meeting shall be confidential.

Article 28.
Secretariat

1. The International Atomic Energy Agency, (hereinafter referred to as the "Agency") shall provide the secretariat for the meetings of the Contracting Parties.
2. The secretariat shall:
   i. convene, prepare and service the meetings of the Contracting Parties;
   ii. transmit to the Contracting Parties information received or prepared in accordance with the provisions of this Convention.

   The costs incurred by the Agency in carrying out the functions referred to in sub-paragraphs i) and (ii) above shall be borne by the Agency as part of its regular budget.

3. The Contracting Parties may, by consensus, request the Agency to provide other services in support of meetings of the Contracting Parties. The Agency may provide such services if they can be undertaken within its programme and regular budget. Should this not be possible, the Agency may provide such services if voluntary funding is provided from another source.

Chapter 4.
FINAL CLAUSES AND OTHER PROVISIONS

Article 29.
Resolution of disagreements

In the event of a disagreement between two or more Contracting Parties concerning the interpretation or application of this Convention, the Contracting Parties shall consult within the framework of a meeting of the Contracting Parties with a view to resolving the disagreement.

Article 30.
Signature, ratification, acceptance, approval, accession

1. This Convention shall be open for signature by all States at the Headquarters of the Agency in Vienna from 20 September 1994 until its entry into force.
2. This Convention is subject to ratification, acceptance or approval by the signatory States.
3. After its entry into force, this Convention shall be open for accession by all States.
4.
    i. This Convention shall be open for signature or accession by regional organizations of an integration or other nature, provided that any such organization is constituted by sovereign States and has competence in respect of the negotiation, conclusion and application of international agreements in matters covered by this Convention.
    ii. In matters within their competence, such organizations shall, on their own behalf, exercise the rights and fulfil the responsibilities which this Convention attributes to States Parties
    iii. When becoming party to this Convention, such an organization shall communicate to the Depositary referred to in Article 34, a declaration indicating which States are members thereof, which articles of this Convention apply to it, and the extent of its competence in the field covered by those articles.
    iv. Such an organization shall not hold any vote additional to those of its Member States.
5. Instruments of ratification, acceptance, approval or accession shall be deposited with the Depositary.

Article 31.
Entry into force

1. This Convention shall enter into force on the ninetieth day after the date of deposit with the Depositary of the twenty- second instrument of ratification, acceptance or approval, including the instruments of seventeen States, each having at least one nuclear installation which has achieved criticality in a reactor core.
2. For each State or regional organization of an integration of other nature which ratifies, accepts, approves or accedes to this Convention after the date of deposit of the last instrument required to satisfy the conditions set forth in paragraph 1, this Convention shall enter into force on the ninetieth day after the date of deposit with the Depositary of the appropriate instrument by such a State or organization.

Article 32.
Amendments to the convention

1. Any Contracting party may propose an amendment to this Convention. Proposed amendments shall be considered at a review meeting or an extraordinary meeting.
2. The text of any proposed amendment and the reasons for it shall be provided to the Depositary who shall communicate the proposal to the Contracting Parties promptly and at least ninety days before the meeting for which it is submitted for consideration. Any comments received on such a proposal shall be circulated by the Depositary to the Contracting Parties.
3. The Contracting Parties shall decide after consideration of the proposed amendment whether to adopt it by consensus, or, in the absence of consensus, to submit it to a Diplomatic Conference. A decision to submit a proposed amendment to a Diplomatic Conference shall require a two-thirds majority vote of the Contracting parties present and voting at the meeting, provided that at least one half of the Contracting Parties are present at the time of voting. Abstentions shall be considered as voting.
4. The Diplomatic Conference to consider and adopt amendments to this Convention shall be convened by the Depositary and held no later than one year after the appropriate decision taken in accordance with paragraph 3 of this Article. The Diplomatic Conference shall make every effort to ensure amendments are adopted by consensus. Should this not be possible, amendments shall be adopted with a two-thirds majority of all Contracting Parties.
5. Amendments to this Convention adopted pursuant to paragraphs 3 and 4 above shall be subject to ratification, acceptance, approval, or confirmation by the Contracting Parties and shall enter into force for those Contracting Parties which have ratified, accepted, approved or confirmed them on the ninetieth day after the receipt by the Depositary of the relevant instruments by at least three fourths of

the Contracting Parties. For a Contracting Party which subsequently ratifies, accepts, approves or confirms the said amendments, the amendments will enter into force on the ninetieth day after that Contracting Party has deposited its relevant instrument.

Article 33.
Denunciation

1. Any Contracting Party may denounce this Convention by written notification to the Depositary.
2. Denunciation shall take effect one year following the date of the receipt of the notification by the Depositary, or on such later date as may be specified in the notification.

Article 34.
Depositary

1. The Director General of the Agency shall be the Depositary of this Convention.
2. The Depositary shall inform the Contracting Parties of:
   i. the signature of this Convention and of the deposit of instruments of ratification, acceptance, approval or accession, in accordance with Article 30;
   ii. the date on which the Convention enters into force, in accordance with Article 31;
   iii. the notifications of denunciation of the Convention and the date thereof, made in accordance with Article 33;
   iv. the proposed amendments to this Convention submitted by Contracting Parties, the amendments adopted by the relevant Diplomatic Conference or by the meeting of the Contracting Parties, and the date of entry into force of the said amendments, in accordance with Article 32.

Article 35.
Authentic texts

The original of this Convention of which the Arabic, Chinese, English, French, Russian and Spanish texts are equally authentic, shall be deposited with the Depositary, who shall send certified copies thereof to the Contracting Parties.

THE IAEA JOINT CONVENTION ON THE SAFETY OF SPENT FUEL MANAGEMENT AND ON THE SAFETY OF RADIOACTIVE WASTE MANAGEMENT

(Vienna, 5 September 1997)

In the course of the negotiations for the Nuclear Safety Convention (see preceding pages) the safe management of radioactive waste had indeed been considered for inclusion in the scope of that Convention. Further discussion, however, led to the decision to leave it out for the very important reason that it was believed to deserve a specific separate instrument. At the same time, an agreement was reached that negotiations for such instrument should be started within the shortest possible delay. This held certainly true, since the new convention was adopted only three years later, bearing in mind that negotiations were protracted for longer than originally expected since it was found that the convention should cover also spent fuel, equally needing to be governed by an international regime pertaining to its safe management.

The new regime addresses spent fuel and waste from nuclear installations, including those originally intended for military or defence programmes which are declared (by the contracting Party) as transferred permanently to and managed within exclusively civilian programmes. The Convention basically aims at ensuring that adequate measures are taken to protect individuals, society and the environment from any potential risk arising from the spent fuel and the waste in point. To this purpose, the Convention requires the laying down of national legislation and licensing and inspection systems, as well as the clear allocation of responsibilities of the bodies involved in the various steps of the safe management to be pursued. It is important to recall that also institutional measures to be taken after closure of a disposal facility (that is, once all operations after emplacement of the fuel or the waste in the facility are completed) are required by the Convention. This addresses also the trans-boundary movement of the materials under consideration. A "peer review" mechanism similar to that set up by the Nuclear safety Convention is finally provided for, based again on submission of national reports to the meetings of the contracting parties.

For the entry into force of the Convention, which was adopted on 5 September 1997, twenty-five ratifications were necessary, fifteen of which by States each having at least one nuclear installation in operation. The Convention entered into force on 18 June, 2001 and has 33 contracting parties.

PREAMBLE

The Contracting Parties

i. Recognizing that the operation of nuclear reactors generates spent fuel and radioactive waste and that other applications of nuclear technologies also generate radioactive waste;
ii. Recognizing that the same safety objectives apply both to spent fuel and radioactive waste management;
iii. Reaffirming the importance to the international community of ensuring that sound practices are planned and implemented for the safety of spent fuel and radioactive waste management;
iv. Recognizing the importance of informing the public on issues regarding the safety of spent fuel and radioactive waste management;
v. Desiring to promote an effective nuclear safety culture worldwide;
vi. Reaffirming that the ultimate responsibility for ensuring the safety of spent fuel and radioactive waste management rests with the State;
vii. Recognizing that the definition of a fuel cycle policy rests with the State, some States considering spent fuel as a valuable resource that may be reprocessed, others electing to dispose of it;
viii. Recognizing that spent fuel and radioactive waste excluded from the present Convention because they are within military or defence programmes should be managed in accordance with the objectives stated in this Convention;
ix. Affirming the importance of international co-operation in enhancing the safety of spent fuel and radioactive waste management through bilateral and multilateral mechanisms, and through this incentive Convention;
x. Mindful of the needs of developing countries, and in particular the least developed countries, and of States with economies in transition and of the need to facilitate existing mechanisms to assist in the fulfillment of their rights and obligations set out in this incentive Convention;
xi. Convinced that radioactive waste should, as far as is compatible with the safety of the management of such material, be disposed of in the State in which it was generated, whilst recognizing that, in certain circumstances, safe and efficient management of spent fuel and radioactive waste might be fostered through agreements among Contracting Parties to use facilities in one of them for the benefit of the other Parties, particularly where waste originates from joint projects;
xii. Recognizing that any State has the right to ban import into its territory of foreign spent fuel and radioactive waste;
xiii. Keeping in mind the Convention on Nuclear Safety (1994), the Convention on Early Notification of a Nuclear Accident (1986), the Convention on Assistance

in the Case of a Nuclear Accident or Radiological Emergency (1986), the Convention on the Physical Protection of Nuclear Material (1980), the Convention on the Prevention of Marine Pollution by Dumping of Wastes and Other Matter as amended (1994) and other relevant international instruments;

xiv. Keeping in mind the principles contained in the interagency "International Basic Safety Standards for Protection against Ionizing Radiation and for the Safety of Radiation Sources" (1996), in the IAEA Safety Fundamentals entitled "The Principles of Radioactive Waste Management" (1995), and in the existing international standards relating to the safety of the transport of radioactive materials;

xv. Recalling Chapter 22 of Agenda 21 by the United Nations Conference on Environment and Development in Rio de Janeiro adopted in 1992, which reaffirms the paramount importance of the safe and environmentally sound management of radioactive waste;

xvi. Recognizing the desirability of strengthening the international control system applying specifically to radioactive materials as referred to in Article 1(3) of the Basel Convention on the Control of Transboundary Movements of Hazardous Wastes and Their Disposal (1989);

Have agreed as follows:

Chapter 1.
OBJECTIVES, DEFINITIONS AND SCOPE OF APPLICATION

Article 1.
Objectives

The objectives of this Convention are:

i. to achieve and maintain a high level of safety worldwide in spent fuel and radioactive waste management, through the enhancement of national measures and international co-operation, including where appropriate, safety-related technical co-operation;

ii. to ensure that during all stages of spent fuel and radioactive waste management there are effective defences against potential hazards so that individuals, society and the environment are protected from harmful effects of ionizing radiation, now and in the future, in such a way that the needs and aspirations of the present generation are met without compromising the ability of future generations to meet their needs and aspirations;

iii. to prevent accidents with radiological consequences and to mitigate their consequences should they occur during any stage of spent fuel or radioactive waste management.

Article 2.
Definitions

For the purposes of this Convention:

a. *"closure"* means the completion of all operations at some time after the emplacement of spent fuel or radioactive waste in a disposal facility. This includes the final engineering or other work required to bring the facility to a condition that will be safe in the long term;
b. *"decommissioning"* means all steps leading to the release of a nuclear facility, other than a disposal facility, from regulatory control. These steps include the processes of decontamination and dismantling;
c. *"discharges"* means planned and controlled releases into the environment, as a legitimate practice, within limits authorized by the regulatory body, of liquid or gaseous radioactive materials that originate from regulated nuclear facilities during normal operation;
d. *"disposal"* means the emplacement of spent fuel or radioactive waste in an appropriate facility without the intention of retrieval;
e. *"licence"* means any authorization, permission or certification granted by a regulatory body to carry out any activity related to management of spent fuel or of radioactive waste;
f. *"nuclear facility"* means a civilian facility and its associated land, buildings and equipment in which radioactive materials are produced, processed, used, handled, stored or disposed of on such a scale that consideration of safety is required;
g. *"operating lifetime"* means the period during which a spent fuel or a radioactive waste management facility is used for its intended purpose. In the case of a disposal facility, the period begins when spent fuel or radioactive waste is first emplaced in the facility and ends upon closure of the facility;
h. *"radioactive waste"* means radioactive material in gaseous, liquid or solid form for which no further use is foreseen by the Contracting Party or by a natural or legal person whose decision is accepted by the Contracting Party, and which is controlled as radioactive waste by a regulatory body under the legislative and regulatory framework of the Contracting Party;
i. *"radioactive waste management"* means all activities, including decommissioning activities, that relate to the handling, pretreatment, treatment, conditioning, storage, or disposal of radioactive waste, excluding off-site transportation. It may also involve discharges;
j. *"radioactive waste management facility"* means any facility or installation the primary purpose of which is radioactive waste management, including a nuclear facility in the process of being decommissioned only if it is designated by the Contracting Party as a radioactive waste management facility;

k. *"regulatory body"* means any body or bodies given the legal authority by the Contracting Party to regulate any aspect of the safety of spent fuel or radioactive waste management including the granting of licences;
l. *"reprocessing"* means a process or operation, the purpose of which is to extract radioactive isotopes from spent fuel for further use;
m. *"sealed source"* means radioactive material that is permanently sealed in a capsule or closely bonded and in a solid form, excluding reactor fuel elements;
n. *"spent fuel"* means nuclear fuel that has been irradiated in and permanently removed from a reactor core;
o. *"spent fuel management"* means all activities that relate to the handling or storage of spent fuel, excluding off-site transportation. It may also involve discharges;
p. *"spent fuel management facility"* means any facility or installation the primary purpose of which is spent fuel management;
q. *"State of destination"* means a State to which a transboundary movement is planned or takes place;
r. *"State of origin"* means a State from which a transboundary movement is planned to be initiated or is initiated;
s. *"State of transit"* means any State, other than a State of origin or a State of destination, through whose territory a transboundary movement is planned or takes place;
t. *"storage"* means the holding of spent fuel or of radioactive waste in a facility that provides for its containment, with the intention of retrieval;
u. *"transboundary movement"* means any shipment of spent fuel or of radioactive waste from a State of origin to a State of destination.

Article 3.
Scope of Application

1. This Convention shall apply to the safety of spent fuel management when the spent fuel results from the operation of civilian nuclear reactors. Spent fuel held at reprocessing facilities as part of a reprocessing activity is not covered in the scope of this Convention unless the Contracting Party declares reprocessing to be part of spent fuel management.
2. This Convention shall also apply to the safety of radioactive waste management when the radioactive waste results from civilian applications. However, this Convention shall not apply to waste that contains only naturally occurring radioactive materials and that does not originate from the nuclear fuel cycle, unless it constitutes a disused sealed source or it is declared as radioactive waste for the purposes of this Convention by the Contracting Party.
3. This Convention shall not apply to the safety of management of spent fuel or radioactive waste within military or defence programmes, unless declared as spent

fuel or radioactive waste for the purposes of this Convention by the Contracting Party. However, this Convention shall apply to the safety of management of spent fuel and radioactive waste from military or defence programmes if and when such materials are transferred permanently to and managed within exclusively civilian programmes.

4. This Convention shall also apply to discharges as provided for in Articles 4, 7, 11, 14, 24 and 26.

Chapter 2.
SAFETY OF SPENT FUEL MANAGEMENT

Article 4.
General Safety Requirements

Each Contracting Party shall take the appropriate steps to ensure that at all stages of spent fuel management, individuals, society and the environment are adequately protected against radiological hazards.
In so doing, each Contracting Party shall take the appropriate steps to:

i. ensure that criticality and removal of residual heat generated during spent fuel management are adequately addressed;
ii. ensure that the generation of radioactive waste associated with spent fuel management is kept to the minimum practicable, consistent with the type of fuel cycle policy adopted;
iii. take into account interdependencies among the different steps in spent fuel management;
iv. provide for effective protection of individuals, society and the environment, by applying at the national level suitable protective methods as approved by the regulatory body, in the framework of its national legislation which has due regard to internationally endorsed criteria and standards;
v. take into account the biological, chemical and other hazards that may be associated with spent fuel management;
vi. strive to avoid actions that impose reasonably predictable impacts on future generations greater than those permitted for the current generation;
vii. aim to avoid imposing undue burdens on future generations.

Article 5.
Existing Facilities

Each Contracting Party shall take the appropriate steps to review the safety of any spent fuel management facility existing at the time the Convention enters into force for that

Contracting Party and to ensure that, if necessary, all reasonably practicable improvements are made to upgrade the safety of such a facility.

Article 6.
Siting of Proposed Facilities

1. Each Contracting Party shall take the appropriate steps to ensure that procedures are established and implemented for a proposed spent fuel management facility:
   i. to evaluate all relevant site-related factors likely to affect the safety of such a facility during its operating lifetime;
   ii. to evaluate the likely safety impact of such a facility on individuals, society and the environment;
   iii. to make information on the safety of such a facility available to members of the public;
   iv. to consult Contracting Parties in the vicinity of such a facility, insofar as they are likely to be affected by that facility, and provide them, upon their request, with general data relating to the facility to enable them to evaluate the likely safety impact of the facility upon their territory.
2. In so doing, each Contracting Party shall take the appropriate steps to ensure that such facilities shall not have unacceptable effects on other Contracting Parties by being sited in accordance with the general safety requirements of Article 4.

Article 7.
Design and Construction of Facilities

Each Contracting Party shall take the appropriate steps to ensure that:

i. the design and construction of a spent fuel management facility provide for suitable measures to limit possible radiological impacts on individuals, society and the environment, including those from discharges or uncontrolled releases;

ii. at the design stage, conceptual plans and, as necessary, technical provisions for the decommissioning of a spent fuel management facility are taken into account;

iii. the technologies incorporated in the design and construction of a spent fuel management facility are supported by experience, testing or analysis.

Article 8.
Assessment of Safety of Facilities

Each Contracting Party shall take the appropriate steps to ensure that:

i. before construction of a spent fuel management facility, a systematic safety assessment and an environmental assessment appropriate to the hazard presented by the facility and covering its operating lifetime shall be carried out;

ii. before the operation of a spent fuel management facility, updated and detailed versions of the safety assessment and of the environmental assessment shall be prepared when deemed necessary to complement the assessments referred to in paragraph (i).

Article 9.
Operation of Facilities

Each Contracting Party shall take the appropriate steps to ensure that:

i. the licence to operate a spent fuel management facility is based upon appropriate assessments as specified in Article 8 and is conditional on the completion of a commissioning programme demonstrating that the facility, as constructed, is consistent with design and safety requirements;
ii. operational limits and conditions derived from tests, operational experience and the assessments, as specified in Article 8, are defined and revised as necessary;
iii. operation, maintenance, monitoring, inspection and testing of a spent fuel management facility are conducted in accordance with established procedures;
iv. engineering and technical support in all safety-related fields are available throughout the operating lifetime of a spent fuel management facility;
v. incidents significant to safety are reported in a timely manner by the holder of the licence to the regulatory body;
vi. programmes to collect and analyse relevant operating experience are established and that the results are acted upon, where appropriate;
vii. decommissioning plans for a spent fuel management facility are prepared and updated, as necessary, using information obtained during the operating lifetime of that facility, and are reviewed by the regulatory body.

Article 10.
Disposal of Spent Fuel

If, pursuant to its own legislative and regulatory framework, a Contracting Party has designated spent fuel for disposal, the disposal of such spent fuel shall be in accordance with the obligations of Chapter 3 relating to the disposal of radioactive waste.

Chapter 3.
SAFETY OF RADIOACTIVE WASTE MANAGEMENT

Article 11.
General Safety Requirements

Each Contracting Party shall take the appropriate steps to ensure that at all stages of radioactive waste management individuals, society and the environment are adequately protected against radiological and other hazards.

In so doing, each Contracting Party shall take the appropriate steps to:

i. ensure that criticality and removal of residual heat generated during radioactive waste management are adequately addressed;
ii. ensure that the generation of radioactive waste is kept to the minimum practicable;
iii. take into account interdependencies among the different steps in radioactive waste management;
iv. provide for effective protection of individuals, society and the environment, by applying at the national level suitable protective methods as approved by the regulatory body, in the framework of its national legislation which has due regard to internationally endorsed criteria and standards;
v. take into account the biological, chemical and other hazards that may be associated with radioactive waste management;
vi. strive to avoid actions that impose reasonably predictable impacts on future generations greater than those permitted for the current generation;
vii. aim to avoid imposing undue burdens on future generations.

Article 12.
Existing Facilities and Past Practices

Each Contracting Party shall in due course take the appropriate steps to review:

i. the safety of any radioactive waste management facility existing at the time the Convention enters into force for that Contracting Party and to ensure that, if necessary, all reasonably practicable improvements are made to upgrade the safety of such a facility;
ii. the results of past practices in order to determine whether any intervention is needed for reasons of radiation protection bearing in mind that the reduction in detriment resulting from the reduction in dose should be sufficient to justify the harm and the costs, including the social costs, of the intervention.

Article 13.
Siting of Proposed Facilities

1. Each Contracting Party shall take the appropriate steps to ensure that procedures are established and implemented for a proposed radioactive waste management facility:
   i. to evaluate all relevant site-related factors likely to affect the safety of such a facility during its operating lifetime as well as that of a disposal facility after closure;
   ii. to evaluate the likely safety impact of such a facility on individuals, society and the environment, taking into account possible evolution of the site conditions of disposal facilities after closure;
   iii. to make information on the safety of such a facility available to members of the public;
   iv. to consult Contracting Parties in the vicinity of such a facility, insofar as they are likely to be affected by that facility, and provide them, upon their request, with general data relating to the facility to enable them to evaluate the likely safety impact of the facility upon their territory.
2. In so doing, each Contracting Party shall take the appropriate steps to ensure that such facilities shall not have unacceptable effects on other Contracting Parties by being sited in accordance with the general safety requirements of Article 11.

Article 14.
Design and Construction of Facilities

Each Contracting Party shall take the appropriate steps to ensure that:

i. the design and construction of a radioactive waste management facility provide for suitable measures to limit possible radiological impacts on individuals, society and the environment, including those from discharges or uncontrolled releases;
ii. at the design stage, conceptual plans and, as necessary, technical provisions for the decommissioning of a radioactive waste management facility other than a disposal facility are taken into account;
iii. at the design stage, technical provisions for the closure of a disposal facility are prepared;
iv. the technologies incorporated in the design and construction of a radioactive waste management facility are supported by experience, testing or analysis.

Article 15.
Assessment of Safety of Facilities

Each Contracting Party shall take the appropriate steps to ensure that:

i. before construction of a radioactive waste management facility, a systematic safety assessment and an environmental assessment appropriate to the hazard presented by the facility and covering its operating lifetime shall be carried out;

ii. in addition, before construction of a disposal facility, a systematic safety assessment and an environmental assessment for the period following closure shall be carried out and the results evaluated against the criteria established by the regulatory body;

iii. before the operation of a radioactive waste management facility, updated and detailed versions of the safety assessment and of the environmental assessment shall be prepared when deemed necessary to complement the assessments referred to in paragraph (i).

Article 16.
Operation of Facilities

Each Contracting Party shall take the appropriate steps to ensure that:

i. the licence to operate a radioactive waste management facility is based upon appropriate assessments as specified in Article 15 and is conditional on the completion of a commissioning programme demonstrating that the facility, as constructed, is consistent with design and safety requirements;

ii. operational limits and conditions, derived from tests, operational experience and the assessments as specified in Article 15 are defined and revised as necessary;

iii. operation, maintenance, monitoring, inspection and testing of a radioactive waste management facility are conducted in accordance with established procedures. For a disposal facility the results thus obtained shall be used to verify and to review the validity of assumptions made and to update the assessments as specified in Article 15 for the period after closure;

iv. engineering and technical support in all safety-related fields are available throughout the operating lifetime of a radioactive waste management facility;

v. procedures for characterization and segregation of radioactive waste are applied;

vi. incidents significant to safety are reported in a timely manner by the holder of the licence to the regulatory body;

vii. programmes to collect and analyse relevant operating experience are established and that the results are acted upon, where appropriate;

viii. decommissioning plans for a radioactive waste management facility other than a disposal facility are prepared and updated, as necessary, using information obtained during the operating lifetime of that facility, and are reviewed by the regulatory body;

ix. plans for the closure of a disposal facility are prepared and updated, as necessary, using information obtained during the operating lifetime of that facility and are reviewed by the regulatory body.

Article 17.
Institutional Measures After Closure

Each Contracting Party shall take the appropriate steps to ensure that after closure of a disposal facility:

i. records of the location, design and inventory of that facility required by the regulatory body are preserved;
ii. active or passive institutional controls such as monitoring or access restrictions are carried out, if required; and
iii. if, during any period of active institutional control, an unplanned release of radioactive materials into the environment is detected, intervention measures are implemented, if necessary.

Chapter 4.
GENERAL SAFETY PROVISIONS

Article 18.
Implementing Measures

Each Contracting Party shall take, within the framework of its national law, the legislative, regulatory and administrative measures and other steps necessary for implementing its obligations under this Convention.

Article 19.
Legislative and Regulatory Framework

1. Each Contracting Party shall establish and maintain a legislative and regulatory framework to govern the safety of spent fuel and radioactive waste management.
2. This legislative and regulatory framework shall provide for:
   i. the establishment of applicable national safety requirements and regulations for radiation safety;
   ii. a system of licensing of spent fuel and radioactive waste management activities;

iii. a system of prohibition of the operation of a spent fuel or radioactive waste management facility without a licence;
iv. a system of appropriate institutional control, regulatory inspection and documentation and reporting;
v. the enforcement of applicable regulations and of the terms of the licences;
vi. a clear allocation of responsibilities of the bodies involved in the different steps of spent fuel and of radioactive waste management.

3. When considering whether to regulate radioactive materials as radioactive waste, Contracting Parties shall take due account of the objectives of this Convention.

Article 20.
Regulatory Body

1. Each Contracting Party shall establish or designate a regulatory body entrusted with the implementation of the legislative and regulatory framework referred to in Article 19, and provided with adequate authority, competence and financial and human resources to fulfil its assigned responsibilities.
2. Each Contracting Party, in accordance with its legislative and regulatory framework, shall take the appropriate steps to ensure the effective independence of the regulatory functions from other functions where organizations are involved in both spent fuel or radioactive waste management and in their regulation.

Article 21.
Responsibility of the Licence Holder

1. Each Contracting Party shall ensure that prime responsibility for the safety of spent fuel or radioactive waste management rests with the holder of the relevant licence and shall take the appropriate steps to ensure that each such licence holder meets its responsibility.
2. If there is no such licence holder or other responsible party, the responsibility rests with the Contracting Party which has jurisdiction over the spent fuel or over the radioactive waste.

Article 22.
Human and Financial Resources

Each Contracting Party shall take the appropriate steps to ensure that:

i. qualified staff are available as needed for safety-related activities during the operating lifetime of a spent fuel and a radioactive waste management facility;

ii. adequate financial resources are available to support the safety of facilities for spent fuel and radioactive waste management during their operating lifetime and for decommissioning;
iii. financial provision is made which will enable the appropriate institutional controls and monitoring arrangements to be continued for the period deemed necessary following the closure of a disposal facility.

Article 23.
Quality Assurance

Each Contracting Party shall take the necessary steps to ensure that appropriate quality assurance programmes concerning the safety of spent fuel and radioactive waste management are established and implemented.

Article 24.
Operational Radiation Protection

1. Each Contracting Party shall take the appropriate steps to ensure that during the operating lifetime of a spent fuel or radioactive waste management facility:
   i. the radiation exposure of the workers and the public caused by the facility shall be kept as low as reasonably achievable, economic and social factors being taken into account;
   ii. no individual shall be exposed, in normal situations, to radiation doses which exceed national prescriptions for dose limitation which have due regard to internationally endorsed standards on radiation protection; and
   iii. measures are taken to prevent unplanned and uncontrolled releases of radioactive materials into the environment.
2. Each Contracting Party shall take appropriate steps to ensure that discharges shall be limited:
   i. to keep exposure to radiation as low as reasonably achievable, economic and social factors being taken into account; and
   ii. so that no individual shall be exposed, in normal situations, to radiation doses which exceed national prescriptions for dose limitation which have due regard to internationally endorsed standards on radiation protection.
3. Each Contracting Party shall take appropriate steps to ensure that during the operating lifetime of a regulated nuclear facility, in the event that an unplanned or uncontrolled release of radioactive materials into the environment occurs, appropriate corrective measures are implemented to control the release and mitigate its effects.

Article 25.
Emergency Preparedness

1. Each Contracting Party shall ensure that before and during operation of a spent fuel or radioactive waste management facility there are appropriate on-site and, if necessary, off-site emergency plans. Such emergency plans should be tested at an appropriate frequency.
2. Each Contracting Party shall take the appropriate steps for the preparation and testing of emergency plans for its territory insofar as it is likely to be affected in the event of a radiological emergency at a spent fuel or radioactive waste management facility in the vicinity of its territory.

Article 26.
Decommissioning

Each Contracting Party shall take the appropriate steps to ensure the safety of decommissioning of a nuclear facility. Such steps shall ensure that:

i. qualified staff and adequate financial resources are available;
ii. the provisions of Article 24 with respect to operational radiation protection, discharges and unplanned and uncontrolled releases are applied;
iii. the provisions of Article 25 with respect to emergency preparedness are applied; and
iv. records of information important to decommissioning are kept.

Chapter 5.
MISCELLANEOUS PROVISIONS

Article 27.
Transboundary Movement

1. Each Contracting Party involved in transboundary movement shall take the appropriate steps to ensure that such movement is undertaken in a manner consistent with the provisions of this Convention and relevant binding international instruments.

   In so doing:
   i. a Contracting Party which is a State of origin shall take the appropriate steps to ensure that trans-boundary movement is authorized and takes place only with the prior notification and consent of the State of destination;

ii. trans-boundary movement through States of transit shall be subject to those international obligations which are relevant to the particular modes of transport utilized;
iii. a Contracting Party which is a State of destination shall consent to a trans-boundary movement only if it has the administrative and technical capacity, as well as the regulatory structure, needed to manage the spent fuel or the radioactive waste in a manner consistent with this Convention;
iv. a Contracting Party which is a State of origin shall authorize a trans-boundary movement only if it can satisfy itself in accordance with the consent of the State of destination that the requirements of subparagraph (iii) are met prior to trans-boundary movement;
v. a Contracting Party which is a State of origin shall take the appropriate steps to permit re-entry into its territory, if a trans-boundary movement is not or cannot be completed in conformity with this Article, unless an alternative safe arrangement can be made.

2. A Contracting Party shall not licence the shipment of its spent fuel or radioactive waste to a destination south of latitude 60 degrees South for storage or disposal.
3. Nothing in this Convention prejudices or affects:
   i. the exercise, by ships and aircraft of all States, of maritime, river and air navigation rights and freedoms, as provided for in international law;
   ii. rights of a Contracting Party to which radioactive waste is exported for processing to return, or provide for the return of, the radioactive waste and other products after treatment to the State of origin;
   iii. the right of a Contracting Party to export its spent fuel for reprocessing;
   iv. rights of a Contracting Party to which spent fuel is exported for reprocessing to return, or provide for the return of, radioactive waste and other products resulting from reprocessing operations to the State of origin.

Article 28.
Disused Sealed Sources

1. Each Contracting Party shall, in the framework of its national law, take the appropriate steps to ensure that the possession, remanufacturing or disposal of disused sealed sources takes place in a safe manner.
2. A Contracting Party shall allow for re-entry into its territory of disused sealed sources if, in the framework of its national law, it has accepted that they be returned to a manufacturer qualified to receive and possess the disused sealed sources.

Chapter 6.
MEETINGS OF THE CONTRACTING PARTIES

Article 29.
Preparatory Meeting

1. A preparatory meeting of the Contracting Parties shall be held not later than six months after the date of entry into force of this Convention.
2. At this meeting, the Contracting Parties shall:
   i. determine the date for the first review meeting as referred to in Article 30. This review meeting shall be held as soon as possible, but not later than thirty months after the date of entry into force of this Convention;
   ii. prepare and adopt by consensus Rules of Procedure and Financial Rules;
   iii. establish in particular and in accordance with the Rules of Procedure:
      a. guidelines regarding the form and structure of the national reports to be submitted pursuant to Article 32;
      b. a date for the submission of such reports;
      c. the process for reviewing such reports.
3. Any State or regional organization of an integration or other nature which ratifies, accepts, approves, accedes to or confirms this Convention and for which the Convention is not yet in force, may attend the preparatory meeting as if it were a Party to this Convention.

Article 30.
Review Meetings

1. The Contracting Parties shall hold meetings for the purpose of reviewing the reports submitted pursuant to Article 32.
2. At each review meeting the Contracting Parties:
   i. shall determine the date for the next such meeting, the interval between review meetings not exceeding three years;
   ii. may review the arrangements established pursuant to paragraph 2 of Article 29, and adopt revisions by consensus unless otherwise provided for in the Rules of Procedure. They may also amend the Rules of Procedure and Financial Rules by consensus.
3. At each review meeting each Contracting Party shall have a reasonable opportunity to discuss the reports submitted by other Contracting Parties and to seek clarification of such reports.

Article 31.
Extraordinary Meetings

An extraordinary meeting of the Contracting Parties shall be held:

i. if so agreed by a majority of the Contracting Parties present and voting at a meeting; or
ii. at the written request of a Contracting Party, within six months of this request having been communicated to the Contracting Parties and notification having been received by the secretariat referred to in Article 37 that the request has been supported by a majority of the Contracting Parties.

Article 32.
Reporting

1. In accordance with the provisions of Article 30, each Contracting Party shall submit a national report to each review meeting of Contracting Parties. This report shall address the measures taken to implement each of the obligations of the Convention. For each Contracting Party the report shall also address its:
   i. spent fuel management policy;
   ii. spent fuel management practices;
   iii. radioactive waste management policy;
   iv. radioactive waste management practices;
   v. criteria used to define and categorize radioactive waste.
2. This report shall also include:
   i. a list of the spent fuel management facilities subject to this Convention, their location, main purpose and essential features;
   ii. an inventory of spent fuel that is subject to this Convention and that is being held in storage and of that which has been disposed of. This inventory shall contain a description of the material and, if available, give information on its mass and its total activity;
   iii. a list of the radioactive waste management facilities subject to this Convention, their location, main purpose and essential features;
   iv. an inventory of radioactive waste that is subject to this Convention that:
      a. is being held in storage at radioactive waste management and nuclear fuel cycle facilities;
      b. has been disposed of; or
      c. has resulted from past practices.

This inventory shall contain a description of the material and other appropriate information available, such as volume or mass, activity and specific radio-nuclides;

v. a list of nuclear facilities in the process of being decommissioned and the status of decommissioning activities at those facilities.

Article 33.
Attendance

1. Each Contracting Party shall attend meetings of the Contracting Parties and be represented at such meetings by one delegate, and by such alternates, experts and advisers as it deems necessary.
2. The Contracting Parties may invite, by consensus, any intergovernmental organization which is competent in respect of matters governed by this Convention to attend, as an observer, any meeting, or specific sessions thereof. Observers shall be required to accept in writing, and in advance, the provisions of Article 36.

Article 34.
Summary Reports

The Contracting Parties shall adopt, by consensus, and make available to the public a document addressing issues discussed and conclusions reached during meetings of the Contracting Parties.

Article 35.
Languages

1. The languages of meetings of the Contracting Parties shall be Arabic, Chinese, English, French, Russian and Spanish unless otherwise provided in the Rules of Procedure.
2. Reports submitted pursuant to Article 32 shall be prepared in the national language of the submitting Contracting Party or in a single designated language to be agreed in the Rules of Procedure. Should the report be submitted in a national language other than the designated language, a translation of the report into the designated language shall be provided by the Contracting Party.
3. Notwithstanding the provisions of paragraph 2, the secretariat, if compensated, will assume the translation of reports submitted in any other language of the meeting into the designated language.

Article 36.
Confidentiality

1. The provisions of this Convention shall not affect the rights and obligations of the Contracting Parties under their laws to protect information from disclosure. For the purposes of this Article, "information" includes, inter alia, information relating to national security or to the physical protection of nuclear materials, information protected by intellectual property rights or by industrial or commercial confidentiality, and personal data.
2. When, in the context of this Convention, a Contracting Party provides information identified by it as protected as described in paragraph 1, such information shall be used only for the purposes for which it has been provided and its confidentiality shall be respected.
3. With respect to information relating to spent fuel or radioactive waste falling within the scope of this Convention by virtue of paragraph 3 of Article 3, the provisions of this Convention shall not affect the exclusive discretion of the Contracting Party concerned to decide:
   i. whether such information is classified or otherwise controlled to preclude release;
   ii. whether to provide information referred to in sub-paragraph (i) above in the context of the Convention; and
   iii. what conditions of confidentiality are attached to such information if it is provided in the context of this Convention.
4. The content of the debates during the reviewing of the national reports at each review meeting held pursuant to Article 30 shall be confidential.

Article 37.
Secretariat

1. The International Atomic Energy Agency, (hereinafter referred to as "the Agency") shall provide the secretariat for the meetings of the Contracting Parties.
2. The secretariat shall:
   i. convene, prepare and service the meetings of the Contracting Parties referred to in Articles 29, 30 and 31;
   ii. transmit to the Contracting Parties information received or prepared in accordance with the provisions of this Convention.

   The costs incurred by the Agency in carrying out the functions referred to in sub-paragraphs (i) and (ii) above shall be borne by the Agency as part of its regular budget.

3. The Contracting Parties may, by consensus, request the Agency to provide other services in support of meetings of the Contracting Parties. The Agency may provide such services if they can be undertaken within its programme and regular budget. Should this not be possible, the Agency may provide such services if voluntary funding is provided from another source.

Chapter 7.
FINAL CLAUSES AND OTHER PROVISIONS

Article 38.
Resolution of Disagreements

In the event of a disagreement between two or more Contracting Parties concerning the interpretation or application of this Convention, the Contracting Parties shall consult within the framework of a meeting of the Contracting Parties with a view to resolving the disagreement. In the event that the consultations prove unproductive, recourse can be made to the mediation, conciliation and arbitration mechanisms provided for in international law, including the rules and practices prevailing within the IAEA.

Article 39.
Signature, Ratification, Acceptance, Approval, Accession

1. This Convention shall be open for signature by all States at the Headquarters of the Agency in Vienna from 29 September 1997 until its entry into force.
2. This Convention is subject to ratification, acceptance or approval by the signatory States.
3. After its entry into force, this Convention shall be open for accession by all States.
4. This Convention shall be open for signature subject to confirmation, or accession by regional organizations of an integration or other nature, provided that any such organization is constituted by sovereign States and has competence in respect of the negotiation, conclusion and application of international agreements in matters covered by this Convention.
   i. In matters within their competence, such organizations shall, on their own behalf, exercise the rights and fulfil the responsibilities which this Convention attributes to States Parties.
   ii. When becoming party to this Convention, such an organization shall communicate to the Depositary referred to in Article 43, a declaration indicating which States are members thereof, which Articles of this Convention apply to it, and the extent of its competence in the field covered by those Articles.

    iii. Such an organization shall not hold any vote additional to those of its Member States.
5. Instruments of ratification, acceptance, approval, accession or confirmation shall be deposited with the Depositary.

Article 40.
Entry Into Force

1. This Convention shall enter into force on the ninetieth day after the date of deposit with the Depositary of the twenty-fifth instrument of ratification, acceptance or approval, including the instruments of fifteen States each having an operational nuclear power plant.
2. For each State or regional organization of an integration or other nature which ratifies, accepts, approves, accedes to or confirms this Convention after the date of deposit of the last instrument required to satisfy the conditions set forth in paragraph 1, this Convention shall enter into force on the ninetieth day after the date of deposit with the Depositary of the appropriate instrument by such a State or organization.

Article 41.
Amendments to the Convention

1. Any Contracting Party may propose an amendment to this Convention. Proposed amendments shall be considered at a review meeting or at an extraordinary meeting.
2. The text of any proposed amendment and the reasons for it shall be provided to the Depositary who shall communicate the proposal to the Contracting Parties at least ninety days before the meeting for which it is submitted for consideration. Any comments received on such a proposal shall be circulated by the Depositary to the Contracting Parties.
3. The Contracting Parties shall decide after consideration of the proposed amendment whether to adopt it by consensus, or, in the absence of consensus, to submit it to a Diplomatic Conference. A decision to submit a proposed amendment to a Diplomatic Conference shall require a two-thirds majority vote of the Contracting Parties present and voting at the meeting, provided that at least one half of the Contracting Parties are present at the time of voting.
4. The Diplomatic Conference to consider and adopt amendments to this Convention shall be convened by the Depositary and held no later than one year after the appropriate decision taken in accordance with paragraph 3 of this Article. The Diplomatic Conference shall make every effort to ensure amendments are adopted

by consensus. Should this not be possible, amendments shall be adopted with a two-thirds majority of all Contracting Parties.

5. Amendments to this Convention adopted pursuant to paragraphs 3 and 4 above shall be subject to ratification, acceptance, approval, or confirmation by the Contracting Parties and shall enter into force for those Contracting Parties which have ratified, accepted, approved or confirmed them on the ninetieth day after the receipt by the Depositary of the relevant instruments of at least two thirds of the Contracting Parties. For a Contracting Party which subsequently ratifies, accepts, approves or confirms the said amendments, the amendments will enter into force on the ninetieth day after that Contracting Party has deposited its relevant instrument.

Article 42.
Denunciation

1. Any Contracting Party may denounce this Convention by written notification to the Depositary.
2. Denunciation shall take effect one year following the date of the receipt of the notification by the Depositary, or on such later date as may be specified in the notification.

Article 43.
Depositary

1. The Director General of the Agency shall be the Depositary of this Convention.
2. The Depositary shall inform the Contracting Parties of:
   i. the signature of this Convention and of the deposit of instruments of ratification, acceptance, approval, accession or confirmation in accordance with Article 39;
   ii. the date on which the Convention enters into force, in accordance with Article 40;
   iii. the notifications of denunciation of the Convention and the date thereof, made in accordance with Article 42;
   iv. the proposed amendments to this Convention submitted by Contracting Parties, the amendments adopted by the relevant Diplomatic Conference or by the meeting of the Contracting Parties, and the date of entry into force of the said amendments, in accordance with Article 41.

Article 44.
Authentic Texts

The original of this Convention of which the Arabic, Chinese, English, French, Russian and Spanish texts are equally authentic, shall be deposited with the Depositary, who shall send certified copies thereof to the Contracting Parties.

IN WITNESS WHEREOF THE UNDERSIGNED, BEING DULY AUTHORIZED TO THAT EFFECT, HAVE SIGNED THIS CONVENTION.

Done at Vienna on the fifth day of September, one thousand nine hundred and ninety-seven.

THE EC REGULATIONS ON CONTAMINATED ITEMS ORIGINATING IN THIRD COUNTRIES FOLLOWING THE CHERNOBYL ACCIDENT – THE EURATOM REGULATIONS ON MAXIMUM PERMITTED LEVELS OF CONTAMINATION AFTER A NUCLEAR ACCIDENT – OTHER REGULATIONS (1960-2003)

Among the measures taken at the European Community level as a consequence of the Chernobyl accident, a distinction must be drawn between those (EEC) intended to face the consequences of that specific event (hence referred to as the post-Chernobyl Regulations), and those (EURATOM) adopted later on (and not directly related to Chernobyl) to cope with any future possible nuclear accident or radiological emergency.

In general, it should be pointed out that the "regulation" as the most suitable tool (see under Euratom in Chapter One) was chosen given its direct and immediate application, thus allowing for uniform conditions over the whole territory of the European Community, which is understandably more than desirable under the circumstances addressed by the regulations in point. However, it should be also pointed out that they were adopted on a different legal basis, i.e. the European Economic Community Treaty and the Euratom Treaty. The reasons for this are the following: in the case of the actual after-Chernobyl situation, the regulations adopted were based on the EEC Treaty, since the event thereby associated (occurred outside the Community) led the competent bodies to consider that the measures to be taken should be placed within the framework of trade policy (in that they pertained to the exchanges between the Community and third countries), while the Euratom regulations addressed health protection issues within the Community, hence their proper legal basis being offered by the Euratom Treaty (see anyway case law in Appendix to the volume)..

On account of the above, in the following pages only the text of Euratom regulations may be found, while as to the (E)EC regulations we confine ourselves to listing the main ones below as a matter of information, since they are not concerned with radiation protection as it is the object of this Chapter Two. On the other hand, the Euratom regulations under consideration, as specified at the very outset of this presentation, include the radiation protection measures adopted to keep the contamination levels in foodstuffs and feedingstuffs under control after a nuclear accident.

*EEC (Council) Regulation 86/1707 on maximum permissible levels of contamination for all agricultural products originating in third countries

*EEC (Council) Regulation 89/2219 on special conditions for exporting foodstuffs and feeding-stuffs following a nuclear accident

*EC (Commission) Regulation 99/1661 laying down detailed rules for the application of Council Regulation 90/737

*EEC (Council) Regulation 90/737 on the conditions governing imports of agricultural products originating in third countries following the Chernobyl accident, as amended by EC Regulation 2000/616

*EC (Commission) Regulation 00/1609 establishing a list of products excluded from the application of Council Regulation (EEC) 90/737

*EC (Commission) Regulation 01/1621, amending EC Regulation 99/1661 (previously amended by EC Regulation 00/1627) as regards the export certificate required for agricultural products and the list of customs offices permitting the declaration of products for free circulation in the Community.

Finally, it is recalled that the post-Chernobyl Regulations, when not extended in time given persisting contamination levels, are the object of periodic amendments taking into account the evolving situation in terms of (decreasing) radioactive contamination in connection with given radioisotopes and products.

COUNCIL REGULATION (87/3954/EURATOM) OF 22 DECEMBER 1987 LAYING DOWN MAXIMUM PERMITTED LEVELS OF RADIOACTIVE CONTAMINATION OF FOODSTUFFS AND OF FEEDINGSTUFFS FOLLOWING A NUCLEAR ACCIDENT OR ANY OTHER CASE OF RADIOLOGICAL EMERGENCY

This very basic Regulation is an indirect consequence of the Chernobyl accident, which had stressed quite acutely the need not only for specific measures strictly related to the accident, but also more in general for "permanent" maximum permissible contamination levels to be established for the eventuality of any nuclear accident or radiological emergency.

Indeed, it should be recalled that the Euratom Directives on radiological protection (basic standards) did already provide for specific measures to be adopted in that eventuality. Chernobyl offered the decisive impulse for the setting up of a "permanent system" by means of a more stringent tool such as a regulation. Its adoption was based on article 31 of the Euratom Treaty, taking into account also the provisions under article 2b) of the Treaty concerning the laying down of uniform standards in the Community for the health protection of workers and the public against ionising radiation. The Regulation is moreover intended to preserve unity within the Community. The levels so established are adapted to the actual evolving situation whenever necessary. The Regulation also empowers the Commission to adopt certain provisions facilitating the application of the levels following information collected by the Commission itself about accidents or emergencies, mainly on the basis of a Decision adopted (1987) by the Council (addressed further on in the volume) and of the Iaea Convention on Early Notification of a nuclear accident (see preceding pages). Examples of this competence given to the Commission are: Regulation 89/944/Euratom (of 12 April 1989), laying down maximum permitted levels of radioactive contamination in minor foodstuffs (i.e. those making only a marginal contribution to food consumption by the population) following a nuclear accident or an emergency, and: Regulation 90/770/Euratom (of 29 March 1990) laying down contamination levels for feeding-stuffs taking into consideration the caesium radioisotopes, which scientific investigations had shown to be the only ones relevant in the particular case.

Article 7 (special procedure for adopting application modalities) of Regulation 3954 was amended by Regulation 2218/89 addressed in the following pages.

The choice of the Euratom Treaty as a legal basis for the adoption of Regulation 3954/87 gave rise in the past years to some important litigation before the Court of Justice (Luxembourg), which is reported on in the Appendix to the volume.

THE COUNCIL OF THE EUROPEAN COMMUNITIES,

Having regard to the Treaty establishing the European Atomic Energy Community, and in particular Article 31 thereof,
Having regard to the proposal from the Commission, drawn up after obtaining the opinion of a group of experts appointed by the Scientific and Technical Committee (1),
Having regard to the opinion of the European Parliament (2),
Having regard to the opinion of the Economic and Social Committee (3),
Whereas Article 2 (b) of the Treaty requires that the Council shall establish uniform safety standards to protect the health of workers and of the general public and ensure that they are applied, as further set out in Title Two, Chapter III of the Treaty;
Whereas, on 2 February 1959, the Council adopted Directives (4), laying down basic safety standards the text of which was replaced by that of Directive 80/836/Euratom (5), as amended by Directive 84/467/Euratom (6), and whereas Article 45 of that Directive requires Member States to stipulate intervention levels in the event of accidents;
Whereas, following the accident at the Chernobyl nuclear power-station on 26 April 1986, considerable quantities of radioactive materials were released into the atmosphere, contaminating foodstuffs and feeding-stuffs in several European countries to levels significant from the health point of view;
Whereas, the Community adopted measures (7) to ensure that certain agricultural products are only introduced into the Community according to the common arrangements which safeguard the health of the population while maintaining the unified nature of the market and avoiding deflections of trade;
Whereas the need arises to set up a system allowing the Community, following a nuclear accident or any other case of radiological emergency which is likely to lead or has led to a significant radioactive contamination of foodstuffs and feeding-stuffs, to fix maximum permitted levels of radioactive contamination in order to protect the population;
Whereas the Commission will be informed of a nuclear accident or of unusually high levels of radioactivity according to the Council Decision of 14 December 1987 on Community arrangements for the early exchange of information in the event of radiological emergency (8), or under the Convention on Early Notification of a Nuclear Accident of 26 September 1986;
Whereas the Commission will, if the circumstances so require, immediately adopt a Regulation rendering applicable pre-established maximum permitted levels;

Whereas, on the basis of current data available in the field of radiation protection, derived reference levels have been established and these may be used as a basis for the fixing of maximum permitted levels of radioactive contamination to be applied immediately following a nuclear accident or any other case of radiological emergency which is likely to lead or has led to significant radioactive contamination of foodstuffs and feeding-stuffs;
Whereas such maximum permitted levels take due account of the latest scientific advice as presently available on an international scale whilst reflecting the need for reassuring the public and avoiding divergences in international regulatory practice;
Whereas, however, it is necessary to take due account of the particular conditions applying and, therefore, to establish a procedure allowing the rapid adaptation of these pre-established levels to maximum permitted levels appropriate to the circumstances of any particular nuclear accident or any other case of radiological emergency which is likely to lead or has led to significant radioactive contamination of foodstuffs and feeding-stuffs;
Whereas the adoption of a Regulation rendering applicable maximum permitted levels would also maintain the unity of the Common Market and avoid deflections of trade within the Community;
Whereas, in order to facilitate the adaptation of maximum permitted levels, procedures should be provided for allowing the consultation of experts including the Group of Experts referred to in Article 31 of the Treaty;
Whereas compliance with the maximum permitted levels will have to be the subject of appropriate checks,

HAS ADOPTED THIS REGULATION:

Article 1

1. This Regulation lays down the procedure for determining the maximum permitted levels of radioactive contamination of foodstuffs and of feeding-stuffs which may be placed on the market following a nuclear accident or any other case of radiological emergency which is likely to lead to or has led to significant radioactive contamination of foodstuffs and feeding-stuffs.
2. For the purposes of this Regulation, 'foodstuffs' means products which are intended for human consumption either immediately or after processing and 'feeding-stuffs' means products which are intended only for animal nutrition.

Article 2

1. In the event of the Commission receiving – in particular according to either the Community arrangements for the early exchange of information in case of a radio-

logical emergency or under the IEA Convention of 26 September 1986 on early notification of a nuclear accident – official information on accidents or on any other case of radiological emergency, substantiating that the maximum permissible levels in the Annex are likely to be reached or have been reached, it will immediately adopt, if the circumstances so require, a Regulation rendering applicable those maximum permissible levels.
2. The period of validity of any Regulation within the meaning of paragraph 1 shall be as short as possible and shall not exceed three months subject to the provisions of Article 3 (4).

Article 3

1. After consultation with experts, which shall include the Article 31 Group of Experts, the Commission shall submit to the Council a proposal for a Regulation to adapt or confirm the provisions of the Regulation referred to in Article 2 (1) within one month of its adoption.
2. The Commission shall when submitting the proposal for a Regulation referred to in paragraph 1 take into account the basic standards laid down in accordance with Articles 30 to 31 of the Treaty including the principle that all exposures shall be kept as low as reasonably achievable, taking the aspect of the protection of the health of the general public and economic and social factors into account.
3. The Council shall, acting by a qualified majority, take a decision on the proposal for a Regulation referred to in paragraphs 1 and 2 within the time limit set out in Article 2 (2).
4. In the event that the Council does not decide within this time limit, the levels set out in the Annex shall continue to apply until the Council does decide or until the Commission withdraws its proposal because the conditions set out in Article 2 (1) no longer apply.

Article 4

The period of validity of any Regulation within the meaning of Article 3 shall be limited. This period may be revised at the request of a Member State or on the initiative of the Commission in accordance with the procedure laid down in Article 3.

Article 5

1. In order to ensure that the maximum permitted levels laid down in the Annex take account of any new scientific data becoming available, the Commission shall from time to time, seek the opinion of experts, which shall include the Article 31 Group of Experts.

2. At the request of a Member State or the Commission, the maximum permitted levels laid down in the Annex may be revised or supplemented, upon the submission of a proposal from the Commission to the Council in accordance with the procedure laid down in Article 31 of the Treaty.

Article 6

1. Foodstuffs or feeding-stuffs not in compliance with the maximum permitted levels laid down in a Regulation adopted in accordance with Articles 2 or 3 shall not be placed on the market. For the purposes of applying this Regulation, foodstuffs or feeding-stuffs imported from third countries shall be considered to be placed on the market if, on the customs territory of the Community, they undergo a customs procedure other than a transit procedure.
2. Each Member State shall provide the Commission with all information concerning the application of this Regulation, in particular concerning cases of non-compliance with the maximum permitted levels. The Commission shall communicate such information to the other Member States.

Article 7

Rules for applying this Regulation and a list of minor foodstuffs together with the maximum levels to be applied thereto shall be adopted in accordance with the procedure laid down in Article 30 of Regulation (EEC) No 804/68 (1), which shall apply by analogy. To this end an ad hoc Committee shall be set up.

Article 8

This Regulation shall enter into force on the third day following that of its publication in the Official Journal of the European Communities.
This Regulation shall be binding in its entirety and directly applicable in all Member States.

Done at Brussels, 22 December 1987.
For the Council
The President
N. WILHJELM

(1) OJ No C 174, 2. 7. 1987, p. 6.
(2) Opinion delivered on 16 December 1987 (not yet published in the Official Journal).
(3) OJ No C 180, 8. 7. 1987, p. 20.
(4) OJ No 11, 20. 2. 1959, p. 221/59.

(4) OJ No L 246, 17. 9. 1980, p. 1.
(6) OJ No L 265, 5. 10. 1984, p. 4.
(7) Council Regulations (EEC) No 1707/86, (OJ No L 146, 31. 5. 1986, p. 88;) (EEC) No 3020/86, (OJ No L 280, 1. 10. 1986, p. 79;) (EEC) No 624/87, (OJ No L 58, 28. 2. 1987, p. 101;) (EEC) No 3955/87, (See page 14 of the Official Journal).
(8) See page 76 of the Official Journal.
(1) OJ No L 148, 28. 6. 1968, p. 13.

ANNEX

MAXIMUM PERMITTED LEVELS FOR FOODSTUFFS AND FEEDINGSTUFFS (Bq/kg or Bq/l)
1.2.3.4.5.6 // // // // // // // // Baby foods (1) // Dairy Produce (2) (3) // Other foodstuffs except minor foodstuffs (4) // Liquid foodstuffs (5) // Feeding-stuffs (6) // // // // // // // Isotopes of strontium, notably Sr-90 // // 125 // 750 // // // Isotopes of iodine notably I-131 // // 500 // 2 000 // // // Alpha-emitting isotopes of plutonium and trans-plutonium elements, notably Pu-239, Am-241 // // 20 // 80 // // // All other nuclides of half-life greater than 10 days, notably Cs-134, Cs-137 (7) // // 1 000 // 1 250 // // // // // // // //
(1) Baby foods are defined as those foodstuffs intended for the feeding of infants during the first four to six months of life, which meet, in themselves, the nutritional requirements of this category of person and are put up for retail sale in packages which are clearly identified and labelled 'food preparation for infants'. Values to be established.
(2) Dairy produce is defined as milk falling within headings Nos 04.01 and 04.02 of the Common Customs Tariff, and the corresponding headings of the combined nomenclature as from 1 January 1988.
(3) The level applicable to concentrated or dried products shall be calculated on the basis of the reconstituted product as ready for consumption.
(4) Minor foodstuffs and the corresponding levels to be applied to them will be as defined in accordance with Article 7.
(5) Liquid foodstuffs as defined by Chapters 20 and 22 of the Common Customs Tariff and by the corresponding Chapter of the combined nomenclature as from 1 January 1988. Values are calculated taking into account consumption of tap-water and the same values should be applied to drinking water supplies at the discretion of competent authorities in Member States. Values for liquid foodstuffs to be established.
(6) Values to be established.
(7) Carbon 14 and tritium are not included in this group.

COUNCIL REGULATION (89/2218/EURATOM) OF 18 JULY 1989 AMENDING REGULATION 87/3954/EURATOM LAYING DOWN MAXIMUM PERMITTED LEVELS OF RADIOACTIVE CONTAMINATION OF FOODSTUFFS AND OF FEEDINGSTUFFS FOLLOWING A NUCLEAR ACCIDENT OR ANY OTHER CASE OF RADIOLOGICAL EMERGENCY

This Regulation amends article 7 of the 1987 Regulation, by extending the scope of this provision to cover also the laying down of maximum permissible levels for feeding-stuffs. The amendments to the Annex consist in the introduction of levels the determination of which had been postponed when the 1987 Regulation was adopted, since the relevant technical-scientific investigations were still under way.

THE COUNCIL OF THE EUROPEAN COMMUNITIES,

Having regard to the Treaty establishing the European Atomic Energy Community, and in particular Article 31 thereof,
Having regard to the proposal from the Commission, drawn up after obtaining the opinion of a group of experts appointed by the Scientific and Technical Committee (1),
Having regard to the opinion of the European Parliament (2),
Having regard to the opinion of the Economic and Social Committee (3),
Whereas the Annex to Regulation (Euratom) No 3954/87 (4) contains headings for the maximum permitted levels for foodstuffs and feeding-stuffs;
Whereas, however, no maximum levels were laid down for some of those headings pending a decision to be taken by the Council at a later stage following additional work to be carried out mainly by scientific experts;
Whereas the Commission submitted two communications to the Council on 14 June and 9 December 1988 respectively which were intended to supplement the Annex to the abovementioned Regulation and were drafted after consultation of the group of experts referred to in Article 31 of the Treaty;
Whereas the Annex to that Regulation should therefore be supplemented;
Whereas some other information in the said Annex should also be adapted in the light of the latest scientific work in the field;
Whereas it therefore seems advisable to consolidate the levels and the other information in the said Annex in a single table;

Whereas it also seems advisable, since further work is to be carried out, to stipulate that the procedure provided for in Article 7 of Regulation (Euratom) No 3954/87 should also apply for fixing the maximum permitted levels for feeding-stuffs; whereas that Regulation should be supplemented accordingly,

HAS ADOPTED THIS REGULATION:

Article 1

The Annex to Regulation (Euratom) No 3954/87 is hereby replaced by the Annex hereto.

Article 2

Article 7 of Regulation (Euratom) No 3954/87 is hereby replaced by the following:
'Article 7
Rules for applying this Regulation, a list of minor foodstuffs together with the maximum levels to be applied thereto, and the maximum levels for feeding-stuffs shall be adopted in accordance with the procedure laid down in Article 30 of Regulation (EEC) No 804/68, which shall apply by analogy. To this end an ad hoc Committee shall be set up.'

Article 3

This Regulation shall enter into force on the third day following that of its publication in the Official Journal of the European Communities.
This Regulation shall be binding in its entirety and directly applicable in all Member States.

Done at Brussels, 18 July 1989.
For the Council
The President
R. DUMAS

(1) OJ No C 174, 2. 7. 1987, p. 6.
(2) OJ No C 13, 18. 1. 1988, p. 61.
(3) OJ No C 180, 8. 7. 1987, p. 20.
(4) OJ No L 371, 30. 12. 1987, p. 11.

ANNEX

MAXIMUM PERMITTED LEVELS FOR FOODSTUFFS AND FEEDINGSTUFFS (Bq/kg)
1.2,5.6 // // // // // Foodstuffs (1) // Feeding-stuffs (2) // // // 1.2.3.4.5.6 // // Baby foods (3) // Dairy produce (4) // Other foodstuffs except minor foodstuffs (5) // Liquid foodstuffs (6) // // // // // // // // // Isotopes of strontium, notably Sr-90 // 75 // 125 // 750 // 125 // // Isotopes of iodine, notably I-131 // 150 // 500 // 2 000 // 500 // // Alpha-emitting isotopes of plutonium and trans-plutonium elements, notably Pu-239, Am-241 // 1 // 20 // 80 // 20 // // All other nuclides of half-life greater than 10 days, notably Cs-134, Cs-137 (7) // 400 // 1 000 // 1 250 // 1 000 // // // // // // //

(1) The level applicable to concentrated or dried products is calculated on the basis of the reconstituted product as ready for consumption. Member States may make recommendations concerning the diluting conditions in order to ensure that the maximum permitted levels laid down in this Regulation are observed.

(2) Maximum permitted levels for feeding-stuffs will be defined in accordance with Article 7, since such levels are intended to contribute to the observance of the permitted maximum levels for foodstuffs, do not alone guarantee such observance in all circumstances and do not lessen the requirement for monitoring levels in animal products destined for human consumption.

(3) Baby foods are defined as those foodstuffs intended for the feeding of infants during the first four to six months of life, which meet, in themselves, the nutritional requirements of this category of person and are put up for retail sale in packages which are clearly identified and labelled "food preparation for infants".

(4) Dairy produce is defined as those products falling within the following CN codes including, where appropriate, any adjustments which might be made to them later: 0401, 0402 (except 0402 29 11).

(5) Minor foodstuffs and the corresponding levels to be applied to them will be defined in accordance with Article 7.

(6) Liquid foodstuffs as defined in the heading 2009 and in chapter 22 of the combined nomenclature. Values are calculated taking into account consumption of tap-water and the same values should be applied to drinking water supplies at the discretion of competent authorities in Member States.

(7) Carbon 14, tritium and potassium 40 are not included in this group.'

COUNCIL DECISION (87/600/EURATOM) OF 14 DECEMBER 1987 ON COMMUNITY ARRANGEMENTS FOR THE EARLY EXCHANGE OF INFORMATION IN THE EVENT OF A RADIOLOGICAL EMERGENCY

This Decision was adopted to make it possible for Member States to be informed rapidly about a radiological emergency which might occur, in order to apply uniform protection measures on the whole territory of the European Community, helping at the same time the Commission in the accomplishment of its tasks. To this end, one of the main elements of the Decision is that the information should be received promptly in an agreed format. It should be added that modalities for the exchange of information had already been agreed bilaterally between certain Member States, all of whom are signatories to the Iaea Convention on Early Notification (see preceding pages). Moreover, both the Euratom Treaty and the 1980 Euratom Basic Standards on radiological protection provided for checks on radioactivity levels in the environment and for information about accidents within the Community.

The 1987 Decision indicates installations and activities on which the exchange of information is to be ensured; it also requires competent national authorities and contact points (at the Commission as well) to be permanently on call.

THE COUNCIL OF THE EUROPEAN COMMUNITIES,

Having regard to the Treaty establishing the European Atomic Energy Community, and in particular Article 31 thereof,
Having regard to the proposal from the Commission, submitted after obtaining the opinion of the group of persons appointed by the Scientific and Technical Committee,
Having regard to the opinion of the European Parliament (1),
Having regard to the opinion of the Economic and Social Committee (2),
Whereas Article 2 (b) of the Treaty requires the Community to establish uniform safety standards to protect the health of workers and of the general public;
Whereas, on 2 February 1959, the Council adopted Directives laying down basic standards for the protection of the health of workers and the general public against the dangers arising from ionizing radiations (3), which were last amended by Directive 80/836/Euratom (4) and Directive 84/467/Euratom (5);
Whereas Article 45 (5) of Directive 80/836/Euratom already requires that any accident involving exposure of the population be notified as a matter of urgency, when the circumstances so require, to neighbouring Member States and to the Commission;

Whereas Articles 35 and 36 of the Treaty already provide that Member States are to establish the facilities necessary to carry out continuous monitoring of the level of radioactivity in the air, water and soil and to communicate such information to the Commission so that it is kept informed of the levels of radioactivity to which the public is exposed;
Whereas Article 13 of Directive 80/836/Euratom requires Member States regularly to transmit to the Commission results of reviews and estimates referred to in that Article;
Whereas the accident at the nuclear power station at Chernobyl in the Soviet Union demonstrated that, in the event of a radiological emergency and in order to fulfil its tasks, the Commission needs to receive promptly all relevant information in an agreed format;
Whereas some bilateral arrangements have been agreed upon by Member States and whereas all Member States have signed the IAEA Convention on Early Notification of a Nuclear Accident;
Whereas these Community arrangements will ensure that all Member States are promptly informed in the event of a radiological emergency in order to provide that the uniform standards for protection of the population as is laid down in the Directives made pursuant to Title Two, Chapter III, of the Treaty are applied throughout the Community;
Whereas the establishment of Community arrangements for the early exchange of information does not affect the rights and obligations of Member States under bilateral and multilateral treaties or conventions;
Whereas, in furtherance of international cooperation, the Community will participate in the IAEA Convention on Early Notification of a Nuclear Accident,

HAS ADOPTED THIS DECISION:

Article 1

1. These arrangements shall apply to the notification and provision of information whenever a Member State decides to take measures of a wide-spread nature in order to protect the general public in case of a radiological emergency following:
(a) an accident in its territory involving facilities or activities referred to in paragraph 2 from which a significant release of radioactive material occurs or is likely to occur; or
(b) the detection, within or outside its own territory, of abnormal levels of radioactivity which are likely to be detrimental to public health in that Member State; or
(c) accidents other than those specified in (a) involving facilities or activities referred to in paragraph 2 from which a significant release of radioactive material occurs or is likely to occur; or

(d) other accidents from which a significant release of radioactive materials occurs or is likely to occur.
2. The facilities or activities referred to in paragraph 1 (a) and 1 (c) are the following:
(a) any nuclear reactor, wherever located;
(b) any other nuclear fuel cycle facility;
(c) any radioactive waste management facility;
(d) the transport and storage of nuclear fuels or radio- active wastes;
(e) the manufacture, use, storage, disposal and transport of radioisotopes for agricultural, industrial, medical and related scientific and research purposes; and
(f) the use of radioisotopes for power generation in space objects.

Article 2

1. When a Member State decides to take measures as referred to in Article 1, that Member State shall:
(a) forthwith notify the Commission and those Member States which are, or are likely to be, affected of such measures and the reasons for taking them;
(b) promptly provide the Commission and those Member States which are, or are likely to be, affected with available information relevant to minimizing the foreseen radiological consequences, if any, in those States.
2. A Member State should whenever possible provide the Commission and those Member States which are likely to be affected with notification of its intention to take without delay measures as referred to in Article 1.

Article 3

1. The information to be provided pursuant to Article 2 (1) (b) shall, without jeopardy to matters of national security, include, as far as practicable and appropriate, the following:
(a) the nature and time of the event, its exact location and the facility or the activity involved;
(b) the assumed or established cause and the foreseeable development of the accident relevant to the release of the radioactive materials;
(c) the general characteristics of the radioactive release, including the nature, probable physical and chemical form and the quantity, composition and effective height of the radioactive release;
(d) information on current and forecast meteorological and hydrological conditions, necessary for forecasting the dispersion of the radioactive release;
(e) the results of environmental monitoring;
(f) the results of measurements of foodstuffs, feedingstuffs and drinking water;
(g) the protective measures taken or planned;

(h) the measures taken, or planned, to inform the public;
(i) the predicted behaviour over time of the radioactive release.
2. The information shall be supplemented at appropriate intervals by further relevant information, including the development of the emergency situation and its foreseeable or actual termination.
3. The Member State referred to in Article 1 shall, in accordance with Article 36 of the Treaty, continue to inform the Commission at appropriate intervals of the levels of radioactivity as laid down in paragraph 1 (e) and (f).

Article 4

Any Member State, upon receipt of the information set out in Articles 2 and 3, shall:
(a) promptly inform the Commission of the measures taken and recommendations issued following the receipt of such information;
(b) inform the Commission, at appropriate intervals, of the levels of radioactivity measured by their monitoring facilities in foodstuffs, feedingstuffs, drinking water and the environment.

Article 5

1. Upon receipt of the information referred to in Articles 2, 3 and 4, the Commission shall, subject to Article 6, immediately forward it to the competent authorities of all other Member States. Likewise the Commission shall forward to all Member States any information it receives about significant increases in the level of radioactivity or about nuclear accidents in non-Community countries and especially those adjacent to the Community.
2. Detailed procedures for the transmission of the information referred to in Articles 1 to 4 shall be agreed by the Commission and the competent authorities of the Member States and tested at regular intervals.
3. Each Member State shall indicate to the Commission the competent national authorities and points of contact designated to forward or receive the information set out in Articles 2 to 5. The Commission shall in turn communicate this and details of the designated Commission service to the competent authorities of the other Member States.
4. Points of contact and the designated Commission service shall be available on a 24 hour basis.

Article 6

1. Information received pursuant to Articles 2, 3 and 4 may be used without restrictions except when such information is provided in confidence by the notifying Member State.

2. Information received by the Commission relating to an establishment of the Joint Research Centre will not be circulated or released without the agreement of the host Member State.

Article 7

This Decision does not affect the reciprocal rights and obligations of the Member States resulting from bilateral or multilateral agreements or Conventions existing or to be concluded in the field covered by this Decision and in accordance with its object and purpose.

Article 8

Member States shall take the measures necessary to comply with this Decision within three months of the date of its notification.

Article 9

This Decision is addressed to the Member States.

Done at Brussels, 14 December 1987.
For the Council
The President
U. ELLEMANN-JENSEN
(1) OJ No C 318, 30. 11. 1987.
(2) OJ No C 105, 21. 4. 1987, p. 9.
(3) OJ No 11, 20. 2. 1959, p. 221/59.
(4) OJ No L 246, 17. 9. 1980, p. 1.
(5) OJ No L 265, 5. 10. 1984, p. 4.

COUNCIL REGULATION (93/1493/EURATOM) OF 8 JUNE 1993 ON SHIPMENTS OF RADIOACTIVE SUBSTANCES BETWEEN MEMBER STATES

From the viewpoint of substance, this Regulation has certain links with the Euratom Directive 92/3 on the shipments of radioactive waste which is addressed further on in this Chapter. The Regulation in fact deals also with radioactive substances other than waste, stipulating a number of obligations aimed at keeping them under control when they are shipped from one country to another within the European Community. The above mentioned Directive differs however from the 1993 Regulation, in that the former addresses the shipment of waste not only between Member States, but also into and out of the Community.

From a strictly legal viewpoint, this Regulation (based on article 31 of the Euratom Treaty) was intended to fill the gap between its entry into force and the implementation at the national levels of the 92/3 Directive, for which the prescribed deadline was 1 January 1994. Obviously, this action would have covered only radioactive waste but, as to the other radioactive substances, it was envisaged that the provisions on the controls over their shipments would be incorporated in the Euratom Directives on radiological protection (1980 Basic Standards) which were under revision at the time.

The Regulation in point pursued also the objective of taking into account the evolving situation in connection with the entry into force of the Single Market in the European Community as of 1 January 1994. This entailed the abolition of frontiers and relevant checks within the Community, which were consequently conferred on national authorities to perform them over the respective territories. By virtue of the Regulation, therefore, border controls on radioactive substances were suppressed; its second main feature was the introduction of a declaration (by the consignee to the holder of substances who intended to carry out a shipment) that the former had complied (in the Member State of destination) with all applicable provisions on safe storage, use or disposal of those substances.

On account of what is pointed out above, the Regulation ceased to apply to radioactive waste as of January 1, 1994.

THE COUNCIL OF THE EUROPEAN COMMUNITIES,

Having regard to the Treaty establishing the European Atomic Energy Community, and in particular Articles 31 and 32 thereof,

Having regard to the proposal from the Commission (1), drawn up after obtaining the opinion of a group of persons appointed by the Scientific and Technical Committee from among scientific experts in the Member States,
Having regard to the opinion of the European Parliament (2),
Having regard to the opinion of the Economic and Social Committee (3),
Whereas on 2 February 1959 the Council adopted directives laying down the basic standards for the protection of the health of workers and the general public against the dangers arising from ionizing radiation (4), amended in particular by Directive 80/836/Euratom (5);
Whereas, pursuant to Article 3 of Directive 80/836/Euratom, each Member State must make compulsory the reporting of activities which involve a hazard arising from ionizing radiation; whereas, in the light of possible dangers and other relevant considerations, these activities are subject to prior authorization in cases decided upon by each Member State;
Whereas Member States have consequently set up systems within their territories in order to meet the requirements of Article 3 of Directive 80/836/Euratom; whereas, therefore, by means of the internal controls that Member States apply on the basis of national rules consistent with existing Community and any relevant international requirements, Member States continue to ensure a comparable level of protection within their territories;
Whereas shipments of radioactive waste between Member States and into and out of the Community are subject to the specific measures laid down by Directive 92/3/Euratom (6); whereas Member States are required to bring into force not later than 1 January 1994 the laws, regulations and administrative provisions necessary to comply with Directive 92/3/Euratom; whereas each Member State should be responsible for ensuring that its own radioactive waste is properly managed;
Whereas the removal of frontier controls in the Community as from 1 January 1993 has deprived the competent authorities of Member States of information previously received through those controls on shipments of radioactive substances; whereas there is a need for the competent authorities concerned to receive the same level of information as before to continue implementing their controls for radiation protection purposes; whereas a Community system of declaration and provision of information would facilitate the maintenance of radiation protection control; whereas a system of prior declaration is needed for shipments of sealed sources and radioactive waste;
Whereas special fissile materials as defined by Article 197 of the EAEC Treaty are subject to the provisions of Title II, Chapter VII – Safeguards of that Treaty; whereas the transport of such materials is subject to the obligations of the Member States and the Commission pursuant to the International Convention on the Physical Protection of Nuclear Materials (IAEA.1980);
Whereas this Regulation is without prejudice to provision of information and to controls imposed for reasons other than radiation protection,

HAS ADOPTED THIS REGULATION:

Article 1

1. This Regulation shall apply to shipments, between Member States, of sealed sources and other relevant sources, whenever the quantities and concentrations exceed the levels laid down in Article 4 (a) and (b) of Directive 80/836/Euratom. It shall also apply to shipments of radioactive waste, between Member States, as covered by Directive 92/3/Euratom.
2. In the case of nuclear materials, each Member State carries out all necessary controls, within its own territory, in order to ensure that each consignee of such materials, which are the subject of a shipment from another Member State, complies with the national provisions implementing Article 3 of Directive 80/836/Euratom.

Article 2

For the purposes of this Regulation:

- shipment means transport operations from the place of origin to the place of destination, including loading and unloading of radioactive substances,
- the holder of radioactive substances means any natural or legal person who, before carrying out a shipment, has the legal responsibility under national law for such materials and intends to carry out shipment to a consignee,
- the consignee of radioactive substances means any natural or legal person to whom such material is shipped,
- sealed source has the meaning given to it in Directive 80/836/Euratom,
- other relevant source means any radioactive substance not being a sealed source intended for direct or indirect use of the ionizing radiation it emits for medical, veterinary, industrial, commercial, research or agricultural applications,
- radioactive waste has the meaning given to it in Directive 92/3/Euratom,
- nuclear materials means the special fissile materials, the source materials and the ores as defined in Article 197 of the EAEC Treaty,
- competent authorities means any authority responsible in the Member State for the application or administration of this Regulation or of any other authority designated by the Member State,
- activity has the meaning given to it in Directive 80/836/Euratom.

Article 3

Controls of shipments of sealed sources, other relevant sources and radioactive waste between Member States, pursuant to Community or national law, for the purpose of radiation protection shall be performed as part of the control procedures applied in a non-discriminatory manner throughout the territory of the Member State.

Article 4

1. A holder of sealed sources or radioactive waste who intends to carry out a shipment of such sources or waste, or to arrange for such a shipment to be carried out, shall obtain a prior written declaration by the consignee of the radioactive substances to the effect that the consignee has complied, in the Member State of destination, with all applicable provisions implementing Article 3 of Directive 80/836/Euratom and with relevant national requirements for safe storage, use or disposal of that class of source or waste.
The declaration shall be made by means of the standard documents set out in Annexes I and II to this Regulation.
2. The declaration referred to in paragraph 1 shall be sent by the consignee to the competent authority of the Member State to which the shipment is to be made. The competent authority shall confirm with its stamp on the document that it has taken note of the declaration and the declaration shall then be sent by the consignee to the holder.

Article 5

1. The declaration referred to in Article 4 may refer to more than one shipment, provided that:
- the sealed sources or radioactive waste to which it relates have essentially the same physical and chemical characteristics,
- the sealed sources or radioactive waste to which it relates do not exceed the levels of activity set out in the declaration, and
- the shipments are to be made from the same holder to the same consignee and involve the same competent authorities.

2. The declaration shall be valid for a period of not more than three years from the date of stamping by the competent authority as referred to in Article 4 (2).

Article 6

A holder of sealed sources, other relevant sources and radioactive waste who has carried out a shipment of such sources or waste, or arranged for such a shipment to be carried out, shall, within 21 days of the end of each calendar quarter, provide the competent authorities in the Member State of destination with the following information in respect of deliveries during the quarter:

- names and addresses of consignees,
- the total activity per radio-nuclide delivered to each consignee and the number of such deliveries made,
- the highest single quantity of each radio-nuclide delivered to each consignee,
- the type of substance: sealed source, other relevant source or radioactive waste.

The first such return shall cover the period 1 July to 30 September 1993.

Article 7

The competent authorities of Member States shall cooperate in ensuring the application and enforcement of this Regulation.

Article 8

Member States shall forward to the Commission not later than 1 July 1993 the name(s) and the address(es) of the competent authorities as defined in Article 2 and all necessary information for rapidly communicating with such authorities.
Member States shall forward to the Commission any changes to such data.
The Commission shall communicate this information, and any changes thereto, to all competent authorities in the Community and shall publish it, and any changes thereto, in the Official Journal of the European Communities.

Article 9

Nothing in this Regulation shall effect existing national provisions and international agreements on the transport, including transit, of radioactive material.

Article 10

Nothing in this Regulation shall affect the obligations and rights resulting from Directive 92/3/Euratom.

Article 11

1. The Regulation shall enter into force on the 20th day following its publication in the Official Journal of the European Communities.
2. This Regulation shall cease to apply to radioactive waste on 1 January 1994.

This Regulation shall be binding in its entirety and directly applicable in all Member States.

Done at Luxembourg, 8 June 1993.
For the Council
The President
N. HELVEG PETERSEN

(1) OJ No C 347, 31. 12. 1992, p. 17.
(2) OJ No 150, 31. 5. 1993,
(3) OJ No C 19, 25. 1. 1993, p. 13.
(4) OJ No L 11, 20. 2. 1959, p. 221/59.
(5) OJ No L 246, 17. 9. 1980, p. 1. Directive as amended by Directive 84/467/Euratom (OJ No L 265, 5. 10. 1984, p. 4).
(6) OJ No L 35, 12. 2. 1992, p. 24.

ANNEX I
SHIPMENT OF SEALED SOURCES BETWEEN THE MEMBER STATES OF THE EUROPEAN COMMUNITY
Standard document to be used pursuant to Council Regulation (EEC) No 1493/93 Notice

– The consignee of sealed sources must complete boxes 1 to 5 and send this form to the relevant competent authority in his country.
– The competent authority of the consignee Member State must fill in box 6 and return this form to the consignee.
– The consignee must then send this form to the holder in the forwarding country prior to the shipment of the sealed sources.
– All sections of this form must be completed and boxes ticked, where appropriate.
1. THIS DECLARATION CONCERNS: ONE SHIPMENT (This form is valid until the shipment is completed unless otherwise stated in box 6)
expected date of shipment (if available):
SEVERAL SHIPMENTS (This form is valid for three years unless otherwise stated in box 6)

2. DESTINATION OF THE SOURCE(S)
Name of consignee:
Person to contact:
Address:
Tel.: Fax:

3. HOLDER OF THE SOURCE(S) IN THE FORWARDING COUNTRY
Name of holder:
Person to contact:

Address:
Tel.: Fax:

4. DESCRIPTION OF THE SOURCE(S) INVOLVED IN THE SHIPMENT(S)
(a) Radio-nuclide(s):

(b) Maximum activity of individual source (MBq):

(c) Number of sources:
(d) If this (these) sealed source(s) is (are) mounted in (a) machinery/device/equipment, short description of the machinery/device/equipment:
(e) Indicate (if available and requested by the competent authorities):
– national or international technical standard with which the sealed source(s) complies(y) and certificate number:
– date of expiry of certification:
– name of the manufacturer and catalogue reference:

5. DECLARATION OF THE AUTHORIZED OR RESPONSIBLE PERSON
– I, the consignee, hereby certify that the information provided in this form is correct.
– I, the consignee, hereby certify that I am licensed, authorized or otherwise permitted to receive the source(s) described in this form.
– Licence, authorization or other permission number (if applicable) and validity date thereof:
– I, the consignee, hereby certify that I comply with all the relevant national requirements, such as those relating to the safe storage, use or disposal of the source(s) described in this form.
Name: Signature: Date:

6. CONFIRMATION BY THE COMPETENT AUTHORITY OF THE CONSIGNEE COUNTRY THAT IT HAS TAKEN NOTE OF THIS DECLARATION.
Stamp: Name of the authority:
Address:
Tel.: Fax:
Date:
This declaration is valid until (if applicable):
Please see box 1, page 1, for guidance on the length of time this form is valid.

ANNEX II
SHIPMENT OF RADIOACTIVE WASTE BETWEEN THE MEMBER STATES OF THE EUROPEAN COMMUNITY
Standard document to be used pursuant to Council Regulation (Euratom) No 1493/93 Notice

– The consignee of radioactive waste must complete boxes 1 to 6 and send this form to the relevant competent authority of his country.
– The competent authority of the consignee Member State must fill in box 7 and return this form to the consignee.
– The consignee must then send this form to the holder in the forwarding country prior to the shipment of the radioactive waste.
– All sections of this form must be completed and boxes ticked, where appropriate.
– This document will no longer apply from 1 January 1994.

1. THIS DECLARATION CONCERNS: ONE SHIPMENT
expected date of shipment (if available):
SEVERAL SHIPMENTS

2. DESTINATION OF THE RADIOACTIVE WASTE
Name of consignee:
Person to contact:
Address:
Tel.: Fax:

3. HOLDER OF THE RADIOACTIVE WASTE IN THE FORWARDING COUNTRY
Name of holder:
Person to contact:
Address:
Tel.: Fax:

4. NATURE OF THE RADIOACTIVE WASTE
(a) Description of waste:
(b) Origin of the waste: (e.g. medical, research, power production, etc.)
(c) Principal radio-nuclides:
(d) Maximum alpha activity of the shipment(s) (Bq):
(e) Maximum beta/gamma activity of the shipment(s) (Bq):
(f) Maximum quantity of waste of the shipment(s), volume or mass (m3 or kg):
(g) Number of shipments:

5. PURPOSE OF SHIPMENT
(waste conditioning, storage, disposal, etc.)

6. DECLARATION OF THE AUTHORIZED OR RESPONSIBLE PERSON
– I, the consignee, hereby certify that the information provided in this form is correct.
– I, the consignee, hereby certify that I am licensed, authorized or otherwise permitted to receive the radioactive waste described in this form.
– Licence, authorization or other permission number (if applicable) and validity date thereof:
– I, the consignee, hereby certify that I comply with all the relevant national requirements relating to the safe storage or disposal of the waste described in this form.
Name: Signature: Date:

7. CONFIRMATION BY THE COMPETENT AUTHORITY OF THE CONSIGNEE COUNTRY THAT IT HAS TAKEN NOTE OF THIS DECLARATION
Stamp: Name of the authority:
Address:
Tel.: Fax:
Date:
This declaration is valid until (if applicable):
Please see notice, page 1, for guidance on the length of time this form is valid

COUNCIL REGULATION (9/60/EURATOM) OF 2 FEBRUARY 1960 DEFINING THE CONCENTRATION OF ORES IN ACCORDANCE WITH ARTICLE 197, PARAGRAPH 4, OF THE TREATY ESTABLISHING THE EUROPEAN ATOMIC ENERGY COMMUNITY

Article 197 of the Euratom Treaty defines, for the purposes of the Treaty, various terms like "special fissile materials",, "source materials" and "ores" (as well as uranium enriched in uranium-235 or 233). Under the same provision, the main technical features relating to these notions are specified by the Council following a proposal from the Commission. As to ores in particular, the Council Regulation in point is concerned with the average concentration of substances from which the source materials of above may be obtained by the appropriate chemical and physical processing.

The Regulation is published here, given its relevance for the application of the Treaty.

THE COUNCIL OF THE EUROPEAN ATOMIC ENERGY COMMUNITY,

Having regard to the provisions of the Treaty, and in particular Article 197(4) and Article 161 thereof;
Having regard to the proposal from the Commission;
Whereas the average concentrations in ores must be defined, on the basis of current scientific and technological knowledge, in such a way that the provisions of the Treaty may be applied in accordance with the general objectives laid down for the Community, in particular as regards co-ordination of investment, supply and safeguards;

HAS ADOPTED THIS REGULATION:

Article 1

For the purposes of applying Article 197 (4) of the Treaty, average concentrations are the ratio between the weight of the uranium (U) or thorium (Th) contained, in any form whatsoever, in a given quantity of ore and the weight of that same quantity of ore.

Article 2

The average concentration is defined as follows:
– uranium-bearing ores:
any average concentration of 0,1% or more uranium;
– thorium-bearing ores-except monazites:
any average concentration of 3% or more thorium;
– monazites:
any average concentration of 10% or more thorium or 0,1% or more uranium.

Article 3

This Regulation shall enter into force on the twentieth day following its publication in the Official Journal of the European Communities.

This Regulation shall be binding in its entirety and directly applicable in all Member States.

Done at Brussels, 2 February 1960.

COUNCIL REGULATION (99/2587/EURATOM) OF 2 DECEMBER 1999 DEFINING THE INVESTMENT PROJECTS TO BE COMMUNICATED TO THE COMMISSION IN ACCORDANCE WITH ARTICLE 41 OF THE TREATY ESTABLISHING THE EUROPEAN ATOMIC ENERGY COMMUNITY

Under article 41 of the Euratom Treaty, persons and undertakings engaged in industrial activities shall communicate to the Commission investment projects relating to new installations which fulfil the criteria as to type and size determined by the Council following a proposal from the Commission. These criteria were laid down for the first time in Regulation no. 4 of September 15, 1958, and threshold values relating to projects were established for the purpose of the communication to be sent to the Commission. This would enable it to publish periodically, as stipulated under article 40 of the E.T., indicative programmes, so as to facilitate coordinated development of investments in the nuclear field. The 1958 Regulation was repealed and replaced by the 1999 Regulation, in order to update the threshold values referred to above.

A Commission (EC) Regulation was adopted in 2000 to determine the procedures for carrying out the obligations (i.e. the communications prescribed under article 41) imposed on the persons and undertakings of above. Further provisions were adopted by the Commission in 2003 (Reg. 1352 of July 23), clarifying procedures regarding the application of the 1999 Regulation. Although not directly relevant for safety and protection, Regulation 2587 is published here with its Annex where the industrial activities and the related costs are identified for the purposes of the Regulation.

THE COUNCIL OF THE EUROPEAN UNION,

Having regard to the provisions of the Treaty establishing the European Atomic Energy Community, and in particular Article 41(1) thereof,

Having regard to the proposal from the Commission,

Whereas:
(1) In order to attain the objectives laid down in the Treaty, the Commission must be notified of investment projects concerning new installations and of replacements or conversions involved in the industrial activities listed in Annex II to the Treaty when

such projects are sufficiently extensive and are likely to have a direct influence on production or productivity while respecting nuclear safety;
(2) It is the responsibility of the Commission to publish periodically, in accordance with Article 40 of the Treaty, illustrative programmes and to facilitate a coordinated development of these investments and to make its point of view known about them;
(3) The investments made in the entire fuel cycle, including waste management and decomissioning are basically necessary for a correct and responsible operation of the nuclear industry;
(4) The threshold values in Regulation No 4 should be updated and replaced by new threshold values;
(5) Regulation No 4 should be repealed and replaced by this Regulation,

HAS ADOPTED THIS REGULATION:

Article 1

1. Persons or undertakings engaged in the industrial activities listed in Annex II to the Treaty shall communicate to the Commission, within the time limits laid down in Article 42 of the Treaty, their investment projects aimed at:
(a) creating a production capacity;
(b) maintaining quantitative and qualitative production capacity;
(c) directly increasing production capacity;
(d) directly increasing productivity;
(e) improving the quality of production;
(f) creating facilities for the management of spent fuel or radioactive waste, including treatment, interim or final storage and/or disposal;

when, in the industrial activities listed in column I of the table in the Annex, the cost exceeds the corresponding amount in column II of the table in the Annex for new installations and that in column III of the table in the Annex for replacements and conversions.

2. Investment projects aiming at decommissioning installations shall be notified, when the cost exceeds the corresponding amount in column III of the table in the Annex through a declaration which may be limited to essential characteristics; the procedure laid down in Article 43 of the Treaty need not be applied.

3. Investment projects aiming at decommissioning installations, where the costs are lower than the threshold values in column III of the table in the Annex, may be notified on a voluntary basis; the procedure laid down in Article 43 of the Treaty need not be applied.

4. Projects for new installations for nuclear reactors of any type and for any purpose and projects concerning the replacement, transformation, modernisation or power increase of such installations, where the costs are lower than the threshold values of the table in the Annex, may be notified on a voluntary basis through a simple declaration giving only their essential characteristics; the procedure laid down in Article 43 of the Treaty need not be applied.

Article 2

For the purpose of calculating the costs referred to in Article 1 all expenditure arising directly from the carrying out of the investment projects shall be taken into account, irrespective of the time at which such expenditure is incurred.

Article 3

Communication of projects pursuant to Article 1(1) of this Regulation shall include and be limited to the details required for the discussion provided for in Article 43 of the Treaty and in particular all the information relating to:
(a) the type of products or activity and the production or storage capacity;
(b) the total amount of expenditure directly chargeable to the project under consideration;
(c) the length of time likely to be required for carrying out the project;
(d) the prospects as regards supplies for and operation of the installation.

Article 4

Regulation No 4 of the Council of the European Atomic Energy Community of 15 September 1958 shall be repealed.

Article 5

This Regulation shall enter into force on the day of its publication in the *Official Journal of the European Communities.*

It shall apply three months after the date of its entry into force.

This Regulation shall be binding in its entirety and directly applicable in all Member States.

Done at Brussels, 2 December 1999.

For the Council The President
E. TUOMIOJA

ANNEX

Table

(EUR million)

I Sectors	II New installations	III Replacements and conversions
1. Mining of uranium and thorium ore	40	20
2. Concentration of such ores	40	20
3. Chemical processing and refining of uranium and thorium concentrates	40	20
4. Preparation of nuclear fuels, in any form	20	10
5. Fabrication of nuclear fuel elements	20	10
6. Production of uranium hexafluoride	20	10
7. Production of enriched uranium	140	70
8. Processing of irradiated fuels for the purpose of separating some or all of the elements contained therein	140	70
9. Production of reactor moderators	40	20
10. Production of hafnium-free zirconium or components thereof	20	10
11. Nuclear reactors of all types and for all purposes	100	40
12. Facilities for the industrial processing of radioactive waste, set up in conjunction with one or more of the facilities specified in this list	50	20
13. Semi-industrial installations intended to prepare the way for the construction of plants involved in any of activities in sectors 3 to 10	20	10

Notes on the Table
Preparation of nuclear fuels, in any form (sector No 4), includes chemical processing and conversion of source materials or special fissile materials.

Defluorination processes for effluents/wastes after enrichment pertain to sectors No 4, 6, 8 and 12.

Facilities for treatment, storage or disposal of radioactive waste or used fuels pertain to sector No 12, even if these facilities are not located on the site of any other nuclear industrial facility mentioned in Annex II to the Euratom Treaty.

THE EURATOM DIRECTIVES AND OTHER INSTRUMENTS AND ACTS RELATING TO RADIATION PROTECTION (1959-2003)

It should be stressed preliminarily that the legislative action by the European Community in the domain of radiation protection was started in the late 1950's, that is soon after the stipulation of the Euratom Treaty (see under previous Chapter One) from which all these directives stem as "derived" legislation. The first Euratom Basic Standards date back to 1959, and have been amended several times (1962, 1966, 1976, 1980, 1984 and lately 1996). The other directives on specific areas were adopted between 1989 and 2003, in part as an indirect consequence of the Chernobyl nuclear accident, but more generally in order to strengthen the existing radiation protection regime. Another factor which has had an impact on this legislation is the creation and entry into force (as of 1994) of the European Single Market, which entails the free movement within the Community of goods, persons etc. This extends understandably to radioactive sources, workers employed in nuclear activities etc.

The various instruments (including the "directives") made available by the Euratom Treaty for the adoption of radiation protection provisions at Community level are addressed in the previous Chapter One. Here it is recalled that the Treaty deals with radiation protection in article 2 b) (as regards the establishment within the Community of "uniform safety standards to protect the health of workers and of the general public...") and more extensively in Title II, Chapter 3 (Health and Safety). In the present context, it is important to refer to articles 30 to 33, concerned respectively with the object of the Basic Standards, the procedure for their elaboration and adoption, as well as their revision, and the checking by the Commission on compliance of national provisions with the Basic Standards, in order to ensure harmonisation of such provisions.

The other directives are equally based on the Euratom Treaty and intended to supplement the Basic Standards by introducing provisions on particular areas or activities where radiation protection also applies, taking into account their specific features and needs.

Finally, attention is drawn to the fact that the Basic Standards have their technical-scientific matrix in the "recommendations" issued by ICRP (International Commission on Radiological Protection, described further on in this Chapter) and are consistent with the International Basic Safety Standards for Protection against Ionising Radiation and for Safety of Radiation Sources sponsored by the International Atomic Energy Agency and jointly sponsored by other five International Organisations with competence in radiation protection (see again further on in this Chapter).

All the main features of the "directives" are reflected in national legislation of Member States (although realised by varying solutions given the flexibility accorded to them as to the form and methods) all such solutions being equivalent in terms of the radiation protection objectives indicated in the "directives". These normally stipulate a deadline within which they must be implemented in national legislation. The Euratom Treaty contains provisions (esp. article 141) addressing the non-respect of the Treaty and derived legislation.

THE EURATOM BASIC STANDARDS ON RADIATION PROTECTION (1959-1996)

The second half of the 1950s marked the beginning of the nuclear era in terms of international action intended to set up a regulatory framework for nuclear activities. As one can see under the previous Chapter One in connection with the creation of international organisation acting in the nuclear field, their normative role provided a considerable impulse to the intensive and rapid development of the regulatory framework above mentioned. The normative output (which indeed had its initial thrust also in the late 1950's) of IAEA, NEA and of non-exclusively nuclear international organisations is described further on in the present Chapter. Here the history and development of the Euratom Basic Standards are resumed, which are one of the mainstays of radiation protection in the European Union. Moreover, they have a considerable importance in connection with the enlargement of the Union (an on-going process), which now includes also a number of Central and Eastern European countries.

Among the many versions of the Basic Standards, the first one ever dating back to 1959 is obviously of capital importance. This holds true also because, throughout their several amendments and despite the specifications and adaptations especially to keep apace with the latest developments in radiological protection (expressed in the ICRP Recommendations, see further on in this Chapter) they have preserved their basic structure resting on four sets of provisions concerned with a) reporting and prior authorisation system, b) maximum permissible doses [dose limits] compatible with adequate safety, c) physical and medical surveillance of workers and the public, d) inspection to ensure compliance with radiation protection laws and regulations.

The Basic Standards stem from the Euratom Treaty and are adopted by means of "directives", which are addressed to Member States and indirectly binding on them, that is as to the result to be achieved. Not all the amendments made after 1959 pertain to the substance, in fact some of them touched essentially upon the technical annexes (1962) or particular radiation protection principles and issues (1984); on the other hand, the 1966 text took into account the latest technical-scientific developments concerning exceptional irradiation of workers; the 1976 version was deeply innovative especially where it reflected the presence in the Community of three new Member States (Denmark, Great Britain and Ireland); the 1980 Standards introduced expressly for the first time the basic principles of justification and optimisation in radiation protection; finally, the 1996 new Standards addressed (again, for the first time) natural radioactivity and certain other activities and practices of radiation protection concern, such as aircraft operation involving exposure to cosmic radiation of air crew; besides, they take into account the latest ICRP recommen-

dations as to the (more conservative) dose limits for workers and the public, as well as the specific needs associated with the entering into force of the Single European Market as of 1994; lastly, they provide more in detail for co-operation especially among Member States in relation to possible radiological emergencies. It should be added that the Basic Standards are particularly important also because since the 1959 version they provided for the creation of two specialists (to be formally recognised and with very few counterparts in fields other than the nuclear) in radiation protection, that is the qualified expert (for physical control) and the approved medical practitioner (for medical surveillance).

The deadline for implementation of the latest Basic Standards (Council Directive 96/29/Euratom of 13 May 1996) in national legislation was 13 May 2000, and it may be said that by now such implementation has been achieved in Member States. A Commission Communication (98/C 133/03) supplements the Basic Standards and provides elements intended to facilitate their implementation. It is recalled that the Standards are and remain the only binding instrument and therefore the Communication is meant to be merely a useful tool for a better understanding and practical implementation of the provisions concerned.

The text of Directive 96/29 (without its many technical annexes) and of the Communication may be found in the following pages.

COUNCIL DIRECTIVE 96/29/EURATOM OF 13 MAY 1996 LAYING DOWN BASIC SAFETY STANDARDS FOR THE PROTECTION OF THE HEALTH OF WORKERS AND THE GENERAL PUBLIC AGAINST THE DANGERS ARISING FROM IONIZING RADIATION

THE COUNCIL OF THE EUROPEAN UNION,

Having regard to the Treaty establishing the European Atomic Energy Community, and in particular Articles 31 and 32 thereof,
Having regard to the proposal from the Commission, drawn up after obtaining the opinion of a group of persons appointed by the Scientific and Technical Committee from among scientific experts in the Member States,
Having regard to the opinion of the European Parliament (1),
Having regard to the opinion of the Economic and Social Committee (2)
Whereas Article 2b of the Treaty provides for the establishment of uniform basic safety standards to protect the health of workers and of the general public;
Whereas Article 30 of the Treaty defines the »basic standards« for the protection of the health of workers and the general public against the dangers arising from ionizing radiation as:
(a) maximum permissible doses compatible with adequate safety;
(b) maximum permissible levels of exposure and contamination;
(c) the fundamental principles governing the health surveillance of workers;
Whereas Article 33 of the Treaty requires each Member State to lay down the appropriate provisions, whether by legislation, regulation or administrative action, to ensure compliance with the basic standards which have been established and shall take the necessary measures with regard to teaching, education and vocational training;
Whereas in order to perform its task the Community laid down basic standards for the first time in 1959 pursuant to Article 218 of the Treaty by means of Directives of 2 February 1959 laying down the basic standards for the protection of the health of workers and the general public against the dangers arising from ionizing radiations (3); whereas the Directives were revised in 1962 by Directive of 5 March 1962 (4), in 1966 by Directive 66/45/Euratom (5), in 1976 by Directive 76/579Euratom (6), in 1979 by Directive 79/343/Euratom (7), in 1980 by Directive 80/836/Euratom (8) and in 1984 by Directive 84/467/Euratom (9);
Whereas the basic standards directives have been supplemented by Council Directive 84/466/Euratom of 3 September 1984 laying down basic measures for the radiation protection of persons undergoing medical examination or treatment (10); Council

Decision 87/600/Euratom of 14 December 1987 on Community arrangements for the early exchange of information in the event of a radiological emergency (11); Council Regulation (Euratom) No 3954/87 of 22 December 1987 laying down maximum permitted levels of radioactive contamination of foodstuffs and of feedingstuffs following a nuclear accident or any other case of radiological emergency (12); Council Directive 89/618Euratom of 27 November 1989 on informing the general public about health protection measures to be applied and steps to be taken in the event of a radiological emergency (13); Council Directive 90/641/Euratom of 4 December 1990 on the operational protection of outside workers exposed to the risk of ionizing radiation during their activities in controlled areas (14); Council Directive 92/3/Euratom of 3 February 1992 on the supervision and control of shipments of radioactive waste between Member States and into and out of the Community (15); and Council Regulation (Euratom) No 1493/93 of 8 June 1993 on shipments of radioactive substances between Member States (16);

Whereas the development of scientific knowledge concerning radiation protection, as expressed in particular in Recommendation No 60 of the International Commission on Radiological Protection, makes it convenient to revise the basic standards and to lay them down in a new legal instrument;

Whereas the basic standards are of special significance as to ionizing radiation risks with regard to other Directives concerned with other types of risks and it is important to make progress in applying them in a uniform manner within the Community;

Whereas it is desirable to take into account in the scope of the basic standards the practices or work activities which may result in a significant increase in exposure for workers and members of the public, which cannot be disregarded from the radiation protection point of view, due to ionizing radiation from artificial radiation sources or natural radiation sources, as well as appropriate protection in cases of intervention;

Whereas the Member States, in order to ensure compliance with the basic standards, are required to submit certain practices involving a hazard from ionizing radiation to a system of reporting and prior authorization or to prohibit certain practices;

Whereas a system of radiation protection for practices should continue to be based on the principles of justification of exposure, optimization of protection and dose limitation; whereas, limitations of doses must be fixed taking into account the particular situation of the different groups of persons exposed such as workers, apprentices, students and members of the public;

Whereas the operational protection of exposed workers, apprentices and students requires the implementation of measures at the workplace; whereas these measures must include prior evaluation of the hazard involved, classification of workplaces and workers, monitoring of areas and working conditions and medical surveillance;

Whereas the Member States should be required to identify work activities involving significantly increased levels of exposure for workers or members of the public to natural radiation sources which cannot be disregarded from a radiation protection

point of view; whereas the Member States should take appropriate protective measures in respect of the work activities declared to be of concern;
Whereas the operational protection of the population in normal circumstances requires the establishment by Member States of a system of inspection to keep under review the radiation protection of the population and to check compliance with the basic standards;
Whereas the Member States should be prepared for the likelihood of potential radiological emergencies on their territory and should cooperate with other Member States and with third countries in order to facilitate the preparedness and management of those situations;
Whereas the basic standards directives as last revised by Directive 84/467/Euratom should be repealed with effect from the date that this Directive becomes applicable,

HAS ADOPTED THIS DIRECTIVE:

TITLE I
DEFINITIONS

Article 1

For the purpose of this Directive, the following terms have the meaning hereby assigned to them.

Absorbed dose (D): the energy absorbed per unit mass where

[GRAPHICS]

is the mean energy imparted by ionizing radiation to the matter in a volume element,

– dm is the mass of the matter in this volume element.

In this Directive absorbed dose denotes the dose averaged over a tissue or an organ. The unit for absorbed dose is the gray.

Accelerator: apparatus or installation, in which particles are accelerated, emitting ionizing radiation with an energy higher than 1 mega-electron volt (MeV).

Accidental exposure: an exposure of individuals as a result of an accident. It does not include emergency exposure.

Activation: process through which a stable nuclide is transformed into a radionuclide by irradiating with particles or high-energy gamma rays the material in which it is contained.

Activity (A): the activity, A, of an amount of a radionuclide in a particular energy state at a given time is the quotient of dN by dt, where dN is the expectation value of the number of spontaneous nuclear transitions from that energy state in the time interval dt: A=dN/dt

The unit of activity is the becquerel.

Apprentice: a person receiving training or instruction within an undertaking with a view to exercising a specific skill.

Approved dosimetric service: a body responsible for the calibration, reading or interpretation of individual monitoring devices, or for the measurement of radioactivity in the human body or in biological samples, or for assessment of doses, whose capacity to act in this respect is recognized by the competent authorities.

Approved medical practioner: a medical practitioner responsible for the medical surveillance of category A workers, as defined in Article 21, whose capacity to act in that respect is recognized by the competent authorities.

Approved occupational health services: a body or bodies to which may be assigned responsibility for the radiation protection of exposed workers and/or medical surveillance of category A workers. Its capacity to act in that respect is recognized by the competent authorities.

Artificial sources: radiation sources other than natural radiation sources.

Authorization: a permission granted in a document by the competent authority, on application, or granted by national legislation, to carry out a practice or any other action within the scope of this Directive.

Becquerel (Bq): the special name of the unit of activity. One becquerel is equivalent to one transition per second:

1 Bq = 1 s-1

Clearance levels: values, established by national competent authorities, and expressed in terms of activity concentrations and/or total activity, at or below which radioactive substances or materials containing radioactive substances arising from any practice subject to the requirement of reporting or authorization may be released from the requirements of this Directive.

Committed effective dose: (E(ô)): the sum of the committed organ or tissue equivalent dowes (HT(ô)) resulting from an intake, each multiplied by the appropriate tissue weighting factor wT. It is defined by:

[GRAPHICS]

In specifying E(ô), ô is given in the number of years over which the integration is made. The unit for committed effective dose is the sievert.

Committed equivalent dose (HT(ô)): the integral over time (t) of the equivalent dose rate in tissue or organ T that will be received by an individual as a result of an intake. It is given by:

[GRAPHICS] for an intake at time t0 where

T(t) is the relevant equivalent dose rate in organ or tissue T at time t,

– ô is the time over which the integration is performed.

In specifying HT(ô), ô is given in years. When ô is not given, a period of 50 years is assumed for adults and up to age 70 for children. The unit for committed equivalent dose is the sievert.

Competent authorities: any authority designated by a Member State.

Controlled area: an area subject to special rules for the purpose of protection against ionizing radiation or of preventing the spread of radioactive contamination and to which access is controlled.

Disposal: the emplacement of waste in a repository, or a given location, without the intention of retrieval. Disposal also covers the approved direct discharge of wastes into the environment, with subsequent dispersion.

Dose constraint: a restriction on the prospective doses to individuals which may result from a defined source, for use at the planning stage in radiation protection whenever optimization is involved.

Dose limits: maximum references laid down in Title IV for the doses resulting from the exposure of workers, apprentices and students and members of the public to ionizing radiation covered by this Directive that apply to the sum of the relevant doses from external exposures in the specified period and the 50-year committed doses (up to age 70 for children) from intakes in the same period.

Effective dose (E): the sum of the weighted equivalent doses in all the tissues and organs of the body specified in Annex II from internal and external irradiation. It is defined by the expression:

[GRAPHICS]

where

- DT,R is the absorbed dose averaged over tissue or organ T, due to radiation R,
- wR is the radiation weighting factor and
- wT is the tissue weighting factor for tissue or organ T.

The appropriate wT and wR values are specified in Annex II. The unit for effective dose is the sievert.

Emergency exposure: an exposure of individuals implementing the necessary rapid action to bring help to endangered individuals, prevent exposure of a large number of people or save a valuable installation or goods, whereby one of the individual dose limits equal to that laid down for exposed workers could be exceeded. Emergency exposure shall apply only to volunteers.

Equivalent dose (HT): the absorbed dose, in tissue or organ T weighted for the type and quality of radiation R. It is given by:

HT,R = wR DT,R

where
- DT,R is the absorbed dose averaged over tissue or organ T, due to radiation R,
- wR is the radiation weighting factor.

When the radiation field is composed of types and energies with different values of WR, the total equivalent dose, HT, is given by:

[GRAPHICS]

The appropriate wR values are specified in Annex II. The unit for equivalent dose is the sievert.

Exposed workers: persons, either self-employed or working for an employer, subject to an exposure incurred at work from practices covered by this Directive and liable to result in doses exceeding one or other of the dose levels equal to the dose limits for members of the public.

Exposure: the process of being exposed to ionizing radiation.

Gray (Gy): the special name of the unit of absorbed dose. One gray is equal to one joule per kilogram:

1 Gy = 1 J kg-1

Health detriment: an estimate of the risk of reduction in length and quality of life occurring in a population following exposure to ionizing radiations. This includes loss arising from somatic effects, cancer and severe genetic disorder.

Intake: the activities of radionuclides entering the body from the external environment.

Intervention: a human activity that prevents or decreases the exposure of individuals to radiation from sources which are not part of a practice or which are out of control, by acting on sources, transmission pathways and individuals themselves.

Intervention level: a value of avertable equivalent dose, avertable effective dose or a derived value, at which intervention measures should be considered. The avertable dose or derived value is solely that associated with the exposure pathway to which the intervention measure is to be applied.

Ionizing radiation: the transfer of energy in the form of particles or electromagnetic waves of a wavelength of 100 nanometer or less or a frequency of 3 ×1015 Hertz or more capable of producing ions directly or indirectly.

Members of the public: individuals in the population, excluding exposed workers, apprentices and students during their working hours and individuals during the exposures referred to in Article 6(4)(a), (b) and (c).

Natural radiation sources: sources of ionizing radiation from natural terrestrial or cosmic origin.

Potential exposure: exposure, that is not expected to be delivered with certainty, with a probability of occurrence that can be estimated in advance.

Practice: a human activity that can increase the exposure of individuals to radiation from an artificial source, or from a natural radiation source where natural radionuclides are processed for their radioactive, fissile or fertile properties, except in the case of an emergency exposure.

Qualified experts: Persons having the knowledge and training needed to carry out physical, technical or radiochemical tests enabling doses to be assessed, and to give advice in order to ensure effective protection of individuals and the correct operation of protective equipment, whose capacity to act as a qualified expert is recognized by the competent authorities. A qualified expert may be assigned the technical responsibility for the tasks of radiation protection of workers and members of the public.

Radioactive contamination: the contamination of any material, surface or environment or of an individual by radioactive substances. In the specific case of the human body, this radioactive contamination includes both external skin contamination and internal contamination, irrespective of route of intake.

Radioactive substance: any substance that contains one or more radionuclides the activity or concentration of which cannot be disregarded as far as radiation protection is concerned.

Radiological emergency: a situation that requires urgent action in order to protect workers, members of the public or the population either partially or as a whole.

Reference group of the population: a group comprising individuals whose exposure to a source is reasonably uniform and representative of that of the individuals in the population who are the more highly exposed to that source.

Reporting: requirement of submitting a document to the competent authority to notify the intention to carry out a practice or any other action within the scope of this Directive.

Sealed source: a source whose structure is such as to prevent, under normal conditions of use, any dispersion of the radioactive substances into the environment.

Sievert: the special name of the unit of equivalent or effective dose. One sievert is equivalent to one joule per kilogram:

1 Sv = 1 J kg-1

Source: an apparatus, a radioactive substance or an installation capable of emitting ionizing radiation or radioactive substances.

Supervised area: an area subject to appropriate supervision for the purpose of protection against ionizing radiation.

Undertaking: any natural or legal person who carries out the practices or work activities referred to in Article 2 of this Directive and who has the legal responsibility under national law for such practices or work activities.

TITLE II
SCOPE

Article 2

1. This Directive shall apply to all practices which involve a risk from ionizing radiation emanating from an artificial source or from a natural radiation source in cases where natural radionuclides are or have been processed in view of their radioactive, fissile or fertile properties, namely:
(a) the production, processing, handling, use, holding, storage, transport, import to and export from the Community and disposal of radioactive substances;
(b) the operation of any electrical equipment emitting ionizing radiation and containing components operating at a potential difference of more than 5 kV;
(c) any other practice specified by the Member State.

2. In accordance with Title VII it shall also apply to work activities which are not covered by paragraph 1 but which involve the presence of natural radiation sources and lead to a significant increase in the exposure of workers or members of the public which cannot be disregarded from the radiation protection point of view.

3. In accordance with Title IX it shall also apply to any intervention in cases of radiological emergencies or in cases of lasting exposure resulting from the after-effects of a radiological emergency or a past or old practice or work activity.

4. This Directive shall not apply to exposure to radon in dwellings or to the natural level of radiation, i.e. to radionuclides contained in the human body, to cosmic radiation prevailing at ground level or to aboveground exposure to radionuclides present in the undisturbed earth's crust.

TITLE III
REPORTING AND AUTHORIZATION OF PRACTICES

Article 3
Reporting

1. Each Member State shall require the carrying out of the practices referred to in Article 2 (1) to be reported, except as provided for in this Article.

2. No reporting need be required for practices involving the following:
(a) radioactive substances where the quantities involved do not exceed in total the exemption values set out in column 2 of Table A to Annex I or, in exceptional circumstances in an individual Member State, different values authorized by the competent authorities that nevertheless satisfy the basic general criteria set out in Annex I; or
(b) radioactive substances where the concentration of activity per unit mass do not exceed the exemption values set out in column 3 of Table A to Annex I or, in exceptional circumstances in an individual Member State, different values authorized by the competent authorities that nevertheless satisfy the basic general criteria set out in Annex I; or
(c) apparatus containing radioactive substances exceeding the quantities or concentration values specified in subparagraphs (a) or (b), provided that:
(i) it is of a type approved by the competent authorities of the Member State; and
(ii) it is constructed in the form of a sealed source; and
(iii) it does not cause, in normal operating conditions, a dose rate exceeding 1 μSv h-1 at a distance of 0,1 m from any accessible surface of the apparatus; and
(iv) conditions for disposal have been specified by the competent authorities; or
(d) the operation of any electrical apparatus to which this Directive applies, other than that referred to in subparagraph (e) provided that:
(i) it is of a type approved by the competent authorities of the Member State; and
(ii) it does not cause, in normal operating conditions, a dose rate exceeding 1 μSv h-1 at a distance of 0,1 m from any accessible surface of the apparatus; or
(e) the operation of any cathode ray tube intended for the display of visual images, or other electrical apparatus operating at a potential difference not exceeding 30 kV, provided that this operation does not cause, in normal operating conditions, a dose rate exceeding 1 μSv h-1 at a distance of 0,1 m from any accessible surface of the apparatus; or
(f) material contaminated with radioactive substances resulting from authorized releases which competent authorities have declared not to be subject to further controls.

Article 4
Authorization

1. Except as provided for in this Article, each Member State shall require prior authorization for the following practices:
(a) operation and decommissioning of any facility of the nuclear fuel cycle and exploitation and closure of uranium mining;
(b) the deliberate addition of radioactive substances in the production and manufacture of medicinal products and the import or export of such goods;
(c) the deliberate addition of radioactive substances in the production and manufacture of consumer goods and the import or export of such goods;
(d) the deliberate administration of radioactive substances to persons and, in so far as radiation protection of human beings is concerned, animals for the purpose of medical or veterinary diagnosis, treatment or research;
(e) the use of X-ray sets or radioactive sources for industrial radiography or processing of products or research of the exposure of persons for medical treatment and the use of accelerators except electron microscopes;

2. Prior authorization may be required for practices other than those listed in paragraph 1.

3. Member States may specify that a practice shall not require authorization where:
(a) in the case of the practices described in paragraph 1 (a), (c) and (e), the practice is exempt from reporting; or
(b) in cases where a limited risk of exposure of human beings does not necessitate the examination of individual cases the practice is undertaken in accordance with conditions laid down in national legislation.

Article 5
Authorization and clearance for disposal, recycling or reuse

1. The disposal, recycling or reuse of radioactive substances or materials containing radioactive substances arising from any practice subject to the requirement of reporting or authorization is subject to prior authorization.

2. However, the disposal, recycling or reuse of such substances or materials may be released from the requirements of this Directive provided they comply with clearance levels established by national competent authorities. These clearance levels shall follow the basic criteria used in Annex I and shall take into account any other technical guidance provided by the Community.

TITLE IV
JUSTIFICATION, OPTIMIZATION AND DOSE LIMITATION FOR PRACTICES

Chapter I
GENERAL PRINCIPLES

Article 6

1. Member States shall ensure that all new classes or types of practice resulting in exposure to ionizing radiation are justified in advance of being first adopted or first approved by their economic, social or other benefits in relation to the health detriment they may cause.

2. Existing classes or types of practice may be reviewed as to justification whenever new and important evidence about their efficacy or consequences is acquired.

3. In addition each Member State shall ensure that:
(a) in the context of optimization all exposures shall be kept as low as reasonably achievable, economic and social factors being taken into account;
(b) without prejudice to Article 12, the sum of the doses from all relevant practices shall not exceed the dose limits laid down in this Title for exposed workers, apprentices and students and members of the public.

4. The principle set out in paragraph 3 (a) shall apply to all exposures to ionizing radiation resulting from the practices referred to in Article 2 (1). The principle set out in paragraph 3 (b) shall not apply to any of the following exposures:
(a) exposure of individuals as part of their own medical diagnosis or treatment;
(b) exposure of individuals knowingly and willingly helping (other than as part of their occupation) in the support and comfort of patients undergoing medical diagnosis or treatment;
(c) exposure of volunteers participating in medical and biomedical research programmes.

5. Member States shall permit neither the deliberate addition of radioactive substances in the production of foodstuffs, toys, personal ornaments and cosmetics nor the import or export of such goods.

Article 7
Dose constraints

1. Dose constraints should be used, where appropriate, within the context of optimization of radiological protection.

2. Guidance established by each Member State on the appropriate procedures to be applied to individuals exposed in accordance with Article 6 (4) (b) and (c) may include dose constraints.

Chapter II
LIMITATION OF DOSES

Article 8
Age limit for exposed workers

Subject to Article 11 (2), persons under 18 years of age may not be assigned to any work which would result in their being exposed workers.

Article 9
Dose limits for exposed workers

1. The limit on effective dose for exposed workers shall be 100 millisieverts ('mSv') in a consecutive five-year period, subject to a maximum effective dose of 50 mSv in any single year. Member States may decide an annual amount.

2. Without prejudice to paragraph 1:
(a) the limit on equivalent dose for the lens of the eye shall be 150 mSv in a year;
(b) the limit on equivalent dose for the skin shall be 500 mSv in a year. This limit shall apply to the dose averaged over any area of 1 cm^2, regardless of the area exposed;
(c) the limit on equivalent dose for the hands, forearms, feet and ankles shall be 500 mSv in a year.

Article 10
Special protection during pregnancy and breastfeeding

1. As soon as a pregnant woman informs the undertaking, in accordance with national legislation and/or national practice, of her condition, the protection of the child to be born shall be comparable with that provided for members of the public. The conditions for the pregnant woman in the context of her employment shall therefore be such that the equivalent dose to the child to be born will be as low as reasonably achievable

and that it will be unlikely that this dose will exceed 1 mSv during at least the remainder of the pregnancy.

2. As soon as a nursing woman informs the undertaking of her condition she shall not be employed in work involving a significant risk of bodily radioactive contamination.

Article 11
Dose limits for apprentices and students

1. The dose limits for apprentices aged 18 years or over and students aged 18 years or over who, in the course of their studies, are obliged to use sources shall be the same as the dose limits for exposed workers laid down in Article 9.

2. The limit for effective dose for apprentices aged between 16 and 18 years and for students aged between 16 and 18 years who, in the course of their studies, are obliged to use sources shall be 6 mSv per year.

Without prejudice to this dose limit:
(a) the limit on equivalent dose for the lens of the eye shall be 50 mSv in a year;
(b) the limit on equivalent dose for the skin shall be 150 mSv in a year. This limit shall apply to the dose averaged over any area of 1 cm^2, regardless of the area exposed;
(c) the limit on equivalent dose for the hands, forearms, feet and ankles shall be 150 mSv in a year.

3. The dose limits for apprentices and students who are not subject to the provisions of paragraphs 1 and 2 shall be the same as the dose limits for members of the public specified in Article 13.

Article 12
Specially authorized exposures

1. In exceptional circumstances, excluding radiological emergencies and evaluated case by case, the competent authorities may, where some specific operation so requires, authorize individual occupational exposures of some identified workers exceeding the dose limits set out in Article 9, provided that such exposures are limited in time, confined to certain working areas and within maximum exposure levels defined for the particular case by the competent authorities. The following conditions shall be taken into account:
(a) only category A workers as defined in Article 21 may be subject to specially authorized exposures;

(b) apprentices, students, pregnant women and breastfeeding women who are likely to be bodily contaminated shall be excluded from such exposures;
(c) the undertaking shall carefully justify these exposures in advance and thoroughly discuss them with the voluntary workers, their representatives, the approved medical practitioner, the approved occupational health services or the qualified expert;
(d) information about the risks involved and the precautions to be taken during the operation shall be provided to the relevant workers in advance;
(e) all doses relating to such exposures shall be separately recorded in the medical record referred to in Article 34 and the individual record referred to in Article 28.

2. The exceeding of dose limits as a result of specially authorized exposures shall not necessarily constitute a reason by the employer for excluding from his usual occupation or relocating the worker, without the agreement of the worker.

Article 13
Dose limits for members of the public

1. Without prejudice to Article 14, the dose limits for members of the public shall be as laid down in paragraphs 2 and 3.

2. The limit for effective dose shall be 1 mSv in a year. However, in special circumstances, a higher effective dose may be authorized in a single year, provided that the average over five consecutive years does not exceed 1 mSv per yeare.

3. Without prejudice to paragraph 2:
(a) the limit on equivalent dose for the lens of the eye shall be 15 mSv in a year;
(b) the limit on equivalent dose for the skin shall be 50 mSv in a year averaged over any 1 cm^2 area of skin, regardless of the area exposed.

Article 14
Exposure of the population as a whole

Each Member State shall take reasonable steps to ensure that the contribution to the exposure of the population as a whole from practices is kept as low as reasonably achievable, economic and social factors being taken into account.
The total of all such contributions shall be regularly assessed.

TITLE V
ESTIMATION OF EFFECTIVE DOSE

Article 15

For the estimation of effective and equivalent doses the values and relationships referred to in this Title shall be used. The competent authorities may authorize the use of equivalent methods.

Article 16

Without prejudice to the provisions of Article 15:
(a) For external radiation, the values and relationships given in Annex II shall be used to estimate the relevant effective and equivalent doses;
(b) For internal exposure from a radionuclide or from a mixture of radionuclides, the values and relationships given in Annexes II and III may be used to estimate the effective doses.

TITLE VI
FUNDAMENTAL PRINCIPLES GOVERNING OPERATIONAL PROTECTION OF EXPOSED WORKERS, APPRENTICES AND STUDENTS FOR PRACTICES

Article 17

Operational protection of exposed workers shall be based in particular on the following principles:
(a) prior evaluation to identify the nature and magnitude of the radiological risk to exposed workers and implementation of the optimization of radiation protection in all working conditions;
(b) classification of workplaces into different areas, where appropriate, by reference to an assessment of the expected annual doses and the probability and magnitude of potential exposures;
(c) classification of workers into different categories;
(d) implementation of control measures and monitoring relating to the different areas and working conditions, including, where necessary, individual monitoring;
(e) medical surveillance.

Chapter I
MEASURES FOR THE RESTRICTION OF EXPOSURE

Section 1
Classification and delineation of areas

Article 18
Arrangements in workplaces

1. For the purposes of radiation protection, arrangements shall be made as regards all workplaces where there is a possibility of exposure to ionizing radiation in excess of 1 mSv per year on an equivalent dose of 10 of the dose limits for the lens of the eyes, skin and extremities laid down in Article 9 (2). Such arrangements must be appropriate to the nature of the installations and sources and to the magnitude and nature of the risks. The scope of the precautions and monitoring, as well as their type and quality, must be appropriate to the risks associated with the work involving exposure to ionizing radiation.

2. A distinction shall be made between controlled areas and supervised areas.

3. The competent authorities shall establish guidance on the classification of controlled and supervised areas which is relevant to the particular circumstances.

4. The undertaking shall keep under review the working conditions in controlled and supervised areas.

Article 19
Requirements for controlled areas

1. The minimum requirements for a controlled area are as follows:
(a) the controlled area shall be delineated and access to it shall be restricted to individuals who have received appropriate instructions and shall be controlled in accordance with written procedures provided by the undertaking. Wherever there is a significant risk of the spread of radioactive contamination, specific arrangements shall be made, including access and exit of individuals and goods;
(b) taking into account the nature and extent of radiological risks in the controlled area, radiological surveillance of the working environment shall be organized in accordance with the provisions of Article 24;
(c) signs indicating type of area, nature of the sources and their inherent risks shall be displayed;

(d) working instructions appropriate to the radiological risk associated with the sources and the operations involved shall be laid down.

2. The implementation of these duties will be carried out under the responsibility of the undertaking following consultations with the approved occupational health services or the qualified experts.

Article 20
Requirements for supervised areas

1. The requirements for a supervised area are as follows:
(a) as a minimum, taking into account the nature and extent of radiological risks in the supervised area, radiological surveillance of the working environment shall be organized in accordance with the provisions of Article 24;
(b) if appropriate, signs indicating type of area, nature of the sources and their inherent risks shall be displayed;
(c) if appropriate, working instructions appropriate to the radiological risk associated with the sources and the operations involved shall be laid down.

2. The implementation of these duties will be carried out under the responsibility of the undertaking following consultations with the qualified experts or the approved occupational health services.

Section 2
Classification of exposed workers, apprentices and students

Article 21
Categorization of exposed workers

For the purposes of monitoring and surveillance, a distinction shall be made between two categories of exposed workers:
(a) category A: those exposed workers who are liable to receive an effective dose greater than 6 mSv per year or an equivalent dose greater than 3/10 of the dose limits for the lens of the eye, skin and extremities laid down in Article 9 (2);
(b) category B: those exposed workers who are not classified as exposed category A workers.

Article 22
Information and training

1. Member States shall require the undertaking to inform exposed workers, apprentices and students who, in the course of their studies, are obliged to use sources on:

(a) the health risks involved in their work:

- the general radiation protection procedures and precautions to be taken and, in particular, those involved with operational and working conditions in respect of both the practice in general and each type of work station or job to which they may be assigned,
- the importance of complying with the technical, medical and administrative requirements;

(b) in the case of women, the need for early declaration of pregnancy in view of the risks of exposure for the child to be born and the risk of contaminating the nursing infant in case of bodily radioactive contamination.

2. Member States shall require the undertaking to arrange for relevant training in the field of radiation protection to be given to exposed workers, apprentices and students.

Section 3
Assessment and implementation of arrangements for the radiological protection of exposed workers

Article 23

1. The undertaking shall be responsible for assessing and implementing arrangements for the radiological protection of exposed workers.

2. Member States shall require the undertaking to consult the qualified experts or the approved occupational health services on the examination and testing of protective devices and measuring instruments comprising in particular:

(a) prior critical examination of plans for installations from the point of view of radiation protection;

(b) the acceptance into service of new or modified sources from the point of view of radiation protection;

(c) regular checking of the effectiveness of protective devices and techniques;

(d) regular calibration of measuring instruments and regular checking that they are serviceable and correctly used.

Chapter II
ASSESSMENT OF EXPOSURE

Section 1
Monitoring of the workplace

Article 24

1. The radiological surveillance of the working environment referred to in Articles 19 (1) (b) and 20 (1) (a) shall comprise, where appropriate:
(a) the measurement of external dose rates, indicating the nature and quality of the radiation in question;
(b) the measurement of air activity concentration and surface density of contaminating radioactive substances, indicating their nature and their physical and chemical states.

2. The results of these measurements shall be recorded and shall be used, if necessary, for estimating individual doses, as provided for in Article 25.

Section 2
Individual monitoring

Article 25
Monitoring – General

1. Individual monitoring shall be systematic for exposed category A workers. This monitoring shall be based on individual measurements which are established by an approved dosimetric service. In cases where category A workers are liable to receive significant internal contamination an adequate system for monitoring should be set up; the competent authorities may provide general guidance for identifying such workers.

2. Monitoring for category B workers shall be at least sufficient to demonstrate that such workers are correctly classified in category B. Member States may require individual monitoring and if necessary individual measurements, established by an approved dosimetric service, for category B workers.

3. In cases where individual measurements are impossible or inadequate, the individual monitoring shall be based on an estimate arrived at either from individual measurements made on other exposed workers or from the results of the surveillance of the workplace provided for in Article 24.

Section 3
Monitoring in the case of accidental or emergency exposure

Article 26

In the case of accidental exposure the relevant doses and their distribution in the body shall be assessed.

Article 27

In the case of emergency exposure, individual monitoring or assessment of the individual doses shall be carried out as appropriate to the circumstances.

Section 4
Recording and reporting of results

Article 28

1. A record containing the results of the individual monitoring, shall be made for each exposed category A worker.

2. For the purposes of paragraph 1 the following shall be retained during the working life involving exposure to ionizing radiation of exposed workers, and afterwards until the individual has or would have attained the age of 75 years, but in any case not less than 30 years from the termination of the work involving exposure:
(a) a record of the exposures measured or estimated, as the case may be, of individual doses pursuant to Articles 12, 25, 26 and 27;
(b) in the case of exposures referred to in Articles 26 and 27, the reports relating to the circumstances and the action taken;
(c) the results of workplace monitoring used to assess individual doses where necessary.

3. Exposure referred to in Articles 12, 26 and 27 shall be recorded separately in the dose record referred to in paragraph 1.

Article 29

1. The results of the individual monitoring required by Articles 25, 26 and 27 shall be:
(a) made available to the competent authorities, and to the undertaking;
(b) made available to the worker concerned in accordance with Article 38 (2);

(c) submitted to the approved medical practitioner or approved occupational health services in order to interpret their implications for human health, as provided for in Article 31.

2. Member States shall determine the arrangements under which the results of individual monitoring are conveyed.

3. In the case of an accidental or emergency exposure, the results of individual monitoring shall be submitted without delay.

Chapter III
MEDICAL SURVEILLANCE OF EXPOSED WORKERS

Article 30

The medical surveillance of exposed workers shall be based on the principles that govern occupational medicine generally.

Section 1
Medical surveillance of category A workers

Article 31
Medical surveillance

1. Notwithstanding the overall responsibility of the undertaking, the medical surveillance of category A workers shall be the responsibility of approved medical practitioners or approved occupational health services.
This medical surveillance must allow for ascertaining the state of health of workers under surveillance as regards their fitness for the tasks assigned to them. To this end the approved medical practitioner or approved occupational health services must have access to any relevant information they require including the environmental conditions existing in the working premises.

2. Medical surveillance shall include:
(a) a medical examination prior to employment or classification as category A worker. The purpose of this thorough examination shall be to determine the worker's fitness for a post as category A worker for which he is being considered;
(b) periodic reviews of health.
The state of health of each category A worker shall be reviewed at least once a year, in order to determine whether they remain fit to perform their duties. The nature of these reviews, which can be performed as many times as the approved medical practi-

tioner considers necessary, shall depend on the type of work and on the individual worker's state of health.

3. The approved medical practitioner or approved occupational health services may indicate the need for medical surveillance to continue after cessation of work for as long as they consider it necessary to safeguard the health of the person concerned.

Article 32
Medical classification

The following medical classification shall be adopted with respect to fitness for work as a category A worker:
(a) fit;
(b) fit, subject to certain conditions;
(c) unfit.

Article 33

No worker may be employed or classified for any period in a specific post as a category A worker if the medical findings deem him unfit for that specific post.

Article 34
Medical records

1. A medical record shall be opened for each category A worker and kept up to date so long as he remains a worker of that category. Thereafter it shall be retained until the individual has or would have attained the age of 75 years, but in any case not less than 30 years from the termination of the work involving exposure to ionizing radiation.
2. The medical record shall include information regarding the nature of the employment, the results of the medical examinations prior to employment or classification as category A worker, the periodic reviews of health and the record of doses required by Article 28.

Section 2
Special surveillance of exposed workers

Article 35

1. Special medical surveillance shall be provided in each case where one of the dose limits laid down in Article 9 has been exceeded.

2. Subsequent conditions of exposure shall be subject to the agreement of the approved medical practitioner or approved occupational health services.

Article 36

In addition to the medical surveillance of exposed workers provided for in Articles 30 and 31, provision shall be made for any further action in relation to the health protection of the exposed individual considered necessary by the approved medical practitioner or approved occupational health services such as further examinations, decontamination measures or urgent remedial treatment.

Section 3
Appeals

Article 37

Each Member State shall lay down the procedure for appeal against the findings and decisions made in pursuance of Articles 32, 33 and 35.

Chapter IV
TASKS OF MEMBER STATES IN RESPECT OF PROTECTION OF EXPOSED WORKERS

Article 38

1. Each Member State shall establish a system or systems of inspection to enforce the provisions introduced in compliance with this Directive and to initiate surveillance and intervention measures wherever necessary.

2. Each Member State shall require that workers have access at their request to the results of their individual monitoring, including the results of measurements which may have been used in estimating them, or of the assessments of their doses made as a result of workplace measurements.

3. Each Member State shall make the necessary arrangements to recognize, as appropriate, the capacity of:
- the approved medical practitioners,
- the approved occupational health services,
- the approved dosimetric services,
- the qualified experts.

To this end, each Member State shall ensure that the training of such specialists is arranged.

4. Each Member State shall require that the means necessary for proper radiation protection are placed at the disposal of the units responsible. A specialized radiation protection unit, distinct from production and operation units in the case of an internal unit, authorized to perform radiation protection tasks and provide specific advice shall be required for the installations which the competent authorities consider necessary. This unit may be shared by several installations.

5. Each Member State shall facilitate the exchange amongst competent authorities, or approved medical practitioners, or approved occupational health services, or qualified experts, or approved dosimetric services within the European Community of all relevant information on the doses previously received by a worker in order to perform the medical examination prior to employment or classification as a category A worker pursuant to Article 31 and to control the further exposure of workers.

Chapter V
OPERATIONAL PROTECTION OF APPRENTICES AND STUDENTS

Article 39

1. The exposure conditions and operational protection of apprentices and students aged 18 years or over referred to in Article 11 (1) shall be equivalent to that of exposed workers of category A or B as appropriate.

2. The exposure conditions and operational protection of apprentices and students aged between 16 and 18 years referred to in Article 11 (2) shall be equivalent to that of exposed workers of category B.

TITLE VII
SIGNIFICANT INCREASE IN EXPOSURE DUE TO NATURAL RADIATION SOURCES

Article 40
Application

1. This Title shall apply to work activities not covered by Article 2 (1) within which the presence of natural radiation sources leads to a significant increase in the exposure of workers or of members of the public which cannot be disregarded from the radiation protection point of view.

2. Each Member State shall ensure the identification, by means of surveys or by any other appropriate means, of work activities which may be of concern. These include, in particular:
(a) work activities where workers and, where appropriate, members of the public and exposed to thoron or radon daughters or gamma radiation or any other exposure in workplaces such as spas, caves, mines, underground workplaces and aboveground workplaces in identified areas;
(b) work activities involving operations with, and storage of, materials, not usually regarded as radioactive but which contain naturally occurring radionuclides, causing a significant increase in the exposure of workers and, where appropriate, members of the public;
(c) work activities which lead to the production of residues not usually regarded as radioactive but which contain naturally occurring radionuclides, causing a significant increase in the exposure of members of the public and, where appropriate, workers;
(d) aircraft operation.

3. Articles 41 and 42 shall apply to the extent that the Member States have declared that exposure to natural radiation sources due to work activities identified in accordance with paragraph 2 of this Article needed attention and had to be subject to control.

Article 41
Protection against exposure from terrestrial natural radiation sources

For each work activity declared by them to be of concern, the Member States shall require the setting-up of appropriate means for monitoring exposure and as necessary:
(a) the implementation of corrective measures to reduce exposure pursuant to all or part of Title IX;
(b) the application of radiation protection measures pursuant to all or part of Titles III, IV, V, VI and VIII.

Article 42
Protection of air crew

Each Member State shall make arrangements for undertakings operating aircraft to take account of exposure to cosmic radiation of air crew who are liable to be subject to exposure to more than 1 mSv per year. The undertakings shall take appropriate measures, in particular:

- to assess the exposure of the crew concerned,
- to take into account the assessed exposure when organizing working schedules with a view to reducing the doses of highly exposed aircrew,

- to inform the workers concerned of the health risks their work involves,
- to apply Article 10 to female air crew.

TITLE VIII
IMPLEMENTATION OF RADIATION PROTECTION FOR THE POPULATION IN NORMAL CIRCUMSTANCES

Article 43
Basic principles

Each Member State shall create the conditions necessary to ensure the best possible protection of the population based on the principles set out in Article 6 and to apply the fundamental principles governing operational protection of the population.

Article 44
Conditions for authorization of practices involving a risk from ionizing radiation for the population

Operational protection of the population in normal circumstances from practices subject to prior authorization means all arrangements and surveys for detecting and eliminating the factors which, in the course of any operation involving exposure to ionizing radiation, are liable to create a risk of exposure for the population which cannot be disregarded from the radiation protection point of view. Such protection shall include the following tasks:
(a) examination and approval of plans for installations involving an exposure risk, and of the proposed siting of such installations within the territory concerned, from the point of view of radiation protection;
(b) acceptance into service of such new installations subject to adequate protection being provided against any exposure or radioactive contamination liable to extend beyond the perimeter, taking into account, if relevant, demographic, meteorological, geological, hydrological and ecological conditions;
(c) examination and approval of plans for the discharge of radioactive effluents.
These tasks shall be carried out in accordance with rules laid down by the competent authorities on the basis of the extent of the exposure risk involved.

Article 45
Estimates of population doses

The competent authorities shall:
(a) ensure that dose estimates from practices referred to in Article 44 are made as realistic as possible for the population as a whole and for reference groups of the population in all places where such groups may occur;

(b) decide on the frequency of assessments and take all necessary steps to identify the reference groups of the population, taking into account the effective pathways of transmission of the radioactive substances;
(c) ensure, taking into account the radiological risks, that the estimates of the population doses include:
- assessment of the doses due to external radiation, indicating, where appropriate, the quality of the radiation in question,
- assessment of the intake of radionuclides, indicating the nature of the radionuclides and, where necessary, their physical and chemical states, and determination of the activity and concentrations of these radionuclides,
- assessment of the doses that the reference groups of the population are liable to receive and specification of the characteristics of these groups.

(d) require records to be kept relating to measurements of external exposure, estimates of intakes of radionuclides and radioactive contamination as well as the results of the assessment of the doses received by reference groups and by the population.

Article 46
Inspection

As regards health protection of the population each Member State shall establish a system of inspection to enforce the provisions introduced in compliance with this Directive and to initiate surveillance in the area of radiation protection.

Article 47
Responsibilities of undertakings

1. Each Member State shall require the undertaking responsible for practices as referred to in Article 2 to conduct them in accordance with the principles of health protection of the population in the area of radiation protection and in particular to carry out the following tasks within its installations:
(a) achieving and maintaining an optimal level of protection of the environment and the population;
(b) checking the effectiveness of technical devices for protecting the environment and the population;
(c) acceptance into service, from the point of view of surveillance of radiation protection, of equipment and procedures for measuring and assessing, as appropriate, exposure and radioactive contamination of the environment and the population;
(d) regular calibration of measuring instruments and regular checking that they are serviceable and correctly used.

2. Qualified experts and, as appropriate, the specialized radiation protection unit referred to in Article 38 (4) shall be concerned in the discharge of these duties.

TITLE IX
INTERVENTION

Article 48
Application

1. This Title shall apply to intervention in cases of radiological emergencies or in cases of lasting exposure resulting from the after-effects of a radiological emergency or a past or old practice or work activity.

2. The implementation and extent of any intervention shall be considered in compliance with the following principles:
- intervention shall be undertaken only if the reduction in detriment due to radiation is sufficient to justify the harm and costs, including social costs, of the intervention,
- the form, scale and duration of the intervention shall be optimized so that the benefit of the reduction in health detriment less the detriment associated with the intervention, will be maximized,
- dose limits, as laid down in Articles 9 and 13, shall not apply to intervention; however, the intervention levels established in application of Article 50 (2) constitute indications as to the situations in which intervention is appropriate; furthermore, in cases of long term exposure covered by Article 53, the dose limits set out in Article 9 should normally be appropriate for workers involved in interventions.

Section 1
Intervention in cases of radiological emergency

Article 49
Potential exposures

The Member States shall, where appropriate, require:
- that the possibility of radiological emergencies resulting from practices subject to the system of reporting or authorization laid down in Title III be considered,
- that the spatial and temporal distribution of the radioactive substances dispersed in the event of a possible radiological emergency be assessed,
- that the corresponding potential exposures be assessed.

Article 50
Intervention preparation

1. Each Member State shall ensure that account is taken of the fact that radiological emergencies may occur in connection with practices on or outside its territory and affect it.

2. Each Member State shall ensure that appropriate intervention plans, taking account of the general principles of radiation protection for intervention referred to in Article 48 (2) and of the appropriate intervention levels established by the competent authorities, are drawn up at national or local level, including within installations, in order to deal with various types of radiological emergency and that such plans are tested to an appropriate extent at regular intervals.

3. Each Member State shall ensure, where appropriate, that provision is made for the creation and appropriate training of special teams for technical, medical and health intervention.

4. Each Member State shall seek to cooperate with other Member States or non-Member States in relation to possible radiological emergencies at installations on its own territory which may affect other Member States or non-Member States, in order to facilitate the organization of radiological protection in these States.

Article 51
Implementation of intervention

1. Each Member State shall make provision for the immediate notification to its competent authorities by the undertaking responsible for the practices involved of any radiological emergency occurring in its territory and shall require all appropriate action to reduce the consequences.

2. Each Member State shall ensure that in the event of a radiological emergency on its own territory, the undertaking responsible for the practices involved makes an initial provisional assessment of the circumstances and consequences of the emergency and assists with intervention.

3. Each Member State shall ensure that provision is made, if the situation so requires, for intervention related to:
- the source, to reduce or stop the direct radiation and emission of radionuclides,
- the environment, to reduce the transfer of radioactive substances to individuals,
- individuals, to reduce exposure and organize the treatment of victims.

4. In the event of a radiological emergency on or outside its territory, each Member State shall require:
(a) the organization of appropriate intervention, taking account of the real characteristics of the emergency;
(b) the assessment and recording of the consequences of the radiological emergency and of the effectiveness of the intervention.

5. Each Member State shall, in the event of a radiological emergency occurring at an installation on its territory or being likely to have radiological consequences on its territory, establish relations to obtain cooperation with any other Member State or non-Member State which may be involved.

Article 52
Emergency occupational exposure

1. Each Member State shall make provision for situations where workers or intervention personnel involved in different kinds of intervention are liable to be subjected to emergency exposure resulting in doses in excess of the dose limits for exposed workers. To this end, each Member State shall establish exposure levels taking into account the technical obligations and health risks. These levels shall be operational guides. An exposure above these special levels may be admitted exceptionally to save human lives and only for volunteers who are informed about the risks involved in their intervention.

2. Each Member State shall require radiological monitoring and medical surveillance of the special emergency intervention teams.

Section II
Intervention in cases of lasting exposure

Article 53

Where the Member States have identified a situation leading to lasting exposure resulting from the after-effects of a radiological emergency or a past practice, they shall, if necessary and to the extent of the exposure risk involved, ensure that:
(a) the area concerned is demarcated;
(b) arrangements for the monitoring of exposure are made;
(c) any appropriate intervention is implemented, taking account of the real characteristics of the situation;
(d) access to or use of land or buildings situated in the demarcated area is regulated.

TITLE X
FINAL PROVISIONS

Article 54

1. This Directive establishes the basic safety standards for the protection of the health of workers and the general public against the dangers arising from ionizing radiation with the aim of their uniform implementation by Member States. If a Member State is to adopt dose limits which are stricter than those laid down in this Directive, it shall inform the Commission and the Member States.

Article 55
Implementation

1. Member States shall bring into force the laws, regulations and administrative provisions necessary to comply with this Directive before 13 May 2000. They shall forthwith inform the Commission thereof.

When Member States adopt these provisions, they shall contain a reference to this Directive or shall be accompanied by such reference on the occasion of their official publication. The methods of making such reference shall be laid down by Member States.

2. Member States shall communicate to the Commission the text of the main laws, regulations or administrative provisions which they adopt in the field governed by this Directive.

Article 56
Repeals

The Directives of 2 February 1959, the Directive of 5 March 1962, Directives 66/45/Euratom, 76/579/Euratom, 79/343/Euratom, 80/836/Euratom and 84/467/Euratom shall be repealed with effect from 13 May 2000.

Article 57

This Directive is addressed to the Member States.

Done at Brussels, 13 May 1996.

For the Council
The President
S. AGNELLI

(1) OJ No C 128, 9. 5. 1994, p. 209.
(2) OJ No C 108, 19. 4. 1993, p. 48.
(3) OJ No 11, 20. 2. 1959, p. 221/59.
(4) OJ No 57, 6. 7. 1962, p. 1633/62.
(5) OJ No 216, 26. 11. 1966, p. 3693/66.
(6) OJ No L 187, 12. 7. 1976, p. 1.
(7) OJ No L 83, 3. 4. 1979, p. 18.
(8) OJ No L 246, 17. 9. 1980, p. 1.
(9) OJ No L 265, 5. 10. 1984, p. 4.
(10) OJ No L 265, 5. 10. 1984, p. 1.
(11) OJ No L 371, 30. 12. 1987, p. 76.
(12) OJ No L 371, 30. 12. 1987, p. 11. Regulation as amended by Regulation (Euratom) No 2218/89 (OJ No L 211, 22. 7. 1989, p. 19).
(13) OJ No L 357, 7. 12. 1989, p. 31.
(14) OJ No L 349, 13. 12. 1990, p. 21. Directive as amended by the 1994 Act of Accession.

COMMUNICATION FROM THE COMMISSION CONCERNING THE IMPLEMENTATION OF COUNCIL DIRECTIVE 96/29/EURATOM LAYING DOWN BASIC SAFETY STANDARDS FOR THE PROTECTION OF THE HEALTH OF THE WORKERS AND THE GENERAL PUBLIC AGAINST THE DANGERS ARISING FROM IONISING RADIATION (98/C 133/03)

Note: *Footnotes and annexes to this Communication are omitted both for the sake of brevity and since most footnotes refer to instruments and acts dealt with in the volume.*

For the purposes of implementing Council Directive 96/29/Euratom of 13 May 1996 laying down basic safety standards for the protection of the health of the workers and the general public against the dangers arising from ionising radiation, the Commission, having consulted the group of scientific experts referred to in Article 31 of the Euratom Treaty, wishes to communicate the following information:

I. General remarks

The purpose of this communication is to assist the Member States in transposing into national law Council Directive 96/29/Euratom of 13 May 1996 laying down basic safety standards for the protection of the health of the workers and the general public against the dangers arising from ionising radiation, hereinafter called 'the Directive'. The Directive repeals, with effect from 13 May 2000, the previously established Basic Safety Standards Directives.

It should be regarded as a reference document since Member States are bound only by the provisions of the Directive.

Exposure to ionising radiation can lead to detrimental health effects in human beings. The Directive sets out requirements designed for the protection of workers and the general public against the dangers of ionising radiation without unduly limiting the beneficial uses of the practices giving rise to radiation exposure. The Commission recognises that all those concerned with radiation protection have to make value judgements about the relative importance of different kinds of risks and about the balancing of risks and benefits.

The European Community is required by Article 30 of the Treaty establishing the European Atomic Energy Community to lay down basic standards for the protection of workers and the general public against the dangers of ionising radiation. These standards have been laid down in the form of Council Directives.

Those Directives have always made use of the recommendations of the International Commission on Radiological Protection (ICRP) and the International Commission on Radiation Units and Measurements (ICRU). Those organisations are internationally recognised for their assessments of the state of the art in their respective fields.

The ICRP publication on which the 1996 Directive is based is ICRP Publication No 60 that contains the latest general recommendations issued by the ICRP to take account of the continuing development in scientific knowledge and administrative experience. This development has been of an evolutionary nature and it did not fundamentally change the system of protection recommended by ICRP Publication no. 26 on which the 1980/1984 Directive was based.

Until 1984 the Basic Safety Standards Directive has been the only instrument of derived legislation based on Article 31 of the Euratom Treaty. Since then, although it remained together with the Euratom Treaty itself, the central element of the European Community radiation protection system, it has been supplemented by a number of specific legal instruments.

The Directive does not affect general obligations relating to the protection of those at work as given for example in Directive 89/391/EEC on the introduction of measures to encourage improvements in the safety and health of workers at work. In the case of mutually exclusive dispositions the Euratom Directive is given priority over EC Directives.

One of the major new features of the Directive is the distinction between practices and interventions. Practices relate to those human activities that can increase radiation exposure; interventions are those human activities that prevent or decrease radiation exposure. Other new features are the increased recognition of the fact that some exposures due to work activities involving natural radiation sources are significant enough to warrant attention, the use of dose constraints in optimisation of protection, the concepts of clearance and of potential exposures. The development of scientific knowledge led to new concepts and quantities in dosimetry and radiation protection. It also led to lower dose limits, to redefined values for the application of the requirements on reporting and authorisation of practices and to new parameters for the estimation of doses from external radiation, notably from neutrons, and from intakes of radio-nuclides.

II. Comments on some Articles of the Directive

a) TITLE I
DEFINITIONS

Article 1

The definitions relate to terms used in the Directive. Further definitions are given in Annex II. Where necessary, guidance on their interpretation is given below in the comments on the Articles in question.

(i) 'Accidental exposure' is no longer limited to exposures whereby one of the dose limits laid down for exposed workers is exceeded.

(ii) 'Emergency exposure' should not be confused with 'Specially authorised exposures'; an emergency exposure is the exposure of a volunteer actively implementing urgent protective actions (Article 52). A specially authorised exposure is the carefully planned exposure of a category A worker who should be a volunteer for carrying out specific operations in exceptional circumstances (Article 12).

(iii) 'Equivalent dose' and 'Effective dose'. The Directive uses the protection quantities recommended by ICRP Publication No 60. They replace the previous quantities 'Dose equivalent' and 'Effective dose (equivalent)'. It is noted that the ICRP recommends that 'it is appropriate to treat as additive the weighted quantities used by the ICRP but assessed at different times, despite the use of different values of weighting factors. The ICRP does not recommend that any attempt be made to correct earlier values. It is also appropriate to add values of dose equivalent to equivalent dose and values of effective dose equivalent to effective dose without any adjustment'.

(iv) The newly introduced concept of 'Health detriment' includes the probability of fatal cancer, of severe hereditary effects, of non-fatal cancer and the relative length of life lost.

(v) 'Qualified expert'. Advice on basic and additional training for qualified experts is given in Annex I of this communication.

(vi) 'Undertaking'. The obligations set out in Title VI for the protection of exposed workers and related to requirements for working areas are linked to the undertaking which has the legal responsibility for the practice. In a given working area more than one practice can be carried out by various undertakings or employers. In this context it should be noted that the Directive does not affect employers' obligations required by Council Directive 89/391/EEC of 12 June 1989 on the introduction of measures to encourage improvements in the safety and health of workers at work.

b) TITLE II
SCOPE

Article 2

The Directive does not apply to radon in dwellings, for which a Commission recommendation exists, nor to exposures to natural radiation sources essentially not controllable.

c) TITLE III
REPORTING AND AUTHORISATION OF PRACTICES

Article 3

Reporting means the submission of a document to notify or inform the competent authorities of the intention to undertake a practice. Article 3(2) and Annex I specify the circumstances under which competent authorities may decide that reporting is not required. Member States are allowed to deviate from the values in Table A of Annex I, in exceptional circumstances and subject to specified conditions.

Article 4

Prior authorisation is the permission granted by the competent authority in individual written notification or in a legislative act that is individual in character, to carry out a practice. It implies the prior examination by the competent authorities of individual submitted cases.

Member States need not require such prior authorisation in the case of certain practices, exempted from the requirement to report as stated in Article 3(2) and in Article 4(3)(a), and in the case of practices, permitted according to conditions laid down in national legislation, where examination of individual cases is not considered necessary as a result of limited risk of exposure of human beings as stated in Article 4(3)(b). In compliance with Article 3(1) such latter practices are reported to the competent authorities.

Authorisation is needed under any circumstances for the practices referred to in Article 4(1)(b) and in Article 4(1)(d).

Article 6(5) identifies practices which are not permitted under any circumstances.

Article 5

This Article deals with the disposal, recycling or reuse of radioactive substances or materials.

The disposal, recycling or reuse of materials containing radioactive substances which have been involved in practices subject to reporting or prior authorisation is subject to prior authorisation. Such materials may nevertheless be released from the requirements of the Directive subject to compliance with clearance levels established by national competent authorities. Such clearance levels shall be established following the basic criteria in Annex I. They may be generic or be established in individual cases. The term 'clearance' refers to material previously subject to regulatory control as part of the operations that gave rise to this disposal, recycling or reuse. On the other hand exemption from reporting according to Article 3(2) refers to material which does not need to become subject to regulatory control.

Article 3(2)(f) ensures that human activities involving materials contaminated as a result of authorised releases need not be reported.

In view of the internal market, a harmonised approach to the development of clearance levels is highly desirable. The Commission will therefore give technical guidance for national competent authorities on the establishment of clearance levels. The Commission, with the support of the group of scientific experts referred to in Article 31 of the Euratom Treaty, is working on a revised version of the technical guide (1988) on clearance levels for the recycling of material coming from the decommissioning of nuclear installations. Other technical guides will follow.

d) TITLE IV
JUSTIFICATION, OPTIMISATION AND DOSE LIMITATION FOR PRACTICES

Article 6

This Article sets out the basic principles of radiation protection and thus requires Member States to base their procedures on these principles, namely justification, optimisation and dose limitation.

Determination of the justification of any new classes or types of practice is the duty of the Member State. It should take place before the introduction of the class or type of practice and as early as possible to reduce the influence of the already incurred costs in balancing economic and social factors against health detriment. Compliance with this principle can be safely assumed in respect of a new class or type of practice by the existence or laying down of regulations specifically concerning the class or type of practice. Paragraph 5 gives a list of practices considered a priori as not justifiable under any circumstances. The newly introduced proviso of Article 6(2) reflects that there might be the need to review the justification of existing classes or types of practices. If an existing practice should be considered unjustified a transitional period could still be tolerated on the basis of a carefully weighted balance between economic, social or other benefits and the health detriment.

Optimisation requires that exposures from practices shall be kept as low as reasonably achievable below the prescribed limits, economic and social factors being taken into account. The techniques for judging the need for further reductions in exposure in the light of what is reasonable are very diverse. They include formal aids to decision-making such as cost-benefit analyses, but they are more usually based on professional judgment. The principle should be applied from the design stage, throughout all other stages to eventual decommissioning or disposal of sources.

The third principle requires that the sum of the doses to an individual from all relevant practices shall not exceed specified dose limits. The considerations which led to the establishment of the dose limits are presented in ICRP Publication No 60. The dose limits are intended to protect the most highly exposed individuals which, in the case of members of the public, are defined as the 'reference group of the population' (Article 1).

Article 7

The concept of dose constraint has been introduced in ICRP Publication No 60 within the context of optimisation of protection. Dose constraints should not be confused with dose limits. They are essentially a ceiling to the predicted values of individual doses from a source, practice or task which could be determined to be acceptable in the process of optimisation of protection for that source, practice or task.

Dose constraints may be established and used by undertakings as a help for optimising protection in the design or in the planning stage. They may also be established by authorities, particularly in the context of public exposure. They may be matters for discussions between undertakings and authorities.

A guide on the utilisation of the newly introduced concept is given in a report by a joint group of experts from the OECD Nuclear Energy Agency and from the European Commission, published by the OECD in 1996.

Article 9

The Directive has decreased the effective dose limit for exposed workers from 50 mSv in a year to 100 mSv in a consecutive five-year period, subject to a maximum effective dose of 50 mSv in any single year.

While respecting the limit of 100 mSv in a consecutive five-year period Member States are entitled to decide instead on an annual amount. In this case the effective dose limit

would be 20 mSv in a year. Member States which wish to adopt stricter dose limits shall comply with Article 54.
The equivalent dose limits for the lens of the eye, the skin, the hands, forearms, feet and ankles remain unchanged. Their purpose is to protect against deterministic effects, for which scientific information indicates no need for change. However, the limit for the skin now applies to the dose averaged over any 1 cm^2 of skin, regardless of the area exposed. Compliance with the effective dose limit alone is not always sufficient to prevent the occurrence of deterministic effects on some organs or tissues. It is therefore necessary to ensure compliance with both the effective dose limit and the equivalent dose limits.

Article 10

Article 10 aims at protecting the suckling child or the child to be born, via the working conditions of the nursing or the pregnant woman.
Article 22(1)(b) identifies the additional information that women should be given.

Article 12

Specially authorised exposures replace the planned special exposures from Directive 80/836/Euratom. Experience on the application of planned special exposure under the terms of the 1980 Directive has shown that they have been applied very seldom if at all. A specially authorised exposure would involve an exposure above one of the dose limits for exposed workers established by national legislation in compliance with Article 9.
The Directive requires maximum exposure levels resulting from specially authorised exposures to be defined for each particular case by the competent authorities. No ceiling is given for such levels as it might be interpreted as a generally tolerable value. Article 12(2) should be read in conjunction with Articles 35 and 36 on the special surveillance of exposed workers.

Article 13

The Directive has decreased the effective dose limit for members of the public from 5 mSv to 1 mSv in a year; in special circumstances, a higher effective dose may be authorised in a single year, provided that the average over five consecutive years does not exceed 1 mSv per year.
The equivalent dose limits for the lens of the eye and for the skin are unchanged. Their purpose is to protect against deterministic effects, for which scientific information indicates no need for change. However, the limit for the skin now applies to the dose averaged over any 1 cm^2 of skin, regardless of the area exposed. Equivalent dose limits

for the hands, forearms, feet and ankles are no longer seen as necessary. Compliance with the effective dose limit alone is not always sufficient to prevent the occurrence of deterministic effects on some organs or tissues. It is therefore necessary to ensure compliance with both the effective dose limit and the equivalent dose limits.
The dose limits apply to the sum of the doses to members of the public due to exposure to all relevant sources received in one year, through all exposure pathways.

Article 14

This Article requires optimisation of protection to be made not only with respect to individuals but also to the population as a whole.
The second paragraph requires regular assessments of the total of contributions to the exposure of the population from practices. The objective is to enable competent authorities and undertakings to identify trends in the pattern of exposures in particular where actions to reduce doses might be warranted. See also Article 45.

e) TITLE V
ESTIMATION OF EFFECTIVE DOSE

Articles 15 and 16

This Title refers to the values and relationships given in Annex II and the dose coefficients given in Annex III to be used for the estimation of effective and equivalent doses. The information contained in these annexes and the additional tables annexed to this Communication are taken from the most recent relevant work of ICRU and ICRP and reflect the current status of scientific knowledge. While competent authorities may authorise the use of equivalent methods (Article 15), it is recommended that these be kept in line with internationally recognised scientific guidance.
With regard to the estimation of effective dose for internal exposure, Annex III gives dose coefficients for different chemical and physical forms that have been considered for the listed radio-nuclides and corresponding parameter values. If specific information is not available, the indicated default parameters may be used. On the other hand, whenever information is available which permits a better estimation of the parameter values and corresponding dose coefficients, competent authorities may authorise the use of such information to calculate effective dose to workers and to members of the public.
In the above context, the last paragraph of Part B of Annex III relates to the choice of parameter values for inhalation dose coefficients for members of the public. The international scientific guidance referred to is now identified in Table 1 in Annex II to this Communication.

In the first paragraph of Part B of Annex III it is stated that dose coefficients for members of the public also relate to apprentices and students aged between 16 and 18 years. While this makes allowance for the age dependence of dose coefficients, in some circumstances it may be useful to look into whether the default parameters used for members of the public are suitable for the physical and chemical forms in which radio-nuclides occur in the workplace. Article 15 allows Member States to authorise the use of dose coefficients for workers whenever these are more appropriate.

f) TITLE VI
FUNDAMENTAL PRINCIPLES GOVERNING OPERATIONAL PROTECTION OF EXPOSED WORKERS, APPRENTICES AND STUDENTS FOR PRACTICE

Article 17

Consistent with Council Directive 89/391/EEC of 12 June 1989 on the introduction of measures to encourage improvements in the safety and health of workers at work, Article 17(a) requires a prior evaluation of the radiological risk to exposed workers. This should be seen as the first step in identifying the protection measures required including the classification of workplaces and workers.

Article 17(b), dealing with classification of workplaces into different areas, introduces the concept of potential exposure, as defined in Article 1. An example of potential exposure is that resulting from the failure of the operation of an interlock preventing access to the beam of an irradiation facility. Any exposure resulting from such an event would be considered as accidental. Exposures that may result from events having a relatively high probability of occurrence, and contributing only small increments to the doses inherent in the normal working conditions, can be considered as resulting from the normal working conditions. An example of such exposures are those resulting from the spillage of a radio-pharmaceutical in a nuclear medicine laboratory.

Articles 18 to 20

These Articles give the requirements to implement Article 17. Article 18(2) requires a distinction to be made between controlled and supervised areas. This distinction is primarily a management matter. It aims at facilitating the practical organisation of radiation protection commensurate with the radiological risk. It also draws the attention of the workers to the particular conditions of the workplace and makes them aware of their responsibilities as regards radiation protection.

Controlled areas should be established where workers are required to follow rules specially related to radiological protection rather than simply on the basis of a defined fraction of the dose limit. Special rules are required based on considerations of

radiological risk, including expected dose to workers, possible spread of contamination and potential exposures.
The Directive does not require a controlled area to be surrounded by a supervised area; nor does it require that supervised areas only exist at the border of controlled areas.

Article 21

The classification of exposed workers in Category A and Category B workers is maintained. It is intended to simplify working arrangements and to ensure that workers are aware both of their own status and of the likely conditions in their place of work. It also contributes to ensure that radiation protection arrangements for workers are appropriate to the risks linked with their work and working conditions.

Article 28

The Directive requires a record of the results of the individual monitoring to be retained only for Category A workers. Member States, however, are free to require such records to be kept for other persons who are individually monitored.

The individual dose record shall contain the estimated or measured doses separated into:
- those received routinely (Article 25),
- those received as specially authorised exposures (Article 12),
- those due to accidents (Article 26),
- those received as emergency exposures (Article 27) and,
- those received from natural radiation sources in a work activity declared to be of concern (Article 41),
  when decided by Member States.

The individual dose record shall also contain reports relating to the circumstances of an accident or emergency exposure and actions taken (Article 28(2)(b)).
A separate medical record shall be opened for each Category A worker as specified by Article 34.

Article 29

Article 29(2) requires Member States to determine the arrangements for conveying the results of individual monitoring following their national regulations concerning confidentiality and privacy.

Articles 31 to 37

One of the aims of medical surveillance of Category A workers is to ensure that they are and continue to be medically fit for their duties. The approved medical practitioner conducting the surveillance must therefore have relevant information about these duties and the conditions in which they are carried out.

The nature of the periodic reviews shall depend on the type of work that is undertaken and the state of health of the worker.

For example, special consideration may be needed in situations:

- where workers are required to use respiratory protective equipment,
- where workers with skin diseases or skin damage are required to handle radioactive substances which are not in the form of sealed sources,
- where workers are known to have psychological disorders.

(g) TITLE VII
SIGNIFICANT INCREASE IN EXPOSURE DUE TO NATURAL RADIATION SOURCES

Articles 40 to 42

In some cases, the exposures of workers and members of the public to natural radiation sources owing to work activities are sufficiently high to warrant the introduction of radiation protection measures to monitor, control and reduce them. Examples are radon exposures in identified working places and exposures due to work with large amounts of materials with activity concentrations significantly above the normal levels of natural radio-nuclides in the earth's crust. Materials with elevated activity concentrations might include phosphate rock, rare earth materials, scales and residues from oil and gas industries. The potential to apply protection measures regarding these exposures may vary considerably depending for example on working conditions within and between Member States; therefore the Directive leaves significant discretion to the Member States as regards actions to be taken.

The Directive sets up a four-step system to deal with exposures due to natural radiation sources:

(i) the use of surveys or other appropriate means to identify work activities which may lead to a significant increase in the exposure of workers or members of the public;
(ii) the setting-up of appropriate means for monitoring exposures, and the evaluation of the related doses in identified workplaces;
(iii) the implementation, as necessary, of corrective measures to reduce exposure,
(iv) in total or partial application, as necessary, of radiation protection measures for practices (Title III, IV, V, VI and VIII).

Advice on the implementation of Title VII of the Directive concerning significant increase in exposure due to natural radiation sources, prepared with the support of the group of scientific experts referred to in Article 31 of the Euratom Treaty has been issued by the Commission.
The advice covers protection of air crew.

(i) TITLE IX
INTERVENTION

Articles 48 to 53

A clear distinction between practices and interventions is one of the main modifications introduced by the Directive. Therefore, Title IX includes a section on the various phases for intervention in cases of a radiological emergency:
- preventive consideration of possible radiological emergency,
- preventive preparation of the intervention,
- implementation of the intervention, should an emergency occur.

Article 48(2) sets out the radiation protection principles for interventions. It makes clear that dose limits do not apply to interventions; however, they should normally be appropriate for workers involved in interventions. Intervention levels established by the competent authorities constitute indications as to the situations in which intervention would be appropriate.
Mainly following the Chernobyl accident a number of measures in relation to possible radiological emergencies have been adopted by the Community.
- Regulation laying down maximum permitted levels of radioactive contamination of foodstuffs and feeding-stuffs following a nuclear accident or any other case of radiological emergency, including a Council Regulation on the special conditions for exporting foodstuffs and feeding-stuffs following a nuclear accident or any other case of radiological emergency,
- Council Decision 87/600/Euratom of 14 December 1987 on Community arrangements for the early exchange of information in the event of a radiological emergency,
- Council Directive 89/618/Euratom of 27 November 1989 on informing the general public about the health protection measures to be applied and steps to be taken in the event of a radiological emergency.

Following Council conclusions of 27 November 1989 experts from the Member States meet regularly on issues of cooperation between Member States in the event of a radiological emergency.
The Commission, with the support of the Group of Experts referred to in Article 31 of the Euratom Treaty, issued guidance on the radiological protection principles for relocation and return of people in the event of accidental releases of radioactive

material and on the radiological protection principles for emergency countermeasures to protect the public in the event of accidental releases of radioactive material.
Title IX also emphasises the importance of international cooperation to ensure protection of the population concerned in the event of radiological emergencies and sets requirements on the Member States. These measures complement the obligations stemming from two international conventions adopted in 1986 which deal respectively with the early notification of a nuclear accident and mutual assistance in the event of a nuclear accident. The two conventions have been signed by all Member States.
Article 49 deals with potential exposures. The concept is to be used essentially in the preventive phase.
Article 53 deals with lasting exposure situations resulting from the after-effects of a radiological emergency or a past practice.

(j) TITLE X
FINAL PROVISIONS

Article 54

Under Article 33(3) of the Euratom Treaty, the Member States are required to communicate to the Commission any draft legislative, regulatory and administrative provision intended to ensure compliance with the basic safety standards.
As a result of Article 54 of the Directive, in the case a Member State is to adopt stricter dose limits, it has also to inform the other Member States. The Commission would normally be notified under Article 33 of the Treaty.

ANNEXES TO THE DIRECTIVE

Annex I

The exemption levels, which apply to practices, are worked out using scenarios, pathways and formulae presented in a report published by the Commission.

Annex II

The values and relationships given in Annex II for external radiations are those required for the protection quantities defined by the International Commission on Radiological Protection in Publication No 60 and the International Commission on Radiation Units and Measurement in Report 51.
During the preparation of the Directive some small changes were introduced by the ICRP in the composition of some tissues and organs used to work out the effective dose, in particular as regards the colon and the remaining tissues and organs. Com-

petent authorities may authorise the use of the updated ICRP guidance, as an equivalent method under the terms of Article 15.
The dose limits given in the Directive are expressed in terms of effective dose and equivalent dose. The need for measurable quantities that can be related to these protection quantities has led to the development of the operational quantities. The operational quantities for area monitoring are ambient dose equivalent and directional dose equivalent. The operational quantity for use in individual monitoring is the personal dose equivalent at a specified depth.

Annex III

The requirements on doses in the Directive apply to the sum of the relevant doses from external and internal radiation exposure. In the case of internal exposure, the calculation is based on the use of dose coefficients which are the committed effective doses per unit intake of the relevant radio-nuclide. Tables in Annex III give the appropriate dose coefficients for workers and members of the public. These are based on parameters that generally apply. The Directive permits competent authorities to use other methods that are equivalent. For example, where information is available on the actual chemical, physical or biological behaviour of a particular form of radio-nuclide the competent authorities may authorise the use of specially derived dose coefficients.
Annual limits of intake (ALI) are no longer used in the Directive. If required, they can be derived from the dose coefficients and the relevant dose limits.
Dose coefficients of Annex III are taken from ICRP Publication No 68 (for workers) and ICRP Publication No 72 (for members of the public).
Inhalation dose coefficients for workers are given both for 1 micrometer activity median aerodynamic diameter (AMAD) and for 5 micrometers AMAD. The advice from ICRP is that the default value for the AMAD is 5 micrometers and this should be used in the absence of specific information. Inhalation dose coefficients for members of the public are based on 1 micrometer AMAD. For inhalation by workers, materials categorised as lung absorption classes D, W and Y (days, weeks and years respectively, indications of the residence time) in ICRP Publication No 30 were assigned to lung absorption types F, M and S (fast, moderate and slow) in the model of ICRP Publication No 66.
Three tables, relevant for the estimation of doses from intakes or from exposure to inert gases are given in Annex II to this Communication.
Table 1 indicates the relevant ICRP publications for the source of information on lung absorption types and biokinetics models for systematic activity used to calculate the coefficients in Table B of Annex III to the Directive. For a number of elements, lung absorption type G has also been retained, which refers to their occurrence in specific chemical forms as soluble or reactive gases and vapours. The corresponding dose coefficients for soluble or reactive gases and vapours for the different age classes are

given in Table 2. The values for adults are appropriate for both workers and members of the public and thus the table complements the list of chemical forms for which dose coefficients for workers are given in Table (C.2) of Annex III of the Directive.
Table 3 gives effective doses for exposure of adults to inert gases. For most nuclides, internal exposure resulting from gases absorbed in body tissues or contained in the lungs is negligible compared to external exposure of skin and other organs when a person is submerged in a radioactive gas. Hence the dose coefficients, which apply to workers and members of the public, are expressed per unit integrated air concentration. Doses from the exposure to radon (i.e. radon-222) and thoron (i.e. radon-220) arise principally from the inhalation of their short-lived progeny, the data for which is given in paragraph C of Annex III of the Directive. Data for the parent radio-nuclides (radon and thoron) has therefore not been included in Table 3.

COUNCIL DIRECTIVE (89/618/EURATOM) OF 27 NOVEMBER 1989 ON INFORMING THE GENERAL PUBLIC ABOUT HEALTH PROTECTION MEASURES TO BE APPLIED AND STEPS TO BE TAKEN IN THE EVENT OF A RADIOLOGICAL EMERGENCY

The factors leading to the adoption of this Directive are manifold. The main and more specific one lies in the obligation put by the 1980 Euratom Basic Standards on Member States to establish intervention levels and measures to be taken for the eventuality of a nuclear accident. Secondly, it had been found necessary to add further elements to the information made available to the public in areas other than those covered by the Directives on environmental impact assessment (EEC/85/337) and on major industrial hazards (EEC/82/501) and to encourage the population affected by an accident to take the actions likely to increase the effectiveness of the emergency measures. Finally, the new provisions were aimed at laying down common principles and specific measures, in an adequate and on-going manner, addressing radiological emergencies.

The Directive strengthens measures and practices already in place nationally, and contains provisions addressing information both for the eventuality of an accident and for the case of an actual one.

A Commission Communication (91/C/103/3) supplements the Directive and provides elements intended to facilitate its implementation in Member States, bearing in mind that the latter remains the only binding instrument. Both texts may be found in the following pages.

THE COUNCIL OF THE EUROPEAN COMMUNITIES,

Having regard to the Treaty establishing the European Atomic Energy Community, and in particular Article 31 thereof,
Having regard to the proposal from the Commission, submitted following consultation with a group of persons appointed by the Scientific and Technical Committee from among scientific experts in the Member States, as laid down in that Article,
Having regard to the opinion of the European Parliament (1),
Having regard to the opinion of the Economic and Social Committee (2),
Whereas Article 2 (b) of the Treaty lays down that the Community shall establish uniform safety standards to protect the health of workers and of the general public;

Whereas, on 2 February 1959, the Council adopted Directives laying down the basic standards for the protection of the health of workers and the general public against the dangers arising from ionizing radiations (1), as last amended by Directives 80/836/Euratom (2) and 84/467/Euratom (3);
Whereas, pursuant to Article 24 of Directive 80/836/Euratom, all Member States must ensure that exposed workers received adequate information on radiation protection;
Whereas, pursuant to Article 45 (4) of the said Directive, each Member State must, in the event of an accident, stipulate the intervention levels and measures to be taken by the competent authorities and the necessary resources both in personnel and equipment to enable action to be taken to safeguard and maintain the health of the general public;
Whereas, at Community level, further elements should be added to the information made available to the public over and above the areas already covered by Article 6 (2) of Council Directive 85/337/EEC of 27 June 1985 on the assessment of the effects of certain public and private projects on the environment (1) and by Article 8 (1) of Council Directive 82/501/EEC of 24 June 1982 on the major accident hazards of certain industrial activities (2), as amended by Directive 88/610/EEC (3);
Whereas all Member States have signed the International Atomic Energy Agency (IAEA) Convention on Early Notification of a Nuclear Accident;
Whereas Council Decision 87/600/Euratom of 14 December 1987 on Community arrangements for the early exchange of information in the event of a radiological emergency (4) requires all Member States which decide to take emergency measures to protect the general public, either as a result of abnormally high levels of radioactivity in the environment, or following an accident from which a significant release of radioactive material occurs or is likely to occur, to notify the Commission and the Member States which are, or are likely to be, affected, of the protective measures which they have taken or planned and also of any measures which they have taken or planned and also of any measures which they have taken or planned to inform the general public;
Whereas some Member States have already concluded bilateral agreements on information, coordination and mutual assistance in the event a nuclear accident;
Whereas, in the event of an accident in a nuclear installation in a Member State, the population affected should be encouraged to take appropriate action likely to increase the effectiveness of the emergency measures taken or planned;
Whereas the sections of the population likely to be affected by the radiological emergency should therefore be given in advance appropriate and continuing information on the planned health protection measures relating to them and the action they should take in the event of a radiological emergency; whereas certain joint principles and specific provisions for informing such sections of the population should be drawn up for this purpose at Community level;

Whereas joint principles and specific provisions for informing the population actually affected by a real radiological emergency should also be drawn up;
Whereas account must also be taken, in the information supplied, of those sections of the population living in frontier areas;
Whereas, moreover, efforts should be made to strengthen the measures and practices for informing the general public already in force at national level in the event of a radiological emergency,

HAS ADOPTED THIS DIRECTIVE:

TITLE I
OBJECTIVES AND DEFINITIONS

Article 1

This Directive is intended to define, at Community level, common objectives with regard to measures and procedures for informing the general public for the purpose of improving the operational health protection provided in the event of a radiological emergency.

Article 2

For the purposes of this Directive, 'a radiological emergency' means any situation:
1. that follows:
(a) an accident in the territory of a Member State involving facilities or activities referred to in point 2 which a significant release of radioactive material occurs or is likely to occur; or
(b) the detection, within or outside its own territory, of abnormal levels of radioactivity which are likely to be detrimental to public health in that Member State; or
(c) accidents other than those specified in (a) involving facilities or activites referred to in point 2 from which a significant of radioactive material occurs or is likely to occur; or
(d) other accidents from which a significant release of radioactive material occurs or is likely to occur;

2. that is attributable to the facilities or activities referred to in point 1 (a) and (c), viz.:
(a) any nuclear reactor, wherever located;
(b) any other nuclear-fuel-cycle facility:
(c) any radioactive-waste management facility;
(d) the transport and storage of nuclear fuels or radioactive wastes;

(e) the manufacture, use, storage, disposal and transport of radioisotopes for agricultural, industrial, medical and related scientific and research purposes; and
(f) the use of radioisotopes for power generation in space vehicles.

Article 3

For the purposes of applying this Directive, the terms 'significant release of radioactive material' and 'abnormal levels of radioactivity which are likely to be detrimental to public health' are to be understood as covering situations likely to result in members of the public being exposed to doses in excess of the dose limits prescribed under the Directives laying down basic Community safety standards for radiological protection (1).

Article 4

For the purposes of this Directive the following terms shall have the meanings hereby assigned:
(a) population likely to be affected in the event of a radiological emergency:
any population group for which Member States have drawn up intervention plans in the event of a radiological emergency;
(b) population actually affected in the event of a radiological emergency:
any population group for which specific protection measures are taken as soon as a radiological emergency occurs.

TITLE II
PRIOR INFORMATION

Article 5

1. Member States shall ensure that the population likely to be affected in the event of a radiological emergency is given information about the health-protection measures applicab le to it and about the action it should take in the event of such an emergency.

2. The information supplied shall at least include the elements set out in Annex I.

3. This information shall be communicated to the population referred to in paragraph 1 without any request being made.

4. Member States shall update the information and circulate it at regular intervals and whenever significant changes in the arrangements that it describes take place. This information shall be permanently available to the public.

TITLE III
INFORMATION IN THE EVENT OF A RADIOLOGICAL EMERGENCY

Article 6

1. Member States shall ensure that, when a radiological emergency occurs, the population actually affected is informed without delay of the facts of the emergency, of the steps to be taken and, as appropriate to the case in point, of the health-protection measures applicable to it.

2. The information provided shall cover the points contained in Annex II which are relevant to the type of radiological emergency.

TITLE IV
INFORMATION OF PERSONS WHO MIGHT BE INVOLVED IN THE ORGANIZATION OF EMERGENCY ASSISTANCE IN THE EVENT OF A RADIOLOGICAL EMERGENCY

Article 7

1. Member States shall ensure that any persons who are not on the staff of the facilities and/or not engaged in the activities defined in Article 2 (2) but who might be involved in the organization of emergency assistance in the event of a radiological emergency are given adequate and regularly updated information on the health their intervention might involve and on the precautionary measures to be taken in such an event; this information shall take into account the range of potential radiological emergencies.

2. As soon as a radiological emergency occurs, this information shall be supplemented appropriately, having regard to the specific circumstances.

TITLE V
IMPLEMENTATION PROCEDURES

Article 8

The information referred to in Articles 5, 6 and 7 shall also mantion the authorities responsible for implementing the measures referred to in those Articles.

Article 9

Procedures for circulating the information referred to in Articles 5, 6 and 7 and those to whom the information shall be addressed (natural and legal persons shall be determined in each Member State.

Article 10

1. The information referred to in Article 5 shall be notified to the Commission, if it so requests, without prejudice to the Member States' right to notify this information to other States.

2. The information circulated by a Member State, pursuant to Article 6, shall be notified to the Commission and to those Member which are, or are likely to be, affected.

3. With respect to the information referred to in Article 7, the data relevant to the radiological emergency shall be notified to the Commission, at its request, as soon as possible and in so far as this is feasible.

TITLE VI
FINAL PROVISIONS

Article 11

This Directive shall not affect the right of the Member States to apply or adopt measures to provide information additional to that required under this Directive.

Article 12

Member States shall take the measures necessary to comply with this Directive not later than 24 months after its adoption. They shall forthwith inform the Commission thereof as well as of any further amendments thereto.

Article 13

This Directive is addressed to the Member States.

Done at Brussels, 27 November 1989.

For the Council
The President
R. DUMAS

(1) OJ No C 158, 26. 6. 1989, p. 403.
(2) OJ No C 337, 31. 12. 1988, p. 67.
(3) OJ No 11, 20. 2. 1959, p. 221/59.
(4) OJ No L 246, 17. 9. 1980, p. 1.
(5) OJ No L 265, 5. 10. 1984, p. 4.
(6) OJ No L 175, 5. 7. 1985, p. 40.
(7) OJ No L 230, 5. 8. 1982, p. 1.
(8) OJ No L 336, 7. 12. 1988, p. 14.
(9) OJ No L 371, 30. 12. 1987, p. 76.
(1) See in particular Article 12 of Directive 80/836/Euratom.

ANNEX I
PRIOR INFORMATION REFERRED TO IN ARTICLE 5

1. Basic facts about radioactivity and its effects on human beings and on the environment.
2. The various types of radiological emergency covered and their consequences for the general public and the environment.
3. Emergency measures envisaged to alert, protect and assist the general public in the event of a radiological emergency.
4. Appropriate information on action to be taken by the general public in the event of a radiological emergency.

ANNEX II
INFORMATION IN THE EVENT OF A RADIOLOGICAL EMERGENCY REFERRED TO IN ARTICLE 6

1. On the basis of the intervention plans previously drawn up in the Member States, the population actually affected in the event of a radiological emergency will rapidly and regularly receive:
(a) information on the type of emergency which has occurred and, where possible, its characteristics (e.g. its origin, extent and probable development);
(b) advice on protection which, depending on the type of emergency, might:
- cover the following: restrictions on the consumption of certain foodstuffs likely to be contaminated, simple rules on hygiene and decontamination, recommendations to stay indoors, distribution and use of protective substances, evacuation arrangements,

- be accompanied, where necessary, by special warnings for certain population groups;

(c) announcements recommending cooperation with instructions or requests by the competent authorities.

2. If the emergency is preceded by a pre-alarm phase, the population likely to be affected in the event of a radiological emergency should already receive information and advice during that phase, such as:
- an invitation to the population concerned to tune in to radio or television,
- preparatory advice to establishments with particular collective responsibilities,
- recommendations to occupational groups particularly affected.

3. This information and advice will be supplemented if time permits by a reminder of the basic facts about radioactivity and its effects on human beings and on the environment.

COMMISSION COMMUNICATION ON THE IMPLEMENTATION OF COUNCIL DIRECTIVE 89/618/EURATOM OF 27 NOVEMBER 1989 ON INFORMING THE GENERAL PUBLIC ABOUT HEALTH PROTECTION MEASURES TO BE APPLIED AND STEPS TO BE TAKEN IN THE EVENT OF A RADIOLOGICAL EMERGENCY (91/C 103/03)

For the purposes of implementing Council Directive 89/618/Euratom of 27 November 1989 on informing the general public about health protection measures to be applied and steps to be taken in the event of a radiological emergency[1], the Commission, having consulted the group of scientific experts referred to in Article 31 of the Euratom Treaty, wishes to communicate the following information concerning Articles 5 and 6 of the said Directive and the Annexes thereto:

I. GENERAL REMARKS

1. The purpose of this communication is to help the Member States in transposing the Directive into national law.
It should be regarded as a reference document since Member States are bound only by the provisions of the Directive.
In order to be as helpful as possible some examples are quoted as to ways in which the objectives are achieved in some Member States.
2. The aim of the Council in adopting this Directive on 27 November 1989 was to supplement Council Directive 80/836/Euratom of 15 July 1980 amending the Directives laying down the basic safety standards for the health protection of the general public and workers against the dangers of ionising radiation[2], especially Article 45 which requires Member States to stipulate intervention levels and the necessary resources to safeguard the health of the population in the event of an accident.

3. Directive 89/618/Euratom lays down two types of action:
- prior information to be given in a normal situation to the population likely to be affected (Article 5 of the Directive),
- information to be given in the event of a radiological emergency to the population actually affected (Article 6 of the Directive).

These two types of information are complementary and should therefore both be given whenever it is possible to do so; this should always be the case for fixed plant or facilities covered by Article 2. For transport or nuclear powered satellite accidents it will often not be possible to give 'prior Information', but in many situations it may be possible to give 'early Information' during a pre-alarm phase, e.g. as when a satellite begins a descent which will last several days or even weeks, or when a ship is beached but the containers of the radioactive materials it is carrying are not breached. In such a pre-alarm phase 'early Information' could be given as preparation for any necessary further information if the event does proceed to a significant release of radioactivity.

4. The two types of information laid down by the Directive cover not only the protection measures and behaviour to be adopted in the event of an emergency but also the basic facts about radioactivity and its effects.

5. Experience in implementing Article 8 of Council Directive 82/501/EEC of 24 June 1982 on the major-accident hazards of certain industrial activities[3], which is known as the 'Seveso' Directive and concerns information to be supplied to the persons liable to be affected on the hazards of major accidents other than nuclear accidents, has shown that in order to be effective any policy for providing information to the general public on technological hazards must ensure that:

- there is a high degree of cooperation between the parties involved (national, regional and local authorities and plant operators).
  Agreements can be concluded with the parties concerned regarding the division of responsibilities, methods and timetable for communicating information and the content of the information,
- the provision of information to the general public forms an integral part of emergency planning.

6. Where similar advice is given about emergency plans for other serious industrial accidents, it may be beneficial to include all the advice in one document, to avoid confusing and annoying the general public.

II. PRIOR INFORMATION

A. Organization of the dissemination of information (Article 5)

1. A clear distinction must be made between regional or local populations, for which there are regional or local intervention plans relating to fixed installations, and the population as a whole, for which a national intervention plan may be drawn up to deal also with accidents outside national borders or resulting from activities not related to fixed installations (e.g. accidents during the transport of radioactive materials).

The prior information which must be given to these two categories of population under Article 5 is of two different types. The information given to the persons in the vicinity of fixed installations could be more detailed than that given to the population as a whole, since the latter is less likely to be affected by a radiological emergency.
One of the functions of the information provided at regional or local level should be to 'prepare the ground' by giving specific information in advance to those playing a key role in the dissemination of information, e.g. plant personnel, local politicians and journalists, as well as to those with direct responsibilities for carrying out the intervention plan.

2. The creation of local committees including, for example, representatives of local authorities, competent national authorities and relevant organizations could play a decisive role in providing adequate and detailed information to the local population concerned.

3. The basic intervention plan is, perhaps, one of the most effective information tools. It could be published in an appropriate form and made widely available for the general public.
Also the public could be allowed to consult their regional or local intervention plans under conditions determined by the competent authorities taking into account confidentiality and national security needs.

4. Information could also be provided as part of the curricula adopted in schools at all levels.

5. The Member States must provide information to the general public on their own initiative, without receiving a request to do so (Article 5 (3) of the Directive).

6. The competent authorities in the Member States should decide how individuals are to receive the information – for example by means of a letter or information leaflet addressed to them – and set out in detail how to inform the local population, as a community – for example by displaying public notices within a certain radius, placing notices in local newspapers, radio or television, organizing exhibitions providing plans, literature, illustrations and models, arranging visits to installations and holding public meetings.
In a public announcement or in the information disseminated by letter or information leaflet the authorities could specify the places and bodies where additional information may be consulted or obtained.
The Member States may also wish to consider incorporating prior information in other publications that are more likely to remain available in case of need, e.g. in telephone directories.

7. The Member States are responsible for laying down the intervals at which information is to be distributed. The intervals must be sufficiently close to ensure that up to date information is available at all times, e.g. every two or three years.

8. Whatever the normal frequency of re-issue, the information distributed should also be updated whenever major changes made to intervention plans have a practical impact on the population. For example, these would include changes affecting the system of alert, the protection measures and the area covered by the intervention plan.

B. Determining the content of the information (Annex I to the Directive)

TRANSPARENCY CREATES CONFIDENCE

1. In normal circumstances the information provided should be primarily instructive and aimed at reassuring the general public that emergency plans exist, both at national level for hazards associated also with non-fixed installations or originating outside national borders, and at regional or local level for fixed installations.
In order to ensure that the general public takes the message seriously without exaggerating the scale of the hazard, the information should be credible and allow the general public to see that the emergency plans drawn up would be implemented in the event of a real emergency.

2. The four points set out in Annex I must be covered by the prior information, even in the case of the information given to the entire population in a national information plan.
The information disseminated by the Member States may include other items not laid down in Annex I. This principle is set out in Article 11 of the Directive.
It is also important to provide information on radiation protection, not just in relation to the hazards of nuclear energy but covering all radiation sources that may give rise to a radiological emergency.

3. Basic facts about radioactivity and its effects
The following aspects could be covered in the prior information communicated:
The basic facts on radioactivity
Paying particular attention to the terminology used, scientific concepts should cover the physical and dosimetric aspects of radiation:
- explanations of 'activity' and 'dose',
- the scientific units connected with these quantities concepts (mention only Becquerels and Sieverts),
- a comparison between natural radioactivity and artificial radioactivity.

Effects on human beings and on the environment
- Explain the difference between irradiation and contamination.
- Explain the distinction between immediate effects and delayed effects.
- Pathways to man including transfer through the food chain.

It would also be advisable to include the general principles of radiation protection with this general information.

4. The various types of radiological emergency and their consequences for the population and the environment
The information for the population living near an installation should cover:
- a simple explanation of the work carried out at the installation,
- the unlikely possibility of an accident having any impact on the population,
- the types of emissions (gas, dust, liquid) which would be released from the installation in the event of an accident, and how far and how quickly they would spread. The International Nuclear Event Scale (INES) could be very useful for explaining the consequences of the various situations.

5. Emergency measures envisaged to alert, protect and assist the population in the event of a radiological emergency
- Specify the means used to give the alert (sirens, radio, television, police).
- For local intervention plans, give a general description of how they are organized and of the protection measures.

6. Appropriate information on action to be taken by the population in the event of a radiological emergency
The information on action in the short-term (from the first hours to the first days following the accident) could include listening for the alert, sheltering, listening to the radio and awaiting instructions.
The information on action in the longer term could cover self-protection measures and observance of the decontamination instructions and, for example, conditions for consumption of foodstuffs and drinking water.

III. INFORMATION IN THE EVENT OF A RADIOLOGICAL EMERGENCY

A. Organization of the dissemination of information (Article 6 of the Directive)

1. In the event of a real radiological emergency, information must be provided systematically, rapidly and openly in order to encourage the population actually affected to adopt the appropriate behaviour.
This cannot be achieved without obtaining the confidence of the population.

The credibility of the information depends very much on the time taken to provide it and how dissemination is organized.
As laid down in Article 6 (1), the information must be provided without delay, since lack of information and ignorance of the facts may produce anxiety and unforeseeable reactions on the part of the general public. The Member States can therefore, if appropriate, begin informing the population at the pre-alarm phase (see Annex II (2)).
The most direct sources of information should be used (national, regional and local press and radio, television, direct answers by telephone and, if appropriate, computerized magazines such as teletexts).
Every step should be taken to ensure that sources of information are not giving contradictory information, e.g. by creating or appointing a national information dissemination agency with a coordinating function.

2. The requirement for the Member States to provide information in a real radiological emergency applies to any situation likely to result in the general public receiving a dose during a period of one year following the accident in excess of the annual dose limit specified by the Directive laying down the Community's basic safety standards on radiation protection (see Article 12 of Directive 80/836/Euratom).

B. Determining the content of the information (Annex II to the Directive)

1. The information must be appropriate to the situation in question and need not necessarily cover all the points set out in Annex II. There are various types of situation which might arise:
- pre-alarm situations (Annex II (2)),
- situations where the type of accident is known (Annex II (1) (a)),
- situations where protective measures and action are required (Annex II (1) (b) and (c): list of options depending on the circumstances).

2. The Directive defines common objectives with regard to information aspects of the emergency plans:
- the broad outlines of intervention plans should be made known to the general public in advance,
- they should also include arrangements for providing information in an accident situation in accordance with Annex II to the Directive.

3. Depending on the type of radiological emergency, the information provided should cover the following:
Information on the radiological emergency:
- the location, date and time of the accident,
- the type of radiological emergency,

- the main characteristics of the radioactive substances released,
- the area under threat,
- the probable development of the situation and the influence of climatic and meteorological factors.

Advice on protection:

- moving around outside and staying indoors,
- conditions for consuming food and drinking water (dilution, cleaning),
- restrictions and warnings on consumption,
- if appropriate, arrangements for supplying uncontaminated food and water,
- use of clothing and footwear,
- personal hygiene,
- distribution of iodine tablets,
- evacuation arrangements:
- public transport (stops and timetable),
- routes for private vehicles and road traffic restrictions,
- shelters and their capacities,
- medical centres and arrangements for providing medical care.

4. Special instructions for certain population groups
If appropriate, additional information may be disseminated for children and pregnant women (advice on food consumption, information on exposure of the embryo and foetus) and farmers (advice on harvesting conditions and protecting livestock).
Where doctors, teachers and journalists are channels of information they should therefore receive fuller details, right from the pre-alarm phase if such a phase is announced. The heads of educational establishments, social institutions (e.g. homes for the aged), health institutions and industrial establishments should also receive information and advice at the pre-alarm phase on the action to be taken by the groups for which they are responsible.

5. Advice to the population to follow the instructions given
The population should be encouraged to follow the instructions of competent authorities in the event of a radiological emergency (e.g. staying indoors or being evacuated).

6. Basic facts about radioactivity and its effects
In practice it may prove difficult, during the first days following an accident, to distribute relevant supplementary information on radioactivity and its effects. Such information should therefore be provided subsequently.

FINAL REMARKS

1. The Commission suggests that the Member States take due account of this communication when introducing or adapting the regulations and administrative practices that are suitable for transposing the Directive into national law.

2. The Commission points out that Article 33 of the Euratom Treaty requires Member States to communicate to the Commission any draft provisions to be laid down, whether by legislation, regulation or administrative action, to ensure compliance with the basic standards so as to enable the Commission to make appropriate recommendations. The main consequence of this is that any draft regulations on the right of the population to receive information on radiation hazards or on the intervention plan must be subject to the aforementioned procedure to ensure their compliance with the Directive in question.

COUNCIL DIRECTIVE (90/641/EURATOM) OF 4 DECEMBER 1990 ON THE OPERATIONAL PROTECTION OF OUTSIDE WORKERS EXPOSED TO THE RISK OF IONISING RADIATION DURING THEIR ACTIVITIES IN CONTROLLED AREAS

Specific studies and investigations within the Community carried out until the late 1980's had shown that the radiation protection of "outside workers" (i.e. workers employed temporarily or permanently by an outside undertaking, or self employed) was not always ensured in a satisfactory way. Besides, problems relating to such workers had become more important given both their increasing employment for highly qualified operations, maintenance etc., and their performing of activities in different countries, where administration, organisation and other factors may differ from one country to another. Last but not least, the entering into force of the Single European Market, entailing also the free movement of workers within the Community, created the need for avoiding obstacles to that free movement and, at the same time, for ensuring uniform and in any case equivalent radiation protection to that afforded by exposed workers under the Euratom Basic Standards.

This Directive therefore addressed for the first time the "itinerant" and "trans-frontier" workers, by supplementing the Basic Standards and by optimising operational radiation protection at Community level for workers exposed to ionising radiation notably in the so called "controlled areas" (i.e. those entailing a higher risk). The new provisions address also the respective responsibilities of the undertaking to which normally the worker belongs and of the operator for whom the outside worker performs the activity. Finally, the Directive provides for the creation of a uniform protection computerised system at Community level, while in the meantime a centralised national network or an individual radiological monitoring document may be used. This is made compulsory immediately by the Directive as far as trans-frontier workers are concerned.

Following is the text of the Directive.

THE COUNCIL OF THE EUROPEAN COMMUNITIES,

Having regard to the Treaty establishing the European Atomic Energy Community, and in particular Articles 31 and 32 thereof,
Having regard to the proposal from the Commission, submitted following consultation with a group of persons appointed by the Scientific and Technical Committee from among scientific experts in the Member States, as laid down in Article 31 of the Treaty,

Having regard to the opinion of the European Parliament (1),
Having regard to the opinion of the Economic and Social Committee (2),
Whereas, Article 2 (b) of the Treaty provides that the Community shall establish uniform safety standards to protect the health of workers and of the general public and ensure that they are applied in accordance with the procedures laid down in Chapter III of Title II of the Treaty;
Whereas, on 2 February 1959, the Council adopted Directives laying down the basic standards for the protection of the health of workers and of the general public against the dangers arising from ionizing radiations (3), as amended by Directives 80/836/Euratom (4) and 84/467/Euratom (5);
Whereas Title VI of Directive 80/836/Euratom lays down the fundamental principles governing operational protection of exposed workers;
Whereas Article 40 (1) of that Directive provides that each Member State shall take all necessary measures to ensure the effective protection of exposed workers;
Whereas Article 20 and 23 of that Directive establish a classification of areas of work and categories of exposed workers according to the level of exposure;
Whereas the workers performing activities in a controlled area within the meaning of the said Articles 20 and 23 can belong to the personnel of the operator or be outside workers;
Whereas Article 3 of Directive 80/836/Euratom concerning the activities referred to in Article 2 of that Directive provides that they should be reported or subject to prior authorization in cases decided upon by each Member State;
Whereas outside workers are liable to be exposed to ionizing radiation in several controlled areas in succession in one and the same Member State or in different Member States; whereas these specific working conditions require an appropriate radiological monitoring system;
Whereas any radiological monitoring system for outside workers must provide protection equivalent to that offered the operator's established workers, by means of common provisions;
Whereas, pending the introduction of a uniform Community-wide system, account should also be taken of the radiological monitoring systems for outside workers which may exist in the Member States;
Whereas, to optimize the protection of outside workers, it is necessary to define clearly the obligations of outside undertakings and operators, without prejudice to the contribution that outside workers themselves have to make to their own protection;
Whereas the system for the radiological protection of outside workers also applies as far as practicable to the case of a self-employed worker with the status of outside undertaking,

HAS ADOPTED THIS DIRECTIVE:

TITLE I
PURPOSE AND DEFINITIONS

Article 1

The purpose of this Directive is to supplement Directive 80/836/Euratom thereby optimizing at Community level operational protection arrangements for outside workers performing activities in controlled areas.

Article 2

For the purposes of this Directive:
- 'controlled area' means any area subject to special rules for the purposes of protection against ionizing radiation and to which access is controlled, as specified in Article 20 of Directive 80/836/Euratom;
- 'operator' means any natural or legal person who under national law, is responsible for a controlled area in which an activity required to be reported under Article 3 of Directive 80/836/Euratom is carried on;
- 'outside undertaking' means any natural or legal person, other than the operator, including members of his staff, performing an activity of any sort in a controlled area;
- 'outside worker' means any worker of category A, as defined in Article 23 of Directive 80/836/Euratom, performing activities of any sort in a controlled area, whether employed temporarily or permanently by an outside undertaking, including trainees, apprentices and students within the meaning of Article 10 of that Directive, or whether he provides services as a self-employed worker;
- 'radiological monitoring system' means measures to apply the arrangements set out in Directive 80/836/Euratom, and in particular in Title VI thereof, during the activities of outside workers.
- 'activities carried out by a worker' means any service or services provided by an outside worker in a controlled area for which an operator is responsible.

TITLE II
OBLIGATIONS OF MEMBER STATES' COMPETENT AUTHORITIES

Article 3

Each Member State shall make the performance of the activities referred to in Article 2 of Directive 80/836/Euratom by outside undertakings subject to reporting or prior authorization as laid down in accordance with Title II of the aforementioned Directive, in particular Article 3 thereof.

Article 4

1. Each Member State shall ensure that the radiological monitoring system affords outside workers equivalent protection to that for workers employed on a permanent basis by the operator.

2. Pending the establishment, at Community level, of a uniform system for the radiological protection of outside workers, such as a computer network, recourse shall be had:
(a) on a transitional basis, in accordance with the common provisions set out in Annex I, to – a centralized national network, or – the issuing of an individual radiological monitoring document to every outside worker, in which case the common provisions of Annex II shall also apply;
(b) in the case of cross-frontier outside workers, and until the date of establishment of a system within the meaning of paragraph 2, to the individual document referred to in (a).

TITLE III
OBLIGATIONS OF OUTSIDE UNDERTAKINGS AND OPERATORS

Article 5

Outside undertakings shall, either directly or through contractual agreements with the operators, ensure the radiological protection of their workers in accordance with the relevant provisions of Titles III to VI of Directive 80/836/Euratom, and in particular:
(a) ensure compliance with the general principles and the limitation of doses referred to in Articles 6 to 11 thereof;
(b) provide the information and training in the field of radiation protection referred to in Article 24 thereof;
(c) guarantee that their workers are subject to assessment of exposure and medical surveillance under the conditions laid down in Articles 26 and 28 to 38 thereof;
(d) ensure that the radiological data of the individual exposure monitoring of each of their workers within the meaning of Annex I, part II to this Directive are kept up to date in the networks and individual documents referred to in Article 4 (2).

Article 6

1. The operator of a controlled area in which outside workers perform activities shall be responsible, either directly or through contractual agreements, for the operational aspects of their radiological protection which are directly related to the nature of the controlled area and of the activities.

2. In particular, for each outside worker performing activities in a controlled area, the operator must:
(a) check that the worker concerned has been passed as medically fit for the activities to be assigned to him;
(b) ensure that, in addition to the basic training in radiation protection referred to in Article 5 (1) (b), he has received specific training in connection with the characteristics of both the controlled area and the activities;
(c) ensure that he has been issued with the necessary personal protective equipment;
(d) also ensure that he receives individual exposure monitoring appropriate to the nature of the activities, and any operational dosimetric monitoring that may be necessary;
(e) ensure compliance with the general principles and limitation of doses referred to in Articles 6 to 11 of Directive 80/836/Euratom;
(f) ensure or take all appropriate steps to ensure that after every activity the radiological data of individual exposure monitoring of each outside worker within the meaning of Annex I, Part III, are recorded.

TITLE IV
OBLIGATIONS OF OUTSIDE WORKERS

Article 7

Every outside worker shall be obliged to make his own contribution as far as practicable towards the protection that the radiological monitoring system referred to in Article 4 is intended to afford him.

TITLE V
FINAL PROVISIONS

Article 8

1. Member States shall bring into force not later than 31 December 1993, the laws, regulations and administrative provisions necessary to comply with this Directive. They shall forthwith inform the Commission thereof.

2. When Member States adopt the measures referred to in paragraph 1, they shall contain a reference to this Directive or shall be accompanied by such reference on the occasion of their official publication. The methods of making such a reference shall be laid down by the Member States.

3. Member States shall communicate to the Commission the main provisions of domestic law which they adopt in the field governed by this Directive.

Article 9

This Directive is addressed to the Member States.

Done at Brussels, 4 December 1990.
For the Council
The President G. DE MICHELIS

ANNEX I
PROVISIONS COMMON TO THE NETWORKS AND INDIVIDUAL DOCUMENTS REFERRED TO IN ARTICLE 4 (2)

PART I
1. Any radiological monitoring system of the Member States for outside workers must comprise the following three sections:
- particulars concerning the outside workers' identity;
- particulars to be supplied before the start of any activity;
- particulars to be supplied after the end of any activity.

2. The competent authorities of the Member States shall take the measures necessary to prevent any forgery or misuse of, or illegal tampering with, the radiological monitoring system.
3. Data on the outside worker's identity must also include the worker's sex and date of birth.

PART II Before the start of any activity, the data to be supplied via the radiological monitoring system to the operator or his approved medical practitioner by the outside undertaking or an authority empowered to that end must be as follows:
- the name and address of the outside undertaking;
- the medical classification of the outside worker in accordance with Article 35 of Directive 80/836/Euratom;
- the date of the last periodic health review;
- the results of the outside worker's individual exposure monitoring.

PART III The data which the operator must record or have recorded by the authority empowered to that end in the radiological monitoring system after the end of any activity must be as follows:

- the period covered by the activity;
- an estimate of any effective dose received by the outside worker;
- in the event of non-uniform exposure, an estimate of the dose-equivalent in the different parts of the body;
- in the event of internal contamination, an estimate of the activity taken in or the committed dose.

ANNEX II
PROVISIONS ADDITIONAL TO THOSE OF ANNEX I CONCERNING THE INDIVIDUAL RADIOLOGICAL MONITORING DOCUMENT

1. The individual radiological monitoring document issued by the Member States' competent authorities for outside workers shall be a non-transferable document.

2. Pursuant to Annex I, Part I (2), individual documents shall be issued by the Member States' competent authorities, which shall give each individual document an identification number.

COUNCIL DIRECTIVE (92/3/EURATOM) OF 3 FEBRUARY 1992 ON THE SUPERVISION AND CONTROL OF SHIPMENTS OF RADIOACTIVE WASTE BETWEEN MEMBER STATES AND INTO AND OUT OF THE COMMUNITY

There are two main reasons at the root of this Directive: one is submitting the shipments of radioactive waste to a prior authorisation system, in order to protect the health of workers and of the public; the second one, ensuring a follow-up to the European Parliament Resolution of 6 July 1988, calling for Community rules on trans-frontier movements of nuclear waste, such as strict controls and authorisations from their point of origin to their point of storage.

Other existing Directives and Conventions addressed in fact hazardous waste other than radioactive. The 1992 Directive lays down a detailed authorisation and reporting procedure for waste shipments between Member States and into and out of the Community, as well as for the returning of sources containing fissile materials to the shipper (for some connections with this Directive, see under the Euratom Regulation 93/1493 illustrated in the preceding pages of this Chapter). The Directive considers also the case of waste in transit. The use of uniform documentation on the necessary operations is required. A Commission Decision (93/552/Euratom) of 1 October 1993 establishes the standard document for the supervision and control of shipments referred to by article 20 of the Directive. Both texts are published in the following pages (not including however the numerous technical annexes to the standard document). A Commission Communication (94/C224/02) set out the names and addresses of national competent authorities for rapidly communicating with such authorities and acquiring the necessary information, as required by article 17 of the Directive.

Member States must inform the Commission every two years on the state of implementation of the Directive and on the movements of waste on their respective territories.

It is noted that this Directive is going through a revision process especially on the basis of experience acquired during its application so far, and an amended text might be adopted in 2006.

THE COUNCIL OF THE EUROPEAN COMMUNITIES,

Having regard to the Treaty establishing the European Atomic Energy Community, and in particular Articles 31 and 32 thereof,
Having regard to the proposal from the Commission (1), drawn up after obtaining the opinion of a group of persons appointed by the Scientific and Technical Committee from among scientific experts in the Member States,
Having regard to the opinion of the European Parliament (2),
Having regard to the opinion of the Economic and Social Committee (3),
Whereas on 2 February 1959 the Council adopted Directives laying down the basic standards for the protection of the health of workers and the general public against the dangers arising from ionizing radiation (4), as amended by Directive 80/836/Euratom (5) and Directive 84/467/Euratom (6);
Whereas, pursuant to Article 2 of Directive 80/836/Euratom, these basic safety standards apply inter alia to the transport of natural and artificial radioactive substances;
Whereas, pursuant to Article 3 of Directive 80/836/Euratom, each Member State must make compulsory the reporting of activities which involve a hazard arising from ionizing radiation; whereas, in the light of possible dangers and other relevant considerations these activities are subject to prior authorization in cases decided upon by each Member State;
Whereas Member States have consequently set up systems within their territories in order to meet the requirements of Article 3 of Directive 80/836/Euratom laying down basic standards in accordance with Article 30 of the Euratom Treaty; whereas, therefore, by means of the internal controls that Member States apply on the basis of national rules consistent with existing Community and any relevant international requirements, Member States continue to ensure a comparable level of protection within their territories;
Whereas the protection of the health of workers and the general public requires that shipments of radioactive waste between Member States and into and out of the Community be subjet to a system of prior authorization; whereas this requirement is in line with the Community's policy of subsidiarity;
Whereas the European Parliament resolution of 6 July 1988 on the findings of the Committee of Inquiry into the Handling and Transport of Nuclear Materials (7) calls inter alia, for comprehensive Community rules to make trans-frontier movements of nuclear waste subject to a system of strict controls and authorizations from their point of origin to their point of storage;
Whereas Council Directive 84/631/EEC of 6 December 1984 on the supervision and control within the European Community of the trans-frontier shipment of hazardous waste (8) does not apply to radioactive waste;

Whereas by Decision No 90/170/EEC (9) the Council has decided that the Community should be Party to the Basel Convention on the control of trans-boundary movements of hazardous wastes and their disposal of 22 March 1989; whereas that Convention does not apply to radioactive waste;
Whereas all the Member States have subscribed to the International Atomic Energy Agency (IAEA) code of good practice on the international trans-boundary movement of radioactive waste;
Whereas the management of radioactive waste necessitates supervision and control including a compulsory and common notification procedure for shipments of such waste;
Whereas measures ensuring post-factum control of shipments are necessary;
Whereas the competent authorities of the Member States of destination of radioactive waste should be able to raise objections to shipments of radioactive waste;
Whereas it is also desirable for the competent authorities of the Member State of origin and of the Member State(s) of transit to be able, subject to certain criteria, to lay down conditions in respect of the shipment of radioactive waste on their territory;
Whereas, to protect human health and the environment against dangers arising from such waste, account must be taken of risks occurring outside the Community; whereas, therefore, in the case of radioactive waste entering and/or leaving the Community, the third country of destination or origin and any third country or countries of transit must be consulted and informed and must have given their consent;
Whereas the Fourth ACP-EEC Convention signed at Lomé on 15 December 1989 contains specific provisions governing the export of radioactive waste from the Community to non-member States party to that Convention;
Whereas radioactive waste may contain nuclear materials as defined by Commission Regulation (Euratom) No 3227/76 of 19 October 1976 concerning the application of the provisions on Euratom safeguards (10) and the transport of such substances must be subjected to the International Convention on the physical protection of nuclear materials (IAEA, 1980),

HAS ADOPTED THIS DIRECTIVE:

TITLE I
SCOPE

Article 1

1. This Directive shall apply to shipments of radioactive waste between Member States and into and out of the Community whenever the quantities and concentration exceed the levels laid down in Articles 4 (a) and (b) of Directive 80/836/Euratom.

2. Specific provisions concerning reshipment of such waste are set out in Title IV.

Article 2

For the purpose of this Directive:
- 'radioactive waste' means any material which contains or is contaminated by radionuclides and for which no use is foreseen,
- 'shipment' means transport operations from the place of origin to the place of destination, including loading and unloading, of radioactive waste,
- the 'holder' of radioactive waste means any natural or legal person who, before carrying out a shipment, has the legal responsibility for such materials and intends to carry out shipment to a consignee,
- the 'consignee' of radioactive waste means any natural or legal person to whom such material is shipped,
- 'place of origin' and 'place of destination' mean places situated in two different countries, either Member States of the Community or third countries, accordingly called 'country of origin' and 'country of destination',
- 'competent authorities' means any authority which, under the law or regulations of the countries of origin, transit or destination, are empowered to implement the system of supervision and control defined in Titles I to IV inclusive; these competent authorities shall be designated in accordance with Article 17,
- 'sealed source' has the meaning given to it in Directive 80/836/Euratom.

Article 3

The transport operations necessary for shipment shall comply with Community and national provisions and with international agreements on the transport of radioactive material.

TITLE II
SHIPMENTS BETWEEN MEMBER STATES

Article 4

A holder of radioactive waste who intends to carry out a shipment of such waste or to arrange for such a shipment to be carried out shall submit an application for authorization to the competent authorities of the country of origin. These competent authorities shall send such applications for approval to the competent authorities of the country of destination and of the country or countries of transit, if any.
For this purpose they shall use the standard document referred to in Article 20.

The sending of that document shall in no way affect the subsequent decision referred to in Article 7.

Article 5

1. Any application may be sent in respect of more than one shipment, provided that:
- the radioactive waste to which it relates essentially has the same physical, chemical and radioactive characteristics, and
- the shipments are to be made from the same holder to the same consignee and involve the same competent authorities, and
- where shipments involve third countries, such transit is via the same frontier post of entry to and/or exit from the Community and via the same frontier post of the third country or countries concerned, unless otherwise agreed between the competent authorities concerned.

2. The authorization shall be valid for a period of not more than three years.

Article 6

1. Not later than two months after receipt of the duly completed application, the competent authorities of the country of destination and of any country of transit shall notify the competent authorities of the country of origin of their acceptance or of the conditions which they consider necessary or of their refusal to grant approval.
For this purpose they shall use the standard document referred to in Article 20.

2. Any conditions required by the competent authorities of the Member States, whether they are the country of transit or of destination, may not be more stringent than those laid down for similar shipments within those States and must comply with existing international agreements.
Reasons shall be given for any refusal to grant approval, or the attaching of conditions to approval, in accordance with Article 3.

3. However, the competent authorities of the country of destination or of any country of transit may request a further period of not more than one month in addition to the period referred to in paragraph 1 to make their position known.

4. If upon expiry of the periods referred to in paragraph 1 and, if appropriate, paragraph 3, no reply has been received from the competent authorities of the country of destination and/or the intended countries of transit, those countries shall be deemed to have given their approval for the shipment requested, unless they have informed

the Commission, in accordance with Article 17, that they do not accept this automatic approval procedure in general.

Article 7

If all the approvals necessary for shipment have been granted, the competent authorities of the Member State of origin shall be entitled to authorize the holder of the radioactive waste to ship it and inform the competent authorities of the country of destination and of the country or countries of transit, if any.
For that purpose, they shall use the standard document referred to in Article 20. Any additional requirements for such shipments shall be attached to this document.
This authorization shall not in any way affect the responsibility of the holder, the transporter, the owner, the consignee or any other natural or legal person involved in the shipment.

Article 8

Without prejudice to any other accompanying documents required under other relevant legal provisions, the documents referred to in Articles 4 and 6 shall accompany each shipment falling under the scope of this Directive, including the cases of approval of more than one transfer referred to in Article 5.
Where shipments are made by rail, these documents shall be available to the competent authorities of all the countries concerned.

Article 9

1. Within 15 days of receipt, the consignee of the radioactive waste shall send the competent authorities of its Member State an acknowledgement of receipt, using the standard document referred to in Article 20.

2. The competent authorities of the country of destination shall send copies of the acknowledgment to the other countries involved in the operation. The competent authorities of the country of origin shall send a copy of the acknowledgement to the original holder.

TITLE III
IMPORTS INTO AND EXPORTS OUT OF THE COMMUNITY

Article 10

1. Where waste falling within the scope of this Directive is to enter the Community from a third country and the country of destination is a Member State, the consignee

shall submit an application for authorization to the competent authorities of that Member State using the standard document referred to in Article 20. The consignee shall act as the holder and the competent authorities of the country of destination shall act as if they were the competent authorities of the country of origin referred to in Title II in respect of the country or countries of transit.

2. Where waste falling within the scope of this Directive is to enter the Community from a third country and the country of destination is not a Member State, then the Member State in whose territory the waste is first to enter the Community shall be deemed to be the country of origin for the purposes of that shipment.

3. With regard to shipments falling within paragraph 1, the intended consignee of the shipment within the Community, and with regard to shipments falling within paragraph 2, the person within the Member State in whose territory the waste is first to enter the Community who has responsibility for managing the shipment within that Member State shall inform his competent authorities in order to initiate the appropriate procedures.

Article 11

The competent authorities of Member States shall not authorize shipments:
1. either to:
(a) a destination south of latitude 60° south;
(b) a State party to the Fourth ACP-EEC Convention which is not a member of the Community, taking account, however, of Article 14;

2. or to a third country which, in the opinion of the competent authorities of the country of origin, in accordance with the criteria referred to in Article 20, does not have the technical, legal or administrative resources to manage the radioactive waste safely.

Article 12

1. Where radioactive waste is to be exported from the Community to a third country, the competent authorities of the Member State of origin shall contact the authorities of the country of destination regarding such a shipment.

2. If all the conditions for shipment are fulfilled, the competent authorities of the Member State of origin shall authorize the holder of radioactive waste to ship it and shall inform the authorities of the country of destination about this shipment.

3. This authorization shall not in any way affect the responsibility of the holder, the transporter, the owner, the consignee or any other natural or legal person involved in the shipment.

4. For the purpose of the shipment, the standard documents referred to in Article 20 shall be used.

5. The holder of the radioactive waste shall notify the competent authorities of the country of origin that the waste has reached its destination in the third country within two weeks of the date of arrival and shall indicate the last customs post in the Community through which the shipment passed.

6. This notification shall be substantiated by a declaration or certification of the consignee of the radioactive waste stating that the waste has reached its proper destination and indicating the customs post of entry in the third country.

TITLE IV
RESHIPMENT OPERATIONS

Article 13

Where a sealed source is returned by its user to the supplier of the source in another country, its shipment shall not fall within the scope of this Directive.
However, this exemption shall not apply to sealed sources containing fissile material.

Article 14

This Directive shall not affect the right of a Member State or an undertaking in the Member State to which waste is to be exported for processing to return the waste after treatment to its country of origin. Nor shall it affect the right of a Member State or an undertaking in that Member State to which irradiated nuclear fuel is to be exported for reprocessing to return to its country of origin waste and/or other products of the reprocessing operation.

Article 15

1. Where a shipment of radioactive waste cannot be completed or if the conditions for shipment are not complied with in accordance with the provisions under Title II, the competent authorities of the Member State of dispatch shall ensure that the radioactive waste in question is taken back by the holder of that waste.

2. In case of shipments of radioactive waste from a third country to a destination within the Community, the competent authorities of the Member State of destination shall ensure that the consignee of that waste negotiates a clause with the holder of the waste established in the third country obliging that holder to take back the waste where a shipment cannot be completed.

Article 16

The Member State or States which approved transit for the initial shipment may not refuse to approve reshipment in the cases referred to:

- in Article 14, if the reshipment concerns the same material after treatment or reprocessing and if all relevant legislation is respected,
- in Article 15, if the reshipment is undertaken on the same conditions and with the same specifications.

TITLE V
PROCEDURAL PROVISIONS

Article 17

Member States shall forward to the Commission not later than 1 January 1994 the name(s) and the address(es) of the competent authorities and all necessary information for rapidly communicating with such authorities, as well as their possible non-acceptance of the automatic approval procedure referred to in Article 6 (4).
Member States shall regularly forward to the Commission any changes to such data.
The Commission shall communicate this information, and any changes thereto, to all the competent authorities in the Community.

Article 18

Every two years, and for the first time on 31 January 1994, Member States shall forward to the Commission reports on the implementation of this Directive.
They shall supplement these reports by information on the situation with regard to shipments within their respective territories.
On the basis of these reports, the Commission shall prepare a summary report for the European Parliament, the Council and the Economic and Social Committee.

Article 19

The Commission shall be assisted in performing the tasks laid down in Articles 18 and 20 by a Committee of an advisory nature composed of representatives of the Member States and chaired by the representative of the Commission.
The representative of the Commission shall submit to the Committee a draft of the measures to be taken. The Committee shall deliver its opinion on the draft within a time limit which the Chairman may lay down according to the urgency of the matter, if necessary by taking a vote.
The opinion shall be recorded in the minutes; in addition, each Member State shall have the right to ask to have its position recorded in the minutes.
The Commission shall take the utmost account of the opinion delivered by the Committee. It shall inform the Committee of the manner in which its opinion has been taken into account.

Article 20

The procedure laid down in Article 19 shall in particular apply to:
- the preparation and possible updating of the standard document for applications for authorization referred to in Article 4,
- the preparation and possible updating of the standard document for granting approval referred to in Article 6 (1),
- the preparation and possible updating of the standard document for acknowledgment of receipt referred to in Article 9 (1),
- the establishment of criteria enabling Member States, to evaluate whether requirements for exports of radioactive waste are met, as provided for in Article 11 (2),
- the preparation of the summary report referred to in Article 18.

TITLE VI
FINAL PROVISIONS

Article 21

1. Member States shall bring into force not later than 1 January 1994 the laws, regulations and administrative provisions necessary to comply with this Directive. They shall forthwith inform the Commission thereof.

2. When Member States adopt the measures referred to in paragraph 1, they shall contain a reference to this Directive or shall be accompanied by such reference on the occasion of their official publication. The methods of making such reference shall be laid down by the Member States.

3. Member States shall communicate to the Commission the main provisions of domestic law which they adopt in the field governed by this Directive.

Article 22

This Directive is addressed to the Member States.

Done at Brussels, 3 February 1992. For the Council
The President
Joao PINHEIRO
(1) OJ No C 210, 23. 8. 1990, p. 7. (2) OJ No C 267, 14. 10. 1991, p. 210. (3) OJ No C 168, 10. 7. 1990, p. 18. (4) OJ No 11, 20. 2. 1959, p. 221/59. (5) OJ No L 246, 17. 9. 1980, p. 1. (6) OJ No L 265, 5. 10. 1984, p. 4. (7) OJ No C 235, 12. 9. 1988, p. 70. (8) OJ No L 326, 13. 12. 1984, p. 31. Directive as last amended by Directive 86/279/EEC (OJ No L 181, 4. 7. 1986, p. 13). (9) OJ No L 92, 7. 4. 1990, p. 52. (10) OJ No L 363, 31. 12. 1976, p. 1. Regulation as amended by Regulation (Euratom) No 220/90 (OJ No L 22, 27. 1. 1990, p. 56).

COMMISSION DECISION OF 1 OCTOBER 1993 ESTABLISHING THE STANDARD DOCUMENT FOR THE SUPERVISION AND CONTROL OF SHIPMENTS OF RADIOACTIVE WASTE REFERRED TO IN COUNCIL DIRECTIVE 92/3/EURATOM (93/552/EURATOM)

THE COMMISSION OF THE EUROPEAN COMMUNITIES,

Having regard to the Treaty establishing the European Atomic Energy Community,
Having regard to Council Directive 92/3/Euratom of 3 February 1992 on the supervision and control of shipments of radioactive waste between Member States and into and out of the Community (1), and in particular Article 20 thereof,
Whereas by virtue of Directive 92/3/Euratom the Commission is required to establish a standard document;
Whereas that Directive applies not only to shipments of radioactive waste between Member States but also to imports into and exports out of the Community of such waste and to its transit through the Community from a third country to another third country;
Whereas under certain circumstances an application may be sent in respect of more than one shipment;
Whereas it is appropriate to include all these cases in a uniform document, with a number of sections reflecting the various cases envisaged by the Directive;
Whereas the measures provided for in this Decision are in accordance with the opinion of the Committee instituted under Article 19 of that Directive,

HAS ADOPTED THIS DECISION:

Article 1

The standard document contained in the Annex shall be used in respect of any shipments of radioactive waste between Member States or into and out of the Community within the scope of Directive 92/3/Euratom.

Article 2

The standard document must be completed in accordance with the notes contained in its different sections.

Article 3

1. The standard document shall be printed in black ink on white paper, weighing at least 40 grams per square metre, and its strength should be such that in normal use it does not easily tear or crease.
2. The standard document shall measure 210 by 297 mm (A4) with a maximum tolerance as to length of 5 mm less and 8 mm more.
3. Member States may require that the forms show the name and address of the printer or a mark enabling the printer to be identified. They may also make private printing of the forms conditional on prior approval.

Article 4

Member States shall take the measures necessary to comply with this Decision not later than 1 January 1994.

Article 5

This Decision is addressed to the Member States.

Done at Brussels, 1 October 1993.
For the Commission
Yannis PALEOKRASSAS
Member of the Commission

(1) OJ No L 35, 12. 2. 1992, p. 24.

(Date and place) Stamp
(Signature)

SECTION 3 Registration No:
(to be completed by the authorities responsible for issuing the shipment authorization)
STANDARD DOCUMENT FOR MONITORING RADIOACTIVE WASTE SHIPMENTS (DIRECTIVE 92/3/EURATOM)
SHIPMENT AUTHORIZATION NOTE
The competent authorities responsible for issuing the shipment authorization:
1. complete this section, bearing in mind, when filling in box number 22, that the maximum period of validity for the authorization is three years;

2. send it to the applicant together with the other sections necessary for the procedure (that is, sections 1, 3, 4 and 5);
3. send copies of this section to the other competent authorities consulted.
21 Competent authorities responsible for issuing the shipment authorization
Depending on the type of shipment, these authorities are:
Type A: the authorities of the country of origin;
Type B: the authorities of the country of destination;
Type C: the authorities of the country of origin;
Type D: the authorities of the Member State by way of which the waste enters the Community.
Name of the competent authorities:
Contact person: Mr/Ms
Address:
Post code: Town: Country:
Tel.: Fax: Telex:

22 Authorization
Yes Valid for a single shipment
No Valid for several shipments
Date of expiry of the authorization:

23 Sequential list of the countries involved in the shipment
(the first country is that where the waste is held and the last the country of destination)

Country Conditions Country Conditions
Yes No Yes No

1 5
2 6
3 7
4 8

24 List of conditions
(indicating the country imposing the conditions and any references to attached documents) Reason for the refusal

Section 3 page 2
25 The decision adopted and recorded in this section has been reached in accordance with the provisions of Directive 92/3/Euratom

The competent authorities consulted are informed that the authorization for radioactive waste shipment has been granted or refused.

(Date and place) Stamp
(Signature of the person responsible) N.B.
1. This authorization in no way diminishes the responsibility of the holder, carrier, owner, consignee or any other physical or legal person involved in the shipment.
2. The wastes shipped must be accompanied by sections 1, 3 and 4, duly completed.

SECTION 4 Registration No:
(to be completed by the authorities responsible for issuing the shipment authorization)
STANDARD DOCUMENT FOR MONITORING RADIOACTIVE WASTE SHIPMENTS (DIRECTIVE 92/3/EURATOM)
LIST OF PACKAGES NOTE
This list must be completed by the holder of the radioactive waste before each shipment (even if the authorization relates to several shipments). Like sections 1 and 3 of the standard document, it accompanies the waste while it is being shipped. It is then attached to the acknowledgement of receipt.

26 Holder (trade name):
Contact person: Mr/Ms
Address:
Post code: Town: Country:
Tel.: Fax: Telex:

27 The authorization covers a single shipment
several shipments Serial number of the shipment:

28 Nature of the waste:
Physico-chemical characteristics:
Main radionuclides:
Maximum alpha activity/package: (GBq)
Maximum beta/gamma activity/package: (GBq)
Model of packages containing the waste (e.g. plastic bags, metal drums of 200 litres' capacity, ISO transport containers, etc.):

29 Total alpha activity: (GBq)
Total beta/gamma activity: (GBq)
Total number of packages:
Total net weight of the waste: (Kg)
Total gross weight: (Kg)
Total volume (optional):

30 Identification of the packages containing the waste
(identification number of each package, gross weight (Kg)/package, net weight (Kg)/package, activity (GBq)/package)

See attached list (if the space provided above is inadequate), or (if preferred) the attached document containing the abovementioned data.

31 Date of dispatch:
I hereby certify that the information provided in this section (and the attached list) is correct to the best of my knowledge.

(Date and place) Stamp
(Signature of the holder)

SECTION 5 Registration No:
(to be completed by the authorities responsible for issuing the shipment authorization)
STANDARD DOCUMENT FOR MONITORING RADIOACTIVE WASTE SHIPMENTS (DIRECTIVE 92/3/EURATOM)
ACKNOWLEDGEMENT OF RECEIPT OF THE WASTE NOTE
This section must be filled in by the consignee, any necessary additions being made by the applicant. However, a consignee located outside the European Community may acknowledge receipt of the waste by means of a declaration separate from the standard document.
Depending on whether the authorization is for one or several shipments, the procedure to be adopted is as follows.
Authorization for a single shipment
1. Shipment of type A or B
Within 15 days of receiving the waste, the consignee must complete boxes 32, 33 and 35, and submit sections 4 and 5 to the competent authorities of the Member State of destination.
The competent authorities of the Member State of destination then forward copies of sections 4 and 5 to the other competent authorities consulted (and, where appropriate, the original of these two sections to the competent authorities which issued the authorization).
For shipments between Member States, the competent authorities of the Member State of origin must send a copy of the acknowledgement of receipt to the holder.
2. Shipment of type C or D
The applicant must ensure that the consignee located outside the European Community sends him section 4 and section 5 with boxes 32 to 35 duly completed immediately

on receipt of the waste. Section 5 may be replaced by a declaration on the part of the consignee providing at least the information contained in boxes 34 and 35.
Within 15 days after receipt of the waste, the applicant must forward section 4, section 5 (if the consignee did not use section 5, the applicant must complete it with the exception of box 34) and, where applicable, the consignee's declaration, to the competent authorities which issued the authorization.
These authorities must then send copies of sections 4 and 5, and, where applicable, the consignee's declaration, to the other competent authorities consulted.
Authorization for several shipments
1. Shipment of type A or B
The consignee completes boxes 32, 33 and 35 of section 5 after each shipment (having made several copies of a blank section 5 for this purpose) and submits this section direct to the competent authorities which issued the authorization. He attaches the section 4 relating to the same shipment.

Section 5 page 2
2. Shipment of type C or D
The applicant must ensure that after each shipment the consignee located outside the European Communities completes boxes 32 to 35 on a copy of a blank Section 5 and returns it to him together with the appropriate section 4.
The applicant must complete box 36 of section 5 and forward sections 4 and 5 to the authorities which issued the authorization.
3. Shipments of all types
When all the shipments covered by an authorization have been carried out, the final acknowledgement of receipt is completed and submitted as if the authorization were valid for a single shipment only (see above) except that:
- it is stated in box 33 of section 5 that the shipment in question is the last shipment covered by the authorization;
- any declaration made by a consignee located outside the European Communities must state that all the waste covered by the shipping authorization has indeed arrived;
- to provide an overview, the sections 4 for each of the shipments covered by the authorization must be attached to the final acknowledgement of receipt.

Section 5 page 3
32 Consignee (trade name):
Contact person: Mr/Ms
Address:
Post code: Town: Country:
Tel.: Fax: Telex:

Place where the waste is held:
Contact person: Mr/Ms
Address:
Post code: Town: Country:
Tel.: Fax: Telex:

33 Authorization granted for:
A single shipment
Several shipments Serial number of shipment:
Last shipment covered by the authorization: Yes No

34 To be completed for shipments of type C or D only:
(this item may be replaced by a separate declaration)
Frontier post of entry to the third country of destination:
Country:
Post:

35 Date of receipt of the waste:

Date of dispatch of the acknowledgement of receipt together with section 4:
depending on the type of shipment, the acknowledgement of receipt must be sent:
– type A or B: to the competent authorities of the Member State of destination,
– type C or D: to the applicant (type C: to the holder; type D: to the person responsible for the shipment in the Member State by way of which the waste enters the Community).

I hereby certify that the information provided above is correct to the best of my knowledge.
Stamp
(Signature of the consignee)

Section 5 page 4
36 For shipments of type C or D only:
Forwarding by the applicant of the acknowledgement of receipt and, where appropriate, the consignee's declaration (see note below) to the authority which issued the authorization:
Date of forwarding of the acknowledgement of receipt (together with section 4):
Frontier post of exit from the Community:
Country:
Post:

Stamp
(Signature of the applicant)

NB:
1. A consignee located outside the European Communities may acknowledge receipt of the waste by means of a declaration or certificate providing at least the information contained in boxes 32 to 35.
2. The competent authorities which receive the original acknowledgement of receipt must send copies of it to the other competent authorities.
3. The originals of sections 4 and 5 must be sent finally to the competent authority which issued the authorization.
4. For shipments between Member States, the competent authorities of the Member State of origin must send a copy of the acknowledgement of receipt to the holder.

COUNCIL DIRECTIVE (97/43/EURATOM) OF 30 JUNE 1997 ON HEALTH PROTECTION OF INDIVIDUALS AGAINST THE DANGERS OF IONISING RADIATION IN RELATION TO MEDICAL EXPOSURE

This Directive repeals a previous one (n.466 of 1984) which had been adopted to cover radiation protection of patients in nuclear medicine and radiology. The 1984 Directive was the first one on this matter, since the Euratom Basic Standards contained only few and very basic provisions on radiation protection in medical exposures; the 1984 Directive provided then for a "vertical" development of the Basic Standards by applying them to all the possible extent to such exposures. It was also important in that it expanded on the justification and optimisation principles, the application of which to medical exposure had been merely enunciated in the existing Basic Standards. Later on (1996 Basic Standards) it was stipulated that the specific provisions applying to patients should also apply to other categories such as persons (outside professionals) supporting and comforting them, as well as those participating voluntarily in medical and biomedical research programmes. These aspects, together with the developments in radiological protection as reflected in the 1990 ICRP Recommendations (see further on in this Chapter) are at the root of the 97/43 Directive.

The main amendments to the 1984 Directive, which is published in the following pages, are resumed hereunder.

The scope is widened to cover exposure of persons in the framework of medical-legal procedure and of insurance; the provisions relating to the application of the justification and optimisation principles are strengthened; it is stressed that ionising radiation in medical practice must be used under the responsibility of a practitioner, although certain tasks of an executive nature may be delegated to persons habilitated to this effect; quality assurance programmes for installations and relevant checks must be established; specific additional rules must be laid down for exposures of children, pregnant women and voluntaries. It is also provided for the qualification of the staff involved in medical exposures. It should be pointed out that workers exposed to ionising radiation in these practices and the members of the public do not fall within the scope of this Directive, since they are addressed by the Basic Standards; besides, it should be noted that the safety aspects in the conception, fabrication of and trade in medical equipment relevant to radiation protection are addressed by another specific Directive (of 1993, on medical equipment in general).

THE COUNCIL OF THE EUROPEAN UNION,

Having regard to the Treaty establishing the European Atomic Energy Community, and in particular Article 31 thereof,
Having regard to the proposal from the Commission, drawn up after obtaining the opinion of a group of persons appointed by the Scientific and Technical Committee,
Having regard to the opinion of the European Parliament (1),
Having regard to the opinion of the Economic and Social Committee (2),
(1) Whereas the Council has adopted Directives laying down the basic safety standards for the protection of the health of workers and the general public against the dangers arising from ionizing radiation, as last amended by Directive 96/29/Euratom (3);
(2) Whereas in accordance with Article 33 of the Treaty, each Member State is to lay down the appropriate provisions, whether by legislation, regulation or administrative action, to ensure compliance with the basic standards which have been established and take the necessary measures with regard to teaching, education and vocational training;
(3) Whereas, on 3 September 1984 the Council adopted Directive 84/466/Euratom laying down the basic measures for the radiation protection of persons undergoing medical examination or treatment (4);
(4) Whereas, as in 1984, medical exposure continues to constitute the major source of exposure to artificial sources of ionizing radiation of European Union citizens; whereas the use of ionizing radiation has enabled great progress to be made in many aspects of medicine; whereas practices causing medical exposure need to be carried out in optimized radiation protection conditions;
(5) Whereas, recognizing the development of scientific knowledge in the field of radiation protection applied to medical exposure, the International Commission on Radiological Protection reviewed the subject in its 1990 and 1996 recommendations;
(6) Whereas such developments make it necessary to repeal Directive 84/466/Euratom;
(7) Whereas Directive 96/29/Euratom lays down basic safety standards for the protection of the workers administering the medical exposure and of the members of the public; whereas the same Directive ensures that the total of contributions to the exposure of the population as a whole, is kept under review;
(8) Whereas health and safety requirements, including radiation protection aspects, regarding the design, manufacture and placing on the market of the medical devices are dealt with by Council Directive 93/42/EEC of 14 June 1993 concerning medical devices (5); whereas pursuant to Article 1 (8) of that Directive, the relevant Directives adopted under the Euratom Treaty are not to be affected by its provisions; whereas it is necessary to set out radiation protection requirements for the medical use of radiological installations from the date of the commencement of their operation;

(9) Whereas provisions need to be adapted for the protection as regards exposure incurred by volunteers and persons knowingly and willingly helping persons undergoing medical examination or treatment;
(10) Whereas the Committee of Ministers of the Council of Europe adopted on 6 February 1990 Recommendation R(90)3 on medical research on human beings, concerning inter alia the setting up of an ethics committee;
(11) Whereas detailed requirements are needed for the correct application of the justification and optimization principles in relation to exposure within the scope of this Directive;
(12) Whereas responsibilities for administering medical exposure need to be set out;
(13) Whereas appropriate training for the staff involved, the establishment of quality assurance and audit programmes, and inspections by the competent authorities are necessary to ensure that medical exposure is delivered under good radiation protection conditions;
(14) Whereas specific provisions are necessary as regards special practice, pregnant and breastfeeding females, volunteers in research and helping persons;
(15) Whereas potential exposure needs to be taken into account,

HAS ADOPTED THIS DIRECTIVE:

Article 1
Purpose and scope

1. This Directive supplements Directive 96/29/Euratom and lays down the general principles of the radiation protection of individuals in relation to the exposure referred to in paragraphs 2 and 3.
2. This Directive shall apply to the following medical exposure:
(a) the exposure of patients as part of their own medical diagnosis or treatment;
(b) the exposure of individuals as part of occupational health surveillance;
(c) the exposure of individuals as part of health screening programmes;
(d) the exposure of healthy individuals or patients voluntarily participating in medical or biomedical, diagnostic or therapeutic, research programmes;
(e) the exposure of individuals as part of medico-legal procedures.
3. This Directive shall also apply to exposure of individuals knowingly and willingly helping (other than as part of their occupation) in the support and comfort of individuals undergoing medical exposure.

Article 2
Definitions

For the purpose of this Directive, the following terms have the meaning hereby assigned them:

- Clinical audit: a systematic examination or review of medical radiological procedures which seeks to improve the quality and the outcome of patient care through structured review whereby radiological practices, procedures and results are examined against agreed standards for good medical radiological procedures, with modification of practices where indicated and the application of new standards if necessary.
- Clinical Responsibility: responsibility regarding individual medical exposures attributed to a practitioner, notably: justification; optimization; clinical evaluation of the outcome; cooperation with other specialists and the staff, as appropriate, regarding practical aspects; obtaining information, if appropriate, of previous examinations; providing existing radiological information and/or records to other practitioners and/or prescribers, as required; giving information on the risk of ionizing radiation to patients and other individuals involved, as appropriate.
- Competent Authorities: any authority designated by a Member State.
- Diagnostic Reference Levels: dose levels in medical radiodiagnostic practices or, in the case of radio-pharmaceuticals, levels of activity, for typical examinations for groups of standard-sized patients or standard phantoms for broadly defined types of equipment. These levels are expected not to be exceeded for standard procedures when good and normal practice regarding diagnostic and technical performance is applied.
- Dose Constraint: a restriction on the prospective doses to individuals which may result from a defined source, for use at the planning stage in radiation protection whenever optimization is involved.
- Exposure: the process of being exposed to ionizing radiation.
- Health screening: a procedure using radiological installations for early diagnosis in population groups at risk.
- Holder: any natural or legal person who has the legal responsibility under national law for a given radiological installation.
- Individual Detriment: clinically observable deleterious effects that are expressed in individuals or their descendants, the appearance of which is either immediate or delayed and, in the latter case, implies a probability rather than a certainty of appearance.
- Inspection: inspection is an investigation by any competent authority to verify compliance with national provisions on radiological protection for medical radiological procedures, equipment in use or radiological installations.

- Medical Physics Expert: an expert in radiation physics or radiation technology applied to exposure, within the scope of this Directive, whose training and competence to act is recognized by the competent authorities; and who, as appropriate, acts or gives advice on patient dosimetry, on the development and use of complex techniques and equipment, on optimization, on quality assurance, including quality control, and on other matters relating to radiation protection, concerning exposure within the scope of this Directive.
- Medical Radiological Procedure: any procedure concerning medical exposure.
- Medico-legal procedures: procedures performed for insurance or legal purposes without a medical indication.
- Occupational health surveillance: the medical surveillance for workers as specified by Member States or competent authorities.
- Patient dose: the dose, concerning patients or other individuals undergoing medical exposure.
- Patient dosimetry: the dosimetry concerning patients or other individuals undergoing medical exposure.
- Practical Aspects: the physical conduct of any of the exposure referred to in Article 1 (2) and any supporting aspects including handling and use of radiological equipment, and the assessment of technical and physical parameters including radiation doses, calibration and maintenance of equipment, preparation and administration of radio-pharmaceuticals and the development of films.
- Practitioner: a medical doctor, dentist or other health professional, who is entitled to take clinical responsibility for an individual medical exposure in accordance with national requirements.
- Prescriber: a medical doctor, dentist or other health professional, who is entitled to refer individuals for medical exposure to a practitioner, in accordance with national requirements.
- Quality Assurance: all those planned and systematic actions necessary to provide adequate confidence that a structure, system, component or procedure will perform satisfactorily complying with agreed standards.
- Quality control: is a part of quality assurance. The set of operations (programming, coordinating, implementing) intended to maintain or to improve quality. It covers monitoring, evaluation and maintenance at required levels of all characteristics of performance of equipment that can be defined, measured, and controlled.
- Radiological: pertaining to radiodiagnostic and radiotherapeutic procedures, and interventional radiology or other planning and guiding radiology.
- Radiological installation: a facility containing radiological equipment.
- Radiodiagnostic: pertaining to in vivo diagnostic nuclear medicine, medical diagnostic radiology, and dental radiology.
- Radiotherapeutic: pertaining to radiotherapy including nuclear medicine for therapeutic purposes.

Article 3
Justification

1. Medical exposure referred to in Article 1 (2) shall show a sufficient net benefit, weighing the total potential diagnostic or therapeutic benefits it produces, including the direct health benefits to an individual and the benefits to society, against the individual detriment that the exposure might cause, taking into account the efficacy, benefits and risks of available alternative techniques having the same objective but involving no or less exposure to ionizing radiation.
In particular:
(a) – all new types of practices involving medical exposure shall be justified in advance before being generally adopted,
– existing types of practices involving medical exposure may be reviewed whenever new, important evidence about their efficacy or consequences is acquired.
(b) all individual medical exposures shall be justified in advance taking into account the specific objectives of the exposure and the characteristics of the individual involved.
If a type of practice involving a medical exposure is not justified in general, a specific individual exposure of this type could be justified in special circumstances, to be evaluated on a case-by-case basis.
The prescriber and the practitioner as specified by Member States, shall seek, where practicable, to obtain previous diagnostic information or medical records relevant to the planned exposure and consider these data to avoid unnecessary exposure.
(c) medical exposure for biomedical and medical research shall be examined by an ethics committee, set up in accordance with national procedures and/or by the competent authorities.
(d) special attention shall be given to the justification of those medical exposures where there is no direct health benefit for the person undergoing the exposure and especially for those exposures on medico-legal grounds.

2. Exposure referred to in Article 1 (3) shall show a sufficient net benefit, taking into account also the direct health benefits to a patient, the benefits to individuals referred to in Article 1 (3) and the detriment that the exposure might cause.

3. If an exposure can not be justified, it should be prohibited.

Article 4
Optimization

1. (a) All doses due to medical exposure for radiological purposes except radiotherapeutic procedures referred to in Article 1 (2) shall be kept as low as reasonably

achievable consistent with obtaining the required diagnostic information, taking into account economic and social factors.
(b) For all medical exposure of individuals for radiotherapeutic purposes, as mentioned in Article 1 (2) (a), exposures of target volumes shall be individually planned; taking into account that doses of non-target volumes and tissues shall be as low as reasonably achievable and consistent with the intended radiotherapeutic purpose of the exposure.

2. Member States shall:
(a) promote the establishment and the use of diagnostic reference levels for radiodiagnostic examinations, as referred to in Article 1 (2) (a), (b), (c) and (e), and the availability of guidance for this purpose having regard to European diagnostic reference levels where available;
(b) ensure that for each biomedical and medical research project as mentioned in Article 1 (2) (d):
- the individuals concerned shall participate voluntarily,
- these individuals shall be informed about the risks of this exposure,
- a dose constraint is established for individuals for whom no direct medical benefit is expected from this exposure,
- in the case of patients, who voluntarily accept to undergo an experimental diagnostic or therapeutic practice and who are expected to receive a diagnostic or therapeutical benefit from this practice, the target levels of doses shall be planned on an individual basis by the practitioner and/or prescriber;

(c) ensure that special attention be given, to keep the dose arising from the medico-legal exposure referred to in Article 1 (2) (e) as low as reasonably achievable.

3. The optimization process shall include the selection of equipment, the consistent production of adequate diagnostic information or therapeutic outcome as well as the practical aspects, quality assurance including quality control and the assessment and evaluation of patient doses or administered activities, taking into account economic and social factors.

4. Member States shall ensure that:
(a) dose constraints are established for exposure, as referred to in Article 1 (3), of those individuals knowingly and willingly helping (other than as part of their occupation) in the support and comfort of patients undergoing medical diagnosis or treatment where appropriate;
(b) appropriate guidance is established for exposure as referred to in Article 1 (3);
(c) in the case of a patient undergoing a treatment or diagnosis with radionuclides, where appropriate the practitioner or the holder of the radiological installation provides the patient or legal guardian with written instructions, with a view to the

restriction of doses to persons in contact with the patient as far as reasonably achievable and to provide information on the risks of ionizing radiation.
These instructions shall be handed out before leaving the hospital or clinic or a similar institution.

Article 5
Responsibilities

1. The prescriber as well as the practitioner shall be involved as specified by Member States in the justification process at the appropriate level.

2. Member States shall ensure that any medical exposure referred to in Article 1 (2) is effected under the clinical responsibility of a practitioner.

3. The practical aspects for the procedure or part of it may be delegated by the holder of the radiological installation or the practitioner, as appropriate, to one or more individuals entitled to act in this respect in a recognized field of specialization.

4. Member States shall ensure the laying down of procedures to be observed in case of medico-legal examinations.

Article 6
Procedures

1. Written protocols for every type of standard radiological practice shall be established for each equipment.

2. Member States shall ensure that recommendations concerning referral criteria for medical exposure, including radiation doses, are available to the prescribers of medical exposure.

3. In radiotherapeutic practices, a medical physics expert shall be closely involved. In standardized therapeutical nuclear medicine practices and in diagnostic nuclear medicine practices, a medical physics expert shall be available. For other radiological practices, a medical physics expert shall be involved, as appropriate, for consultation on optimization including patient dosimetry and quality assurance including quality control, and also to give advice on matters relating to radiation protection concerning medical exposure, as required.

4. Clinical audits shall be carried out in accordance with national procedures.

5. Member States shall ensure that appropriate local reviews are undertaken whenever diagnostic reference levels are consistently exceeded and that corrective actions are taken where appropriate.

Article 7
Training

1. Member States shall ensure that practitioners and those individuals mentioned in Articles 5 (3) and 6 (3) have adequate theoretical and practical training for the purpose of radiological practices, as well as relevant competence in radiation protection. For this purpose Member States shall ensure that appropriate curricula are established and shall recognize the corresponding diplomas, certificates or formal qualifications.

2. Individuals undergoing relevant training programmes may participate in practical aspects for the procedures mentioned in Article 5 (3).

3. Member States shall ensure that continuing education and training after qualification is provided and, in the special case of the clinical use of new techniques, the organization of training related to these techniques and the relevant radiation protection requirements.

4. Member States shall encourage the introduction of a course on radiation protection in the basic curriculum of medical and dental schools.

Article 8
Equipment

1. Member States shall take such steps as they may consider necessary with a view to avoiding unnecessary proliferation of radiological equipment.

2. Member States shall ensure that:
- all radiological equipment in use is kept under strict surveillance regarding radiation protection,
- an up-to-date inventory of radiological equipment for each radiological installation is available to the competent authorities,
- appropriate quality assurance programmes including quality control measures and patient dose or administered activity assessments are implemented by the holder of the radiological installation, and
- acceptance testing is carried out before the first use of the equipment for clinical purposes, and thereafter performance testing on a regular basis, and after any major maintenance procedure.

3. Competent authorities shall take steps to ensure that necessary measures are taken by the holder of the radiological installation to improve inadequate or defective features of the equipment. They shall also adopt specific criteria of acceptability for equipment in order to indicate when appropriate remedial action is necessary, including, if appropriate, taking the equipment out of service.

4. In the case of fluoroscopy, examinations without an image intensification or equivalent techniques are not justified and shall therefore be prohibited.

5. Fluoroscopic examinations without devices to control the dose rate shall be limited to justified circumstances.

6. If new radiodiagnostical equipment is used, it shall have, where practicable, a device informing the practitioner of the quantity of radiation produced by the equipment during the radiological procedure.

Article 9
Special Practices

1. Member States shall ensure that appropriate radiological equipment, practical techniques and ancillary equipment are used for the medical exposure
- of children,
- as part of a health screening programme,
- involving high doses to the patient, such as interventional radiology, computed tomography or radiotherapy.

Special attention shall be given to the quality assurance programmes, including quality control measures and patient dose or administered activity assessment, as mentioned in Article 8, for these practices.

2. Member States shall ensure that practitioners and those individuals referred to in Article 5 (3) performing the exposure referred to in the first paragraph obtain appropriate training on these radiological practices as required by Article 7 (1) and (2).

Article 10
Special protection during pregnancy and breastfeeding

1. (a) In the case of a female of childbearing age, the prescriber and the practitioner shall inquire as specified by Member States whether she is pregnant, or breastfeeding, if relevant; and

(b) if pregnancy cannot be excluded, depending on the type of medical exposure, in particular if abdominal and pelvic regions are involved, special attention shall be given to the justification, particularly the urgency, and to the optimization of the medical exposure taking into account the exposure both of the expectant mother and the unborn child.

2. In the case of breastfeeding females, in nuclear medicine depending on the type of medical examination or treatment, special attention shall be given to the justification, particularly the urgency, and to the optimization of the medical exposure, taking into account the exposure both for the mother and the child.

3. Without prejudice to Article 10 (1) and (2), any measure contributing to increasing the awareness of women subject to this Article, such as public notices in appropriate places, could be helpful.

Article 11
Potential exposure

Member States shall ensure that all reasonable steps to reduce the probability and the magnitude of accidental or unintended doses of patients from radiological practices are taken, economic and social factors being taken into account.
The main emphasis in accident prevention should be on the equipment and procedures in radiotherapy, but some attention should be paid to accidents with diagnostic equipment.
Working instructions and written protocols as referred to in Article 6 (1) and quality assurance programmes as referred to in Article 8 (2) and the criteria referred to in Article 8 (3) are of particular relevance for this purpose.

Article 12
Estimates of population doses

Member States shall ensure that the distribution of individual dose estimates from medical exposure referred to in Article 1 (2) is determined for the population and for relevant reference groups of the population as may be deemed necessary by the Member State.

Article 13
Inspection

Member States shall ensure that a system of inspection as defined in Article 2 enforces the provisions introduced in compliance with this Directive.

Article 14
Transposition into Member State law

1. Member States shall bring into force the laws, regulations and administrative provisions necessary to comply with this Directive before 13 May 2000. They shall forthwith inform the Commission thereof.
When Member States adopt these measures, they shall contain a reference to this Directive or shall be accompanied by such reference on the occasion of their official publication. The methods of making such reference shall be adopted by Member States.

2. Member States shall communicate to the Commission the text of the main laws, regulations or administrative provisions which they adopt in the field covered by this Directive.

Article 15
Repeal

Directive 84/466/Euratom is hereby repealed with effect from 13 May 2000.

Article 16
This Directive is addressed to the Member States.

Done at Luxembourg, 30 June 1997.
For the Council
The President
A. NUIS

(1) OJ No C 167, 2. 6. 1997.
(2) OJ No C 212, 22. 7. 1996, p. 32.
(3) OJ No L 159, 29. 6. 1996, p. 1.
(4) OJ No L 265, 5. 10. 1984, p. 1.
(5) OJ No L 169, 12. 7. 1993, p. 1.
(6) OJ No C 167, 2. 6. 1997.
(7) OJ No C 212, 22. 7. 1996, p. 32.
(8) OJ No L 159, 29. 6. 1996, p. 1.
(9) OJ No L 265, 5. 10. 1984, p. 1.
(10) OJ No L 169, 12. 7. 1993, p. 1.

COUNCIL DIRECTIVE (2003/122/EURATOM) OF DECEMBER 2003 ON THE CONTROL OF HIGH-ACTIVITY SEALED RADIOACTIVE SOURCES AND ORPHAN SOURCES

Radioactive sources are used all over the world for a variety of purposes (industry, medicine, research etc.) and the risk associated with their planned use is well known. These sources are subject to legal and regulatory requirements, which ensure their keeping under control. In the European Union their use is governed by the radiation protection legislation adopted pursuant to the Euratom Treaty. In recent years, however, a number of events often resulting in accidents have drawn the European Commission's attention to the problem of sources which for various reasons had escaped control. The likelihood that these sources be recovered by persons (workers or members of the public) unaware of the possible risks, is a potential for serious radiation injuries and in some cases death. It should be added that at the root of the problems associated with the sources in point there are their often small size, their number and their mobility. However, the risk is bound to increase when the sources are no longer actively used, therefore stored or left unattended fore long periods.

A particular reason of concern is attached to the so called "orphan sources", i.e. those not under regulatory control, having been lost, abandoned, misplaced etc.

Although the Euratom Basic Standards Directives on radiation protection (see previous pages in this Chapter) have always been of general application, already in the past it was found necessary to complement them with measures addressing specific purposes. Outside legislation proper, an intensive international action (involving the European Commission, the Iaea, the Interpol, the World Custom Organization and the UN Economic Commission for Europe) was carried out since 1998 by means of symposia, reports and an IAEA Code of Conduct on the safety and security of radioactive sources.

On account of the above, the Commission felt that it would be appropriate to adopt specific EU legislation supplementing the Basic Standards, which would strengthen the control by competent national authorities on the sources entailing the major risk, and to emphasize the responsibility of holders of such sources. The strengthening and harmonizing of regulatory practices applied in Member States leads to a very important acquisition in the framework of the enlarged European Union (as of May 2004).

Following is the text of the Directive.

THE COUNCIL OF THE EUROPEAN UNION,

Having regard to the Treaty establishing the European Atomic Energy Community, and in particular Articles 31(2) and 32 thereof,
Having regard to the proposal from the Commission, drawn up after obtaining the opinion of a group of persons appointed by the Scientific and Technical Committee from among scientific experts in the Member States, in accordance with Article 31 of the Treaty,
After consulting the European Economic and Social Committee,
Having regard to the opinion of the European Parliament(1),
Whereas:
(1) Article 30 of the Treaty requires basic standards to be laid down within the Community for the protection of the health of workers and the general public against the dangers arising from ionising radiation.
(2) Council Directive 96/29/Euratom of 13 May 1996 laying down basic safety standards for the protection of the health of workers and the general public against the dangers arising from ionising radiation(2), continues the line of directives laying down basic safety standards since 1959.
(3) Article 4(1)(e) of Directive 96/29/Euratom requires prior authorisation for, amongst other practices, the use of radioactive sources for industrial radiography or processing of products or research or the exposure of persons for medical treatment. It is appropriate to extend this requirement to all practices involving high-activity radioactive sources in order further to reduce the likelihood of accidents involving such sources.
(4) Prior to authorisation, adequate arrangements and provision for the safe management of sources should exist.
(5) The International Atomic Energy Agency (IAEA) issues regulations for the safe transport of radioactive material that include activity limits for the requirements of the regulations, which should provide an appropriate basis for defining high-activity sealed radioactive sources within the scope of this Directive(3).
(6) In Directive 96/29/Euratom exemption values were laid down for the reporting of a practice to the authorities. These values were defined in that Directive on the basis of a negligible level of risk. As the requirements of this Directive should not put an administrative burden on the holders of small sources that is not commensurate with the possible health detriment, the definition of high activity radioactive sources should not be extended to the exemption levels of Directive 96/29/Euratom.
(7) Shipments of sealed sources between Member States are subject to the procedure established by Council Regulation (Euratom) No 1493/93 of 8 June 1993 on shipments of radioactive substances between Member States(4).
(8) Although the legal requirements deriving from existing legislation at Community and at national level ensure basic protection, high-activity sources still imply consi-

derable potential risks for human health and for the environment and therefore need to be subject to a strict control from the time they are manufactured to the time they are placed in a recognised installation for their long-term storage or disposal.
(9) Prevention of radiological accidents and injuries requires the location of each high-activity source to be known, recorded and verified from the time the source is manufactured or imported into the Community to the time it is placed in a recognised installation for its long-term storage or disposal or it is exported from the Community. Changes in the situation of a high-activity source, e.g. its location or use, should also be recorded and notified. Physical or financial obstacles should not hinder any appropriate reuse, recycling or disposal of such sources when disused under any reasonably foreseeable circumstances.
(10) Cases of unintentional exposure should be notified to the competent authority.
(11) Movements within the Community of high-activity sources make it necessary to harmonise the control of and information on such sources through the application of minimum criteria.
(12) Experience shows that, despite the existence of an appropriate regulatory framework, control of high-activity sources may nevertheless be lost. Furthermore, the existence of orphan sources resulting from past activities requires that specific initiatives be undertaken.
(13) Accordingly, it is necessary to provide for the identification, marking and recording of each high-activity source as well as for the specific training and informing of all those involved in activities relating to the use of sources. However, the marking of existing high-activity sources by engraving or stamping by persons other than the manufacturer could be problematic and should be avoided. It is also advisable to provide appropriate training and information for those who may deal accidentally with orphan sources.
(14) It is also necessary to provide for suitable means of dealing with orphan high-activity sources for international cooperation and exchange of information in this area, for inspection and, finally, for making financial provision for cases in which the original holder either cannot be identified or, even if identified, is found to be insolvent.
(15) The Member States should lay down rules on penalties applicable to infringements of the provisions of this Directive and ensure that they are implemented; those penalties should be effective, proportionate and dissuasive,

HAS ADOPTED THIS DIRECTIVE:

Article 1
Purpose and scope

1. The purpose of this Directive is to prevent exposure of workers and the public to ionising radiation arising from inadequate control of high-activity sealed radioactive

sources and orphan sources and to harmonise controls in place in the Member States by defining specific requirements ensuring that each such source is kept under control.

2. This Directive applies to high-activity sources as defined in Article 2. Member States may exclude sources from the scope of this Directive once their activity has fallen below the exemption levels specified in Directive 96/29/Euratom.

3. The minimum obligations resulting from this Directive supplement those set out in Directive 96/29/Euratom.

Article 2
Definitions

For the purpose of this Directive, the following definitions shall apply:
(a) "orphan source" means a sealed source, the activity level of which, at the time of its discovery, is above the exemption level referred to in Article 3(2)(a) of Directive 96/29/Euratom, and which is not under regulatory control, either because it has never been under regulatory control or because it has been abandoned, lost, misplaced, stolen or transferred, without proper notification of the competent authority, to a new holder or without informing the recipient;
(b) "high-activity source", hereinafter referred to as "source", means a sealed source containing a radio-nuclide whose activity at the time of manufacture or, if this is not known, of the first placing on the market is equal to or exceeds the relevant activity level specified in Annex I;
(c) "practice" has the meaning given to it by Directive 96/29/Euratom;
(d) "authorisation" means permission granted in a document by competent authorities, on request, to carry out a practice involving a source;
(e) "competent authority" means any authority designated by a Member State to carry out tasks in accordance with this Directive;
(f) "disused source" means a source which is no longer used or intended to be used for the practice for which authorisation was granted;
(g) "holder" means any natural or legal person who is responsible under national law for a source, including manufacturers, suppliers and users of sources but excluding "recognised installations";
(h) "manufacturer" means any natural or legal person who manufactures a source;
(i) "recognised installation" means a facility located in the territory of a Member State authorised by the competent authorities of that State in accordance with national law for the long-term storage or disposal of sources or an installation duly authorised under national law for the interim storage of sources;
(j) "exposed worker" has the meaning given to it by Directive 96/29/Euratom;

(k) "sealed source" has the meaning given to it by Directive 96/29/Euratom and includes the capsule, where applicable, enclosing the radioactive material as an integral part of the source;
(l) "supplier" means any natural or legal person who supplies or makes available a source;
(m) "transfer" of a source means a transfer of a source from one holder to another one;
(n) "source container" means the containment of a sealed source not being an integral part of the source, but meant for transport, handling, etc.

Article 3
Authorisation

1. Member States shall require the holder to obtain prior authorisation for any practice involving a source, including taking possession of a source.

2. Member States shall ensure that, before issuing authorisation:
(a) adequate arrangements, including those arising from this Directive, have been made for the safe management of sources, including when they become disused sources. These latter arrangements may provide for the transfer of these sources to the supplier or their placement in a recognised installation or an obligation for the manufacturer or the supplier to receive these sources;
(b) adequate provision, by way of a financial security or any other equivalent means appropriate to the source in question, have been made for the safe management of sources when they become disused sources, including the case where the holder becomes insolvent or goes out of business.

3. Member States shall ensure that the authorisation covers:
(a) responsibilities;
(b) minimum staff competencies, including information and training;
(c) minimum source, source container and additional equipment performance criteria;
(d) requirements for emergency procedures and communication links;
(e) work procedures to be followed;
(f) maintenance of equipment, sources and containers;
(g) adequate management of disused sources, including agreements regarding the transfer, if appropriate, of disused sources to a supplier, another authorised holder or a recognised installation.

Article 4
Transfers

Member States shall set up a system to enable them to be adequately informed of individual transfers of sources.

Article 5
Records

1. The holder shall keep records of all sources under his responsibility, their location and their transfer. The records shall include the information set out in Annex II. This information may be recorded on a standard record sheet pursuant to paragraph 5.
2. The holder shall provide the competent authority with an electronic or written copy of all or part of the records referred to in paragraph 1, as required by the Member State concerned,
- without undue delay, at the time of the establishment of such records, which should be as soon as possible after the source is acquired,
- at intervals, to be determined by Member States/competent authorities, of not more than 12 months thereafter,
- if the situation indicated on the information sheet has changed,
- without undue delay on the closure of the records for a specific source when the holder no longer holds this source; in this case the name of the holder or recognised installation to which the source is transferred shall be included,
- without undue delay on the closure of such records when the holder no longer holds any sources, and
- whenever so requested by the competent authority.

The holder's records shall be available for inspection by the competent authority.
3. The competent authorities shall keep records of authorised holders and of the sources they hold. These records shall include the radio-nuclide involved, the activity at the time of manufacture, or if this activity is not known, the activity at the time of the first placing on the market or at the time the holder acquired the source, and the type of source.
4. The competent authorities shall keep the records up to date, taking transfers into account, among other factors.
5. The Commission shall make available in electronic format the standard record sheet for the records set out in Annex II.
6. The Commission may, in accordance with the procedure referred to in Article 17, update the required information set out in Annex II and the standard record sheet for the records set out in Annex II.

Article 6
Requirements for holders

Each holder of sources shall:
(a) ensure that suitable tests, such as leak tests based on international standards, are undertaken regularly in order to check and maintain the integrity of each source;
(b) regularly verify, at specific intervals which may be determined by Member States, that each source and, where relevant, the equipment containing the source, is still present and in apparently good condition at its place of use or of storage;
(c) ensure that each fixed and mobile source is subject to adequate documented measures, such as written protocols and procedures, aimed at preventing unauthorised access to or loss or theft of the source or its damage by fire;
(d) promptly notify the competent authority of any loss, theft or unauthorised use of a source, arrange for a check on the integrity of each source after any event, including fire, that may have damaged the source and, if appropriate, inform the competent authority thereof and of the measures taken;
(e) return each disused source to the supplier or place it in a recognised installation or transfer it to another authorised holder unless otherwise agreed by the competent authority, without undue delay after termination of the use;
(f) ascertain that, before a transfer is made, the recipient holds appropriate authorisation;
(g) promptly notify the competent authority of any incident or accident resulting in unintentional exposure of a worker or a member of the public.

Article 7
Identification and marking

1. The manufacturer shall identify or, in the case of sources imported from outside the Community, the supplier shall ensure that each source is identified by a unique number. This number shall be engraved or stamped on the source, where practicable. This number shall also be engraved or stamped on the source container. If this is not feasible or in the case of reusable transport containers, the source container shall at least have information on the nature of the source.
The manufacturer or the supplier shall ensure that the source container and, where practicable, the source are marked and labelled with an appropriate sign to warn people of the radiation hazard.
The manufacturer shall provide a photograph of each manufactured source design type and of the typical source container.
2. The holder shall ensure that each source is accompanied by written information indicating that the source is identified and marked in compliance with paragraph 1 and that the markings and labels referred to in paragraph 1 remain legible. The

information shall include photographs of the source, source container, transport packaging, device and equipment as appropriate.

Article 8
Training and information

1. When arranging information and training in the field of radiation protection in compliance with Article 22 of Directive 96/29/Euratom, the holder shall ensure that such training includes specific requirements for the safe management of sources.
The information and training shall place particular emphasis on the necessary safety requirements and shall contain specific information on possible consequences of the loss of adequate control of sources.
The information and training shall be repeated at regular intervals and documented, with a view to preparing the relevant workers adequately for such events.
The relevant information and training shall be addressed to exposed workers.
2. Member States shall provide encouragement to ensure that the management and workers in installations where orphan sources are most likely to be found or processed (e.g. large metal scrap yards and major metal scrap recycling plants), and the management and workers in significant nodal transit points (e.g. customs posts), are
(a) informed of the possibility that they may be confronted with a source;
(b) advised and trained in the visual detection of sources and of their containers;
(c) informed of basic facts about ionising radiation and its effects;
(d) informed of and trained in the action to be taken on site in the event of the detection or suspected detection of a source.

Article 9
Orphan sources

1. Member States shall ensure that the competent authorities are prepared, or have made provision, including assignment of responsibilities, to recover orphan sources and to deal with radiological emergencies due to orphan sources and have drawn up appropriate response plans and measures.
2. Member States shall ensure that specialised technical advice and assistance is promptly made available to the persons, not normally involved in operations subject to radiation protection requirements, who suspect the presence of an orphan source. The primary aim of advice and assistance shall be the protection of workers and members of the public from radiation and the safety of the source.
3. Member States shall encourage the establishment of systems aimed at detecting orphan sources in places such as large metal scrap yards and major metal scrap recycling installations where orphan sources may generally be encountered, or at significant nodal transit points, wherever appropriate, such as customs posts.

4. Member States shall ensure that campaigns are organised, as appropriate, to recover orphan sources left behind from past activities.
The campaigns may include the financial participation of Member States in the costs of recovering, managing and disposing of the sources and may also include surveys of historical records of authorities, such as customs, and of holders, such as research institutes, material testing institutes or hospitals.

Article 10
Financial security for orphan sources

Member States shall ensure that, on the basis of arrangements to be decided by Member States, a system of financial security is established or any other equivalent means to cover intervention costs relating to the recovery of orphan sources and which may result from implementation of the requirements set out in Article 9.

Article 11
International cooperation and information exchange

Each Member State shall promptly exchange information and cooperate with other relevant Member States or third countries and with relevant international organisations as regards loss, removal, theft or discovery of sources and as regards related follow-up or investigations, without prejudice to relevant confidentiality requirements and relevant national regulations.

Article 12
Inspections

Member States shall establish or maintain a system of inspection to enforce the provisions introduced in compliance with this Directive.

Article 13
Competent authority

1. Member States shall designate the competent authority to carry out tasks in accordance with this Directive.
2. Member States shall forward to the Commission the name and the address of the competent authority and all necessary information for rapidly communicating with such authorities.
3. Where Member States have more than one competent authority, they shall designate one point of contact to act as an interface with correspondents in other Member States.

4. Member States shall forward to the Commission any changes to the data referred to in paragraphs 2 and 3.
5. The Commission shall communicate the information referred to in paragraphs 2, 3 and 4 to all competent authorities in the Community and shall publish it periodically in the Official Journal of the European Union, at intervals of no more than two years.

Article 14
Report on experience

By 31 December 2010, Member States shall report to the Commission on the experience gained in the implementation of this Directive, including consideration of any effect which Article 1(2) may have had.
On that basis, the Commission shall submit a report to the European Parliament, the Council and the European Economic and Social Committee.

Article 15
Penalties

Member States shall determine the penalties applicable to breaches of the national provisions adopted pursuant to this Directive. The penalties shall be effective, proportionate and dissuasive.

Article 16
Transposition

1. Member States shall bring into force the laws, regulations and administrative provisions necessary to comply with this Directive before 31 December 2005.
Member States may provide, as regards sources placed on the market before the date referred to in the first subparagraph, that:
(a) Articles 3 to 6 shall not apply until 31 December 2007;
(b) Article 7 shall not apply, with the exception of the following requirements which shall apply by 31 December 2007 at the latest:
- the holder shall ensure that, if practicable, each such source and the source container are accompanied by written information to identify the source and its nature,
- the holder shall ensure that, if practicable, each such source, if practicable, and the source container are labelled with an appropriate sign to warn people of the radiation hazard.

Where these measures are adopted by the Member States, they shall contain a reference to this Directive or shall be accompanied by such reference on the occasion of their

official publication. The methods of making such reference shall be laid down by Member States.
2. Member States shall communicate to the Commission the text of the main provisions of national law which they adopt in the field covered by this Directive, together with a table showing how the provisions of this Directive correspond to the national provisions adopted.

Article 17
Committee

The Commission shall be assisted in performing the tasks laid down in Article 5(6) by an Advisory Committee composed of the representatives of the Member States and chaired by the representative of the Commission.
The representative of the Commission shall submit to the Committee a draft of the measures to be taken. The Committee shall deliver its opinion on the draft within a time limit which the Chairman may lay down according to the urgency of the matter, if necessary by taking a vote.
The opinion of the Committee shall be recorded in the minutes; in addition, each Member State shall have the right to ask to have its position recorded in the minutes.
The Commission shall take the utmost account of the opinion delivered by the Committee. It shall inform the Committee of the manner in which its opinion has been take into account.

Article 18
Entry into force

This Directive shall enter into force on the day of its publication in the Official Journal of the European Union.

Article 19
This Directive is addressed to the Member States.

Done at Brussels, 22 December 2003.

For the Council
The President
A. Matteoli

(1) Opinion of 18 November 2003
(2) OJ L 159, 29.6.1996, p. 1.

(3) IAEA Safety Standards Series No TS-R-1 (ST, Revised), Vienna, 2000.
(4) OJ L 148, 19.6.1993, p. 1.

ANNEX I
ACTIVITY LEVELS

For radio-nuclides not listed in the table below, but referred to in Annex I, Table A, of Directive 96/29/Euratom, the relevant activity level is one hundredth of the corresponding A1 value given in the IAEA Regulations for the safe transport of radioactive materials(1).

>TABLE POSITION>

(1) No TS-R-1 (ST-1, revised) – International Atomic Energy Agency, Vienna 2000.

ANNEX II (*Records under article 5*)

COUNCIL RESOLUTION (2002/C 119/05) ON THE ESTABLISHMENT OF NATIONAL SYSTEMS FOR SURVEILLANCE AND CONTROL OF THE PRESENCE OF RADIOACTIVE MATERIALS IN THE RECYCLING OF METALLIC MATERIALS IN THE MEMBER STATES

This Resolution is important not only per se but also on account of the context in which it has been conceived, in order to meet specific needs related to the safety of the environment and the health of people, let alone certain economic implications.

The use of ionising radiation is covered by a detailed and strict regulatory system in all member States of the European Union. However, despite this, the presence of uncontrolled sources or materials contaminated with natural or artificial radioactive substances has been detected among metal scrap, i.e. metallic materials intended for recycling. This situation was enhanced, in general, by the so called "globalisation" process and, more specifically, by the geo-political changes occurred in the Central and Eastern European countries mainly in connection with the fall of the Soviet "block".

The uncontrolled circulation of the above-mentioned materials may understandably entail serious consequences for the environment and for the health of individuals, as indeed it is shown by many accidents occurred in these last years, which in some cases resulted even in the death of persons.

The Resolution aims at creating the basis for additional prevention measures in respect of the risk just referred to, as well as of the need to accommodate public concern, taking into account also the importance that the materials in point have for the metallurgical industry in many countries. The actions taken following the Resolution should therefore be carried out uniformly in the various countries and especially in the European Union where no border restrictions are applied, and in addition the related radiological protection should rely on a common basis. National initiatives (which are already in place in certain countries) should be developed "within a more global context", so as to ensure consistency among measures and decisions adopted by different countries of the Union.

The Resolution invites both member States and the Commission to study and adopt the most adequate measures, and to join their efforts in order to achieve all the possible "homogeneity" between national systems governing the area under consideration.

THE COUNCIL OF THE EUROPEAN UNION,

Considering that:

(1) The use of radiation technologies in the Member States is subject to a specific regulatory system that includes strict control measures contemplating the control of cross-border movements, and that despite these controls the presence of uncontrolled radiation sources or materials contaminated with radio-nuclides of natural or artificial origin has been detected among metallic materials destined for recycling.

(2) The presence of radioactive materials among metals may have serious consequences for the economy of companies, the safety of the environment and, in certain cases, the health of people as happened in the case of several accidents.

(3) As a complementary measure to the provisions already in place, and in order to reduce the probability of such accidents being repeated, it is appropriate to adopt additional, specific and adequate prevention measures, since there are radiation sources that were used prior to the current control systems or because there is always the possibility of a source escaping from the control systems established or even because such systems are not necessarily applicable.

(4) The prevention of radiological risk in the recycling of metallic materials cannot lose sight of the great economic and social importance of the metallurgical industry in most countries, and especially in the Member States.

(5) The presence of radioactive materials in metals originates outside of the metallurgical industry.

(6) In minimising radiological risk in the metallurgical industry consideration should be given to the safety standards applied in this field, which in general are not subject to any system regulating radiological aspects. The measures to be adopted should therefore include, among their basic requirements, the self-protection of the metallurgical industry against this type of risk, preventing, to the extent possible, the entry into the metallurgical field of quantities of radioactive material that might damage its products and its market. Therefore, they should be implemented as soon as possible within the whole commercial system in that industry with respect to raw materials needed in metal processing plants. This could be supplemented by adequate controls and surveillance of final products.

(7) The prevention of radiological risk in the recycling of metals is an activity located at the interface between two industrial fields that are traditionally weakly linked, and that it would, therefore, appear to be appropriate that implementation be accomplished taking into account the capacities, needs and interests of both fields, and considering in this respect that the design of the prevention measures should be the result of collaboration between the different agents involved in the two industrial sectors, including the authorities responsible for decision-making, the regulators and the metallurgical, recovery and radioactive waste management sectors.

(8) The market for metallic products intended for recycling is strongly international in nature, and that any action taken should take this circumstance into account, and in particular that the minimisation of radiological risk should be undertaken homogeneously in the different countries, especially in the case of the Member States, between which there are no frontier restrictions, and in which the radiological protection standards share a common basis.
(9) These measures may contribute very positively to responding to the public concerns that have arisen as a result of the accidents that have occurred in steelyards and scrap-processing centres in recent years.
(10) There is growing concern at international level regarding the illicit trafficking of radioactive material and that, although the prevention of radiological risk in the recycling of metals is not directly related to such activities, the implementation of systems of this type might make an additional contribution towards alleviating the consequences of such illegal activities.
(11) In recent years, and as a result of the radiological accidents that have occurred in the metallic materials recycling sector, various international organisations, among them the International Atomic Energy Agency (IAEA), the World Customs Organisation (WCO), the International Criminal Police Organisation (ICPO-Interpol) and the Economic Commission of the United Nations for Europe (ECE), in collaboration with the Bureau of International Recycling (BIR), have adopted initiatives aimed at minimising radiological risk in this industrial sector.
(12) The existing Community legislation includes basic standards for the protection of the health of workers and the general public against the dangers arising from ionising radiation and that the basic standards include provisions on clearance levels to be established by national competent authorities.
(13) The Commission has also taken several initiatives to minimise the risks deriving from the presence of radioactive materials among metallic materials intended for recycling, among which are the commitment to propose a Council Directive aimed at improving the control over high activity sealed radioactive sources in the Member States, the publication of guidance on the practical use of the concepts of clearance and exemption and the establishment of a group of experts from the Member States on radioactive contamination of scrap metals.
(14) The conclusions of the Council of June 1999 in relation to the monitoring of metal recycling, and the conclusions of the Meeting on Preventing Radiological Risk in Metal Recycling, held in Seville in January 2002, attended by representatives from radiological protection and metallurgical sectors.
(15) Various Member States, echoing the concerns expressed by the business associations and trade unions in the metallurgical sector, have manifested to the Commission their concern regarding this issue, with the objective of the latter's undertaking some type of measures at Community level.

(16) In certain countries additional steps have been taken, with the installation of radiation monitoring systems at steelyards and scrap storage facilities, and that other complementary measures have been adopted to prevent the occurrence of this type of incident and to manage the radioactive materials detected among the metallic products destined for recycling.
(17) In certain cases, these national actions have led to a specific integrated plan contemplating legal, administrative, financial, operational, materials management, training and information measures, the implementation of such integrated systems having proved to be efficient for the detection and control of uncontrolled radiation sources.
(18) Some of these national systems are based on various measures including voluntary action by the industrial sector and that such actions, based in turn on the responsibility of an industrial sector that has well-established practices, have proved to be simple to apply and to provide efficient results.
(19) The two fields involved, the metallurgical field and the nuclear or radiation protection regulated field, have repeatedly manifested their desire that national systems be implemented.
(20) The trans-national nature of the market for metallic materials makes it advisable to develop such national initiatives within a more global context, in order for the measures and decisions adopted by the different countries to be coherent, this being especially relevant in the case of the European Community, where there are no internal frontiers and where merchandise may freely circulate without border controls,

1. INVITES Member States to examine the measures required to minimise the radiological risks deriving from the presence of radioactive materials among metallic materials destined for recycling with a view to supplementing, if appropriate, their regulations implementing Euratom legislation, notably the basic safety standards directive(1).
2. To that effect, INVITES the Commission, in collaboration with Member States, to compile the existing measures in this field.
3. UNDERSTANDS that the operability and efficiency of these radiological risk prevention measures are based on a series of elements, among which are the adoption of voluntary measures, such as voluntary agreements, the implementation of technical or legal measures or a combination of both, the assignment of resources, the training of the agents involved, the development of appropriate procedures and information paths, including public information, preparedness for action against situations of imminent risk and the analysis of the experience acquired in order to improve the measures adopted.
4. ENCOURAGES Member States to adopt the measures required to establish systems minimising radiological risk in the recycling of metal at national level and preventing, to the extent possible, the presence of radioactive materials.

5. INVITES the Commission to promote and facilitate homogeneity between the different national systems, to facilitate the exchange of information between the agents of the national systems, systematically to compile, in collaboration with Member States, the information submitted by the different national plans such that it may be used as a reference for updating and improvement, and to identify possible improvements in order to bring cross-border control aspects into harmony.
6. ENCOURAGES each Member State to adopt measures to reduce to a minimum and to the extent possible the existence of radioactive materials significant from a radiation protection point of view in imports of metallic materials, to place whatever radioactive materials might be detected in imported shipments under proper control and to facilitate the safe return of whatever radioactive materials might be detected in another country in shipments originating in their territories, especially in the case of intra-Community movements of merchandise.
7. INVITES the Commission to continue its studies on how to reduce the presence of radioactive materials in imports of metallic materials and to facilitate their safe return after the appropriate detection.
8. NOTES that the technical, legal and administrative resources of the country of origin to manage the radioactive materials safely should be evaluated before returning radioactive materials to the country of origin.
9. ENCOURAGES Member States to ensure the establishment and the implementation of arrangements to facilitate the management of contaminated materials constituting radioactive sources, discovered in the recycling loop, with clear assignment of responsibilities, in order to encourage the detection and the proper treatment of such radioactive materials.
10. STRESSES the importance of taking the appropriate steps to ensure that orphan radiation sources are placed under proper supervision.
11. ENCOURAGES Member States to collaborate, with the assistance of the Commission, in the exchange of experiences, information and technology for the development of the national systems for the prevention of radiological risk in the recycling of metallic products, in particular the risk of having radioactive materials being mixed with scrap metals intended for recycling and SUGGESTS in this respect that each Member State and the Commission appoint an organisation for each party that will be responsible for coordinating the prevention system.
12. ADVISES Member States and the Commission to use the information arising from the implementation of these prevention systems to collaborate with the systems established internationally to prevent the illicit trafficking of radioactive materials.

(1) *Council Directive 96/29/Euratom of 13 May 1996 laying down basic safety standards for the protection of the health of workers and the general public against the danger arising from ionising radiation (OJ L 159, 29.6.1996, p. 1).*

COUNCIL DIRECTIVE (85/337/EC) ON THE ASSESSMENT OF THE EFFECTS OF CERTAIN PUBLIC AND PRIVATE PROJECTS ON THE ENVIRONMENT, AND RELATED AMENDMENTS

In 1985 the first EC Directive on the environmental impact assessment (EIA) was adopted, putting a number of obligations on Member States as to the procedure to be applied nationally addressing the potential impact on the environment of certain public and private projects. These included also various categories of nuclear installations such as power stations, research reactors etc. The relevance of this Directive hardly needs to be stressed, especially as far as its main objective to prevent pollution "at source" from the activities involved is concerned.

On the basis of practical application as well as developments in environmental impact issues, the 1985 Directive was amended importantly twelve years later, also taking into account the commitments taken by the European Community when signing to the 1991 (25 February) Convention on the environmental impact in a trans-boundary context (see Part Two, Section Three of the volume). Similarly to the previous one, the 1997 Directive ((97/11/EC of March 3) basically addresses in annexes I and II the projects for which an EIA is compulsory and optional respectively. As regards the nuclear sphere, a significant innovation is the introduction in annex I of installations in the course of decommissioning; in second place, installations for the treatment of irradiated fuel, formerly belonging to Annex II, under the 1997 Directive are subject to compulsory EIA, together with installations for the production or enrichment of nuclear fuel, for final disposal of irradiated nuclear fuel and waste, and for the long-term storage of these when originating from a site other than the production site. Annex II allows for less flexibility than under the 1985 Directive, in that it makes the projects susceptible to undergo an EIA dependent on certain criteria (their nature, siting, potential impact) determined in an Annex III, while such criteria were previously left to Member States. The latest amendments are included in the EC Directive 2003/35, in order to take into account certain provisions of the 1998 Aarhus Convention (which addresses access to information and involvement of the public in decision-making pertaining to the environment sector). The 2003 Directive is also aimed at making the provisions of EC Directive 96/61 (concerning integrated pollution prevention and control) compatible with the Aarhus Convention.

As part of the EIA procedure, it is worth mentioning the obligation on the builder(s) to submit to the competent authorities the main possible solutions examined and to explain the reason for the solution opted for; in addition, information of the public about a project submitted for authorisation must be ensured before this is granted. These two sets of provisions go further than the previous ones and are geared to a better prevention of any undue impact on the environment.

Given the size of the texts and the information provided above, none of these Directives are published here.

COMMISSION RECOMMENDATION (90/143/EURATOM) OF 21 FEBRUARY 1990 ON THE PROTECTION OF THE PUBLIC AGAINST INDOOR EXPOSURE TO RADON

In previous times the Commission had carried out investigations on radon gas, the presence of which in buildings and premises is the object of attention, both in Community and other countries, given its implications for human health. On the basis of a series of technical checks carried out within the Community, the Commission decided to adopt this Recommendation addressing protection of the public from indoor exposure to radon gas. This decision was made also taking into account that ICRP (the International Commission on Radiological Protection, see further on in this Chapter) had already adopted (1987) some specific recommendations in order to limit that exposure.

It is pointed out that the Recommendation does not consider radon present at workplaces, which was to be taken up later on by the 1996 Euratom Basic Standards. The Recommendation covers both existing buildings and future constructions. It indicates the reference levels above which measures are needed to reduce the emissions of radon, that the degree of urgency of the constructions to be realised should be established in connection with the radioactivity levels involved, and that the public ought to be adequately informed where certain measures are necessary to protect it.

Building and premises should be constructed in such a way as to ensure that the recommended levels are not exceeded. Finally, national authorities are invited to lay down building criteria to be observed where the risk of exposure could be higher.

THE COMMISSION OF THE EUROPEAN COMMUNITIES,

Having regard to the Treaty establishing the European Atomic Energy Community, and in particular Article 33, second paragraph, thereof,
Having consulted the group of experts appointed by the Scientific and Technical Committee pursuant to Article 31 of the Treaty,
Whereas:

I. In many Member States there is increasing awareness of the significance of indoor exposure of the population to radon. Several countries already have or are drawing up dose-control policies;

It is the task of the Commission to harmonize Member States' provisions for the application of the basic safety standard for the health protection of the general public against the dangers arising from ionizing radiation;
The Commission, therefore, asked the group of experts, set up under the terms of Article 31 of the Treaty, to examine the problem and to draw up proposals for any appropriate action;
The group has now reported to the Commission and the present recommendation is based on its report;
This is without prejudice to the Commission's ongoing work of developing a global approach to the problems of indoor pollution;

II. Radon is a naturally occurring radioactive gas, the most significant isotope of which is radon-222 with a half life of 3,82 days. This is a member of the uranium-238 decay series and its presence in the environment is associated mainly with the trace amounts of its immediate parent, radium-226, in rocks and soils. The major contributor to radon concentration in dwellings is soil gas which may enter indoor air spaces through floors by pressure-driven or concentration-driven flow; in most countries, the contribution from building materials, except in special cases, is usually minor by comparison;
Recent surveys in Member States have shown average concentrations indoors of some 20 to 50 Bq/m3, with typical outdoor values an order of magnitude lower. Compared to other forms of natural radiation the chief characteristic of indoor radon levels is their variability; in many countries some dwellings exhibit radon levels more than an order of magnitude above the average;
The dose from inhaled radon gas is low in comparison to that from its short-lived radioactive daughters, which are isotopes of polonium, lead and bismuth. When inhaled, these deposit on surfaces of the human respiratory tract and the most significant doses arise from alpha irradiation of the bronchial epithelium. A task group of the International Commission on Radiological Protection (ICRP), set up to study the lung cancer risk from indoor exposure to radon daughters, reported on these doses in 1987 (1). On the basis of current exposure models it implied a conversion coefficient around 20 Bq/m3 per mSv/year between the time-averaged activity concentration of radon gas and the annual effective dose equivalent for indoor exposure of members of the public. Consequently, typical annual doses in dwellings in the Community lie in the range 1 to 2,5 mSv with a small percentage of the population in some countries receiving more than 20 mSv per year. For comparison, the current annual dose limit for exposure of members of the public to man-made radiation, as laid down in the Community basic safety standards (2), is 5 mSv;
Exposure to radon is not a new phenomenon and epidemiological studies of various groups of minors exposed to elevated concentrations at work have revealed an excess of lung cancer deaths. While at present there is no firm evidence of the effect of indoor

radon exposure on the general public, on the available evidence it appears prudent for the Commission to make recommendations for limiting such exposure, as indeed the ICRP has already done (3);
It must be noted that indoor radon is controllable in the physical or engineering sense. Therefore, criteria of radiological safety would allow the development of practical guidelines for remedial action in existing buildings. For future buildings preventive measures are required based upon appropriate design and construction specifications. Such a preventive approach justifies the adoption of a design level which is lower than the reference level for remedial action in existing buildings;
Simple metrological procedures should be established to ensure that measurements of indoor radon yield data of the appropriate quality and reliability;
To promote the control of exposure to indoor radon in the Community, the Article 31 group of experts drew up detailed guidance which as been incorporated in the present recommendation and is consistent with the guidance provided by ICRP. It is achievable in a practical sense;
Finally, it must also be mentioned that due to the special characteristics of the problem adequate public information is an important element both in improving the controllability of exposure and on assuring a positive public response,

HEREBY RECOMMENDS:

1. An appropriate system be established for reducing any exposure to indoor radon concentrations. Within this system adequate public information and response to public concern deserve particular attention.
2. For existing buildings:
(a) a reference level for consideration of remedial action be used: where exceeded, it should be cause for consideration of simple but effective measures aimed at reducing the radon level;
(b) the reference level be an effective dose equivalent of 20 mSv per annum, which for practical purposes, may be taken as equivalent to an annual average radon gas concentration of 400 Bq/m3;
(c) the urgency of the remedial action take account of the extent to which this reference level is exceeded;
(d) where remedial actions are considered necessary, the public concerned be informed on the radon levels it is exposed to and on the remedies available to reduce such levels.
3. For future constructions:
(a) a design level be used to aid the relevant authorities in establishing regulations, standards, or codes of construction practices for circumstances under which the design level might otherwise be exceeded;

(b) the design level be an effective dose equivalent of 10 mSv per annum, which for practical purposes, may be taken as equivalent to an annual average radon gas concentration of 200 Bq/m3;
(c) information be provided to those involved in the construction of new buildings, as relevant, on possible radon exposure levels, and on preventive measures which could be taken.
4. When remedial or preventative measures are being determined, the principles of optimization be applied in accordance with the Community basic safety standards (4).
5. Because of diurnal and seasonal variations of indoor radon levels, radiation protection decisions should in general be based on the annually-averaged measurements of radon gas or daughters in affected buildings using integrating techniques. The competent authorities should ensure that the quality and reliability of measurements are adequate.
6. Criteria be developed for identifying regions, sites and building characteristics likely to be associated with high indoor radon levels. Investigation levels for the underlying parameters (i.e. activity in soil and building materials, permeability of ground, etc.) could be used to identify such exposure circumstances.

This recommendation is addressed to the Member States.

Done at Brussels, 21 February 1990.
For the Commission
Carlo RIPA DI MEANA
Member of the Commission
(1) Lung cancer risks from indoor exposures to radon daughters. Annals of the ICRP, Vol. 17, No 1, 1987, Publication 50, Pergamon Press.
(2) Council Directive 80/836/Euratom of 15 July 1980 amending the Directive laying down the basic safety standards for the health protection of the general public and workers against the dangers of ionizing radiation, OJ No L 246, 17. 9. 1980, p. 1.
(3) Principles for limiting exposure of the public to natural sources of radiation. Annals of the ICRP, Vol. 14, No 1, 1984, Publication 39, Pergamon Press.
(4) Commission communication concerning the implementation of Council Directives 80/836/Euratom of 15 July 1980 amending the Directives laying down the basic safety standards for the health protection of the general public and workers against the dangers of ionizing radiation and 84/467/Euratom of 3 September 1984 amending Directive 80/836/Euratom, OJ No C 347, 31. 12. 1985, p. 9.

COMMISSION RECOMMENDATION (91/444/EURATOM) OF 26 JULY 1991 ON THE APPLICATION OF THE THIRD AND FOURTH PARAGRAPH OF ARTICLE 33 OF THE EURATOM TREATY

Article 33 of the Euratom Treaty stipulates that, in order to make it possible for the Commission to carry out its checks on compliance of national legislation with the Euratom Basic Standards, as well as to ensure all the possible harmonisation of the corresponding national legislation, Member States must notify the Commission of any national provision (legal, regulatory, administrative) implementing the Basic Standards. This implies that such provisions must be submitted when they are still in a draft form, thus giving the Commission the possibility to express its opinion as required by Article 33, which is to be done within ninety days.

Experience after many years had shown that Member States do not always comply with Article 33, both as to a timely submission and to the nature of the draft provisions notified. The Recommendation is therefore intended to invite States to take into account these basic principles of Article 33 more strictly, together with the need to notify also the provisions once finally adopted and any future amendment thereto.

In order to facilitate the States' task, in an annex to the Recommendation the provisions are indicated which should be considered in relation to Article 33. They include especially provisions concerning intervention plans to cope with radiological emergencies, training programmes for workers as well as for the specialists in charge of physical control and medical surveillance, the inventory of medical radiological equipment as under the Euratom Directive on radiation protection of patients (see previous pages), and the programmes for informing the public and other persons involved in emergencies as under the relevant Euratom Directive (see again previous pages).

THE COMMISSION OF THE EUROPEAN COMMUNITIES,

Having regard to the Treaty establishing the European Atomic Energy Community, and in particular Articles 33, second paragraph, and 124, second indent, thereof,
Whereas Article 2 (b) of the Treaty provides for the establishment of uniform safety standards to protect the health of the general public and workers against the dangers arising from ionizing radiation;
Whereas, in order to achieve this objective, Article 31 of the Treaty entrusts to the Council the task of establishing the basic standards in the area of radiation protection;

Whereas the Council and the Commission have adopted a number of legal acts pursuant to this Article relating to the health protection of the general public and workers (1);

Whereas the basic standards are intended to evolve and may be supplemented on the basis of Article 32;

Whereas, pursuant to the first paragraph of Article 33 of the Treaty, each Member State is required to lay down the appropriate provisions, by legislation, regulation or administrative action, to ensure compliance with the basic standards which have been established, and to take the necessary measures with regard to teaching, education and vocational training;

Whereas, on the basis of the second paragraph of Article 33, the Commission makes appropriate recommendations for harmonizing the provisions applicable in this field in the Member States;

Whereas, pursuant to the third paragraph of Article 33 of the Treaty, each Member State is required to communicate to the Commission the draft laws, regulations and administrative provisions mentioned above; whereas, pursuant to the fourth paragraph of

Article 33, the Commission may issue recommendations within three months of the date on which such provisions are communicated;

Whereas this procedure is designed to ensure that the uniform nature of the basic standards is reflected in the national provisions of the Member States and to bring about the harmonization of their legislation for the protection of the health of the general public and workers against ionizing radiation;

Whereas the Commission's recommendations are designed to ensure that the draft laws, regulations and administrative provisions are adapted to take account of the basic standards;

Whereas the Commission's recommendations can be fully effective only if they are addressed to the Member States before the latter adopt their draft provisions;

Whereas the Member States should therefore not finally adopt any draft provisions until the period of three months granted to the Commission under Article 33, fourth paragraph, of the Treaty has elapsed;

Whereas it is essential that the Member States, in accordance with the spirit of Article 192 of the Treaty and with a view to facilitating the work of the Commission, communicate to the Commission the provisions as finally adopted in order to make it possible for the Commission to ensure, pursuant to Article 124 of the Treaty, that the provisions of Community law are applied;

Whereas, in order to ensure correct application of the procedure provided for in Article 33, it is useful to define the draft provisions which must be communicated to the Commission for this purpose;

Whereas experience has been gained in the application of the third and fourth paragraphs of Article 33 of the Treaty,

HEREBY RECOMMENDS:

1. The Member States, after completion of the consultation procedure provided for in the national decision-making process and, in any event, at the last three months before their adoption, communicate to the Commission, in accordance with the third paragraph of Article 33 of the Treaty establishing the European Atomic Energy Community, the draft laws, regulations and administrative provisions, defined in the Annex, which are designed to ensure compliance with the basic standards.
2. The Member States refrain from finally adopting any draft provisions before the Commission has communicated its recommendations to them or, in any event, before the period of three months mentioned in the fourth paragraph of Article 33 of the Treaty, starting from the date on which the Commission receives the draft provisions, has elapsed.
3. Any major amendment to draft provisions which have already been presented to the Commission for recommendations be communicated to the Commission.
4. The Member States communicate to the Commission the text adopted and the date on which it enters into force.

This recommendation is addressed to the Member States. Done at Brussels, 26 July 1991.

For the Commission
Carlo RIPA DI MEANA
Member of the Commission

Directive 80/836/Euratom (OJ No L 246, 17. 9. 1980, p. 1). Directive 84/466/Euratom (OJ No L 265, 5. 10. 1984, p. 1). Directive 84/467/Euratom (OJ No L 265, 5. 10. 1984, p. 4). Directive 89/618/Euratom (OJ No L 357, 7. 12. 1989, p. 31). Directive 90/641/Euratom (OJ No L 349, 13. 12. 1990, p. 21). Decision 87/600/Euratom (OJ No L 371, 30. 12. 1987, p. 76). Regulation (Euratom) No 3954/87 (OJ No L 371, 30. 12. 1987, p. 11). Regulation (Euratom) No 2218/89 (OJ No L 211, 22. 7. 1989, p. 1). Regulation (Euratom) No 944/89 (OJ No L 101, 13. 4. 1989, p. 17). Regulation (Euratom) No 770/90 (OJ No L 83, 30. 3. 1990, p. 78).

ANNEX

'Provisions, whether by legislation, regulation or administrative action', as referred to in the first paragraph of Article 33 of the Treaty establishing the European Atomic Energy Community, are taken to mean:

- all laws and all other acts which are legally binding,
- circulars, directives and codes of practice of a general nature which are not legally binding but are binding on the administrative body concerned,
- national, regional or local emergency plans, depending on the organization adopted in the Member States, for dealing with a radiological emergency within the meaning of Council Directives 80/836/Euratom and 89/618/Euratom,
- in so far as the contents of the following have not been laid down in the above-mentioned acts:
- the training programmes for workers, approved medical practitioners and qualified experts within the meaning of Articles 24 and 40 (3) of Directive 80/836/Euratom and for doctors, dental practitioners and other practitioners and assistants within the meaning of Article 2 of Directive 84/466/Euratom,
- the programmes for informing the general public and the persons likely to be involved in organizing assistance in the event of a radiological emergency within the meaning of Directive 89/618/Euratom,
- the inventory of medical radiological equipment within the meaning of Article 3 of Directive 84/466/Euratom,

  which are appropriate to ensure compliance with the standards laid down in the Directives adopted pursuant to Article 31 of the Treaty.

COMMISSION RECOMMENDATION (99/669/EC/EURATOM) OF 15 SEPTEMBER 1999 ON A CLASSIFICATION SYSTEM FOR SOLID RADIOACTIVE WASTE

This Recommendation was adopted having regard to articles 155 of the EC Treaty and 124 of the Euratom Treaty (addressing the Commission's powers to ensure the proper functioning and development of the Common Market, as well as the development of nuclear energy). Besides, article 174 of the EC Treaty calls for international measures to preserve, protect and improve the quality of the environment, and a Council Resolution (92/C 158/02 of 15 June 1992) requires that the Commission will provide the Council with periodical analyses of the situation in the field of radioactive waste management, with special reference to safety and environmental protection.

The main aim of the Recommendation is to ease up an approximation of national practices and regulations in the field of safe disposal of the various categories of waste in point, bearing in mind that the relevant Community Action Plan (addressed by the 1992 Council Resolution referred to above) calls for "concerted action on the safe management of radioactive waste". Since the classification system varies from one country to another (in terms of approach and of application modalities, on account of national nuclear programmes and of the difficulties in assessing amounts of "bordering" categories etc.), the Recommendation encourages Member States and their industries to adopt a common classification system: this concerns the purpose (and management) of information, both nationally and internationally, intended for the public and institutions. The proposed classification (to be adopted as of 2002, but in the meantime usable in parallel with existing national systems) includes "transition", low-intermediate and high level waste. The system is not meant to replace technical criteria which might be required for specific safety needs.

The text of the Recommendation is published here without paragraph 4 of its annex, containing a description of classification systems in many countries which might change in the course of time.

THE COMMISSION OF THE EUROPEAN COMMUNITIES,

Having regard to the Treaty establishing the European Community, and in particular Article 155 thereof, having regard to the Treaty establishing the European Atomic Energy Community, and in particular Article 124 thereof,

(1) Whereas under Article 174 of the Treaty establishing the European Community calls for promoting measures at international level to preserve, protect and improve the quality of the environment;
(2) Whereas Council Directive 90/313/EEC of 7 June 1990 on the freedom of access to information on the environment(1) requires under Article 7 that "Member States shall take the necessary steps to provide general information to the public on the state of the environment by such means as the periodic publication of descriptive reports";
(3) Whereas Council Resolution 92/C 158/02 of 15 June 1992 on the renewal of the Community plan of action in the field of radioactive waste(2) under point 1 "Continuous analysis of the situation" of the Annex, requires that the Commission will periodically provide the Council with an analysis of the situation and prospects in the field of radioactive waste management in the Member States, with special reference to safety and environmental protection requirements and the requirements of nuclear programmes and activities involving radioisotopes. The Commission will also keep the European Parliament informed of this analysis;
(4) Whereas the Community action plan in the field of radioactive waste(3) calls for, "Concerted action on the safe management of radioactive waste" which should make it possible to "approximate national practices and regulations in the field of safety of disposal, with particular reference to the different waste categories";
(5) Whereas the Committee of the Regions under Article 11 of Resolution 98/C 251/06 on nuclear safety and local/regional democracy(4) "considers that many of the issues relating to the consideration of proposals for disposal of radioactive waste are complex and not subject to widespread public understanding and for this reason believes that it is crucial to ensure access to all relevant information to the public, to involve local and regional authorities, and the public in decision-making and to seek public confidence in the principles that govern the safety of repositories and in waste management programmes",

HEREBY RECOMMENDS:

on the base of the explanatory statements provided in the Annex;
that the Member States and their nuclear industry adopt a common classification system of radioactive waste for national and international communication purposes as well as to facilitate information management in this field;
that this classification system should be used for providing information concerning solid radioactive waste to the public, the national and international institutions and the non-governmental organisations. It would not replace technical criteria where required for specific safety considerations such as licensing of facilities or other operations;

that this classification system could be used by Member States. During the period to 1 January 2002 it could be used in parallel with existing national systems; the proposed classification is summarised as follows:

1. Transition radioactive waste
Type of radioactive waste (mainly from medical origin) which will decay within the period of temporary storage and may then be suitable for management outside of the regulatory control system subject to compliance with clearance levels.

2. Low and intermediate level waste (LILW)
In LILW the concentration of radio-nuclides is such that generation of thermal power during its disposal is sufficiently low. These acceptable thermal power values are site-specific following safety assessments.
2.1. Short-lived waste (LILW-SL)
This category includes radioactive waste with nuclides half-life less than or equal to those of Cs137 and Sr90 (around 30 years) with a restricted alpha long-lived radio-nuclide concentration (limitation of long-lived alpha emitting radio-nuclides to 4000 Bq/g in individual waste packages and to an overall average of 400 Bq/g in the total waste volume).
2.2. Long-lived waste (LILW-LL)
Long-lived radio-nuclides and alpha emitters whose concentration exceeds the limits for short-lived waste.

3. High level waste
Waste with such a concentration of radio-nuclides that generation of thermal power shall be considered during its storage and disposal (The thermal power generation level is site-specific and this waste is mainly forthcoming from treatment/conditioning of sent nuclear fuel).

4. This Recommendation is addressed to the Member States.

Done at Brussels, 15 September 1999.

For the Commission
Ritt BJERREGAARD
Member of the Commission

(1) OJ L 158, 23.6.1990, p. 56.
(2) OJ C 158, 25.6.1992, p. 3.
(3) OJ C 158, 25.6.1992, p. 3.
(4) OJ C 251, 10.8.1998, p. 34.

ANNEX

1. Introduction

Radioactive waste comprises a great variety of materials, with different physical, chemical and radioactive characteristics. This diversity results in widely different potential hazards.

The classification systems for radioactive waste in use across the European Union vary widely in approach and application. Some are used purely for communication purposes, while others are dictated by the disposal route.

Member States' radioactive waste classification systems are based on activity concentration, total activity, waste source or disposal route.

One of the main differences is between countries which have nuclear power generation and those that do not. In addition the borderlines between the categories are not always easily quantifiable and hence can vary widely from one country to another.

Differences in radioactive waste classifications may make cooperation between Member States difficult within the framework of the single market and the free movement of goods and services. For instance in the optimisation of disposal facilities and in return of wastes following treatment and/or conditioning, a common language defining the different radioactive waste categories could be very useful.

A European Union classification system should also be useful for providing comparative information concerning solid radioactive waste to the public, the national and international institutions and the non-governmental organisations.

This explanatory statement outlines the reasons and need for harmonisation, discussses the requirements and describes the proposed classification system.

2. Background

The Community action plan in the field of radioactive waste(1) calls for "concerted action on the safe management of radioactive waste" which should make it possible:

1. develop a common approach and work towards harmonisation at Community level on radioactive waste management strategies and practices wherever possible,
2. approximate national practices and regulations in the field of safety of disposal, with particular reference to the different waste categories,
3. draw up recommendations regarding safety assessment in the storage of radioactive waste and establish the relevant criteria,
4. to achieve, generally speaking, an equivalent and satisfactory degree of protection at the highest practical safety level for workers, members of the public and the environment.

In general terms, as a consequence of industrial, research and medical activities, residual materials containing radio-nuclides are produced. Following potential segregation, reuse in the nuclear industry and treatment, there are, in principle, two cate-

gories of such materials left. The main distinction between the two categories is established as follows:
>TABLE POSITION>
Material of category 1 can be released by national authorities provided they comply with clearance levels established using the basic criteria laid down in Annex 1 of Directive 96/29/Euratom(2). National authorities shall take into account technical guidance provided by the Community. It should be noted however that there is as yet no common basis for the harmonisation of category 1.

Only category 2 materials are regarded as "radioactive waste", and this recommendation is only concerned with the latter. Two basic management alternatives can be defined:

1. storage for a limited period of time until they can be either assigned to category 1 or disposed;
2. disposal following well-established routes (surface or near-surface disposal, or deep disposal).

In general, the factors considered most relevant to the definition of radioactive waste classification systems as well as management procedures are: type of radionuclides, total activity, activity concentration, half-life, dose rate, heat generation and other physical/chemical properties.

International bodies, national authorities and waste operators have established radioactive waste classification systems in their sectors of competence or responsibility (waste treatment, transport, waste disposal, communication within international scientific community and with the public, etc.), grouping in the same category wastes with similar characteristics and hazards, with a view to facilitate management and thereby improve safety.

Most national needs of the Member States are adequately covered by the national classifications they have developed (see Section 4, "Current position"). However, since these systems have been developed independently and for different purposes, they can vary significantly, some being based on activity concentration, others on source or disposal route.

The use by all countries of the international IAEA classification of radioactive waste packages is a suitable base to develop a common classification system for the Member States of the European Union. Definition of a reference classification system may provide useful guidance for specific countries in developing their own management strategies, whilst at the same time facilitating general and commercial communications. Concerning safety, however, while such a reference classification system may be useful for generic and basic considerations, it cannot replace specific safety assessments performed for specific management purposes, including the selection of disposal routes.

3. The purpose of a European Union waste classification system.

A classification system's primary purpose is to improve communication and facilitate information management by providing a good descriptive tool enabling holdings of radioactive waste within the Community to be described to politicians and the public in a standard and easily understood manner.

A more difficult issue is the relationship between the classification system and the way in which waste itself is handled and eventually disposed of in practice. Therefore the Commission services shared the view that the classification system should be indicative (qualitative) rather than prescriptive.

The key consideration is that any such qualitative classification system could never pre-empt the role of national regulatory authorities in the control of handling and disposal of radioactive waste at specific sites. The detailed safety assessments which they employ in light of their own specific management and regulatory arrangements and capabilities require much more detailed information concerning the individual waste streams than a classification system can provide. The different current waste classification systems used in practice within the Member States rarely feature in the wording of national legislation or regulatory procedures.

The divergence of current plans for final radioactive waste disposal within individual Member States also complicates the linkage of waste classification to eventual disposal routes. Some Member States have firm plans for both deep and surface disposal facilities for different types of waste. Other are likely to opt for only one of these types of facility, and some are undecided.

Some Member States believe that a suitably constructed classification system could provide basic guidance as to how radioactive waste management, in particular disposal, could be better structured in general terms. For example in those Member States where both surface and deep underground disposal options were available it might give some indication of the groups of waste streams which would go to each type of disposal site.

In light of the current diversity of national waste classification systems, a European Community classification system could be used initially in parallel with existing national systems until 1 January 2002. It would also need to be capable of dealing with all current and anticipated future waste streams in order to allow comprehensive reporting of holdings. It will serve regulatory purposes and improve communication to the public, for example on free access to environmental information (Directive 90/313/EEC).

4. *(omitted)* Current position on classification systems in various countries

(1) Council Resolution of 15 June 1992 on the renewal of the Community plan of action in the field of radioactive waste (OJ C 158, 25.6.1992, p. 2).

(2) Council Directive Euratom 96/29 of 13 May 1996 laying down basic safety standards for the health protection of the general public and workers against the danger of ionising radiation (OJ L 159, of 29.6.1996, p. 1).

(3) Radioactive waste categories. Current Position (98) in the EU Member States and in the Baltic and central European countries. 1998 EUR-OP Luxembourg EUR 18324.
(4) IAEA Safety Series No 111-G-1.1 Classification of radioactive waste, A safety guide. Vienna 1994.
(5) OJ L 35, 12.2.1992, p. 24

COMMISSION RECOMMENDATION (99/829/EURATOM) OF 6 DECEMBER 1999 ON THE APPLICATION OF ARTICLE 37 OF THE EURATOM TREATY

This Recommendation is not in fact the first concerning the application of Article 37, similar ones having been indeed adopted three times in the past (1960, 1982 and 1991). This kind of acts is revised periodically on the basis of experience acquired from practical application. On the other hand, it should be pointed out that the 1991 revision is also associated with a particularly significant event, i.e. the European Court of Justice's ruling (1988) on the so called "Cattenom Case" which is described in the Appendix to this volume.

It is recalled that Article 37 stipulates that each Member State must notify the Commission of the general data concerning every project for the disposal of radioactive waste, enabling it to determine whether such project is likely to pollute the environment of another member State. The Commission is to express an advice accordingly within six months.

The latest Recommendation takes into account the adoption of the 1996 Euratom Basic Standards, the need for determining beforehand those operations which are not likely to contaminate another State and for assessing the projects in a consistent manner, by identifying specifically the operations entailing waste disposal relevant for the purposes of Article 37. A list of 14 types of operations is included, for which the nature of information to be provided in terms of "general data" (also described in the Recommendation) is supplied in the technical Annexes (not published here). Each Member State is responsible for this information, as well as for the measures to be adopted following the Commission's advice.

THE COMMISSION OF THE EUROPEAN COMMUNITIES,

Having regard to the Treaty establishing the European Atomic Energy Community, and in particular Articles 37 and 124 thereof,

Having consulted the group of persons appointed in accordance with Article 31 of the Treaty by the Scientific and Technical Committee,

(1) Whereas Article 37 requires that each Member State is to provide the Commission with such general data relating to any plan for the disposal of radioactive waste in whatever form as will make it possible to determine whether the implementation of such plan is liable to result in the radioactive contamination of the water, soil or

airspace of another Member State. The Commission is to deliver its opinion within six months, after consulting the group of experts referred to in Article 31;

(2) Considering the experience acquired in the application of the Commission Recommendations of 16 November 1960, 82/181/ Euratom and 91/4/Euratom concerning the application of Article 37 of the Treaty;

(3) Whereas the Court of Justice of the European Communities in its judgement of 22 September 1988 in Case 187/87 ruled as follows: 'Article 37 of the Treaty of 25 March 1957 establishing the European Atomic Energy Community must be interpreted as meaning that the Commission of the European Communities must be provided with general data relating to any plan for the disposal of radioactive waste before such disposal is authorised by the competent authorities of the Member State concerned';

(4) Whereas in the same judgement the Court stated that, 'Consequently, it must be acknowledged that, where a Member State makes the disposal of radioactive waste subject to authorisation, the Commission's opinion must, in order to be rendered fully effective, be brought to the notice of that State before the issue of any such authorisation';

(5) Whereas Article 37 has as its objective to forestall any possibility of radioactive contamination of another Member State; whereas the Commission, having consulted the abovementioned group of experts, has deemed disposal of radioactive waste associated with certain operations to be not liable to result in the radioactive contamination of another Member State;

(6) Whereas in exceptional cases due to information received, the Commission may call for general data to be submitted for a plan for the disposal of radioactive waste, otherwise deemed not to be liable to result in the radioactive contamination of another Member State on the basis of the present Recommendation; whereas the Commission's opinion may then pertain to an authorisation which has been granted at an earlier stage;

(7) Whereas the basic safety standards for the health protection of the general public and workers against the dangers of ionising radiation have been revised by Directive 96/29/Euratom and the application of Article 37 should reflect these revisions where appropriate;

(8) Whereas to appraise disposal plans in a consistent manner, it is necessary to specify which types of operation may result in the disposal of radioactive waste within the meaning of Article 37 of the treaty, and to specify for the different types of operation which information is to be supplied as the general data;

(9) Whereas all Member States have now declared that they will desist from sea dumping,

HEREBY RECOMMENDS:

1. That the 'disposal of radioactive waste' within the meaning of Article 37 of the Treaty should cover any planned disposal or accidental release of radioactive substance associated with the operations listed below, in gaseous, liquid or solid form in or to the environment.
1. The operation of nuclear reactors.
2. The reprocessing of irradiated nuclear fuel.
3. The mining, milling and conversion of uranium and thorium.
4. U-235 enrichment of uranium.
5. The fabrication of nuclear fuel.
6. The storage of irradiated nuclear fuel in dedicated facilities.
7. The handling and processing of radioactive substances on an industrial scale.
8. The processing or storage of radioactive waste arising from operations (1) to (7) and (9).
9. The dismantling of nuclear reactors and reprocessing plants.
10. The emplacement above or under the ground of radioactive wastes without the intention of retrieval.
11. The sea dumping of radioactive waste.
12. The sub-seabed burial of radioactive wastes.
13. Work activities involving natural radiation sources and identified under the terms of Title VII of the Basic Safety Standards by the Member States involved as being of concern with regard to the resulting disposal of radioactive wastes and as requiring to be subject to prior authorisation.
14. All other operations.

2. That 'general data' within the meaning of Article 37 of the Treaty be understood to mean:
- for operations (1) to (8) the information set out in Annex 1
- for operations listed under (9) the information set out in Annex 2
- for operations listed under (10) the information set out in Annex
- for operations listed under (11) and (12) such information as will be required by the Commission on a case-by-case basis
- for operations listed under (13) the relevant parts of the information set out in Annex 1, as required for the specific work activity (Chapters 6 and 7 are normally not applicable).

3. That operations falling within the scope of point 1(14) are deemed not to be liable to result in the radioactive contamination of another Member State, significant from the point of view of health, unless in any specific case the Commission calls for such general data to be provided.

4. That, if a Member State envisages modifying a plan for the disposal of radioactive waste, the submission of general data be governed by the following conditions:

4.1.(a) If a Member State envisages modifying a plan for the disposal of radioactive waste, on which an opinion has already been given under the terms of Article 37, a submission of general data containing at least the information set out in a standard form in Annex 4 is necessary if the authorised limits or associated requirements for the disposal of radioactive waste are less restrictive than in the existing plan or if the potential consequences of the reference accident(s) evaluated in the licensing procedure are increased.
(b) Unless the Commission calls for general data to be communicated, no submission of general data is necessary if no new authorisation or licence is required.
or if:
- the modification of the plan for the disposal of radioactive waste envisages unchanged or more restrictive authorised limits and associated requirements than in the existing plan and
- the potential consequences of the reference accident(s) are unchanged or decreased.

4.2. In the case of a plan for the disposal of radioactive waste on which no opinion has already been given under the terms of Article 37, a submission of the general data is necessary unless the Member State provides the Commission with a statement demonstrating that the conditions outlined in point 4.1.(b) are met.

5. That, the 'general data' be submitted to the Commission:

5.1. whenever possible one year but not less than six months
- before any authorisation for the disposal of radioactive waste is granted by competent authorities, or
- before start-up of those operations for which no disposal authorisation is foreseen, or
- for operations (9), if the proposed authorised limits and associated requirements for the disposal of radioactive waste are less restrictive than those in the plan for the existing installation, or if the potential consequences of reference accident(s) are increased, before any corresponding new authorisation for the disposal of radioactive waste is granted by the competent authorities, and,

5.2. in cases where the Commission has called for general data in accordance with point 3, no later than six months after the request, without prejudice to any authorisation duly granted by the competent authorities pending receipt of the Commission's request. Any authorisation granted before the Commission called for general data shall be reviewed in the light of the Commission's subsequent opinion.

6. That, since submission of a plan for the disposal of radioactive waste is the responsibility of the relevant Member State, that State accepts responsibility for all information submitted to the Commission in respect of such a plan.

7. That the Member State concerned informs the Commission of the actions it envisages in response to any recommendation given in an opinion of the Commission on a disposal plan.

8. That Member States communicate to the Commission for information:
(a) the authorisation(s) for disposal of radioactive waste for comparison with the information in the general data on which its opinion was based;
(b) preferably annually and at least every two years, a statement on the radioactive liquid and atmospheric waste discharges to the environment from nuclear power reactors and reprocessing plants and, where appropriate, revisions of the authorisation(s) for disposal of radioactive waste that occurred during the period covered. This statement should be provided within nine months of that period.

This recommendation is addressed to the Member States.
It replaces Recommendation 91/4/Euratom.
Done at Brussels, 6 December 1999.
For the Commission
Margot WALLSTRÖM
Member of the Commission

COMMISSION RECOMMENDATION (2000/473/EURATOM) OF 8 JUNE 2000 ON THE APPLICATION OF ARTICLE 36 OF THE EURATOM TREATY CONCERNING THE MONITORING OF THE LEVELS OF RADIOACTIVITY IN THE ENVIRONMENT FOR THE PURPOSE OF ASSESSING THE EXPOSURE OF THE POPULATION AS A WHOLE

It is recalled preliminarily that the recommendation adopted for the application of Article 36 is to be regarded in relation to its links with Article 35 of the Euratom Treaty, requiring each Member State to carry out regular monitoring of the level of radioactivity in the environment, with a view to ensuring compliance with the Euratom Basic Standards. In particular, these stipulate that contribution to the exposure of the public as a whole from all practices be regularly assessed. Under Article 36, national authorities are required to keep the Commission periodically informed on the checks prescribed by Article 35. This makes it possible for the Commission to have a timely and uniform picture of the levels of radioactivity to which the public is exposed in Member States.

In connection with the above, the Recommendation indicates a number of requirements which should be met in terms of monitoring networks, sampling strategies and media, types of measurements and periodicity. The Recommendation addresses also the procedure for reporting to the Commission, as regards for example the treatment of data, the means of transmission and the integration of reporting practices. Four annexes (not published here) deal with sample types and measurements, country partitions and codes, reporting levels, and minimum requirements per data record.

THE COMMISSION OF THE EUROPEAN COMMUNITIES,

Having regard to the Treaty establishing the European Atomic Energy Community, and in particular Article 124 and Article 36 thereof,
Having consulted the group of persons appointed in accordance with Article 31 of the Euratom Treaty by the Scientific and Technical Committee,
Whereas:
(1) Article 35 of the Euratom Treaty requires each Member State to establish the facilities necessary to carry out continuous monitoring of the level of radioactivity in the air, water and soil and to ensure compliance with the basic standards.

(2) Article 36 of the Euratom Treaty requires the appropriate authorities periodically to communicate information on the checks referred to in Article 35 of the Euratom Treaty to the Commission so that it is kept informed of the level of radioactivity to which the public is exposed.
(3) Experience has been gained in the application of Article 36 of the Euratom Treaty. It is current practice for the Commission to publish annual monitoring reports, on the basis of quality controlled data received by the Commission in application of Article 36 and Article 39 of the Euratom Treaty. The Commission should continue to publish such annual monitoring reports.
(4) To ensure that the exposure of the population is kept under review it is important that the Commission be informed in a timely fashion and on a uniform basis of the levels of radioactivity to which the population as a whole is exposed in every Member State.
(5) Article 14 of Council Directive 96/29/Euratom of 13 May 1996 laying down basic safety standards for the protection of the health of workers and the general public against the dangers arising from ionising radiation(1) (the Basic Safety Standards) requires contribution to the exposure of the population as a whole from all practices to be regularly assessed.
(6) Article 45 of the Basic Safety Standards requires the competent authorities to ensure that dose estimates for the population as a whole are made as realistic as possible.
(7) Without prejudice to the requirements of Article 35 of the Euratom Treaty, it is sufficient for the review of the exposure of the population as a whole to provide a defined set of specific monitoring results.
(8) To ensure compliance with the Basic Safety Standards it is important that, in addition to air, water and soil, levels of radioactivity be determined in biological samples and in particular in foodstuffs, and that, to assess external exposure, the ambient dose rates be monitored.
(9) The monitoring of levels of radioactivity in soil does not allow a direct assessment of the exposure of the population. The exposure related to soil contamination is more directly assessed on the basis of ambient dose rate and foodstuff contamination. Experience has shown that the incorporation of soil data in the monitoring serves little useful purpose.
(10) It is necessary to keep under review which sampling media and which radionuclide categories are relevant indicators of actual and potential levels of radioactivity in the environment and of exposure of the population.
(11) There is consensus among Member States as to the adequacy of current monitoring programmes. Such monitoring may change in function of the evolution of levels of radioactivity, measurement technology, and the needs in view of emergency response. The Commission will keep under review the adequacy of monitoring programmes and will involve the group of experts established under Article 31 of the Euratom Treaty in this process.

(12) In the framework of Article 37 of the Euratom Treaty, the data on discharges of radionuclides to the environment from nuclear power plants and reprocessing plants are already requested in Commission Recommendation 1999/829/Euratom of 6 December 1999 on the application of Article 37 of the Euratom Treaty(2).
(13) Council Directive 98/83/EC of 3 November 1998 on the quality of water intended for human consumption(3) provides for indicator parameters for radioactivity. This Recommendation is without prejudice to specific requirements under Annex II and Annex III to that Directive.
(14) The uniformity, comparability, transparency and timeliness of data reported in accordance with Article 36 of the Euratom Treaty should be ensured.

HEREBY RECOMMENDS:

1. In order to discharge their obligation under Article 36 of the Euratom Treaty periodically to communicate information on the results of the monitoring of the levels of radioactivity which they are bound to perform under the terms of Article 35 of that Treaty, the Member States should forward to the Commission, in accordance with the time periods set out in point 5(c), the monitoring results listed in Annex I. In case of an elevated concentration of a radionuclide not specified in Annex I, appropriate date should also be forwarded.

2. For the purposes of this Recommendation, the following definitions apply:
(a) "continuous monitoring" means the existence and implementation of a continuing monitoring programme. Depending on the medium monitored, this is achieved as appropriate through:
(i) continuous sampling and assessment;
(ii) continuous sampling and periodic assessment;
(iii) periodic sampling and periodic assessment;
(iv) direct continuous measurement;
(b) "facilities" means the monitoring programme, the direct measurement and sampling and analysis equipment and procedures (including quality control and the reporting and archiving of all relevant data), and the laboratories necessary to implement continuous monitoring of the levels of radioactivity;
(c) "monitoring network" means the combination of each medium of the sampling and direct measurement locations, as appropriate, used for the monitoring of that specific medium;
(d) "dense monitoring network" means a monitoring network comprising sampling locations distributed throughout the Member State's territory such as to allow the Commission to compute regional averages for radioactivity levels in the Community;
(e) "sparse monitoring network" means a monitoring network comprising for every region and for every sampling medium at least one location representative of that

region. At such locations high sensitivity measurements should be performed thus giving a transparent representation of actual levels and trends of radioactivity levels;
(f) "region" means each representative area of a Member State for the assessment of the radiological exposure of the population as a whole under consideration of the radiological impact by emissions and ambient dose and the population distribution. The regions currently defined in the Commission monitoring reports are given in Annex II.

3. Member States should notify to the Commission the appropriate authorities referred to in Article 36 of the Euratom Treaty.

4. The following requirements should be met:
(a) Monitoring networks
(i) Each Member State should define representative geographical regions for its own territory.
(ii) Each Member State should define for each type of medium a sparse monitoring network and a dense monitoring network.
(iii) The sites comprising a network should be representative of the regional situation taking into account, where appropriate, the population distribution within the region.
(b) Sampling media, types of measurements, and periodicity
(i) The sampling media and types of measurements are listed in Annex I. Except where otherwise specified in this Recommendation, measurements should preferably be carried out for the sparse network on a monthly basis and for the dense network quarterly.
(ii) For the sparse monitoring network, the detection limits and sensitivities of the measurement instruments should allow the actual levels to be quantified.
(iii) For the dense monitoring network, the detection limits of the measurement devices should be lower than the reporting levels defined in Annex III.
(iv) The Member States should inform the Commission of the detection limits and of the uncertainties taken into account.
(v) The Member States should retain measurement techniques that have proven reliable and ensure quality control of the results.
(vi) Member State laboratories supplying data under the terms of this Recommendation should periodically participate in intercomparison exercises, in particular those organised by the Commission, so as to ensure the intercomparability of the data reported.
(c) Sampling strategies and measurements in relation to each of the required sampling media
(i) Airborne particulates
Measurements of gamma emitting radionuclides should be performed on a routine basis to detect and measure man-made radioisotopes as well as naturally occurring

radionuclides. Beryllium-7 should be reported as a qualitative check of the methods used. Where gross beta activity(4) measurements are recorded these should also be reported.
Sampling locations should be in the vicinity of densely populated areas; adequate geographical coverage should be ensured by the choice of at least one sampling location per geographical region.
Sampling should be performed by systems operating continuously.
(ii) External ambient gamma dose rates should be measured continuously. No reporting level is defined.
(iii) Surface water
Samples should be taken from major inland waters of the Member States' territory and, if relevant, from coastal waters.
In the case of river water, sampling should be carried out, where practicable, at locations for which flow rate measurements are available. In such cases, the average flow rate during the sampling period should be reported to improve the representativeness of the mean values calculated by the Commission.
Gamma emitting radionuclides should be monitored. Where residual beta activity(5) measurements are recorded these should also be reported.
(iv) Water intended for human consumption
Monitoring of levels of radioactivity in drinking water should be such as to ensure compliance with the requirements of Directive 98/83/EC.
For the purposes of compliance with Article 36 of the Euratom Treaty, values should be reported for major ground or surface water supplies and for water distribution networks such as to ensure a representative coverage of the Member State.
The corresponding volumes of water distributed or produced in a year should be reported to improve the representativeness of the mean values calculated by the Commission.
(v) Milk
Milk samples should be taken from dairies. The necessary statistical information on production rates should be reported to improve the representativeness of the mean values calculated by the Commission. The spread of dairies should be sufficient to ensure representative coverage of the Member State.
Gamma emitters and strontium-90 should be monitored; potassium-40 should be reported as a qualitative check of the methods used.
(vi) Mixed diet
Due to the trade in foodstuffs, the mixed diet is not necessarily representative of the regional or national environmental contamination but is an indicator of public exposure.
Where appropriate, foodstuffs are measured as separate ingredients; in this case the Member State should report to the Commission the results of measurements of the individual ingredients and the composition of the diet. The sampling programme

should take into consideration regional variations in dietary patterns. Individual ingredients should be from market places or local distribution centres providing food products to large population groups. Appropriate account should be taken of products from natural or semi-natural ecosystems, to the extent that the fallout from the Chernobyl accident may still affect such systems.

In addition, Member States should sample complete meals to give a representative figure for the average level of radioactivity in mixed diet. Actual meal samples should be taken from large consumption centres such as canteens or restaurants.

Gamma emitters and strontium-90 should be monitored; the measurements should be not less frequent than quarterly. Where carbo-14 measurements are performed, these should also be reported.

5. The procedure for reporting to the Commission should be as follows:

(a) Treatment of data

The Member States should forward to the Commission data which have been subject to quality control and cleared for public release. The data set should contain all details listed in Annex IV.

The Member States should forward the data in the format defined by the Commission and preferably use the specialised software provided by the Commission.

Tndividual non-aggregated measurement data should be transmitted for each medium and each site rather than average values. However, if the data correspond to direct continuous measurements, then the monthly averages for each site should be communicated.

(b) Means of transmission

Data should be forwarded in a digital form using the most appropriate electronic media.

(c) Periodicity

All available data should be forwarded to the Commission as soon as they are validated in order to allow for a prompt assessment by the Commission of the impact of environmental radioactivity on public health. All data for a calendar year should be submitted no later than 30 June of the following year.

(d) Transmission of other data

In addition to the data transmitted under point (a), Member States should transmit to the Commission their national monitoring reports to allow a fuller understanding of the significance of the data referred to in Annex I in relation to the national monitoring programmes. The Commission's annual monitoring reports will list references to those national reports.

(e) Integration of reporting practices

Data regularly reported under Article 36 of the Euratom Treaty, data voluntarily reported other than national monitoring reports and large amounts of data of types potentially relevant in emergency situations should be forwarded through the same communication means and channels and in the same format in order to simplify reporting practices and to avoid duplication of efforts and to conduct regular exercises of the emergency arrangements.

6. This Recommendation is addressed to the Member States.

Done at Brussels, 8 June 2000.

For the Commission
Margot Wallström
Member of the Commission

(1) OJ L 159, 29.6.1996, p. 1.
(2) OJ L 324, 16.12.1999, p. 23.
(3) OJ L 330, 5.12.1998, p. 32.
(4) The total measured beta activity in a sample; depending on the measurement methodology tritium and in general very low energy beta emitters are normally not included and short lived radon daughters are excluded through a sufficient delay time (e.g. five days) before counting.
(5) The total measured beta acitivity minus potassium-40 activity.

COMMISSION RECOMMENDATION (2001/928/EURATOM) OF 20 DECEMBER 2001 ON PROTECTION OF THE PUBLIC AGAINST EXPOSURE TO RADON IN DRINKING WATER SUPPLIES

It is recalled that in the past radon gas had already been addressed in international and European Community recommendations and directives (dealt with in this Chapter), concerning its presence both at working places and in the common environment. In particular, the Euratom Basic Standards on radiation protection (Directive 96/29), and the EC Directive 98/83 lay down respectively the radiation protection principles applicable also to drinking water, and the requirements of water intended for human consumption. Nevertheless, the latter Directive (not published here) addresses the concentration of natural radio-nuclides in drinking water excepting radon and its decay products. Besides, other directives concern natural mineral water as well as water intended for medical use, which are therefore outside the scope of the Recommendation in point.

Given the increasing awareness in many member States about the implications of exposure to radon in drinking water, the main aims of the Recommendation are to foster the development of adequate systems to reduce any significant such exposure of the public, to keep it appropriately informed on account of the specific features of the issue, and to establish simple and reliable procedure for measuring radon and its decay products in drinking water. The Recommendation addresses water not only for individual consumption, but also as part of a commercial supply system, and contemplates investigations suitable for assessing levels and nature of exposures. Furthermore, it considers methods to be adopted in member States in order to eliminate radon from drinking water and remedial actions to be taken to protect human health accordingly. Finally, the application of Title VII of the Euratom Basic Standards recalled above is stressed (on exposure of workers to radon at workplaces where significant amounts of radon may be contained in water, such as spas, pools, etc.).

THE COMMISSION OF THE EUROPEAN COMMUNITIES,

Having regard to the Treaty establishing the European Atomic Energy Community, and in particular Article 30, the second paragraph of Article 33, the first paragraph of Article 38, and the second indent of Article 124 thereof,
Having regard to the opinion of the Group of Experts appointed by the Scientific and Technical Committee pursuant to Article 31 of the Treaty,

Whereas:
(1) Council Directive 96/29/Euratom of 13 May 1996 laying down basic safety standards for the protection of the health of workers and the general public against the dangers arising from ionising radiation(1) lays down a framework for controlling exposures to natural radiation sources arising from work activities. Title VII of the Directive applies to work activities within which the presence of natural radiation sources leads to a significant increase in the exposure of workers or of members of the public. Member States are required to identify work activities which may be of concern.
(2) In view of the large geographical variability in the natural occurrence of radon and in the extent to which the population and water supplies are affected, a flexible approach is needed to allow Member States to apply the concept of optimisation, while ensuring protection of the most highly exposed part of the population. Such an approach is in accordance with Article 6(3)(a) of Directive 96/29/Euratom.
(3) The Group of Experts set up under Article 31 of the Euratom Treaty has provided technical guidance(2) for the implementation of Title VII of Directive 96/29/Euratom(3). The guidance includes the protection of workers to inhaled radon in establishments where significant amounts of radon may be released from water into indoor air.
(4) Commission Recommendation 90/143/Euratom of 21 February 1990 on the protection of the public against indoor exposure to radon(4) introduces reference and design levels for indoor radon. The reference level for consideration of remedial action is 400 Bq/m3 and the design level for future constructions is 200 Bq/m3.
(5) Surveys in Member States have shown elevated concentrations of radon in some ground waters, particularly in regions with crystalline rocks. There are circumstances under which radon concentrations in drinking water are radiologically significant as they expose the population to enhanced doses and should not be disregarded from the radiation-protection point of view. High concentrations are often related to individual drilled wells, but sometimes also to waterworks utilising rock or soil aquifers.
(6) In many Member States there is increasing awareness of the significance of exposure of the population to radon in drinking water. Several countries have already or are drawing up dose-control policies. In many cases the control policies are drawn up in accordance with the protection principles established by the Council Directives 96/29/Euratom and 98/83/EC of 3 November 1998 on the quality of water intended for human consumption(5).
(7) Radon is a naturally occurring radioactive noble gas, the most significant isotope of which is radon-222 with a half life of 3,82 days. This isotope is a member of the uranium-238 decay series and its presence in the environment is associated mainly with the trace amounts of its immediate parent, radium-226, in rocks and soil. Because radon is an inert gas, it can move rather freely through porous media such as soil or fragmented rock. Where the pores are saturated with water, as in soil and rock under

the water table, radon is dissolved into the water and is then transported by it. Water-saturated soil with a porosity of 20% and a radium concentration of 40 Bq/kg, which is the world-wide average in the earth's crust, causes at equilibrium a radon concentration in ground water of the order of 50 Bq/l.

(8) Surveys in Member States have shown that radon concentrations in surface waters are very low, usually well below 1 Bq/l. Concentrations in ground water vary from 1 to 50 Bq/l for rock aquifers in sedimentary rocks, to 10 to 300 Bq/l for wells dug in soil, and to 100 Bq/l to 50000 Bq/l in crystalline rocks. The highest concentrations are usually associated with high uranium concentrations in the bedrock. A characteristic of radon concentrations in rock aquifers are their variability; within a region with fairly uniform rock types some wells exhibit concentrations far above the average for that region. Significant seasonal variations in concentrations have also been observed.

(9) Radon in domestic water supplies causes human exposure through ingestion and inhalation pathways. Radon can be ingested by direct consumption of tap or fresh bottled water. Radon is released from tap water into indoor air which causes exposure to radon by inhalation.

(10) In its report of 1993, the United Nations Scientific Committee on the Effects of Atomic Radiation (UNSCEAR)(6) estimated that the committed effective dose from ingestion of radon in water is 10-8 Sv/Bq for an adult and somewhat higher for a child and an infant. In 1998, the National Research Council, a committee in the United States, presented a conversion factor of 0.35.10-8 Sv/Bq(7). The committee did not find sufficient scientific evidence to introduce separate dose estimations for different age groups. In addition to the conversion factor, the ingestion dose depends also on the annual consumption of water. Estimates on the annual committed effective dose absorbed by an adult by the ingestion of water containing 1000 Bq/l vary between 0,2 mSv and 1,8 mSv, depending on the annual water consumption and the range of conversion factors used.

(11) The increase in indoor radon concentration caused by tap water depends on various parameters such as the total consumption of water in the house, the volume of the house and the ventilation rate. Both the UNSCEAR and the National Research Council estimate that 1000 Bq/l of radon in tap water will on the average increase the indoor air radon concentration by 100 Bq/m3.

(12) Radon in drinking water is controllable in the physical and engineering sense; effective methods for removing radon from drinking water have been developed(8) and are commercially available. Accordingly, an appropriate system needs to be established for reducing significant exposures. An important part of the system is the adoption of reference levels for consideration of remedial or preventive action.

(13) The methods and equipment used for removing radon and long-lived radon decay products from water do not significantly differ in techniques or in costs between an existing water supply and a new supply planned for future use. Consequently, the same

criteria, including the reference levels, may be used for remedial action on the existing water supplies and for setting preventive requirements for new water supplies.

(14) For an individual water supply, whereby no water is supplied as part of a commercial or public activity, the exposure caused by radon in water is a phenomenon fairly similar to that of radon in dwellings. Accordingly, similar radiological protection criteria should be applied. Considering both the ingestion and inhalation pathways, the annual effective dose caused by water containing 1000 Bq/l radon is, according to current knowledge, very comparable to that caused by an indoor radon concentration of 200 Bq/m3, the design level established in Recommendation 90/143/Euratom.

(15) Where water is supplied as part of a commercial or public activity, such as through a waterworks, the consumer does not have the same opportunity to control the received dose as an owner of an individual supply. It follows that the consumer must be confident that the water does not pose any risk to human health. In addition, remedial action taken on that water affects a large number of people, which makes the action more cost-effective at lower radon concentrations than is the case with an individual supply. Consequently, it is justified to adopt a more stringent control policy, including a lower reference level, for water supplied as part of a commercial or public activity than for an individual supply. Small amounts of radon in water are ubiquitous and therefore no remedial action should be required if the concentration is less than 100 Bq/l. National surveys might show that a higher reference level needs to be adopted for implementing a practical radon programme. However, it is unlikely that public or commercial distribution water with a radon concentration exceeding 1000 Bq/l could be considered justifiable from the radiation protection point of view.

(16) The radon concentration of water at the point of delivery is unlikely to be greater than that at the source, as in the case of a waterworks. Usually a measurement at the source is sufficient to demonstrate compliance with the reference concentration and no separate measurements are needed at the various points of use. However, the radioactive decay and possible aeration of radon during delivery may need to be taken into account, for example, in assessing the doses.

(17) Directive 98/83/EC requires the Member States to monitor the concentrations of natural radio-nuclides in drinking water, but in addition to radon, radon decay products are also excluded from the scope of the Directive. There are circumstances under which polonium-210 and lead-210 (long-lived decay products of radon) in drinking water pose a comparable or a higher radiation risk than some natural radionuclides monitored in accordance with the Directive. Accordingly, polonium-210 and lead-210 should not be disregarded in monitoring and in taking action to reduce exposures caused by natural radio-nuclides in drinking water. Reference concentrations for polonium-210 and lead-210 should be established and they should be monitored according to the principles set for natural radio-nuclides by the Directive. The indicative dose of 0,1 mSv and the principles of dose calculation established in the Directive should be used for deriving the reference concentrations.

(18) High radon concentrations indicate a potential presence of other radio-nuclides of the uranium decay series in the water, although the correlation is not always unambiguous. When remedial action is taken to reduce radon concentration, the presence of other natural radio-nuclides should be screened and, where appropriate, be analysed in more detail so that a suitable technique can be chosen to remove all the radiologically significant natural radio-nuclides from the water at the same time, in a cost effective way.
(19) Specific guidance should be made available to the waterworks and to the owners of public water supplies on the different methods available for removing radon and long-lived radon decay products from water. The guidance should include, in particular, instructions on the handling and disposal of accrued radioactive waste and on the ways of minimising possible exposure due to radon released from a removal device or by the increase in external gamma radiation in the vicinity of a removal device.
(20) Simple metrological procedures should be established to ensure that measurements of radon and radon decay products in water yield data of the appropriate quality and reliability.
(21) Owing to the special characteristics of the problem, adequate public information is an important element both in improving the controllability of exposure and in securing a positive public response.
(22) The purpose of this Recommendation is to provide guidance to the Member States for setting controls on exposures caused by radon and radon decay products in drinking water,

HEREBY RECOMMENDS:

1. This Recommendation concerns the radiological quality of drinking water supplies regarding radon and long-lived radon decay products.

2. An appropriate system should be established for reducing exposures to radon and long-lived radon decay products in domestic drinking water supplies. Within this system adequate public information and response to public concern deserve particular attention. Under the system attention should concentrate on the highest exposures and on those areas where action is most likely to be effective.

3. For the purpose of this Recommendation, "drinking water" shall mean:
(a) all water either in its original state or after treatment, intended for drinking, cooking, food preparation or other domestic purposes, regardless of its origin and whether it is supplied from a distribution network, from a tanker, or in bottles or containers,
(b) all water used in any food-production undertaking for the manufacture, processing, preservation or marketing of products or substances intended for human

consumption unless the competent national authorities are satisfied that the quality of the water cannot affect the wholesomeness of the foodstuff in its finished form. Natural mineral waters covered by Council Directive 80/777/EEC(9) and waters which are medical products according to Council Directive 65/65/EEC(10) are excluded from the scope of this Recommendation, since special rules for those types of water have been established.

4. Representative surveys should be undertaken to determine the scale and nature of exposures caused by radon and long-lived radon decay products in domestic drinking water supplies originating from different types of ground water sources and wells in different geological areas unless this information is already available. The surveys should be designed in such a way that underlying parameters, and especially the geology and hydrology of the area, radioactivity of rock or soil, and well type, can be identified and used later for directing further action on the highest exposures. The surveys should cover, in particular:
(a) drilled wells, especially those in crystalline rock areas,
(b) waterworks using rock or soil aquifers.

5. For water supplied as part of a commercial or public activity, the following action should be taken:
(a) above a concentration of 100 Bq/l, Member States should set a reference level for radon to be used for consideration whether remedial action is needed to protect human health. A level higher than 100 Bq/l may be adopted if national surveys show that this is necessary for implementing a practical radon programme. For concentrations in excess of 1000 Bq/l, remedial action is deemed to be justified on radiological protection grounds;
(b) measurements of radon concentration should be required if there is a specific reason to suspect, on the basis of the results of representative surveys or other reliable information, that the reference level might be exceeded;
(c) where significant concentrations of polonium-210 and lead-210 are suspected, on the basis of the results of representative surveys or other reliable information, monitoring of these nuclides should be arranged in conjunction with the monitoring of other natural radio-nuclides required by Directive 98/83/EC;
(d) above a reference concentration of 0,1 Bq/l for polonium-210 and 0,2 Bq/l for lead-210, consideration should be given to whether remedial action is needed to protect human health.

6. For an individual water supply, from which no water is supplied as part of any commercial or public activity, the following action should be taken:
(a) a level of 1000 Bq/l should be used for consideration of remedial action;

(b) the urgency of the remedial action should be commensurate with the extent to which the reference concentration is exceeded;
(c) where remedial action is considered necessary because of radon, the levels of other natural radio-nuclides should be screened and where appropriate as a result of the screening, other natural radio-nuclides should be analysed and removed from the drinking water with the same remedial action;
(d) where remedial action is considered necessary, the consumers concerned should be informed of the radon levels of the water and of the remedies available to reduce such levels.

7. Where measurements indicate that the radon in tap water contributes significantly to exceeding the threshold set for indoor radon, remedial action on this source should be considered.

8. Drinking water distributed in public premises such as residential homes, schools, and hospitals should comply with the principles of point 5.

9. Measurements should be made with appropriate methods and equipment which have undergone approved calibration and quality assurance programmes.

10. Member States should provide guidance on different methods available for removing radon and long-lived radon decay products from water. Member States should provide instructions on the handling and disposal of radioactive waste generated by the removal process and on ways to minimise possible exposure caused by radon released from a removal device or by the increase in external gamma radiation in the vicinity of a removal device.

11. The exposure of workers to inhaled radon in establishments where significant amounts of radon may be released from water into indoor air, in particular in water-works, spas and swimming pools, should be controlled according to Title VII of the Directive 96/29/Euratom and according to the Recommendations, "Radiation Protection 88", made in 1997 for the implementation of that Title by the Group of Experts established under Article 31 of the Euratom Treaty.

12. Member States should consider to what extent the intentional use of radon-bearing water for its prospective therapeutic effects is justified by its economic, social or other benefits when set against the health detriment it may cause.

This Recommendation is addressed to the Member States.

Done at Brussels, 20 December 2001.

For the Commission
Margot Wallström
Member of the Commission

(1) OJ L 159, 29.6.1996, p. 1.
(2) Radiation Protection 88. Recommendations for the implementation of Title VII of the European Basic Safety Standards Directive (BSS) concerning the significant increase in exposure due to natural radiation sources. European Commission, Luxembourg, 1997.
(3) OJ L 159, 29.6.1996, p. 1.
(4) OJ L 80, 27.3.1990, p. 26.
(5) OJ L 330, 5.12.1998, p. 32.
(6) UNSCEAR 1993 report. Sources and effects of ionising radiation. United Nations Scientific Committee on the Effects of Atomic Radiation, New York, 1993.
(7) Risk Assessment of Radon in Drinking Water. Committee on Risk Assessment of Exposure to Radon in Drinking Water, Board on Radiation Effects Research, Commission of Life Sciences, NRC (National Research Council). National Academy Press, Washington DC, 1999.
(8) The Commission has funded and is funding several research projects on the risk of exposure to radon. The TENEWA project (Treatment Techniques for Removing Natural Radio-nuclides from Drinking Water) carried out under the CEC contract No FI4PCT960054 has produced a significant amount of information on the removal techniques, including information on the possible radiological hazards caused by removal devices.
(9) OJ L 229, 30.8.1980, p. 1.
(10) OJ Special Edition 1965-1966, p. 20.

COMMISSION RECOMMENDATION (2003/274/EURATOM) OF 14 APRIL 2003 ON THE PROTECTION AND INFORMATION OF THE PUBLIC WITH REGARD TO THE CONTINUED CONTAMINATION OF CERTAIN WILD FOOD PRODUCTS FOLLOWING THE CHERNOBYL ACCIDENT

This Recommendation is concerned with the possible exposure resulting from the continued radioactive caesium contamination of the wild food of above, as a consequence of the accident at the Chernobyl nuclear power station in 1986. EU member States are invited to take appropriate measures to ensure that the maximum permitted levels in terms of caesium-134 and caesium-137 are respected in the Community for the placing on the market of the wild food in point, and to inform the public in affected regions of the health risks involved. To this effect, member States are also invited to use an EC Regulation of 2002 (on Community Rapid Alert System) for the exchange of information on recorded cases of maximum permitted levels being exceeded.

Given the very specific and clearly limited scope, the text of the Recommendation is omitted here.

COMMISSION RECOMMENDATION (2004/2/EURATOM) OF 18 DECEMBER 2003 ON STANDARDIZED INFORMATION ON RADIOACTIVE AIRBORNE AND LIQUID DISCHARGES INTO THE ENVIRONMENT FROM NUCLEAR POWER REACTORS AND REPROCESSING PLANTS IN NORMAL OPERATIONS

This recommendation mainly takes into account another Commission recommendation on the application of article 37 of the Euratom Treaty (1999/829, see in this Chapter) following which member States regularly communicate to the Commission a statement on radioactive liquid and airborne discharges into the environment from nuclear power reactors and reprocessing plants. The 1999 recommendation does not specify the content of the information to be provided in the statement, which is therefore done in the 2003 one. Standardized information on the domain in point is needed "to achieve comparable measurement results of radioactive discharges on a Community scale" and to ensure that minimum analysing standards are applied in the Community. The recommendation does not cover dismantling operations, given their different nature and the type of waste they produce. The information to be provided under the recommendation is also aimed at enhancing the significance and transparency of the reports addressing the radiological impact on the population of the European Union from the operations under consideration, that the Commission publishes regularly. The two technical annexes (not published here) deal with the detection limits for radio-nuclides addressed by the recommendation and with the information to be provided in the format of compilation sheets.

THE COMMISSION OF THE EUROPEAN COMMUNITIES,

Having regard to the Treaty establishing the European Atomic Energy Community, and in particular Article 124 thereof,
Having consulted the group of persons appointed in accordance with Article 31 of the Treaty by the Scientific and Technical Committee,
Whereas:
(1) Under Title II, Chapter 3, of the Euratom Treaty, Member States regularly report to the Commission on assessed levels of environmental radioactivity.
(2) Article 35 of the Euratom Treaty requires each Member State to establish the facilities necessary to carry out continuous monitoring of the level of radioactivity in the air, water and soil and to ensure compliance with the basic standards.

(3) Article 36 of the Euratom Treaty requires the appropriate authorities to periodically communicate to the Commission information on the environmental checks referred to in Article 35, so that it is kept informed on the level of radioactivity to which the public is exposed. The information on the checks referred to in Article 35 also concerns information on levels of radioactivity in discharges as this is necessary for the assessment of the environmental impact of such discharges. This aspect was not within the scope of Commission Recommendation 2000/473/Euratom of 8 June 2000 on the application of Article 36 of the Euratom Treaty concerning the monitoring of the levels of radioactivity in the environment for the purpose of assessing the exposure of the population as a whole(1). It is appropriate to define and specify such information.
(4) Following Commission Recommendation 1999/829/Euratom of 6 December 1999 on the application of Article 37 of the Euratom Treaty(2), Member States regularly communicate to the Commission a statement on radioactive liquid and airborne discharges into the environment from nuclear power reactors and reprocessing plants. However, Recommendation 1999/829/Euratom does not specify the content of the information to be provided in the statement. This Recommendation defines and specifies that information.
(5) Article 45 of Council Directive 96/29/Euratom of 13 May 1996 laying down basic safety standards for the protection of the health of workers and the general public against the dangers of ionising radiation(3) requires the competent authorities of Member States to ensure that estimates of doses to the population from practices subject to prior authorisation are made as realistic as possible; nuclide-specific information on radioactive discharges into the environment is needed for the assessment of such doses.
(6) Standardised information on radio-nuclides discharged into the environment from nuclear power reactors and reprocessing plants during normal operation is needed to achieve comparable measurement results of radioactive discharges on a Community scale and to ensure that minimum standards for the analysis methods are met across the Community. For this purpose, for each category of radioactive discharges and each type of nuclear installation considered, it is appropriate to identify key nuclides to which requirements for detection limits should apply. These key nuclides should represent categories of radio-nuclides or a specific type of radiation, be significant in terms of radiological impact and be suitable measurement sensitivity indicators.
(7) The Commission regularly publishes reports on annual radioactive effluents from nuclear power stations and nuclear fuel reprocessing plants in the European Community and on assessment of the radiological impact on the population of the European Union from European Union nuclear sites. The significance and transparency of the Commission's reports would be enhanced if they were based on standardised information.
(8) It is important to ensure at this stage, as a first step towards harmonisation at Community level, the comparability of the information provided on levels of radio-

activity in discharges from nuclear power reactors and nuclear fuel reprocessing plants in normal operation. Dismantling operations should not be covered by this Recommendation, as these are of a different nature and give rise to different types of waste,

HEREBY RECOMMENDS:

1. This Recommendation defines information selected for monitoring and reporting to the European Commission on radio-nuclides discharged or liable to be discharged from nuclear power reactors and reprocessing plants in normal operation.

2. For the purpose of this Recommendation, the following definition apply:
(a) "normal operation": normal activities relating to the operation of a nuclear power reactor or reprocessing plant, including the decommissioning phase (shutdown and containment and surveillance operations), but not the dismantling phase;
(b) "key nuclide": suitable measurement sensitivity indicator, selected for each radio-nuclide category;
(c) "detection limit": smallest true value of the measure and that is detectable, with a given probability of error, by the measuring method;
(d) "decision threshold": the fixed value of the decision quantity (random variable for the decision whether the physical effect to be measured is present or not) by which, when exceeded by the result of an actual measurement of a measure and quantifying a physical effect, it is decided that the physical effect is present.

3. For airborne and liquid discharges from nuclear power reactors and reprocessing plants, Member States should assess the discharged activity of all radio-nuclides considered in column 1 of Annex I.

4. In situations where measured values are below detection limits, for key nuclides identified in column 2 of Annex I, the detection limits achieved should not exceed the corresponding requirements defined in column 3 of Annex I.

5. In situations where a similar accuracy can be achieved by the calculation of discharges for specific radio-nuclides on the basis of operational data, or on the basis of measurement results for other radio-nuclides, such calculated discharge values may be used as a substitute for direct measurements.

6. The determination of detection limits, decision thresholds, and the expression of results should comply with international standard ISO/IS 11929-7. For practical reasons, even though technically the decision threshold is below half the detection limit actually achieved for a measurement, the decision threshold may conservatively be taken to be equal to one half of the detection limit.

7. Where measurement outcomes are below the decision threshold, these outcomes should conservatively be substituted by one half of the decision threshold. However, if repeated measurement outcomes in the period considered are all below the decision threshold, then it is reasonable to assume that the true value is zero, i.e. that the radio-nuclide is not present in the discharge.

8. Member States should report the following information on radioactive discharges to the Commission in the format of the compilation sheets outlined in Annex II:
(a) annual discharge values for each radio-nuclide listed in column 1 of Annex I for which there is at least one measurement outcome above the decision threshold in the period considered, or for which a calculated assessment has been made in the same period;
(b) for each key nuclide, the highest value of the detection limit that has been obtained among all the measurements for the period considered;
(c) estimates of radio-nuclide discharges based on calculation, as a substitute for measurement, when measurement is technically not feasible;
(d) as far as available, the chemical/physical form of tritium, carbon-14 and iodine discharges to the atmosphere;
(e) the time basis for the reported values, and where appropriate information on the summation method used, including the substitutes for values below decision threshold, which have been used in estimating summation results;
(f) the sampling method for the effluent streams.
The information referred to in (d), (e) and (f) should be provided in the commentaries. Estimated values as referred to in (c) should be identified as such in a commentary together with an indication of the method used and, where appropriate, any relevant detection limit

9. The period of reporting information on radioactive discharges should be one calendar year. Information on radioactive discharges should be submitted no later than 30 September of the following year.

10. This Recommendation is addressed to the Member States.

Done at Brussels, 18 December 2003.

For the Commission
Loyola De Palacio
Vice-President

COUNCIL DECISION OF 15 DECEMBER 2003 AMENDING THE COUNCIL DECISION OF 7 DECEMBER 1998 APPROVING THE ACCESSION OF THE EUROPEAN ATOMIC ENERGY COMMUNITY TO THE NUCLEAR SAFETY CONVENTION WITH REGARD TO THE DECLARATION ATTACHED THERETO

This Decision is published here with no Introductory Material. See case law no. 5 in the Appendix to the volume as to the reasons leading to the amended Decision.

THE COUNCIL OF THE EUROPEAN UNION,

Having regard to the Treaty establishing the European Atomic Energy Community, and in particular Article 101 thereof,

Having regard to the proposal from the Commission,
Whereas:

(1) Council Decision of 7 December 1998[1] approved the accession of the European Atomic Energy Community to the Nuclear Safety Convention. Attached to this Decision was a Declaration by the European Atomic Energy Community in accordance with the provisions of Article 30(4)(iii) of that Convention.
(2) In its judgement of 10 December 2002 in Case C-29/99[2], the Court of Justice annulled the third paragraph of this Declaration in so far as Articles 7, 14, 16(1) and (3) and Articles 17 to 19 of the Convention are not referred to therein.
(3) The second paragraph of the Declaration is also incomplete because it fails to mention all the Articles that apply to the Community.
(4) It is therefore necessary to amend the Decision of 7 December 1998 accordingly,

HAS DECIDED AS FOLLOWS:

Sole Article

The Declaration to be submitted by the European Atomic Energy Community pursuant to Article 30(4)(iii) of the Nuclear Safety Convention, which is attached to the

1 Not published.
2 Commission v. Council, ECR [2002] page I-11221.

Council Decision of 7 December 1998 approving the accession of the European Atomic Energy Community to the Nuclear Safety Convention, shall be replaced by the Declaration set out in the Annex.

Done at Brussels,

For the Council
The President

ANNEX
DECLARATION BY THE EUROPEAN ATOMIC ENERGY COMMUNITY PURSUANT TO ARTICLE 30(4)(III) OF THE NUCLEAR SAFETY CONVENTION

The following States are at present members of the European Atomic Energy Community: the Kingdom of Belgium, the Kingdom of Denmark, the Federal Republic of Germany, the Hellenic Republic, the Kingdom of Spain, the French Republic, Ireland, the Italian Republic, the Grand Duchy of Luxembourg, the Kingdom of the Netherlands, the Republic of Austria, the Portuguese Republic, the Republic of Finland, the Kingdom of Sweden, the United Kingdom of Great Britain and Northern Ireland.

The Community declares that Articles 1 to 5, Article 7 and Articles 14 to 35 of the Convention apply to it.

The Community possesses competences, shared with the abovementioned Member States, in the fields covered by Article 7 and Articles 14 to 19 of the Convention as provided for by the Treaty establishing the European Atomic Energy Community in Article 2(b) and the relevant Articles of Title II, Chapter 3, entitled "Health and Safety".

THE IAEA STANDARDS ON NUCLEAR SAFETY AND RADIATION PROTECTION

Under Article III of its statute IAEA is empowered inter alia "to establish or adopt ....standards of safety for protection of health and minimisation of danger to life and property......" in connection with the peaceful use of ionising radiation. The "standards" in general are defined to include "norms, regulations or recommendations", besides, three types of "Agency's standards" are foreseen, that is a) basic safety standards, b) specialized regulations, c) codes of practice, those under b) and c) being considered as detailed operational standards. There exist in addition the so called "related instruments" (to the standards), which include manuals and guides, notes and addenda, and reports. All the above gives a good idea of the IAEA's extremely vast and articulated normative output, which ranges from basic to specific ones on particular activities and practices. Given the impossibility of publishing here these innumerable and massive documents, we refer to them as published by IAEA itself.

Although it is recalled that all these norms belong as a whole to the category of "recommendations", i.e. not legally binding, their technical and scientific relevance should be stressed, which means they are as a rule taken into account in national regimes independently of their non-binding nature. Moreover, it should be pointed out that the Agency's standards mentioned above are promulgated under the authority of the IAEA Board of Governors (i.e. approved by it) given their importance in regulating fundamental issues or activities, such as basic safety standards for radiation protection, safe transport of radioactive materials, safe handling of radio-nuclides , etc.

Independently of their qualification among the various standards referred to above, a considerable part of them has been adopted in a "Safety Series" numbered progressively, concerned with the safety issue and covering practically the whole range of nuclear safety and radiation protection requirements.

The standards are often adopted, where appropriate, in consultation and/or jointly with other international organisations such as the OECD Nuclear Energy Agency, the World Health Organisation, etc. The scientific basis to the IAEA's standards on radiation protection is provided by the ICRP recommendations (see further on in this volume).

THE NEA STANDARDS ON RADIATION PROTECTION

Under Article 11 of its statute, NEA (formerly ENEA, see introductory material) is to promote the elaboration and harmonisation of legislation governing nuclear energy in Member States of the Agency, in particular as regards, inter alia, protection of public health and prevention of accidents in nuclear industry. Similarly to the IAEA, also the NEA's technical standards belong to the category of "recommendations", i.e. non-binding norms, and they are commonly acknowledged as highly important standards, in fact often the sole reference standards in certain practices of nuclear industry and ionising radiation.

It is useful to point out that, although there seems to be some sort of overlapping in the normative action carried out by international organisations, in actual fact these work in close co-operation not only for the purpose of ensuring consistency among their standards, but also to the effect of addressing areas, activities and practices without creating "duplications". It should be added that, on one hand the respective "institutional framework" in which these organisations act, and practical experience on the other hand, result in a sort of "tacit agreement" by which certain areas have been/are traditionally addressed by one organisation, while other areas (e.g. some specific issues) are left to the other organisation to deal with. This is the case of NEA, whose standards are mostly concerned with particular issues such as for example the use of products containing radio-nuclides available to the public.

As for the EAEC (Euratom) and IAEA, also the NEA basic standards (Radiation Protection Norms) are regarded as an important reference text, which is largely consistent with other similar standards. Indeed, both the radiation protection norms and a number of other specific standards are to the extent necessary laid down in co-operation with IAEA, WHO, FAO, etc. Although the NEA's normative output (Radiation Protection Norms, guides, manuals and reports) is not comparable in vastness to IAEA's, it was deemed opportune to omit its publication in this volume, and simply stress that they represent a very useful (although non-binding) reference set of radiation protection standards in the activities and practices they consider.

THE ILO NORMS ON HEALTH PROTECTION OF WORKERS

As the highest international organisation and specialised United Nations institution responsible for the development of legislation on working conditions and protection of workers, the International Labour Organisation (ILO, headquartered in Geneva, Switzerland)) is also concerned with the particular problems associated to the various applications of nuclear energy and ionising radiation.

An important legal instrument was in fact adopted on June 22, 1960, on protection of workers against ionising radiation, known as Convention 115, and entered into force on June 17, 1962. This Convention was supplemented by Recommendation 114 (adopted jointly on the same date) and was amended in 1973. These texts are published in the following pages given their original importance in the radiation protection arena, though it should be added that, given the existence of more specific and similarly binding instruments (such as, for example, the Euratom Basic Standards) addressing radiation protection of workers, the Convention may be considered "de facto" superseded at least as far as the European Union is concerned. However, its application is certainly not discontinued as to the other countries in the world which are parties to the Convention, especially those which are not bound to any other international instrument governing radiation protection of workers.

Apart from collaborating with the IAEA in laying down the Agency's Basic Safety Standards, ILO has moreover adopted some guides, codes, reports etc. on specific activities and practices involving radiation protection of workers.

THE WHO RECOMMENDATIONS ON HEALTH PROTECTION OF THE PUBLIC

These Recommendations are adopted by the World Health Organization (WHO) in the framework of its general competence in the domain of public health. WHO (headquartered in Geneva, Switzerland) is a specialised agency of the United Nations and its recommendations on radiation protection are often adopted in co-operation with the IAEA (Basic Safety Standards), NEA, ILO, the Food and Agriculture Organization (FAO) and ICRP (the International Commission on Radiological Protection, see further on in this volume). Again in order to avoid overburdening the volume, we simply refer to the recommendations as published by WHO itself.

THE ICRP RECOMMENDATIONS ON RADIOLOGICAL PROTECTION (1959-2004)

The International Commission on Radiological Protection is a non-governmental organisation headquartered in London. As briefly mentioned several times in the preceding pages mainly in connection with radiation protection standards adopted by Euratom, IAEA and NEA, the ICRP has a guiding role in laying down the "philosophy" of and in reflecting the most recent scientific developments in radiological protection. Its Recommendations provide therefore the scientific background to international and national standards and legislation, all the more since they address not only basic principles and criteria, but also the very many practices involving ionising radiation and radiation protection related thereto. Despite their non-binding nature, these Recommendations have therefore a considerable impact on the corresponding standards adopted by the international governmental organisations and a large influence also on national legal and regulatory regimes of radiological protection.

The origin of ICRP dates back to 1928, when an International Committee for Protection against X-rays and Radium was created, following a decision by the Second International Conference on Radiology. In 1950 the Committee was restructured and took the present name, the former event being related to the need for coping with radiological protection issues arising from the new applications of nuclear energy and ionising radiation. Since then, ICRP has been engaged in a more and more intensive work reflected in its Recommendations, which by now cover an extremely wide range of activities and practices. These norms are contained in publications which are numbered progressively. The members of the Commission are very highly qualified experts in the various disciplines relating to radiation protection, such as radiology, nuclear medicine, biology, radiobiology, physics, chemistry, hygiene, public health and so on.

It should be pointed out that among the vast output of recommendations adopted, the publications devoted to general principles and criteria in radiological protection occupy an outstanding place. The first set of recommendations (Publication 1) appeared in 1959, followed by Publication 6 in 1964, Publication 9 in 1966, Publication 26 in 1977 and lastly Publication 60 in 1990. It is also important to add that ICRP works in close collaboration with ICRU (International Commission on Radiation Units and Measurements), a twin organisation headquartered in Washington, and has official relations with the WHO and IAEA. Besides, it has important links with the ILO, UNSCEAR (the United Nations Scientific Committee on the Effects of Atomic Radiation), the Commission of the European

Communities, the NEA, the IRPA (the International Radiological Protection Association) etc.

Due to the considerable size and number of the Publications in point, here we must yet stress the special importance of Publication no. 60 as the latest comprehensive set of recommendations on radiation protection as a whole. It is noted that ICRP is currently working on a further revision of this basic document, which should be issued in the course of 2006.

CHAPTER THREE
NUCLEAR THIRD PARTY LIABILITY

INTERNATIONAL CONVENTIONS ON NUCLEAR THIRD PARTY LIABILITY, OTHER RELATED INSTRUMENTS AND ACTS (1960-2004)

The reasons for creating a special regime of third party liability for compensation of damage resulting from a nuclear incident are manifold. First, it did not seem possible to apply unlimited liability to nuclear operators indefinitely; secondly, it was considered necessary to overcome, by introducing a qualitatively stricter regime for operators (causal liability), the serious difficulties for the victims of an incident to prove nuclear damage and its cause, given the extremely sophisticated safety standards applied to nuclear installations; in third place, it was also necessary to protect legally all those associated with the construction or operation of nuclear installations (suppliers of services, equipment, materials). In the absence of a specific regime, the ordinary tort law would apply, with imaginable consequences on the persons directly or indirectly concerned with the construction or operation of nuclear installations, as well as on the compensation aspects: all this would neither help the victims of a nuclear incident, nor a regular and smooth development of nuclear energy.

The special regime in point set up a system envisaging a liability which is strict (i.e. "channelled" onto the operator) and absolute (i.e. irrespective of fault, therefore without any burden of proof being put on the victims). At the same time, an obligation was put on the operator to cover the installation by means of financial security up to a certain (minimum) amount for the eventuality of an incident. A second level of coverage was envisaged up to a higher (minimum) amount, for the case where the consequences of an incident would be such that they could not be covered by the operator's security: this second amount would be dealt with by the State where the installation causing the incident is situated (referred to as the "the installation State"). Obviously, also the eventuality of an incident with consequences going beyond the coverage ensured by the installation State was considered, which led to a coverage system supplementing the basic one, by the creation of an international fund provided by the States party to such supplementing system.

There are mainly two regimes in place, one "regional" in character and the other one worldwide in scope, based on various conventions adopted under the aegis of the Nuclear Energy Agency in Paris and of the International Atomic Energy Agency in Vienna. Indeed, the first convention ever in this domain is due to the Paris Agency and dates back to 1960. In 1963, two more conventions were adopted, one (the Brussels Convention, supplementary to Paris) together with the latter featuring the "regional" system recalled above, and the other (the Vienna Convention) worldwide in scope, which set up a similar "universal" system. It should be noted that at least so far various countries with a very strong nuclear programme (such as for ex. the United States or Japan) are not contracting parties to any of the existing Conventions on nuclear liability.

A number of amending instruments were adopted in 1964, 1982 (amendments to the Paris Convention and the Brussels Supplementary Convention), 1988 (Joint Protocol to Paris and Vienna), 1997 (amendments to the Vienna Convention) and 2004 (further amendments to the Paris and Brussels Conventions). This covered a very long time-span during which important changes were made, in order to adjust those instruments to the pertinent developments occurred and to ensure as much uniformity as possible internationally; besides and more importantly, the Chernobyl incident (1986), an event entailing large-scale damage, did show that the existing liability regime was inadequate to ensure compensation in a rapid and equitable manner. However, the basic principles remain unchanged throughout the several amendments and indeed represent the fundamental features of the system. This applies also to some specific Conventions on liability of operators of nuclear ships (1962) and on civil liability in the field of maritime carriage of nuclear material (1971).

In the following pages the instruments in point are published. It is barely necessary to recall that reading the respective introductory material is essential to secure a better understanding of the relevant links and problems. It should be borne in mind that, at least as far as the Paris and the Brussels Supplementary Conventions are concerned, the previous instruments will obviously continue to be the only applicable ones until the entry into force of their respective amending Protocols. The Introductory Material to the instruments published here highlights the main changes contained in such Protocols.

PROTOCOL TO AMEND THE PARIS CONVENTION ON THIRD PARTY LIABILITY IN THE FIELD OFNUCLEAR ENERGY

(Paris, 12 February 2004)

1. A few months after the adoption of the amending Protocol to the Vienna Convention (1997) the contracting Parties (now 15) to the Paris Convention (PC), decided to revise it mainly on account of two reasons: the significant impact which the revision of the Vienna Convention would have on States party, who were also parties to the Joint Protocol (1988), to the two basic conventions, and the need to ensure the possibility for such States party wishing to do so to accede to the Supplementary Compensation Convention (1997). More in general, it was found necessary to ensure as much uniformity as possible over the relevant international regime.

When embarking on the task, the contracting Parties (to the PC) believed that it would be more effective and expedient to carry out the revision work as an "ad hoc" group within the NEA. Such work, which occupied nearly four years, was regular and intensive since many and often complex issues had to be tackled. It required also some informal sessions and multilateral consultations/negotiations, in order to find ways and means to accommodate certain specific needs of the different parties, and to adjust the new text to the changed reality since after the previous amendments (1982).

The main aims of the revision were to ensure greater financial compensation of damage in case of an incident (i.e. to compensate a larger number of victims, and to cover a broader range of damages suffered). Moreover, a number of modifications were agreed to implement decisions, recommendations or interpretations concerning the application of the Convention as they had been adopted by the NEA Steering Committee since the 1982 revision. Finally, the modifications were intended to make the new Paris (and Brussels) regime(s) compatible with the other equally new instruments such as the Protocol to amend the Vienna Convention and the Supplementary Compensation Convention.

The major improvement in the revised Convention is the increase in the liability amounts, in particular those for which the operator will be liable: such amounts (minimum, to accommodate some countries which have established a national regime of unlimited liability for nuclear operators) are in the amended text 700 million euros as compared to (a maximum of) 15 million Special Drawing Rights, SDR (previously adopted under the International Monetary Fund). This considerable increase is due not only to the need for creating more uniform conditions vis-à-vis the revised Vienna Convention, but also to other factors such as the increased capacity of the insurance market, the expanded concept of nuclear damage and the expanded geographical scope. The revision includes also a change to the Convention's unit of account, the **euro** *having become the single currency in the European Monetary Union as of January 2002 (exception made for Denmark, Sweden and the United Kingdom). The minimum amount of 5 million SDR for incidents arising from low-risk installations and from the transport of nuclear substances is raised to (a minimum of) 70 million and 80 million euros respectively.*

It should be pointed out that, following the amendments, some specific phasing-in provisions make it possible for States joining the Convention to limit the operator's liability amount to 350 million euros for a limited time period. Clearly, such provisions are intended to attract those States with less ample financial resources. However, a State intending to make use of the phasing-in "benefit" must ensure that, where necessary, it will make funds available to cover the difference up to 700 million euros.

Attention is also drawn to the more detailed definition of "nuclear damage" (obviously of paramount importance when applying the Convention to an actual incident) and to the extension of the geographical scope. As to the former, the inclusion of new heads of damage entails that national regimes will have to provide for correspondingly, although some flexibility is accorded to the law of the (national) competent court in determining the extent of damage in terms of economic (and certain other) losses or the cost of (reasonable) preventive measures also for reinstating an impaired environment. This new approach is one of the consequences of the Chernobyl incident, which showed how such damage was likely to be a major resulting portion. As regards the geographical scope, it is recalled that the amended Convention applies also to non-contracting State (including maritime zone or on board a ship or aircraft registered by that State), provided that it is a party to the Vienna Convention and to the Joint Protocol, or it has no nuclear installation on its own territory, or it has nuclear liability legislation affording equivalent reciprocal benefits.

It should be added that the new definition of nuclear installation includes radioactive waste disposal facilities both in their pre-closure and post-closure phase. The prescription/extinction period for nuclear damage claims is extended to 30 years (formerly 10) in case of loss of life and personal injury, while for other types of damage the period of 10 years is retained.
The text of the amending Protocol (entry into force after ratification by at least 5 countries) is published in the following pages.

2. While the Paris Convention was being revised, three instruments, pertaining to European Union law and the implications of which are certainly worth recalling here, became relevant in respect of the regime laid down by the Convention. Two were adopted in 2001 and 2004, the third one was still under discussion at the time of finalization of this volume.

2.1. In connection with the 2001 instrument just mentioned, the problem arose when the revision work of the Paris Convention (PC) had reached its pre-final stage. In mid-2001 the Council of the European (Economic) Community adopted a Regulation (no. 44/01) on jurisdiction, which confers exclusive external competence upon the European Community in matters of jurisdiction and recognition and enforcement of judgements. The result is that the EC member States are no longer competent to negotiate and adopt, in their international agreements, jurisdiction rules differing from those set out in the Regulation. Although Denmark put a reservation that it would not be bound by the Regulation, this was an instrument intended to create uniform conditions in the matter of jurisdiction within the Union. On the other hand, the PC itself had traditionally been concerned with jurisdiction, by stipulating that the courts of the State where the nuclear incident takes place (the "Installation State") are the only ones competent to judge on the damage and associated compensation as the case may be. In addition, a Recommendation (see further on in this Chapter) was adopted by the NEA Steering Committee in 1990, whereby contracting Parties were called upon to provide, in national legislation, for a single court to rule on compensation claims. Indeed, the revised Convention does include provisions to the effect recommended in 1990, the reason for this being to "protect" victims more strongly by avoiding their having to apply to more than one court and being confronted with the associated uncertainties. The Regulation, on the contrary, contemplates the competence of the State where the victims of an incident are located or, more in general, where the damage has occurred.

The conflict was triggered by the fact that the revised Convention, similarly to what is stipulated by the Amending Protocol to the Vienna Convention, includes provisions granting jurisdiction to the (contracting) Party in whose Exclusive Economic Zone (EEZ, in general the maritime zone between the boundary of the territorial sea of a given country and the 200 miles line offshore) a nuclear incident has taken place. It would seem clear enough that the introduction of the "new" notion of EEZ, not appearing in the previous Convention since it had not yet been addressed by international law, represents no real innovation to the jurisdiction principle traditionally recognised not only in the PC, but also in the other existing international instruments on nuclear third party liability. In fact, the provisions on jurisdiction relating to the EEZ were regarded by the contracting Parties to the PC as a simple extension of the Convention basic principle to the EEZ. The Parties also felt that applying the EC Regulation provisions to rule on jurisdiction under the Convention would upset a regime already in force for over forty years, where the competence of the "Installation State" had been a pillar of this special regime. Moreover, it should be borne in mind that some States (Austria, Ireland, Luxembourg) in the European Union are not contracting Parties to the PC. Last, but not least, the Regulation does include a provision to the effect that the international agreements are not affected by the new EC regime on jurisdiction: however, the interpretation of this provision is not crystal clear as to whether it will apply only to existing or to future instruments as well.

Several months were spent in a debate involving, on the one side, the EC services insisting on full application of the Regulation and, on the other side, the contracting Parties pleading for the full preservation of the special regime and stressing the need for not paving the way to complications and indeed potential detriment to the victims of an incident. During this long debate, in which also the Civil Law Committee of the European Union Council was involved, mainly two possible alternative solutions were eventually considered, one providing for authorization of the EU member States at the same time contracting Parties to the PC to sign the amending Protocol "in the interest" of the Community, the other for authorization of those EU members/contracting Parties to ratify or to accede to the Protocol also "on behalf" of the Community. This option would have entailed that contracting Parties/EU member States would not be bound to judicial decisions taken in non-contracting Parties/EU members States, a perspective clearly in contrast with the uniformity pursued by the Regulation. Nor would the relations between contracting Parties to the PC and to the Vienna Convention have benefited from that option, given the links existing between these conventions by virtue of the 1988 Joint Protocol.

Further consultations and reflection led finally to opting for the former solution, based on EC rules governing judicial co-operation in civil matters and the procedures to be followed for conclusion of agreements between the Community and one or more States or international organizations. The instrument found mostly suitable in the end consists in a Council Decision (no. 882/EC, adopted on November 27, 2003) authorizing member States also contracting Parties to the PC to sign the Protocol in the interest of the European Community (without prejudice to the position of Austria, Ireland and Luxembourg for the reasons recalled above). As a second step, another Council Decision (no.294/EC, March 8, 2004) was adopted to authorize the above member States/contracting Parties to ratify (or accede to) the PC in the interest of the Community. These two Decisions are not published here for the sake of brevity, but their importance is stressed since they set up a precedent in EU legislation.

2.2. Another instrument seems to be the source of a potential conflict with the Paris Convention (PC), and that is the (Council and European Parliament) draft Regulation known as "Rome II" addressing the applicable law on non-contractual obligations. Discussions on this draft Regulation were still in full spate while this volume was being prepared; therefore attention is drawn here to the possible problems arising from the draft text under discussion. The "Rome II" Regulation addresses civil and commercial cases involving a conflict of laws.

Firstly, it is noted that in principle the application of the future Regulation to non-contractual obligations arising from nuclear damage is excluded: indeed, the explanatory memorandum to the Regulation refers to such exclusion on account of the important economic and state interests at stake, as well as the of the contribution by member States to measures for compensating nuclear damage within the international third party liability framework as per the relevant conventions. On the other hand, the memorandum stresses that exclusions should be interpreted in a restrictive sense.

Thus, in the absence of a specific exclusion relating to the nuclear sector, circumstances falling within the scope of the PC would give rise to conflicting provisions in various respects, namely:

- *Based on article 14(b) of the PC, the competent court would apply not only this Convention but also its own legislation to cases not specifically covered by it: this means that a conflict would arise if such legislation were not the same as that of the country where the damage had occurred, since the Regulation does not take into account the legislation of the country where damage was originated (as stipulated by the Convention);*

- *Based on article 13(b) of the PC, where the place of the incident may not be determined with certainty, jurisdiction pertains to the courts of the contracting Party on whose territory the installation of the liable operator is located: again, one would be faced with conflicting provisions, unless that operator were subject to the same jurisdiction of the place where the damage was originated;*

- *Based on article 25 of the (draft) Regulation, this is applied without prejudice to international conventions to which member States of the EU are contracting Parties when the Regulation is adopted and which, in relation to specific matters, stipulate provisions on the conflict of laws concerning non-contractual obligations: although this seems to preserve the application of the conventions mentioned above, it is not altogether clear whether the "exemption" refers to all international conventions, since the explanatory memorandum only recalls two (non nuclear-related) instruments intended specifically to harmonize provisions of conflict of laws in specific legal matters. Yet, the PC does provide (articles 13-14) for jurisdiction proper as well as for applicable law, and therefore it should in principle benefit from the "exemption" under article 25 of the Regulation.*

So far we have been referring to the PC in its present form, but it should be pointed out that the potential conflict such as illustrated would affect also the amending Protocol to the PC. Indeed, if the in principle exclusion recalled at the outset of this paragraph were not to be kept in the final text of the Regulation, its article 25 would have no impact on the Convention: in fact, unless the aforesaid Protocol enters into force prior to the adoption of the Regulation in point (which is quite improbable since the former obviously requires the necessary number of ratifying countries) article 25 would not apply; secondly, given that article 14(b) of the amended Convention excludes the application of national provisions addressing the conflict of laws, such Convention does not appear to be among international conventions to which article 25 would definitely apply.

As for the issue discussed in the previous paragraph, it is clear that an adequate solution needs to be found in order to avoid problems when both the amended Convention and the Regulation become effective.

2.3. The third instrument having a potential impact on the PC is the (Council and European Parliament) draft Directive on environmental liability and compensation for damage to the environment. The problem is related to potential conflicting obligations (between the Directive and the PC) resulting from the inclusion of activities involving ionising radiation within the scope of the Directive.

Originally, the draft Directive included a "nuclear exclusion clause", to the effect that the directive would not apply to nuclear risk or damage to the environment in respect of which liability or compensation is covered by international instruments listed in an Annex V to the directive, which included the existing conventions on nuclear liability addressed in this Chapter. This exclusion was intended to preserve a specific regime (which had been in force for several decades), thus avoiding overlapping and/or conflicting provisions, and at the same time preserving the uniformity which that regime aims at ensuring as far as possible internationally (also bearing in mind that not all the contracting Parties to the PC are members of the EU). It is recalled (see above Introductory Material) that the revised Convention does address damage to the environment, although subject to certain conditions.

Following discussions and amendments to the draft directive within the EU Council and the European Parliament (the latter, as for the Regulation discussed under para. 2.2, sharing legislative powers with the Council in this matter), the application of the Directive was however extended to cases where the relevant international convention (on nuclear liability) has not yet entered into force. Consequently, the exclusion mentioned before would not apply to the Protocol amending the PC (unless this enters into force before the directive takes effect, an unlikely event for the reasons recalled in previous para. 2). The amendments provided also for a "gap analysis" to be developed (following the entry into force of the Directive) by the European Commission, which might lead to proposals on the application of the Directive to environmental damage where the relevant international conventions do not require liability for that damage.

As a further step, the Council adopted a so called "common position" (September 2003), hopefully to be shared by the Parliament, on the draft Directive, by which nuclear activities would be in principle excluded from its scope and Annex V (see above) would be retained. In addition, "a review clause" would require the European Commission to submit both to the Parliament and the Council a report on the application of the nuclear exclusion clause (the report including also the extent to which the conventions under Annex V have entered into force and been modified). The issue became even more important when considering that, besides EU member States that were also parties to the PC, there were States acceding to the EU which were parties to the Vienna Convention. It seemed fairly clear that if the Protocol(s) amending the PC (and the Brussels Supplementary Convention) had been duly ratified and had taken effect, the adequacy of the international nuclear liability regime vis-à-vis the Directive could have been considered more favourably. This obviously implied that the latter should not refer to amendments to the Paris and the Vienna conventions. In any case, clearly what was needed was a solution which would avoid difficulties in the interpretation and above all the overlapping of regimes within the contracting Parties to the conventions. The persisting difference in the approach between Council and Parliament led to the "conciliation procedure" provided for by EC rules under such circumstances. This procedure was started in early 2004 and resulted in an agreement largely based on the "common position" recalled before, which excludes nuclear risks from the Directive (EC/2004/35), and the deadline for the Commission's report was set at ten years after its entry into force (30 April 2004).

PROTOCOL

TO AMEND THE CONVENTION ON THIRD PARTY LIABILITY IN THE FIELD OF NUCLEAR ENERGY OF 29 JULY 1960, AS AMENDED BY THE ADDITIONAL PROTOCOL OF 28 JANUARY 1964 AND BY THE PROTOCOL OF 16 NOVEMBER 1982

THE GOVERNMENTS of the Federal Republic of Germany, the Kingdom of Belgium, the Kingdom of Denmark, the Kingdom of Spain, the Republic of Finland, the French Republic, the Hellenic Republic, the Italian Republic, the Kingdom of Norway, the Kingdom of the Netherlands, the Portuguese Republic, the United Kingdom of Great Britain and Northern Ireland, the Republic of Slovenia, the Kingdom of Sweden, the Swiss Confederation and the Republic of Turkey;

CONSIDERING that it is desirable to amend the Convention on Third Party Liability in the Field of Nuclear Energy, concluded at Paris on 29 July 1960 within the framework of the Organisation for European Economic Co-operation, now the Organisation for Economic Co-operation and Development, as amended by the Additional Protocol signed at Paris on 28 January 1964 and by the Protocol signed at Paris on 16 November 1982;

HAVE AGREED as follows:

I.

The Convention on Third Party Liability in the Field of Nuclear Energy of 29 July 1960, as amended by the Additional Protocol of 28 January 1964 and by the Protocol of 16 November 1982, shall be amended as follows:

A. Sub-paragraphs (*i*) and (*ii*) of paragraph (*a*) of Article 1 shall be replaced by the following text:

i) "A nuclear incident" means any occurrence or series of occurrences having the same origin which causes nuclear damage.
ii) "Nuclear installation" means reactors other than those comprised in any means of transport; factories for the manufacture or processing of nuclear substances; factories for the separation of isotopes of nuclear fuel; factories for the reprocessing of irradiated nuclear fuel; facilities for the storage of nuclear substances other than storage incidental to the carriage of such substances; installations for the disposal of nuclear substances; any such reactor, factory, facility or installation that is in the course of being decommissioned; and such other installations in which there are nuclear fuel or radioactive products or waste as the Steering Committee for Nuclear Energy of the Organisation (hereinafter referred to as the "Steering Committee") shall from time to time determine; any Contracting Party may determine that two or more nuclear installations of one operator which are located on the same site shall, together with any other premises on that site where nuclear fuel or radioactive products or waste are held, be treated as a single nuclear installation.

B. Four new sub-paragraphs (*vii*), (*viii*), (*ix*) and (*x*), shall be added to paragraph (*a*) of Article 1 as follows:

vii) "Nuclear damage" means,
1. loss of life or personal injury;
2. loss of or damage to property;
and each of the following to the extent determined by the law of the competent court,
3. economic loss arising from loss or damage referred to in sub-paragraph *1* or *2* above insofar as not included in those sub-paragraphs, if incurred by a person entitled to claim in respect of such loss or damage;

4. the costs of measures of reinstatement of impaired environment, unless such impairment is insignificant, if such measures are actually taken or to be taken, and insofar as not included in sub-paragraph *2* above;
5. loss of income deriving from a direct economic interest in any use or enjoyment of the environment, incurred as a result of a significant impairment of that environment, and insofar as not included in sub-paragraph *2* above;
6. the costs of preventive measures, and further loss or damage caused by such measures,
in the case of sub-paragraphs *1* to *5* above, to the extent that the loss or damage arises out of or results from ionising radiation emitted by any source of radiation inside a nuclear installation, or emitted from nuclear fuel or radioactive products or waste in, or of nuclear substances coming from, originating in, or sent to, a nuclear installation, whether so arising from the radioactive properties of such matter, or from a combination of radioactive properties with toxic, explosive or other hazardous properties of such matter.

viii) "Measures of reinstatement" means any reasonable measures which have been approved by the competent authorities of the State where the measures were taken, and which aim to reinstate or restore damaged or destroyed components of the environment, or to introduce, where reasonable, the equivalent of these components into the environment. The legislation of the State where the nuclear damage is suffered shall determine who is entitled to take such measures.

ix) "Preventive measures" means any reasonable measures taken by any person after a nuclear incident or an event creating a grave and imminent threat of nuclear damage has occurred, to prevent or minimise nuclear damage referred to in sub-paragraphs *(a)(vii) 1* to *5*, subject to any approval of the competent authorities required by the law of the State where the measures were taken.

x) "Reasonable measures" means measures which are found under the law of the competent court to be appropriate and proportionate, having regard to all the circumstances, for example:

1. the nature and extent of the nuclear damage incurred or, in the case of preventive measures, the nature and extent of the risk of such damage;
2. the extent to which, at the time they are taken, such measures are likely to be effective; and
3. relevant scientific and technical expertise.

C. Article 2 shall be replaced by the following text:

a) This Convention shall apply to nuclear damage suffered in the territory of, or in any maritime zones established in accordance with international law of, or, except in the territory of a non-Contracting State not mentioned under (*ii*) to (*iv*) of this paragraph, on board a ship or aircraft registered by,
i) a Contracting Party;
ii) a non-Contracting State which, at the time of the nuclear incident, is a Contracting Party to the Vienna Convention on Civil Liability for Nuclear Damage of 21 May 1963 and any amendment thereto which is in force for that Party, and to the Joint Protocol relating to the Application of the Vienna Convention and the Paris Convention of 21 September 1988, provided however, that the Contracting Party to the Paris Convention in whose territory the installation of the operator liable is situated is a Contracting Party to that Joint Protocol;
iii) a non-Contracting State which, at the time of the nuclear incident, has no nuclear installation in its territory or in any maritime zones established by it in accordance with international law; or
iv) any other non-Contracting State which, at the time of the nuclear incident, has in force nuclear liability legislation which affords equivalent reciprocal benefits, and which is based on principles identical to those of this Convention, including, inter alia, liability without fault of the operator liable, exclusive liability of the operator or a provision to the same effect, exclusive jurisdiction of the competent court, equal treatment of all victims of a nuclear incident, recognition and enforcement of judgements, free transfer of compensation, interests and costs.

b) Nothing in this Article shall prevent a Contracting Party in whose territory the nuclear installation of the operator liable is situated from providing for a broader scope of application of this Convention under its legislation.

D. Article 3 shall be replaced by the following text:

a) The operator of a nuclear installation shall be liable, in accordance with this Convention, for nuclear damage other than:
i) damage to the nuclear installation itself and any other nuclear installation, including a nuclear installation under construction, on the site where that installation is located; and
ii) damage to any property on that same site which is used or to be used in connection with any such installation,
upon proof that such damage was caused by a nuclear incident in such installation or involving nuclear substances coming from such installation, except as otherwise provided for in Article 4.

b) Where nuclear damage is caused jointly by a nuclear incident and by an incident other than a nuclear incident, that part of the damage which is caused by such other incident, shall, to the extent that it is not reasonably separable from the nuclear damage caused by the nuclear incident, be considered to be nuclear damage caused by the nuclear incident. Where nuclear damage is caused jointly by a nuclear incident and by an emission of ionising radiation not covered by this Convention, nothing in this Convention shall limit or otherwise affect the liability of any person in connection with that emission of ionising radiation.

E. Paragraphs (*c*) and (*d*) of Article 4 shall be renumbered as paragraphs (*d*) and (*e*) respectively and a new paragraph (*c*) shall be added to read as follows:

c) The transfer of liability to the operator of another nuclear installation pursuant to paragraphs (*a*)(*i*) and

(*ii*) and (*b*)(*i*) and (*ii*) of this Article may only take place if that operator has a direct economic interest in the nuclear substances that are in the course of carriage.

F. Paragraphs (*b*) and (*d*) of Article 5 shall be replaced by the following text:

b) Where, however, nuclear damage is caused by a nuclear incident occurring in a nuclear installation and involving only nuclear substances stored therein incidentally to their carriage, the operator of the nuclear installation shall not be liable where another operator or person is liable pursuant to Article 4.

d) If nuclear damage gives rise to liability of more than one operator in accordance with this Convention, the liability of these operators shall be joint and several, provided that where such liability arises as a result of nuclear damage caused by a nuclear incident involving nuclear substances in the course of carriage in one and the same means of transport, or, in the case of storage incidental to the carriage, in one and the same nuclear installation, the maximum total amount for which such operators shall be liable shall be the highest amount established with respect to any of them pursuant to Article 7. In no case shall any one operator be required, in respect of a nuclear incident, to pay more than the amount established with respect to him pursuant to Article 7.

G. Paragraphs (*c*), (*e*) and (*g*) of Article 6 shall be replaced by the following text:

c) *i*) Nothing in this Convention shall affect the liability:
1. of any individual for nuclear damage caused by a nuclear incident for which the operator, by virtue of Article 3(*a*) or Article 9, is not liable under this Convention and

which results from an act or omission of that individual done with intent to cause damage;
2. of a person duly authorised to operate a reactor comprised in a means of transport for nuclear damage caused by a nuclear incident when an operator is not liable for such damage pursuant to Article 4(*a*)(*iii*) or (*b*)(*iii*).
ii) The operator shall incur no liability outside this Convention for nuclear damage caused by a nuclear incident.

e) If the operator proves that the nuclear damage resulted wholly or partly either from the gross negligence of the person suffering the damage or from an act or omission of such person done with intent to cause damage, the competent court may, if national law so provides, relieve the operator wholly or partly from his obligation to pay compensation in respect of the damage suffered by such person.

g) If the operator has a right of recourse to any extent pursuant to paragraph (*f*) of this Article against any person, that person shall not, to that extent, have a right against the operator under paragraph (*d*) of this Article.

H. Article 7 shall be replaced by the following text:

a) Each Contracting Party shall provide under its legislation that the liability of the operator in respect of nuclear damage caused by any one nuclear incident shall not be less than 700 million euro.

b) Notwithstanding paragraph (*a*) of this Article and Article 21(*c*), any Contracting Party may,
i) having regard to the nature of the nuclear installation involved and to the likely consequences of a nuclear incident originating therefrom, establish a lower amount of liability for that installation, provided that in no event shall any amount so established be less than 70 million euro; and
ii) having regard to the nature of the nuclear substances involved and to the likely consequences of a nuclear incident originating therefrom, establish a lower amount of liability for the carriage of nuclear substances, provided that in no event shall any amount so established be less than 80 million euro.

c) Compensation for nuclear damage caused to the means of transport on which the nuclear substances involved were at the time of the nuclear incident shall not have the effect of reducing the liability of the operator in respect of other nuclear damage to an amount less than either 80 million euro, or any higher amount established by the legislation of a Contracting Party.

d) The amount of liability of operators of nuclear installations in the territory of a Contracting Party established in accordance with paragraph (*a*) or (*b*) of this Article or with Article 21(*c*), as well as the provisions of any legislation of a Contracting Party pursuant to paragraph (*c*) of this Article shall apply to the liability of such operators wherever the nuclear incident occurs.

e) A Contracting Party may subject the transit of nuclear substances through its territory to the condition that the maximum amount of liability of the foreign operator concerned be increased, if it considers that such amount does not adequately cover the risks of a nuclear incident in the course of the transit, provided that the maximum amount thus increased shall not exceed the maximum amount of liability of operators of nuclear installations situated in its territory.

f) The provisions of paragraph *(e)* of this Article shall not apply:
i)...to carriage by sea where, under international law, there is a right of entry in case of urgent distress into the ports of such Contracting Party or a right of innocent passage through its territory; or
ii)..to carriage by air where, by agreement or under international law, there is a right to fly over or land on the territory of such Contracting Party.

g) In cases where the Convention is applicable to a non-Contracting State in accordance with Article 2 (*a*)(*iv*), any Contracting Party may establish in respect of nuclear damage amounts of liability lower than the minimum amounts established under this Article or under Article 21(*c*) to the extent that such State does not afford reciprocal benefits of an equivalent amount.

h) Any interest and costs awarded by a court in actions for compensation under this Convention shall not be considered to be compensation for the purposes of this Convention and shall be payable by the operator in addition to any sum for which he is liable in accordance with this Article.

i) The sums mentioned in this Article may be converted into national currency in round figures.

j) Each Contracting Party shall ensure that persons suffering damage may enforce their rights to compensation without having to bring separate proceedings according to the origin of the funds provided for such compensation.

I. Article 8 shall be replaced by the following text:

a) The right of compensation under this Convention shall be subject to prescription or extinction if an action is not brought,
i) with respect to loss of life and personal injury, within thirty years from the date of the nuclear incident;
ii) with respect to other nuclear damage, within ten years from the date of the nuclear incident.

b) National legislation may, however, establish a period longer than that set out in sub-paragraph (*i*) or (*ii*) of paragraph (*a*) of this Article, if measures have been taken by the Contracting Party within whose territory the nuclear installation of the operator liable is situated to cover the liability of that operator in respect of any actions for compensation begun after the expiry of the period set out in sub-paragraph (*i*) or (*ii*) of paragraph (*a*) of this Article and during such longer period.

c) If, however, a longer period is established in accordance with paragraph (*b*) of this Article, an action for compensation brought within such period shall in no case affect the right of compensation under this Convention of any person who has brought an action against the operator,
i) within a thirty year period in respect of personal injury or loss of life;
ii) within a ten year period in respect of all other nuclear damage.

d) National legislation may establish a period of not less than three years for the prescription or extinction of rights of compensation under the Convention, determined from the date at which the person suffering nuclear damage had knowledge, or from the date at which that person ought reasonably to have known of both the nuclear damage and the operator liable, provided that the periods established pursuant to paragraphs (*a*) and (*b*) of this Article shall not be exceeded.

e) Where the provisions of Article 13(*f*) (*ii*) are applicable, the right of compensation shall not, however, be subject to prescription or extinction if, within the time provided for in paragraphs (*a*), (*b*) and (*d*) of this Article,
i) prior to the determination by the Tribunal referred to in Article 17, an action has been brought before any of the courts from which the Tribunal can choose; if the Tribunal determines that the competent court is a court other than that before which such action has already been brought, it may fix a date by which such action has to be brought before the competent court so determined; or
ii) a request has been made to a Contracting Party concerned to initiate a determination by the Tribunal of the competent court pursuant to Article 13(*f*) (*ii*) and an action is brought subsequent to such determination within such time as may be fixed by the Tribunal.

f) Unless national law provides to the contrary, any person suffering nuclear damage caused by a nuclear incident who has brought an action for compensation within the period provided for in this Article may amend his claim in respect of any aggravation of the nuclear damage after the expiry of such period, provided that final judgement has not been entered by the competent court.

J. Article 9 shall be replaced by the following text:

The operator shall not be liable for nuclear damage caused by a nuclear incident directly due to an act of armed conflict, hostilities, civil war, or insurrection.

K. Article 10 shall be replaced by the following text:

a) To cover the liability under this Convention, the operator shall be required to have and maintain insurance or other financial security of the amount established pursuant to Article 7(*a*) or 7(*b*) or Article 21(*c*) and of such type and terms as the competent public authority shall specify.

b) Where the liability of the operator is not limited in amount, the Contracting Party within whose territory the nuclear installation of the liable operator is situated shall establish a limit upon the financial security of the operator liable, provided that any limit so established shall not be less than the amount referred to in Article 7(*a*) or 7(*b*).

c) The Contracting Party within whose territory the nuclear installation of the liable operator is situated shall ensure the payment of claims for compensation for nuclear damage which have been established against the operator by providing the necessary funds to the extent that the insurance or other financial security is not available or sufficient to satisfy such claims, up to an amount not less than the amount referred to in Article 7(*a*) or Article 21(*c*).

d) No insurer or other financial guarantor shall suspend or cancel the insurance or other financial security provided for in paragraph (*a*) or (*b*) of this Article without giving notice in writing of at least two months to the competent public authority or, in so far as such insurance or other financial security relates to the carriage of nuclear substances, during the period of the carriage in question.

e) The sums provided as insurance, reinsurance, or other financial security may be drawn upon only for compensation for nuclear damage caused by a nuclear incident.

L. Article 12 shall be replaced by the following text:

Compensation payable under this Convention, insurance and reinsurance premiums, sums provided as insurance, reinsurance, or other financial security required pursuant to Article 10, and interest and costs referred to in Article 7(*h*), shall be freely transferable between the monetary areas of the Contracting Parties.

M. Article 13 shall be replaced by the following text:

a) Except as otherwise provided in this Article, jurisdiction over actions under Articles 3, 4 and 6(*a*) shall lie only with the courts of the Contracting Party in whose territory the nuclear incident occurred.

b) Where a nuclear incident occurs within the area of the exclusive economic zone of a Contracting Party or, if such a zone has not been established, in an area not exceeding the limits of an exclusive economic zone were one to be established, jurisdiction over actions concerning nuclear damage from that nuclear incident shall, for the purposes of this Convention, lie only with the courts of that Party, provided that the Contracting Party concerned has notified the Secretary-General of the Organisation of such area prior to the nuclear incident. Nothing in this paragraph shall be interpreted as permitting the exercise of jurisdiction or the delimitation of a maritime zone in a manner which is contrary to the international law of the sea.

c) Where a nuclear incident occurs outside the territory of the Contracting Parties, or where it occurs within an area in respect of which no notification has been given pursuant to paragraph (*b*) of this Article, or where the place of the nuclear incident cannot be determined with certainty, jurisdiction over such actions shall lie with the courts of the Contracting Party in whose territory the nuclear installation of the operator liable is situated.

d) Where a nuclear incident occurs in an area in respect of which the circumstances of Article 17(*d*) apply, jurisdiction shall lie with the courts determined, at the request of a Contracting Party concerned, by the Tribunal referred to in Article 17 as being the courts of that Contracting Party which is most closely related to and affected by the consequences of the incident.

e) The exercise of jurisdiction under this Article as well as the notification of an area made pursuant to paragraph (*b*) of this Article shall not create any right or obligation or set a precedent with respect to the delimitation of maritime areas between States with opposite or adjacent coasts.

f) Where jurisdiction would lie with the courts of more than one Contracting Party by virtue of paragraph (*a*), (*b*) or (*c*) of this Article, jurisdiction shall lie,

i) if the nuclear incident occurred partly outside the territory of any Contracting Party and partly in the territory of a single Contracting Party, with the courts of that Contracting Party; and
ii) in any other case, with the courts determined, at the request of a Contracting Party concerned, by the Tribunal referred to in Article 17 as being the courts of that Contracting Party which is most closely related to and affected by the consequences of the incident.

g) The Contracting Party whose courts have jurisdiction shall ensure that in relation to actions for compensation of nuclear damage:
i) any State may bring an action on behalf of persons who have suffered nuclear damage, who are nationals of that State or have their domicile or residence in its territory, and who have consented thereto; and
ii) any person may bring an action to enforce rights under this Convention acquired by subrogation or assignment.

h) The Contracting Party whose courts have jurisdiction under this Convention shall ensure that only one of its courts shall be competent to rule on compensation for nuclear damage arising from any one nuclear incident, the criteria for such selection being determined by the national legislation of such Contracting Party.

i) Judgements entered by the competent court under this Article after trial, or by default, shall, when they have become enforceable under the law applied by that court, become enforceable in the territory of any of the other Contracting Parties as soon as the formalities required by the Contracting Party concerned have been complied with. The merits of the case shall not be the subject of further proceedings. The foregoing provisions shall not apply to interim judgements.

j) If an action is brought against a Contracting Party under this Convention, such Contracting Party may not, except in respect of measures of execution, invoke any jurisdictional immunities before the court competent in accordance with this Article.

N. Paragraph (*b*) of Article 14 shall be replaced by the following text:

b) "National law" and "national legislation" mean the law or the national legislation of the court having jurisdiction under this Convention over claims arising out of a nuclear incident, excluding the rules on conflict of laws relating to such claims. That law or legislation shall apply to all matters both substantive and procedural not specifically governed by this Convention.

O. Paragraph (*b*) of Article 15 shall be replaced by the following text:

b) In so far as compensation for nuclear damage is in excess of the 700 million euro referred to in Article 7(*a*), any such measure in whatever form may be applied under conditions which may derogate from the provisions of this Convention.

P. A new Article 16bis shall be added after Article 16 as follows:

Article 16bis

This Convention shall not affect the rights and obligations of a Contracting Party under the general rules of public international law.

Q. Article 17 shall be replaced by the following text:

a) In the event of a dispute arising between two or more Contracting Parties concerning the interpretation or application of this Convention, the parties to the dispute shall consult with a view to settling the dispute by negotiation or other amicable means.

b) Where a dispute referred to in paragraph (*a*) is not settled within six months from the date upon which such dispute is acknowledged to exist by any party thereto, the Contracting Parties shall meet in order to assist the parties to the dispute to reach a friendly settlement.

c) Where no resolution to the dispute has been reached within three months of the meeting referred to in paragraph (*b*), the dispute shall, upon the request of any party thereto, be submitted to the European Nuclear Energy Tribunal established by the Convention of 20 December 1957 on the Establishment of a Security Control in the Field of Nuclear Energy.

d) Disputes concerning the delimitation of maritime boundaries are outside the scope of this Convention.

R. Article 18 shall be replaced by the following text:

a) Reservations to one or more of the provisions of this Convention may be made at any time prior to ratification, acceptance or approval of, or accession to, this Convention or prior to the time of notification under Article 23 in respect of any territory or territories mentioned in the notification, and shall be admissible only if the terms of these reservations have been expressly accepted by the Signatories.

b) Such acceptance shall not be required from a Signatory which has not itself ratified, accepted or approved this Convention within a period of twelve months after the date of notification to it of such reservation by the Secretary-General of the Organisation in accordance with Article 24.

c) Any reservation admitted in accordance with this Article may be withdrawn at any time by notification addressed to the Secretary-General of the Organisation.

S. Article 19 shall be replaced by the following text:

a) This Convention shall be subject to ratification, acceptance or approval. Instruments of ratification, acceptance or approval shall be deposited with the Secretary-General of the Organisation.

b) This Convention shall come into force upon the deposit of instruments of ratification, acceptance or approval by not less than five of the Signatories. For each Signatory ratifying, accepting or approving thereafter, this Convention shall come into force upon the deposit of its instrument of ratification, acceptance or approval.

T. Article 20 shall be replaced by the following text:

Amendments to this Convention shall be adopted by mutual agreement of all the Contracting Parties. They shall come into force when ratified, accepted or approved by two-thirds of the Contracting Parties. For each Contracting Party ratifying, accepting or approving thereafter, they shall come into force at the date of such ratification, acceptance or approval.

U. A new paragraph (*c*) shall be added to Article 21 to read as follows:

c) Notwithstanding Article 7(*a*), where a Government which is not a Signatory to this Convention accedes to this Convention after 1 January 1999, it may provide under its legislation that the liability of an operator in respect of nuclear damage caused by any one nuclear incident may be limited, for a maximum period of five years from the date of the adoption of the Protocol of 12 February 2004 to amend this Convention, to a transitional amount of not less than 350 million euro in respect of a nuclear incident occurring within that period.

V. Paragraph (*c*) of Article 22 shall be renumbered as paragraph (*d*) and a new paragraph (*c*) shall be added to read as follows:

c) The Contracting Parties shall consult each other at the expiry of each five year period following the date upon which this Convention comes into force, upon all problems of common interest raised by the application of this Convention, and in particular, to consider whether increases in the liability and financial security amounts under this Convention are desirable.

W. Paragraph (*b*) of Article 23 shall be replaced by the following text:

b) Any Signatory or Contracting Party may, at the time of signature, ratification, acceptance or approval of, or accession to, this Convention or at any later time, notify the Secretary-General of the Organisation that this Convention shall apply to those of its territories, including the territories for whose international relations it is responsible, to which this Convention is not applicable in accordance with paragraph (*a*) of this Article and which are mentioned in the notification. Any such notification may, in respect of any territory or territories mentioned therein, be withdrawn by giving twelve months' notice to that effect to the Secretary-General of the Organisation.

X. Article 24 shall be replaced with the following text:

The Secretary-General of the Organisation shall give notice to all Signatories and acceding Governments of the receipt of any instrument of ratification, acceptance, approval, accession or withdrawal, of any notification under Articles 13(*b*) and 23, of decisions of the Steering Committee under Article 1(*a*)(*ii*), 1(*a*)(*iii*) and 1(*b*), of the date on which this Convention comes into force, of the text of any amendment thereto and the date on which such amendment comes into force, and of any reservation made in accordance with Article 18.

Y. The term "damage" appearing in the following articles shall be replaced by the term "nuclear damage":

Article 4(*a*) and (*b*)
Article 5(*a*) and (*c*)
Article 6(*a*), (*b*), (*d*), (*f*) and (*h*)

Z. In the first sentence of Article 4 of the French text the word "stockage" shall be replaced by the word "entreposage", and in this same Article the word "transportées" is replaced by the words "en cours de transport". In paragraph (*h*) of Article 6 of the English text, the word "workmen's" shall be replaced by the word "workers'".

AA. Annex II of the Convention shall be deleted.

II.

a) The provisions of this Protocol shall, as between the Parties thereto, form an integral part of the Convention on Third Party Liability in the Field of Nuclear Energy of 29 July 1960, as amended by the Additional Protocol of 28 January 1964 and by the Protocol of 16 November 1982 (hereinafter referred to as the "Convention"), which shall be known as the "Convention on Third Party Liability in the Field of Nuclear Energy of 29 July 1960, as amended by the Additional Protocol of 28 January 1964, by the Protocol of 16 November 1982 and by the Protocol of 12 February 2004".

b) This Protocol shall be subject to ratification, acceptance or approval. An instrument of ratification, acceptance or approval shall be deposited with the Secretary-General of the Organisation for Economic Cooperation and Development.

c) The Signatories of this Protocol who have already ratified or acceded to the Convention express their intention to ratify, accept or approve this Protocol as soon as possible. The other Signatories of this Protocol undertake to ratify, accept or approve it at the same time as they ratify the Convention.

d) This Protocol shall be open for accession in accordance with the provisions of Article 21 of the Convention. Accessions to the Convention will be accepted only if they are accompanied by accession to this Protocol.

e) This Protocol shall come into force in accordance with the provisions of Article 20 of the Convention.

f) The Secretary-General of the Organisation for Economic Co-operation and Development shall give notice to all Signatories and acceding Governments of the receipt of any instrument of ratification, acceptance, approval or accession to this Protocol.

PROTOCOL TO AMEND THE BRUSSELS CONVENTION SUPPLEMENTARY TO THE PARIS CONVENTION

(Brussels, 12 February 2004)

Negotiations for the latest revision of the Brussels Convention (BSC) started at the beginning of 2000 (that is some two years after the negotiations for the revision of the Paris Convention, PC, had started) when the 11 contracting Parties (now 12) recognized that undertaking this task was necessary to ensure compatibility between the two conventions, and in particular to increase the supplementary funds to be made available, also considering the adoption of the Convention on Supplementary Compensation (CSC, 1997, see following pages) under the aegis of IAEA. The revision exercise was obviously carried out in parallel with the amendments to the PC.

In fact, given the similarities between the BSC and the CSC, various parts of the former are based on the latter: for example, the geographic scope of application in the amended BSC is expanded by similar provisions, including the Exclusive Economic Zone (EEZ) and the continental shelf of a contracting Party in connection with the exploitation or the exploration on the natural resources of that EEZ or shelf.

A "renovated" feature of the revised Paris/Brussels system as a whole in connection with the liability amounts, is that the revised BSC (unlike the previous and still applicable one, which provided for the third tier to be made available by its contracting Parties) provides for three tiers: the first one, equalling the 700 million euros of the revised PC and to be distributed according to that Convention; the second one, as previously from public funds, to be provided by the State where the accident has occurred (the "Installation State") from 700 up to 1,200 million euros; the third one, again from public funds, covering the difference between this sum and 1,500 million euros, this last amount thus being the total compensation available according to the Paris/Brussels system. It should be pointed out that since the second and third tiers are basically "public" money, they are intended only for potential victims in contracting States to the BSC. In case of use of the phasing-in provisions under the PC, the same conditions apply (see Introductory Material to PC) to the State involved.

Another important change under the revised Convention concerns the method of calculating the financial contribution to the third tier (which, it is worth stressing, is not pre-established but is mobilized only if the need arises, i.e. in the case of an actual incident). Such method was based on 50% of the gross domestic product and 50% of the installed nuclear capacity, whereas these figures are now 35% and 65% respectively, to reflect the degree of commitment on the part of individual States as far as nuclear power generation is concerned.

One more issue deserves to be recalled, i.e. the so called "reciprocity principle". Since the amount of compensation is determined by the liability amount imposed on the operator under national law, a victim might receive a higher or lower compensation from a foreign operator than he/she would from his/her own national operator. This would tamper with the non-discrimination provisions in the PC. On the other hand, although the PC itself provides also for derogation from such provisions in case of public funds intended to compensate damage above the liability amounts laid down for the operator (the so called "reference amounts"), in countries with an unlimited regime the funds to be distributed in application of the non-discrimination rule are still private (i.e. the operator's) funds. In order to overcome what was regarded as an unfair perspective, and at the same time to avoid that the "excess funds" be distributed contrary to the interests of the contracting Parties as a whole, an OECD Council Recommendation adopted together with the amending Protocol to the Convention is intended to avoid discrimination against victims of contracting States with no nuclear installation on their territory, or affording equivalent reciprocal benefits if having at least one nuclear installation.

The text of the amending Protocol (entry into force after ratification by 6 countries) is published here, the previous Convention remaining applicable until entry into force of the Protocol.

PROTOCOL

TO AMEND THE CONVENTION OF 31 JANUARY 1963 SUPPLEMENTARY TO THE PARIS CONVENTION OF 29 JULY 1960 ON THIRD PARTY LIABILITY IN THE FIELD OF NUCLEAR ENERGY, AS AMENDED BY THE ADDITIONAL PROTOCOL OF 28 JANUARY 1964 AND BY THE PROTOCOL OF 16 NOVEMBER 1982

THE GOVERNMENTS of the Federal Republic of Germany, the Kingdom of Belgium, the Kingdom of Denmark, the Kingdom of Spain, the Republic of Finland, the French Republic, the Italian Republic, the Kingdom of Norway, the Kingdom of the Netherlands, the United Kingdom of Great Britain and Northern Ireland, the Republic of Slovenia, the Kingdom of Sweden and the Swiss Confederation;

CONSIDERING that certain provisions of the Convention of 29 July 1960 on Third Party Liability in the Field of Nuclear Energy, as amended by the Additional Protocol of 28 January 1964 and by the Protocol of 16 November 1982, have been amended by the Protocol concluded at Paris on .12 February 2004, and of which they are Signatories;

CONSIDERING that it is desirable to amend also the Convention of 31 January 1963 Supplementary to the Paris Convention of 29 July 1960, as amended by the Additional Protocol of 28 January 1964 and by the Protocol of 16 November 1982;

HAVE AGREED as follows:

I.

The Convention of 31 January 1963 Supplementary to the Paris Convention of 29 July 1960 on Third Party Liability in the Field of Nuclear Energy, as amended by the Additional Protocol of 28 January 1964 and by the Protocol of 16 November 1982, is amended as follows:

A. The second paragraph of the Preamble shall be replaced by the following text:

BEING PARTIES to the Convention of 29 July 1960 on Third Party Liability in the Field of Nuclear Energy, concluded within the framework of the Organisation for European Economic Co-operation, now the Organisation for Economic Co-operation and Development, and as amended by the Additional Protocol concluded at Paris on 28 January 1964, by the Protocol concluded at Paris on 16 November 1982 and by the Protocol concluded at Paris on 12 February 2004 (hereinafter referred to as the "Paris Convention");

B. Article 2 shall be replaced by the following text:

Article 2

a) The system of this Convention shall apply to nuclear damage for which an operator of a nuclear installation, used for peaceful purposes, situated in the territory of a Contracting Party to this Convention (hereinafter referred to as a "Contracting Party"), is liable under the Paris Convention, and which is suffered:
i) in the territory of a Contracting Party; or
ii) in or above maritime areas beyond the territorial sea of a Contracting Party
1. on board or by a ship flying the flag of a Contracting Party, or on board or by an aircraft registered in the territory of a Contracting Party, or on or by an artificial island, installation or structure under the jurisdiction of a Contracting Party, or
2. by a national of a Contracting Party,

excluding damage suffered in or above the territorial sea of a State not Party to this Convention; or
iii) in or above the exclusive economic zone of a Contracting Party or on the continental shelf of a Contracting Party in connection with the exploitation or the exploration of the natural resources of that exclusive economic zone or continental shelf,
provided that the courts of a Contracting Party have jurisdiction pursuant to the Paris Convention.
b) Any Signatory or acceding Government may, at the time of signature of or accession to this Convention or on the deposit of its instrument of ratification, acceptance or approval declare that, for the purposes of the application of paragraph (*a*)(*ii*) *2* of this Article, individuals or certain categories thereof, considered under its law as having their habitual residence in its territory, are assimilated to its own nationals.
c) In this Article, the expression "a national of a Contracting Party" shall include a Contracting Party or any of its constituent sub-divisions, or a partnership, or any public or private body whether corporate or not, established in the territory of a Contracting Party.

C. Article 3 shall be replaced by the following text:

Article 3

a) Under the conditions established by this Convention, the Contracting Parties undertake that compensation in respect of nuclear damage referred to in Article 2 shall be provided up to the amount of 1 500 million euro per nuclear incident, subject to the application of Article 12bis.
b) Such compensation shall be provided as follows:
i) up to an amount of at least 700 million euro, out of funds provided by insurance or other financial security or out of public funds provided pursuant to Article 10(*c*) of the Paris Convention, such amount to be established under the legislation of the Contracting Party in whose territory the nuclear installation of the operator liable is situated, and to be distributed, up to 700 million euro, in accordance with the Paris Convention;
ii) between the amount referred to in paragraph (*b*)(*i*) of this Article and 1 200 million euro out of public funds to be made available by the Contracting Party in whose territory the nuclear installation of the operator liable is situated;
iii) between 1 200 million euro and 1 500 million euro, out of public funds to be made available by the Contracting Parties according to the formula for contributions referred to in Article 12, subject to such amount being increased in accordance with the mechanism referred to in Article 12bis.

c) For this purpose, each Contracting Party shall either:

i) establish under its legislation that the liability of the operator shall not be less than the amount referred to in paragraph (*a*) of this Article, and provide that such liability shall be covered by all the funds referred to in paragraph (*b*) of this Article; or

ii) establish under its legislation the liability of the operator at an amount at least equal to that established pursuant to paragraph (*b*)(*i*) of this Article or Article 7(*b*) of the Paris Convention, and provide that, in excess of such amount and up to the amount referred to in paragraph (*a*) of this Article, the public funds referred to in paragraphs (*b*)(*i*), (*ii*) and (*iii*) of this Article shall be made available by some means other than as cover for the liability of the operator, provided that the rules of substance and procedure laid down in this Convention are not thereby affected.

d) The obligation of the operator to pay compensation, interest or costs out of public funds made available pursuant to paragraphs (*b*)(*ii*) and (*iii*) and (*g*) of this Article shall only be enforceable against the operator as and when such funds are in fact made available.

e) Where a State makes use of the option provided for under Article 21(*c*) of the Paris Convention, it may only become a Contracting Party to this Convention if it ensures that funds will be available to cover the difference between the amount for which the operator is liable and 700 million euro.

f) The Contracting Parties, in carrying out this Convention, undertake not to make use of the right provided for in Article 15(*b*) of the Paris Convention to apply special conditions, other than those laid down in this Convention, in respect of compensation for nuclear damage provided out of the funds referred to in paragraph (*a*) of this Article.

g) The interest and costs referred to in Article 7(*h*) of the Paris Convention are payable in addition to the amounts referred to in paragraph (*b*) of this Article, and shall be borne in so far as they are awarded in respect of compensation payable out of the funds referred to in:

i) paragraph (*b*)(*i*) of this Article, by the operator liable;

ii) paragraph (*b*)(*ii*) of this Article, by the Contracting Party in whose territory the installation of the operator liable is situated to the extent of the funds made available by that Contracting Party;

iii) paragraph (*b*)(*iii*) of this Article, by the Contracting Parties together.

h) The amounts mentioned in this Convention shall be converted into the national currency of the Contracting Party whose courts have jurisdiction in accordance with the value of that currency at the date of the incident, unless another date is fixed for a given incident by agreement between the Contracting Parties.

D. Article 4 shall be deleted.

E. Article 5 shall be replaced by the following text:

Article 5

Where the operator liable has a right of recourse pursuant to Article 6(*f*) of the Paris Convention, the Contracting Parties to this Convention shall have the same right of recourse, to the extent that public funds have been made available pursuant to Article 3(b) and (g).

F. Article 6 shall be replaced by the following text:

Article 6

In calculating the public funds to be made available pursuant to this Convention, account shall be taken only of those rights to compensation exercised within thirty years from the date of the nuclear incident in the case of loss of life or personal injury, and ten years from the date of the nuclear incident in the case of all other nuclear damage. Such period is, moreover, extended in the cases and under the conditions laid down in Article 8(*e*) of the Paris Convention. Amendments made to claims after the expiry of this period, under the conditions laid down in Article 8(*f*) of the Paris Convention, shall also be taken into account.

G. Article 7 shall be replaced by the following text:

Article 7

Where a Contracting Party makes use of the right provided for in Article 8(*d*) of the Paris Convention, the period which it establishes shall be a period of prescription of at least three years either from the date at which the person suffering damage has knowledge or from the date at which he ought reasonably to have known of both the damage and the operator liable.

H. Article 8 shall be replaced by the following text:

Article 8

Any person who is entitled to benefit from the provisions of this Convention shall have the right to full compensation in accordance with national law for nuclear damage suffered, provided that where the amount of such damage exceeds or is likely to exceed 1 500 million euro, a Contracting Party may establish equitable criteria for apportioning the amount of compensation that is available under this Convention. Such criteria shall be applied whatever the origin of the funds and, subject to the provisions of Article 2, without discrimination based on the nationality, domicile or residence of the person suffering the damage.

I. Article 9 shall be replaced by the following text:

Article 9

a) The system of payment of public funds made available pursuant to this Convention shall be that of the Contracting Party whose courts have jurisdiction.
b) Each Contracting Party shall ensure that persons suffering nuclear damage may enforce their rights to compensation without having to bring separate proceedings according to the origin of the funds provided for such compensation.
c) A Contracting Party shall be required to make available the funds referred to in Article 3(*b*)(*iii*) once the amount of compensation under this Convention reaches the total of the amounts referred to in Article 3(*b*)(*i*) and (*ii*), irrespective of whether funds to be provided by the operator remain available or whether the liability of the operator is not limited in amount.

J. Article 10 shall be replaced by the following text:

Article 10

a) The Contracting Party whose courts have jurisdiction shall be required to inform the other Contracting Parties of a nuclear incident and its circumstances as soon as it appears that the nuclear damage caused by such incident exceeds, or is likely to exceed the sum of the amounts provided for under Article 3(*b*)(*i*) and (*ii*). The Contracting Parties shall, without delay, make all the necessary arrangements to settle the procedure for their relations in this connection.
b) Only the Contracting Party whose courts have jurisdiction shall be entitled to request the other Contracting Parties to make available the public funds required under Article 3(*b*)(*iii*) and (*g*) and shall have competence to disburse such funds.
c) Such Contracting Party shall, when the occasion arises, exercise the right of recourse provided for in Article 5 on behalf of the other Contracting Parties who have made available public funds pursuant to Article 3(*b*)(*iii*) and (*g*).
d) Settlements effected in respect of the payment of compensation for nuclear damage out of the public funds referred to in Article 3(*b*)(*ii*) and (*iii*) in accordance with the conditions established by national legislation shall be recognised by the other Contracting Parties, and judgements entered by the competent courts in respect of such compensation shall become enforceable in the territory of the other Contracting Parties in accordance with the provisions of Article 13(*i*) of the Paris Convention.

K. Article 11 shall be replaced by the following text:

Article 11

a) If the courts having jurisdiction are those of a Contracting Party other than the Contracting Party in whose territory the nuclear installation of the operator liable is situated, the public funds required under Article 3(*b*)(*ii*) and (*g*) shall be made available by the first-named Contracting Party. The Contracting Party in whose territory the nuclear installation of the operator liable is situated shall reimburse to the other Contracting Party the sums paid. These two Contracting Parties shall agree on the procedure for reimbursement.
b) If more than one Contracting Party is required to make available public funds pursuant to Article 3(*b*)(*ii*) and (*g*), the provisions of paragraph (*a*) of this Article shall apply mutatis mutandis. Reimbursement shall be based on the extent to which each operator has contributed to the nuclear incident.
c) In adopting all legislative, regulatory or administrative provisions, after the nuclear incident has occurred, concerning the nature, form and extent of the compensation, the procedure for making available the public funds required under Article 3(*b*)(*ii*) and (*g*) and, if necessary, the criteria for the apportionment of such funds, the Contracting Party whose courts have jurisdiction shall consult the Contracting Party in whose territory the nuclear installation of the operator liable is situated. It shall further take all measures necessary to enable the latter to intervene in proceedings and to participate in any settlement concerning compensation.

L. Article 12 shall be replaced by the following text:

Article 12

a) The formula for contributions according to which the Contracting Parties shall make available the public funds referred to in Article 3(*b*)(*iii*) shall be determined as follows:

i) as to 35%, on the basis of the ratio between the gross domestic product at current prices of each Contracting Party and the total of the gross domestic products at current prices of all Contracting Parties as shown by the official statistics published by the Organisation for Economic Co-operation and Development for the year preceding the year in which the nuclear incident occurs;

ii) as to 65%, on the basis of the ratio between the thermal power of the reactors situated in the territory of each Contracting Party and the total thermal power of the reactors situated in the territories of all the Contracting Parties. This calculation shall be made on the basis of the thermal power of the reactors shown at the date of the nuclear incident in the lists referred to in Article 13, provided that for the purposes of this calculation, a reactor shall only be taken into consideration as from the date when it first reaches criticality and a reactor shall be excluded from the calculation when all nuclear fuel has been removed permanently from the reactor core and has been stored safely in accordance with approved procedures.

b) For the purposes of this Convention, "thermal power" means:

i) before the issue of a final operating licence, the planned thermal power;

ii) after the issue of such licence, the thermal power authorised by the competent national authorities.

M. A new Article 12bis shall be added after Article 12 as follows:

Article 12*bis*

a) In case of accession to this Convention, the public funds mentioned in Article 3(*b*)(*iii*) are increased by:

i) 35% of an amount determined by applying to the above-mentioned sum the ratio between the gross domestic product at current prices of the acceding Party and the total of the gross domestic products at current prices of all the Contracting Parties, excluding that of the acceding Party, and

ii) 65% of an amount determined by applying to the above-mentioned sum the ratio between the thermal power of the reactors situated in the territory of the acceding Party and the total thermal power of the reactors situated in the territories of all the Contracting Parties, excluding that of the acceding Party.

b) The increased amount referred to in paragraph (a) shall be rounded up to the nearest amount expressed in thousands of euro.

c) The gross domestic product of the acceding Party shall be determined in accordance with the official statistics published by the Organisation for Economic Co-operation and Development for the year preceding the year in which the accession comes into force.

d) The thermal power of the acceding Party shall be determined in accordance with the list of nuclear installations communicated by that Government to the Belgian Government pursuant to Article 13(*b*), provided that for the purpose of calculating the contributions under paragraph (*a*)(*ii*) of this Article, a reactor shall only be taken into consideration as from the date when it first reaches criticality and a reactor shall be excluded from the calculation when all nuclear fuel has been removed permanently from the reactor core and has been stored safely in accordance with approved procedures.

N. Paragraphs (a), (b), (f) and (i) of Article 13 shall be replaced by the following text:

Article 13

a) Each Contracting Party shall ensure that all nuclear installations used for peaceful purposes situated in its territory, and falling within the definition in Article 1 of the Paris Convention, appear on a list.

b) For this purpose, each Signatory or acceding Government shall, on the deposit of its instrument of ratification, acceptance, approval or accession, communicate to the Belgian Government full particulars of such installations.

f) If a Contracting Party is of the opinion that the particulars, or any modification to be made to the list, communicated by another Contracting Party do not comply with the provisions of this Article, it may raise objections thereto only by addressing them to the Belgian Government within three months from the date on which it has received notice pursuant to paragraph (*h*) of this Article.

i) The list referred to in this Article shall consist of all the particulars and modifications referred to in paragraphs (*b*), (*c*), (*d*) and (*e*) of this Article, it being understood that objections submitted pursuant to paragraphs (*f*) and (*g*) of this Article shall have effect retrospective to the date on which they were raised, if they are sustained.

O. Article 14 shall be replaced by the following text:

Article 14

a) Except in so far as this Convention otherwise provides, each Contracting Party may exercise the powers vested in it by virtue of the Paris Convention, and any provisions made thereunder may be invoked against the other Contracting Parties in order that the public funds referred to in Article 3(*b*)(*ii*) and (*iii*) be made available.
b) Any such provisions made by a Contracting Party pursuant to Article 2(*b*) of the Paris Convention as a result of which the public funds referred to in Article 3(*b*)(*ii*) and (*iii*) are required to be made available may not be invoked against any other Contracting Party unless it has consented thereto.
c) Nothing in this Convention shall prevent a Contracting Party from making provisions outside the scope of the Paris Convention and of this Convention, provided that such provisions shall not involve any further obligation on the part of the Contracting Parties in so far as their public funds are concerned.
d) Where all of the Contracting Parties to this Convention ratify, accept, approve or accede to any other international agreement in the field of supplementary compensation for nuclear damage, a Contracting Party to this Convention may use the funds to be provided pursuant to Article 3(*b*)(*iii*) of this Convention to satisfy any obligation

it may have under such other international agreement to provide supplementary compensation for nuclear damage out of public funds.

P. Article 15 shall be replaced by the following text:

Article 15

a) Any Contracting Party may conclude an agreement with a State which is not a Party to this Convention
concerning compensation out of public funds for damage caused by a nuclear incident. Any Contracting Party intending to conclude such an agreement shall notify the other Contracting Parties of its intention. Agreements concluded shall be notified to the Belgian Government.
b) To the extent that the conditions for payment of compensation under any such agreement are not more favourable than those which result from the measures adopted by the Contracting Party concerned for the application of the Paris Convention and of this Convention, the amount of damage caused by a nuclear incident covered by this Convention and for which compensation is payable by virtue of such an agreement may be taken into consideration, where the proviso to Article 8 applies, in calculating the total amount of damage caused by that incident.
c) The provisions of paragraphs (*a*) and (*b*) of this Article shall in no case affect the obligations under Article 3(*b*)(*ii*) and (*iii*) of those Contracting Parties which have not given their consent to such agreement.

Q. Article 17 shall be replaced by the following text:

Article 17

a) In the event of a dispute arising between two or more Contracting Parties concerning the interpretation or application of this Convention, the parties to the dispute shall consult with a view to settling the dispute by negotiation or other amicable means.
b) Where a dispute referred to in paragraph (*a*) is not settled within six months from the date upon which such dispute is acknowledged to exist by any party thereto, the Contracting Parties shall meet in order to assist the parties to the dispute to reach a friendly settlement.
c) Where no resolution to the dispute has been reached within three months of the meeting referred to in paragraph (*b*), the dispute shall, upon the request of any party thereto, be submitted to the European Nuclear Energy Tribunal established by the Convention of 20th December 1957 on the Establishment of a Security Control in the Field of Nuclear Energy.

d) Where a nuclear incident gives rise to a dispute between two or more Contracting Parties concerning the interpretation or application of the Paris Convention and of this Convention, the procedure for resolving such dispute shall be the procedure provided for under Article 17 of the Paris Convention.

R. Article 18 shall be replaced by the following text:

Article 18

a) Reservations to one or more of the provisions of this Convention may be made at any time prior to ratification, acceptance or approval of this Convention if the terms of these reservations have been expressly accepted by all Signatories or, at the time of accession or of the application of the provisions of Articles 21 and 24, if the terms of these reservations have been expressly accepted by all Signatories and acceding Governments.
b) Such acceptance shall not be required from a Signatory which has not itself ratified, accepted or approved this Convention within a period of twelve months after the date of notification to it of such reservation by the Belgian Government in accordance with Article 25.
c) Any reservation accepted in accordance with the provisions of paragraph (*a*) of this Article may be withdrawn at any time by notification addressed to the Belgian Government.

S. Article 20 shall be replaced by the following text:

Article 20

a) The Annex to this Convention shall form an integral part thereof.
b) This Convention shall be subject to ratification, acceptance or approval. Instruments of ratification, acceptance or approval shall be deposited with the Belgian Government.
c) This Convention shall come into force three months after the deposit of the sixth instrument of ratification, acceptance or approval.
d) For each Signatory ratifying, accepting or approving this Convention after the deposit of the sixth instrument of ratification, acceptance or approval, it shall come into force three months after the date of the deposit of its instrument of ratification, acceptance or approval.

T. Article 21 shall be replaced by the following text:

Article 21

Amendments to this Convention shall be adopted by agreement among all the Contracting Parties. They shall come into force on the date when all Contracting Parties have ratified, accepted or approved them.

U. Article 25 shall be replaced by the following text:

Article 25

The Belgian Government shall notify all Signatories and acceding Governments of the receipt of any instrument of ratification, acceptance, approval, accession or withdrawal, and shall also notify them of the date on which this Convention comes into force, the text of any amendment thereto and the date on which such amendment comes into force, any reservations made in accordance with Article 18, any increase in the compensation to be provided under Article 3(*a*) as a result of the application of Article 12bis, and all notifications which it has received.

V. The Annex shall be replaced by the following text:

ANNEX
TO THE CONVENTION OF 31 JANUARY 1963 SUPPLEMENTARY TO THE PARIS CONVENTION OF 29 JULY 1960 ON THIRD PARTY LIABILITY IN THE FIELD OF NUCLEAR ENERGY, AS AMENDED BY THE ADDITIONAL PROTOCOL OF 28 JANUARY 1964, BY THE PROTOCOL OF 16 NOVEMBER 1982 AND BY THE PROTOCOL OF 12 FEBRUARY 2004

THE GOVERNMENTS OF THE CONTRACTING PARTIES declare that compensation for nuclear damage caused by a nuclear incident not covered by the Supplementary Convention solely by reason of the fact that the relevant nuclear installation, on account of its utilisation, is not on the list referred to in Article 13 of the Supplementary Convention (including the case where such installation is considered by one or more but not all of the Governments to be outside the Paris Convention):
- shall be provided without discrimination among the nationals of the Contracting Parties to the Supplementary Convention; and
- shall not be limited to less than 1 500 million euro.

In addition, if they have not already done so, they shall endeavour to make the rules for compensation of persons suffering damage caused by such incidents as similar as possible to those established in respect of nuclear incidents occurring in connection with nuclear installations covered by the Supplementary Convention.

II.

a) The provisions of this Protocol shall, as between the Parties thereto, form an integral part of the Convention of 31 January 1963 Supplementary to the Paris Convention of 29 July 1960 on Third Party Liability in the Field of Nuclear Energy, as amended by the Additional Protocol of 28 January 1964 and by the Protocol of 16 November 1982 (hereinafter referred to as the "Convention"), which shall be known as the "Convention of 31 January 1963 Supplementary to the Paris Convention of 29 July 1960, as amended by the Additional Protocol of 28 January 1964, by the Protocol of 16 November 1982 and by the Protocol of .12 February 2004".

b) This Protocol shall be subject to ratification, acceptance or approval. Instruments of ratification, acceptance or approval of this Protocol shall be deposited with the Belgian Government.

c) The Signatories of this Protocol who have already ratified or acceded to the Convention express their intention to ratify, accept or approve this Protocol as soon as possible. The other Signatories of this Protocol undertake to ratify, accept or approve it at the same time as they ratify the Convention.

d) This Protocol shall be open for accession in accordance with the provisions of Article 22 of the Convention. Accessions to the Convention will be accepted only if they are accompanied by accession to this Protocol.

e) This Protocol shall come into force in accordance with the provisions of Article 21 of the Convention.

f) The Belgian Government shall give notice to all Signatories and acceding Governments of the receipt of any instrument of ratification, acceptance, approval or accession.

PROTOCOL TO AMEND THE VIENNA CONVENTION ON CIVIL LIABILITY FOR NUCLEAR DAMAGE

(Vienna, 12 September 1997)

Although the basic Vienna Convention (May 21, 1963) had been adopted not long after the first one ever (Paris Convention) in the domain of nuclear third party liability, its success in terms of States becoming contracting Parties to it had been for very many years rather modest. It is recalled that, while the "Paris system" was "regional" in nature, the "Vienna system" was worldwide in scope, which means that the latter was potentially addressed to a much higher number of countries than those belonging to the "Paris system". The Vienna Convention entered into force on 12 February 1978 and has so far 32 contracting Parties.

During the second half of the eighties, the Chernobyl incident on one hand and the fall of the Soviet block on the other, created conditions for a number of countries (especially in Central and Eastern Europe) to accede to the "Vienna system". However, although this was a significant step forward as far as a wider application of the international nuclear third party liability regime was concerned, there were still certain intrinsic elements to the Convention which were regarded as unsatisfactory, such as for example the very low liability amounts thereby provided (5 million dollars, a largely inadequate figure even over forty years ago).

Such being basically the reasons for a revision of this Convention, the relevant work was started at the IAEA and occupied nearly eight years of complex negotiations. Nevertheless, the long period needed must be put down to the fact that, at the same time, parallel negotiations were carried out in order to set up a supplementary compensation regime, again worldwide in scope, similar to the "regional" one existing on the strength of the 1963 Brussels Convention (see previous pages). The "parallel" negotiations led to the adoption of the Convention on Supplementary Compensation dealt with further on in this Chapter.

The amending Protocol to the Vienna Convention (adopted in the framework of the 1997 IAEA General Conference) improves the previous regime in various ways. For example, the Convention is now clearly applicable also to non-contracting Parties, although national law may derogate to this. A second innovation touches upon compensation of damage to the environment: as a matter of fact damage had been defined by the former Convention (while no such definition was included in the 1960 Paris Convention) but compensation of damage to the environment had been left in rather vague terms. The amending Protocol provides for a better structured definition covering also the latter, although it should be pointed out that the provisions concerned refer to the measures to be adopted to prevent or minimise damage to the environment after an incident, leaving however to national courts any decision as to the extent of compensation to be accorded.

In third place, the liability amounts have been considerably increased, thus providing a far more acceptable basis than before, with a view to ensuring an equitable compensation of victims should the need arise. Lastly, a "phasing-in" mechanism is established making it possible for States with a less strong economy to adopt lower liability amounts than those laid down in the Convention. This possibility is accorded for a maximum of 15 years as of the entry into force of the Protocol.

As regards this last point more in general, is recalled that, in order to ensure the entry into force of the Protocol within the shortest possible delay and at the same time attract the highest possible number of countries, only five ratifications are required. It is obvious in any case that the success of the new Convention is very much dependent on the ratification by countries carrying more weight, which would be an important incentive for other countries to do the same.

While the 1963 Convention remains obviously in force for those Parties that do not wish to be bound by the amending Protocol of 1997 (in force as of October 4, 2003) the latter text is published here. The contracting Parties to the Protocol are now five.

THE STATES PARTIES TO THIS PROTOCOL,

CONSIDERING that it is desirable to amend the Vienna Convention on Civil Liability for Nuclear Damage of 21 May 1963, to provide for broader scope, increased amount of liability of the operator of a nuclear installation and enhanced means for securing adequate and equitable compensation,

HAVE AGREED as follows,

Article 1

The Convention which the provisions of this Protocol amend is the Vienna Convention on Civil Liability for Nuclear Damage of 21 May 1963, hereinafter referred to as the "1963 Vienna Convention".

Article 2

Article I of the 1963 Vienna Convention is amended as follows:

1. Paragraph 1(j) is amended as follows:
a. the word "and" is deleted at the end of sub-paragraph (ii) and is inserted at the end of sub-paragraph (iii).
b. a new sub-paragraph (iv) is added as follows:

(iv) such other installations in which there are nuclear fuel or radioactive products or waste as the Board of Governors of the International Atomic Energy Agency shall from time to time determine;

2. Paragraph 1(k) is replaced by the following text:

(k) "Nuclear Damage" means -
i. loss of life or personal injury;
ii. loss of or damage to property;

and each of the following to the extent determined by the law of the competent court;
iii. economic loss arising from loss or damage referred to in sub-paragraph (i) or (ii), insofar as not included in those sub-paragraphs, if incurred by a person entitled to claim in respect of such loss or damage;
iv. the costs of measures of reinstatement of impaired environment, unless such impairment is insignificant, if such measures are actually taken or to be taken, and insofar as not included in sub-paragraph (ii);
v. loss of income deriving from an economic interest in any use or enjoyment of the environment, incurred as a result of a significant impairment of that environment, and insofar as not included in sub-paragraph (ii);
vi. the costs of preventive measures, and further loss or damage caused by such measures;
vii. any other economic loss, other than any caused by the impairment of the environment, if permitted by the general law on civil liability of the competent court,

in the case of subparagraphs (i) to (v) and (vii) above, to the extent that the loss or damage arises out of or results from ionizing radiation emitted by any source of radiation inside a nuclear installation, or emitted from nuclear fuel or radioactive products or waste in, or of nuclear material coming from, originating in, or sent to, a nuclear installation, whether so arising from the radioactive properties of such matter, or from a combination of radioactive properties with toxic, explosive or other hazardous properties of such matter.

3. Paragraph 1(l) is replaced by the following text:

(l) "Nuclear incident" means any occurrence or series of occurrences having the same origin which causes nuclear damage or, but only with respect to preventive measures, creates a grave and imminent threat of causing such damage.

4. After paragraph 1(l) four new paragraphs 1(m), 1(n), 1(o) and 1(p) are added as follows:

(m) "Measures of reinstatement" means any reasonable measures which have been approved by the competent authorities of the State where the measures were taken, and which aim to reinstate or restore damaged or destroyed components of the environment, or to introduce, where reasonable, the equivalent of these components into the environment. The law of the State where the damage is suffered shall determine who is entitled to take such measures.

(n) "Preventive measures" means any reasonable measures taken by any person after a nuclear incident has occurred to prevent or minimize damage referred to in subparagraphs (k)(i) to (v) or (vii), subject to any approval of the competent authorities required by the law of the State where the measures were taken.

(o) "Reasonable measures" means measures which are found under the law of the competent court to be appropriate and proportionate having regard to all the circumstances, for example –

i. the nature and extent of the damage incurred or, in the case of preventive measures, the nature and extent of the risk of such damage;
ii the extent to which, at the time they are taken, such measures are likely to be effective; and
iii. relevant scientific and technical expertise.

(p) "Special Drawing Right", hereinafter referred to as SDR, means the unit of account defined by the International Monetary Fund and used by it for its own operations and transactions.

5. Paragraph 2 is replaced by the following text:

2. An Installation State may, if the small extent of the risks involved so warrants, exclude any nuclear installation or small quantities of nuclear material from the application of this Convention, provided that–

a. with respect to nuclear installations, criteria for such exclusion have been established by the Board of Governors of the International Atomic Energy Agency and any exclusion by an Installation State satisfies such criteria; and

b. with respect to small quantities of nuclear material, maximum limits for the exclusion of such quantities have been established by the Board of Governors of the International Atomic Energy Agency and any exclusion by an Installation State is within such established limits.

The criteria for the exclusion of nuclear installations and the maximum limits for the exclusion of small quantities of nuclear material shall be reviewed periodically by the Board of Governors.

Article 3

After Article I of the 1963 Vienna Convention two new Articles I A and I B are added as follows:

Article I A

1. This Convention shall apply to nuclear damage wherever suffered.

2. However, the legislation of the Installation State may exclude from the application of this Convention damage suffered –

a. in the territory of a non-Contracting State; or

b. in any maritime zones established by a non-Contracting State in accordance with the international law of the sea.

3. An exclusion pursuant to paragraph 2 of this Article may apply only in respect of a non-Contracting State which at the time of the incident –

a. has a nuclear installation in its territory or in any maritime zones established by it in accordance with the international law of the sea; and

b. does not afford equivalent reciprocal benefits.

4. Any exclusion pursuant to paragraph 2 of this Article shall not affect the rights referred to in sub-paragraph (a) of paragraph 2 of Article IX and any exclusion pursuant to paragraph 2(b) of this Article shall not extend to damage on board or to a ship or an aircraft.

Article I B

This Convention shall not apply to nuclear installations used for non-peaceful purposes.

Article 4

Article II of the 1963 Vienna Convention is amended as follows:

1. At the end of paragraph 3(a) the following text is added:

The Installation State may limit the amount of public funds made available per incident to the difference, if any, between the amounts hereby established and the amount established pursuant to paragraph 1 of Article V.

2. At the end of paragraph 4 the following text is added:

The Installation State may limit the amount of public funds made available as provided for in sub-paragraph (a) of paragraph 3 of this Article.

3. Paragraph 6 is replaced by the following text:

6. No person shall be liable for any loss or damage which is not nuclear damage pursuant to sub-paragraph (k) of paragraph 1 of Article I but which could have been determined as such pursuant to the provisions of that sub-paragraph.

Article 5

After the first sentence in Article III of the 1963 Vienna Convention the following text is added:

However, the Installation State may exclude this obligation in relation to carriage which takes place wholly within its own territory.

Article 6

Article IV of the 1963 Vienna Convention is amended as follows:

1. Paragraph 3 is replaced by the following text:

3. No liability under this Convention shall attach to an operator if he proves that the nuclear damage is directly due to an act of armed conflict, hostilities, civil war or insurrection.

2. Paragraph 5 is replaced by the following text:

5. The operator shall not be liable under this Convention for nuclear damage –
a. to the nuclear installation itself and any other nuclear installation, including a nuclear installation under construction, on the site where that installation is located; and
b. to any property on that same site which is used or to be used in connection with any such installation.

3. Paragraph 6 is replaced by the following text:

6. Compensation for damage caused to the means of transport upon which the nuclear material involved was at the time of the nuclear incident shall not have the effect of reducing the liability of the operator in respect of other damage to an amount less than either 150 million SDRs, or any higher amount established by the legislation of a Contracting Party, or an amount established pursuant to sub-paragraph (c) of paragraph 1 of Article V.

4. Paragraph 7 is replaced by the following text:

7. Nothing in this Convention shall affect the liability of any individual for nuclear damage for which the operator, by virtue of paragraph 3 or 5 of this Article, is not liable under this Convention and which that individual caused by an act or omission done with intent to cause damage.

Article 7

1. The text of Article V of the 1963 Vienna Convention is replaced by the following text:

1.The liability of the operator may be limited by the Installation State for any one nuclear incident, either –
a. to not less than 300 million SDRs; or
b. to not less than 150 million SDRs provided that in excess of that amount and up to at least 300 million SDRs public funds shall be made available by that State to compensate nuclear damage; or
c. for a maximum of 15 years from the date of entry into force of this Protocol, to a transitional amount of not less than 100 million SDRs in respect of a nuclear incident occurring within that period. An amount lower than 100 million SDRs may be established, provided that public funds shall be made available by that State to compensate nuclear damage between that lesser amount and 100 million SDRs.

2. Notwithstanding paragraph 1 of this Article, the Installation State, having regard to the nature of the nuclear installation or the nuclear substances involved and to the likely consequences of an incident originating therefrom, may establish a lower amount of liability of the operator, provided that in no event shall any amount so established be less than 5 million SDRs, and provided that the Installation State ensures that public funds shall be made available up to the amount established pursuant to paragraph 1.

3. The amounts established by the Installation State of the liable operator in accordance with paragraphs 1 and 2 of this Article and paragraph 6 of Article IV shall apply wherever the nuclear incident occurs.

2. After Article V, four new Articles V A, V B, V C and V D are added as follows:

Article V A

1. Interest and costs awarded by a court in actions for compensation of nuclear damage shall be payable in addition to the amounts referred to in Article V.

2. The amounts mentioned in Article V and paragraph 6 of Article IV may be converted into national currency in round figures.

Article V B

Each Contracting Party shall ensure that persons suffering damage may enforce their rights to compensation without having to bring separate proceedings according to the origin of the funds provided for such compensation.

Article V C

1. If the courts having jurisdiction are those of a Contracting Party other than the Installation State, the public funds required under sub-paragraphs (b) and (c) of paragraph 1 of Article V and under paragraph 1 of Article VII, as well as interest and costs awarded by a court, may be made available by the first-named Contracting Party. The Installation State shall reimburse to the other Contracting Party any such sums paid. These two Contracting Parties shall agree on the procedure for reimbursement.

2. If the courts having jurisdiction are those of a Contracting Party other than the Installation State, the Contracting Party whose courts have jurisdiction shall take all measures necessary to enable the Installation State to intervene in proceedings and to participate in any settlement concerning compensation.

Article V D

1. A meeting of the Contracting Parties shall be convened by the Director General of the International Atomic Energy Agency to amend the limits of liability referred to in Article V if one-third of the Contracting Parties express a desire to that effect.

2. Amendments shall be adopted by a two-thirds majority of the Contracting Parties present and voting, provided that at least one-half of the Contracting Parties shall be present at the time of the voting.

3. When acting on a proposal to amend the limits, the meeting of the Contracting Parties shall take into account, inter alia, the risk of damage resulting from a nuclear incident, changes in the monetary values, and the capacity of the insurance market.
a. Any amendment adopted in accordance with paragraph 2 of this Article shall be notified by the Director General of the IAEA to all Contracting Parties for acceptance. The amendment shall be considered accepted at the end of a period of 18 months after it has been notified provided that at least one-third of the Contracting Parties at the time of the adoption of the amendment by the meeting have communicated to the Director General of the IAEA that they accept the amendment. An amendment accepted in accordance with this paragraph shall enter into force 12 months after its acceptance for those Contracting Parties which have accepted it.
b. If, within a period of 18 months from the date of notification for acceptance, an amendment has not been accepted in accordance with sub-paragraph (a), the amendment shall be considered rejected.

4. For each Contracting Party accepting an amendment after it has been accepted but not entered into force or after its entry into force in accordance with paragraph 4 of this Article, the amendment shall enter into force 12 months after its acceptance by that Contracting Party.

5. A State which becomes a Party to this Convention after the entry into force of an amendment in accordance with paragraph 4 of this Article shall, failing an expression of a different intention by that State –
a. be considered as a Party to this Convention as so amended; and
b. be considered as a Party to the unamended Convention in relation to any State Party not bound by the amendment.

Article 8

Article VI of the 1963 Vienna Convention is amended as follows:

1. Paragraph 1 is replaced by the following text:

a. Rights of compensation under this Convention shall be extinguished if an action is not brought within –
i. with respect to loss of life and personal injury, thirty years from the date of the nuclear incident;
ii. with respect to other damage, ten years from the date of the nuclear incident.

b. If, however, under the law of the Installation State, the liability of the operator is covered by insurance or other financial security including State funds for a longer period, the law of the competent court may provide that rights of compensation against the operator shall only be extinguished after such a longer period which shall not exceed the period for which his liability is so covered under the law of the Installation State.

c. Actions for compensation with respect to loss of life and personal injury or, pursuant to an extension under sub-paragraph (b) of this paragraph with respect to other damage, which are brought after a period of ten years from the date of the nuclear incident shall in no case affect the rights of compensation under this Convention of any person who has brought an action against the operator before the expiry of that period.

2. Paragraph 2 is deleted.

3. Paragraph 3 is replaced by the following text:

3. Rights of compensation under the Convention shall be subject to prescription or extinction, as provided by the law of the competent court, if an action is not brought within three years from the date on which the person suffering damage had knowledge or ought reasonably to have had knowledge of the damage and of the operator liable for the damage, provided that the periods established pursuant to sub-paragraphs (a) and (b) of paragraph 1 of this Article shall not be exceeded.

Article 9

Article VII is amended as follows:

1. In paragraph 1, the following two sentences are added at the end of the paragraph and the paragraph so amended becomes sub-paragraph (a) of that paragraph:

Where the liability of the operator is unlimited, the Installation State may establish a limit of the financial security of the operator liable, provided that such limit is not lower than 300 million SDRs. The Installation State shall ensure the payment of claims for compensation for nuclear damage which have been established against the operator to the extent that the yield of the financial security is inadequate to satisfy such claims, but not in excess of the amount of the financial security to be provided under this paragraph.

2. A new sub-paragraph (b) is added to paragraph 1 as follows:

(b) Notwithstanding sub-paragraph (a) of this paragraph, where the liability of the operator is unlimited, the Installation State, having regard to the nature of the nuclear installation or the nuclear substances involved and to the likely consequences of an incident originating therefrom, may establish a lower amount of financial security of the operator, provided that in no event shall any amount so established be less than 5 million SDRs, and provided that the Installation State ensures the payment of claims for compensation for nuclear damage which have been established against the operator by providing necessary funds to the extent that the yield of insurance or other financial security is inadequate to satisfy such claims, and up to the limit provided pursuant to sub-paragraph (a) of this paragraph.

3. In paragraph 3, the words "or sub-paragraphs (b) and (c) of paragraph 1 of Article V" are inserted after the words "of this Article".

Article 10

Article VIII of the 1963 Vienna Convention is amended as follows:

1. The text of Article VIII becomes paragraph 1 of that Article.

2. A new paragraph 2 is added as follows:

2. Subject to application of the rule of sub-paragraph (c) of paragraph 1 of Article VI, where in respect of claims brought against the operator the damage to be compensated under this Convention exceeds, or is likely to exceed, the maximum amount made available pursuant to paragraph 1 of Article V, priority in the distribution of the compensation shall be given to claims in respect of loss of life or personal injury.

Article 11

In Article X of the 1963 Vienna Convention, a new sentence is added at the end of the Article as follows:

The right of recourse provided for under this Article may also be extended to benefit the Installation State insofar as it has provided public funds pursuant to this Convention.

Article 12

Article XI of the 1963 Vienna Convention is amended as follows:

1. A new paragraph 1bis is added as follows:

1bis. Where a nuclear incident occurs within the area of the exclusive economic zone of a Contracting Party or, if such a zone has not been established, in an area not exceeding the limits of an exclusive economic zone, were one to be established, jurisdiction over actions concerning nuclear damage from that nuclear incident shall, for the purposes of this Convention, lie only with the courts of that Party. The preceding sentence shall apply if that Contracting Party has notified the Depositary of such area prior to the nuclear incident. Nothing in this paragraph shall be interpreted as permitting the exercise of jurisdiction in a manner which is contrary to the international law of the sea, including the United Nations Convention on the Law of the Sea.

2. Paragraph 2 is replaced by the following text:

2. Where a nuclear incident does not occur within the territory of any Contracting Party, or within an area notified pursuant to paragraph 1bis, or where the place of the nuclear incident cannot be determined with certainty, jurisdiction over such actions shall lie with the courts of the Installation State of the operator liable.

3. In paragraph 3, first line, and in sub-paragraph (b), after the figure "1", insert ", 1bis".

4. A new paragraph 4 is added as follows:

4. The Contracting Party whose courts have jurisdiction shall ensure that only one of its courts shall have jurisdiction in relation to any one nuclear incident.

Article 13

After Article XI a new Article XI A is added as follows:

Article XI A

The Contracting Party whose courts have jurisdiction shall ensure that in relation to actions for compensation of nuclear damage -

a. any State may bring an action on behalf of persons who have suffered nuclear damage, who are nationals of that State or have their domicile or residence in its territory, and who have consented thereto; and

b. any person may bring an action to enforce rights under this Convention acquired by subrogation or assignment.

Article 14

The text of Article XII of the 1963 Vienna Convention is replaced by the following text:

Article XII

1. A judgment that is no longer subject to ordinary forms of review entered by a court of a Contracting Party having jurisdiction shall be recognized, except –

a. where the judgment was obtained by fraud;

b. where the party against whom the judgment was pronounced was not given a fair opportunity to present his case; or

c. where the judgment is contrary to the public policy of the Contracting Party within the territory of which recognition is sought, or is not in accord with fundamental standards of justice.

2. A judgment which is recognized under paragraph 1 of this Article shall, upon being presented for enforcement in accordance with the formalities required by the law of the Contracting Party where enforcement is sought, be enforceable as if it were a judgment of a court of that Contracting Party. The merits of a claim on which the judgment has been given shall not be subject to further proceedings.

Article 15

Article XIII of the 1963 Vienna Convention is amended as follows:

1. The text of Article XIII becomes paragraph 1 of that Article.

2. A new paragraph 2 is added as follows:

2. Notwithstanding paragraph 1 of this Article, insofar as compensation for nuclear damage is in excess of 150 million SDRs, the legislation of the Installation State may derogate from the provisions of this Convention with respect to nuclear damage suffered in the territory, or in any maritime zone established in accordance with the international law of the sea, of another State which at the time of the incident, has a nuclear installation in such territory, to the extent that it does not afford reciprocal benefits of an equivalent amount.

Article 16

The text of Article XVIII of the 1963 Vienna Convention is replaced by the following text:

This Convention shall not affect the rights and obligations of a Contracting Party under the general rules of public international law.

Article 17

After Article XX of the 1963 Vienna Convention a new Article XX A is added as follows:

Article XX A

1. In the event of a dispute between Contracting Parties concerning the interpretation or application of this Convention, the parties to the dispute shall consult with a view to the settlement of the dispute by negotiation or by any other peaceful means of settling disputes acceptable to them.

2. If a dispute of this character referred to in paragraph 1 of this Article cannot be settled within six months from the request for consultation pursuant to paragraph 1 of this Article, it shall, at the request of any party to such dispute, be submitted to arbitration or referred to the International Court of Justice for decision. Where a dispute is submitted to arbitration, if, within six months from the date of the request, the parties to the dispute are unable to agree on the organization of the arbitration, a party may request the President of the International Court of Justice or the Secretary-General of the United Nations to appoint one or more arbitrators. In cases of conflicting requests by the parties to the dispute, the request to the Secretary-General of the United Nations shall have priority.

3. When ratifying, accepting, approving or acceding to this Convention, a State may declare that it does not consider itself bound by either or both of the dispute settlement

procedures provided for in paragraph 2 of this Article. The other Contracting Parties shall not be bound by a dispute settlement procedure provided for in paragraph 2 of this Article with respect to a Contracting Party for which such a declaration is in force.

4. A Contracting Party which has made a declaration in accordance with paragraph 3 of this Article may at any time withdraw it by notification to the depositary.

Article 18

1. Articles XX to XXV, paragraphs 2, 3 and paragraph number "1." of Article XXVI, Articles XXVII and XXIX of the 1963 Vienna Convention are deleted.

2. The 1963 Vienna Convention and this Protocol shall, as between the Parties to this Protocol, be read and interpreted together as one single text that may be referred to as the 1997 Vienna Convention on Civil Liability for Nuclear Damage.

Article 19

1. A State which is a Party to this Protocol but not a Party to the 1963 Vienna Convention shall be bound by the provisions of that Convention as amended by this Protocol in relation to other States Parties hereto, and failing an expression of a different intention by that State at the time of deposit of an instrument referred to in Article 20 shall be bound by the provisions of the 1963 Vienna Convention in relation to States which are only Parties thereto.

2. Nothing in this Protocol shall affect the obligations of a State which is a Party both to the 1963 Vienna Convention and to this Protocol with respect to a State which is a Party to the 1963 Vienna Convention but not a Party to this Protocol.

Article 20

1. This Protocol shall be open for signature by all States at the Headquarters of the International Atomic Energy Agency in Vienna from 29 September 1997 until its entry into force.

2. This Protocol is subject to ratification, acceptance or approval by States which have signed it.

3. After its entry into force, any State which has not signed this Protocol may accede to it.

4. The instruments of ratification, acceptance, approval or accession shall be deposited with the Director General of the International Atomic Energy Agency, who shall be the depositary of this Protocol.

Article 21

1. This Protocol shall enter into force three months after the date of deposit of the fifth instrument of ratification, acceptance or approval.

2. For each State ratifying, accepting, approving or acceding to this Protocol after the deposit of the fifth instrument of ratification, acceptance or approval, this Protocol shall enter into force three months after the date of deposit by such State of the appropriate instrument.

Article 22

1. Any Contracting Party may denounce this Protocol by written notification to the depositary.

2. Denunciation shall take effect one year after the date on which the notification is received by the depositary.

3. As between the Parties to this Protocol, denunciation by any of them of the 1963 Vienna Convention in accordance with its Article XXVI shall not be construed in any way as denunciation of the 1963 Vienna Convention as amended by this Protocol.

4. Notwithstanding a denunciation of this Protocol by a Contracting Party pursuant to this Article, the provisions of this Protocol shall continue to apply to any nuclear damage caused by a nuclear incident occurring before such denunciation takes effect.

Article 23

The depositary shall promptly notify States Parties and all other States of:
a. each signature of this Protocol;
b. each deposit of an instrument of ratification, acceptance, approval or accession;
c. the entry into force of this Protocol;
d. any notification received pursuant to paragraph 1bis of Article XI;
e. requests for the convening of a revision conference pursuant to Article XXVI of the 1963 Vienna Convention and for a meeting of the Contracting Parties pursuant to Article V D of the 1963 Vienna Convention as amended by this Protocol;

f. notifications of denunciations received pursuant to Article 22 and other pertinent notifications relating to this Protocol.

Article 24

1. The original of this Protocol, of which Arabic, Chinese, English, French, Russian and Spanish texts are equally authentic, shall be deposited with the depositary.

2. The International Atomic Energy Agency shall establish the consolidated text of the 1963 Vienna Convention as amended by this Protocol in the Arabic, Chinese, English, French, Russian and Spanish languages as set forth in the annex to this Protocol.

3. The depositary shall communicate to all States the certified true copies of this Protocol together with the consolidated text of the 1963 Vienna Convention as amended by this Protocol.

IN WITNESS WHEREOF the undersigned, being duly authorized thereto, have signed this Protocol.

Done at Vienna, the twelfth day of September, one thousand nine hundred and ninety-seven.

JOINT PROTOCOL RELATING TO THE APPLICATION OF THE VIENNA CONVENTION AND THE PARIS CONVENTION

(Vienna, 21 September 1988)

The problem of relations between the above two Conventions had been under consideration since 1974, and it acquired more importance especially after the Chernobyl incident. Given the similarities between the Paris and the Vienna "systems", the need for a better definition of such relations became increasingly stronger, mainly in order to establish criteria for the application of these Conventions, thus avoiding their simultaneous application which would create serious difficulties also to national courts.

For these reasons, an instruments linking the Paris (PC) and Vienna (VC) conventions was believed to be necessary, with a view to laying down conditions for the application of either Convention (to the exclusion of the other) on a reciprocity basis. In other words, if a nuclear incident had occurred in a country party to the PC and had affected a country party to the VC, the former country would be considered as if it were a party (however without acquiring the status of a party) to the latter Convention, and vice-versa. Understandably, this was intended to create conditions for compensation of victims in any case, which is the main objective of the nuclear liability regime.

The instrument conceived to ensure the above was the so called "Joint Protocol" published hereafter, adopted on 21 September 1988 under the aegis of the NEA and IAEA, the sponsoring organisations of the basic Conventions affected by the Joint Protocol. The number of ratifying countries necessary for its entry into force was deliberately kept low (five for each of the two basic Conventions), in order to ensure practical application of the Protocol within a short time. This entered into force on 27 April 1992. Its application to the countries concerned in case of an incident obviously implies that they are parties both to the Protocol and to either Convention. The number of contracting Parties is now 24.

THE CONTRACTING PARTIES

HAVING REGARD to the Vienna Convention on Civil Liability for Nuclear Damage of 21 May 1963;

HAVING REGARD to the Paris Convention on Third Party Liability in the Field of Nuclear Energy of 29 July 1960 as amended by the Additional Protocol of 28 January 1964 and by the Protocol of 16 November 1982;

CONSIDERING that the Vienna Convention and the Paris Convention are similar in substance and that no State is at present a Party to both Conventions;

CONVINCED that adherence to either Convention by Parties to the other Convention could lead to difficulties resulting from the simultaneous application of both Conventions to a nuclear incident; and

DESIROUS to establish a link between the Vienna Convention and the Paris Convention by mutually extending the benefit of the special regime of civil liability for nuclear damage set forth under each Convention and to eliminate conflicts arising from the simultaneous applications of both Conventions to a nuclear incident;

HAVE AGREED as follows:

Article I

In this Protocol:

"Vienna Convention" means the Vienna Convention on Civil Liability for Nuclear Damage of 21 May 1963 and any amendment thereto which is in force for a Contracting Party to this Protocol;

"Paris Convention" means the Paris Convention on Third Party Liability in the Field of Nuclear Energy of 29 July 1960 and any amendment thereto which is in force for a Contracting Party to this Protocol.

Article II

For the purpose of this Protocol:

The operator of a nuclear installation situated in the territory of a Party to the Vienna Convention shall be liable in accordance with that Convention for nuclear damage suffered in the territory of a Party to both the Paris Convention and this Protocol;

The operator of a nuclear installation situated in the territory of a Party to the Paris Convention shall be liable in accordance with that Convention for nuclear damage suffered in the territory of a Party to both the Vienna Convention and this Protocol.

Article III

Either the Vienna Convention or the Paris Convention shall apply to a nuclear incident to the exclusion of the other.

In the case of a nuclear incident occurring in a nuclear installation, the applicable Convention shall be that to which the State is a Party within whose territory that installation is situated.

In the case of a nuclear incident outside a nuclear installation and involving nuclear material in the course of carriage, the applicable Convention shall be that to which the State is a Party within whose territory the nuclear installation is situated whose operator is liable pursuant to either Article II.1(b) and (c) of the Vienna Convention or Article 4(a) and (b) of the Paris Convention.

Article IV

1..Articles I to XV of the Vienna Convention shall be applied, with respect to the Contracting Parties to this Protocol which are Parties to the Paris Convention, in the same manner as between Parties to the Vienna Convention.

2..Articles 1 to 14 of the Paris Convention shall be applied, with respect to the Contracting Parties to this Protocol which are Parties to the Vienna Convention, in the same manner as between Parties to the Paris Convention.

Article V

This Protocol shall be open for signature, from 21 September 1988 until the date of its entry into force, at the Headquarters of the International Atomic Energy Agency by all States which have signed, ratified or acceded to either the Vienna Convention or the Paris Convention.

Article VI

This Protocol is subject to ratification, acceptance, approval or accession. Instruments of ratification, acceptance or approval shall only be accepted from States party to either the Vienna Convention or the Paris Convention. Any such State which has not signed this Protocol may accede to it.

The instruments of ratification, acceptance, approval or accession shall be deposited with the Director General of the International Atomic Energy Agency, who is hereby designated as the depositary of this Protocol.

Article VII

1. This Protocol shall come into force three months after the date of deposit of instruments of ratification, acceptance, approval or accession by at least five States Party to the Vienna Convention and five States Party to the Paris Convention. For each State ratifying, accepting, approving or acceding to this Protocol after the deposit of the above- mentioned instruments this Protocol shall enter into force three months after the date of deposit of the instrument of ratification, acceptance, approval or accession.

2. This Protocol shall remain in force as long as both the Vienna Convention and the Paris Convention are in force.

Article VIII

1.. Any Contracting Party may denounce this Protocol by written notification to the depositary.

2.. Denunciation shall take effect one year after the date on which the notification is received by the depositary.

Article IX

1.. Any Contracting Party which ceases to be a Party to either the Vienna Convention or the Paris Convention shall notify the depositary of the termination of the application of that Convention with respect to it and of the date such termination takes effect.

2.. This Protocol shall cease to apply to a Contracting Party which has terminated application of either the Vienna Convention or the Paris Convention on the date such termination takes effect.

Article X

The depositary shall promptly notify Contracting Parties and States invited to the Conference on the relationship between the Paris Convention and the Vienna Convention as well as the Secretary General of the Organisation for Economic Co-operation and Development of:

Each signature of this Protocol;
Each deposit of an instrument of ratification, acceptance, approval or accession concerning this Protocol;
The entry into force of this Protocol;
Any denunciation; and
Any information received pursuant to Article IX.

Article XI

The original of this Protocol, of which the Arabic, Chinese, English, French, Russian and Spanish texts are equally authentic, shall be deposited with the depositary, who shall send certified copies to Contracting Parties and States invited to the Conference on the relationship between the Paris Convention and the Vienna Convention as well as the Secretary General of the Organisation for Economic Co-operation and Development.

IN WITNESS WHEREOF the undersigned being duly authorized by their respective Governments for that purpose have signed the present Joint Protocol.

DONE at Vienna this twenty-first day of September, one thousand nine hundred and eighty-eight.

CONVENTION ON SUPPLEMENTARY COMPENSATION FOR NUCLEAR DAMAGE

(Vienna, 12 September 1997)

As recalled in the Introductory Material to the Protocol amending the Vienna Convention, this new instrument on supplementary compensation was the object of long negotiations in parallel to those for that Protocol, and indeed was adopted on the same date during the IAEA General Conference. However, contrary to the amending Protocol which clearly stems from the basic text of 1963, the new Convention is intended to create an independent system of supplementary compensation, although its conceptual links with the Vienna Convention are evident (e.g. the notions of incident, of damage etc.).

As a matter of fact, among the various proposals originally submitted one was indeed conceived as an instrument supplementing that Convention (similarly to the "Paris/Brussels system", but worldwide in scope). However, during the negotiations it was found that the new instrument would meet more success if designed in a way which would encourage accession also by countries not parties to any of the existing Conventions, and not only by those anyway interested in an international nuclear liability regime covering extremely serious incidents. On account of this it was agreed that the new Convention would be open for accession also to countries not parties to the other existing conventions on nuclear liability, on condition that their corresponding legislation would have to be in line with the fundamental principles (strict and absolute liability) on which such conventions are based.

The main objectives pursued by the Convention on Supplementary Compensation (CSC, published hereafter) are to create a) obligations between States party or not to the "Paris/Brussels system", and b) an international fund (in which the States party to the SCC contribute) beside or instead of that established by the Brussels Convention (or by any other "regional" instrument). The fund is made available up to 50% for national damage (i.e. occurred on the territory of the State where the installation giving rise to the incident is situated) and for trans-frontier damage; the remaining 50% is made available exclusively for the latter. The fund is not actually set up in its amount by the Convention, which only lays down criteria for contributing in the fund (installed nuclear capacity and gross domestic product).

Similarly to the amending Protocol to the Vienna Convention, a "phasing-in" mechanism is provided for by which States with a less strong economy may contribute in the fund with a lower amount, for a maximum of 10 years as of the signature (therefore not the entry into force, as for the above mentioned Protocol) of the Convention.

Finally and again similarly to the Protocol, the number of ratifying countries allowing for the entry into force of the new Convention is five; however, there is an additional condition attached, i.e. the total installed nuclear capacity which must be 400 thousand MW. In perspective and understandably, such high capacity is not so much important as a figure in itself, but rather in connection with the weight carried by the ratifying countries as an incentive to further ratifications. There are so far only 3 contracting Parties to the CSC.

THE CONTRACTING PARTIES,

RECOGNIZING the importance of the measures provided in the Vienna Convention on Civil Liability for Nuclear Damage and the Paris Convention on Third Party Liability in the Field of Nuclear Energy as well as in national legislation on compensation for nuclear damage consistent with the principles of these Conventions;

DESIROUS of establishing a worldwide liability regime to supplement and enhance these measures with a view to increasing the amount of compensation for nuclear damage;

RECOGNIZING further that such a worldwide liability regime would encourage regional and global co-operation to promote a higher level of nuclear safety in accordance with the principles of international partnership and solidarity;

HAVE AGREED as follows:

Chapter I
GENERAL PROVISIONS

Article I
Definitions

For the purposes of this Convention:

a. "Vienna Convention" means the Vienna Convention on Civil Liability for Nuclear Damage of 21 May 1963 and any amendment thereto which is in force for a Contracting Party to this Convention.

b. "Paris Convention" means the Paris Convention on Third Party Liability in the Field of Nuclear Energy of 29 July 1960 and any amendment thereto which is in force for a Contracting Party to this Convention.

c. "Special Drawing Right", hereinafter referred to as SDR, means the unit of account defined by the International Monetary Fund and used by it for its own operations and transactions.

d. "Nuclear reactor" means any structure containing nuclear fuel in such an arrangement that a self-sustaining chain process of nuclear fission can occur therein without an additional source of neutrons.

e. "Installation State", in relation to a nuclear installation, means the Contracting Party within whose territory that installation is situated or, if it is not situated within the territory of any State, the Contracting Party by which or under the authority of which the nuclear installation is operated.

f. "Nuclear Damage" means:
i. loss of life or personal injury;
ii. loss of or damage to property;
and each of the following to the extent determined by the law of the competent court:
iii. economic loss arising from loss or damage referred to in sub-paragraph (i) or (ii), insofar as not included in those sub-paragraphs, if incurred by a person entitled to claim in respect of such loss or damage;
iv. the costs of measures of reinstatement of impaired environment, unless such impairment is insignificant, if such measures are actually taken or to be taken, and insofar as not included in sub-paragraph (ii);
v. loss of income deriving from an economic interest in any use or enjoyment of the environment, incurred as a result of a significant impairment of that environment, and insofar as not included in sub-paragraph (ii);
vi. the costs of preventive measures, and further loss or damage caused by such measures;
vii. any other economic loss, other than any caused by the impairment of the environment, if permitted by the general law on civil liability of the competent court,
in the case of sub-paragraphs (i) to (v) and (vii) above, to the extent that the loss or damage arises out of or results from ionizing radiation emitted by any source of radiation inside a nuclear installation, or emitted from nuclear fuel or radioactive products or waste in, or of nuclear material coming from, originating in, or sent to, a nuclear installation, whether so arising from the radioactive properties of such matter, or from a combination of radioactive properties with toxic, explosive or other hazardous properties of such matter.

g. "Measures of reinstatement" means any reasonable measures which have been approved by the competent authorities of the State where the measures were taken, and which aim to reinstate or restore damaged or destroyed components of the environment, or to introduce, where reasonable, the equivalent of these components into the environment. The law of the State where the damage is suffered shall determine who is entitled to take such measures.

h. "Preventive measures" means any reasonable measures taken by any person after a nuclear incident has occurred to prevent or minimize damage referred to in sub-paragraphs (f)(i) to (v) or (vii), subject to any approval of the competent authorities required by the law of the State where the measures were taken.

i. "Nuclear incident" means any occurrence or series of occurrences having the same origin which causes nuclear damage or, but only with respect to preventive measures, creates a grave and imminent threat of causing such damage.

j. "Installed nuclear capacity" means for each Contracting Party the total of the number of units given by the formula set out in Article IV.2; and "thermal power" means the maximum thermal power authorized by the competent national authorities.

k. "Law of the competent court" means the law of the court having jurisdiction under this Convention, including any rules of such law relating to conflict of laws.

l. "Reasonable measures" means measures which are found under the law of the competent court to be appropriate and proportionate, having regard to all the circumstances, for example:
i. the nature and extent of the damage incurred or, in the case of preventive measures, the nature and extent of the risk of such damage;
ii. the extent to which, at the time they are taken, such measures are likely to be effective; and.
iii. relevant scientific and technical expertise

Article II
Purpose and Application

1. The purpose of this Convention is to supplement the system of compensation provided pursuant to national law which:
a. implements one of the instruments referred to in Article I (a) and (b); or
b. complies with the provisions of the Annex to this Convention.

2. The system of this Convention shall apply to nuclear damage for which an operator of a nuclear installation used for peaceful purposes situated in the territory of a Contracting Party is liable under either one of the Conventions referred to in Article I or national law mentioned in paragraph 1(b) of this Article.

3. The Annex referred to in paragraph 1(b) shall constitute an integral part of this Convention.

Chapter II
COMPENSATION

Article III
Undertaking

1. Compensation in respect of nuclear damage per nuclear incident shall be ensured by the following means:
a.
i. the Installation State shall ensure the availability of 300 million SDRs or a greater amount that it may have specified to the Depositary at any time prior to the nuclear incident, or a transitional amount pursuant to sub-paragraph (ii);
ii. a Contracting Party may establish for the maximum of 10 years from the date of the opening for signature of this Convention, a transitional amount of at least 150 million SDRs in respect of a nuclear incident occurring within that period.
b. beyond the amount made available under sub-paragraph (a), the Contracting Parties shall make available public funds according to the formula specified in Article IV.

2.
a. Compensation for nuclear damage in accordance with paragraph 1(a) shall be distributed equitably without discrimination on the basis of nationality, domicile or residence, provided that the law of the Installation State may, subject to obligations of that State under other conventions on nuclear liability, exclude nuclear damage suffered in a non-Contracting State.
b. Compensation for nuclear damage in accordance with paragraph 1(b), shall, subject to Articles V and XI.1(b), be distributed equitably without discrimination on the basis of nationality, domicile or residence.

3. If the nuclear damage to be compensated does not require the total amount under paragraph 1(b), the contributions shall be reduced proportionally.

4. The interest and costs awarded by a court in actions for compensation of nuclear damage are payable in addition to the amounts awarded pursuant to paragraphs 1(a) and (b) and shall be proportionate to the actual contributions made pursuant to paragraphs 1(a) and (b), respectively, by the operator liable, the Contracting Party in whose territory the nuclear installation of that operator is situated, and the Contracting Parties together.

Article IV
Calculation of Contributions

1. The formula for contributions according to which the Contracting Parties shall make available the public funds referred to in Article III.1(b) shall be determined as follows:

a.

i. the amount which shall be the product of the installed nuclear capacity of that Contracting Party multiplied by 300 SDRs per unit of installed capacity; and

ii. the amount determined by applying the ratio between the United Nations rate of assessment for that Contracting Party as assessed for the year preceding the year in which the nuclear incident occurs, and the total of such rates for all Contracting Parties to 10% of the sum of the amounts calculated for all Contracting Parties under sub-paragraph (i).

b. Subject to sub-paragraph (c), the contribution of each Contracting Party shall be the sum of the amounts referred to in sub-paragraphs (a)(i) and (ii), provided that States on the minimum United Nations rate of assessment with no nuclear reactors shall not be required to make contributions.

c. The maximum contribution which may be charged per nuclear incident to any Contracting Party, other than the Installation State, pursuant to sub-paragraph (b) shall not exceed its specified percentage of the total of contributions of all Contracting Parties determined pursuant to sub-paragraph (b). For a particular Contracting Party, the specified percentage shall be its UN rate of assessment expressed as a percentage plus 8 percentage points. If, at the time an incident occurs, the total installed capacity represented by the Parties to this Convention is at or above a level of 625,000 units, this percentage shall be increased by one percentage point. It shall be increased by one additional percentage point for each increment of 75,000 units by which the capacity exceeds 625,000 units.

2. The formula is for each nuclear reactor situated in the territory of the Contracting Party, 1 unit for each MW of thermal power. The formula shall be calculated on the basis of the thermal power of the nuclear reactors shown at the date of the nuclear incident in the list established and kept up to date in accordance with Article VIII.

3. For the purpose of calculating the contributions, a nuclear reactor shall be taken into account from that date when nuclear fuel elements have been first loaded into the nuclear reactor. A nuclear reactor shall be excluded from the calculation when all fuel elements have been removed permanently from the reactor core and have been stored safely in accordance with approved procedures.

Article V
Geographical Scope

1. The funds provided for under Article III.1(b) shall apply to nuclear damage which is suffered:

a. in the territory of a Contracting Party; or

b. in or above maritime areas beyond the territorial sea of a Contracting Party:

i. on board or by a ship flying the flag of a Contracting Party, or on board or by an aircraft registered in the territory of a Contracting Party, or on or by an artificial island, installation or structure under the jurisdiction of a Contracting Party; or

ii. by a national of a Contracting Party;

excluding damage suffered in or above the territorial sea of a State not Party to this Convention; or

c. in or above the exclusive economic zone of a Contracting Party or on the continental shelf of a Contracting Party in connection with the exploitation or the exploration of the natural resources of that exclusive economic zone or continental shelf; provided that the courts of a Contracting Party have jurisdiction pursuant to Article XIII.

2. Any signatory or acceding State may, at the time of signature of or accession to this Convention or on the deposit of its instrument of ratification, declare that for the purposes of the application of paragraph 1(b)(ii), individuals or certain categories thereof, considered under its law as having their habitual residence in its territory, are assimilated to its own nationals.

3. In this article, the expression "a national of a Contracting Party" shall include a Contracting Party or any of its constituent sub-divisions, or a partnership, or any public or private body whether corporate or not established in the territory of a Contracting Party.

Chapter III
ORGANIZATION OF SUPPLEMENTARY FUNDING

Article VI
Notification of Nuclear Damage

Without prejudice to obligations which Contracting Parties may have under other international agreements, the Contracting Party whose courts have jurisdiction shall inform the other Contracting Parties of a nuclear incident as soon as it appears that the damage caused by such incident exceeds, or is likely to exceed, the amount available under Article III.1(a) and that contributions under Article III.1(b) may be required. The Contracting Parties shall without delay make all the necessary arrangements to settle the procedure for their relations in this connection.

Article VII
Call for Funds

1. Following the notification referred to in Article VI, and subject to Article X.3, the Contracting Party whose courts have jurisdiction shall request the other Contracting Parties to make available the public funds required under Article III.1(b) to the extent and when they are actually required and shall have exclusive competence to disburse such funds.

2. Independently of existing or future regulations concerning currency or transfers, Contracting Parties shall authorize the transfer and payment of any contribution provided pursuant to Article III.1(b) without any restriction.

Article VIII
List of Nuclear Installations

1. Each Contracting State shall, at the time when it deposits its instrument of ratification, acceptance, approval or accession, communicate to the Depositary a complete listing of all nuclear installations referred to in Article IV.3. The listing shall contain the necessary particulars for the purpose of the calculation of contributions.

2. Each Contracting State shall promptly communicate to the Depositary all modifications to be made to the list. Where such modifications include the addition of a nuclear installation, the communication must be made at least three months before the expected date when nuclear material will be introduced into the installation.

3. If a Contracting Party is of the opinion that the particulars, or any modification to be made to the list communicated by a Contracting State pursuant to paragraphs

1 and 2, do not comply with the provisions, it may raise objections thereto by addressing them to the Depositary within three months from the date on which it has received notice pursuant to paragraph 5. The Depositary shall forthwith communicate this objection to the State to whose information the objection has been raised. Any unresolved differences shall be dealt with in accordance with the dispute settlement procedure laid down in Article XVI.

4. The Depositary shall maintain, update and annually circulate to all Contracting States the list of nuclear installations established in accordance with this Article. Such list shall consist of all the particulars and modifications referred to in this Article, it being understood that objections submitted under this Article shall have effect retrospective to the date on which they were raised, if they are sustained.

5. The Depositary shall give notice as soon as possible to each Contracting Party of the communications and objections which it has received pursuant to this Article.

Article IX
Rights of Recourse

1. Each Contracting Party shall enact legislation in order to enable both the Contracting Party in whose territory the nuclear installation of the operator liable is situated and the other Contracting Parties who have paid contributions referred to in Article III.1(b), to benefit from the operator's right of recourse to the extent that he has such a right under either one of the Conventions referred to in Article I or national legislation mentioned in Article II.1(b) and to the extent that contributions have been made by any of the Contracting Parties.

2. The legislation of the Contracting Party in whose territory the nuclear installation of the operator liable is situated may provide for the recovery of public funds made available under this Convention from such operator if the damage results from fault on his part.

3. The Contracting Party whose courts have jurisdiction may exercise the rights of recourse provided for in paragraphs 1 and 2 on behalf of the other Contracting Parties which have contributed.

Article X
Disbursements, Proceedings

1. The system of disbursements by which the funds required under Article III.1 are to be made available and the system of apportionment thereof shall be that of the Contracting Party whose courts have jurisdiction.

2. Each Contracting Party shall ensure that persons suffering damage may enforce their rights to compensation without having to bring separate proceedings according to the origin of the funds provided for such compensation and that Contracting Parties may intervene in the proceedings against the operator liable.

3. No Contracting Party shall be required to make available the public funds referred to in Article III.1(b) if claims for compensation can be satisfied out of the funds referred to in Article III.1(a).

Article XI
Allocation of Funds

The funds provided under Article III.1(b) shall be distributed as follows:
a. 50% of the funds shall be available to compensate claims for nuclear damage suffered in or outside the Installation State;
b. 50% of the funds shall be available to compensate claims for nuclear damage suffered outside the territory of the Installation State to the extent that such claims are uncompensated under sub-paragraph (a).
c. In the event the amount provided pursuant to Article III.1(a) is less than 300 million SDRs:
i. the amount in paragraph 1(a) shall be reduced by the same percentage as the percentage by which the amount provided pursuant to Article III.1(a) is less than 300 million SDRs; and
ii. the amount in paragraph 1(b) shall be increased by the amount of the reduction calculated pursuant to sub-paragraph (i).
d. If a Contracting Party, in accordance with Article III.1(a), has ensured the availability without discrimination of an amount not less than 600 million SDRs, which has been specified to the Depositary prior to the nuclear incident, all funds referred to in Article III.1(a) and (b) shall, notwithstanding paragraph 1, be made available to compensate nuclear damage suffered in and outside the Installation State.

Chapter IV
EXERCISE OF OPTIONS

Article XII

1. Except insofar as this Convention otherwise provides, each Contracting Party may exercise the powers vested in it by virtue of the Vienna Convention or the Paris Convention, and any provisions made thereunder may be invoked against the other Contracting Parties in order that the public funds referred to in Article III.1(b) be made available.

2. Nothing in this Convention shall prevent any Contracting Party from making provisions outside the scope of the Vienna or the Paris Convention and of this Convention, provided that such provision shall not involve any further obligation on the part of the other Contracting Parties, and provided that damage in a Contracting Party having no nuclear installations within its territory shall not be excluded from such further compensation on any grounds of lack of reciprocity.
a. Nothing in this Convention shall prevent Contracting Parties from entering into regional or other agreements with the purpose of implementing their obligations under Article III.1(a) or providing additional funds for the compensation of nuclear damage, provided that this shall not involve any further obligation under this Convention for the other Contracting Parties.
b. A Contracting Party intending to enter into any such agreement shall notify all other Contracting Parties of its intention. Agreements concluded shall be notified to the Depositary.

Chapter V
JURISDICTION AND APPLICABLE LAW

Article XIII
Jurisdiction

1. Except as otherwise provided in this article, jurisdiction over actions concerning nuclear damage from a nuclear incident shall lie only with the courts of the Contracting Party within which the nuclear incident occurs.

2. Where a nuclear incident occurs within the area of the exclusive economic zone of a Contracting Party or, if such a zone has not been established, in an area not exceeding the limits of an exclusive economic zone, were one to be established by that Party, jurisdiction over actions concerning nuclear damage from that nuclear incident shall, for the purposes of this Convention, lie only with the courts of that Party. The preceding sentence shall apply if that Contracting Party has notified the Depositary of such area prior to the nuclear incident. Nothing in this paragraph shall be interpreted as permitting the exercise of jurisdiction in a manner which is contrary to the international law of the sea, including the United Nations Convention on the Law of the Sea. However, if the exercise of such jurisdiction is inconsistent with the obligations of that Party under Article XI of the Vienna Convention or Article 13 of the Paris Convention in relation to a State not Party to this Convention jurisdiction shall be determined according to those provisions.

3. Where a nuclear incident does not occur within the territory of any Contracting Party or within an area notified pursuant to paragraph 2, or where the place of a

nuclear incident cannot be determined with certainty, jurisdiction over actions concerning nuclear damage from the nuclear incident shall lie only with the courts of the Installation State.

4. Where jurisdiction over actions concerning nuclear damage would lie with the courts of more than one Contracting Party, these Contracting Parties shall determine by agreement which Contracting Party's courts shall have jurisdiction.

5. A judgment that is no longer subject to ordinary forms of review entered by a court of a Contracting Party having jurisdiction shall be recognized except:
a. where the judgment was obtained by fraud;
b. where the party against whom the judgment was pronounced was not given a fair opportunity to present his case; or
c. where the judgment is contrary to the public policy of the Contracting Party within the territory of which recognition is sought, or is not in accord with fundamental standards of justice.

6. A judgment which is recognized under paragraph 5 shall, upon being presented for enforcement in accordance with the formalities required by the law of the Contracting Party where enforcement is sought, be enforceable as if it were a judgment of a court of that Contracting Party. The merits of a claim on which the judgment has been given shall not be subject to further proceedings.

7. Settlements effected in respect of the payment of compensation out of the public funds referred to in Article III.1(b) in accordance with the conditions established by national legislation shall be recognized by the other Contracting Parties.

Article XIV
Applicable Law

1. Either the Vienna Convention or the Paris Convention or the Annex to this Convention, as appropriate, shall apply to a nuclear incident to the exclusion of the others.

2. Subject to the provisions of this Convention, the Vienna Convention or the Paris Convention, as appropriate, the applicable law shall be the law of the competent court.

Article XV
Public International Law

This Convention shall not affect the rights and obligations of a Contracting Party under the general rules of public international law.

Chapter VI
DISPUTE SETTLEMENT

Article XVI

1. In the event of a dispute between Contracting Parties concerning the interpretation or application of this Convention, the parties to the dispute shall consult with a view to the settlement of the dispute by negotiation or by any other peaceful means of settling disputes acceptable to them.

2. If a dispute of this character referred to in paragraph 1 cannot be settled within six months from the request for consultation pursuant to paragraph 1, it shall, at the request of any party to such dispute, be submitted to arbitration or referred to the International Court of Justice for decision. Where a dispute is submitted to arbitration, if, within six months from the date of the request, the parties to the dispute are unable to agree on the organization of the arbitration, a party may request the President of the International Court of Justice or the Secretary-General of the United Nations to appoint one or more arbitrators. In cases of conflicting requests by the parties to the dispute, the request to the Secretary-General of the United Nations shall have priority.

3. When ratifying, accepting, approving or acceding to this Convention, a State may declare that it does not consider itself bound by either or both of the dispute settlement procedures provided for in paragraph 2. The other Contracting Parties shall not be bound by a dispute settlement procedure provided for in paragraph 2 with respect to a Contracting Party for which such a declaration is in force.

4. A Contracting Party which has made a declaration in accordance with paragraph 3 may at any time withdraw it by notification to the Depositary.

Chapter VII
FINAL CLAUSES

Article XVII
Signature

This Convention shall be open for signature, by all States at the Headquarters of the International Atomic Energy Agency in Vienna from 29 September 1997 until its entry into force.

Article XVIII
Ratification, Acceptance, Approval

1. This Convention shall be subject to ratification, acceptance or approval by the signatory States. An instrument of ratification, acceptance or approval shall be accepted only from a State which is a Party to either the Vienna Convention or the Paris Convention, or a State which declares that its national law complies with the provisions of the Annex to this Convention, provided that, in the case of a State having on its territory a nuclear installation as defined in the Convention on Nuclear Safety of 17 June 1994, it is a Contracting State to that Convention.

2. The instruments of ratification, acceptance or approval shall be deposited with the Director General of the International Atomic Energy Agency who shall act as the Depositary of this Convention.

3. A Contracting Party shall provide the Depositary with a copy, in one of the official languages of the United Nations, of the provisions of its national law referred to in Article II.1 and amendments thereto, including any specification made pursuant to Article III.1(a), Article XI.2, or a transitional amount pursuant to Article III.1(a)(ii). Copies of such provisions shall be circulated by the Depositary to all other Contracting Parties.

Article XIX
Accession

1. After its entry into force, any State which has not signed this Convention may accede to it. An instrument of accession shall be accepted only from a State which is a Party to either the Vienna Convention or the Paris Convention, or a State which declares that its national law complies with the provisions of the Annex to this Convention, provided that, in the case of a State having on its territory a nuclear installation as defined in the Convention on Nuclear Safety of 17 June 1994, it is a Contracting State to that Convention.

2. The instruments of accession shall be deposited with the Director General of the International Atomic Energy Agency.

3. A Contracting Party shall provide the Depositary with a copy, in one of the official languages of the United Nations, of the provisions of its national law referred to in Article II.1 and amendments thereto, including any specification made pursuant to Article III.1(a), Article XI.2, or a transitional amount pursuant to Article III.1(a)(ii).

Copies of such provisions shall be circulated by the Depositary to all other Contracting Parties.

Article XX
Entry Into Force

1. This Convention shall come into force on the ninetieth day following the date on which at least 5 States with a minimum of 400,000 units of installed nuclear capacity have deposited an instrument referred to in Article XVIII.

2. For each State which subsequently ratifies, accepts, approves or accedes to this Convention, it shall enter into force on the ninetieth day after deposit by such State of the appropriate instrument.

Article XXI
Denunciation

1. Any Contracting Party may denounce this Convention by written notification to the Depositary.

2. Denunciation shall take effect one year after the date on which the notification is received by the Depositary.

Article XXII
Cessation

1. Any Contracting Party which ceases to be a Party to either the Vienna Convention or the Paris Convention shall notify the Depositary thereof and of the date of such cessation. On that date such Contracting Party shall have ceased to be a Party to this Convention unless its national law complies with the provisions of the Annex to this Convention and it has so notified the Depositary and provided it with a copy of the provisions of its national law in one of the official languages of the United Nations. Such copy shall be circulated by the Depositary to all other Contracting Parties.

2. Any Contracting Party whose national law ceases to comply with the provisions of the Annex to this Convention and which is not a Party to either the Vienna Convention or the Paris Convention shall notify the Depositary thereof and of the date of such cessation. On that date such Contracting Party shall have ceased to be a Party to this Convention.

3. Any Contracting Party having on its territory a nuclear installation as defined in the Convention on Nuclear Safety which ceases to be Party to that Convention shall notify the depositary thereof and of the date of such cessation. On that date, such Contracting Party shall, notwithstanding paragraphs 1 and 2, have ceased to be a Party to the present Convention.

Article XXIII
Continuance of Prior Rights and Obligations

Notwithstanding denunciation pursuant to Article XXI or cessation pursuant to Article XXII, the provisions of this Convention shall continue to apply to any nuclear damage caused by a nuclear incident which occurs before such denunciation or cessation.

Article XXIV
Revision and Amendments

1. The Depositary, after consultations with the Contracting Parties, may convene a conference for the purpose of revising or amending this Convention.

2. The Depositary shall convene a conference of Contracting Parties for the purpose of revising or amending this Convention at the request of not less than one-third of all Contracting Parties.

Article XXV
Amendment by Simplified Procedure

1. A meeting of the Contracting Parties shall be convened by the Depositary to amend the compensation amounts referred to in Article III.1(a) and (b) or categories of installations including contributions payable for them, referred to in Article IV.3, if one-third of the Contracting Parties express a desire to that effect.

2. Decisions to adopt a proposed amendment shall be taken by vote. Amendments shall be adopted if no negative vote is cast.

3. Any amendment adopted in accordance with paragraph 2 shall be notified by the Depositary to all Contracting Parties. The amendment shall be considered accepted if within a period of 36 months after it has been notified, all Contracting Parties at the time of the adoption of the amendment have communicated their acceptance to the Depositary. The amendment shall enter into force for all Contracting Parties 12 months after its acceptance.

4. If, within a period of 36 months from the date of notification for acceptance the amendment has not been accepted in accordance with paragraph 3, the amendment shall be considered rejected.

5. When an amendment has been adopted in accordance with paragraph 2 but the 36 months period for its acceptance has not yet expired, a State which becomes a Party to this Convention during that period shall be bound by the amendment if it comes into force. A State which becomes a Party to this Convention after that period shall be bound by any amendment which has been accepted in accordance with paragraph 3. In the cases referred to in the present paragraph, a Contracting Party shall be bound by an amendment when that amendment enters into force, or when this Convention enters into force for that Contracting Party, whichever date is the later.

Article XXVI
Functions of the Depositary

In addition to functions in other Articles of this Convention, the Depositary shall promptly notify Contracting Parties and all other States as well as the Secretary-General of the Organization for Economic Co-operation and Development of:
a. each signature of this Convention;
b. each deposit of an instrument of ratification, acceptance, approval or accession concerning this Convention;
c. the entry into force of this Convention;
d. declarations received pursuant to Article XVI;
e. any denunciation received pursuant to Article XXI, or notification received pursuant to Article XXII;
f. any notification under paragraph 2 of Article XIII;
g. other pertinent notifications relating to this Convention.

Article XXVII
Authentic Texts

The original of this Convention, of which Arabic, Chinese, English, French, Russian and Spanish texts are equally authentic, shall be deposited with the Director General of the International Atomic Energy Agency who shall send certified copies thereof to all States.

IN WITNESS WHEREOF, THE UNDERSIGNED, BEING DULY AUTHORIZED THERETO, HAVE SIGNED THIS CONVENTION.

Done at Vienna, this twelfth day of September, one thousand nine hundred ninety-seven.

ANNEX

A Contracting Party which is not a Party to any of the Conventions mentioned in Article I(a) or (b) of this Convention shall ensure that its national legislation is consistent with the provisions laid down in this Annex insofar as those provisions are not directly applicable within that Contracting Party. A Contracting Party having no nuclear installation on its territory is required to have only that legislation which is necessary to enable such a Party to give effect to its obligations under this Convention.

Article 1
Definitions

1. In addition to the definitions in Article I of this Convention, the following definitions apply for the purposes of this Annex:
a. "Nuclear Fuel" means any material which is capable of producing energy by a self-sustaining chain process of nuclear fission.
b. "Nuclear Installation" means:
i. any nuclear reactor other than one with which a means of sea or air transport is equipped for use as a source of power, whether for propulsion thereof or for any other purpose;
ii. any factory using nuclear fuel for the production of nuclear material, or any factory for the processing of nuclear material, including any factory for the re-processing of irradiated nuclear fuel; and
iii. any facility where nuclear material is stored, other than storage incidental to the carriage of such material;
provided that the Installation State may determine that several nuclear installations of one operator which are located at the same site shall be considered as a single nuclear installation.
c. "Nuclear material" means:
i. nuclear fuel, other than natural uranium and depleted uranium, capable of producing energy by a self-sustaining chain process of nuclear fission outside a nuclear reactor, either alone or in combination with some other material; and
ii. radioactive products or waste.
d. "Operator", in relation to a nuclear installation, means the person designated or recognized by the Installation State as the operator of that installation.
e. "Radioactive products or waste" means any radioactive material produced in, or any material made radioactive by exposure to the radiation incidental to, the production or utilization of nuclear fuel, but does not include radioisotopes which have

reached the final stage of fabrication so as to be usable for any scientific, medical, agricultural, commercial or industrial purpose.

2 . An Installation State may, if the small extent of the risks involved so warrants, exclude any nuclear installation or small quantities of nuclear material from the application of this Convention, provided that:
a. with respect to nuclear installations, criteria for such exclusion have been established by the Board of Governors of the International Atomic Energy Agency and any exclusion by an Installation State satisfies such criteria; and
b. with respect to small quantities of nuclear material, maximum limits for the exclusion of such quantities have been established by the Board of Governors of the International Atomic Energy Agency and any exclusion by an Installation State is within such established limits.
The criteria for the exclusion of nuclear installations and the maximum limits for the exclusion of small quantities of nuclear material shall be reviewed periodically by the Board of Governors.

Article 2
Conformity of Legislation

1. The national law of a Contracting Party is deemed to be in conformity with the provisions of Articles 3, 4, 5 and 7 if it contained on 1 January 1995 and continues to contain provisions that:
a. provide for strict liability in the event of a nuclear incident where there is substantial nuclear damage off the site of the nuclear installation where the incident occurs;
b. require the indemnification of any person other than the operator liable for nuclear damage to the extent that person is legally liable to provide compensation; and
c. ensure the availability of at least 1000 million SDRs in respect of a civil nuclear power plant and at least 300 million SDRs in respect of other civil nuclear installations for such indemnification.

2. If in accordance with paragraph 1, the national law of a Contracting Party is deemed to be in conformity with the provision of Articles 3, 4, 5 and 7, then that Party:
a. may apply a definition of nuclear damage that covers loss or damage set forth in Article I(f) of this Convention and any other loss or damage to the extent that the loss or damage arises out of or results from the radioactive properties, or a combination of radioactive properties with toxic, explosive or other hazardous properties of nuclear fuel or radioactive products or waste in, or of nuclear material coming from, originating in, or sent to, a nuclear installation; or other ionizing radiation emitted by any source of radiation inside a nuclear installation, provided that such application does

not affect the undertaking by that Contracting Party pursuant to Article III of this Convention; and

b. may apply the definition of nuclear installation in paragraph 3 of this Article to the exclusion of the definition in Article 1.1(b) of this Annex.

3. For the purpose of paragraph 2 (b) of this Article, "nuclear installation" means:

a. any civil nuclear reactor other than one with which a means of sea or air transport is equipped for use as a source of power, whether for propulsion thereof or any other purpose; and

b. any civil facility for processing, reprocessing or storing:

i. irradiated nuclear fuel; or

ii. radioactive products or waste that:

1. result from the reprocessing of irradiated nuclear fuel and contain significant amounts of fission products; or

2. contain elements that have an atomic number greater than 92 in concentrations greater than 10 nano-curies per gram.

c. any other civil facility for processing, reprocessing or storing nuclear material unless the Contracting Party determines the small extent of the risks involved with such an installation warrants the exclusion of such a facility from this definition.

4. Where that national law of a Contracting Party which is in compliance with paragraph 1 of this Article does not apply to a nuclear incident which occurs outside the territory of that Contracting Party, but over which the courts of that Contracting Party have jurisdiction pursuant to Article XIII of this Convention, Articles 3 to 11 of the Annex shall apply and prevail over any inconsistent provisions of the applicable national law.

Article 3
Operator Liability

1. The operator of a nuclear installation shall be liable for nuclear damage upon proof that such damage has been caused by a nuclear incident:

a. in that nuclear installation; or

b. involving nuclear material coming from or originating in that nuclear installation, and occurring:

i. before liability with regard to nuclear incidents involving the nuclear material has been assumed, pursuant to the express terms of a contract in writing, by the operator of another nuclear installation;

ii. in the absence of such express terms, before the operator of another nuclear installation has taken charge of the nuclear material; or

iii. where the nuclear material is intended to be used in a nuclear reactor with which a means of transport is equipped for use as a source of power, whether for propulsion thereof or for any other purpose, before the person duly authorized to operate such reactor has taken charge of the nuclear material; but
iv. where the nuclear material has been sent to a person within the territory of a non-Contracting State, before it has been unloaded from the means of transport by which it has arrived in the territory of that non-Contracting State;
c. involving nuclear material sent to that nuclear installation, and occurring:
i. after liability with regard to nuclear incidents involving the nuclear material has been assumed by the operator pursuant to the express terms of a contract in writing, from the operator of another nuclear installation;
ii. in the absence of such express terms, after the operator has taken charge of the nuclear material; or
iii. after the operator has taken charge of the nuclear material from a person operating a nuclear reactor with which a means of transport is equipped for use as a source of power, whether for propulsion thereof or for any other purpose; but
iv. where the nuclear material has, with the written consent of the operator, been sent from a person within the territory of a non-Contracting State, only after it has been loaded on the means of transport by which it is to be carried from the territory of that State;

2. Provided that, if nuclear damage is caused by a nuclear incident occurring in a nuclear installation and involving nuclear material stored therein incidentally to the carriage of such material, the provisions of sub-paragraph (a) shall not apply where another operator or person is solely liable pursuant to sub-paragraph (b) or (c).

3. The Installation State may provide by legislation that, in accordance with such terms as may be specified in that legislation, a carrier of nuclear material or a person handling radioactive waste may, at such carrier or such person's request and with the consent of the operator concerned, be designated or recognized as operator in the place of that operator in respect of such nuclear material or radioactive waste respectively. In this case such carrier or such person shall be considered, for all the purposes of this Convention, as an operator of a nuclear installation situated within the territory of that State.

4. The liability of the operator for nuclear damage shall be absolute.

5. Whenever both nuclear damage and damage other than nuclear damage have been caused by a nuclear incident or jointly by a nuclear incident and one or more other occurrences, such other damage shall, to the extent that it is not reasonably separable from the nuclear damage, be deemed to be nuclear damage caused by that nuclear

incident. Where, however, damage is caused jointly by a nuclear incident covered by the provisions of this Annex and by an emission of ionizing radiation not covered by it, nothing in this Annex shall limit or otherwise affect the liability, either as regards any person suffering nuclear damage or by way of recourse or contribution, of any person who may be held liable in connection with that emission of ionizing radiation.

6.
a. No liability shall attach to an operator for nuclear damage caused by a nuclear incident directly due to an act of armed conflict, hostilities, civil war or insurrection.
b. Except insofar as the law of the Installation State may provide to the contrary, the operator shall not be liable for nuclear damage caused by a nuclear incident caused directly due to a grave natural disaster of an exceptional character.

7. National law may relieve an operator wholly or partly from the obligation to pay compensation for nuclear damage suffered by a person if the operator proves the nuclear damage resulted wholly or partly from the gross negligence of that person or an act or omission of that person done with the intent to cause damage.

8. The operator shall not be liable for nuclear damage:
a. to the nuclear installation itself and any other nuclear installation, including a nuclear installation under construction, on the site where that installation is located; and
b. to any property on that same site which is used or to be used in connection with any such installation;
c. unless otherwise provided by national law, to the means of transport upon which the nuclear material involved was at the time of the nuclear incident. If national law provides that the operator is liable for such damage, compensation for that damage shall not have the effect of reducing the liability of the operator in respect of other damage to an amount less than either 150 million SDRs, or any higher amount established by the legislation of a Contracting Party.

9. Nothing in this Convention shall affect the liability outside this Convention of the operator for nuclear damage for which by virtue of paragraph 7(c) he is not liable under this Convention.

10. The right to compensation for nuclear damage may be exercised only against the operator liable, provided that national law may permit a direct right of action against any supplier of funds that are made available pursuant to provisions in national law to ensure compensation through the use of funds from sources other than the operator.

11. The operator shall incur no liability for damage caused by a nuclear incident outside the provisions of national law in accordance with this Convention.

Article 4
Liability Amounts

1. Subject to Article III.1(a)(ii), the liability of the operator may be limited by the Installation State for any one nuclear incident, either:
a. to not less than 300 million SDRs; or
b. to not less then 150 million SDRs provided that in excess of that amount and up to at least 300 million SDRs public funds shall be made available by that State to compensate nuclear damage.

2. Notwithstanding paragraph 1, the Installation State, having regard to the nature of the nuclear installation or the nuclear substances involved and to the likely consequences of an incident originating therefrom, may establish a lower amount of liability of the operator, provided that in no event shall any amount so established be less than 5 million SDRs, and provided that the Installation State ensures that public funds shall be made available up to the amount established pursuant to paragraph 1.

3. The amounts established by the Installation State of the liable operator in accordance with paragraphs 1 and 2, as well as the provisions of any legislation of a Contracting Party pursuant to Article 3.7(c) shall apply wherever the nuclear incident occurs.

Article 5
Financial Security

1.
a. The operator shall be required to have and maintain insurance or other financial security covering his liability for nuclear damage in such amount, of such type and in such terms as the Installation State shall specify. The Installation State shall ensure the payment of claims for compensation for nuclear damage which have been established against the operator by providing the necessary funds to the extent that the yield of insurance or other financial security is inadequate to satisfy such claims, but not in excess of the limit, if any, established pursuant to Article 4. Where the liability of the operator is unlimited, the Installation State may establish a limit of the financial security of the operator liable provided that such limit is not lower than 300 million SDRs. The Installation State shall ensure the payment of claims for compensation for nuclear damage which have been established against the operator to the extent that

yield of the financial security is inadequate to satisfy such claims, but not in excess of the amount of the financial security to be provided under this paragraph.
b. Notwithstanding sub-paragraph (a), the Installation State, having regard to the nature of the nuclear installation or the nuclear substances involved and to the likely consequences of an incident originating therefrom, may establish a lower amount of financial security of the operator, provided that in no event shall any amount so established be less than 5 million SDRs, and provided that the Installation State ensures the payment of claims for compensation for nuclear damage which have been established against the operator by providing necessary funds to the extent that the yield of insurance or other financial security is inadequate to satisfy such claims, and up to the limit provided in sub-paragraph (a).

2. Nothing in paragraph 1 shall require a Contracting Party or any of its constituent sub-divisions to maintain insurance or other financial security to cover their liability as operators.

3. The funds provided by insurance, by other financial security or by the Installation State pursuant to paragraph 1 or Article 4.1(b) shall be exclusively available for compensation due under this Annex.

4. No insurer or other financial guarantor shall suspend or cancel the insurance or other financial security provided pursuant to paragraph 1 without giving notice in writing of at least two months to the competent public authority or, in so far as such insurance or other financial security relates to the carriage of nuclear material, during the period of the carriage in question.

Article 6
Carriage

1. With respect to a nuclear incident during carriage, the maximum amount of liability of the operator shall be governed by the national law of the Installation State.

2. A Contracting Party may subject carriage of nuclear material through its territory to the condition that the amount of liability of the operator be increased to an amount not to exceed the maximum amount of liability of the operator of a nuclear installation situated in its territory.

3. The provisions of paragraph 2 shall not apply to:
a. carriage by sea where, under international law, there is a right of entry in cases of urgent distress into ports of a Contracting Party or a right of innocent passage through its territory;

b. carriage by air where, by agreement or under international law, there is a right to fly over or land on the territory of a Contracting Party.

Article 7
Liability of More Than One Operator

1. Where nuclear damage engages the liability of more than one operator, the operators involved shall, in so far as the damage attributable to each operator is not reasonably separable, be jointly and severally liable. The Installation State may limit the amount of public funds made available per incident to the difference, if any, between the amounts hereby established and the amount established pursuant to Article 4.1.

2. Where a nuclear incident occurs in the course of carriage of nuclear material, either in one and the same means of transport, or, in the case of storage incidental to the carriage, in one and the same nuclear installation, and causes nuclear damage which engages the liability of more than one operator, the total liability shall not exceed the highest amount applicable with respect to any one of them pursuant to Article 4.

3. In neither of the cases referred to in paragraphs 1 and 2 shall the liability of any one operator exceed the amount applicable with respect to him pursuant to Article 4.

4. Subject to the provisions of paragraphs 1 to 3, where several nuclear installations of one and the same operator are involved in one nuclear incident, such operator shall be liable in respect of each nuclear installation involved up to the amount applicable with respect to him pursuant to Article 4. The Installation State may limit the amount of public funds made available as provided for in paragraph 1.

Article 8
Compensation Under National Law

1. For purposes of this Convention, the amount of compensation shall be determined without regard to any interest or costs awarded in a proceeding for compensation of nuclear damage.

2. Compensation for damage suffered outside the Installation State shall be provided in a form freely transferable among Contracting Parties.

3. Where provisions of national or public health insurance, social insurance, social security, workmen's compensation or occupational disease compensation systems include compensation for nuclear damage, rights of beneficiaries of such systems and

rights of recourse by virtue of such systems shall be determined by the national law of the Contracting Party in which such systems have been established or by the regulations of the intergovernmental organization which has established such systems.

Article 9
Period of Extinction

1. Rights of compensation under this Convention shall be extinguished if an action is not brought within ten years from the date of the nuclear incident. If, however, under the law of the Installation State the liability of the operator is covered by insurance or other financial security or by State funds for a period longer than ten years, the law of the competent court may provide that rights of compensation against the operator shall only be extinguished after a period which may be longer than ten years, but shall not be longer than the period for which his liability is so covered under the law of the Installation State.

2. Where nuclear damage is caused by a nuclear incident involving nuclear material which at the time of the nuclear incident was stolen, lost, jettisoned or abandoned, the period established pursuant to paragraph 1 shall be computed from the date of that nuclear incident, but the period shall in no case, subject to legislation pursuant to paragraph 1, exceed a period of twenty years from the date of the theft, loss, jettison or abandonment.

3. The law of the competent court may establish a period of extinction or prescription of not less than three years from the date on which the person suffering nuclear damage had knowledge or should have had knowledge of the damage and of the operator liable for the damage, provided that the period established pursuant to paragraphs 1 and 2 shall not be exceeded.

4. If the national law of a Contracting Party provides for a period of extinction or prescription greater than ten years from the date of a nuclear incident, it shall contain provisions for the equitable and timely satisfaction of claims for loss of life or personal injury filed within ten years from the date of the nuclear incident.

Article 10
Right of Recourse

National law may provide that the operator shall have a right of recourse only:
a. if this is expressly provided for by a contract in writing; or
b. if the nuclear incident results from an act or omission done with intent to cause damage, against the individual who has acted or omitted to act with such intent.

Article 11
Applicable Law

Subject to the provisions of this Convention, the nature, form, extent and equitable distribution of compensation for nuclear damage caused by a nuclear incident shall be governed by the law of the competent court.

CONVENTION ON THE LIABILITY OF OPERATORS OF NUCLEAR SHIPS

(Brussels, 25 May 1962)

The Paris and Vienna Conventions (see previous pages) on nuclear third party liability, as adopted in 1960 and 1963 respectively, did not include provisions covering damage from incidents occurred in the operation of nuclear ships (i.e. equipped with a nuclear power plant). The main reason for this is that at the time of adoption of those Conventions, there was no immediate need to lay down a specific international regime on liability of operators of nuclear ships. These were in fact built and put into operation some years later in the Usa (the "Savannah") and in the Federal Republic of Germany (the "Otto Hahn"). Other existing international instruments such as the SOLAS Convention of 1960 (see Part II, Section II of this volume) did address conditions for the operation of nuclear ships, but not for third party liability in case of an incident.

On the occasion of the 1962 Diplomatic Conference on Maritime Law held in Brussels, the IAEA in co-operation with the Intergovernmental Maritime Consultative Organisation (IMCO, now IMO) promoted the adoption of a Convention (at the end of the 12th session of the conference) specifically addressing the liability of operators of (commercial) nuclear ships. The depositary of the ratification instruments is the Belgian Government, the entry into force of the Convention requiring the deposit of ratification instruments by at least one State which has authorised the operation of a nuclear ship and one other State. This is obviously depending very much on the importance and the urgency of the States' interest in building and putting into operation such ships. Given the problems raised by public opinion in the debate on nuclear safety and on protection of the environment, such interest has gradually but steadily decreased. Consequently, also the interest in the entry into force of the Convention eventually vanished, although some ratifications (by non-licensing States) did ensue in the past years.

The text of the Convention is published in the following pages on account of its "historical" importance.

THE CONTRACTING PARTIES

HAVING RECOGNIZED the desirability of determining by agreement certain uniform rules concerning the liability of operators of nuclear ships,

HAVE DECIDED to conclude a Convention for this purpose, and thereto have agreed as follows:

Article I

For the purposes of this Convention: 1. "Nuclear ship" means any ship equipped with a nuclear power plant. 2. "Licensing State" means the Contracting State which operates or which has authorized the operation of a nuclear ship under its flag. 3. "Person" means any individual or partnership, or any public or private body whether corporate or not, including a State or any of its constituent subdivisions. 4. "Operator" means the person authorized by the licensing State to operate a nuclear ship, or where a Contracting State operates a nuclear ship, that State. 5. "Nuclear fuel" means any material which is capable of producing energy by a self-sustaining process of nuclear fission and which is used or intended for use in a nuclear ship. 6. "Radioactive products or waste" means any material, including nuclear fuel, made radioactive by neutron irradiation incidental to the utilization of nuclear fuel in a nuclear ship. 7. "Nuclear damage" means loss of life or personal injury and loss or damage to property which arises out of or results from the radioactive properties or a combination of radioactive properties with toxic, explosive or other hazardous properties of nuclear fuel or of radioactive products or waste; any other loss, damage or expense so arising or resulting shall be included only if and to the extent that the applicable national law so provides. 8. "Nuclear incident" means any occurrence or series of occurrences having the same origin which causes nuclear damage. 9. "Nuclear power plant" means any power plant in which a nuclear reactor is, or is to be used as, the source of power, whether for propulsion of the ship or for any other purpose. 10. "Nuclear reactor" means any installation containing nuclear fuel in such an arrangement that a self-sustained chain process of nuclear fission can occur therein without an additional source of neutrons. 11. "Warship" means any ship belonging to the naval force of a State and bearing the external marks distinguishing warships of its nationality, under the command of an officer duly commissioned by the Government of such State and whose name appears in the Navy List, and manned by a crew who are under regular naval discipline. 12. "Applicable national law" means the national law of the court having jurisdiction under the Convention including any rules of such national law relating to conflict of laws.

Article II

1. The operator of a nuclear ship shall be absolutely liable for any nuclear damage upon proof that such damage has been caused by a nuclear incident involving the nuclear fuel of, or radioactive products or waste produced in, such ship. 2. Except as otherwise provided in this Convention no person other than the operator shall be liable for such

nuclear damage. 3. Nuclear damage suffered by the nuclear ship itself, its equipment, fuel or stores shall not be covered by the operator's liability as defined in this Convention. 4. The operator shall not be liable with respect to nuclear incidents occurring before the nuclear fuel has been taken in charge by him or after the nuclear fuel or radioactive products or waste have been taken in charge by another person duly authorized by law and liable for any nuclear damage that may be caused by them. 5. If the operator proves that the nuclear damage resulted wholly or partially from an act or omission done with intent to cause damage by the individual who suffered the damage, the competent courts may exonerate the operator wholly or partially from his liability to such individual. 6. Notwithstanding the provisions of paragraph 1 of this Article, the operator shall have a right of recourse; (a) If the nuclear incident results from a personal act or omission done with intent to cause damage, in which even recourse shall lie against the individual who has acted, or omitted to act, with such intent; (b) If the nuclear incident occurred as a consequence of any wreck-raising operation, against the person or persons who carried out such operation without the authority of the operator or persons who carried out such operation without the authority of the operator or of the State HAVING licensed the sunken ship or of the State in whose waters the wreck is situated; (c) If recourse is expressly provided for by contract.

Article III

1. The liability of the operator as regards one nuclear ship shall be limited to 1,500 million francs in respect of any one nuclear incident notwithstanding that the nuclear incident may have resulted from any fault or activity of that operator; such limit shall include neither any interest nor costs awarded by a court in actions for compensation under this Convention. 2. The operator shall be required to maintain insurance, or other financial security covering his liability for nuclear damage, in such amount, of such type and in such terms as the licensing State shall specify. The licensing State shall ensure the payment of claims for compensation for nuclear damage established against the operator by providing the necessary funds up to the limit laid down in paragraph 1 of this Article to the extent that the yield of the insurance or the financial security is inadequate to satisfy such claims. 3. However, nothing in paragraph 2 of this Article shall require any Contracting State or any of its constituent subdivisions, such as States, Republics or Cantons, to maintain insurance or other financial security to cover their liability as operators of nuclear ships. 4. The franc mentioned in paragraph 1 of this Article is a unit of account constituted by sixty-five and one half milligrams of gold of millesimal fineness nine hundred. The amount awarded may be converted into each national currency in round figures. Conversion into national currencies other than gold shall be effected on the basis of their gold value at the date of payment.

Article IV

Whenever both nuclear damage and damage other than nuclear damage have been caused by a nuclear incident or jointly by a nuclear incident and one or more other occurrences and the nuclear damage and such other damage are not reasonably separable, the entire damage shall, for the purposes of this Convention, be deemed to be nuclear damage exclusively caused by the nuclear incident. However, where damage is caused jointly by a nuclear incident covered by this Convention and by an emission of ionizing radiation or by an emission of ionizing radiation in combination with the toxic, explosive or other hazardous properties of the source of radiation not covered by it, nothing in this Convention shall limit or otherwise affect the liability, either as regards the victims or by way of recourse or contribution, of any person who may be held liable in connection with the emission of ionizing radiation or by the toxic, explosive or other hazardous properties of the source of radiation not covered by this Convention.

Article V

1. Rights of compensation under this Convention shall be extinguished if an action is not brought within ten years from the date of the nuclear incident. If, however, under the law of the licensing State the liability of the operator is covered by insurance or other financial security or State indemnification for a period longer than ten years, the applicable national law may provide that rights of compensation against the operator shall only be extinguished after a period which may be longer than ten years, but shall not be longer than the period for which his liability is so covered under the law of the licensing State. However, such extension of the extinction period shall in no case affect the right of compensation under this Convention of any person who has brought an action for loss of life or personal injury against the operator before the expiry of the aforesaid period of ten years. 2. Where nuclear damage is caused by nuclear fuel, radioactive products or waste which were stolen, lost, jettisoned, or abandoned, the period established under paragraph 1 of this Article shall be computed from the date of the nuclear incident causing the nuclear damage, but the period shall in no case exceed a period of twenty years from the date of the theft, loss, jettison or abandonment. 3. The applicable national law may establish a period of extinction or prescription of not less than three years from the date on which the person who claims to have suffered nuclear damage had knowledge or ought reasonably to have had knowledge of the damage and of the person responsible for the damage, provided that the period established under paragraphs 1 and 2 of this Article shall not be exceeded. 4. Any person who claims to have suffered nuclear damage and who has brought an action for compensation within the period applicable under this Article may amend

his claim to take into account any aggravation of the damage, even after the expiry of that period, provided that final judgment has not been entered.

Article VI

Where provisions of national health insurance, social insurance, social security, workmen's compensation or occupational disease compensation systems include compensation for nuclear damage, rights of beneficiaries under such systems and rights of subrogation, or of recourse against the operator, by virtue of such systems, shall be determined by the law of the Contracting State HAVING established such systems. However, if the law of such Contracting State allows claims of beneficiaries of such systems and such rights of subrogation and recourse to be brought against the operator in conformity with the terms of this Convention, this shall not result in the liability of the operator exceeding the amount specified in paragraph 1 of Article III.

Article VII

1. Where nuclear damage engages the liability of more than one operator and the damage attributable to each operator is not reasonably separable, the operators involved shall be jointly and severally liable for such damage. However, the liability of any one operator shall not exceed the limit laid down in Article III. 2. In the case of a nuclear incident where the nuclear damage arises out of or results from nuclear fuel or radioactive products or waste of more than one nuclear ship of the same operator, that operator shall be liable in respect of each ship up to the limit laid down in Article III. 3. In case of joint and several liability, and subject to the provisions of paragraph 1 of this Article: (a) Each operator shall have a right of contribution against the others in proportion to the fault attaching to each of them: (b) Where circumstances are such that the degree of fault cannot be apportioned, the total liability shall be borne in equal parts.

Article VIII

No liability under this Convention shall attach to an operator in respect to nuclear damage caused by a nuclear incident directly due to an act of war, hostilities, civil war or insurrection.

Article IX

The sums provided by insurance, by other financial security or by State indemnification in conformity with paragraph 2 of Article III shall be exclusively available for compensation due under this Convention.

Article X

1. Any action for compensation shall be brought, at the option of the claimant, either before the courts of the licensing State or before the courts of the Contracting State or States in whose territory nuclear damage has been sustained. 2. If the licensing State has been or might be called upon to ensure the payment of claims for compensation in accordance with paragraph 2 of Article III of this Convention, it may intervene as party in any proceedings brought against the operator. 3. Any immunity from legal processes pursuant to rules of national or international law shall be waived with respect to duties or obligations arising under, or for the purpose of, this Convention. Nothing in this Convention shall make warships or other State-owned or State-operated ships on non-commercial service liable to arrest, attachment or seizure or confer jurisdiction in respect of warships on the courts of any foreign State.

Article XI

1. When, HAVING regard to the likelihood of any claims arising out of a nuclear incident exceeding the amount specified in Article III of this Convention, a court of the licensing State, at the request of the operator, a claimant or the licensing State, so certifies, the operator or the licensing State shall make that amount available in that court to pay any such claims; that amount shall be regarded as constituting the limitation fund in respect of that incident. 2. The amount may be made available for the purposes of the preceding paragraph by payment into court or by the provision of security or guarantees sufficient to satisfy the court that the money will be available when required to meet any established claim. 3. After the fund has been constituted in accordance with paragraph 1 of this Article the court of the licensing State shall be exclusively competent to determine all matters relating to the apportionment and distribution of the fund. 4. (a) A final judgment entered by a court HAVING jurisdiction under Article X shall be recognised in the territory of any other Contracting State, except: (i) where the judgment was obtained by fraud; or (ii) the operator was not given a fair opportunity to present his case, (b) A final judgment which is recognized shall, upon being presented for enforcement in accordance with the formalities required by the law of the Contracting State where enforcement is sought, be enforceable as if it were a judgment of a court of that State, (c) The merits of a claim on which the judgment has been given shall not be subject to further proceedings. 5. (a) If a person who is a national of a Contracting State, other than the operator, has paid compensation for nuclear damage under an International Convention or under the law of a non-Contracting State, such person shall, up to the amount which he has paid, acquired by subrogation the rights which the person so compensated would have enjoyed under this Convention. However, no rights shall be so acquired by any person if and to the extent that the operator has a right of recourse or contribution against

such person under this Convention; (b) If a limitation fund has been set up and (i) the operator has paid, prior to its being set up, compensation for nuclear damage; or (ii) the operator has paid, after it has been set up, compensation for nuclear damage under an International Convention or the law of a non-Contracting State, he shall be entitled to recover from the fund, up to the amount which he has paid, the amount which the person so compensated would have obtained in the distribution of the fund; (c) If no limitation fund is set up, nothing in this Convention shall preclude an operator, who has paid compensation for nuclear damage out of funds other than those provided pursuant to paragraph 2 of Article III, from recovering from the person providing financial security under paragraph 2 of Article III or from the licensing State, up to the amount he has paid, the sum which the person so compensated would have obtained under this Convention; (d) In this paragraph the expression "a national of a Contracting State" shall include a Contracting State or any of its constituent subdivisions or a partnership or any public or private body whether corporate or not established in a Contracting State. 6. Where no fund has been constituted under the provisions of this Article, the licensing State shall adopt such measures as are necessary to ensure that adequate sums provided by it or by insurance or other financial security in accordance with paragraph 2 of Article III, shall be available for the satisfaction of any claim established by a judgment of a court of any other Contracting State which would be recognised under paragraph 4 of this Article; the sums shall be made available, at the option of the claimant, either in the licensing State or in the Contracting State in which the damage was sustained or in the Contracting State in which the claimant is habitually resident. 7. After the limitation fund has been constituted in accordance with paragraph 1 of this Article or, where no such fund has been constituted, if the sums provided by the licensing State, or by insurance, or other financial security are available in accordance with paragraph 6 of this Article to meet a claim for compensation, the claimant shall not be entitled to exercise any right against any other asset of the operator in respect of his claim for nuclear damage and any bail or security (other than security for costs) given by or on behalf of that operator in any Contracting State shall be released.

Article XII

1.The Contracting States undertake to adopt such measures as are necessary to ensure implementation of the provisions of this Convention, including any appropriate measures for the prompt and equitable distribution of the sums available for compensation for nuclear damage. 2. The Contracting States undertake to adopt such measures as are necessary to ensure that insurance and reinsurance premiums and sums provided by insurance, reinsurance or other financial security, or provided by them in accordance with paragraph 2 of Article III, shall be freely transferable into the currency of the Contracting State in which the damage was sustained, of the Contracting State in which the claimant is habitually resident or, as regards insurance and reinsurance premiums and payments, in the currencies specified in the insurance or reinsurance contract. 3. This Convention shall be applied without discrimination based upon nationality, domicile or residence.

Article XIII

This Convention applies to nuclear damage caused by a nuclear incident occurring in any part of the world and involving the nuclear fuel of, or radioactive products or waste produced in, a nuclear ship flying the flag of a Contracting State.

Article XIV

This Convention shall supersede any International Conventions in force or open for signature, ratification or accession at the date on which this Convention is opened for signature, but only to the extent that such Conventions would be in conflict with it; however, nothing in this Article shall affect the obligations of Contracting States to non-Contracting States arising under such International Conventions.

Article XV

1. Each Contracting State undertakes to take all measures necessary to prevent a nuclear ship flying its flag from being operated without a licence or authority granted by it. 2. In the event of nuclear damage involving the nuclear fuel of, or radioactive products or waste produced in, a nuclear ship flying the flag of a Contracting State, the operation of which was not at the time of the nuclear incident licensed or authorized by such Contracting State, the owner of the nuclear ship at the time of the nuclear incident shall be deemed to be the operator of the nuclear ship for all the purposes of this Convention, except that his liability shall not be limited in amount. 3. In such an event, the Contracting State whose flag the nuclear ship flies shall be deemed to be the licensing State for all the purposes of this Convention and shall, in particular, be liable for compensation for victims in accordance with the obligations imposed on a licensing State by Article III and up to the limit laid down therein. 4. Each Contracting State undertakes not to grant a licence or other authority to operate a nuclear ship flying the flag of another State. However, nothing in this paragraph shall prevent a Contracting State from implementing the requirements of its national law concerning the operation of a nuclear ship within its internal waters and territorial seas.

Article XVI

This Convention shall apply to a nuclear ship from the date of her launching. Between her launching and the time she is authorized to fly a flag, the nuclear ship shall be deemed to be operated by the owner and to be flying the flag of the State in which she was built.

Article XVII

Nothing in this Convention shall affect any right which a Contracting State may have under international law to deny access to its waters and harbours to nuclear ships licensed by another Contracting State, even when it has formally complied with all the provisions of this Convention.

Article XVIII

An action for compensation for nuclear damage shall be brought against the operator; it may also be brought against the insurer or any person other than the licensing State who has provided financial security to the operator pursuant to paragraph 2 of Article III, if the right to bring an action against the insurer or such other person is provided under the applicable national law.

Article XIX

Notwithstanding the termination of this Convention or the termination of its application to any Contracting State pursuant to Article XXVII, the provisions of the Convention shall continue to apply with respect to any nuclear damage caused by a nuclear incident involving the nuclear fuel of, or radioactive products or waste produced in, a nuclear ship licensed or otherwise authorized for operation by any Contracting State prior to the date of such termination, provided the nuclear incident occurred prior to the date of such termination or, in the event of a nuclear incident occurring subsequent to the date of such termination, prior to the expiry of a period of twenty-five years after the date of such licensing or other authorization to operate such ship.

Article XX

Without prejudice to Article X any dispute between two or more Contracting Parties concerning the interpretation or application of this Convention which cannot be settled through negotiation, shall, at the request of one of them, be submitted to arbitration. If within six months from the date of the request for arbitration the Parties are unable to agree on the organization of the arbitration, any one of those Parties may refer the dispute to the International Court of Justice by request in conformity with the Statute of the Court.

Article XXI

1. Each Contracting Party may at the time of signature or ratification of this Convention or accession thereto, declare that it does not consider itself bound by Article XX of the Convention. The other Contracting Parties shall not be bound by this Article with respect to any Contracting Party having made such a reservation. 2. Any Contracting Party having made a reservation in accordance with paragraph 1 may at any time withdraw this reservation by notification to the Belgian Government.

Article XXII

This Convention shall be open for signature by the States represented at the eleventh session (1961-1962) of the Diplomatic Conference on Maritime Law.

Article XXIII

This Convention shall be ratified and the instruments of ratification shall be deposited with the Belgian Government.

Article XXIV

1. This Convention shall come into force three months after the deposit of an instrument of ratification by at least one licensing State and one other State. 2. This Convention shall come into force, in respect of each signatory State which ratifies it after its entry into force as provided in paragraph 1 of this Article, three months after the date of deposit of the instrument of ratification of that State.

Article XXV

1. States Members of the United Nations, Members of the specialized agencies and of the International Atomic Energy Agency not represented at the eleventh session of the Diplomatic Conference on Maritime Law, may accede to this Convention. 2. The instruments of accession shall be deposited with the Belgian Government. 3. The Convention shall come into force in respect of the acceding State three months after the date of deposit of the instrument of accession of that State, but not before the date of entry into force of the Convention as established by Article XXIV.

Article XXVI

1. A conference for the purpose of revising this Convention shall be convened by the Belgian Government and the International Atomic Energy Agency after the Conven-

tion has been in force five years. 2. Such a conference shall also be convened by the Belgian Government and the International Atomic Energy Agency before the expiry of this term or thereafter, if one-third of the Contracting States express a desire to that effect.

Article XXVII

1. Any Contracting State may denounce this Convention by notification to the Belgian Government at any time after the first revision Conference held in accordance with the provisions of Article XXVI.1. 2. This denunciation shall take effect one year after the date on which the notification has been received by the Belgian Government.

Article XXVIII

The Belgian Government shall notify the States represented at the eleventh session of the Diplomatic Conference on Maritime Law, and the States acceding to this Convention, of the following: 1. Signatures, ratifications and accessions received in accordance with Articles XXII, XXIII and XXV. 2. The date on which the Convention will come into force in accordance with Article XXIV. 3. Denunciations received in accordance with Article XXVII.

IN WITNESS WHEREOF, the undersigned Plenipotentiaries, whose credentials have been found in order, have signed this Convention.

DONE at Brussels, this twenty-fifth day of May, one thousand nine hundred and sixty-two, in the English, French, Russian and Spanish languages in a single copy, which shall remain deposited in the archives of the Belgian Government which shall issue certified copies. In case of any disparity in the texts, the English and French versions shall be authentic.

CONVENTION RELATING TO CIVIL LIABILITY IN THE FIELD OF MARITIME CARRIAGE OF NUCLEAR MATERIAL

(Brussels, 17 December 1971)

The aim of this Convention is to extend the regime of the basic Paris (PC) and Vienna (VC) conventions on nuclear third party liability to this mode of transport. The need for such extension stemmed from two main reasons: on one hand, the PC and the VC provided for derogations from their special regime where international agreements existed governing transports, on the other hand, the maritime conventions stipulated an unlimited liability of the shipper in case of damage to third parties caused by incidents during transport. Nuclear operators or ship-owners were therefore in difficulty as regards shipments of nuclear materials by sea, unless they were able to provide basically unlimited financial security covering possible incidents in the course of transports.

This Brussels Convention stipulates then that anybody resulting liable for damages caused during such transports on the strength of international agreements or of national provisions on maritime law, is exempted from liability if the nuclear operator concerned with the transport is directly liable either under the PC or the VC, or under national provisions on nuclear third party liability which are at least as favourable to the victims as are those Conventions.

The Convention was adopted at the end of a diplomatic conference convened by IMCO (Intergovernmental Maritime Consultative Organisation, now IMO), the (E)NEA and the IAEA. The conference was held from 29 November to 2 December 1971. The Secretary general of IMO in London is the depositary of the ratification instruments. The Convention entered into force on July 15, 1975 and has now 16 contracting Parties.

THE HIGH CONTRACTING PARTIES,

CONSIDERING that the Paris Convention of 29 July 1960 on Third Party Liability in the Field of Nuclear Energy and its Additional Protocol of 28 January 1964 (hereinafter referred to as "the Paris Convention") and the Vienna Convention of 21 May 1963 on Civil Liability for Nuclear Damage (hereinafter referred to as "the Vienna Convention") provide that, in the case of damage caused by a nuclear incident occurring in the course of maritime carriage of nuclear material covered by such Conventions, the operator of a nuclear installation is the person liable for such damage,

CONSIDERING that similar provisions exist in the national law in force in certain States,

CONSIDERING that the application of any preceding international Convention in the field of maritime transport is however maintained,

DESIROUS of ensuring that the operator of a nuclear installation will be exclusively liable for damage caused by a nuclear incident occurring in the course of maritime carriage of nuclear material,

HAVE AGREED as follows:

Article 1

Any person who by virtue of an international convention or national law applicable in the field of maritime transport might be held liable for damage caused by a nuclear incident shall be exonerated from such liability:
(a) if the operator of a nuclear installation is liable for such damage under either the Paris or the Vienna Convention, or
(b) if the operator of a nuclear installation is liable for such damage by virtue of a national law governing the liability for such damage, provided that such law is in all respects as favourable to persons who may suffer damage as either the Paris or the Vienna Convention.

Article 2

1. The exoneration provided for in Article 1 shall also apply in respect of damage caused by a nuclear incident:
(a) to the nuclear installation itself or to any property on the site of that installation which is used or to be used in connexion with that installation, or
(b) to the means of transport upon which the nuclear material involved was at the time of the nuclear incident,
for which the operator of the nuclear installation is not liable because his liability for such damage has been excluded pursuant to the provisions of either the Paris or the Vienna Convention, or, in cases referred to in Article 1(b), by equivalent provisions of the national law referred to therein.

2. The provisions of paragraph 1 shall not, however, affect the liability of any individual who has caused the damage by an act or omission done with intent to cause damage.

Article 3

No provision of the present Convention shall affect the liability of the operator of a nuclear ship in respect of damage caused by a nuclear incident involving the nuclear fuel of or radioactive products or waste produced in such ship.

Article 4

The present Convention shall supersede any international Conventions in the field of maritime transport which, at the date on which the present Convention is opened for signature, are in force or open for signature, ratification or accession but only to the extent that such Conventions would be in conflict with it; however, nothing in this Article shall affect the obligations of the Contracting Parties to the present Convention to non-Contracting States arising under such international Conventions.

Article 5

1. The present Convention shall be opened for signature in Brussels and shall remain open for signature in London at the Headquarters of the Intergovernmental Maritime Consultative Organization (hereinafter referred to as "the Organization") until 31 December 1972 and shall thereafter remain open for accession.

2. States Members of the United Nations or any of the Specialized Agencies or of the International Atomic Energy Agency or Parties to the Statute of the International Court of Justice may become Parties to the present Convention by:
(a) signature without reservation as to ratification, acceptance or approval;
(b) signature subject to ratification, acceptance or approval followed by ratification, acceptance or approval; or
(c) accession.

3. Ratification, acceptance, approval or accession shall be effected by the deposit of a formal instrument to that effect with the Secretary-General of the Organization.

Article 6

1. The present Convention shall enter into force on the ninetieth day following the date on which five States have either signed it without reservation as to ratification, acceptance or approval or have deposited instruments of ratification, acceptance, approval or accession with the Secretary-General of the Organization.

2. For any State which subsequently signs the present Convention without reservation as to ratification, acceptance or approval, or deposits its instrument of ratification, acceptance, approval or accession, the Convention shall come into force on the ninetieth day after the date of such signature or deposit.

Article 7

1. The present Convention may be denounced by any Contracting Party to it at any time after the date on which the Convention comes into force for that State.

2. Denunciation shall be effected by a notification in writing delivered to the Secretary-General of the Organization.

3. A denunciation shall take effect one year, or such longer period as may be specified in the notification, after its receipt by the Secretary-General of the Organization.

4. Notwithstanding a denunciation by a Contracting Party pursuant to this Article the provisions of the present Convention shall continue to apply to any damage caused by a nuclear incident occurring before the denunciation takes effect.

Article 8

1. The United Nations where it is the administering authority for a territory, or any Contracting Party to the present Convention responsible for the international relations of a territory, may at any time by notification in writing to the Secretary-General of the Organization declare that the present Convention shall extend to such territory.

2. The present Convention shall, from the date of receipt of the notification or from such other date as may be specified in the notification, extend to the territory named therein.

3. The United Nations, or any Contracting Party which had made a declaration under paragraph 1 of this Article may at any time after the date on which the Convention has been so extended to any territory declare by notification in writing to the Secretary-General of the Organization that the present Convention shall cease to extend to any such territory named in the notification.

4. The present Convention shall cease to extend to any territory mentioned in such notification one year, or such longer period as may be specified therein, after the date of receipt of the notification by the Secretary-General of the Organization.

Article 9

1. A Conference for the purpose of revising or amending the present Convention may be convened by the Organization.

2. The Organization shall convene a Conference of the Contracting Parties to the present Convention for revising or amending it at the request of not less than one-third of the Contracting Parties.

Article 10

A Contracting Party may make reservations corresponding to those which it has validly made to the Paris or Vienna Convention. A reservation may be made at the time of signature, ratification, acceptance, approval or accession

Article 11

1. The present Convention shall be deposited with the Secretary-General of the Organization.

2. The Secretary-General of the Organization shall:
(a) inform all States which have signed or acceded to the present Convention of:
(i) each new signature and each deposit of an instrument together with the date thereof;
(ii) any reservation made in conformity with the present Convention;
(iii) the date of entry into force of the present Convention;
(iv) any denunciation of the present Convention and the date on which it takes effect;
(v) the extension of the present Convention to any territory under paragraph 1 of Article 8 and of the termination of any such extension under the provisions of paragraph 4 of that Article stating in each case the date on which the present Convention has been or will cease to be so extended,
(b) transmit certified true copies of the present Convention to all Signatory States and to all States which have acceded to the present Convention.

3. As soon as the present Convention comes into force, a certified true copy thereof shall be transmitted by the Secretary-General of the Organization to the Secretariat of the United Nations for registration and publication in accordance with Article 102 of the Charter of the United Nations.

Article 12

The present Convention is established in a single original in the English and French languages, both texts being equally authentic. Official translations in the Russian and Spanish languages shall be prepared by the Secretariat of the Organization and deposited with the signed original.

IN WITNESS WHEREOF the undersigned being duly authorized by their respective Governments for that purpose have signed the present Convention.

DONE at Brussels this seventeenth day of December 1971.

DECISIONS, RECOMMENDATIONS AND INTERPRETATIONS RELATING TO THE PARIS CONVENTION

These decisions, recommendations and interpretations have been adopted to ensure a better understanding of the Paris Convention (PC) and to facilitate its implementation at national levels. These acts stem from the powers accorded to the OECD Council and the NEA Steering Committee under article 1 (a)(ii), (iii) and (b) of the PC; the NEA Steering Committee, on the basis of the general powers conferred on it by the NEA Statute, may adopt decisions, recommendations and interpretations relating to the PC (and the same applies to the OECD Council's general powers to adopt recommendations, under the 1960 Convention establishing the OECD, concerning the application of the PC). The recommendations and interpretations are not legally binding.

Among these various acts, it is worth recalling the 1971 Recommendation on the extension of the territorial scope, the 1977 Decisions on the exclusion of small quantities of nuclear substances outside a nuclear installation and of certain kinds of nuclear substances, the 1981 Recommendation on damage to nuclear substances in the course of carriage, the 1982 Recommendation on fixing a lower liability amount, the 1990 Decision on the possibility of excluding installations being decommissioned, the 1990 Recommendation on raising and harmonizing liability amounts, and the 1990 Recommendation on a single competent court. Over time, given the entry into force of certain pertinent instruments (like the 1982 amending Protocol) some of the earlier acts in point were superseded.

For the text of all these acts, we refer to them as published by the NEA itself.

CHAPTER FOUR
SCIENTIFIC, INDUSTRIAL AND COMMERCIAL CO-OPERATION AGREEMENTS

This Chapter deals with a number of international agreements, both **multilateral and bilateral**, concluded in order to carry out joint technical-scientific, industrial and commercial programmes, thus ensuring the development of nuclear energy and its peaceful applications. The co-operation entailed by these agreements consists in the exchange of know-how and experience, the realisation of joint projects, the free movement of specialists, materials and equipment, the improvement of nuclear safety and protection etc. The Chapter refers to agreements concluded among States (i.e. their governments), between States and international organizations and between these organizations. It is useful to point out that for the conclusion of an agreement with another international organization or a third State, the European Atomic Energy Community (Euratom) acts according to negotiating directives (see article 101 of the Euratom Treaty) to the Commission, approved by Council Decisions; similarly, the IAEA Governing Board is empowered (article 16 of the Statute) to conclude agreements for the Agency with the prior assent of the General Conference.

A certain number of the above agreements are no longer in force. In the past, OECD sponsored a Convention setting up a European undertaking for the chemical treatment of irradiated fuel (EUROCHEMIC) based in Mol (Belgium). The Convention was adopted on December 20, 1957 and entered into force in 1959. The undertaking was discontinued several years ago, on account of the diminished interest in the above treatment issue on the part of some participating countries.

Another important agreement concluded in the past (Paris, 23 March 1959) and also discontinued even much earlier than Eurochemic, concerned a high-temperature gas-cooled reactor (Dragon) project. The agreement to carry out a joint programme covered not only studies and research, but also the actual construction and operation of such a reactor. Both the OECD and Euratom were associated to the project. This was ended as of March 1976, having the signatories decided not to extend it further.

An agreement between Euratom and the UK on co-operation in the field of the peaceful use of nuclear energy, initially concluded in 1959 and renewed later on, was superseded due to the accession of the UK to the European Community.

Thirdly, mention should be made of a multilateral agreement which, although not strictly falling under the category of instruments considered here as the result of agreements between governments, is of a special importance in the field of nuclear energy from an economic and political standpoint. This agreement (concluded in Paris on 27 November 1973 and still in force) concerns EURODIF, a company set up under French law (participants being Belgium, France, Spain and Italy) for the construction and operation (at Tricastin, in the Rhone valley, France) of an installation for the enrichment of uranium by the gaseous diffusion processing.

Finally, the Euratom-KEDO agreement is worth recalling, given the importance attached to it by the signatories especially with a view to contributing to non-proliferation in the nuclear field. The agreement, concluded for a five year period in the mid-nineties, was concerned with the construction of two light water type reactors (basically of USA technology) in South Korea, replacing two heavy water type reactors of Soviet design. It involved Euratom on one side, and Japan, South Korea and the USA on the other, these countries being members of the Korean Energy Development Organization (KEDO). The project (financed also by Euratom) addressed by the agreement was carried out for five years, and extended for the same period of time (i.e. until 2005). However, in early 2003 relations between North Korea and Japan (never actually smooth) became even more difficult, besides the former decided to withdraw from the Non-Proliferation Treaty and to put back into operation some reactors which had been shut down in previous years. These events had consequences also on the project in point, which in the following time was gradually but definitely discontinued. Thought was given to the possibility of converting the project into some other activity, but nothing concrete came out of that. At any rate, since Summer 2003 the prevailing orientation by the concerned bodies was to suspend the project (provisionally for a year, this measure far more likely to become "for good").
For all the rather extensive agreements (whether superseded or still in existence) considered in this Chapter, it became necessary to provide only introductory material in order to avoid overburdening the volume.

SECTION ONE
MULTILATERAL AGREEMENTS

CONVENTION ESTABLISHING A EUROPEAN ORGANIZATION FOR NUCLEAR RESEARCH (CERN)

(Paris, 1 July 1953)

CERN is an international institution grouping 12 countries of Western Europe, intended to address basic research in the domain of nuclear energy (excepting industrial applications) and to promote progress of nuclear physics in the broader context of applied sciences, as well as co-operation of European States in the field.

The Convention was open to signature from July to December 1953 and entered into force (together with it Financial Protocol) on September 29, 1954. The Convention was amended in 1954 and 1971 (the latter in connection with the planned construction of a 300 GeV installation intended for the research mentioned above. The first such installation realized at CERN was the largest one of its kind worldwide until 1965. In more recent years, it was decided to focus on research in the domain of sub-nuclear physics, carried out by means of an LHC (Large Hadron Collider) to study the behaviour of certain particles (hadrons).

CERN is based in Geneva (Switzerland), the relevant accession instruments being deposited with the United Nations.

AGREEMENT ON THE JOINT OPERATION OF THE HALDEN BOILING WATER REACTOR

(Oslo, 11 June 1958)

In 1955 the Norwegian Institute for Atomic Energy started the construction of a boiling water reactor near Halden. During that time, studies undertaken within OECD in the field of experimental reactors had revealed the interest of certain member countries of the Organization in participating in research in connection with the operation of boiling water reactors. Thus the Institute decided to make its own reactor available for the execution of a joint programme of research and experiments.

An agreement was therefore signed between governments (Austria, Switzerland) and nuclear bodies of the interested countries (Norway, Denmark, Sweden and the United Kingdom). The Commission of the European Atomic Energy Community (Euratom) also participated in the agreement, concluded initially for three years but open for extension in time and for accession by other countries under prior consent by the signatories. The agreement has been extended several times and is still in force, focusing on nuclear research (including safety) mainly applied to power stations.

JOINT EUROPEAN THORUS (JET) JOINT UNDERTAKING

(Brussels, 30 May 1978)

JET was set up as a joint undertaking by virtue of a Council of the European Communities' Decision adopted on the date indicated above. The purposes of the undertaking are the construction and operation of a Tokamak type and ancillary installations. These actions are taken in the framework of the Euratom research programme in thermonuclear fusion for the benefit of the participants in the programme. The relevant tests are performed under conditions similar to those necessary for a thermonuclear reactor.

The project is operated at Culham (United Kingdom) and is open also to non member States of the European Community. In more recent years activities are focused mainly on research in the domain of plasma and the study of its behaviour at extremely high temperatures.

SECTION TWO
BILATERAL AGREEMENTS

The number of agreements between the EAEC (Euratom) and other ***international organizations*** *or* ***third countries*** *is considerable. Some of such agreements were concluded for the first time back in the late fifties, some other were initialled in the second half of the nineties, some have been renewed several times, and a certain number of them are under way or approaching conclusion. For the purposes of this volume, it was deemed opportune only to provide some basic overall information, focusing on their object and current status, and recalling that they are negotiated by the European Commission following ad hoc directives by the Council.*

Concerning other ***international organizations****, an agreement was concluded by Euratom with the International Labour Organization (ILO) since January 26, 1961. This agreement aimed at creating a satisfactory basis for co-operation in the field of health protection of workers and the public, contributing to economic expansion, the development of energy resources and improving living and working condition. A similar agreement had been concluded by the International Atomic Energy Agency (IAEA) with ILO in 1958, whereby the two organizations stressed the need to act within the respective competences to the common end of ensuring the best conditions in the various peaceful applications of nuclear energy. Besides, the IAEA concluded a co-operation agreement with Euratom on December 1, 1975, with a view to strengthening such co-operation in promoting the peaceful use of nuclear energy.*

As to the agreements with ***third countries****, the current situation is summarized below, since the main aim is to give an idea of the activity carried out in this domain and of the areas covered. The scope of most agreements is technical-scientific co-operation in the peaceful use of nuclear energy: in this case only the date of entry into force is indicated in brackets (as to Australia, Canada and the USA, for which agreements have been in existence for very many years, the date indicates the entry into force of the agreement as it was last renewed). In some other cases the agreements address matters (indicated in brackets with the date of entry into force) related to the co-operation referred to above. Where no date is indicated, negotiations were still under way or in any case approaching conclusion while this volume was being finalized:*

Argentina (1997), Canada (1998), Australia (1999), China, Japan, Kazakhstan (nuclear fusion and nuclear safety, 2003), Russian Federation (nuclear fusion and nuclear safety, 2002, and nuclear trade), Ukraine (nuclear fusion and nuclear safety, 2002), United States (1996), Uzbekistan (signed in 2003, not yet in force).

PART TWO
PROVISIONS GOVERNING THE PEACEFUL USE, DENUCLEARIZATION AND RADIOACTIVE POLLUTION

STRUCTURE OF PART TWO

This Part is devoted to international instruments and acts aiming to ensure the peaceful use of nuclear energy and in general to prevent radioactive pollution of the environment at large. These instruments and acts pertain to many different issues, ranging from diversion of nuclear energy from peaceful use to non-peaceful or military purposes and the proliferation of nuclear weapons (specifically addressed by the IAEA and Euratom systems of safeguards, security and physical protection of nuclear materials), to the so called "de-nuclearization" of certain parts of the globe and to the prevention of pollution of the environment (both issues addressed mostly by treaties and conventions, though not all of them dealing exclusively with radioactive materials and contamination).

The variety and nature of the instruments and acts in point suggested the adoption of a structure based on three sections, Section One dealing with **safeguards and security** (treaties, regulations, agreements etc.), Section Two addressing treaties and other instruments intended to ensure that certain areas of the globe are kept free from nuclear weapons and materials (**de-nuclearization**), and Section Three devoted to international conventions on **protection of the environment and pollution prevention**.

Similarly to the treaties, the (fewer in number) conventions are not concerned solely with nuclear energy and radioactive pollution. Besides, the extent to which these areas are addressed varies from one instrument to another. Consequently and again for reasons similar to those pointed out for some other parts of this volume, a selective approach had to be adopted. This applies eminently to the instruments addressed in Sections Two and Three. Indeed, a certain number of such instruments have been supplemented or amended by protocols (not published in the volume, although mentioned in the relevant introductory material). This material is provided for all treaties and conventions, while the actual text of such instruments is published in the volume, with a few exceptions, only where they address the nuclear matter. It is recalled that some of these instruments draw on the so-called "precautionary principle", which was affirmed especially in the Rio Declaration (Principle 15) at the Earth Summit of June 1992. According to it, whenever there is a risk of serious or irreversible damage, the absence of an absolute scientific certainty about that risk must not become a pretext for delaying the adoption of effective measures aimed at preventing environmental degradation.

It is moreover noted that there exist other conventions, such as for example Geneva (1979, on long distance trans-frontier atmospheric pollution), Marpol (London, 1973, on MARritime POLlution from ships), Montego Bay (1982, on the law of the sea), Lomé (1989, on prohibition of export of hazardous and radioactive waste from the

European Community to any African, Caribbean and Pacific country) and New York (1992, framework convention on climate change) etc., somewhat covering also radioactive pollution but in a more general context. Here it is worth simply recalling that the Marpol Convention (as modified by the 1978 Protocol relating thereto, and incorporating the 1973 Convention) is the main international instrument covering prevention of pollution of the marine environment by ships from operational or accidental causes. Its article 210 calls upon States to prevent, limit and control the dumping of waste (esp. radioactive). The New York Convention includes nuclear activities in its scope and the 1997 Kyoto Protocol to this convention addresses also nuclear energy. It should be pointed out that the Protocol, while not challenging the benefits deriving from this energy source as far as carbon dioxide emissions are concerned, lays down certain conditions excluding nuclear energy as an option to be implemented on the basis of given "flexibility mechanisms" offered to both developed countries and those in economic transition. These mechanisms apply currently to the Protocol compliance period (2008-2012), which means that the benefits from nuclear energy in terms of emissions savings will become more important with the entry into force of the Protocol (not yet achieved at the end of 2004) and after that compliance period.

Finally, mention should be made of the Final Declaration (whereby it was stressed – inter alia – that man and the environment must be preserved from the harmful effects of nuclear weapons) and of the Resolutions adopted at the United Nations Conference on the environment, which took place in Stockholm in June 1972. In particular, Resolution 3(1) of June 14 addressed nuclear weapons tests, by condemning them (especially those carried out in the atmosphere). The Resolution also called upon States intending to carry out such tests to abandon their plans, in order to avoid further contamination of the environment.

SECTION ONE
SAFEGUARDS AGAINST DIVERSIONS TO NON-PEACEFUL OR MILITARY PURPOSES

THE OECD CONVENTION ON THE ESTABLISHMENT OF A SECURITY CONTROL IN THE FIELD OF NUCLEAR ENERGY

(Paris, 20 December 1957)

This Convention was adopted at the same time when the European Nuclear Energy Agency (ENEA, now NEA) was created. Its aim was to establish a security control in the field of nuclear energy, in order to ensure its development for peaceful purposes exclusively, the relevant tasks being conferred on ENEA. More specifically, the control addressed joint enterprises, materials, equipments and services in which this Agency was involved, and aimed at preventing any military use.

The Convention stipulated also the adoption of measures for the case of infringement, by a contracting State, of the obligations arising from this control system, as well as an agreement with Euratom allowing for the control over its Member States to be performed by Euratom itself.

The Convention entered into force on 22 June 1959 and remained applicable until the stipulation of the Non Proliferation Treaty (NPT, see further on in this Section). It is recalled that in the same domain the International Atomic Energy Agency (IAEA) and Euratom have developed, since after the stipulation of the NPT, very strict and particular systems addressing prevention of non peaceful or military purposes. As a consequence, by virtue of a Decision by the NEA Steering Committee of 14th October 1976, the application of the NEA Security Control Regulations (Articles 8 and 10 of the Convention) were suspended until further notice. On account of this, the text of the Convention is not published here, but its historical importance as the first overall international instrument ever in the area of security control must be stressed (although provisions on such control had been included in the Euratom Treaty and the IAEA Statute, see Chapter One).

THE IAEA SAFEGUARDS SYSTEM (1961-1998)

Both the IAEA Statute and the EURATOM Treaty provided for the setting up of similar systems, having in common the final objective of preventing the use of nuclear energy for purposes other than peaceful or for military ones. While referring for more detailed elements to the Introductory Material to each system, here it is worth pointing out that a distinction should be drawn between the Euratom and the IAEA systems: in summary, the difference consists in the former system being addressed to verifying that nuclear materials are not diverted from their intended use as declared by the users (and in fact the Euratom Treaty related provisions do not mention peaceful use or otherwise), while the latter system is aimed to prevent nuclear materials and installations from being used for any military purpose (article III.A.5 of the Statute). Basically the controls in point are carried out according to as uniform procedures as possible, and include mainly the analysis of the installations, checks on accountancy of materials (notably the so called "fissile" materials such as plutonium and uranium) and other forms of international (i.e. "supernational") inspection. It must be stressed that this overall regime implies that States as such (rather than users or operators) are responsible vis-à-vis the international organization (IAEA or Euratom) involved in inspection. This also means that there is little scope left to national provisions in this respect, which therefore may merely address organizational aspects of the inspection.

It is pointed out that for practical and substantive reasons, in the discussion of the IAEA and Euratom systems to be found in the following pages reference is made in both cases to safeguards. Indeed, Chapter VII of the Euratom Treaty is titled "safeguards", although the latter system is often referred to as "security controls".

There are several features attached to the IAEA system. A major one is that during the seventies, in connection with the entry into force of the Non Proliferation Treaty (NPT, 1970), the system was the object of considerable changes both as to character and scope. Secondly, a very important Agreement (the "Verification Agreement") was concluded (1973) pursuant to article III, paragraphs 1 and 4 of the NPT, between IAEA, Euratom and some European Community member States, aimed at checking compliance by member States with the obligations arising from the NPT. On the strength of the 1973 Agreement, under the Euratom Treaty a Regulation (no.3227) was adopted in 1976, which also became part of the overall safeguard system. Lastly, in recent years this system was marked by another significant development, consisting in its strengthening by virtue of appropriate international instruments (the Additional Protocols to the Verification Agreement) adopted in 1998 (Euratom being one of the contracting parties to them). It is noted that, although both the Verification Agreement and the Additional Protocols are actually common to the IAEA and the Euratom systems, for practical reasons here they are dealt with under the Vienna Agency's system.

A few more specific features need to be recalled as to the application of IAEA safeguards. In first place, these are based on information provided by the State about materials or equipment, but the Agency is empowered to carry out special inspections in order to detect any possible undeclared activities. Moreover, any infringement of safeguards obligations cannot be avoided thanks to the mere existence of the system. Remedial actions are possible as the case may be following an inspection, but infringements are reported to the UN Security Council. Finally, safeguards address the existing situation and may not pre-empt on possible States' intentions as to the future.

The texts referred to in the following pages take into account this "chronological" division by which they may be ascribed to the time before and after the stipulation of the NPT. The first document considering safeguards was adopted in 1961, then expanded in 1964 to cover large installations, revised in 1965, supplemented and expanded again to other installations in 1966 and 1968. These texts are incorporated in a document named INFCIRC/66/Rev.2, addressing scope, validity in time and relevant procedures. Attention is drawn to IAEA's INFCIRC documents, by which the Agency informs its member States on matters of general interest (agreements, technical standards, reports etc.). Such documents are not normally binding, although some are of a higher rank in that they have been approved by the Agency's Board of Governors (as it is the case for INFCIRC/66 of above, as well as INFCIRC/153 and 209 dealt with further on in this Section). In various cases, INFCIRC documents are also used as a basis for laying down international instruments at the initiative of IAEA and falling within its competence, as it may be equally found elsewhere in this Section.

INFCIRC/66 Rev.2 remains important since it is still applicable (as a sort of "model agreement") to the stipulation of safeguards agreements between IAEA and member States of the Agency not signatories to the NPT but voluntarily submitting to safeguards. On the basis of this document, IAEA concluded in the past (i.e. before the NPT) agreements with some countries (e.g. France, Indonesia, Japan) specific to particular material or facilities. It is added that the Agency has also stipulated (e.g. with Argentina, Brazil, Columbia and Egypt) safeguards agreements based on a prior non-proliferation commitment, as well as agreements with other countries based on such commitment. Moreover, some nuclear-weapon States (China, USA) have in the past offered voluntary submission to the IAEA for the application of safeguards in those countries.

In connection with the above, another IAEA document, GOV. 1621 of August 1973, is worth mentioning here. This document is intended to ensure a higher degree of uniformity as regards validity in time of agreements stipulated between States and the Agency. Consequently, this also ensures a better application of safeguards measures on the basis of two concepts: time of actual use of materials, equipment etc. subject to safeguards and preservation of rights and duties of the State concerned during the whole time when such materials and equipment are available.

Further on in this Section, the legal instruments belonging to the "post-NPT" era are published with the relevant introductory material. For INFCIRC documents only such material is provided.

TREATY ON THE NON-PROLIFERATION OF NUCLEAR WEAPONS (NPT)

(Washington, London, Moscow, 1 July 1968)

As pointed out in the Introductory Material to the IAEA safeguards system, the stipulation of the NPT must be regarded as a particularly significant event in that it marks a "new era" in the development of that system. The antecedents of the NPT date back to the immediate aftermath of World War II (1946) when the United States proposed to the United Nations Organisation the stipulation of an agreement by which all States would renounce the use of nuclear weapons, and all nuclear activities would be placed under the control of an "International Authority" endowed with "super-national" powers.

After several and various vicissitudes associated with developments in the international situation, the issue was eventually resumed in 1966 by the United States and the Soviet Union, who reached an agreement on a joint draft instrument aimed at limiting the spreading of nuclear weapons. This draft led later on, through various amendments, to a final text in the form of a treaty endorsed by the United Nations General Assembly on 12 June 1968 (Resolution 2373(XII)). The Treaty was opened to signature in Washington, London and Moscow on July 1, 1968, the capitals of the three States whose governments are the depositaries of the ratification instruments. By signing to the Treaty, States undertake among other things to "co-operate in facilitating the application of IAEA safeguards on peaceful activities", on the basis of the principle that benefits from such activities should be available to "all Parties to the Treaty, whether nuclear-weapon or non-nuclear weapon States". Under article IX paragraph 3," a nuclear weapon State is one which has manufactured and exploded a nuclear weapon (or other nuclear explosive device) prior to January 1, 1967". The Treaty was also intended to pave the way to nuclear disarmament, which should be progressively achieved via the cessation of the manufacture of nuclear weapons, the liquidation of existing stockpiles and the elimination of such weapons from national arsenals. It is worth noting that the Preamble to the Treaty recalls another very important instrument which had been adopted in 1963 for the banning of nuclear tests (TBT, see further on in Section Two). Again pursuant to article IX paragraph 3 mentioned above, the conditions for the entry into force of the Treaty required its ratification by the depositaries States and forty other signatory States having deposited their ratification instruments. These conditions were fulfilled within a rather short time, which made it possible for the Treaty to enter into force on 5 March 1970.

In 1995 a Conference was held on NPT Review and Extension, pursuant to article X, paragraph 2 of the Treaty. In this conference the Parties adopted a Resolution on Strengthening the Review Process for the Treaty, to the effect that review conferences should be held regularly (every five years) to address principles and ways to promote full implementation of the NPT as well as its universality. The latest Review and Extension Conference was held in New York in 2000 (24 April-19 May), where the Parties agreed on the indefinite extension of the Treaty. It should be noted that, among other things, the Conference called on Cuba, India, Israel and Pakistan to accede to the Treaty and to accept IAEA safeguards on all their nuclear activities. The contracting Parties to the Treaty are now 189, a considerable number although some important countries are not yet parties to it.

The States concluding this Treaty, hereinafter referred to as the "Parties to the Treaty",

Considering the devastation that would be visited upon all mankind by a nuclear war and the consequent need to make every effort to avert the danger of such a war and to take measures to safeguard the security of peoples,

Believing that the proliferation of nuclear weapons would seriously enhance the danger of nuclear war,

In conformity with resolutions of the United Nations General Assembly calling for the conclusion of an agreement on the prevention of wider dissemination of nuclear weapons,

Undertaking to cooperate in facilitating the application of International Atomic Energy Agency safeguards on peaceful nuclear activities,

Expressing their support for research, development and other efforts to further the application, within the framework of the International Atomic Energy Agency safeguards system, of the principle of safeguarding effectively the flow of source and special fissionable materials by use of instruments and other techniques at certain strategic points,

Affirming the principle that the benefits of peaceful applications of nuclear technology, including any technological by-products which may be derived by nuclear-weapon States from the development of nuclear explosive devices, should be available for peaceful purposes to all Parties of the Treaty, whether nuclear-weapon or non-nuclear weapon States,

Convinced that, in furtherance of this principle, all Parties to the Treaty are entitled to participate in the fullest possible exchange of scientific information for, and to contribute alone or in cooperation with other States to, the further development of the applications of atomic energy for peaceful purposes,

Declaring their intention to achieve at the earliest possible date the cessation of the nuclear arms race and to undertake effective measures in the direction of nuclear disarmament,

Urging the cooperation of all States in the attainment of this objective,

Recalling the determination expressed by the Parties to the 1963 Treaty banning nuclear weapon tests in the atmosphere, in outer space and under water in its Preamble to seek to achieve the discontinuance of all test explosions of nuclear weapons for all time and to continue negotiations to this end,

Desiring to further the easing of international tension and the strengthening of trust between States in order to facilitate the cessation of the manufacture of nuclear weapons, the liquidation of all their existing stockpiles, and the elimination from national arsenals of nuclear weapons and the means of their delivery pursuant to a Treaty on general and complete disarmament under strict and effective international control,

Recalling that, in accordance with the Charter of the United Nations, States must refrain in their international relations from the threat or use of force against the territorial integrity or political independence of any State, or in any other manner inconsistent with the Purposes of the United Nations, and that the establishment and maintenance of international peace and security are to be promoted with the least diversion for armaments of the worlds human and economic resources,

Have agreed as follows:

Article I

Each nuclear-weapon State Party to the Treaty undertakes not to transfer to any recipient whatsoever nuclear weapons or other nuclear explosive devices or control over such weapons or explosive devices directly, or indirectly; and not in any way to assist, encourage, or induce any non-nuclear weapon State to manufacture or otherwise acquire nuclear weapons or other nuclear explosive devices, or control over such weapons or explosive devices.

Article II

Each non-nuclear-weapon State Party to the Treaty undertakes not to receive the transfer from any transferor whatsoever of nuclear weapons or other nuclear explosive devices or of control over such weapons or explosive devices directly, or indirectly; not to manufacture or otherwise acquire nuclear weapons or other nuclear explosive devices; and not to seek or receive any assistance in the manufacture of nuclear weapons or other nuclear explosive devices.

Article III

1. Each non-nuclear-weapon State Party to the Treaty undertakes to accept safeguards, as set forth in an agreement to be negotiated and concluded with the International Atomic Energy Agency in accordance with the Statute of the International Atomic Energy Agency and the Agency's safeguards system, for the exclusive purpose of verification of the fulfilment of its obligations assumed under this Treaty with a view to preventing diversion of nuclear energy from peaceful uses to nuclear weapons or other nuclear explosive devices. Procedures for the safeguards required by this article shall be followed with respect to source or special fissionable material whether it is being produced, processed or used in any principal nuclear facility or is outside any such facility. The safeguards required by this article shall be applied to all source or special fissionable material in all peaceful nuclear activities within the territory of such State, under its jurisdiction, or carried out under its control anywhere.

2. Each State Party to the Treaty undertakes not to provide: (a) source or special fissionable material, or (b) equipment or material especially designed or prepared for the processing, use or production of special fissionable material, to any non-nuclear-weapon State for peaceful purposes, unless the source or special fissionable material shall be subject to the safeguards required by this article.

3. The safeguards required by this article shall be implemented in a manner designed to comply with article IV of this Treaty, and to avoid hampering the economic or technological development of the Parties or international cooperation in the field of peaceful nuclear activities, including the international exchange of nuclear material and equipment for the processing, use or production of nuclear material for peaceful purposes in accordance with the provisions of this article and the principle of safeguarding set forth in the Preamble of the Treaty.

4. Non-nuclear-weapon States Party to the Treaty shall conclude agreements with the International Atomic Energy Agency to meet the requirements of this article either individually or together with other States in accordance with the Statute of the

International Atomic Energy Agency. Negotiation of such agreements shall commence within 180 days from the original entry into force of this Treaty. For States depositing their instruments of ratification or accession after the 180-day period, negotiation of such agreements shall commence not later than the date of such deposit. Such agreements shall enter into force not later than eighteen months after the date of initiation of negotiations.

Article IV

1. Nothing in this Treaty shall be interpreted as affecting the inalienable right of all the Parties to the Treaty to develop research, production and use of nuclear energy for peaceful purposes without discrimination and in conformity with articles I and II of this Treaty.

2. All the Parties to the Treaty undertake to facilitate, and have the right to participate in, the fullest possible exchange of equipment, materials and scientific and technological information for the peaceful uses of nuclear energy. Parties to the Treaty in a position to do so shall also cooperate in contributing alone or together with other States or international organizations to the further development of the applications of nuclear energy for peaceful purposes, especially in the territories of non-nuclear-weapon States Party to the Treaty, with due consideration for the needs of the developing areas of the world.

Article V

Each party to the Treaty undertakes to take appropriate measures to ensure that, in accordance with this Treaty, under appropriate international observation and through appropriate international procedures, potential benefits from any peaceful applications of nuclear explosions will be made available to non-nuclear-weapon States Party to the Treaty on a non-discriminatory basis and that the charge to such Parties for the explosive devices used will be as low as possible and exclude any charge for research and development. Non-nuclear-weapon States Party to the Treaty shall be able to obtain such benefits, pursuant to a special international agreement or agreements, through an appropriate international body with adequate representation of non-nuclear-weapon States. Negotiations on this subject shall commence as soon as possible after the Treaty enters into force. Non-nuclear-weapon States Party to the Treaty so desiring may also obtain such benefits pursuant to bilateral agreements.

Article VI

Each of the Parties to the Treaty undertakes to pursue negotiations in good faith on effective measures relating to cessation of the nuclear arms race at an early date and to nuclear disarmament, and on a Treaty on general and complete disarmament under strict and effective international control.

Article VII

Nothing in this Treaty affects the right of any group of States to conclude regional treaties in order to assure the total absence of nuclear weapons in their respective territories.

Article VIII

1. Any Party to the Treaty may propose amendments to this Treaty. The text of any proposed amendment shall be submitted to the Depositary Governments which shall circulate it to all Parties to the Treaty. Thereupon, if requested to do so by one-third or more of the Parties to the Treaty, the Depositary Governments shall convene a conference, to which they shall invite all the Parties to the Treaty, to consider such an amendment.

2. Any amendment to this Treaty must be approved by a majority of the votes of all the Parties to the Treaty, including the votes of all nuclear-weapon States Party to the Treaty and all other Parties which, on the date the amendment is circulated, are members of the Board of Governors of the International Atomic Energy Agency. The amendment shall enter into force for each Party that deposits its instrument of ratification of the amendment upon the deposit of such instruments of ratification by a majority of all the Parties, including the instruments of ratification of all nuclear-weapon States Party to the Treaty and all other Parties which, on the date the amendment is circulated, are members of the Board of Governors of the International Atomic Energy Agency. Thereafter, it shall enter into force for any other Party upon the deposit of its instrument of ratification of the amendment.

3. Five years after the entry into force of this Treaty, a conference of Parties to the Treaty shall be held in Geneva, Switzerland, in order to review the operation of this Treaty with a view to assuring that the purposes of the Preamble and the provisions of the Treaty are being realized. At intervals of five years thereafter, a majority of the Parties to the Treaty may obtain, by submitting a proposal to this effect to the Depositary Governments, the convening of further conferences with the same objective of reviewing the operation of the Treaty.

Article IX

1. This Treaty shall be open to all States for signature. Any State which does not sign the Treaty before its entry into force in accordance with paragraph 3 of this article may accede to it at any time.

2. This Treaty shall be subject to ratification by signatory States. Instruments of ratification and instruments of accession shall be deposited with the Governments of the United States of America, the United Kingdom of Great Britain and Northern Ireland and the Union of Soviet Socialist Republics, which are hereby designated the Depositary Governments.

3. This Treaty shall enter into force after its ratification by the States, the Governments of which are designated Depositaries of the Treaty, and forty other States signatory to this Treaty and the deposit of their instruments of ratification. For the purposes of this Treaty, a nuclear-weapon State is one which has manufactured and exploded a nuclear weapon or other nuclear explosive device prior to January 1, 1967.

4. For States whose instruments of ratification or accession are deposited subsequent to the entry into force of this Treaty, it shall enter into force on the date of the deposit of their instruments of ratification or accession.

5. The Depositary Governments shall promptly inform all signatory and acceding States of the date of each signature, the date of deposit of each instrument of ratification or of accession, the date of the entry into force of this Treaty, and the date of receipt of any requests for convening a conference or other notices.

6. This Treaty shall be registered by the Depositary Governments pursuant to article 102 of the Charter of the United Nations.

Article X

1. Each Party shall in exercising its national sovereignty have the right to withdraw from the Treaty if it decides that extraordinary events, related to the subject matter of this Treaty, have jeopardized the supreme interests of its country. It shall give notice of such withdrawal to all other Parties to the Treaty and to the United Nations Security Council three months in advance. Such notice shall include a statement of the extraordinary events it regards as having jeopardized its supreme interests.

2. Twenty-five years after the entry into force of the Treaty, a conference shall be convened to decide whether the Treaty shall continue in force indefinitely, or shall

be extended for an additional fixed period or periods. This decision shall be taken by a majority of the Parties to the Treaty.

Article XI

This Treaty, the English, Russian, French, Spanish and Chinese texts of which are equally authentic, shall be deposited in the archives of the Depositary Governments. Duly certified copies of this Treaty shall be transmitted by the Depositary Governments to the Governments of the signatory and acceding States.

IN WITNESS WHEREOF the undersigned, duly authorized, have signed this Treaty.

DONE in triplicate, at the cities of Washington, London and Moscow, this first day of July one thousand nine hundred sixty-eight.

AGREEMENT BETWEEN IAEA, THE EUROPEAN ATOMIC ENERGY COMMUNITY AND ITS NON-NUCLEAR MEMBER STATES IN IMPLEMENTATION OF ARTICLE III, (1) AND (4) OF THE NON PROLIFERATION TREATY

(Brussels, 5 April 1973)

This agreement was concluded in order to implement article III , paragraphs 1 and 4 of the Non Proliferation Treaty, which stipulate the "purpose of verification of the fulfilment of its obligations [i.e. of each non-nuclear weapon State Party to the NPT] assumed ......with a view to preventing diversion of nuclear energy from peaceful uses to nuclear weapons or other nuclear explosive devices". The agreement is known as the "verification agreement" and involves all Euratom member States, excepting France and the United Kingdom which possess nuclear weapons. The contracting States thus committed themselves to accepting safeguards on all nuclear materials of proliferation significance used on their own territory. The United Kingdom, France, the IAEA and Euratom concluded specific bilateral agreements in 1976 and 1978, providing for "voluntary submission" to safeguards on the part of those two countries (civil nuclear installations remaining however under the control of Euratom). On the basis of these three agreements, the Vienna Agency and Euratom are to co-operate in implementing the required safeguards so as to avoid unnecessary duplication of safeguards activities (as specified in a protocol to each agreement).

The "Verification Agreement" lays down provisions for the implementation of safeguards without prejudice of international co-operation in the peaceful use, nuclear safety, commercial and industrial secrets and confidentiality, technological development in the field of safeguards and so on. Attention is drawn especially to article 3, which stipulates specific conditions for a co-ordinated application of safeguards taking into account the prerogatives of the two international organisations concerned.

It must be finally pointed out that the text of this agreement (which is obviously part of both the IAEA and Euratom systems) is published following presentation of the latter system, because it shows how also this system was affected (albeit indirectly) by the existence of the NPT, and it paved the way to the laying down of the Euratom Regulation no.3227/76 dealt with in the following pages.

The "Verification Agreement" (entered into force on February 21, 1977) is reproduced in the IAEA document INFCIRC/193. The other two agreements with the United Kingdom and France entered into force on August 14, 1978 and September 12, 1981 respectively (IAEA docs. INFCIRC/263 of October 1978 and INFCIRC/290 of December 1981 respectively). These INFCIRC documents are not published here in order to avoid overburdening the volume and given the existence of the main Agreements.

WHEREAS the Kingdom of Belgium, the Kingdom of Denmark, the Federal Republic of Germany, Ireland, the Italian Republic, the Grand Duchy of Luxembourg and the Kingdom of the Netherlands (hereinafter referred to as 'the States') are signatories of the Treaty on the Non-Proliferation of Nuclear Weapons (hereinafter referred to as 'the Treaty') opened for Signature at London, Moscow and Washington on I July 1968 and which entered into force on 5 March 1970;
RECALLING that pursuant to Article IV(l) of the Treaty nothing in the Treaty shall be interpreted as affecting the inalienable right of all the Parties to the Treaty to develop research, production and use of nuclear energy for peaceful purposes without discrimination and in conformity with Articles I and H of the Treaty;
RECALLING that according to Article IV(2) of the Treaty all the Parties to the Treaty undertake to facilitate, and have the right to participate in, the fullest possible exchange of equipment, materials and scientific and technological information for the peaceful uses of nuclear energy;
RECALLING further that under the terms of the same paragraph the Parties to the Treaty in a position to do so shall also cooperate in contributing alone or together with other States or international organisations to the further development of the applications of nuclear energy for peaceful purposes, especially in the territories of non-nuclear-weapon States Party to the Treaty;
WHEREAS Article M(l) of the Treaty provides that each non-nuclear-weapon State Party to the Treaty undertakes to accept safeguards, as set forth in an agreement to be negotiated and concluded with the International Atomic Energy Agency (hereinafter referred to as 'the Agency') in accordance with the Statute of the Agency (hereinafter referred to as 'the Statute') and the Agency's safeguards system, for the exclusive purpose of verification of the fulfilment of its obligations assumed under this Treaty with a view to preventing diversion of nuclear energy from peaceful uses to nuclear weapons or other nuclear explosive devices;
WHEREAS Article 111(4) provides that non-nuclear-weapon States Party to the Treaty shall conclude agreements with the Agency to meet the requirements of the said Article either individually or together with other States in accordance with the Statute;
WHEREAS the States are Members of the European Atomic Energy Community (EURATOM) (hereinafter referred to as 'the Community') and have assigned to institutions common to the European Communities regulatory, executive and judicial powers which these institutions exercise in their own right in those areas for which

they are competent and which may take effect directly within the legal systems of the Member States;
WHEREAS within this institutional framework, the Community has in particular the task of ensuring, through appropriate safeguards, that nuclear materials are not diverted to purposes other than those for which they were intended, and will, from the time of the entry into force of the Treaty within the territories of the States, thus be required to satisfy itself through the system of safeguards established by the EURATOM Treaty, that source and special fissionable material in all peaceful nuclear activities within the territories of the States is not diverted to nuclear weapons or other nuclear explosive devices;
WHEREAS these safeguards include notification to the Community of the basic technical characteristics of nuclear facilities, maintenance and submission of operating records to permit nuclear materials accounting for the Community as a whole, inspections by officials of the Community, and a system of sanctions;
WHEREAS the Community has the task of establishing with other countries and with international organisations relations which may promote progress in the use of nuclear energy for peaceful purposes and is expressly authorized to assume special safeguard obligations in an agreement with a third State or an international organisation;
WHEREAS the Agency's international safeguards system referred to in the Treaty comprises, in particular, provisions for the submission of design information to the Agency, the maintenance of records, the submission of reports on all nuclear material subject to safeguards to the Agency, inspections carried out by the Agency's inspectors, requirements for the establishment and maintenance of a system of accounting for and control of nuclear material by a State, and measures in relation to verification of non-diversion;
WHEREAS the Agency, in the light of its statutory responsibilities and its relationship to the General Assembly and the Security Council of the United Nations, has the responsibility to assure the international community that effective safeguards are being applied under the Treaty;
NOTING that the States which were Members of the Community when they signed the Treaty, made it known on that occasion that safeguards provided for in Article M(l) of the Treaty would have to be set out in a verification agreement between the Community, the States and the Agency and defined in such a way that the rights and obligations of the States and the Community would not be affected;
WHEREAS the Board of Governors of the Agency (hereinafter referred to as 'the Board') has approved a comprehensive set of model provisions for the structure and content of agreements between the Agency and States required in connection with the Treaty to be used as the basis for negotiating safeguards agreements between the Agency and non-nuclear-weapon States Party to the Treaty;

WHEREAS the Agency is authorized under Article III.A.5 of the Statute, to apply safeguards, at the request of the parties, to any bilateral or multilateral arrangement, or at the request of a State, to any of that State's activities in the field of atomic energy;
WHEREAS it is the desire of the Agency, the Community and the States to avoid unnecessary duplication of safeguards activities;

NOW, THEREFORE, the Agency, the Community and the States have agreed as follows:

PART I

Basic Undertaking

Article I

The States undertake, pursuant to Article M(l) of the Treaty, to accept safeguards, in accordance with the terms of this Agreement, on all source or special fissionable material in all peaceful nuclear activities within their territories, under their jurisdiction or carried out under their control anywhere, for the exclusive purpose of verifying that such material is not diverted to nuclear weapons or other nuclear explosive devices.

Application of Safeguards

Article 2

The Agency shall have the right and the obligation to ensure that safeguards will be applied, in accordance with the terms of this Agreement, on all source or special fissionable material in all peaceful nuclear activities within the territories of the States, under their jurisdiction or carried out under their control anywhere for the exclusive purpose of verifying that such material is not diverted to nuclear weapons or other nuclear explosive devices.

Article 3

(a) The Community undertakes, in applying its safeguards on source and special fissionable material in all peaceful nuclear activities within the territories of the States, to cooperate with the Agency, in accordance with the terms of this Agreement, with a view to ascertaining that such source and special fissionable material is not diverted to nuclear weapons or other nuclear explosive devices.

(b) The Agency shall apply its safeguards, in accordance with the terms of this Agreement, in such a manner as to enable it to verify, in ascertaining that there has been no diversion of nuclear material from peaceful uses to nuclear weapons or other nuclear explosive devices, findings of the Community's system of safeguards. The Agency's verification shall include, inter alia, independent measurements and observations conducted by the Agency in accordance with the procedures specified in this Agreement. The Agency, in its verification, shall take due account of the effectiveness of the Community's system of safeguards in accordance with the terms of this Agreement.

Co-operation Between the Agency, the Community and the States

Article 4

The Agency, the Community and the States shall cooperate, in so far as each Party is concerned, to facilitate the implementation of the safeguards provided for in this Agreement and shall avoid unnecessary duplication of safeguards activities.

Implementation of Safeguards

Article 5

The safeguards provided for in this Agreement shall be implemented in a manner designed:
(a) To avoid hampering the economic and technological development in the Community or international cooperation in the field of peaceful nuclear activities, including international exchange of nuclear material;
(b) To avoid undue interference in the peaceful nuclear activities in the Community, and in particular in the operation of facilities; and
(c) To be consistent with prudent management practices required for the economic and safe conduct of nuclear activities.

Article 6

(a) The Agency shall take every precaution to protect commercial and industrial secrets and other confidential information coming to its knowledge in the implementation of this Agreement.
(b) (i) The Agency shall not publish or communicate to any State, organisation or person any information obtained by it in connection with the implementation of this Agreement, except that specific information relating to the implementation thereof may be given to the Board and to such Agency staff members as require such know-

ledge reason of their official duties in connection with safeguards, but only to the extent necessary for the Agency to fulfil its responsibilities in implementing this Agreement;
(ii) Summarized information on nuclear material subject to safeguards under this Agreement may be published upon decision of the Board if the States directly concerned or the Community, in so far as either Party is individually concerned, agree thereto.

Article 7

In implementing safeguards under this Agreement, full account shall be taken of technological development in the field of safeguards, and every effort shall be made to ensure optimum cost-effectiveness and the application of the principle of safeguarding effectively the flow of nuclear material subject to safeguards under this Agreement by use of instruments and other techniques at certain strategic points to the extent that present or future technology permits.
(b) In order to ensure optimum cost-effectiveness, use shall be made, for example, of such means as:
(i) Containment as a means of defining material balance areas for accounting purposes;
(ii) Statistical techniques and random sampling in evaluating the flow of nuclear material; and
(iii) Concentration of verification procedures on those stages in the nuclear fuel cycle involving the production, processing, use or storage of nuclear material from which nuclear weapons or other nuclear explosive devices could readily be made, and minimisation of verification procedures in respect of other nuclear material, on condition that this does not hamper the implementation of this Agreement.

Provision of Information to the Agency

Article 8

(a) In order to ensure the effective implementation of safeguards under this Agreement, the Community shall, in accordance with the provisions set out in this Agreement, provide the Agency with information concerning nuclear material subject to such safeguards and the features of facilities relevant to safeguarding such material.
(b) (i) The Agency shall require only the minimum amount of information and data consistent with carrying out its responsibilities under this Agreement.
(ii) Information pertaining to facilities shall be the minimum necessary for safeguarding nuclear material subject to safeguards under this Agreement.
(c) If the Community so requests, the Agency shall be prepared to examine on premises of the Community design information which the Community regards as being of

particular sensitivity. Such information need not be physically transmitted to the Agency provided that it remains readily available for further examination by the Agency on premises of the Community.

Agency Inspectors

Article 9

(a) (i) The Agency shall secure the consent of the Community and the States to the designation of Agency inspectors to the States.
(ii) If the Community, either upon proposal of a designation or at any other time after a designation has been made, objects to the designation, the Agency shall propose to the Community and the States an alternative designation or designations.
(iii) If, as a result of the repeated refusal of the Community to accept the designation of Agency inspectors, inspections to be conducted under this Agreement would be impeded, such refusal shall be considered by the Board, upon referral by the Director General of the Agency (hereinafter referred to as 'the Director General'), with a view to its taking appropriate action.
(b) The Community and the States concerned shall take the necessary steps to ensure that Agency inspectors can effectively discharge their functions under this Agreement.
(c) The visits and activities of Agency inspectors shall be so arranged as:
(i) To reduce to a minimum the possible inconvenience and disturbance to the Community and the States and to the peaceful nuclear activities inspected; and
(ii) To ensure protection of industrial secrets or any other confidential information coming to the knowledge of Agency inspectors.

Privileges and Immunities

Article 10

Each State shall apply to the Agency, including its property, funds and assets, and to its inspectors and other officials, performing functions under this Agreement, the relevant provisions of the Agreement on the Privileges and Immunities of the International Atomic Energy Agency.

Consumption or Dilution of Nuclear Material

Article 11

Safeguards under this Agreement shall terminate on nuclear material upon determination by the Community and the Agency that the material has been consumed, or has been diluted in such a way that it is no longer usable for any nuclear activity relevant from the point of view of safeguards, or has become practically irrecoverable.

Transfer of Nuclear Material Out of the States

Article 12

The Community shall give the Agency notification of transfers of nuclear material subject to safeguards under this Agreement out of the States, in accordance with the provisions of this Agreement. Safeguards under this Agreement shall terminate on nuclear material when the recipient State has assumed responsibility therefor as provided for in this Agreement. The Agency shall maintain records indicating each transfer and, where applicable, the re-application of safeguards to the transferred nuclear material.

Provisions Relating to Nuclear Material to be Used in Non-Nuclear Activities

Article 13

Where nuclear material subject to safeguards under this Agreement is to be used in non-nuclear activities, such as the production of alloys or ceramics, the Community shall agree with the Agency, before the material is so used, on the circumstances under which the safeguards under this Agreement on such material may be terminated.

Non-Application of Safeguards to Nuclear Material to be Used in Non-Peaceful Activities

Article 14

If a State intends to exercise its discretion to use nuclear material which is required to be safeguarded under this Agreement in a nuclear activity which does not require the application of safeguards under this Agreement, the following procedures shall apply:

(a) The Community and the State shall inform the Agency of the activity, and the State shall make it clear:

(i) That the use of the nuclear material in a non-prescribed military activity will not be in conflict with an undertaking the State may have given and in respect of which Agency safeguards apply, that the material will be used only in a peaceful nuclear activity; and

(ii) That during the period of non-application of safeguards under this Agreement the nuclear material will not be used for the production of nuclear weapons or other nuclear explosive devices;
(b) The Agency and the Community shall make an arrangement so that, only while the nuclear material is in such an activity, the safeguards provided for in this Agreement will not be applied. The arrangement shall identify, to the extent possible, the period or circumstances during which such safeguards will not be applied. In any event, the safeguards provided for in this Agreement shall apply again as soon as the nuclear material is reintroduced into a peaceful nuclear activity. The Agency shall be kept informed of the total quantity and composition of such material in the State or in the States concerned and of any transfer of such material; out of that State or those States; and
(c) Each arrangement shall be made in agreement with the Agency. Such agreement shall be given as promptly as possible and shall relate only to such matters as, inter alia, temporal and procedural provisions and reporting arrangements, but shall not involve any approval or classified knowledge of the military activity or relate to the use of the nuclear material therein.

Finance

Article 15

The Agency, the Community and the States will bear the expenses incurred by each of them in implementing their respective responsibilities under this Agreement. However, if the Community, the States or persons under their jurisdiction, incur extraordinary expenses as a result of a specific request by the Agency, the Agency shall reimburse such expenses provided that it has agreed in advance to do so. In any case, the Agency shall bear the cost of any additional measuring or sampling which Agency inspectors may request.

Third Party Liability for Nuclear Damage

Article 16

The Community and the States shall ensure that any protection against third party liability in respect of nuclear damage, including any insurance or other financial security which may be available under their laws or regulations shall apply to the Agency and its officials for the purpose of the implementation of this Agreement, in the same way as that protection applies to nationals of the States.

International Responsibility

Article 17

Any claim by the Community or a State against the Agency or by the Agency against the Community or a State in respect of any damage resulting from the implementation of safeguards under this Agreement, other than damage arising out of a nuclear incident, shall be settled in accordance with international law.

Measures in Relation to Verification of Non-Diversion

Article 18

If the Board, upon report of the Director General, decides that an action by the Community or a State, in so far as either Party is individually concerned, is essential and urgent in order to ensure verification that nuclear material subject to safeguards under this Agreement is not diverted to nuclear weapons or other nuclear explosive devices, the Board may call upon the Community or that State to take the required action without delay irrespective of whether procedures have been invoked pursuant to Article 22 for the settlement of a dispute.

Article 19

If the Board, upon examination of relevant information reported to it by the Director General, finds that the Agency is not able to verify that there has been no diversion of nuclear material required to be safeguarded under this Agreement, to nuclear weapons or other nuclear explosive devices, it may make the reports provided for in Article XII(C) of the Statute and may also take, where applicable, the other measures provided for in that paragraph. In taking such action, the Board shall take account of the degree of assurance provided by the safeguards measures that have been applied and shall offer the Community or the State, in so far as either Party is individually concerned, every reasonable opportunity to furnish the Board with any necessary reassurance.

Interpretation and Application of the Agreement and Settlement of Disputes

Article 20

At the request of the Agency, the Community or a State, there shall be consultations about any question arising out of the interpretation or application of this Agreement.

Article 21

The Community and the States shall have the right to request that any question arising out of the interpretation or application of this Agreement be considered by the Board. The Board shall invite the Community and the State concerned to participate in the discussion of any such question by the Board.

Article 22

Any dispute arising out of the interpretation or application of this Agreement except a dispute with regard to a finding by the Board under Article 19 or an action taken by the Board pursuant to such a finding, which is not settled by negotiation or another procedure agreed to by the Agency, the Community and the States shall, at the request of any one of them, be submitted to an arbitral tribunal composed of five arbitrators. The Community and the States shall designate two arbitrators and the Agency shall also designate two arbitrators, and the four arbitrators so designated shall elect a fifth, who shall be the Chairman. If, within thirty days of the request for arbitration, the Community and the States, or the Agency, have not designated two arbitrators each, the Community or the Agency may request the President of the International Court of Justice to appoint these arbitrators. The same procedure shall apply if, within thirty days of the designation or appointment of the fourth arbitrator, the fifth arbitrator has not been elected. A majority of the members of the arbitral tribunal shall constitute a quorum, and all decisions shall require the concurrence of at least three arbitrators. The arbitral procedure shall be fixed by the tribunal, The decisions of the tribunal shall be binding on the Agency, the Community, and the States concerned.

Accession

Article 23

(a) This Agreement shall come into force for non-nuclear-weapon States Party to the Treaty which become Members of the Community, upon:
(i) Notification to the Agency by the State concerned that its procedures with respect to the coming into force of this Agreement have been completed; and
(ii) Notification to the Agency by the Community that it is in a position to apply its safeguards in respect of that State for the purposes of this Agreement.
(b) Where the State concerned has concluded other agreements with the Agency for the application of Agency safeguards, upon the coming into force of this Agreement for that State, the application of Agency safeguards under such agreements shall be suspended while this Agreement is in force; provided, however, that the State's

undertaking in those agreements not to use items which are subject thereto in such a way as to further any military purpose shall continue to apply.

Amendment of the Agreement

Article 24

(a) The Agency, the Community and the States shall, at the request of any one of them, consult on amendment to this Agreement.
(b) All amendments shall require the agreement of the Agency, the Community and the States.
(c) The Director General shall promptly inform all Member States of the Agency of any amendment to this Agreement.

Entry into Force and Duration

Article 25

(a) This Agreement shall enter into force on the date upon which the Agency receives from the Community and the States written notification that their own requirements for entry into force have been met. The Director General shall promptly inform all Member States of the Agency of the entry into force of this Agreement.
(b) This Agreement shall remain in force as long as the States are Parties to the Treaty.

Protocol

Article 26

The Protocol attached to this Agreement shall be an integral part thereof. The term 'Agreement' as used in this instrument means the Agreement and the Protocol together.

PART II

Introduction

Article 27

The purpose of this part of the Agreement is to specify, as required, the procedures to be applied in the implementation of the safeguards provisions of Part I.

Objective of Safeguards

Article 28

The objective of the safeguards procedures set forth in this Agreement is the timely detection of diversion of significant quantities of nuclear material from peaceful nuclear activities to the manufacture of nuclear weapons or of other nuclear explosive devices or for purposes unknown, and deterrence of such diversion by the risk of early detection.

Article 29

For the purpose of achieving the objective set forth in Article 28, material accountancy shall be used as a safeguards measure of fundamental importance, with containment and surveillance as important complementary measures.

Article 30

The technical conclusion of the Agency's verification activities shall be a statement, in respect of each material balance area, of the amount of material unaccounted for over a specific period, and giving the limits of accuracy of the amounts stated.

The Community's System of Safeguards

Article 31

Pursuant to Article 3, the Agency, in carrying out its verification activities, shall make full use of the Community's system of safeguards.

Article 32

The Community's system of accounting for and control of nuclear material under this Agreement shall be based on a structure of material balance areas. The Community, in applying its safeguards, will make use of and, to the extent necessary, make provision for, as appropriate and specified in the Subsidiary Arrangements such measures as:
(a) A measurement system for the determination of the quantities of nuclear material received, produced, shipped, lost or otherwise removed from inventory, and the quantities on inventory;
(b) The evaluation of precision and accuracy of measurements and the estimation of measurement uncertainty;

(c) Procedures for identifying, reviewing and evaluating differences in shipper/receiver measurements;
(d) Procedures for taking a physical inventory;
(e) Procedures for the evaluation of accumulations of unmeasured inventory and unmeasured losses;
(f) A system of records and reports showing, for each material balance area, the inventory of nuclear material and the changes in that inventory including receipts into and transfers out of the material balance area;
(g) Provisions to ensure that the accounting procedures and arrangements are being operated correctly; and
(h) Procedures for the provision of reports to the Agency in accordance with Articles 59 to 65 and 67 to 69.

Article 33

Safeguards under this Agreement shall not apply to material in mining or ore processing activities.

Article 34

(a) When any material containing uranium or thorium. which has not reached the stage of the nuclear fuel cycle described in paragraph (c) is directly or indirectly exported to a non-nuclear-weapon State not Party to this Agreement, the Community shall inform the Agency of its quantity, composition and destination, unless the material is exported for specifically non-nuclear purposes;
(b) When any material containing uranium or thorium. which has not reached the stage of the nuclear fuel cycle described in paragraph (c) is imported into the States, the Community shall inform the Agency of its quantity and composition, unless the material is imported for specifically non-nuclear purposes; and
(c) When any nuclear material of a composition and purity suitable for fuel fabrication or for isotopic enrichment leaves the plant or the process stage in which it has been produced, or when such nuclear material, or any other nuclear material produced at a later stage in the nuclear fuel cycle, is imported into the States, the nuclear material shall become subject to the other safeguards procedures specified in this Agreement.

Termination of Safeguards

Article 35

(a) Safeguards under this Agreement shall terminate on nuclear material, under the conditions set forth in Article 111. Where the conditions of that Article are not met,

but the Community considers that the recovery of nuclear material subject to safeguards under this Agreement from residues is not for the time being practicable or desirable, the Agency and the Community shall consult on the appropriate safeguards measures to be applied.
(b) Safeguards under this Agreement shall terminate on nuclear material, under the conditions set forth in Article 13, provided that the Agency and the Community agree that such nuclear material is practicably irrecoverable.

Exemptions from Safeguards

Article 36

At the request of the Community, the Agency shall exempt nuclear material from safeguards under this Agreement, as follows:
(a) Special fissionable material, when it is used in gram quantities or less as a sensing component in instruments;
(b) Nuclear material, when it is used in non-nuclear activities in accordance with Article 13, if such nuclear material is recoverable; and
(c) Plutonium with an isotopic concentration of plutonium-238 exceeding 80 %.

Article 37

At the request of the Community the Agency shall exempt from safeguards under this Agreement nuclear material that would otherwise be subject to such safeguards, provided that the total quantity of nuclear material which has been exempted in the States in accordance with this Article may not at any time exceed:
(a) One kilogram in total of special fissionable material, which may consist of one or more of the following:
(i) Plutonium;
(ii) Uranium with an enrichment of 0.2 (20 %) and above, taken account of by multiplying its weight by its enrichment; and
(iii) Uranium with an enrichment below 0.2 (20 %) and above that of natural uranium, taken account of by multiplying its weight by five times the square of its enrichment;
(b) Ten metric tons in total of natural uranium and depleted uranium with an enrichment above 0.005 (0.5 %);
(c) Twenty metric tons of depleted uranium with an enrichment of 0.005 (0.5 %) or below; and
(d) Twenty metric tons of thorium; or such greater amounts as may be specified by the Board for uniform application.

Article 38

If exempted nuclear material is to be processed or stored together with nuclear material subject to safeguards under this Agreement, provision shall be made for the reapplication of such safeguards thereto.

Subsidiary Arrangements

Article 39

The Community shall make Subsidiary Arrangements with the Agency which shall specify in detail, to the extent necessary to permit the Agency to fulfil its responsibilities under this Agreement in an effective and efficient manner, how the procedures laid down in this Agreement are to be applied. The Subsidiary Arrangements may be extended or changed by agreement between the Agency and the Community without amendment of this Agreement.

Article 40

The Subsidiary Arrangements shall enter into force at the same time as, or as soon as possible after, the entry into force of this Agreement. The Agency, the Community and the States shall make every effort to achieve their entry into force within ninety days of the entry into force of this Agreement; an extension of that period shall require agreement between the Agency, the Community and the States. The Community shall provide the Agency promptly with the information required for completing the Subsidiary Arrangements. Upon the entry into force of this Agreement, the Agency shall have the right to apply the procedures laid down therein in respect of the nuclear material listed in the inventory provided for in Article 41, even if the Subsidiary Arrangements have not yet entered into force.

Inventory

Article 41

On the basis of the initial report referred to in Article 62, the Agency shall establish a unified inventory of all nuclear material in the States subject to safeguards under this Agreement, irrespective of its origin, and shall maintain this inventory on the basis of subsequent reports and of the results of its verification activities. Copies of the inventory shall be made available to the Community at intervals to be agreed.

Design Information-General provisions

Article 42

Pursuant to Article 8, design information in respect of existing facilities shall be provided to the Agency by the Community during the discussion of the Subsidiary Arrangements. The time limits for the provision of design information in respect of the new facilities shall be specified in the Subsidiary Arrangements and such information shall be provided as early as possible before nuclear material is introduced into a new facility.

Article 43

The design information to be provided to the Agency shall include, in respect of each facility, when applicable:
(a) The identification of the facility, stating its general character, purpose, nominal capacity and geographic location, and the name and address to be used for routine business purposes;
(b) A description of the general arrangement of the facility with reference, to the extent feasible, to the form, location and flow of nuclear material and to the general layout of important items of equipment which use, produce or process nuclear material;
(c) A description of features of the facility relating to material accountancy, containment and surveillance; and
(d) A description of the existing and proposed procedures at the facility for nuclear material accountancy and control, with special reference to material balance areas established by the operator, measurements of flow and procedures for physical inventory taking.

Article 44

Other information relevant to the application of safeguards under this Agreement shall also be provided to the Agency in respect of each facility, if so specified in the Subsidiary Arrangements. The Community shall provide the Agency with supplementary information on the health and safety procedures which the Agency shall observe and with which Agency inspectors shall comply at the facility.

Article 45

The Agency shall be provided by the Community with design information in respect of a modification relevant for purposes of safeguards under this Agreement, for examination, and shall be informed of any change in the information provided to it under Article 44, sufficiently in advance for the safeguards procedures to be applied under this Agreement to be adjusted when necessary.

Article 46
Purpose of examination of design information

The design information provided to the Agency shall be used for the following purposes:
(a) To identify the features of facilities and nuclear material relevant to the application of safeguards to nuclear material in sufficient detail to facilitate verification;
(b) To determine material balance areas to be used for accounting purposes under this Agreement and to select those strategic points which are key measurement points and which will be used to determine flow and inventory of nuclear material; in determining such material balance areas the following criteria shall, inter alia, be used:
(i) The size of the material balance area shall be related to the accuracy with which the material balance can be established;
(ii) In determining the material balance area advantage shall be taken of any opportunity to use containment and surveillance to help ensure the completeness of flow measurements and thereby to simplify the application of safeguards and to concentrate measurement efforts at key measurement points;
(iii) A special material balance area may, be established at the request of the Community or of the State concerned around a process step involving commercially sensitive information,
(c) To establish the nominal timing and procedures for taking of physical inventory of nuclear material for accounting purposes under this Agreement;
(d) To establish the records and reports requirements and records evaluation procedures;
(e) To establish requirements and procedures for verification of the quantity and location of nuclear material; and
(f) To select appropriate combinations of containment and material accountancy, containment and surveillance methods and techniques and the strategic and points at which they are to be applied.

The results of the examination of the design information, as agreed upon between the Agency and the Community, shall be included in the Subsidiary Arrangements.

Article 47
Re-examination of design information

Design information shall be re-examined in the light of changes in operating conditions, of developments in safeguards technology or of the experience in the application of verification procedures, with a view to modifying action taken pursuant to Article 46.

Article 48
Verification of design information

The Agency, in cooperation with the Community and the State concerned may send inspectors to facilities to verify the design information provided to the Agency pursuant to Articles 42 to 45 for the purposes stated in Article 46.

Information in Respect of Nuclear Material Outside Facilities

Article 49

The Agency shall be provided by the Community with the following information when nuclear material is to be customarily used outside facilities, as applicable:
(a) A general description of the use of the nuclear material, its geographic location, and the user's name and address for routine business purposes; and
(b) A general description of the existing and proposed procedures for nuclear material accountancy and control, as specified in the Subsidiary Arrangements.

The Agency shall be informed by the Community, on a timely basis, of any change in the information provided to it under this Article.

Article 50

The information provided to the Agency pursuant to Article 49 may be used, to the extent relevant, for the purposes set out in Article 46 (b) to (f).

Records System-General provisions

Article 51

The Community shall arrange that records are kept in respect of each material balance area. The records to be kept shall be described in the Subsidiary Arrangements.

Article 52

The Community shall make arrangements to facilitate the examination of records by Agency inspectors, particularly if the records are not kept in English, French, Russian or Spanish.

Article 53

Records shall be retained for at least five years.

Article 54

Records shall consist, as appropriate, of:
(a) Accounting records of all nuclear material subject to safeguards under this Agreement; and
(b) Operating records for facilities containing such nuclear material.

Article 55

The system of measurements on which the records used for the preparation of reports are based shall either conform to the latest international standards or be equivalent in quality to such standards.

Accounting records

Article 56

The accounting records shall set forth the following in respect of each material balance area:
(a) All inventory changes, so as to permit a determination of the book inventory at any time;
(b) All measurement results that are used for determination of the physical inventory; and
(c) All adjustments and corrections that have been made in respect of inventory changes, book inventories and physical inventories.

Article 57

For all inventory changes and physical inventories the records shall show, in respect of each batch of nuclear material: material identification, batch data and source data. The records shall account for uranium, thorium and plutonium separately in each batch of nuclear material. For each inventory change, the date of the inventory change and, when appropriate, the originating material balance area and the receiving material balance area or the recipient, shall be indicated.

Article 58
Operating records

The operating records shall set forth, as appropriate, in respect of each material balance area:
(a) Those operating data which are used to establish changes in the quantities and composition of nuclear material;
(b) The data obtained from the calibration of tanks and instruments and from sampling and analyses, the procedures to control the quality of measurements and the derived estimates of random and systematic error;
(c) A description of the sequence of the actions taken in preparing for, and in taking, a physical inventory, in order to ensure that it is correct and complete; and
(d) A description of the actions taken in order to ascertain the cause and magnitude of any accidental or unmeasured loss that might occur.

Reports System-General provisions

Article 59

The Community shall provide the Agency with reports as detailed in Articles 60 to 65 and 67 to 69 in respect of nuclear material subject to safeguards under this Agreement.

Article 60

Reports shall be made in English, French, Russian or Spanish, except as otherwise specified in the Subsidiary Arrangements.

Article 61

Reports shall be based on the records kept in accordance with Articles 51 to 56 and shall consist, as appropriate, of accounting reports and special reports.

Accounting reports

Article 62

The Agency shall be provided by the Community with an initial report on all nuclear material subject to safeguards under this Agreement. The initial report shall be dispatched to the Agency within thirty days of the last day of the calendar month in which this Agreement enters into force, and shall reflect the situation as of the last day of that month.

Article 63

The Community shall provide the Agency with the following accounting reports for each material balance area:
(a) Inventory change reports showing all changes in the inventory of nuclear material, the reports shall be dispatched as soon as possible and in any event within the time limits specified in the Subsidiary Arrangements; and
(b) Material balance reports showing the material balance based on a physical inventory of nuclear material actually present in the material balance area. The reports shall be dispatched as soon as possible and in any event within the time limits specified in the Subsidiary Arrangements.

The reports shall be based on data available as of the date of reporting and may be corrected at a later date, as required.

Article 64

Inventory change reports shall specify identification and batch data for each batch of nuclear material, the date of the inventory change and, as appropriate, the originating material balance area and the receiving material balance area or the recipient. These reports shall be accompanied by concise notes:
(a) Explaining the inventory changes, on the basis of the operating data contained in the operating records provided for under Article 56(a); and
(b) Describing, as specified in the Subsidiary Arrangements, the anticipated operational programme, particularly the taking of a physical inventory.

Article 65

The Community shall report each inventory change, adjustment and correction, either periodically in a consolidated list or individually. Inventory changes shall be reported in terms of batches. As specified in the Subsidiary Arrangements, small changes in inventory of nuclear material, such as transfers of analytical samples, may be combined in one batch and reported as one inventory change.

Article 66

The Agency shall provide the Community, for the use of the interested parties, with semi-annual statements of book inventory of nuclear material subject to safeguards under this Agreement, for each material balance area, as based on the inventory change reports for the period covered by each such statement.

Article 67

Material balance reports shall include the following entries unless otherwise agreed by the Agency and the Community:
(a) Beginning physical inventory;
(b) Inventory changes (first increases, then decreases); (c) Ending book inventory;
(d) Shipper/receiver differences;
(e) Adjusted ending book inventory; (f) Ending physical inventory; and
(g) Material unaccounted for.

A statement of the physical inventory, listing all batches separately and specifying material identification and batch data for each batch, shall be attached to each material balance report.

Article 68
Special reports

The Community shall make special reports without delay:
(a) If any unusual incident or circumstances lead the Community to believe that there is or may have been loss of nuclear material that exceeds the limits specified for this purpose in the Subsidiary Arrangements; or
(b) If the containment has unexpectedly changed from that specified in the Subsidiary Arrangements to the extent that unauthorized removal of nuclear material has become possible.

Article 69
Amplification and clarification of reports

If the Agency so requests, the Community shall provide it with amplifications or clarifications of any report, in so far as relevant for the purpose of safeguards under this Agreement.

Inspections

Article 70
General provisions

The Agency shall have the right to make inspections as provided for in this Agreement.

Purpose of Inspections

Article 71

The Agency may make ad hoc inspections in order to:
(a) Verify the information contained in the initial report on the nuclear material subject to safeguards under this Agreement and identify and verify changes in the situation which have occurred between the date of the initial report and the date of the entry into force of the Subsidiary Arrangements in respect of a given facility; and
(b) Identify, and if possible verify the quantity and composition of nuclear material subject to safeguards under this Agreement in accordance with Articles 93 and 96, before its transfer out of or upon its transfer into the States except for transfers within the Community.

Article 72

The Agency may make routine inspections in order to:
(a) Verify that reports are consistent with records;
(b) Verify the location, identity, quantity and composition of all nuclear material subject to safeguards under this Agreement; and
(c) Verify information on the possible causes of material unaccounted for, shipper/receiver differences and uncertainties in the book inventory.

Article 73

Subject to the procedures laid down in Article 77, the Agency may make special inspections:
(a) In order to verify the information contained in special reports; or
(b) If the Agency considers that information made available by the Community including explanations from the Community and information obtained from routine inspections, is not adequate for the Agency to fulfil its responsibilities under this Agreement.

An inspection shall be deemed to be special when it is either additional to the routine inspection effort provided for in this Agreement or involves access to information or locations in addition to the access specified in Article 76 for ad hoc and routine inspections, or both.

Scope of inspections

Article 74

For the purposes specified in Articles 71 to 73, the Agency may:
(a) Examine the records kept pursuant to Articles 51 to 56;
(b) Make independent measurements of all nuclear material subject to safeguards under this Agreement;
(c) Verify the functioning and calibration of instruments and other measuring and control equipment;
(d) Apply and make use of surveillance and containment measures; and
(e) Use other objective methods which have been demonstrated to be technically feasible.

Article 75

Within the scope of Article 74, the Agency shall be enabled:
(a) To observe that samples at key measurement points for material balance accountancy are taken in accordance with procedures which produce representative samples, to observe the treatment and analysis of the samples and to obtain duplicates of such samples;
(b) To observe that the measurements of nuclear material at key measurement points for material balance accountancy are representative, and to observe the calibration of the instruments and equipment involved;
(c) To make arrangements with the Community and to the extent necessary with the State concerned that, if necessary:
(i) Additional measurements are made and additional samples taken for the Agency's use;
(ii) The Agency's standard analytical samples are analysed;
(iii) Appropriate absolute standards are used in calibrating instruments and other equipment; and
(iv) Other calibrations are carried out;
(d) To arrange to use its own equipment for independent measurement and surveillance, and if so agreed and specified in the Subsidiary Arrangements to arrange to install such equipment;
(e) To apply its seals and other identifying and tamper-indicating devices to containments, if so agreed and specified in the Subsidiary Arrangements; and
(f) To make arrangements with the Community or the State concerned for the shipping of samples taken for the Agency's use.

Access for inspections

Article 76

(a) For the purposes specified in Article 71 (a) and until such time as the strategic points have been specified in the Subsidiary Arrangements, the Agency inspectors shall have access to any location where the initial report or any inspections carried out in connection with it indicate that nuclear material subject to safeguards under this Agreement is present;
(b) For the purposes specified in Article 7 1 (b) the Agency inspectors shall have access to any location of which the Agency has been notified in accordance with Articles 92(d)(iii) or 95(d)(iii);
(c) For the purposes specified in Article 72 the inspectors shall have access only to the strategic points specified in the Subsidiary Arrangements and to the records maintained pursuant to Articles 51 to 56; and
(d) In the event of the Community concluding that any unusual circumstances require extended limitations on access by the Agency, the Community and the Agency shall promptly make arrangements with a view to enabling the Agency to discharge its safeguards responsibilities in the light of these limitations. The Director General shall report each such arrangement to the Board.

Article 77

In the circumstances which may lead to special inspections for the purposes specified in Article 73 the Community and the Agency shall consult forthwith. As a result of such consultations the Agency may:
(a) Make inspections in addition to the routine inspection effort provided for in this Agreement; and
(b) Obtain access, in agreement with the Community, to information or locations in addition to those specified in Article 76. Any disagreement shall be resolved in accordance with Articles 21 and 22. In case action by the Community or a State, in so far as either Party is individually concerned, is essential and urgent, Article 18 shall apply.

Frequency and intensity of routine inspections

Article 78

The number, intensity and duration of routine inspections, applying optimum timing, shall be kept to the minimum consistent with the effective implementation of the safeguards procedures set forth in this Agreement, and optimum and most economical use of available inspection resources under the Agreement shall be made.

Article 79

The Agency may carry out one routine inspection per year in respect of facilities and material balance areas outside facilities with a content or annual throughput, whichever is greater, of nuclear material not exceeding five effective kilograms.

Article 80

The number, intensity, duration, timing and mode of routine inspections in respect of facilities with a content or annual throughput of nuclear material exceeding five effective kilograms shall be determined on the basis that in the maximum or limiting case the inspection regime shall be no more intensive than is necessary and sufficient to maintain continuity of knowledge of the flow and inventory of nuclear material, and the maximum routine inspection effort in respect of such facilities shall be determined as follows:

(a) For reactors and sealed storage installations the maximum total of routine inspection per year shall be determined by allowing one sixth of a man-year of inspection for each such facility;

(b) For facilities, other than reactors or sealed storage installations, involving plutonium or uranium enriched to more than 5%, the maximum total of routine inspection per year shall be determined by allowing for each such facility $30 \times \sim E$ man-days of inspection per year, where E is the inventory or annual throughput of nuclear material, whichever is greater, expressed in effective kilograms. The maximum established for any such facility shall not, however, be less than 1.5 man-years of inspection; and

(c) For facilities not covered by paragraphs (a) or (b), the maximum total of routine inspection per year shall be determined by allowing for each such facility one third of a man-year of inspection plus $0.4 \times E$ man-days of inspection per year, where E is the inventory or annual throughput of nuclear material, whichever is greater, expressed in effective kilograms.

The Parties to this Agreement may agree to amend the figures for the maximum inspection effort specified in this Article, upon determination by the Board that such amendment is reasonable.

Article 81

Subject to Articles 76 to 80 the criteria to be used for determining the actual number, intensity, duration, timing and mode of routine inspections in respect of any facility shall include:
(a) The form of the nuclear material, in particular, whether the nuclear material is in bulk form or contained in a number of separate items; its chemical composition and, in the case of uranium, whether it is of low or high enrichment; and its accessibility;
(b) The effectiveness of the Community's safeguards, including the extent to which the operators of facilities are functionally independent of the Community's safeguards; the extent to which the measures specified in Article 32 have been implemented by the Community; the promptness of reports provided to the Agency; their consistency with the Agency's independent verification; and the amount and accuracy of the material unaccounted for, as verified by the Agency;
(c) Characteristics of the nuclear fuel cycle in the States, in particular, the number and types of facilities containing nuclear material subject to safeguards under this Agreement, the characteristics of such facilities relevant to safeguards under this Agreement, notably the degree of containment; the extent to which the design of such facilities facilitates verification of the flow and inventory of nuclear material; and the extent to which information from different material balance areas can be correlated;
(d) International interdependence, in particular, the extent to which nuclear material is received from or sent to other States for use or processing; any verification activities by the Agency in connection therewith; and the extent to which the nuclear activities in each State are interrelated with those in other States; and
(e) Technical developments in the field of safeguards, including the use of statistical techniques and random sampling in evaluating the flow of nuclear material.

Article 82

The Agency and the Community shall consult if the latter considers that the inspection effort is being deployed with undue concentration on particular facilities.

Notice of inspections

Article 83

The Agency shall give advance notice to the Community and to the States concerned before arrival of Agency inspectors at facilities or material balance areas outside facilities, as follows:

(a) For ad hoc inspections pursuant to Article 71(b), at least 24 hours; for those pursuant to Article 71(a) as well as the activities provided for in Article 48, at least one week;
(b) For special inspections pursuant to Article 73, as promptly as possible after the Agency and the Community have consulted as provided for in Article 77, it being understood that notification of arrival normally will constitute part of the consultations; and
(c) For routine inspections pursuant to Article 72, at least 24 hours in respect of the facilities referred to in Article 80(b) and sealed storage installations containing plutonium or uranium enriched to more than 5%, and one week in all other cases.

Such notice of inspections shall include the names of the Agency inspectors and shall indicate the facilities and the material balance areas outside facilities to be visited and the period during which they will be visited. If the Agency inspectors are to arrive from outside the States, the Agency shall also give advance notice of the place and time of their arrival in the States.

Article 84

Notwithstanding the provisions of Article 83, the Agency may, as a supplementary measure, carry out without advance notification a portion of the routine inspections pursuant to Article 80 in accordance with the principle of random sampling. In performing any unannounced inspections, the Agency shall fully take into account any operational programme provided to it pursuant to Article 64(b). Moreover, whenever practicable, and on the basis of the operational programme it shall advise the Community and the State concerned periodically of its general programme of announced and unannounced inspections, specifying the general periods when inspections are foreseen. In carrying out any unannounced inspections, the Agency shall make every effort to minimize any practical difficulties for the Community and the State concerned and for facility operators, bearing in mind the relevant provisions of Articles 44 and 89. Similarly the Community and the State concerned shall make every effort to facilitate the task of Agency inspectors.

Designation of Agency inspectors

Article 85

The following procedures shall apply to the designation of Agency inspectors:
(a) The Director General shall inform the Community and the States in writing of the name, qualifications, nationality, grade and such other particulars as may be relevant,

of each Agency official he proposes for designation as an Agency inspector for the States;
(b) The Community shall inform the Director General within thirty days of the receipt of such a proposal whether the proposal is accepted;
The Director General may designate each official who has been accepted by the Community and the States as one of the Agency inspectors for the States, and shall inform the Community and the States of such designations; and
(d) The Director General, acting in response to a request by the Community or on his own initiative, shall immediately inform the Community and the States of the withdrawal of the designation of any official as an Agency inspector for the States.
However, in respect of Agency inspectors needed for the activities provided for in Article 48 and to carry out ad hoc inspections pursuant to Article 7 1 (a) the designation procedures shall be completed if possible within thirty days after the entry into force of this Agreement. If such designation appears impossible within this time limit, Agency inspectors for such purposes shall be designated on a temporary basis.

Article 86

The States shall grant or renew as quickly as possible appropriate visas, where required, for each Agency inspector designated pursuant to Article 85.

Conduct and visits of Agency inspectors

Article 87

Agency inspectors, in exercising their functions under Articles 48 and 71 to 75, shall carry out their activities in a manner designed to avoid hampering or delaying the construction, commissioning or operation of facilities, or affecting their safety. In particular, Agency inspectors shall not operate any facility themselves or direct the staff of a facility to carry out any operation. If Agency inspectors consider that in pursuance of Articles 71 and 75, particular operations in a facility should be carried out by the operator, they shall make a request therefore.

Article 88

When Agency inspectors require services available in a State, including the use of equipment, in connection with the performance of inspections, the State concerned and the Community shall facilitate the procurement of such services and the use of such equipment by Agency inspectors.

Article 89

The Community and the States concerned shall have the right to have Agency inspectors accompanied during their inspections by its inspectors and their representatives respectively, provided that Agency inspectors shall not thereby be delayed or otherwise impeded in the exercise of their functions.

Statement on the Agency's Verification Activities

Article 90

The Agency shall inform the Community for the use of the interested parties of:
(a) The results of its inspections, at intervals to be specified in the Subsidiary Arrangements; and
(b) The conclusions it has drawn from its verification activities.

Transfers Into or Out of the States

Article 91
General provisions

Nuclear material subject or required to be subject to safeguards under this Agreement which is transferred into or out of the States shall, for purposes of this Agreement, be regarded as being the responsibility of the Community and of the State concerned:
(a) In the case of transfers into the States, from the time that such responsibility ceases to lie with the State from which the material is transferred, and no later than the time at which the material reaches its destination; and
(b) In the case of transfers out of the States up to the time at which the recipient State has such responsibility, and no later than the time at which the nuclear material reaches its destination.

The point at which the transfer of responsibility will take place shall be determined in accordance with suitable arrangements to be made by the Community and the State concerned, on the one hand, and the State to which or from which the nuclear material is transferred, on the other hand. Neither the Community nor a State shall be deemed to have such responsibility for nuclear material merely by reason of the fact that the nuclear material is in transit on or over a State's territory, or that it is being transported on a ship under a State's flag or in the aircraft of a State.

Transfers out of the States

Article 92

(a) The Community shall notify the Agency of any intended transfer out of the States of nuclear material subject to safeguards under this Agreement if the shipment exceeds one effective kilogram, or, for facilities which normally transfer significant quantities to the same State in shipments each not exceeding one effective kilogram, if so specified in the Subsidiary Arrangements.
(b) Such notification shall be given to the Agency after the conclusion of the contractual arrangements leading to the transfer and within the time limit specified in the Subsidiary Arrangements.
(c) The Agency and the Community may agree on different procedures for advance notification.
(d) The notification shall specify:
(i) The identification and, if possible, the expected quantity and the composition of the nuclear material to be transferred, and the material balance area from which it will come;
(ii) The State for which the nuclear material is destined;
(iii) The dates on and locations at which the nuclear material is to be prepared for shipping;
(iv) The approximate dates of dispatch and arrival of the nuclear material; and
(v) At what point of the transfer the recipient State will assume responsibility for the nuclear material for the purpose of this Agreement, and the probable date on which that point will be reached.

Article 93

The notification referred to in Article 92 shall be such as to enable the Agency to make, if necessary, an ad hoc inspection to identify, and if possible verify the quantity and composition of the nuclear material before it is transferred out of the States, except for transfers within the Community and, if the Agency so wishes or the Community so requests, to affix seals to the nuclear material when it has been prepared for shipping. However, the transfer of the nuclear material shall not be delayed in any way by any action taken or contemplated by the Agency pursuant to such a notification.

Article 94

If nuclear material will not be subject to Agency safeguards in the recipient State the Community shall make arrangements for the Agency to receive within three months of the time when the recipient State accepts responsibility for the nuclear material, confirmation by the recipient State of the transfer.

Transfers into the States

Article 95

(a) The Cornmunity shall notify the Agency of any expected transfer into the States of nuclear material required to be subject to safeguards under this Agreement if the shipment exceeds one effective kilogram, or, for facilities to which significant quantities are normally transferred from the same State in shipments each not exceeding one effective kilogram, if so specified in the Subsidiary Arrangements.
(b) The Agency shall be notified as much in advance as possible of the expected arrival of the nuclear material, and in any case within the time limits specified in the Subsidiary Arrangements. (c) The Agency and the Community may agree on different procedures for advance notification. (d) The notification shall specify:
(i) The identification and, if possible, the expected quantity and composition of the nuclear material;
(ii) At what point of the transfer the Community and the State concerned will have responsibility for the nuclear material for the purpose of this Agreement, and the probable date on which that point will be reached; and
(iii) The expected date of arrival, the location where, and the date on which, the nuclear material is intended to be unpacked.

Article 96

The notification referred to in Article 95 shall be such as to enable the Agency to make, if necessary, an ad hoc inspection to identify, and if possible verify the quantity and composition of, the nuclear material transferred into the States, except for transfers within the Community, at the time the consignment is unpacked. However, unpacking shall not be delayed by any action taken or contemplated by the Agency pursuant to such a notification.

Article 97
Special reports

The Community shall make a special report as envisaged in Article 68 if any unusual incident or circumstances lead the Community to believe that there is or may have been loss of nuclear material, including the occurrence of significant delay, during a transfer into or out of the States.

Definitions

Article 98

For the purposes of this Agreement:
1. A. 'Community' means both:
(a) The legal person created by the Treaty establishing the European Atomic Energy Community (EURATOM), Party to this Agreement; and
(b) The territories to which the EURATOM Treaty applies.
B. 'States' means the non-nuclear-weapon States Members of the Community, Party to this Agreement.
2. A. 'Adjustment' means an entry into an accounting record or a report showing a shipper/receiver difference or material unaccounted for.
B. 'Annual throughput' means, for the purposes of Articles 79 and 80, the amount of nuclear material transferred annually out of a facility working at nominal capacity.
C. 'Batch' means a portion of nuclear material handled as a unit for accounting purposes at a key measurement point and for which the composition and quantity are defined by a single set of specifications or measurements. The nuclear material may be in bulk form or contained in a number of separate items.
D. 'Batch' data means the total weight of each element of nuclear material and, in the case of plutonium and uranium, the isotopic composition when appropriate. The units of account shall be as follows:
(a) Grams of contained plutonium;
(b) Grams of total uranium and grams of contained uranium-235 plus uranium-233 for uranium enriched in these isotopes; and
(c) Kilograms of contained thorium, natural uranium or depleted uranium.

For reporting purposes the weights of individual items in the batch shall be added together before rounding to the nearest unit.
E. 'Book inventory' of a material balance area means the algebraic sum of the most recent physical inventory of that material balance area and of all inventory changes that have occurred since that physical inventory was taken.
F. 'Correction' means an entry into an accounting record or a report to rectify an identified mistake or to reflect an improved measurement of a quantity previously entered into the record or report. Each correction must identify the entry to which it pertains.
G. 'Effective kilogram' means a special unit used in safeguarding nuclear material. The quantity in effective kilograms is obtained by taking:
(a) For plutonium, its weight in kilograms;
(b) For uranium with an enrichment of 0.01 (1%) and above, its weight in kilograms multiplied by the square of its enrichment;

(c) For uranium with an enrichment below 0.01 (1%) and above 0.005 (0.5%), its weight in kilograms multiplied by 0.0001; and
(d) For depleted uranium with an enrichment of 0.005 (0.5%) or below, and for thorium, its weight in kilograms multiplied by 0.00005.
H. 'Enrichment' means the ratio of the combined weight of the isotopes uranium-233 and uranium-235 to that of the total uranium in question.
'Facility' means:
(a) A reactor, a critical facility, a conversion plant, a fabrication plant, a reprocessing plant, an isotope separation plant or a separate storage installation; or
(b) Any location where nuclear material in amounts greater than one effective kilogram is customarily used.
J. 'Inventory change' means an increase or decrease, in terms of batches, of nuclear material in a material balance area; such a change shall involve one of the following:
(a) Increases:
(i) Import;
(ii) Domestic receipt: receipts from within the States: from other material balance areas; from a non-safeguarded (non-peaceful) activity; at the starting point of safeguards;
(iii) Nuclear production: production of special fissionable material in a reactor; and
(iv) De-exemption: reapplication of safeguards on nuclear material previously exempted therefrom on account of its use or quantity.
(b) Decreases:
(i) Export;
(ii) Domestic shipment: shipments within the States to other material balance areas or for a non-safeguarded (non-peaceful) activity;
(iii) Nuclear loss: loss of nuclear material due to its transformation into other element(s) or isotope(s) as a result of nuclear reactions;
(iv) Measured discard: nuclear material which has been measured, or estimated on the basis of measurements, and disposed of in such a way that it is not suitable for further nuclear use;
(v) Retained waste: nuclear material generated from processing or from an operational accident, which is deemed to be unrecoverable for the time being but which is stored;
(vi) Exemption: exemption of nuclear material from safeguards on account of its use or quantity; and
(vii) Other loss: for example, accidental loss (that is, irretrievable and inadvertent loss of nuclear material as the result of an operational accident) or theft.
K. 'Key measurement point' means a location where nuclear material appears in such a form that it may be measured to determine material flow or inventory. Key measurement points thus include, but are not limited to, the inputs and outputs (including measured discards) and storages in material balance areas.

L. 'Man-year of inspection' means, for the purposes of Article 80, 300 man-days of inspection, a man-day being a day during which a single inspector has access to a facility at any time for a total of not more than eight hours.

M. 'Material balance area' means an area in or outside of a facility such that:

(a) The quantity of nuclear material in each transfer into or out of each material balance area can be determined; and

(b) The physical inventory of nuclear material in each material balance area can be determined when necessary in accordance with specified procedures. In order that the material balance for Agency safeguards purposes can be established.

N. 'Material unaccounted for' means the difference between book inventory and physical inventory.

0. 'Nuclear material' means any source or any special fissionable material as defined in Article XX of the Statute. The term 'source material' shall not be interpreted as applying to ore or ore residue. Any determination by the Board under Article XX of the Statute after the entry into force of this Agreement which adds to the materials considered to be source material or special fissionable material shall have effect under this Agreement only upon acceptance by the Community and the States.

P. 'Physical inventory' means the sum of all the measured or derived estimates of batch quantities of nuclear material on hand at a given time within a material balance area, obtained in accordance with specified procedures.

Q. 'Shipper/receiver difference' means the difference between the quantity of nuclear material in a batch as stated by the shipping material balance area and as measured at the receiving material balance area.

R. 'Source data' means those data, recorded during measurement or calibration or used to derive empirical relationships, which identify nuclear material and provide batch data. Source data may include, for example, weight of compounds, conversion factors to determine weight of element, specific gravity, element concentration, isotopic ratios, relationship between volume and manometer readings and relationship between plutonium produced and power generated.

S. 'Strategic point' means a location selected during examination of design information where, under normal conditions and when combined with the information from all strategic points taken together, the information necessary and sufficient for the implementation of safeguards measures is obtained and verified; a strategic point may include any location where key measurements related to material balance accountancy are made and where containment and surveillance measures are executed.

PROTOCOL

Article 1

This Protocol amplifies certain provisions of the Agreement and, in particular, specifies the conditions and means according to which cooperation in the application of the safeguards provided for under the Agreement shall be implemented in such a way as to avoid unnecessary duplication of the Community's safeguards activities.

Article 2

The Community shall collect the information on facilities and on nuclear material outside facilities to be provided to the Agency under the Agreement on the basis of the agreed indicative questionnaire annexed to the Subsidiary Arrangements.

Article 3

The Agency and the Community shall carry out jointly the examination of design information provided for in Article 46(a) to (f) of the Agreement and shall include the agreed results thereof in the Subsidiary Arrangements. The verification of design information provided for in Article 48 of the Agreement shall be carried out by the Agency in cooperation with the Community.

Article 4

When providing the Agency with the information referred to in Article 2 of this Protocol, the Community shall also transmit information on the inspection methods which it proposes to use and the complete proposals, including estimates of inspection efforts for the routine inspection activities, for Attachments to the Subsidiary Arrangements for facilities and material balance areas outside facilities.

Article 5

The preparation of the Attachments to the Subsidiary Arrangements shall be performed together by the Community and the Agency –

Article 6

The Community shall collect the reports from the operators, keep centralized accounts on the basis of these reports and proceed with the technical and accounting control and analysis of the information received.

Article 7

Upon completion of the tasks referred to in Article 6 of this Protocol the Community shall, on a monthly basis, produce and provide the Agency with the inventory change reports within the time limits specified in the Subsidiary Arrangements.

Article 8

Further, the Community shall transmit to the Agency the material balance reports and physical inventory listings with frequency depending on the frequency of physical inventory taking as specified in the Subsidiary Arrangements.

Article 9

The form and format of reports referred to in Articles 7 and 8 of this Protocol, as agreed between the Agency and the Community, shall be specified in the Subsidiary Arrangements.

Article 10

The routine inspection activities of the Community and of the Agency, including the inspections referred to in Article 81 of the Agreement, for the purposes of the Agreement, shall be coordinated pursuant to the provisions of Articles 11 to 23 of this Protocol.

Article 11

Subject to Articles 79 and 80 of the Agreement, in determining the actual number, intensity, duration, timing and mode of the Agency inspections in respect of each facility, account shall be taken of the inspection effort carried out by the Community in the framework of its multinational system of safeguards pursuant to the provisions of this Protocol.

Article 12

Inspection efforts under the Agreement for each facility shall be determined by the use of the criteria of Article 81 of the Agreement. Such criteria shall be implemented by using the rules and methods set forth in the Subsidiary Arrangements which have been used for the calculation of the inspection efforts in respect of specific examples attached to the Subsidiary Arrangements. These rules and methods shall be reviewed from time to time, pursuant to Article 7 of the Agreement, to take into account new technological developments in the field of safeguards and experience gained.

Article 13

Such inspection efforts, expressed as agreed estimates of the actual inspection efforts to be applied, shall be set out in the Subsidiary Arrangements together with relevant descriptions of verification approaches and scopes of inspections to be carried out by the Community and by the Agency. These inspection efforts shall constitute, under normal operating conditions and under the conditions set out below, the actual maximum inspection efforts at the facility under the Agreement;
(a) The continued validity of the information on Community safeguards provided for in Article 32 of the Agreement, as specified in the Subsidiary Arrangements;
(b) The continued validity of the information provided to the Agency in accordance with -Article 2 of this Protocol;
(c) The continued provision by the Community of the reports pursuant to Articles 60 and 61, 63 to 65 and 67 to 69 of the Agreement, as specified in the Subsidiary Arrangements;
(d) The continued application of the coordination arrangements for inspections pursuant to Articles 10 to 23 of this Protocol, as specified in the Subsidiary Arrangements; and
(e) The application by the Community of its inspection effort with respect to the facility, as specified in the Subsidiary Arrangements, pursuant to this Article.

Article 14

(a) Subject to the conditions of Article 13 of this Protocol, the Agency inspections shall be carried out simultaneously with the inspection activities of the Community. Agency inspectors shall be present during the performance of certain of the Community inspections.
(b) Subject to the provisions of paragraph (a), whenever the Agency can achieve the purposes of its routine inspections set out in the Agreement, the Agency inspectors shall implement the provisions of Articles 74 and 75 of the Agreement through the observation of the inspection activities of the Community inspectors, provided, however, that:
(i) With respect to inspection activities of Agency inspectors to be implemented other than through the observation of the inspection activities of the Community inspectors, which can be foreseen, these shall be specified in the Subsidiary Arrangements; and
(ii) In the course of an inspection, Agency inspectors may carry out inspection activities other than through the observation of the inspection activities of the Community inspectors where they find this to be essential and urgent, if the Agency

could not otherwise achieve the purposes of its routine inspections and this was unforeseeable.

Article 15

The general scheduling and planning of the Corrimunity inspections under the Agreement shall be established by the Community in cooperation with the Agency.

Article 16

Arrangements for the presence of Agency inspectors during the performance of certain of the Community inspections shall be agreed in advance by the Agency and the Community for each type of facility, and to the extent necessary, for individual facilities.

Article 17

In order to enable the Agency to decide, based on requirements for statistical sampling, as to its presence at a particular Community inspection, the Community shall provide the Agency with an advance statement of the numbers, types and contents of items to be inspected according to the information available to the Community from the operator of the facility.

Article 18

Technical procedures in general for each type of facility and, to the extent necessary, for individual facilities, shall be agreed in advance by the Agency and the Community, in particular with respect to:
(a) The determination of techniques for random selection of statistical samples; and
(b) The checking and identification of standards.

Article 19

The coordination arrangements for each type of facility set out in the Subsidiary Arrangements shall serve as a basis for the coordination arrangements to be specified in each Facility Attachment.

Article 20

The specific coordination actions on matters specified in the Facility Attachments pursuant to Article 19 of this Protocol shall be taken between Community and Agency (c) officials designated for that purpose.

Article 21

The Community shall transmit to the Agency its working papers for those inspections at which Agency inspectors were present and inspection reports for all other Community inspections performed under the Agreement.

Article 22

The samples of nuclear material for the Agency shall be drawn from the same randomly selected batches of items as for the Community and shall be taken together with Community samples, except when the maintenance of or reduction to the lowest practical level of the Agency inspection effort requires independent sampling by the Agency, as agreed in advance and specified in the Subsidiary Arrangements.

Article 23

The frequencies of physical inventories to be taken by facility operators and to be verified for safeguards purposes will be in accordance with those laid down as guidelines in the Subsidiary Arrangements. If additional activities under the Agreement in relation to physical inventories are considered to be essential, they will be discussed in the Liaison Committee provided for in Article 25 of this Protocol and agreed before implementation.

Article 24

Whenever the Agency can achieve the purposes of its ad hoc inspections set out in the Agreement through observation of the inspection activities of Community inspectors. It shall do so.

Article 25

(a) With a view to facilitating the application of the Agreement and of this Protocol, a Liaison Committee shall be established, composed of representatives of the Community and of the Agency.

(b) The Committee shall meet at least once a year:

(i) To review, in particular, the performance of the coordination arrangements provided for in this Protocol, including agreed estimates of inspection efforts;

(ii) To examine the development of safeguards methods and techniques; and

(iii) To consider any questions which have been referred to it by the periodic meetings referred to in paragraph (c).

(c) The Committee shall meet periodically at a lower level to discuss, in particular and to the extent necessary, for individual facilities, the operation of the coordination arrangements provided for in this Protocol, including, in the light of technical and operational developments, up-dating of agreed estimates of inspection efforts with respect to changes in throughput, inventory and facility operational programmes, and the application of inspection procedures in different types of routine inspection activities and, in general terms, statistical sampling requirements. Any questions which could not be settled would be referred to the meetings mentioned in paragraph (b).
(d) Without prejudice to urgent actions which might be required under the Agreement, should problems arise in the application of Article 13 of this Protocol in particular when the Agency considered that the conditions specified therein had not been met, the Committee would meet as soon as possible at the suitable level in order to assess the situation and to discuss the measures to be taken. If a problem could not be settled, the Committee may make appropriate proposals to the Parties, in particular with the view to modifying the estimates of inspection efforts for routine inspection activities.
(e) The Committee shall elaborate proposals, as necessary, with respect to questions which require the agreement of the Parties.

DONE at Brussels in duplicate, on the fifth day of April in the year one thousand nine hundred and seventy-three in the English and French languages, both texts being equally authentic.

ADDITIONAL PROTOCOLS TO THE SAFEGUARDS SYSTEM

(22 September 1998)

In the Introductory Material to the Euratom Regulations on safeguards (see following pages) reference is made to IAEA requesting its member States to provide additional information on a voluntary basis (i.e. information not contemplated in the "Verification Agreement", see again following pages), concerning especially import, export and production of uranium and thorium. These requests had been triggered by the detection in Iraq of undeclared materials likely to be used for a secret military programme, that is in violation of the safeguards regime.

It is obvious that such voluntary submission could not be regarded as a binding system for any State, therefore the need for amending the existing regime became fairly soon evident: the amendments should address both the scope of such regime and the methods by which it should be effectively applied. This entailed a survey of the existing regime against the new controls which had been found necessary, in the framework of a programme named "93+2" (where 93 was meant to indicate the year when the need for strengthening the regime had been drawn attention to, and 2 years the time-span during which such objective would have to be attained). Understandably, though, the difficult preparation of the dossier which was of high "political" significance, the lengthy negotiations and other "technical" reasons caused the deadline to stretch up to 1998. The "programme" was made up of Part I addressing the safeguards measures already in force, and Part II introducing new specific measures aiming at expanding controls making them at the same time more effective, for which a new "ad hoc" legal basis was found to be needed. The new measures consisted in IAEA being entitled to a broader access to sites and activities, in order to detect possible "clandestine" nuclear programmes; the Agency would also be empowered to collect samples in soil, waters and atmosphere of States, as well as to obtain information on the so called "dual use" materials (i.e. not necessarily and exclusively intended for nuclear activities). The latter represents the most important added value associated with the new instruments envisaged.

With a view to incorporating Part II of the programme in a binding instrument, the first problem was to identify the most suitable one to stipulate the new measures, which after the necessary analysis was regarded as an "additional protocol" to the existing system (in particular to the "Verification Agreement", as well as to the other two agreements which had been concluded between IAEA, Euratom and United Kingdom/France (see again under "Verification Agreement"). In 1997, in fact, the IAEA Board of Governors approved a "model protocol" as a basis for the actual instruments to be negotiated and adopted. But apart from and beyond this problem of a "formal" nature, there were substantive ones to be sorted out.

Firstly and in general, it was indispensable to strengthen the regime (IAEA and Euratom) in the shortest possible time on account of the situation detected and of similar perspectives at a broader level, but without putting too much burden on those States who had always fully complied with safeguards provisions, including nuclear weapon States (for whom specific measures were anyway necessary). Secondly, account should be taken of those States who were members of the Agency but not of Euratom, and of the need for co-ordinating the action carried out by the two organisations in order to avoid conflicting competences and duplications of interventions. Thirdly, as far as Euratom as such was concerned, the principles on which the Single Market in the European Union was based, although obviously not involving non-E.U. countries, were of the utmost importance; in addition, one should bear in mind the division of competences relating to safeguards, attributed in different parts to Euratom and to member States respectively, and for another part shared between the former and the latter.

On the basis of the above mentioned "model protocol", negotiations took place in Vienna and Brussels in February and March 1998. Three different Protocols were discussed , i.e. one for the 13 non-nuclear weapon Euratom countries, one for France and one for the United Kingdom, IAEA and Euratom being of course standing parties in the negotiations. These pursued above all the objectives of preserving the best possible co-operation between the two organisations and their respective prerogatives as well as national sovereignties, ensuring effectiveness of the new measures also by appropriate relevant procedures, meeting the special needs of nuclear weapon States, and protecting industrial and commercial confidentiality of certain information (which, as recalled above, covers also non-exclusively nuclear materials).

After an agreement was reached on the texts, a draft "decision" approving the Protocols was submitted by the E.U. Commission to the Council, who approved it on 8 June 1998, while on the same date the IAEA Board of Governors approved the Protocols on behalf of the Agency. It is noted that ratification by all the E.U. member countries, required for the entry into force of the Protocols in the E.U., was achieved at the end of 2003. These new instruments represent no doubt an extremely important step forward to secure the peaceful use of nuclear energy worldwide. Here is published the text of the Protocol concerning the 13 non-nuclear EU member States, without its very many technical annexes.

PREAMBLE

Whereas the Republic of Austria, the Kingdom of Belgium, the Kingdom of Denmark, the Republic of Finland, the Federal Republic of Germany, the Hellenic Republic, Ireland, the Italian Republic, the Grand Duchy of Luxembourg, the Kingdom of the Netherlands, the Portuguese Republic, the Kingdom of Spain, the Kingdom of Sweden (hereinafter referred to as 'the States') and the European Atomic Energy Community (hereinafter referred to as 'the Community') are parties to an Agreement between the States, the Community and the International Atomic Energy Agency (hereinafter referred to as the 'the Agency') in implementation of Article III(1) and (4) of the Treaty on the Non-proliferation of Nuclear Weapons (hereinafter referred to as the 'Safeguards Agreement'), which entered into force on 21 February 1997;

Aware of the desire of the international community to further enhance nuclear non-proliferation by strengthening the effectiveness and improving the efficiency of the Agency's safeguards system;

Recalling that the Agency must take into account in the implementation of safeguards the need to avoid hampering the economic and technological development in the Community or international cooperation in the field of peaceful nuclear activities, to respect health, safety, physical protection and other security provisions in force and the rights of individuals, and to take every precaution to protect commercial, technological and industrial secrets as well as other confidential information coming to its knowledge;

Whereas the frequency and intensity of activities described in this Protocol shall be kept to the minimum consistent with the objective of strengthening the effectiveness and improving the efficiency of Agency safeguards;

Now therefore the Community, the States and the Agency have agreed as follows:

RELATIONSHIP BETWEEN THE PROTOCOL AND THE SAFEGUARDS AGREEMENT

Article 1

The provisions of the Safeguards Agreement shall apply to this Protocol to the extent that they are relevant to and compatible with the provisions of this Protocol. In case of conflict between the provisions of the Safeguards Agreement and those of this Protocol, the provisions of this Protocol shall apply.

PROVISION OF INFORMATION

Article 2

(a) Each State shall provide the Agency with a declaration containing the information identified in sub-paragraphs (i), (ii), (iv), (ix) and (x). The Community shall provide the Agency with a declaration containing the information identified in sub-paragraphs (v), (vi) and (vii). Each State and the Community shall provide the Agency with a declaration containing the information identified in sub-paragraphs (iii) and (viii).
(i) A general description of and information specifying the location of nuclear fuel cycle-related research and development activities not involving nuclear material carried out anywhere that are funded, specifically authorised or controlled by, or carried out on behalf of, the State concerned.
(ii) Information identified by the Agency on the basis of expected gains in effectiveness or efficiency, and agreed to by the State concerned, on operational activities of safeguards relevance at facilities and locations outside facilities where nuclear material is customarily used.
(iii) A general description of each building on each site, including its use and, if not apparent from that description, its contents. The description shall include a map of the site.
(iv) A description of the scale of operations for each location engaged in the activities specified in Annex I to this Protocol.
(v) Information specifying the location, operational status and the estimated annual production capacity of uranium mines and concentration plants and thorium concentration plants in each State, and the current annual production of such mines and concentration plants. The Community shall provide, on request by the Agency, the current annual production of an individual mine or concentration plant. The provision of this information does not require detailed nuclear material accountancy.
(vi) Information regarding source material which has not reached the composition and purity suitable for fuel fabrication or for being isotopically enriched, as follows:
(a) the quantities, the chemical composition, the use or intended use of such material, whether in nuclear or non-nuclear use, for each location in the States at which the material is present in quantities exceeding 10 tonnes of uranium and/or 20 tonnes of thorium, and for other locations with quantities of more than 1 tonne, the aggregate for the States as a whole if the aggregate exceeds 10 tonnes of uranium or 20 tonnes of thorium. The provision of this information does not require detailed nuclear material accountancy;
(b) The quantities, the chemical composition and the destination of each export from the States to a State outside the Community, of such material for specifically non-nuclear purposes in quantities exceeding:

(1) 10 tonnes of uranium, or for successive exports of uranium to the same state, each of less than 10 tonnes, but exceeding a total of 10 tonnes for the year;
(2) 20 tonnes of thorium, or for successive exports of thorium to the same State, each of less than 20 tonnes, but exceeding a total 20 tonnes for the year;
(c) the quantities, chemical composition, current location and use or intended use of each import into the Sates from outside the Community of such material for specifically non-nuclear purposes in quantities exceeding:
(1) 10 tonnes of uranium, or for successive imports of uranium each of less than 10 tonnes, but exceeding a total of 10 tonnes for the year;
(2) 20 tonnes of thorium, or for successive imports of thorium each of less than 20 tonnes, but exceeding a total of 20 tonnes for the year; it being understood that there is no requirement to provide information on such material intended for a non-nuclear use once it is in its non-nuclear end-use form.
(vii) (a) Information regarding the quantities, uses and locations of nuclear material exempted from safeguards pursuant to Article 37 of the Safeguards Agreement;

(b) information regarding the quantities (which may be in the form of estimates) and uses at each location, of nuclear material exempted from safeguards pursuant to Article 36(b) of the Safeguards Agreement but not yet in a non-nuclear end-use form, in quantities exceeding those set out in Article 37 of the Safeguards Agreement. The provision of this information does not require detailed nuclear material accountancy.
(viii) Information regarding the location or further processing of intermediate or high-level waste containing plutonium, high enriched uranium or uranium-233 on which safeguards have been terminated pursuant to Article 11 of the Safeguards Agreement. For the purpose of this paragraph, 'further processing' does not include repackaging of the waste or its further conditioning not involving the separation of elements, for storage or disposal.
(ix) The following information regarding specified equipment and non-nuclear material listed in Annex II:

(a) for each export out of the Community of such equipment and material: the identity, quantity, location of intended use in the receiving State and date or, as appropriate, expected date, of export;
(b) on specific request by the Agency, confirmation by the importing State of information provided to the Agency by a State outside of the Community concerning the export of such equipment and material to the importing State.
(x) General plans for the succeeding 10-year period cycle (including planned nuclear fuel cycle-related research and development activities) when approved by the appropriate authorities in the State.
(b) Each State shall make every reasonable effort to provide the Agency with the following information:

(i) a general description of and information specifying the location of nuclear fuel cycle-related research and development activities not involving nuclear material which are specifically related to enrichment, reprocessing of nuclear fuel or the processing of intermediate or high-level waste containing plutonium, high enriched uranium or uranium-233 that are carried out anywhere in the State concerned but which are not funded, specifically authorised or controlled by, or carried out on behalf of, that State. For the purpose of this paragraph 'processing' of intermediate or high-level waste does not include repackaging of the waste or its conditioning not involving the separation of elements, for storage or disposal relevant to the development of the nuclear fuel.
(ii) A general description of activities and the identity of the person or entity carrying out such activities, at locations identified by the Agency outside a site which the Agency considers might be functionally related to the activities of that site. The provision of this information is subject to a specific request by the Agency. It shall be provided in consultation with the Agency and in a timely fashion.
(c) On request by any or all of the Agency, a State or the Community, as appropriate, shall provide amplifications or clarifications of any information provided under this Article, in so far as relevant for the purpose of safeguards.

Article 3

(a) Each State or the Community, or both, as appropriate, shall provide to the Agency the information identified in Article 2(a)(i), (iii), (iv), (v), (vi)(a), (vii), and (x) and Article 2(b)(i) within 180 days of the entry into force of this Protocol.
(b) Each State or the Community, or both, as appropriate, shall provide to the Agency, by 15 May of each year, updates of the information referred to in paragraph (a) for the period covering the previous calendar year. If there has been no change to the information previously provided, each State or the Community, or both, as appropriate, shall so indicate.
(c) The Community shall provide to the Agency, by 15 May of each year, the information identified in Article 2(a)(vi)(b) and (c) for the period covering the previous calendar year.
(d) Each State shall provide to the Agency on a quarterly basis the information identified in Article 2(a)(ix)(a). This information shall be provided within 60 days of the end of each quarter.
(e) The Community and each State shall provide to the Agency the information identified in Article 2(a)(viii) 180 days before further processing is carried out and, by 15 May of each year, information on changes in location for the period covering the previous calendar year.
(f) Each State and the Agency shall agree on the timing and frequency of the provision of the information identified in Article 2(a)(ii).

(g) Each State shall provide to the Agency the information in Article 2(a)(ix)(b) within 60 days of the Agency's request.

COMPLEMENTARY ACCESS

Article 4

The following shall apply in connection with the implementation of complementary access under Article 5 of this Protocol:

(a)The Agency shall not mechanistically or systematically seek to verify the information referred to in Article 2; however, the Agency shall have access to:

(i) any location referred to in Article 5(a)(i) or (ii) on a selective basis in order to assure the absence of undeclared nuclear material and activities;

(ii) any location referred to in Article 5(b) or (c) to resolve a question relating to the correctness and completeness of the information provided pursuant to Article 2 or to resolve an inconsistency relating to that information;

(iii) any location referred to in Article 5(a)(iii) to the extent necessary for the Agency to confirm, for safeguards purposes, the Community's, or, as appropriate, a State's declaration of the decommissioned status of a facility or location outside facilities where nuclear material was customarily used.

(b) (i) Except as provided in paragraph (ii), the Agency shall give the State concerned, or for access under Article 5(a) or under Article 5(c) where nuclear material is involved, the State concerned and the Community, advance notice of access of at least 24 hours.

(ii) For access to any place on a site that is sought in conjunction with design information verification visits *or ad hoc* or routine inspections on that site, the period of advance notice shall, if the Agency so requests, be at least two hours but, in exceptional circumstances, it may be less than two hours.

(c) Advance notice shall be in writing and shall specify the reasons for access and the activities to be carried out during such access.

(d) In the case of a question or inconsistency, the Agency shall provide the State concerned and, as appropriate, the Community with an opportunity to clarify and facilitate the resolution of the question or inconsistency. Such an opportunity will be provided before a request for access, unless the Agency considers that delay in access would prejudice the purpose for which the access is sought. In any event, the Agency shall not draw any conclusions about the question or inconsistency until the State concerned and, as appropriate, the Community have been provided with such an opportunity.

(e) Unless otherwise agreed to by the State concerned, access shall only take place during regular working hours.

(f) The State concerned, or for access under Article 5(a) or under Article 5(c) where nuclear material is involved, the State concerned and the Community, shall have the right to have agency inspectors accompanied during their access by its representatives and, as appropriate, by Community inspectors provided that Agency inspectors shall not thereby be delayed or otherwise impeded in the exercise of their functions.

Article 5

Each State shall provide the Agency with access to:
(a) (i) any place on a site;
(ii) any location identified under Article 2(a)(v) to (viii);
(iii) any decommissioned facility or decommissioned location outside facilities where nuclear material was customarily used.
(b) Any location identified by the State concerned under Article 2(a)(i), Article 2(a)(iv), Article 2(a)(ix)(b) or Article 2(b), other than those referred to in paragraph (a)(i), provided that if the State concerned is unable to provide such access, that State shall make every reasonable effort to satisfy Agency requirements, without delay, through other means.
(c) Any location specified by the Agency, other than locations referred to in paragraphs (a) and (b), to carry out location-specific environmental sampling, provided that if the State concerned is unable to provide such access, that State shall make every reasonable effort to satisfy Agency requirements, without delay, at adjacent locations or through other means.

Article 6

When implementing Article 5, the Agency may carry out the following activities:
(a) for access in accordance with Article 5(a)(i) or (iii): visual observation; collection of environmental samples; utilisation of radiation detection and measurement devices; application of seals and other identifying and tamper indicating devices specified in Subsidiary Arrangements; and other objective measures which have been demonstrated to be technically feasible and the use of which has been agreed by the Board of Governors (hereinafter referred to as 'the Board') and following consultations between the Agency, the Community and the State concerned.
(b) For access in accordance with Article 5(a)(ii): visual observation; item counting of nuclear material; non-destructive measurements and sampling; utilisation of radiation detection and measurement devices; examination of records relevant to the quantities, origin and disposition of the material; collection of environmental samples; and other objective measures which have been demonstrated to be technically feasible and the use of which has been agreed by the Board and following consultations between the Agency, the Community and the State concerned.

(c) For access in accordance with Article 5(b): visual observation; collection of environmental samples; utilisation of radiation detection and measurement devices; examination of safeguards relevant production and shipping records; and other objective measures which have been demonstrated to be technically feasible and the use of which has been agreed by the Board and following consultations between the Agency and the State concerned.
(d) For access in accordance with Article 5(c), collection of environmental samples and, in the event the results do not resolve the question or inconsistency at the location specified by the Agency pursuant to Article 5(c), utilisation at that location of visual observation, radiation detection and measurement devices, and, as agreed by the State concerned and, where nuclear material is involved, the Community, and the Agency, other objective measures.

Article 7

(a) On request by a State, the Agency and that State shall make arrangements for managed access under this Protocol in order to prevent the dissemination of proliferation sensitive information, to meet safety or physical protection requirements, or to protect proprietary or commercially sensitive information. Such arrangements shall not preclude the Agency from conducting activities necessary to provide credible assurance of the absence of undeclared nuclear materials and activities at the location in question, including the resolution of a question relating to the correctness and completeness of the information referred to in Article 2 or of an inconsistency relating to that information.
(b) A State may, when providing the information referred to in Article 2, inform the Agency of the places at a site or location at which managed access may be applicable.
(c) Pending the entry into force of any necessary Subsidiary Arrangements, a State may have recourse to managed access consistent with the provisions of paragraph (a).

Article 8

Nothing in this Protocol shall preclude a State from offering the Agency access to locations in addition to those referred to in Articles 5 and 9 or from requesting the Agency to conduct verification activities at a particular location. The Agency shall, without delay, make every reasonable effort to act on such a request.

Article 9

Each State shall provide the Agency with access to locations specified by the Agency to carry out wide-area environmental sampling, provided that if a State is unable to provide such access that State shall make every reasonable effort to satisfy Agency requirements at alternative locations. The Agency shall not seek such access until the use of wide-area environmental sampling and the procedural arrangements therefore have been approved by the Board and following consultations between the Agency and the State concerned.

Article 10

(a) The Agency shall inform the State concerned and, as appropriate, the Community of:

(i) the activities carried out under this Protocol, including those in respect of any questions or inconsistencies the Agency had brought to the attention of the State concerned and, as appropriate, the Community within 60 days of the activities being carried out by the Agency.

(ii) The results of activities in respect of any questions or inconsistencies the Agency had brought to the attention of the State concerned and, as appropriate, the Community as soon as possible but in any case within 30 days of the results being established by the Agency.

(b) The Agency shall inform the State concerned and the Community of the conclusions it has drawn from its activities under this Protocol. The conclusions shall be provided annually.

DESIGNATION OF AGENCY INSPECTORS

Article 11

(a) (i) The Director-General shall notify the Community and the States of the Board's approval of any Agency official as a safeguards inspector. Unless the Community advises the Director-General of the rejection of such an official as an inspector for the States within three months of receipt of notification of the Board's approval, the inspector so notified to the Community and the States shall be considered designated to the States.

(ii) The Director-General, acting in response to a request by the Community or on his own initiative, shall immediately inform the Community and the States of the withdrawal of the designation of any official as an inspector for the States.

(b) A notification referred to in paragraph (a) shall be deemed to be received by the Community and the States seven days after the date of the transmission by registered post of the notification by the Agency to the Community and the States.

VISAS

Article 12

Each State shall, within one month of the receipt of a request therefor, provide the designated inspector specified in the request with appropriate multiple entry/exit and/or transit visas, where required, to enable the inspector to enter and remain on the territory of the State concerned for the purpose of carrying out his/her functions. Any visas required shall be valid for at least one year and shall be renewed, as required, to cover the duration of the inspector's designation to the States.

SUBSIDIARY ARRANGEMENTS

Article 13

(a) Where a State or the Community, as appropriate, or the Agency indicate that it is necessary to specify in subsidiary Arrangements how measures laid down in this Protocol are to be applied, that State, or that State and the Community and the Agency shall agree on such Subsidiary Arrangements within 90 days of the entry into force of this Protocol or, where the indication of the need for such Subsidiary Arrangements is made after the entry into force of this Protocol, within 90 days of the date of such indication.
(b) Pending the entry into force of any necessary Subsidiary Arrangements, the Agency shall be entitled to apply the measures laid down in this Protocol.

COMMUNICATIONS SYSTEMS

Article 14

(a) Each State shall permit and protect free communications by the Agency for official purposes between Agency inspectors in that State and Agency Headquarters and/or Regional Offices, including attended and unattended transmission of information generated by Agency containment and/or surveillance or measurement devices. The Agency shall have, in consultation with the State concerned, the right to make use of internationally established systems of direct communications, including satellite systems and other forms of telecommunication, not in use in that State. At the request of a State, or the Agency, details of the implementation of this paragraph in that State with respect to the attended or unattended transmission of information generated by Agency containment and/or surveillance or measurement devices shall be specified in the Subsidiary Arrangements.

(b) Communication and transmission of information as provided for in paragraph (a) shall take due account of the need to protect proprietary or commercially sensitive information or design information which the State concerned regards as being of particular sensitivity.

PROTECTION OF CONFIDENTIAL INFORMATION

Article 15

(a) The Agency shall maintain a stringent regime to ensure effective protection against disclosure of commercial, technological and industrial secrets and other confidential information coming to its knowledge, including such information coming to the Agency's knowledge in the implementation of this Protocol.
(b) The regime referred to in paragraph (a) shall include, among others, provisions relating to:
(i) general principles and associated measures for the handling of confidential information;
(ii) conditions of staff employment relating to the protection of confidential information;
(iii) procedures in cases of breaches or alleged breaches of confidentiality.
(c) The regime referred to in paragraph (a) above shall be approved and periodically reviewed by the Board.

ANNEXES

Article 16

(a) The Annexes to this Protocol shall be an integral part thereof. Except for the purposes of amendment of Annexes I and II, the term 'Protocol' as used in this instrument means this Protocol and the Annexes together.
(b) The list of activities specified in Annex I, and the list of equipment and material specified in Annex II, may be amended by the Board on the advice of an open-ended working group of experts established by the Board. any such amendment shall take effect four months after its adoption by the Board.
(c) Annex III to this Protocol specifies how measures in this Protocol shall be implemented by the Community and the States.

ENTRY INTO FORCE

Article 17

(a) This Protocol shall enter into force on the day on which the Agency receives from the Community and the States written notification that their respective requirements for entry into force have been met.
(b) The States and the Community may, at any date before this Protocol enters into force, declare that
they will apply this Protocol provisionally.
(c) The Director-General shall promptly inform all Member States of the Agency of any declaration of
provisional application of, and of the entry into force of, this Protocol.

DEFINITIONS

Article 18

For the purpose of this Protocol:
(a) 'nuclear fuel cycle-related research and development activities' means those activities which are specifically related to any process or system development aspect of any of the following:
- conversion of nuclear material,
- enrichment of nuclear material,
- nuclear fuel fabrication,
- reactors,
- critical facilities,
- reprocessing of nuclear fuel,
- processing (not including repackaging or conditioning not involving the separation of elements, for storage or disposal) of intermediate or high-level waste containing plutonium, high enriched uranium or uranium-233, but do not include activities related to theoretical or basic scientific research or to research and development on industrial radioisotope applications, medical, hydrological and agricultural applications, health and environmental effects and improved maintenance.

(b) 'Site' means that area delimited by the Community and a State in the relevant design information for a facility, including a closed-down facility, and in the relevant information on a location outside facilities where nuclear material is customarily used, including a closed-down location outside facilities where nuclear material was customarily used (this is limited to locations with hot cells or where activities related to conversion, enrichment, fuel fabrication or reprocessing were carried out). 'Site' shall also include all installations, collocated with the facility or location, for the provision or use of essential services, including: hot cells for processing irradiated materials not containing nuclear material; installations for the treatment, storage and disposal of waste; and buildings associated with specified activities identified by the State concerned under Article 2(a)(iv).

(c) 'Decommissioned facility' or 'decommissioned location outside facilities' means an installation or location at which residual structures and equipment essential for its use have been removed or rendered inoperable so that it is not used to store and can no longer be used to handle, process or utilise nuclear material.

(d) 'Closed-down facility' or 'closed-down location outside facilities' means an installation or location where operations have been stopped and the nuclear material removed but which has not been decommissioned.

(e) 'High enriched uranium' means uranium containing 20% or more of the isotope uranium-235.

(f) 'Location-specific environmental sampling' means the collection of environmental samples (e. g. air, water, vegetation, soil, smears) at, and in the immediate vicinity of, a location specified by the Agency for the purpose of assisting the Agency to draw conclusions about the absence of undeclared nuclear material or nuclear activities at the specified location.

(g) 'Wide-area environmental sampling' means the collection of environmental samples (e. g. air, water, vegetation, soil, smears) at a set of locations specified by the Agency for the purpose of assisting the Agency to draw conclusions about the absence of undeclared nuclear material or nuclear activities over a wide area.

(h) 'Nuclear material' means any source or any special fissionable material as defined in Article XX of the Statute. The term source material shall not be interpreted as applying to ore or ore residue. Any determination by the Board under Article XX of the Statute of the Agency after the entry into force of this Protocol which adds to the materials considered to be source material or special fissionable material shall have effect under this Protocol only on acceptance by the Community and the States.

(i) 'Facility' means:

(i) a reactor, a critical facility, a conversion plant, a fabrication plant, a reprocessing plant, an isotope separation plant or a separate storage installation, or

(ii) any location where nuclear material in amounts greater than one effective kilogram is customarily used.

(j) 'Location outside facilities' means any installation or location, which is not a facility, where nuclear material is customarily used in amounts of one effective kilogram or less.

Done at Vienna in duplicate, on the twenty second day of September 1998 in the Danish, Dutch, English, Finnish, French, German, Greek, Italian, Portuguese, Spanish and Swedish languages, the texts of which are equally authentic except that, in case of divergence, those texts concluded in the official languages of the IAEA Board of Governors shall prevail.

THE STRUCTURE AND CONTENT OF AGREEMENTS BETWEEN THE AGENCY AND STATES REQUIRED IN CONNECTION WITH THE NPT

(INFCIRC/153, June 1972)

This document was adopted by the IAEA Board of Governors as "operational norms" for the conclusion of safeguards agreements pursuant to the Non Proliferation Treaty between the Agency and States. As the title suggests, the document provides elements for the structure and content of a "model agreement" to be followed for the purpose. The main aim of the "model" is to ensure the highest possible uniformity of the various points addressed in an agreement, such as co-operation between the IAEA and the States concerned, practical implementation of safeguards, national accounting systems for and control of materials, international inspection, duration of safeguards, nuclear third party liability, interpretation of the agreements, litigation and so on. Based on this document, the Agency has concluded various agreements, e.g. with Egypt, Euratom and some Member States of the European Community, and Argentina and Brazil.

COMMUNICATIONS RECEIVED FROM MEMBERS REGARDING THE EXPORT OF NUCLEAR MATERIAL AND OF CERTAIN CATEGORIES OF EQUIPMENT AND OTHER MATERIAL

(INFCIRC/209, 3 September 1974)

Similarly to INFCIRC/153 recalled in the preceding pages, this document adopted by the IAEA Board of Governors includes "operational norms" for the application of the NPT. The document is known also as the "Zangger agreement" after the chairman of the working group who prepared it.

Pursuant to the obligations arising from article III paragraph 2 of the NPT (i.e. prohibition to export fissile materials unless they are submitted to safeguards provisions by means of a specific agreement) member States interested in such export inform the IAEA that the respective governments commit themselves to complying with the relevant procedures laid down in the Treaty and to applying the measures required.

The list of items, of equipment or material especially designed or prepared for the processing, use or production of special fissionable (or fissile) material, adopted by the exporting government is referred to as the "Trigger List". The information to the IAEA is ensured by letters with technical attachments. The exporting State requires assurances from the recipient State that the material will not be re-exported to a non-nuclear weapon State not party to NPT, unless this accepts submission to the relevant safeguards provisions.

At present the number of participating countries is 35, a particularly important event consisting in the accession of China (a nuclear-weapon country) to the agreement some years ago.

COMMUNICATIONS RECEIVED FROM CERTAIN MEMBER STATES REGARDING GUIDELINES FOR THE EXPORT OF NUCLEAR MATERIAL, EQUIPMENT OR TECHNOLOGY

(INFCIRC/254, February 1978)

Towards the end of the seventies, a large number of States desirous to prevent any diversion of nuclear material and technology from peaceful use to military purposes, decided jointly to lay down a series of guidelines for the transfer of such material and technology to non-nuclear weapon States (especially those not parties to the NPT). This document is therefore a further tool intended to provide guarantees that nuclear energy is geared to exclusively peaceful use, the main purpose being to harmonise export policies outside the framework of the IAEA safeguards system and the NPT.

These guidelines were first laid down by the so-called "London Group" (its members having originally met in that city in 1975). Later on, the governments of the States participating in it sent a series of letters to the IAEA, by which they confirmed their intention to comply with the guidelines and asked the Agency to inform the governments of other member States accordingly. Both guidelines and letters are collected in the IAEA document INFCIRC/254.

THE EURATOM SAFEGUARDS SYSTEM (1959-2005)

The Euratom safeguards system is applied in co-ordination with the IAEA system and is regarded as a "regional" one, since it was established in 1957 by the Treaty creating the European Atomic Energy Community (Euratom). As recalled when addressing the IAEA system, an element of distinction between the two is that according to the Euratom safeguards requirements, nuclear materials must not be diverted from their intended use as declared by the users (article 77 a) of the Euratom Treaty). Nevertheless, although the respective objectives are worded differently, both measures and procedures under the two systems are ultimately of similar nature (in terms of information to be provided, records, reports and "super-national" inspection).

The Euratom Treaty addresses safeguards in articles 77 to 85; attention is drawn in particular to article 77 which stipulates that the provisions relating to supply and safeguards obligations undertaken by Euratom following an agreement with a third State or an international organisation must be observed (article 77 b)). Like for the IAEA inspection, member States are expected not to create conditions delaying or otherwise hindering the performance of duties conferred on Euratom inspectors.

Article 79 establishes that the nature and extent of the requirements concerning "operating records" to be "kept and produced in order to permit accounting for" the materials subject to safeguards, are defined in a Commission regulation approved by the Council". Pursuant to this provision, in 1959 two Regulations were established (no.7 of 18 February and no.8 of 12 March): the first one laid down modalities for the declarations prescribed by article 78 (on the basic of technical characteristics of the installations concerned), the second addressed the nature and extent of obligations under article 79. These regulations are not published here (although preserving their historical importance as the first instruments implementing this part of the Euratom Treaty) since they were superseded by Euratom (Commission) Regulation no.3227 of 1976, adopted to take into account the increased amount of nuclear materials in the European Community, as well as the experience acquired in this domain. The 1976 Regulation was amended (slightly) in 1993 and was linked to the IAEA safeguards system, given the common final objectives as pointed out above. Further extensive amendments to Regulation 3227/76 are addressed in the Introductory Material to be found in the following pages.

Euratom is a party, together with its members countries, to very important instruments adopted in 1998 to strengthen the safeguards system (see previous pages). These instruments are the Additional Protocols which were negotiated by the Vienna Agency,

Euratom, its non-nuclear weapon member countries and France and Great Britain (nuclear weapon States).

Outside the Euratom system proper, but nevertheless for the sake of completeness mention must be made of EC Regulations addressing a Community regime for the control of exports of "dual-use" goods. These are relevant for the nuclear sector, bearing in mind their potential use also for purposes other than peaceful ones (nuclear weapons or other nuclear explosive devices), hence the need to exert controls over their exports by subjecting them to authorization. A Regulation to this effect was adopted in 1994, amended in 2000 and lastly in 2002, in order to remove certain materials and technologies from controls no longer needed.

COMMISSION REGULATION (2005/302/EURATOM) OF 8 FEBRUARY 2005 CONCERNING THE APPLICATION OF THE PROVISIONS ON EURATOM SAFEGUARDS

As pointed out in the Introductory Material to the Euratom safeguards system, Regulations nos. 7 and 8 of 1959 had laid down for the first time modalities for the application of the obligations deriving from article 78 and 79 of the Euratom Treaty.

The 1976 Regulation (no. 3227, see previous pages) was adopted later in time in order to place such obligations in a framework where controls would be more easily applicable in practice. The safeguards requirements concerned each installation and consisted mainly in a) detailed information by the operator to the Commission on the basic technical characteristics of the installation (manipulation of material and its description, control and accountancy system, possible changes in the above characteristics), b) setting up of an accounting system for materials since their reception and description of their characteristics, c) designation of measurement areas for determining flow and stock of materials, d) regular reporting on planned activities and physical inventory of materials, e) import and export of materials. Anomalies detected give rise to actions by Euratom, ranging from inspections to sanctions (pursuant article 83 of the Treaty) which can go as far as the withdrawal of materials. Specific provisions are applicable in the territories of "nuclear weapon" member States. Several annexes (as an integral part of the Regulation) contained questionnaires and forms to be used by operators on complying with Euratom safeguards obligations.

The 1976 Regulation was amended twice. In 1990 (Regulation 90/220/Euratom of 26 January) the amendment consisted in an addition taking into account the "need to establish an appropriate inventory change for the recording and reporting of nuclear material obtained from substances not subject to safeguards". The second amendment (Regulation 93/2130/Euratom of 27 July 1993) was intended in general to ensure an improved co-ordination between the IAEA and Euratom, in order to achieve a more effective action in safeguards controls: this, also considering that the IAEA had started requesting additional information from its member States (to be provided on a voluntary basis). Since several such States were/are also members of Euratom, the amendments to the 1976 Regulation aimed at making it consistent with the new IAEA "policy", by providing for documents and results concerning Euratom inspections to be made available to the IAEA, as well as for joint inspections (thus limiting duplications and reducing costs).

Further extensive amendments have been made to Regulation 3227/76, generally in order to ensure a better consistency between the Euratom and the IAEA safeguards systems, in particular the Additional Protocols (see previous pages) concluded between the IAEA, Euratom and its member States. The amendments are intended to a) provide a detailed framework allowing the Commission to discharge its obligations especially under the Euratom Treaty and the Verification Agreement, b) provide operators with a detailed presentation of their obligations towards Euratom as to the technical characteristics of their installations and nuclear material record keeping and reporting, c) reflect the changes in the legal framework as resulting from the Additional Protocols, d) update Regulation 3227/76 in the light of changes in the industry and development in information technology. It is important to note that the new Regulation will be accompanied by guidelines (non-binding, the Regulation itself remaining the only binding tool) adopted in compliance with article 37 of the Regulation. They will be adopted as a Commission recommendation, in order to facilitate its implementation by operators and member States.

Since the new Regulation repeals entirely Reg. 3227/76 and was published in the Official Journal of the European Union while the volume was being finalized , as a derogation to the closing date chosen for the volume, the text of the new instrument is published in the following pages (without the very extensive technical annexes). The entry into force is March 20, 2005.

THE COMMISSION OF THE EUROPEAN COMMUNITIES,

Having regard to the Treaty establishing the European Atomic Energy Community, and in particular Articles 77, 78, 79 and 81 thereof,

Having regard to the approval of the Council,

Whereas:
(1) Commission Regulation (Euratom) No 3227/76 of 19 October 1976 concerning the application of the provisions on Euratom safeguards [1] defines the nature and extent of the requirements referred to in Articles 78 and 79 of the Treaty.
(2) In view of the increasing quantities of nuclear materials produced, used, carried and recycled in the Community, of the development of trade in these materials and of the successive enlargements of the European Union, it is essential to ensure the effectiveness of safeguards. The nature and the extent of the requirements referred to in Article 79 of the Treaty and set out in Regulation (Euratom) No 3227/76 should therefore be brought up to date in the light of developments, particularly in the fields of nuclear and information technology.

(3) Belgium, Denmark, Germany, Greece, Spain, Ireland, Italy, Luxembourg, the Netherlands, Austria, Portugal, Finland, Sweden and the European Atomic Energy Community have concluded Agreement 78/164/Euratom [2] with the International Atomic Energy Agency in implementation of Article III(1) and (4) of the Treaty on the Non-Proliferation of Nuclear Weapons. Agreement 78/164/Euratom entered into force on 21 February 1977 and was supplemented by Additional Protocol 1999/188/Euratom [3], which entered into force on 30 April 2004.
(4) Agreement 78/164/Euratom contains a particular undertaking entered into by the Community concerning the application of safeguards on source and special fissile materials in the territories of the Member States which have no nuclear weapons of their own and which are parties to the Treaty on the Non-Proliferation of Nuclear Weapons.
(5) The procedures stipulated by Agreement 78/164/Euratom are the result of wide-ranging international negotiations with the International Atomic Energy Agency on the application of Article III(1) and (4) of the Treaty on the Non-Proliferation of Nuclear Weapons. These procedures were approved by the Board of Governors of that Agency.
(6) The Community, the United Kingdom and the International Atomic Energy Agency are parties to an Agreement for the application of safeguards in the United Kingdom in connection with the Treaty on the Non-Proliferation of Nuclear Weapons [4]. That Agreement entered into force on 14 August 1978, and was supplemented by an Additional Protocol which entered into force on 30 April 2004.
(7) The Community, France and the International Atomic Energy Agency are parties to an Agreement for the application of safeguards in France [5]. That Agreement entered into force on 12 September 1981, and was supplemented by an Additional Protocol which entered into force on 30 April 2004.
(8) In the territories of France and the United Kingdom some installations or parts thereof as well as certain materials are liable to be involved in the production cycle for defence needs. Special safeguard procedures should therefore be applied to take account of these circumstances.
(9) The European Council at its meeting in Lisbon on 23 and 24 March 2000 stressed the need to foster the development of state-of-the-art information technology and other telecom networks as well as the content for those networks.
(10) In response to Additional Protocol 1999/188/Euratom, Member States should be required to communicate certain information to the Commission including a general description of sites, advance notification of the processing of waste and reports on changes of location of certain conditioned waste.
(11) Guidelines adopted for the application of this Regulation should fully respect the Community commitments in this field, in particular those resulting from Additional Protocol 1999/188/Euratom and the Additional Protocols to the Agreement for the application of safeguards in the United Kingdom in connection with the Treaty on

the Non-Proliferation of Nuclear Weapons and to the corresponding Agreement for France.
(12) The provisions on security added to the Commission rules of procedure [6] by Commission Decision 2001/844/EC, ECSC, Euratom [7] should apply to information, knowledge and documents acquired by the parties without prejudice to Council Regulation No 3 of 31 July 1958 implementing Article 24 of the Treaty establishing the European Atomic Energy Community [8].
(13) In the interests of clarity, Regulation (Euratom) No 3227/76 should be replaced by this Regulation,

HAS ADOPTED THIS REGULATION:

Chapter I.
SCOPE AND DEFINITIONS

Article 1.
Scope

This Regulation shall apply to any person or undertaking setting up or operating an installation for the production, separation, reprocessing, storage or other use of source material or special fissile material.
It shall not apply to holders of end products used for non-nuclear purposes which incorporate nuclear materials that are in practice irrecoverable.

Article 2
Definitions

For the purposes of this Regulation, the following definitions shall apply:

1. “non-nuclear-weapon Member States” means Belgium, the Czech Republic, Denmark, Germany, Estonia, Greece, Spain, Ireland, Italy, Cyprus, Latvia, Lithuania, Luxembourg, Hungary, Malta, the Netherlands, Austria, Poland, Portugal, Slovenia, Slovakia, Finland and Sweden;

2. “nuclear-weapon Member States” means France and the United Kingdom;

3. “third country” means any State which is not a member of the European Atomic Energy Community;

4. “nuclear materials” means ores, source materials or special fissile materials as defined in Article 197 of the Treaty;

5. "waste" means nuclear material in concentrations or chemical forms considered as irrecoverable for practical or economic reasons and which may be disposed of;

6. "retained waste" means waste, generated from processing or from an operational accident, measured or estimated on the basis of measurements, which has been transferred to a specific location within the material balance area from which it can be retrieved;

7. "conditioned waste" means waste, measured or estimated on the basis of measurements, which has been conditioned in such a way (for example, in glass, cement, concrete or bitumen) that it is not suitable for further nuclear use;

8. "discards to the environment" means waste, measured or estimated on the basis of measurements, which has been irrevocably discarded to the environment as the result of a planned discharge;

9. "categories" (of nuclear material) are natural uranium, depleted uranium, uranium enriched in uranium-235 or uranium-233, thorium, plutonium, and any other material which the Council may determine, acting by a qualified majority on a proposal from the Commission;

10. "item" means an identifiable unit such as a fuel assembly or a fuel pin;

11. "batch" means a portion of nuclear material handled as a unit for accounting purposes at a key measurement point and for which the composition and quantity are defined by a single set of specifications or measurements. The nuclear material may be in bulk form or contained in a number of items;

12. "batch data" means the total weight of each category of nuclear material and, in the case of plutonium and uranium, the isotopic composition when appropriate. For reporting purposes the weights of individual items in the batch shall be added together before rounding to the nearest unit;

13. "effective kilogram" is a special unit used in safeguarding nuclear material, obtained by taking:
(a) for plutonium, its weight in kilograms;
(b) for uranium with an enrichment of 0,01 (1%) and above, its weight in kilograms multiplied by the square of its enrichment;
(c) for uranium with an enrichment below 0,01 (1%) and above 0,005 (0,5%), its weight in kilograms multiplied by 0,0001;
and

(d) for depleted uranium with an enrichment of 0,005 (0,5%) or below, and for thorium, its weight in kilograms multiplied by 0,00005;

14. "material balance area" means an area such that, for the purpose of establishing the material balance:
(a) the quantity of nuclear material in each transfer into or out of each material balance area can be determined;
and
(b) the physical inventory of nuclear material in each material balance area can be determined when necessary in accordance with specified procedures;

15. "key measurement point" means a location where nuclear material appears in such a form that it may be measured to determine material flow or inventory, including but not limited to, the places where nuclear material enters, leaves or is stored in, material balance areas;

16. "book inventory" of a material balance area means the algebraic sum of the most recent physical inventory of that material balance area, and of all inventory changes that have occurred since that physical inventory was taken;

17. "physical inventory" means the sum of all the measured batch quantities or derived estimates of batch quantities of nuclear material on hand at a given time within a material balance area, obtained in accordance with specified procedures;

18. "material unaccounted for" means the difference between the physical inventory and the book inventory;

19. "shipper/receiver difference" means the difference between the quantity of nuclear material in a batch as measured at the receiving material balance area and the quantity as stated by the shipping material balance area;

20. "source data" means those data, recorded during measurement or calibration or used to derive empirical relationships, which identify nuclear material and provide batch data, including: weight of compounds; conversion factors to determine weight of element; specific gravity; element concentration; isotopic ratios; relationship between volume and manometer readings; and relationship between plutonium produced and power generated;

21. "site" means an area delimited by the Community and the Member State, comprising one or more installations, including closed-down installations, as defined in their relevant basic technical characteristics, whereby:

(a) waste treatment or waste storage installations do not constitute a site in themselves;
(b) in the case of a closed-down installation where source material or special fissile material in quantities less than one effective kilogram was customarily used, the term is limited to locations with hot cells or where activities related to conversion, enrichment, fuel fabrication or reprocessing were carried out;
(c) "site" also includes all plants co-located with the installations which provide or use essential services including hot cells for processing irradiated materials not containing nuclear material; plants for the treatment, storage and disposal of waste; and buildings associated with activities specified in Annex 1 to Additional Protocol 1999/188/Euratom and identified by the State concerned;

22. "site representative" means any person, undertaking or entity designated by the Member Stateas being responsible for the declarations referred to in Article 3(2);

23. "installation" means a reactor, a critical installation, a conversion plant, a fabrication plant, a reprocessing plant, an isotope separation plant, a separate storage installation, a waste treatment or waste storage installation; or any other location where source material or special fissile material is customarily used;

24. "decommissioned installation" means an installation for which it has been verified that residual structures and equipment essential for its use have been removed or rendered inoperable so that it is not used to store and can no longer be used to handle, process or utilise source material or special fissile material;

25. "closed-down installation" means an installation for which it has been verified that operations have been stopped and the nuclear material removed but which has not been decommissioned.

Chapter II
BASIC TECHNICAL CHARACTERISTICS AND PARTICULAR SAFEGUARD PROVISIONS

Article 3
Declaration of the basic technical characteristics

1. Any person or undertaking setting up or operating an installation for the production, separation, reprocessing, storage or other use of source material or special fissile material shall declare to the Commission the basic technical characteristics of the installation, using the relevant questionnaire shown in Annex I.
For the purpose of the first subparagraph "use" of nuclear materials is taken to include, inter alia: power production in reactors, research in critical or zero energy installations,

conversion, fabrication, reprocessing, storage, isotope separation, and ore concentration, as well as treatment or storage of waste.
For ore production, the provisions of Articles 24 and 25 apply.

2. Each Member State being a party to Additional Protocol 1999/188/Euratom, shall designate a site representative for each site on its territory who shall provide to the Commission a declaration containing a general description of the site, using the questionnaire shown in Annex II.
The declaration shall be submitted within 120 days of the date of entry into force of Additional Protocol 1999/188/Euratom in the Member State concerned and updates shall be submitted by 1 April of each year.
The declaration shall fulfil the requirements of Article 2(a)(iii) of Additional Protocol 1999/188/Euratom and shall be separate from the declaration required pursuant to paragraph 1 of this Article.

3. While the site representative carries the responsibility for the timely collection of the relevant information and the submission of the general description of the site to the Commission, the responsibility for the correctness and the completeness of the declarations remains with the persons or the undertakings setting up or operating the installation, and for buildings on a site which do not involve nuclear material with the Member State concerned. As far as possible the declarations provided for in paragraphs 1 and 2 shall be submitted in electronic form if they are kept in such form by the person or undertaking. If information is sent to the Commission both in electronic and in paper form, the paper form shall prevail.

Article 4
Time-limits

The declaration of the basic technical characteristics of new installations shall be communicated to the Commission in accordance with Article 3(1) at least 200 days before the first consignment of nuclear material is due to be received.
For new installations with an inventory or annual throughput of nuclear material of more than one effective kilogram, all relevant information relating to the owner, operator, purpose, location, type, capacity and expected commissioning date shall be communicated to the Commission at least 200 days before construction begins.
Changes in the basic technical characteristics for which advance notification is not required as specified in the particular safeguard provisions set out in Article 6, shall be communicated to the Commission within 30 days after the modification is complete.
Installations in the territory of States acceding to the European Union shall communicate to the Commission their basic technical characteristics within 30 days of the date

of entry into force of this Regulation in that State, except for waste treatment or waste storage installations whose basic technical characteristics shall be communicated within 120 days of the date of entry into force of this Regulation in that State.
Using the questionnaire in Annex I, existing waste treatment or waste storage installations shall communicate to the Commission the basic technical characteristics of their installation within 120 days of the date of entry into force of this Regulation.
For other existing installations any additional information required by the questionnaire in Annex I shall be supplied within 120 days of the date of entry into force of this Regulation.

Article 5
Programme of activities

To enable the Commission to plan its safeguards activities, the persons or undertakings referred to in the first subparagraph of Article 3(1) shall communicate to the Commission the following information:
(a) annually, an outline programme of activities on the basis of Annex XI, indicating, in particular, provisional dates for taking a physical inventory;
(b) at least 40 days before taking a physical inventory, the programme for such work.
Changes affecting the outline programme of activities and, in particular, the taking of physical inventories shall be communicated to the Commission without delay.

Article 6
Particular safeguard provisions

1. Acting on the basis of the basic technical characteristics submitted pursuant to Article 3(1) and Article 4, the Commission shall adopt particular safeguard provisions relating to the matters set out in paragraph 2 of this Article. The particular safeguard provisions shall be drawn up by means of a Commission decision addressed to the person or undertaking concerned, taking account of operational and technical constraints and in close consultation with the person or undertaking concerned and the relevant Member State.
The person or undertaking to whom the decision of the Commission is addressed shall be notified thereof, and a copy of such notification shall be transmitted to the Member State concerned.
Until the Commission decision on particular safeguard provisions is adopted, the person or undertaking concerned shall apply the general provisions of this Regulation.

2. The particular safeguard provisions shall include the following:
(a) the material balance areas and the selection of key measurement points for determining the flow and stocks of nuclear materials;

(b) the changes in basic technical characteristics for which advance notification is required;
(c) the procedures for keeping records of nuclear materials for each material balance area and for drawing up reports;
(d) the frequency of, and procedures for, taking physical inventories for accounting purposes as part of safeguards measures;
(e) the containment and surveillance measures, in accordance with the arrangements agreed upon with the person or undertaking concerned;
(f) the arrangements for sample-taking by the person or undertaking concerned solely for safeguards purposes.

3. The particular safeguard provisions may also specify the content of subsequent communications required under Article 5 as well as the conditions under which shipments and receipts of nuclear material require advance notification.

4. The Commission shall reimburse the person or undertaking concerned the cost of those special services which are provided for in the particular safeguard provisions or which are provided as the result of a special request by the Commission or its inspectors, on the basis of an agreed estimate. The amount of, and arrangements for, the reimbursement shall be jointly determined by the parties concerned and shall be reviewed periodically.

Chapter III
NUCLEAR MATERIAL ACCOUNTANCY

Article 7
Accounting system

The persons or undertakings referred to in the first subparagraph of Article 3(1) shall maintain a system of accountancy and control for nuclear materials. This system shall include accounting and operating records and, in particular, information on the quantities, category, form and composition of these materials as provided for in Article 18, their actual location and the particular safeguards obligation as provided for in Article 17, together with details of the recipient or shipper when nuclear materials are transferred.

The system of measurements on which the records are based shall comply with the most recent international standards or shall be equivalent in quality to those standards. On the basis of these records, which shall be retained for a period of at least five years, it must be possible to draw up and substantiate the declarations made to the Commission. Accounting and operating records shall be made available to the

Commission's inspectors in electronic form if they are kept in this form by the installation. Further details may be specified in the particular safeguard provisions referred to in Article 6 for each installation.

Article 8
Operating records

For each material balance area, the operating records shall include, where appropriate:
(a) the operating data used to determine changes in the quantities and composition of nuclear material;
(b) a list of inventory items, updated to the best extent possible, and their location;
(c) the data, including derived estimates of random and systematic errors, obtained from the calibration of tanks and instruments as well as from sampling and analysis;
(d) the data resulting from quality control measures applied to the nuclear material accountancy system, including derived estimates of random and systematic errors;
(e) a description of the sequence of actions taken to prepare for, and take, a physical inventory, and to ensure that the inventory is correct and complete;
(f) a description of the actions taken in order to ascertain the cause and magnitude of any accidental or unmeasured loss that might have occurred;
(g) the isotopic composition of plutonium, including its decay isotopes, and reference dates, if recorded at the installation for operational needs.
When available, the data referred to in point (g) shall be communicated to the Commission on request.

Article 9
Accounting records

In respect of each material balance area the accounting records shall show the following:
(a) all inventory changes, so that the book inventory can be determined at any time;
(b) all measurement and counting results used to determine the physical inventory;
(c) all corrections made to inventory changes, book inventories and physical inventories.
The accounting records relating to any inventory change and physical inventory shall show the material identification, batch data and source data for each batch. These records shall account separately for uranium, thorium and plutonium, in accordance with the categories listed in Article 18(2)(b). In addition, for each inventory change, the date of the change and, when appropriate, the dispatching material balance area or the shipper and the receiving material balance area or the recipient shall be indicated.

Article 10
Accounting reports

The persons or undertakings referred to in the first subparagraph of Article 3(1) shall provide the Commission with accounting reports.
The accounting reports shall contain the information available on the date of reporting and must be corrected at a later date if necessary. Accounting reports shall be transmitted to the Commission in electronic form, except in cases where the Commission has granted a written derogation, or the transitional arrangements specified in Article 39 apply.
On a reasoned request by the Commission, further details or explanations in connection with these reports shall be supplied within three weeks.

Article 11
Initial book inventory

The persons or undertakings referred to in the first subparagraph of Article 3(1) shall transmit to the Commission, within 30 days of the date of entry into force of this Regulation, an initial book inventory of all nuclear materials they are holding, using the format set out in Annex V. This Article does not apply to the persons or undertakings who have already transmitted an initial book inventory under Regulation (Euratom) No 3227/76, or to waste treatment or waste storage installations.

Article 12
Inventory change report

1. For each material balance area, the persons or undertakings referred to in the first subparagraph of Article 3(1) shall transmit to the Commission inventory change reports in respect of all nuclear materials using the format set out in Annex III.
Unless otherwise specified in the particular safeguard provisions referred to in Article 6 for an installation, these reports shall be sent monthly, at the latest 15 days after the end of the month, and shall state all inventory changes which have occurred or become known during that month.

2. For months in which a physical inventory is taken, and the physical inventory taking date is not the last date of the month, two separate inventory change reports shall be transmitted:
(a) a first inventory change report containing any inventory changes up to and including the physical inventory taking date, which shall be sent at the latest, together with the second inventory change report, or together with the physical inventory listing

and the material balance report if the latter are sent before the second inventory change report;
(b) a second inventory change report containing all inventory changes from the first day after the physical inventory taking date to the end of the month which shall be sent within 15 days of the end of the month.

3. For months in which no inventory changes occur, the persons or undertakings concerned shall send the inventory change report, carrying over the ending book inventory of the previous month.

4. In order that they may be reported as a single inventory change, small inventory changes, such as transfers of samples for purposes of analysis, may be grouped together, as laid down in the particular safeguard provisions referred to in Article 6 for the installation concerned.

5. Inventory change reports may be accompanied by comments explaining the inventory changes.

Article 13
Material balance report and physical inventory listing

For each material balance area, the persons or undertakings referred to in the first subparagraph of Article 3(1) shall transmit to the Commission:
(a) material balance reports, in the format set out in Annex IV, showing:
(i) beginning physical inventory;
(ii) inventory changes (first increases, then decreases);
(iii) ending book inventory;
(iv) ending physical inventory;
(v) material unaccounted for;
(b) a physical inventory listing, in the format set out in Annex V, showing all batches separately.
The reports and the listing shall be transmitted as soon as possible and at the latest within 30 days of the date on which a physical inventory was taken.
Unless otherwise specified in the particular safeguard provisions referred to in Article 6 for an installation, a physical inventory shall be taken every calendar year and the period between two successive physical inventory takings shall not exceed 14 months.

Article 14
Special reports

The persons and undertakings referred to in the first subparagraph of Article 3(1) shall transmit to the Commission a special report whenever the circumstances referred to in Articles 15 or 22 arise.
The type of information to be supplied in such reports shall be specified in the particular safeguard provisions referred to in Article 6.
The special reports, and further details or explanations which may be requested by the Commission in connection with these reports, shall be supplied without delay.

Article 15
Unusual occurrences

A special report shall be made in the following cases:
(a) if, as a result of any unusual incident or circumstances, it is believed that there has been or might be an increase or a loss of nuclear material in excess of the limits specified for these purposes in the particular safeguard provisions referred to in Article 6;
(b) if the containment has unexpectedly changed from that specified in the particular safeguard provisions referred to in Article 6, to a point where an unauthorised removal of nuclear material has become possible.
The persons or undertakings concerned shall submit these reports as soon as they have become aware of any such loss or increase or sudden change in the containment conditions, or of anything which leads them to believe that there has been such an occurrence. The causes shall also be stated as soon as they are known.

Article 16
Reporting of nuclear transformations

In respect of reactors, calculated data on nuclear transformations shall be reported in the inventory change report at the latest when irradiated fuel is transferred from the reactor material balance area. In addition, other procedures for recording and reporting nuclear transformations may be specified in the particular safeguard provisions referred to in Article 6.

Article 17
Particular safeguard obligations

1. Nuclear materials subject to particular safeguard obligations entered into by the Community in an agreement concluded with a third country or an international

organisation shall, unless otherwise stipulated by such an agreement, be identified separately for each obligation in the following notifications:
(a) initial book inventory provided for in Article 11;
(b) inventory change reports, including ending book inventories, provided for in Article 12;
(c) material balance reports and physical inventory listings provided for in Article 13;
(d) intended imports and exports provided for in Articles 20 and 21.
Unless specifically prohibited in any of those agreements, such separate identification shall not preclude the physical mixing of materials.

2. Paragraph 1 shall not apply to the Agreements concluded by the Community and the Member States with the International Atomic Energy Agency.

Article 18
Weight units and categories of nuclear materials

1. In any notification referred to in this Regulation, quantities of materials covered by the Regulation shall be expressed in grams.
The corresponding material accounting records shall be kept in grams or in smaller units. They shall be kept in such a manner as to render them trustworthy and, in particular, to comply with current practices in the Member States.
In the notifications, quantities may be rounded down when the first decimal is 0 to 4 and rounded up when the first decimal is 5 to 9.

2. Unless otherwise provided for in the particular safeguard provisions referred to in Article 6 the notifications shall include the following:
(a) the total weight of the elements uranium, thorium and plutonium, and also, for enriched uranium, the total weight of the fissile isotopes;
(b) separate material balance reports as well as separate line entries in inventory change reports and in physical inventory listings for the following categories of nuclear material:
(i) depleted uranium;
(ii) natural uranium;
(iii) uranium enriched to less than 20%;
(iv) uranium enriched to 20% and above;
(v) plutonium;
(vi) thorium.

Article 19
Derogations

1. The Commission may grant producers and users of nuclear materials a written derogation from the rules governing the form and frequency of the notifications provided for in Articles 10 to 18, in order to take account of any particular circumstances in which safeguarded materials are used or produced.
The derogation shall be granted on submission of a request by the person or undertaking concerned using the form set out in Annex IX.
The derogation shall be granted only for a whole material balance area in which nuclear material is not processed or stored together with nuclear material for which no derogation can be granted.

2. The Commission may grant a derogation for a material balance area holding:
(a) quantities of nuclear material commensurate with those specified in Annex I-G, which are kept in the same state for long periods;
(b) depleted uranium, natural uranium or thorium which is used exclusively in non-nuclear activities;
(c) special fissile materials when used in gram quantities or less as sensing components in instruments;
(d) plutonium with an isotopic concentration of plutonium-238 exceeding 80%.

3. The persons or undertakings to whom a derogation is granted shall transmit an annual report to the Commission by 31 January of each year, using the form set out in Annex X. This report shall describe the situation at the end of the previous calendar year.

4. In the case of exports of nuclear material to a third country, the persons or undertakings to whom a derogation has been granted shall transmit a report to the Commission as soon as possible and, at the latest, within 15 days of the end of the month in which the export occurred, using the form set out in Annex X. This report shall indicate the quantity of nuclear material exported and the stock of nuclear material still subject to derogation.

5. In the case of imports of nuclear material from a third country the persons or undertakings to whom a derogation is granted shall transmit a request to the Commission to add this material to the list of materials in respect of which the derogation applies. The request shall be transmitted to the Commission as soon as the transfer date is known to the person or undertaking and, at the latest, within 15 days of the end of the month in which the transfer occurred, using the form set out in Annex IX.

6. The Commission may define other specific clauses concerning the form and the periodicity of the reports in the particular safeguard provisions referred to in Article 6.

7. If the conditions for derogation are no longer met, the derogation shall be withdrawn by the Commission, acting upon receipt of information from the person or undertaking to whom a derogation is granted.

Chapter IV
TRANSFERS BETWEEN STATES

Article 20
Exports and shipments

1. The persons or undertakings referred to in the first subparagraph of Article 3(1) shall give advance notification to the Commission if any source materials or special fissile materials:
(a) are exported to a third country;
(b) are shipped from a non-nuclear-weapon Member State to a nuclear-weapon Member State;
(c) are shipped from a nuclear-weapon Member State to a non-nuclear-weapon Member State.

2. Advance notification is required only:
(a) where the consignment exceeds one effective kilogram;
or
(b) where an installation transfers a total quantity of materials to the same State that could exceed one effective kilogram in any consecutive period of twelve months, even though no single consignment exceeds one effective kilogram.

3. The notification shall be given after the conclusion of the contractual arrangements leading to the transfer, using the form set out in Annex VI, and shall reach the Commission at least eight working days before the material is to be packed for transfer.

4. If so required for reasons of physical protection, special arrangements concerning the form and transmission of the notification may be agreed upon with the Commission.

5. Exports and shipments of nuclear material contained in waste or ores are not subject to the provisions of paragraphs 1 to 4.

Article 21
Imports and receipts

1. The persons or undertakings referred to in the first subparagraph of Article 3(1) shall give advance notification to the Commission if any source materials or special fissile materials:
(a) are imported from a third country;
(b) are received in a non-nuclear-weapon Member State from a nuclear-weapon Member State;
(c) are received in a nuclear-weapon Member State from a non-nuclear-weapon Member State.

2. Advance notification is required only:
(a) where the consignment exceeds one effective kilogram;
or
(b) where an installation imports or receives a total quantity of materials from the same State that could exceed one effective kilogram in any consecutive period of twelve months, even though no single consignment exceeds one effective kilogram.

3. The notification shall be given as far in advance as possible of the expected arrival of the material and, at the latest, on the date of receipt, using the form set out in Annex VII, and shall reach the Commission at least five working days before the material is unpacked.

4. If so required for reasons of physical protection, special arrangements concerning the form and transmission of the notification may be agreed upon with the Commission.

5. Imports and receipts of nuclear material contained in waste or ores are not subject to the provisions of paragraphs 1 to 4.

Article 22
Loss or delay during transfer

A special report shall be submitted, as provided for in Article 14, by the persons or undertakings notifying a transfer under Articles 20 and 21 where, following exceptional circumstances or an incident, they have received information that nuclear materials have been lost or appear to be lost, or where there has been a considerable delay during transfer.

Article 23
Communication of change of date

Any change of the dates for packing before transfer, transport or unpacking of nuclear materials which have been given in the notifications provided for in Articles 20 and 21, shall be communicated without delay, with an indication of the revised dates if known, unless the change gives rise to a special report.

Chapter V
SPECIFIC PROVISIONS

Article 24
Ore producers

1. Any person or undertaking extracting ores in the territory of a Member State shall declare the basic technical characteristics of the ore extraction operations to the Commission, using the questionnaire in Annex I-J, within 120 days of the date of entry into force of this Regulation, and shall communicate the programme of activities in accordance with Article 5.

2. By way of derogation from Articles 7, 8 and 9, any person or undertaking extracting ores shall keep accounting records thereof indicating, in particular, the quantities of the ore extracted, with the average uranium and thorium content, and the stock of extracted ore at the mine. The records shall also contain details of shipments, stating the date, consignee and quantity in each case.
Such records shall be retained for at least five years.

Article 25
Ore shipment/export reports

By way of derogation from Articles 10 to 18, any person or undertaking extracting ores shall inform the Commission, using the form set out in Annex VIII of:
(a) the amount of material dispatched from each mine, by 31 January of each year for the previous calendar year;
and
(b) exports of ores to third countries, by the date of the dispatch at the latest.

Article 26
Carriers and temporary storage agents

Any person or undertaking engaged, within the territories of the Member States, in transporting, or temporarily storing during transport, nuclear materials shall accept or hand over such materials only against a duly signed and dated receipt. This receipt shall state the names of the parties handing over and receiving the materials and indicate the quantities carried as well as the category, form and composition of the materials.

If so required for reasons of physical protection, the description of the materials transferred may be replaced by a suitable identification of the consignment. Such identification shall be traceable to records held by the persons or undertakings referred to in the first subparagraph of Article 3(1).

Those records shall be retained by the contracting parties for at least five years.

Article 27
Substitute records for carriers and temporary storage agents

Records already held by persons or undertakings in accordance with existing regulations which apply to them in the territory of the Member States in which they operate may take the place of the records referred to in Article 26, provided that such records contain all the information required under that Article.

Article 28
Intermediaries

Any intermediaries taking part in the conclusion of any contract for the supply of nuclear materials, such as authorised agents, brokers or commission agents, shall keep all records relating to the transactions performed by them or on their behalf for at least five years after expiry of the contract. Such records shall contain the names of the contracting parties and indicate the date of the contract as well as the quantity, category, form, composition, origin and destination of the materials.

Article 29
Transmission of information and data

The Commission may transmit to the International Atomic Energy Agency information and data obtained pursuant to this Regulation.

Article 30
Waste initial stock list and accounting records

1. By way of derogation from Article 11, any person or undertaking treating or storing nuclear material that has previously been declared as retained or conditioned waste shall transmit to the Commission within 120 days of the date of entry into force of this Regulation, an initial stock list of all nuclear material by category.

2. Any person or undertaking treating or storing nuclear material that has previously been declared as retained or conditioned waste, shall keep accounting records thereof. By way of derogation from Articles 7 to 11, Article 13 and Article 17(1) for material that has been previously declared as retained waste and Articles 7 to 13 and Article 17(1) for material that has previously been declared as conditioned waste, these records shall include:
(a) the operating data used to determine changes in the quantities and composition of nuclear material;
(b) a stock list to be updated yearly after the physical inventory taking;
(c) a description of the sequence of actions taken to prepare for and take a physical inventory, and to ensure that the inventory is correct and complete;
(d) a description of the actions taken in order to ascertain the cause and magnitude of any accidental loss that might have occurred;
(e) all stock changes, so that the book inventory can be established when requested.
The reporting requirements for the processing of retained waste shall be specified in the particular safeguard provisions referred to in Article 6.

Article 31
Processing of waste

The persons or undertakings referred to in the first subparagraph of Article 3(1) shall give advance notification to the Commission of any processing campaign of material that has previously been declared as retained or conditioned waste, excluding repackaging or further conditioning without separation of elements.
This advance notification, using the form set out in Annex XII, shall include information on the amount of plutonium, high enriched uranium and uranium-233 per batch, the form (glass, high active liquid, etc.), the expected duration of the campaign, and the location of the material before and after the campaign. Such notification shall be communicated to the Commission at least 200 days before the campaign starts.

Article 32
Transfers of conditioned waste

The persons or undertakings referred to in the first subparagraph of Article 3(1) shall submit, by 31 January of each year at the latest, annual reports on:
(a) shipments or exports of conditioned waste to an installation within or outside the territories of the Member States, using the form set out in Annex XIII;
(b) receipts or imports of conditioned waste from an installation without a material balance area code or from an installation outside the territories of the Member States, using the form set out in Annex XIV;
(c) changes in location of conditioned waste containing plutonium, high enriched uranium or uranium-233, using the form set out in Annex XV.

Article 33
International obligations

The provisions of this Regulation, and in particular Article 3(2), Article 31 and point (c) of Article 32, shall be applied in conformity with the obligations of the Community and non-nuclear-weapon Member States, under Additional Protocol 1999/188/Euratom.

Chapter VI
SPECIFIC PROVISIONS APPLICABLE IN THE TERRITORIES OF THE NUCLEAR-WEAPON MEMBER STATES

Article 34
Specific provisions for nuclear-weapon Member States

1. This Regulation shall not apply:
(a) to installations or parts of installations which have been assigned to meet defence requirements and which are situated in the territory of a nuclear-weapon Member State;
or
(b) to nuclear materials which have been assigned to meet defence requirements by that nuclear-weapon Member State.

2. For nuclear materials, installations or parts of installations which are liable to be assigned to meet defence requirements and which are situated in the territory of a nuclear-weapon Member State, the extent of the application of this Regulation and the procedures under it shall be defined by the Commission in consultation and in

agreement with the Member State concerned, taking into account the provisions of the second paragraph of Article 84 of the Treaty.

3. Notwithstanding paragraphs 1 and 2:
(a) the provisions of Articles 3(1), 4 and 6 shall apply to installations or parts of installations which at certain times are operated exclusively with nuclear materials liable to be assigned to meet defence requirements but which at other times are operated exclusively with civil nuclear materials;
(b) the provisions of Articles 3(1), 4 and 6 shall apply, with exceptions for reasons of national security, to installations or parts of installations to which access could be restricted for such reasons but which produce, treat, separate, reprocess or use in any other way, simultaneously, both civil nuclear materials and nuclear materials assigned or liable to be assigned to meet defence requirements;
(c) the provisions of Articles 2 and 5, Articles 7 to 32, paragraphs 1 and 2 of this Article and Articles 35, 36 and 37 shall apply in relation to all civil nuclear materials situated in the installations or parts of installations referred to in points (a) and (b) of this paragraph;
(d) the provisions of Article 3(2), Article 31 and Article 32(c) shall not apply in the territories of nuclear-weapon Member States.

Chapter VII
FINAL PROVISIONS

Article 35
Confidentiality of data

The Commission provisions on security set out in Decision 2001/844/EC/ECSC/Euratom shall apply without prejudice to Regulation No 3 implementing Article 24 of the Treaty establishing the European Atomic Energy Community, to information, knowledge and documents acquired or obtained by the Commission under the present Regulation.
The security of information transmission shall be agreed between the Commission and the person, undertaking or entity concerned, and shall be in accordance with Member State requirements for the transmission of such information.

Article 36
Installations controlled from outside the Community

Where an installation is controlled by a person or undertaking established outside the Community, any obligations imposed by this Regulation shall be fulfilled by the local management of the installation.

Article 37
Guidelines

The Commission shall adopt and publish Guidelines for the application of this Regulation by means of a Recommendation, and, if necessary, update them in the light of the experience gained, in close consultation with the Member States, and after having obtained observations from interested parties.

Article 38
Repeal

Regulation (Euratom) No 3227/76 is repealed.
References to the repealed Regulation shall be construed as references to this Regulation.

Article 39
Transitional period

The Commission may grant an exemption from the obligation to use the reporting formats set out in Annexes III, IV and V. The exemption shall apply to persons or undertakings using the reporting format of Annex II, III and IV of Regulation (Euratom) No 3227/76 on the date of entry into force of this Regulation. It shall be granted for a maximum of five years from that date.
The persons or undertakings referred to in the first subparagraph of Article 3(1) shall, within a period of three years of the date of entry into force of this Regulation, inform the Commission of the date on which they intend to start using the reporting formats set out in Annexes III, IV and V. Upon duly justified request and the presentation of an implementation programme the Commission may, on a case by case basis, extend the period by up to two years.-

Article 40
Entry into force

This Regulation shall enter into force on the twentieth day following its publication in the Official Journal of the European Union.
This Regulation shall be binding in its entirety and directly applicable in all Member States.

Done at Brussels, 8 February 2005.

For the Commission, Andris Piebalgs, Member of the Commission

[1] OJ L 363, 31.12.1976, p. 1. Regulation as last amended by Regulation (Euratom) No 2130/93 (OJ L 191, 31.7.1993, p. 75).
[2] OJ L 51, 22.2.1978, p. 1.
[3] OJ L 67, 13.3.1999, p. 1.
[4] IAEA document INFCIRC/263 dated October 1978.
[5] IAEA document INFCIRC/290 dated December 1981.
[6] OJ L 308, 8.12.2000, p. 26. Rules of procedure as last amended by Decision 2004/563/EC, Euratom (OJ L 251, 27.7.2004, p. 9).
[7] OJ L 317, 3.12.2001. p.1.
[8] OJ 17, 6.10.1958, p. 406/58.

Council/Commission statement

1. Guidelines will be adopted and published by the Commission as provided in Article 37 of the Regulation. They will provide non-binding orientations and guidance to operators so as to facilitate the application of the Regulation. It is understood that the Guidelines will not create any legal rights or obligations and that the Regulation will remain the binding instrument which will prevail in case of any divergence between the Regulation and the Guidelines.

2. It is understood that by following the Guidelines the operators would ensure that they are in compliance with the provisions of the Regulation addressed by the Guidelines.

3. The Commission will follow the developments in the field of safeguards and monitor the application of the Regulation. On this basis, the Commission may, as appropriate, modify the Guidelines. Prior to the adoption of any modification, the Commission will undertake to consult stakeholders and Member States. In adopting such modifications the Commission will take account of the positions expressed in such consultations.

4. It is understood that the Working Party on Atomic Questions, in a suitable composition, will be the forum for the consultation of Member States.

IAEA CONVENTION ON THE PHYSICAL PROTECTION OF NUCLEAR MATERIAL

(Vienna, 3 March 1980)

Physical protection of nuclear and other radioactive materials is based on a set of measures intended to prevent, detect and respond to any voluntary act or event (theft, illicit trafficking, sabotage or other illegal activities) involving such materials and potentially the source of damage to persons, property and the environment at large. It should be pointed out that these measures concern materials not only used or stored at nuclear facilities, but also in transit through States. Since 1972 the IAEA had adopted a set of recommendations, later on revised, updated and collected in document INFCIRC/225 of September 1975. The revision took into account the latest developments in physical protection and related needs arising from the increasing use of nuclear energy for peaceful purposes. The recommendations provided objectives and elements for the States to bear in mind when setting up national physical protection systems.

Not very long afterwards, the States felt that the moment had come to create a more adequate and stringent regime, in order to meet physical protection needs in a rapidly changing reality. This led them to negotiate a Convention which would address the objective of avoiding risks arising from the illicit acquisition and use of nuclear materials intended for peaceful purposes. In actual fact, already in 1975 on the occasion of the first revision conference of the Non Proliferation Treaty (NPT, see previous pages), a common position had emerged on the need to ensure the detection, prevention and repression of the illicit acquisition and use referred to above, as well as the protection of nuclear materials both during international transport and in domestic use. This could be effectively achieved only by means of a broad international co-operation, as one of the most important features of the Convention. A draft convention was ready in 1978, on the basis of which negotiations were carried out and led to its adoption in 1979, the Convention being opened for signature on March 3, 1980 under the aegis of the IAEA (who is the depositary of the ratification instruments). It is noted that the Convention also required the contracting Parties to provide for penalties in connection with a number of defined serious criminal offences involving nuclear materials.

It should be recalled that on the occasion of the 28th IAEA General Conference, a Resolution was adopted on 28 September 1984 in which the hope was expressed for the Convention to enter into force at the nearest possible date and to obtain the widest possible adherence. The Convention entered into force three years later (8 February 1987) following ratification by 21 countries (as required under article 19), a certain number of them having significant nuclear activities. It is worth recalling that the final text of the Convention addressed physical protection of nuclear materials while in international transport, but not domestic use, storage and transit. At present, there are 106 contracting Parties to this Convention. The European Community (Euratom) signed the Convention on June 13, 1980 and acceded to it on October 6, 1991, following a Council Decision (June 9, 1980) to this effect. In connection with European Community's competences in the matter of physical protection, see relevant case law no. 1 in the Appendix to the volume.

The IAEA document INFCIRC/225 of 1975, used as a basis for the negotiations concerning the Convention, was revised a few times in the following years. The latest revision (INFCIRC/225 Rev. 4, April 1999) is of special importance in that it addresses also sabotage and relevant measures to be taken to prevent or minimise its effects. The very significant amendments in INFCIRC/ 225 Rev. 4, together with the rather long time of existence of this Convention and the new physical protection problems emerging also in connection with geo-political "mutations" worldwide, in recent times have led some countries to propose that the Convention be amended, notably in order to cover sabotage and domestic use, storage and transit of nuclear materials. A Group of Legal and Technical Experts was set up and several Group meetings were convened by the Agency in Vienna, the terms of reference being to carry out a survey of the overall current situation as to physical protection, which would suggest a revision of the Convention. The survey was also intended to serve as a basis for identifying the areas mostly concerned with a revision, if a decision to this effect were taken. It must be pointed out that during the meetings a number of countries expressed misgivings (when not an opinion to the contrary) about the revision, instead stressing the need for strengthening the physical protection regime by means of basically technical and organisational measures.

With a view to reaching a compromise position, an agreement was reached on starting a revision exercise which would take into account the areas identified as the object of a possible revision, without pre-empting on the final decision. The revision exercise was carried out by the Expert Group mentioned above, meeting in Vienna and elaborating on a draft text, while further thought was being given to whether the Convention should be revised.

The shocking events occurred on September 11, 2001 in New York marked a significant development in the position of several States whose delegations were involved in the revision exercise, and especially those who had always been reluctant in respect of a revision. Shortly after such events, already at the IAEA many actions were undertaken in response to them, including a message by the Director General in which it was strongly recommended to the contracting Parties to consider seriously a revision in the light of the September 11 events, thus overcoming all the previous misgivings and reservations. In this context, it was also recommended to intensify the revision exercise so as to finalize it in the shortest possible time.

A meeting of the Group was convened for the beginning of October 2001, and was followed by four more, given the many crucial issues at stake which made it necessary to pursue long discussions, in order to achieve the largest possible consensus on all of them. In actual fact, a few basic issues (such as the degree of commitment by States to the Fundamentals Principles of physical protection as endorsed by the IAEA Board of Governors in August 2001, or the inclusion of damage to the environment among punishable offences) remained to some extent open even at the end of negotiations within the Group, and were deferred to the diplomatic conference for the adoption of the amended convention. However, it is fair to say that the outcome of the negotiations had been on the whole positive in creating the basis for the strengthening of the international physical protection regime. In this connection, it is worth summarizing the main qualifying achievements of the new Convention, such as: a) extension of the scope, besides the international transport of nuclear materials, also to national use storage and transport, as well as to sabotage, b) commitment of contracting States to adopt all the necessary measures to ensure physical protection of materials and facilities (i.e. legislation and supervising body), c) introduction of related Fundamental Principles and their practical implementation nationally, d) new international co-operation tools, e) a broader range of offences (esp. sabotage to and contraband in nuclear materials) to be made punishable under the Convention (and national legislation accordingly).

Since the 1980 Convention remains obviously applicable until the new text is first adopted and then enters into force, the 1980 text is published here. The revised Convention should be adopted in the course of 2005.

THE STATES PARTIES TO THIS CONVENTION,

RECOGNIZING the right of all States to develop and apply nuclear energy for peaceful purposes and their legitimate interests in the potential benefits to be derived from the peaceful application of nuclear energy,

CONVINCED of the need for facilitating international co-operation in the peaceful application of nuclear energy,

DESIRING to avert the potential dangers posed by the unlawful taking and use of nuclear material,

CONVINCED that offences relating to nuclear material are a matter of grave concern and that there is an urgent need to adopt appropriate and effective measures to ensure the prevention, detection and punishment of such offences,

AWARE OF THE NEED FOR international co-operation to establish, in conformity with the national law of each State Party and with this Convention, effective measures for the physical protection of nuclear material,
CONVINCED that this Convention should facilitate the safe transfer of nuclear material,
STRESSING also the importance of the physical protection of nuclear material in domestic use, storage and transport,
RECOGNIZING the importance of effective physical protection of nuclear material used for military purposes, and understanding that such material is and will continue to be accorded stringent physical protection,

HAVE AGREED as follows:

Article 1

For the purposes of this Convention:

a. "nuclear material" means plutonium except that with isotopic concentration exceeding 80% in plutonium-238; uranium-233; uranium enriched in the isotope 235 or 233; uranium containing the mixture of isotopes as occurring in nature other than in the form of ore or ore-residue; any material containing one or more of the foregoing;
b. "uranium enriched in the isotope 235 or 233" means uranium containing the isotope 235 or 233 or both in an amount such that the abundance ratio of the sum of these isotopes to the isotope 238 is greater than the ratio of the isotope 235 to the isotope 238 occurring in nature;
c. "international nuclear transport" means the carriage of a consignment of nuclear material by any means of transportation intended to go beyond the territory of the State where the shipment originates beginning with the departure from a facility of the shipper in that State and ending with the arrival at a facility of the receiver within the State of ultimate destination.

Article 2

1. This Convention shall apply to nuclear material used for peaceful purposes while in international nuclear transport.
2. With the exception of articles 3 and 4 and paragraph 3 of article 5, this Convention shall also apply to nuclear material used for peaceful purposes while in domestic use, storage and transport.
3. Apart from the commitments expressly undertaken by States Parties in the articles covered by paragraph 2 with respect to nuclear material used for peaceful purposes while in domestic use, storage and transport, nothing in this Convention shall be

interpreted as affecting the sovereign rights of a State regarding the domestic use, storage and transport of such nuclear material.

Article 3

Each State Party shall take appropriate steps within the framework of its national law and consistent with international law to ensure as far as practicable that, during international nuclear transport, nuclear material within its territory, or on board a ship or aircraft under its jurisdiction insofar as such ship or aircraft is engaged in the transport to or from that State, is protected at the levels described in Annex I.

Article 4

1. Each State Party shall not export or authorize the export of nuclear material unless the State Party has received assurances that such material will be protected during the international nuclear transport at the levels described in Annex I.
2. Each State Party shall not import or authorize the import of nuclear material from a State not party to this Convention unless the State Party has received assurances that such material will during the international nuclear transport be protected at the levels described in Annex I.
3. A State Party shall not allow the transit of its territory by land or internal waterways or through its airports or seaports of nuclear material between States that are not parties to this Convention unless the State Party has received assurances as far as practicable that this nuclear material will be protected during international nuclear transport at the levels described in Annex I.
4. Each State Party shall apply within the framework of its national law the levels of physical protection described in Annex I to nuclear material being transported from a part of that State to another part of the same State through international waters or airspace.
5. The State Party responsible for receiving assurances that the nuclear material will be protected at the levels described in Annex I according to paragraphs 1 to 3 shall identify and inform in advance States which the nuclear material is expected to transit by land or internal waterways, or whose airports or seaports it is expected to enter.
6. The responsibility for obtaining assurances referred to in paragraph 1 may be transferred, by mutual agreement, to the State Party involved in the transport as the importing State.
7. Nothing in this article shall be interpreted as in any way affecting the territorial sovereignty and jurisdiction of a State, including that over its airspace and territorial sea.

Article 5

1. States Parties shall identify and make known to each other directly or through the International Atomic Energy Agency their central authority and point of contact having responsibility for physical protection of nuclear material and for co-ordinating recovery and response operations in the event of any unauthorized removal, use or alteration of nuclear material or in the event of credible threat thereof.
2. In the case of theft, robbery or any other unlawful taking of nuclear material or of credible threat thereof, States Parties shall, in accordance with their national law, provide co-operation and assistance to the maximum feasible extent in the recovery and protection of such material to any State that so requests. In particular:
   a. a State Party shall take appropriate steps to inform as soon as possible other States, which appear to it to be concerned, of any theft, robbery or other unlawful taking of nuclear material or credible threat thereof and to inform, where appropriate, international organizations;
   b. as appropriate, the States Parties concerned shall exchange information with each other or international organizations with a view to protecting threatened nuclear material, verifying the integrity of the shipping container, or recovering unlawfully taken nuclear material and shall:
      i. co-ordinate their efforts through diplomatic and other agreed channels;
      ii. render assistance; if requested;
      iii. ensure the return of nuclear material stolen or missing as a consequence of the above-mentioned events.

   The means of implementation of this co-operation shall be determined by the States Parties concerned.
3. States Parties shall co-operate and consult as appropriate, with each other directly or through international organizations, with a view to obtaining guidance on the design, maintenance and improvement of systems of physical protection of nuclear material in international transport.

Article 6

1. States Parties shall take appropriate measures consistent with their national law to protect the confidentiality of any information which they receive in confidence by virtue of the provisions of this Convention form another State Party or through participation in an activity carried out for the implementation of this Convention. If States Parties provide information to international organizations in confidence, steps shall be taken to ensure that the confidentiality of such information is protected.

2. States Parties shall not be required by this Convention to provide any information which they are not permitted to communicate pursuant to national law or which would jeopardize the security of the State concerned or the physical protection of nuclear material.

Article 7

1. The intentional commission of:
   a. an act without lawful authority which constitutes the receipt, possession, use, transfer, alteration, disposal or dispersal of nuclear material and which causes or is likely to cause death or serious injury to any person or substantial damage to property;
   b. a theft of robbery of nuclear material;
   c. an embezzlement or fraudulent obtaining of nuclear material;
   d. an act constituting a demand for nuclear material by threat or use of force or by any other form of intimidation;
   e. a threat:
      i. to use nuclear material to cause death or serious injury to any person or substantial property damage, or
      ii. to commit an offence described in sub-paragraph (b) in order to compel a natural or legal person, international organization or State to do or to refrain from doing any act;
   f. an attempt to commit any offence described in paragraphs (a), (b) or (c); and
   g. an act which constitutes participation in any offence described in paragraphs (a) to (f)

   shall be made a punishable offence by each State Party under its national law.
2. Each State Party shall make the offences described in this article punishable by appropriate penalties which take into account their grave nature.

Article 8

1. Each State Party shall take such measures as may be necessary to establish its jurisdiction over the offences set forth in article 7 in the following cases;
   a. when the offence is committed in the territory of that State or on board a ship or aircraft registered in that State;
   b. when the alleged offender is a national of that State.
2. Each State Party shall likewise take such measures as may be necessary to establish its jurisdiction over these offences in cases where the alleged offender is presented in its territory and it does not extradite him pursuant to article 11 to any of the States mentioned in paragraph 1.

3. This Convention does not exclude any criminal jurisdiction exercised in accordance with national law.
4. In addition to the States Parties mentioned in paragraphs 1 and 2, each State Party may, consistent with international law, establish its jurisdiction over the offences set forth in article 7 when it is involved in international nuclear transport as the exporting or importing State.

Article 9

Upon being satisfied that the circumstances so warrant, the State Party in whose territory the alleged offender is present shall take appropriate measures, including detention, under its national law to ensure his presence for the purpose of prosecution or extradition. Measures taken according to this article shall be notified without delay to the States required to establish jurisdiction pursuant to article 8 and, where appropriate, all other States concerned.

Article 10

The State Party in whose territory the alleged offender is present shall, if it does not extradite him, submit, without exception whatsoever and without undue delay, the case to its competent authorities for the purpose of prosecution, through proceedings in accordance with the laws of that State.

Article 11

1. The offences in article 7 shall be deemed to be included as extraditable offences in any extradition treaty existing between States Parties. States Parties undertake to include those offences as extraditable offences in every future extradition treaty to be concluded between them.
2. If a State Party which makes extradition conditional on the existence of a treaty receives a request for extradition from another State Party with which it has no extradition treaty, it may at its option consider this Convention as the legal basis for extradition in respect of those offences. Extradition shall be subject to the other conditions provided by the law of the requested State.
3. States Parties which do not make extradition conditional on the existence of a treaty shall recognize those offences as extraditable offences between themselves subject to the conditions provided by the law of the requested State.
4. Each of the offences shall be treated, for the purpose of extradition between States Parties, as if it had been committed not only in the place in which it occurred but also in the territories of the States Parties required to establish their jurisdiction in accordance with paragraph 1 of article 8.

Article 12

Any person regarding whom proceedings are being carried out in connection with any of the offences set forth in article 7 shall be guaranteed fair treatment at all stages of the proceedings.

Article 13

1. States Parties shall afford one another the greatest measure of assistance in connection with criminal proceedings brought in respect of the offences set forth in article 7, including the supply of evidence at their disposal necessary for the proceedings. The law of the State requested shall apply in all cases.
2. The provisions of paragraph 1 shall not affect obligations under any other treaty, bilateral or multilateral, which governs or will govern, in whole or in part, mutual assistance in criminal matters.

Article 14

1. Each State Party shall inform the depositary of its laws and regulations which give effect to this Convention. The depositary shall communicate such information periodically to all States Parties.
2. The State Party where an alleged offender is prosecuted shall, wherever practicable, first communicate the final outcome of the proceedings to the States directly concerned. The State Party shall also communicate the final outcome to the depositary who shall inform all States.
3. Where an offence involves nuclear material used for peaceful purposes in domestic use, storage or transport, and both the alleged offender and the nuclear material remain in the territory of the State Party in which the offence was committed, nothing in this Convention shall be interpreted as requiring that State Party to provide information concerning criminal proceedings arising out of such an offence.

Article 15

The Annexes constitute an integral part of this Convention.

Article 16

1. A conference of States Parties shall be convened by the depositary of five years after the entry into force of this Convention to review the implementation of the

Convention and its adequacy as concerns the preamble, the whole of the operative part and the annexes in the light of the then prevailing situation.

2. At intervals of not less than five years thereafter, the majority of States Parties may obtain, by submitting a proposal to this effect to the depositary, the convening of further conferences with the same objective.

Article 17

1. In the event of a dispute between two or more States Parties concerning the interpretation or application of this Convention, such States Parties shall consult with a view to the settlement of the dispute by negotiation, or by any other peaceful means of settling disputes acceptable to all parties to the dispute.
2. Any dispute of this character which cannot be settled in the manner prescribed in paragraph 1 shall, at the request of any party to such dispute, be submitted to arbitration or referred to the International Court of Justice for decision. Where a dispute is submitted to arbitration, if, within six months from the date of the request, the parties to the dispute are unable to agree on the organization of the arbitration, a party may request the President of the International Court of Justice or the Secretary-General of the United Nations to appoint one or more arbitrators. In case of conflicting requests by the parties to the dispute, the request to the Secretary-General of the United Nations shall have priority.
3. Each State Party may at the time of signature, ratification, acceptance or approval of this Convention or accession thereto declare that it does not consider itself bound by either or both of the dispute settlement procedures provided for in paragraph 2. The other States Parties shall not be bound by a dispute settlement procedure provided for in paragraph 2, with respect to a State Party which has made a reservation to that procedure.
4. Any State Party which has made a reservation in accordance with paragraph 3 may at any time withdraw that reservation by notification to the depositary.

Article 18

1. This Convention shall be open for signature by all States at the Headquarters of the International Atomic Energy Agency in Vienna and at the Headquarters of the United Nations in New York from 3 March 1980 until its entry into force.
2. This Convention is subject to ratification, acceptance or approval by the signatory States.
3. After its entry into force, this Convention will be open for accession by all States.
4. (a) This Convention shall be open for signature or accession by international organizations and regional organizations of an integration or other nature, provided that any such organization is constituted by sovereign States and

has competence in respect of the negotiation, conclusion and application of international agreements in matters covered by this Convention.

(b) In matters within their competence, such organizations shall, on their own behalf, exercise the rights and fulfil the responsibilities which this Convention attributes to States Parties.

(c) When becoming party to this Convention such an organization shall communicate to the depository a declaration indicating which States are members thereof and which articles of this Convention do not apply to it.

(d) Such an organization shall not hold any vote additional to those of its Member States.

5. Instruments of ratification, acceptance, approval or accession shall be deposited with depositary.

Article 19

1. This Convention shall enter into force on the thirtieth day following the date of deposit of the twenty-first instrument of ratification, acceptance or approval with the depositary.
2. For each State ratifying, accepting, approving or acceding to the Convention after the date of deposit of the twenty-first instrument of ratification, acceptance or approval, the Convention shall enter into force on the thirtieth day after the deposit by such State of its instrument of ratification, acceptance, approval or accession.

Article 20

1. Without prejudice to article 16 a State Party may propose amendments to this Convention. The proposed amendment shall be submitted to the depositary who shall circulate it immediately to all States Parties. If a majority of States Parties request the depositary to convene a conference to consider the proposed amendments, the depositary shall invite all States Parties to attend such a conference to being not sooner than thirty days after the invitations are issued. Any amendment adopted at the conference by a two-thirds majority of all States Parties shall be promptly circulated by the depositary to all States Parties.
2. The amendment shall enter into force for each State Party that deposits its instrument of ratification, acceptance or approval of the amendment on the thirtieth day after the date on which two thirds of the States Parties have deposited their instruments of ratification, acceptance or approval with the depositary. Thereafter, the amendment shall enter into force for nay other State Party on the day on which that State Party deposits its instrument of ratification, acceptance or approval of the amendment.

Article 21

1. Any State Party any denounce this Convention by written notification to the depositary.
2. Denunciation shall take effect one hundred and eighty days following the date on which notification is received by the depositary.

Article 22

The depositary shall promptly notify all States of:
a. each signature of this Convention;
b. each deposit of an instrument of ratification, acceptance, approval or accession;
c. any reservation or withdrawal in accordance with article 17;
d. any communication made by an organization in accordance with paragraph 4(c) of article 18;
e. the entry into force of this Convention;
f. the entry into force of any amendment to this Convention; and
g. any denunciation made under article 21.

Article 23

The original of this Convention, of which the Arabic, Chinese, English, French, Russian and Spanish texts are equally authentic, shall be deposited with the Director General of the International Atomic Energy Agency who shall send certified copies thereof to all States.

IN WITNESS WHEREOF, the undersigned, being duly authorized, have signed this Convention, opened for signature at Vienna and at New York on 3 March 1980.

ANNEX 1
LEVELS OF PHYSICAL PROTECTION TO BE APPLIED IN INTERNATIONAL TRANSPORT OF NUCLEAR MATERIALS AS CATEGORIZED IN ANNEX II

1. Levels of physical protection for nuclear material during storage incidental to international nuclear transport include:
   a. For Category III materials, storage within an area to which access is controlled;
   b. For Category II materials, storage within an area under constant surveillance by guards or electronic devices, surrounded by a physical barrier with a limited number of points of entry under appropriate control or any area with an equivalent level of physical protection;

c. For Category I material, storage within a protected area as defined for Category II above, to which, in addition, access is restricted to persons whose trustworthiness has been determined, and which is under surveillance by guards who are in close communication with appropriate responses forces. Specific measures taken in this context should have as their object the detection and prevention of any assault, unauthorized access or unauthorized removal of material.

2. Levels of physical protection for nuclear material during international transport include:

a. For Category II and III materials, transportation shall take place under special precautions including prior arrangements among sender, receiver, and carrier, and prior agreement between natural or legal persons subject to the jurisdiction and regulation of exporting and importing States, specifying time, place and procedures for transferring transport responsibility;

a. For Category I materials, transportation shall take place under special precautions identified above for transportation of Category II and III materials, and in addition, under constant surveillance by escorts and under conditions which assure close communication with appropriate response forces;

b. For natural uranium other than in the form of ore or ore-residue; transportation protection for quantities exceeding 500 kilograms uranium shall include advance notification of shipment specifying mode of transport, expected time of arrival and confirmation of receipt of shipment.

ANNEX II
TABLE: CATEGORIZATION OF NUCLEAR MATERIAL

Material	Form	Category		
		I	II	III[c/]
1. Plutonium[a/]	Unirradiated[b/]	2 kg or more	Less than 2 kg but more than 500 g	500 g or less but more than 15 g
2. Uranium-235	Unirradiated[b/] • uranium enriched to 20% ^{235}U or more • uranium enriched to 10% ^{235}U but less than 20% • uranium enriched above natural, but less than 10% ^{235}U	5 kg or more	Less than 5 kg but more than 1 kg 10 kg or more	1 kg or less but more than 15 g Less than 10 kg but more than 1 kg 10 kg or more
3. Uranium-233	Unirradiated[b/]	2 kg or more	Less than 2 kg but more than 500 kg	500 g or less but more than 15 g
4. Irradiated fuel			Depleted or natural urnaium, thorium or low-enriched fuel (less than 10% fossile content)[d/e/]	

[a/] All plutonium except that with isotopic concentration exceeding 80% in plutonium-238.

[b/] Material not irradiated in a reactor or material irradiated in a reactor but with a radiation level equal to or less than 100 rads/hour at one meter unshielded.

[c/] Quantities not falling in Category III and natural uranium should be protected in accordance

SECTION TWO
INTERNATIONAL TREATIES ON DE-NUCLEARIZATION

ANTARCTIC TREATY

(Washington, 1 December 1959)

This Treaty, which is not solely concerned with nuclear energy, was concluded among a number of countries of all the continents and entered info force on 23 June 1961. The treaty governs the co-operation among contracting parties to it in exploring and exploiting Antarctica for peaceful purposes, and it aims to ensure its "neutral" status.

Article I prohibits, together with military bases and manoeuvres, "the testing of any type of weapons" (therefore including nuclear ones), while article V provides more directly as to the prohibition of nuclear explosions and the disposal of radioactive waste.
Given their historical importance, besides article V, the preamble, articles I (purpose), VI (geographical scope) and XIV (final provisions) art worth recalling here.

A Protocol (not published here) to the Treaty, concerning the protection of the environment, was adopted in 1991, its general scope covering also protection from radioactive pollution. The original number of contracting Parties was 12, and the acceding States have so far become 44.

The Governments of Argentina, Australia, Belgium, Chile, the French Republic, Japan, New Zealand, Norway, the Union of South Africa, the Union of Soviet Socialist Republics, the United Kingdom of Great Britain and Northern Ireland, and the United States of America,

Recognizing that it is in the interest of all mankind that Antarctica shall continue for ever to be used exclusively for peaceful purposes and shall not become the scene or object of international discord;

Acknowledging the substantial contributions to scientific knowledge resulting from international cooperation in scientific investigation in Antarctica;

Convinced that the establishment of a firm foundation for the continuation and development of such cooperation on the basis of freedom of scientific investigation in Antarctica as applied during the International Geophysical Year accords with the interests of science and the progress of all mankind;

Convinced also that a treaty ensuring the use of Antarctica for peaceful purposes only and the continuance of international harmony in Antarctica will further the purposes and principles embodied in the Charter of the United Nations;

Have agreed as follows:

Article I

1. Antarctica shall be used for peaceful purposes only. There shall be prohibited, *inter alia* , any measure of a military nature, such as the establishment of military bases and fortifications, the carrying out of military manoeuvres, as well as the testing of any type of weapon.
2. The present Treaty shall not prevent the use of military personnel or equipment for scientific research or for any other peaceful purpose.

Article V

1. Any nuclear explosions in Antarctica and the disposal there of radioactive waste material shall be prohibited.
2. In the event of the conclusion of international agreements concerning the use of nuclear energy, including nuclear explosions and the disposal of radioactive waste material, to which all of the Contracting Parties whose representatives are entitled to participate in the meetings provided for under Article IX are parties, the rules established under such agreements shall apply in Antarctica.

Article VI

The provisions of the present Treaty shall apply to the area south of 60° South Latitude, including all ice shelves, but nothing in the present Treaty shall prejudice or in any way affect the rights, or the exercise of the rights, of any State under international law with regard to the high seas within that area.

Article XIV

The present Treaty, done in the English, French, Russian and Spanish languages, each version being equally authentic, shall be deposited in the archives of the Government of the United States of America, which shall transmit duly certified copies thereof to the Governments of the signatory and acceding States

TREATY BANNING NUCLEAR WEAPON TESTS IN THE ATMOSPHERE, IN OUTER SPACE AND UNDER WATER (TBT) AND COMPREHENSIVE NUCLEAR TEST BAN TREATY (CTBT)

(Moscow, 5 August 1963, New York, 10 September 1996)

Since the spreading and the intensiveness of nuclear tests, with serious radioactive fallout, had reached in the early sixties a considerable level creating worrying problems in terms of health protection on a worldwide scale, the most advanced nuclear countries at the time (the USA, the Soviet Union and the United Kingdom) decided to conclude an agreement addressing the discontinuation of such tests. The main aim of the agreement was "the speediest possible achievement......of general and complete disarmament under strict international control in accordance with the objective of the United Nations". This was intended to "put an end to the armaments race and eliminate the production and testing of all kind of weapons" including nuclear ones, which in its turn would result in putting an end "to the contamination of man's environment by radioactive substances". The Test Ban Treaty (TBT) was signed on 5 August 1963 by the three countries of above (referred to as "the original parties"), was open for signature to all States and is of unlimited duration. Under article III, its entry into force would occur after ratification by the original parties.

Achieving the ban ***of all nuclear weapon tests for all the time****, however, had been the object of discussions started way back in the early 60's, which had continued at various levels leading eventually to the setting up of a Conference on Disarmament, within which (namely an "ad hoc" committee) the issue of a new instrument on comprehensive banning was formally considered as of 1982. In the meantime, other treaties addressed de-nuclearisation of certain areas of the globe (Tlatelolco Treaty of 1967, Rarotonga Treaty of 1985, see further on in this Section). Besides, the conclusion of the Treaty on the non-proliferation of nuclear weapons (NPT, see Section One) in 1968 had been a landmark in the history of nuclear non-proliferation. In fact, it may be said that the indefinite extension of the NPT in 1995 (see Introductory Material) marked a turning point in the negotiations on a comprehensive nuclear test ban treaty (CTBT), which had started in 1994 and continued for over two years. While disagreement was strong during the first stage of negotiations, these became more intensive on the preliminary draft as of May 1995 and later on (March 1996) on a finalised text proposed by the chairman of the afore-mentioned "ad hoc" committee. Nevertheless, for the actual adoption of the treaty a Resolution of the General Assembly of the United Nations was voted on September 10. It is recalled that, while the Conference on Disarmament decides based on consensus, the*

UN General Assembly may decide based on majority, as indeed was the case for the CTBT (158 countries in favour). This was opened to signature on September 24, 1996.

The entry into force of the Treaty was established at six months after ratification by 44 countries, between those members of the Conference on Disarmament up to 18 June 1996 (i.e. before it was expanded to 61 countries) and those having nuclear power and research reactors, as per a list set up by the IAEA. The contracting Parties to the CTBT are 119. While annexes 1 and 2 are published here, the very extensive Protocol and its annexes are omitted.

Published here is also the text of the 1963 Treaty, given its historical importance in the subject matter.

TREATY BANNING NUCLEAR WEAPON TESTS IN THE ATMOSPHERE, OUTER SPACE AND UNDER WATER

The Governments of the United States of America, the United Kingdom of Great Britain and Northern Ireland, and the Union of Soviet Socialist Republics, hereinafter referred to as the "Original Parties",

Proclaiming as their principal aim the speediest possible achievement of an agreement on general and complete disarmament under strict international control in accordance with the objectives of the United Nations which would put an end to the armaments race and eliminate the incentive to the production and testing of all kinds of weapons, including nuclear weapons,

Seeking to achieve the discontinuance of all test explosions of nuclear weapons for all time, determined to continue negotiations to this end, and desiring to put an end to the contamination of man's environment by radioactive substances,

Have agreed as follows:

Article I

1. Each of the Parties to this Treaty undertakes to prohibit, to prevent, and not to carry out any nuclear weapon test explosion, or any other nuclear explosion, at any place under its jurisdiction or control:

(a) in the atmosphere; beyond its limits, including outer space; or under water, including territorial waters or high seas; or

(b) in any other environment if such explosion causes radioactive debris to be present outside the territorial limits of the State under whose jurisdiction or control such explosion is conducted. It is understood in this connection that the provisions of this subparagraph are without prejudice to the conclusion of a treaty resulting in the permanent banning of all nuclear test explosions, including all such explosions underground, the conclusion of which, as the Parties have stated in the Preamble to this Treaty, they seek to achieve.

2. Each of the Parties to this Treaty undertakes furthermore to refrain from causing, encouraging, or in any way participating in, the carrying out of any nuclear weapon test explosion, or any other nuclear explosion, anywhere which would take place in any of the environments described, or have the effect referred to, in paragraph 1 of this Article.

Article II

1. Any Party may propose amendments to this Treaty. The text of any proposed amendment shall be submitted to the Depositary Governments which shall circulate it to all Parties to this Treaty. Thereafter, if requested to do so by one-third or more of the Parties, the Depositary Governments shall convene a conference, to which they shall invite all the Parties, to consider such amendment.
2. Any amendment to this Treaty must be approved by a majority of the votes of all the Parties to this Treaty, including the votes of all of the Original Parties. The amendment shall enter into force for all Parties upon the deposit of instruments of ratification by a majority of all the Parties, including the instruments of ratification of all of the Original Parties.

Article III

1. This Treaty shall be open to all States for signature. Any State which does not sign this Treaty before its entry into force in accordance with paragraph 3 of this Article may accede to it at any time.
2. This Treaty shall be subject to ratification by signatory States. Instruments of ratification and instruments of accession shall be deposited with the Governments of the Original Parties – the United States of America, the United Kingdom of Great Britain and Northern Ireland, and the Union of Soviet Socialist Republics – which are hereby designated the Depositary Governments.
3. This Treaty shall enter into force after its ratification by all the Original Parties and the deposit of their instruments of ratification.

4. For States whose instruments of ratification or accession are deposited subsequent to the entry into force of this Treaty, it shall enter into force on the date of the deposit of their instruments of ratification or accession.
5. The Depositary Governments shall promptly inform all signatory and acceding States of the date of each signature, the date of deposit of each instrument of ratification of and accession to this Treaty, the date of its entry into force, and the date of receipt of any requests for conferences or other notices.
6. This Treaty shall be registered by the Depositary Governments pursuant to Article 102 of the Charter of the United Nations.

Article IV

This Treaty shall be of unlimited duration.
Each Party shall in exercising its national sovereignty have the right to withdraw from the Treaty if it decides that extraordinary events, related to the subject matter of this Treaty, have jeopardized the supreme interests of its country. It shall give notice of such withdrawal to all other Parties to the Treaty three months in advance.

Article V

This Treaty, of which the English and Russian texts are equally authentic, shall be deposited in the archives of the Depositary Governments. Duly certified copies of this Treaty shall be transmitted by the Depositary Governments to the Governments of the signatory and acceding States.

IN WITNESS WHEREOF the undersigned, duly authorized, have signed this Treaty. DONE in triplicate at the city of Moscow the fifth day of August, one thousand nine hundred and sixty-three.

COMPREHENSIVE NUCLEAR TEST BAN TREATY

PREAMBLE

The States Parties to this Treaty (hereinafter referred to as "the States Parties"),

Welcoming the international agreements and other positive measures of recent years in the field of nuclear disarmament, including reductions in arsenals of nuclear weapons, as well as in the field of the prevention of nuclear proliferation in all its aspects,

Underlining the importance of the full and prompt implementation of such agreements and measures,
Convinced that the present international situation provides an opportunity to take further effective measures towards nuclear disarmament and against the proliferation of nuclear weapons in all its aspects, and declaring their intention to take such measures,
Stressing therefore the need for continued systematic and progressive efforts to reduce nuclear weapons globally, with the ultimate goal of eliminating those weapons, and of general and complete disarmament under strict and effective international control,
Recognizing that the cessation of all nuclear weapon test explosions and all other nuclear explosions, by constraining the development and qualitative improvement of nuclear weapons and ending the development of advanced new types of nuclear weapons, constitutes an effective measure of nuclear disarmament and non-proliferation in all its aspects,
Further recognizing that an end to all such nuclear explosions will thus constitute a meaningful step in the realization of a systematic process to achieve nuclear disarmament,
Convinced that the most effective way to achieve an end to nuclear testing is through the conclusion of a universal and internationally and effectively verifiable comprehensive nuclear test-ban treaty, which has long been one of the highest priority objectives of the international community in the field of disarmament and non-proliferation,
Noting the aspirations expressed by the Parties to the 1963 Treaty Banning Nuclear Weapon Tests in the Atmosphere, in Outer Space and Under Water to seek to achieve the discontinuance of all test explosions of nuclear weapons for all time,
Noting also the views expressed that this Treaty could contribute to the protection of the environment,
Affirming the purpose of attracting the adherence of all States to this Treaty and its objective to contribute effectively to the prevention of the proliferation of nuclear weapons in all its aspects, to the process of nuclear disarmament and therefore to the enhancement of international peace and security,

Have agreed as follows:

Article I
Basic obligations

1. Each State Party undertakes not to carry out any nuclear weapon test explosion or any other nuclear explosion, and to prohibit and prevent any such nuclear explosion at any place under its jurisdiction or control.

2. Each State Party undertakes, furthermore, to refrain from causing, encouraging, or in any way participating in the carrying out of any nuclear weapon test explosion or any other nuclear explosion.

Article II
The organization

A. GENERAL PROVISIONS

1. The States Parties hereby establish the Comprehensive Nuclear-Test-Ban Treaty Organization (hereinafter referred to as "the Organization") to achieve the object and purpose of this Treaty, to ensure the implementation of its provisions, including those for international verification of compliance with it, and to provide a forum for consultation and cooperation among States Parties.
2. All States Parties shall be members of the Organization. A State Party shall not be deprived of its membership in the Organization.
3. The seat of the Organization shall be Vienna, Republic of Austria.
4. There are hereby established as organs of the Organization: the Conference of the States Parties, the Executive Council and the Technical Secretariat, which shall include the International Data Centre.
5. Each State Party shall cooperate with the Organization in the exercise of its functions in accordance with this Treaty. States Parties shall consult, directly among themselves, or through the Organization or other appropriate international procedures, including procedures within the framework of the United Nations and in accordance with its Charter, on any matter which may be raised relating to the object and purpose, or the implementation of the provisions, of this Treaty.
6. The Organization shall conduct its verification activities provided for under this Treaty in the least intrusive manner possible consistent with the timely and efficient accomplishment of their objectives. It shall request only the information and data necessary to fulfil its responsibilities under this Treaty. It shall take every precaution to protect the confidentiality of information on civil and military activities and facilities coming to its knowledge in the implementation of this Treaty and, in particular, shall abide by the confidentiality provisions set forth in this Treaty.
7. Each State Party shall treat as confidential and afford special handling to information and data that it receives in confidence from the Organization in connection with the implementation of this Treaty. It shall treat such information and data exclusively in connection with its rights and obligations under this Treaty.
8. The Organization, as an independent body, shall seek to utilize existing expertise and facilities, as appropriate, and to maximize cost efficiencies, through cooperative arrangements with other international organizations such as the International Atomic Energy Agency. Such arrangements, excluding those of a minor and normal

commercial and contractual nature, shall be set out in agreements to be submitted to the Conference of the States Parties for approval.
9. The costs of the activities of the Organization shall be met annually by the States Parties in accordance with the United Nations scale of assessments adjusted to take into account differences in membership between the United Nations and the Organization.
10. Financial contributions of States Parties to the Preparatory Commission shall be deducted in an appropriate way from their contributions to the regular budget.
11. A member of the Organization which is in arrears in the payment of its assessed contribution to the Organization shall have no vote in the Organization if the amount of its arrears equals or exceeds the amount of the contribution due from it for the preceding two full years. The Conference of the States Parties may, nevertheless, permit such a member to vote if it is satisfied that the failure to pay is due to conditions beyond the control of the member.

B. THE CONFERENCE OF THE STATES PARTIES

Composition, Procedures and Decision-making

12. The Conference of the States Parties (hereinafter referred to as "the Conference") shall be composed of all States Parties. Each State Party shall have one representative in the Conference, who may be accompanied by alternates and advisers.
13. The initial session of the Conference shall be convened by the Depositary no later than 30 days after the entry into force of this Treaty.
14. The Conference shall meet in regular sessions, which shall be held annually, unless it decides otherwise.
15. A special session of the Conference shall be convened:
(a) When decided by the Conference;
(b) When requested by the Executive Council; or
(c) When requested by any State Party and supported by a majority of the States Parties.

The special session shall be convened no later than 30 days after the decision of the Conference, the request of the Executive Council, or the attainment of the necessary support, unless specified otherwise in the decision or request.
16. The Conference may also be convened in the form of an Amendment Conference, in accordance with Article VII.
17. The Conference may also be convened in the form of a Review Conference in accordance with Article VIII.
18. Sessions shall take place at the seat of the Organization unless the Conference decides otherwise.

19. The Conference shall adopt its rules of procedure. At the beginning of each session, it shall elect its President and such other officers as may be required. They shall hold office until a new President and other officers are elected at the next session.
20. A majority of the States Parties shall constitute a quorum.
21. Each State Party shall have one vote.
22. The Conference shall take decisions on matters of procedure by a majority of members present and voting. Decisions on matters of substance shall be taken as far as possible by consensus. If consensus is not attainable when an issue comes up for decision, the President of the Conference shall defer any vote for 24 hours and during this period of deferment shall make every effort to facilitate achievement of consensus, and shall report to the Conference before the end of this period. If consensus is not possible at the end of 24 hours, the Conference shall take a decision by a two-thirds majority of members present and voting unless specified otherwise in this Treaty. When the issue arises as to whether the question is one of substance or not, that question shall be treated as a matter of substance unless otherwise decided by the majority required for decisions on matters of substance.
23. When exercising its function under paragraph 26 (k), the Conference shall take a decision to add any State to the list of States contained in Annex 1 to this Treaty in accordance with the procedure for decisions on matters of substance set out in paragraph 22. Notwithstanding paragraph 22, the Conference shall take decisions on any other change to Annex 1 to this Treaty by consensus.

Powers and Functions

24. The Conference shall be the principal organ of the Organization. It shall consider any questions, matters or issues within the scope of this Treaty, including those relating to the powers and functions of the Executive Council and the Technical Secretariat, in accordance with this Treaty. It may make recommendations and take decisions on any questions, matters or issues within the scope of this Treaty raised by a State Party or brought to its attention by the Executive Council.
25. The Conference shall oversee the implementation of, and review compliance with, this Treaty and act in order to promote its object and purpose. It shall also oversee the activities of the Executive Council and the Technical Secretariat and may issue guidelines to either of them for the exercise of their functions.
26. The Conference shall:
(a) Consider and adopt the report of the Organization on the implementation of this Treaty and the annual programme and budget of the Organization, submitted by the Executive Council, as well as consider other reports;
(b) Decide on the scale of financial contributions to be paid by States Parties in accordance with paragraph 9;
(c) Elect the members of the Executive Council;

(d) Appoint the Director-General of the Technical Secretariat (hereinafter referred to as "the Director-General");
(e) Consider and approve the rules of procedure of the Executive Council submitted by the latter;
(f) Consider and review scientific and technological developments that could affect the operation of this Treaty. In this context, the Conference may direct the Director-General to establish a Scientific Advisory Board to enable him or her, in the performance of his or her functions, to render specialized advice in areas of science and technology relevant to this Treaty to the Conference, to the Executive Council or to States Parties. In that case, the Scientific Advisory Board shall be composed of independent experts serving in their individual capacity and appointed, in accordance with terms of reference adopted by the Conference, on the basis of their expertise and experience in the particular scientific fields relevant to the implementation of this Treaty;
(g) Take the necessary measures to ensure compliance with this Treaty and to redress and remedy any situation that contravenes the provisions of this Treaty, in accordance with Article V;
(h) Consider and approve at its initial session any draft agreements, arrangements, provisions, procedures, operational manuals, guidelines and any other documents developed and recommended by the Preparatory Commission;
(i) Consider and approve agreements or arrangements negotiated by the Technical Secretariat with States Parties, other States and international organizations to be concluded by the Executive Council on behalf of the Organization in accordance with paragraph 38 (h);
(j) Establish such subsidiary organs as it finds necessary for the exercise of its functions in accordance with this Treaty; and
(k) Update Annex 1 to this Treaty, as appropriate, in accordance with paragraph 23.

C. THE EXECUTIVE COUNCIL

Composition, Procedures and Decision-making

27. The Executive Council shall consist of 51 members. Each State Party shall have the right, in accordance with the provisions of this Article, to serve on the Executive Council.
28. Taking into account the need for equitable geographical distribution, the Executive Council shall comprise:
(a) Ten States Parties from Africa;
(b) Seven States Parties from Eastern Europe;
(c) Nine States Parties from Latin America and the Caribbean;
(d) Seven States Parties from the Middle East and South Asia;

(e) Ten States Parties from North America and Western Europe; and
(f) Eight States Parties from South-East Asia, the Pacific and the Far East.

All States in each of the above geographical regions are listed in Annex 1 to this Treaty. Annex 1 to this Treaty shall be updated, as appropriate, by the Conference in accordance with paragraphs 23 and 26 (k). It shall not be subject to amendments or changes under the procedures contained in Article VII.

29. The members of the Executive Council shall be elected by the Conference. In this connection, each geographical region shall designate States Parties from that region for election as members of the Executive Council as follows:

(a) At least one-third of the seats allocated to each geographical region shall be filled, taking into account political and security interests by States Parties in that region designated on the basis of the nuclear capabilities relevant to the Treaty as determined by international data as well as all or any of the following indicative criteria in the order of priority determined by each region:
    (i) Number of monitoring facilities of the International Monitoring System;
    (ii) Expertise and experience in monitoring technology; and
    (iii) Contribution to the annual budget of the Organization;
(b) One of the seats allocated to each geographical region shall be filled on a rotational basis by the State Party that is first in the English alphabetical order among the States Parties in that region that have not served as members of the Executive Council for the longest period of time since becoming States Parties or since their last term, whichever is shorter. A State Party designated on this basis may decide to forgo its seat. In that case, such a State Party shall submit a letter of renunciation to the Director-General, and the seat shall be filled by the State Party following next-in-order according to this sub-paragraph; and
(c) The remaining seats allocated to each geographical region shall be filled by States Parties designated from among all the States Parties in that region by rotation or elections.

30. Each member of the Executive Council shall have one representative on the Executive Council, who may be accompanied by alternates and advisers.

31. Each member of the Executive Council shall hold office from the end of the session of the Conference at which that member is elected until the end of the second regular annual session of the Conference thereafter, except that for the first election of the Executive Council, 26 members shall be elected to hold office until the end of the third regular annual session of the Conference, due regard being paid to the established numerical proportions as described in paragraph 28.

32. The Executive Council shall elaborate its rules of procedure and submit them to the Conference for approval.

33. The Executive Council shall elect its Chairman from among its members.

34. The Executive Council shall meet for regular sessions. Between regular sessions it shall meet as may be required for the fulfilment of its powers and functions.
35. Each member of the Executive Council shall have one vote.
36. The Executive Council shall take decisions on matters of procedure by a majority of all its members. The Executive Council shall take decisions on matters of substance by a two-thirds majority of all its members unless specified otherwise in this Treaty. When the issue arises as to whether the question is one of substance or not, that question shall be treated as a matter of substance unless otherwise decided by the majority required for decisions on matters of substance.

Powers and Functions

37. The Executive Council shall be the executive organ of the Organization. It shall be responsible to the Conference. It shall carry out the powers and functions entrusted to it in accordance with this Treaty. In so doing, it shall act in conformity with the recommendations, decisions and guidelines of the Conference and ensure their continuous and proper implementation.
38. The Executive Council shall:
(a) Promote effective implementation of, and compliance with, this Treaty;
(b) Supervise the activities of the Technical Secretariat;
(c) Make recommendations as necessary to the Conference for consideration of further proposals for promoting the object and purpose of this Treaty ;
(d) Cooperate with the National Authority of each State Party;
(e) Consider and submit to the Conference the draft annual programme and budget of the Organization, the draft report of the Organization on the implementation of this Treaty, the report on the performance of its own activities and such other reports as it deems necessary or that the Conference may request;
(f) Make arrangements for the sessions of the Conference, including the preparation of the draft agenda;
(g) Examine proposals for changes, on matters of an administrative or technical nature, to the Protocol or the Annexes thereto, pursuant to Article VII, and make recommendations to the States Parties regarding their adoption;
(h) Conclude, subject to prior approval of the Conference, agreements or arrangements with States Parties, other States and international organizations on behalf of the Organization and supervise their implementation, with the exception of agreements or arrangements referred to in sub-paragraph (i);
(i) Approve and supervise the operation of agreements or arrangements relating to the implementation of verification activities with States Parties and other States; and
(j) Approve any new operational manuals and any changes to the existing operational manuals that may be proposed by the Technical Secretariat.

39. The Executive Council may request a special session of the Conference.
40. The Executive Council shall:
(a) Facilitate cooperation among States Parties, and between States Parties and the Technical Secretariat, relating to the implementation of this Treaty through information exchanges;
(b) Facilitate consultation and clarification among States Parties in accordance with Article IV; and
(c) Receive, consider and take action on requests for, and reports on, on-site inspections in accordance with Article IV.

41. The Executive Council shall consider any concern raised by a State Party about possible non-compliance with this Treaty and abuse of the rights established by this Treaty. In doing so, the Executive Council shall consult with the States Parties involved and, as appropriate, request a State Party to take measures to redress the situation within a specified time. To the extent that the Executive Council considers further action to be necessary, it shall take, *inter alia*, one or more of the following measures:
(a) Notify all States Parties of the issue or matter;
(b) Bring the issue or matter to the attention of the Conference;
(c) Make recommendations to the Conference or take action, as appropriate, regarding measures to redress the situation and to ensure compliance in accordance with Article V.

D. THE TECHNICAL SECRETARIAT

42. The Technical Secretariat shall assist States Parties in the implementation of this Treaty. The Technical Secretariat shall assist the Conference and the Executive Council in the performance of their functions. The Technical Secretariat shall carry out the verification and other function entrusted to it by this Treaty, as well as those functions delegated to it by the Conference or the Executive Council in accordance with this Treaty. The Technical Secretariat shall include, as an integral part, the International Data Centre.
43. The functions of the Technical Secretariat with regard to verification of compliance with this Treaty shall, in accordance with Article IV and the Protocol, include *inter alia*:
(a) Being responsible for supervising and coordinating the operation of the International Monitoring System;
(b) Operating the International Data Centre;
(c) Routinely receiving, processing, analysing and reporting on International Monitoring System data;
(d) Providing technical assistance in, and support for, the installation and operation of monitoring stations;

(e) Assisting the Executive Council in facilitating consultation and clarification among States Parties;
(f) Receiving requests for on-site inspections and processing them, facilitating Executive Council consideration of such requests, carrying out the preparations for, and providing technical support during, the conduct of on-site inspections, and reporting to the Executive Council;
(g) Negotiating agreements or arrangements with States Parties, other States and international organizations and concluding, subject to prior approval by the Executive Council, any such agreements or arrangements relating to verification activities with States Parties or other States; and
(h) Assisting the States Parties through their National Authorities on other issues of verification under this Treaty.

44. The Technical Secretariat shall develop and maintain, subject to approval by the Executive Council, operational manuals to guide the operation of the various components of the verification regime, in accordance with Article IV and the Protocol. These manuals shall not constitute integral parts of this Treaty or the Protocol and may be changed by the Technical Secretariat subject to approval by the Executive Council. The Technical Secretariat shall promptly inform the States Parties of any changes in the operational manuals.
45. The functions of the Technical Secretariat with respect to administrative matters shall include:
(a) Preparing and submitting to the Executive Council the draft programme and budget of the Organization;
(b) Preparing and submitting to the Executive Council the draft report of the Organization on the implementation of this Treaty and such other reports as the Conference or the Executive Council may request;
(c) Providing administrative and technical support to the Conference, the Executive Council and other subsidiary organs;
(d) Addressing and receiving communications on behalf of the Organization relating to the implementation of this Treaty; and
(e) Carrying out the administrative responsibilities related to any agreements between the Organization and other international organizations.

46. All requests and notifications by States Parties to the Organization shall be transmitted through their National Authorities to the Director-General. Requests and notifications shall be in one of the official languages of this Treaty. In response the Director-General shall use the language of the transmitted request or notification.
47. With respect to the responsibilities of the Technical Secretariat for preparing and submitting to the Executive Council the draft programme and budget of the Organization, the Technical Secretariat shall determine and maintain a clear accounting of

all costs for each facility established as part of the International Monitoring System. Similar treatment in the draft programme and budget shall be accorded to all other activities of the Organization.

48. The Technical Secretariat shall promptly inform the Executive Council of any problems that have arisen with regard to the discharge of its functions that have come to its notice in the performance of its activities and that it has been unable to resolve through consultations with the State Party concerned.

49. The Technical Secretariat shall comprise a Director-General, who shall be its head and chief administrative officer, and such scientific, technical and other personnel as may be required. The Director-General shall be appointed by the Conference upon the recommendation of the Executive Council for a term of four years, renewable for one further term, but not thereafter. The first Director-General shall be appointed by the Conference at its initial session upon the recommendation of the Preparatory Commission.

50. The Director-General shall be responsible to the Conference and the Executive Council for the appointment of the staff and for the organization and functioning of the Technical Secretariat. The paramount consideration in the employment of the staff and in the determination of the conditions of service shall be the necessity of securing the highest standards of professional expertise, experience, efficiency, competence and integrity. Only citizens of States Parties shall serve as the Director-General, as inspectors or as members of the professional and clerical staff. Due regard shall be paid to the importance of recruiting the staff on as wide a geographical basis as possible. Recruitment shall be guided by the principle that the staff shall be kept to the minimum necessary for the proper discharge of the responsibilities of the Technical Secretariat.

51. The Director-General may, as appropriate, after consultation with the Executive Council, establish temporary working groups of scientific experts to provide recommendations on specific issues.

52. In the performance of their duties, the Director-General, the inspectors, the inspection assistants and the members of the staff shall not seek or receive instructions from any Government or from any other source external to the Organization. They shall refrain from any action that might reflect adversely on their positions as international officers responsible only to the Organization. The Director-General shall assume responsibility for the activities of an inspection team.

53. Each State Party shall respect the exclusively international character of the responsibilities of the Director-General, the inspectors, the inspection assistants and the members of the staff and shall not seek to influence them in the discharge of their responsibilities.

E. PRIVILEGES AND IMMUNITIES

54. The Organization shall enjoy on the territory and in any other place under the jurisdiction or control of a State Party such legal capacity and such privileges and immunities as are necessary for the exercise of its functions.

55. Delegates of States Parties, together with their alternates and advisers, representatives of members elected to the Executive Council, together with their alternates and advisers, the Director-General, the inspectors, the inspection assistants and the members of the staff of the Organization shall enjoy such privileges and immunities as are necessary in the independent exercise of their functions in connection with the Organization.

56. The legal capacity, privileges and immunities referred to in this Article shall be defined in agreements between the Organization and the State Parties as well as in an agreement between the Organization and the State in which the Organization is seated. Such agreements shall be considered and approved in accordance with paragraph 26 (h) and (i).

57. Notwithstanding paragraphs 54 and 55, the privileges and immunities enjoyed by the Director-General, the inspectors, the inspection assistants and the members of the staff of the Technical Secretariat during the conduct of verification activities shall be those set forth in the Protocol.

Article III
National implementation measures

1. Each State Party shall, in accordance with its constitutional processes, take any necessary measures to implement its obligations under this Treaty. In particular, it shall take any necessary measures:

(a) To prohibit natural and legal persons anywhere on its territory or in any other place under its jurisdiction as recognized by international law from undertaking any activity prohibited to a State Party under this Treaty;

(b) To prohibit natural and legal persons from undertaking any such activity anywhere under its control; and

(c) To prohibit, in conformity with international law, natural persons possessing its nationality from undertaking any such activity anywhere.

2. Each State Party shall cooperate with other States Parties and afford the appropriate form of legal assistance to facilitate the implementation of the obligations under paragraph 1.

3. Each State Party shall inform the Organization of the measures taken pursuant to this Article.

4. In order to fulfill its obligations under the Treaty, each State Party shall designate or set up a National Authority and shall so inform the Organization upon entry into

force of the Treaty for it. The National Authority shall serve as the national focal point for liaison with the Organization and with other States Parties.

Article IV
Verification

A. GENERAL PROVISIONS

1. In order to verify compliance with this Treaty, a verification regime shall be established consisting of the following elements:
(a) An International Monitoring System;
(b) Consultation and clarification;
(c) On-site inspections; and
(d) Confidence-building measures.
At entry into force of this Treaty, the verification regime shall be capable of meeting the verification requirements of this Treaty.
2. Verification activities shall be based on objective information, shall be limited to the subject matter of this Treaty, and shall be carried out on the basis of full respect for the sovereignty of States Parties and in the least intrusive manner possible consistent with the effective and timely accomplishment of their objectives. Each State Party shall refrain from any abuse of the right of verification.
3. Each State Party undertakes in accordance with this Treaty to cooperate through its National Authority established pursuant to Article III, paragraph 4, with the Organization and with other States Parties to facilitate the verification of compliance with this Treaty by, *inter alia*:
(a) Establishing the necessary facilities to participate in these verification measures and establishing the necessary communication;
(b) Providing data obtained from national stations that are part of the International Monitoring System;
(c) Participating, as appropriate, in a consultation and clarification process;
(d) Permitting the conduct of on-site inspections; and
(e) Participating, as appropriate, in confidence-building measures.
4. All States Parties, irrespective of their technical and financial capabilities, shall enjoy the equal right of verification and assume the equal obligation to accept verification.
5. For the purposes of this Treaty, no State Party shall be precluded from using information obtained by national technical means of verification in a manner consistent with generally recognized principles of international law, including that of respect for the sovereignty of States.
6. Without prejudice to the right of States Parties to protect sensitive installations, activities or locations not related to this Treaty, States Parties shall not interfere with

elements of the verification regime of this Treaty or with national technical means of verification operating in accordance with paragraph 5.
7. Each State Party shall have the right to take measures to protect sensitive installations and to prevent disclosure of confidential information and data not related to this Treaty.
8. Moreover, all necessary measures shall be taken to protect the confidentiality of any information related to civil and military activities and facilities obtained during verification activities.
9. Subject to paragraph 8, information obtained by the Organization through the verification regime established by this Treaty shall be made available to all States Parties in accordance with the relevant provisions of this Treaty and the Protocol.
10. The provisions of this Treaty shall not be interpreted as restricting the international exchange of data for scientific purposes.
11. Each State Party undertakes to cooperate with the Organization and with other States Parties in the improvement of the verification regime, and in the examination of the verification potential of additional monitoring technologies such as electromagnetic pulse monitoring or satellite monitoring, with a view to developing, when appropriate, specific measures to enhance the efficient and cost-effective verification of this Treaty. Such measures shall, when agreed, be incorporated in existing provisions in this Treaty, the Protocol or as additional sections of the Protocol, in accordance with Article VII, or, if appropriate, be reflected in the operational manuals in accordance with Article II, paragraph 44.
12. The States Parties undertake to promote cooperation among themselves to facilitate and participate in the fullest possible exchange relating to technologies used in the verification of this Treaty in order to enable all States Parties to strengthen their national implementation of verification measures and to benefit from the application of such technologies for peaceful purposes.
13. The provisions of this Treaty shall be implemented in a manner which avoids hampering the economic and technological development of the States Parties for further development of the application of atomic energy for peaceful purposes.

Verification Responsibilities of the Technical Secretariat

14. In discharging its responsibilities in the area of verification specified in this Treaty and the Protocol, in cooperation with the State Parties the Technical Secretariat shall, for the purpose of this Treaty:
(a) Make arrangements to receive and distribute data and reporting products relevant to the verification of this Treaty in accordance with its provisions, and to maintain a global communications infrastructure appropriate to this task;
(b) Routinely through its International Data Centre, which shall in principle be the focal point within the Technical Secretariat for data storage and data processing:

(i) Receive and initiate requests for data from the International Monitoring System;
(ii) Receive data, as appropriate, resulting from the process of consultation and clarification, from on-site inspections, and from confidence-building measures; and
(iii) Receive other relevant data from States Parties and international organizations in accordance with this Treaty and the Protocol;

(c) Supervise, coordinate and ensure the operation of the International Monitoring System and its component elements, and of the International Data Centre, in accordance with the relevant operational manuals;
(d) Routinely process, analyse and report on International Monitoring System data according to agreed procedures so as to permit the effective international verification of this Treaty and to contribute to the early resolution of compliance concerns;
(e) Make available all data, both raw and processed, and any reporting products, to all States Parties, each State Party taking responsibility for the use of International Monitoring System data in accordance with Article II, paragraph 7, and with paragraphs 8 and 13 of this Article;
(f) Provide to all States Parties equal, open, convenient and timely access to all stored data;
(g) Store all data, both raw and processed, and reporting products;
(h) Coordinate and facilitate requests for additional data from the International Monitoring system;
(i) Coordinate requests for additional data from one State Party to another State Party;
(j) Provide technical assistance in, and support for, the installation and operation of monitoring facilities and respective communication means, where such assistance and support are required by the State concerned;
(k) Make available to any State Party, upon its request, techniques utilized by the Technical Secretariat and its International Data Centre in compiling, storing, processing, analysing and reporting on data from the verification regime; and
(l) Monitor, assess and report on the overall performance of the International Monitoring System and of the International Data Centre.

15. The agreed procedures to be used by the Technical Secretariat in discharging the verification responsibilities referred to in paragraph 14 and detailed in the Protocol shall be elaborated in the relevant operational manuals.

B. THE INTERNATIONAL MONITORING SYSTEM

16. The International Monitoring System shall comprise facilities for seismological monitoring, radionuclide monitoring including certified laboratories, hydroacoustic

monitoring, infrasound monitoring, and respective means of communication, and shall be supported by the International Data Centre of the Technical Secretariat.

17. The International Monitoring System shall be placed under the authority of the Technical Secretariat. All monitoring facilities of the International Monitoring System shall be owned and operated by the States hosting or otherwise taking responsibility for them in accordance with the Protocol.

18. Each State Party shall have the right to participate in the international exchange of data and to have access to all data made available to the International Data Centre. Each State Party shall cooperate with the International Data Centre through its National Authority.

Funding the International Monitoring System

19. For facilities incorporated into the International Monitoring System and specified in Tables 1-A, 2-A, 3 and 4 of Annex 1 to the Protocol, and for their functioning, to the extent that such facilities are agreed by the relevant State and the Organization to provide data to the International Data Centre in accordance with the technical requirements of the Protocol and relevant operational manuals, the Organization, as specified in agreements or arrangements pursuant to Part I, paragraph 4 of the Protocol, shall meet the costs of:

(a) Establishing any new facilities and upgrading existing facilities unless the State responsible for such facilities meets these costs itself;
(b) Operating and maintaining International Monitoring System facilities, including facility physical security if appropriate, and application of agreed data authentication procedures;
(c) Transmitting International Monitoring System data (raw or processed) to the International Data Centre by the most direct and cost effective means available, including, if necessary, via appropriate communications nodes, from monitoring stations, laboratories, analytical facilities or from national data centres; or such data (including samples where appropriate) to laboratory and analytical facilities from monitoring stations; and
(d) Analysing samples on behalf of the Organization.

20. For auxiliary network seismic stations specified in Table 1-B of Annex 1 to the Protocol the Organization, as specified in agreements or arrangements pursuant to Part I, paragraph 4 of the Protocol, shall meet the costs only of:

(a) Transmitting data to the International Data Centre;
(b) Authenticating data from such stations;
(c) Upgrading stations to the required technical standard, unless the State responsible for such facilities meets these costs itself;

(d) If necessary, establishing new stations for the purposes of this Treaty where no appropriate facilities currently exist, unless the State responsible for such facilities meets these costs itself; and
(e) Any other costs related to the provision of data required by the Organization as specified in the relevant operational manuals.

21. The Organization shall also meet the cost of provision to each State Party of its requested selection from the standard range of International Data Centre reporting products and services, as specified in Part I, Section F of the Protocol. The cost of preparation and transmission of any additional data or products shall be met by the requesting State Party.

22. The agreements or, if appropriate, arrangements concluded with States Parties or States hosting or otherwise taking responsibility for facilities of the International Monitoring System shall contain provisions for meeting these costs. Such provisions may include modalities whereby a State Party meets any of the costs referred to in paragraphs 19 (a) and 20 (c) and (d) for facilities which it hosts or for which it is responsible, and is compensated by an appropriate reduction in its assessed financial contribution to the Organization. Such a reduction shall not exceed 50 percent of the annual assessed financial contribution of a State Party, but may be spread over successive years. A State Party may share such a reduction with another State Party by agreement or arrangement between themselves and with the concurrence of the Executive Council. The agreements or arrangements referred to in this paragraph shall be approved in accordance with Article II, paragraphs 26 (h) and 38 (i).

Changes to the International Monitoring System

23. Any measures referred to in paragraph 11 affecting the International Monitoring System by means of addition or deletion of a monitoring technology shall, when agreed, be incorporated into this Treaty and the Protocol pursuant to Article VII, paragraphs 1 to 6.

24. The following changes to the International Monitoring System, subject to the agreement of those States directly affected, shall be regarded as matters of an administrative or technical nature pursuant to Article VII, paragraphs 7 and 8:
(a) Changes to the number of facilities specified in the Protocol for a given monitoring technology; and
(b) Changes to other details for particular facilities as reflected in the Tables of Annex 1 to the Protocol (including, *inter alia*, State responsible for the facility; location; name of facility; type of facility; and attribution of a facility between the primary and auxiliary seismic networks).

If the Executive Council recommends, pursuant to Article VII, paragraph 8 (d) that such changes be adopted, it shall as a rule also recommend pursuant to Article VII, paragraph 8 (g) that such changes enter into force upon notification by the Director-General of their approval.

25. The Director-General, in submitting to the Executive Council and States Parties information and evaluation in accordance with Article VII, paragraph 8 (b), shall include in the case of any proposal made pursuant to paragraph 24:

(a) A technical evaluation of the proposal;

(b) A statement on the administrative and financial impact of the proposal; and

(c) A report on consultations with States directly affected by the proposal, including indication of their agreement.

Temporary Arrangements

26. In cases of significant or irretrievable breakdown of a monitoring facility specified in the Tables of Annex 1 to the Protocol, or in order to cover other temporary reductions of monitoring coverage, the Director-General shall, in consultation and agreement with those States directly affected, and with the approval of the Executive Council, initiate temporary arrangements of no more than one year's duration, renewable if necessary by agreement of the Executive Council and of the States directly affected for another year. Such arrangements shall not cause the number of operational facilities of the International Monitoring System to exceed the number specified for the relevant network; shall meet as far as possible the technical and operational requirements specified in the operational manual for the relevant network; and shall be conducted within the budget of the Organization. The Director-General shall furthermore take steps to rectify the situation and make proposals for its permanent resolution. The Director-General shall notify all States Parties of any decision taken pursuant to this paragraph.

Cooperating National Facilities

27. States Parties may also separately establish cooperative arrangements with the Organization, in order to make available to the International Data Centre supplementary data from national monitoring stations that are not formally part of the International Monitoring System.

28. Such cooperative arrangements may be established as follows:

(a) Upon request by a State Party, and at the expense of that State, the Technical Secretariat shall take the steps required to certify that a given monitoring facility meets the technical and operational requirements specified in the relevant operational manuals for an International Monitoring System facility, and make arrangements for the authentication of its data. Subject to the agreement of the Executive Council, the Technical Secretariat shall then formally designate such a facility as a cooperating national facility. The Technical Secretariat shall take the steps required to revalidate its certification as appropriate;

(b) The Technical Secretariat shall maintain a current list of cooperating national facilities and shall distribute it to all States Parties and;

(c) The International Data Centre shall call upon data from cooperating national facilities, if so requested by a State Party, for the purposes of facilitating consultation and clarification and the consideration of on-site inspection requests, data transmission costs being borne by that State Party.

The conditions under which supplementary data from such facilities are made available, and under which the International Data Centre may request further or expedited reporting, or clarifications, shall be elaborated in the operational manual for the respective monitoring network.

C. CONSULTATION AND CLARIFICATION

29. Without prejudice to the right of any State Party to request an on-site inspection, States Parties should, whenever possible, first make every effort to clarify and resolve, among themselves or with or through the Organization, any matter which may cause concern about possible non-compliance with the basic obligations of this Treaty.
30. A State Party that receives a request pursuant to paragraph 29 directly from another State Party shall provide the clarification to the requesting State Party as soon as possible, but in any case no later than 48 hours after the request. The requesting and requested States Parties may keep the Executive Council and the Director-General informed of the request and the response.
31. A State Party shall have the right to request the Director-General to assist in clarifying any matter which may cause concern about possible non-compliance with the basic obligations of this Treaty. The Director-General shall provide appropriate information in the possession of the Technical Secretariat relevant to such a concern. The Director-General shall inform the Executive Council of the request and of the information provided in response, if so requested by the requesting State Party.
32. A State Party shall have the right to request the Executive Council to obtain clarification from another State Party on any matter which may cause concern about possible non-compliance with the basic obligations of this Treaty. In such a case, the following shall apply:

(a) The Executive Council shall forward the request for clarification to the requested State Party through the Director-General no later than 24 hours after its receipt;

(b) The requested State Party shall provide the clarification to the Executive Council as soon as possible, but in any case no later than 48 hour after receipt of the request;

(c) The Executive Council shall take note of the clarification and forward it to the requesting State Party no later than 24 hours after its receipt;

(d) If the requesting State Party deems the clarification to be inadequate, it shall have the right to request the Executive Council to obtain further clarification from the requested State Party.

The Executive Council shall inform without delay all other States Parties about any request for clarification pursuant to this paragraph as well as any response provided by the requested State Party.

33. If the requesting State Party considers the clarification obtained under paragraph 32 (d) to be unsatisfactory, it shall have the right to request a meeting of the Executive Council in which States Parties involved that are not members of the Executive Council shall be entitled to take part. At such a meeting, the Executive Council shall consider the matter and may recommend any measure in accordance with Article V.

D. ON-SITE INSPECTIONS

Request for an On-Site Inspection

34. Each State Party has the right to request an on-site inspection in accordance with the provisions of this Article and Part II of the Protocol in the territory or in any other place under the jurisdiction or control of any State Party, or in any area beyond the jurisdiction or control of any State.

35. The sole Purpose of an on-site inspection shall be to clarify whether a nuclear weapon test explosion or any other nuclear explosion has been carried out in violation of Article I and, to the extent possible, to gather any facts which might assist in identifying any possible violator.

36. The requesting State Party shall be under the obligation to keep the on-site inspection request within the scope of this Treaty and to provide in the request information in accordance with paragraph 37. The requesting State Party shall refrain from unfounded or abusive inspection requests.

37. The on-site inspection request shall be based on information collected by the International Monitoring System, on any relevant technical information obtained by national technical means of verification in a manner consistent with generally recognized principles of international law, or on a combination thereof. The request shall contain information pursuant to Part II, paragraph 41 of the Protocol.

38. The requesting State Party shall present the on-site inspection request to the Executive Council and at the same time to the Director-General for the latter to begin immediate processing.

Follow-up After Submission of an On-Site Inspection Request

39. The Executive Council shall begin its consideration immediately upon receipt of the on-site inspection request.

40. The Director-General, after receiving the on-site inspection request, shall acknowledge receipt of the request to the requesting State Party within two hours and communicate the request to the State Party sought to be inspected within six hours. The Director-General shall ascertain that the request meets the requirements specified in Part II, paragraph 41 of the Protocol, and, if necessary, shall assist the requesting State Party in filing the request accordingly, and shall communicate the request to the Executive Council and to all other states Parties within 24 hours.
41. When the on-site inspection request fulfils the requirements, the Technical Secretariat shall begin preparations for the on-site inspection without delay.
42. The Director-General, upon receipt of an on-site inspection request referring to an inspection area under the jurisdiction or control of a State Party, shall immediately seek clarification from the State Party sought to be inspected in order to clarify and resolve the concern raised in the request.
43. A State Party that receives a request for clarification pursuant to paragraph 42 shall provide the Director-General with explanations and with other relevant information available as soon as possible, but no later than 72 hours after receipt of the request for clarification.
44. The Director-General, before the Executive Council takes a decision on the on-site inspection request, shall transmit immediately to the Executive Council any additional information available from the International Monitoring System or provided by any State Party on the event specified in the request, including any clarification provided pursuant to paragraphs 42 and 43, as well as any other information from within the Technical Secretariat that the Director-General deems relevant or that is requested by the Executive Council.
45. Unless the requesting State Party considers the concern raised in the on-site inspection request to be resolved and withdraws the request, the Executive Council shall take a decision on the request in accordance with paragraph 46.

Executive Council Decisions

46. The Executive Council shall take a decision on the on-site inspection request no later than 96 hours after receipt of the request from the requesting State Party. The decision to approve the on-site inspection shall be made by at least 30 affirmative votes of members of the Executive Council. If the Executive Council does not approve the inspection, preparations shall be stopped and no further action on the request shall be taken.
47. No later than 25 days after the approval of the on-site inspection in accordance with paragraph 46, the inspection team shall transmit to the Executive Council, through the Director-General, a progress inspection report. The continuation of the inspection shall be considered approved unless the Executive Council, no later than 72 hours after receipt of the progress inspection report, decides by a majority of all

its members not to continue the inspection. If the Executive Council decides not to continue the inspection, the inspection shall be terminated, and the inspection team shall leave the inspection area and the territory of the inspected State Party as soon as possible in accordance with Part II, paragraphs 109 and 110 of the Protocol.

48. In the course of the on-site inspection, the inspection team may submit to the Executive Council, through the Director-General, a proposal to conduct drilling. The Executive Council shall take a decision on such a proposal no later than 72 hours after receipt of the proposal. The decision to approve drilling shall be made by a majority of all members of the Executive Council.

49. The inspection team may request the Executive Council, through the Director-General, to extend the inspection duration by a maximum of 70 days beyond the 60-day time-frame specified in Part II, paragraph 4 of the Protocol, if the inspection team considers such an extension essential to enable it to fulfil its mandate. The inspection team shall indicate in its request which of the activities and techniques listed in Part II, paragraph 6 of the Protocol it intends to carry out during the extension period. The Executive Council shall take a decision on the extension request no later than 72 hours after receipt of the request. The decision to approve an extension of the inspection duration shall be made by a majority of all members of the Executive Council.

50. Any time following the approval of the continuation of the on-site inspection in accordance with paragraph 47, the inspection team may submit to the Executive Council, through the Director-General, a recommendation to terminate the inspection. Such a recommendation shall be considered approved unless the Executive Council, no later than 72 hours after receipt of the recommendation, decides by a two-thirds majority of all its members not to approve the termination of the inspection. In case of termination of the inspection, the inspection team shall leave the inspection area and the territory of the inspected State Party as soon as possible in accordance with Part II, paragraphs 109 and 110 of the Protocol.

51. The requesting State Party and the State Party sought to be inspected may participate in the deliberations of the Executive Council on the on-site inspection request without voting. The requesting State Party and the inspected State Party may also participate without voting in any subsequent deliberations of the Executive Council related to the inspection.

52. The Director-General shall notify all States Parties within 24 hours about any decision by and reports, proposals, requests and recommendations to the Executive Council pursuant to paragraphs 46 to 50.

Follow-up after Executive Council Approval of an On-Site Inspection

53. An on-site inspection approved by the Executive Council shall be conducted without delay by an inspection team designated by the Director-General and in accordance with the provisions of this Treaty and the Protocol. The inspection team

shall arrive at the point of entry no later than six days following the receipt by the Executive Council of the on-site inspection request from the requesting State Party.

54. The Director-General shall issue an inspection mandate for the conduct of the on-site inspection. The inspection mandate shall contain the information specified in Part II, paragraph 42 of the Protocol.

55. The Director-General shall notify the inspected State Party of the inspection no less than 24 hours before the planned arrival of the inspection team at the point of entry, in accordance with Part II, paragraph 43 of the Protocol.

The Conduct of an On-Site Inspection

56. Each State Party shall permit the Organization to conduct an on-site inspection on its territory or at places under its jurisdiction or control in accordance with the provisions of this Treaty and the Protocol. However, no State Party shall have to accept simultaneous on-site inspections on its territory or at places under its jurisdiction or control.

57. In accordance with the provisions of this Treaty and the Protocol, the inspected State Party shall have:

(a) The right and the obligation to make every reasonable effort to demonstrate its compliance with this Treaty and, to this end, to enable the inspection team to fulfil its mandate;

(b) The right to take measures it deems necessary to protect national security interests and to prevent disclosure of confidential information not related to the purpose of the inspection;

(c) The obligation to provide access within the inspection area for the sole purpose of determining facts relevant to the purpose of the inspection, taking into account sub-paragraph (b) and any constitutional obligations it may have with regard to proprietary rights or searches and seizures;

(d) The obligation not to invoke this paragraph or Part II, paragraph 88 of the Protocol to conceal any violation of its obligations under Article I; and

(e) The obligation not to impede the ability of the inspection team to move within the inspection area and to carry out inspection activities in accordance with this Treaty and the Protocol.

Access, in the context of an on-site inspection, means both the physical access of the inspection team and the inspection equipment to, and the conduct of inspection activities within, the inspection area.

58. The on-site inspection shall be conducted in the least intrusive manner possible, consistent with the efficient and timely accomplishment of the inspection mandate, and in accordance with the procedures set forth in the Protocol. Wherever possible, the inspection team shall begin with the least intrusive procedures and then proceed to more intrusive procedures only as it deems necessary to collect sufficient informa-

tion to clarify the concern about possible non-compliance with this Treaty. The inspectors shall seek only the information and data necessary for the purpose of the inspection and shall seek to minimize interference with normal operations of the inspected State Party.

59. The inspected State Party shall assist the inspection team throughout the on-site inspection and facilitate its task.

60. If the inspected State Party, acting in accordance with Part II, paragraphs 86 to 96 of the Protocol, restricts access within the inspection area, it shall make every reasonable effort in consultations with the inspection team to demonstrate through alternative means its compliance with this Treaty.

Observer

61. With regard to an observer, the following shall apply:
(a) The requesting State Party, subject to the agreement of the inspected State Party, may send a representative, who shall be a national either of the requesting State Party or of a third State Party, to observe the conduct of the on-site inspection;
(b) The inspected State Party shall notify its acceptance or non-acceptance of the proposed observer to the Director-General within 12 hours after approval of the on-site inspection by the Executive Council;
(c) In case of acceptance, the inspected State Party shall grant access to the observer in accordance with the Protocol;
(d) The inspected State Party shall, as a rule, accept the proposed observer, but if the inspected State Party exercises a refusal, that fact shall be recorded in the inspection report.

There shall be no more than three observers from an aggregate of requesting States Parties.

Reports of an On-Site Inspection

62. Inspection reports shall contain:
(a) A description of the activities conducted by the inspection team;
(b) The factual findings of the inspection team relevant to the purpose of the inspection,
(c) An account of the cooperation granted during the on-site inspection;
(d) A factual description of the extent of the access granted, including the alternative means provided to the team, during the on-site inspection; and
(e) Any other details relevant to the purpose of the inspection.

Differing observations made by inspectors may be attached to the report.

63. The Director-General shall make draft inspection reports available to the inspected State Party. The inspected State Party shall have the right to provide the Director-

General within 48 hours with its comments and explanations, and to identify any information and data which, in its view, are not related to the purpose of the inspection and should not be circulated outside the Technical Secretariat. The Director-General shall consider the proposals for changes to the draft inspection report made by the inspected State Party and shall wherever possible incorporate them. The Director-General shall also annex the comments and explanations provided by the inspected State Party to the inspection report.

64. The Director-General shall promptly transmit the inspection report to the requesting State Party, the inspected State Party, the Executive Council and to all other States Parties. The Director-General shall further transmit promptly to the Executive Council and to all other States Parties any results of sample analysis in designated laboratories in accordance with Part II, paragraph 104 of the Protocol, relevant data from the International Monitoring System, the assessments of the requesting and inspected States Parties, as well as any other information that the Director-General deems relevant. In the case of the progress inspection report referred to in paragraph 47, the Director-General shall transmit the report to the Executive Council within the time-frame specified in that paragraph.

65. The Executive Council, in accordance with its powers and functions, shall review the inspection report and any material provided pursuant to paragraph 64, and shall address any concerns as to:

(a) Whether any non-compliance with this Treaty has occurred; and
(b) Whether the right to request an on-site inspection has been abused.

66. If the Executive Council reaches the conclusion, in keeping with its powers and functions, that further action may be necessary with regard to paragraph 65, it shall take the appropriate measures in accordance with Article V.

Frivolous or Abusive On-Site Inspection Requests

67. If the Executive Council does not approve the on-site inspection on the basis that the on-site inspection request is frivolous or abusive, or if the inspection is terminated for the same reasons, the Executive Council shall consider and decide on whether to implement appropriate measures to redress the situation, including the following:

(a) Requiring the requesting State Party to pay for the cost of any preparations made by the Technical Secretariat;
(b) Suspending the right of the requesting State Party to request an on-site inspection for a period of time, as determined by the Executive Council; and
(c) Suspending the right of the requesting State Party to serve on the Executive Council for a period of time.

E. CONFIDENCE-BUILDING MEASURES

68. In order to:
(a) Contribute to the timely resolution of any compliance concerns arising from possible misinterpretation of verification data relating to chemical explosions, and
(b) Assist in the calibration of the stations that are part of the component networks of the International Monitoring System,

each State Party undertakes to cooperate with the Organization and with other States Parties in implementing relevant measures as set out in Part III of the Protocol.

Article V
Measures to redress a situation and to ensure compliance, including sanctions

1. The Conference, taking into account, *inter alia*, the recommendations of the Executive Council, shall take the necessary measures, as set forth in paragraphs 2 and 3, to ensure compliance with this Treaty and to redress and remedy any situation which contravenes the provisions of this Treaty.
2. In cases where a State Party has been requested by the Conference or the Executive Council to redress a situation raising problems with regard to its compliance and fails to fulfil the request within the specified time, the Conference may, *inter alia*, decide to restrict or suspend the State Party from the exercise of its rights and privileges under this Treaty until the Conference decides otherwise.
3. In cases where damage to the object and purpose of this Treaty may result from non-compliance with the basic obligations of this Treaty, the Conference may recommend to States Parties collective measures which are in conformity with international law.
4. The Conference, or alternatively, if the case is urgent, the Executive Council, may bring the issue, including relevant information and conclusions to the attention of the United Nations.

Article VI
Settlement of disputes

1. Disputes that may arise concerning the application or the interpretation of this Treaty shall be settled in accordance with the relevant provisions of this Treaty and in conformity with the provisions of the Charter of the United Nations.
2. When a dispute arises between two or more States Parties, or between one or more States Parties and the Organization, relating to the application or interpretation of this Treaty, the parties concerned shall consult together with a view to the expeditious settlement of the dispute by negotiation or by other peaceful means of the parties' choice, including recourse to appropriate organs of this Treaty and, by mutual consent,

referral to the International Court of Justice in conformity with the Statute of the Court. The parties involved shall keep the Executive Council informed of actions being taken.

3. The Executive Council may contribute to the settlement of a dispute that may arise concerning the application or interpretation of this Treaty by whatever means it deems appropriate, including offering its good offices, calling upon the States Parties to a dispute to seek a settlement through a process of their own choice, bringing the matter to the attention of the Conference and recommending a time-limit for any agreed procedure.

4. The Conference shall consider questions related to disputes raised by States Parties or brought to its attention by the Executive Council. The Conference shall, as it finds necessary, establish or entrust organs with tasks related to the settlement of these disputes in conformity with Article II, paragraph 26 (j).

5. The Conference and the Executive Council are separately empowered, subject to authorization from the General Assembly of the United Nations, to request the International Court of Justice to give an advisory opinion on any legal question arising within the scope of the activities of the Organization. An agreement between the Organization and the United Nations shall be concluded for this purpose in accordance with Article II, paragraph 38 (h).

6. This Article is without prejudice to Articles IV and V.

Article VII
Amendments

1. At any time after the entry into force of this Treaty, any State Party may propose amendments to this Treaty, the Protocol, or the Annexes to the Protocol. Any State Party may also propose changes, in accordance with paragraph 7, to the Protocol or the Annexes thereto. Proposals for amendments shall be subject to the procedures in paragraphs 2 to 6. Proposals for changes, in accordance with paragraph 7, shall be subject to the procedures in paragraph 8.

2. The proposed amendment shall be considered and adopted only by an Amendment Conference.

3. Any proposal for an amendment shall be communicated to the Director-General, who shall circulate it to all States Parties and the Depositary and seek the views of the States Parties on whether an Amendment Conference should be convened to consider the proposal. If a majority of the States Parties notify the Director-General no later than 30 days after its circulation that they support further consideration of the proposal, the Director-General shall convene an Amendment Conference to which all States Parties shall be invited.

4. The Amendment Conference shall be held immediately following a regular session of the Conference unless all States Parties that support the convening of an Amend-

ment Conference request that it be held earlier. In no case shall an Amendment Conference be held less than 60 days after the circulation of the proposed amendment.
5. Amendments shall be adopted by the Amendment Conference by a positive vote of a majority of the States Parties with no State Party casting a negative vote.
6. Amendments shall enter into force for all States Parties 30 days after deposit of the instruments of ratification or acceptance by all those States Parties casting a positive vote at the Amendment Conference.
7. In order to ensure the viability and effectiveness of this Treaty, Parts I and III of the Protocol and Annexes 1 and 2 to the Protocol shall be subject to changes in accordance with paragraph 8, if the proposed changes are related only to matters of an administrative or technical nature. All other provisions of the Protocol and the Annexes thereto shall not be subject to changes in accordance with paragraph 8.
8. Proposed changes referred to in paragraph 7 shall be made in accordance with the following procedures:
(a) The text of the proposed changes shall be transmitted together with the necessary information to the Director-General. Additional information for the evaluation of the proposal may be provided by any State Party and the Director-General. The Director-General shall promptly communicate any such proposals and information to all States Parties, the Executive Council and the Depositary;
(b) No later than 60 days after its receipt, the Director-General shall evaluate the proposal to determine all its possible consequences for the provisions of this Treaty and its implementation and shall communicate any such information to all States Parties and the Executive Council;
(c) The Executive Council shall examine the proposal in the light of all information available to it, including whether the proposal fulfils the requirements of paragraph 7. No later than 90 days after its receipt, the Executive Council shall notify its recommendation, with appropriate explanations, to all States Parties for consideration. States Parties shall acknowledge receipt within 10 days;
(d) If the Executive Council recommends to all States Parties that the proposal be adopted, it shall be considered approved if no State Party objects to it within 90 days after receipt of the recommendation. If the Executive Council recommends that the proposal be rejected, it shall be considered rejected if no State Party objects to the rejection within 90 days after receipt of the recommendation;
(e) If a recommendation of the Executive Council does not meet with the acceptance required under sub-paragraph (d), a decision on the proposal, including whether it fulfils the requirements of paragraph 7, shall be taken as a matter of substance by the Conference at its next session;
(f) The Director-General shall notify all States Parties and the Depositary of any decision under this paragraph;
(g) Changes approved under this procedure shall enter into force for all States Parties 180 days after the date of notification by the Director-General of their

approval unless another time period is recommended by the Executive Council or decided by the Conference.

Article VIII
Review of the Treaty

1. Unless otherwise decided by a majority of the States Parties, ten years after the entry into force of this Treaty a Conference of the States Parties shall be held to review the operation and effectiveness of this Treaty, with a view to assuring itself that the objectives and purposes in the Preamble and the provisions of the Treaty are being realized. Such review shall take into account any new scientific and technological developments relevant to this Treaty. On the basis of a request by any State Party, the Review Conference shall consider the possibility of permitting the conduct of underground nuclear explosions for peaceful purposes. If the Review Conference decides by consensus that such nuclear explosions may be permitted, it shall commence work without delay, with a view to recommending to States Parties an appropriate amendment to this Treaty that shall preclude any military benefits of such nuclear explosions. Any such proposed amendment shall be communicated to the Director-General by any State Party and shall be dealt with in accordance with the provisions of Article VII.
2. At intervals of ten years thereafter, further Review Conferences may be convened with the same objective, if the Conference so decides as a matter of procedure in the preceding year. Such Conferences may be convened after an interval of less than ten years if so decided by the Conference as a matter of substance.
3. Normally, any Review Conference shall be held immediately following the regular annual session of the Conference provided for in Article II.

Article IX
Duration and withdrawal

1. This Treaty shall be of unlimited duration.
2. Each State Party shall, in exercising its national sovereignty, have the right to withdraw from this Treaty if it decides that extraordinary events related to the subject matter of this Treaty have jeopardized its supreme interests.
3. Withdrawal shall be effected by giving notice six months in advance to all other States Parties, the Executive Council, the Depositary and the United Nations Security Council. Notice of withdrawal shall include a statement of the extraordinary event or events which a State Party regards as jeopardizing its supreme interests.

Article X
Status of the Protocol and the annexes

The Annexes to this Treaty, the Protocol, and the Annexes to the Protocol form an integral part of the Treaty. Any reference to this Treaty includes the Annexes to this Treaty, the Protocol and the Annexes to the Protocol.

Article XI
Signature

This Treaty shall be open to all States for signature before its entry into force.

Article XII
Ratification

This Treaty shall be subject to ratification by signatory States according to their respective constitutional processes.

Article XIII
Accession

Any State which does not sign this Treaty before its entry into force may accede to it at any time thereafter.

Article XIV
Entry into force

1. This Treaty shall enter into force 180 days after the date of deposit of the instruments of ratification by all States listed in Annex 2 to this Treaty, but in no case earlier than two years after its opening for signature.
2. If this Treaty has not entered into force three years after the date of the anniversary of its opening for signature, the Depositary shall convene a Conference of the States that have already deposited their instruments of ratification on the request of a majority of those States. That Conference shall examine the extent to which the requirement set out in paragraph 1 has been met and shall consider and decide by consensus what measures consistent with international law may be undertaken to accelerate the ratification process in order to facilitate the early entry into force of this Treaty.
3. Unless otherwise decided by the Conference referred to in paragraph 2 or other such conferences, this process shall be repeated at subsequent anniversaries of the opening for signature of this Treaty, until its entry into force.

4. All States Signatories shall be invited to attend the Conference referred to in paragraph 2 and any subsequent conferences as referred to in paragraph 3, as observers.
5. For States whose instruments of ratification or accession are deposited subsequent to the entry into force of this Treaty, it shall enter into force on the 30th day following the date of deposit of their instruments of ratification or accession.

Article XV
Reservations

The Articles of and the Annexes to this Treaty shall not be subject to reservations. The provisions of the Protocol to this Treaty and the Annexes to the Protocol shall not be subject to reservations incompatible with the object and purpose of this Treaty.

Article XVI
Depositary

1. The Secretary-General of the United Nations shall be the Depositary of this Treaty and shall receive signatures, instruments of ratification and instruments of accession.
2. The Depositary shall promptly inform all States Signatories and acceding States of the date of each signature, the date of deposit of each instrument of ratification or accession, the date of the entry into force of this Treaty and of any amendments and changes thereto, and the receipt of other notices.
3. The Depositary shall send duly certified copies of this Treaty to the Governments of the States Signatories and acceding States.
4. This Treaty shall be registered by the Depositary pursuant to Article 102 of the Charter of the United Nations.

Article XVII
Authentic texts

This Treaty, of which the Arabic, Chinese, English, French, Russian and Spanish texts are equally authentic, shall be deposited with the Secretary-General of the United Nations.

ANNEX 1 TO THE TREATY
LIST OF STATES PURSUANT TO ARTICLE II, PARAGRAPH 28

Africa

Algeria, Angola, Benin, Botswana, Burkina Faso, Burundi, Cameroon, Cape Verde, Central African Republic, Chad, Comoros, Congo, Cote d'Ivoire, Djibouti, Egypt,

Equatorial Guinea, Eritrea, Ethiopia, Gabon, Gambia, Ghana, Guinea, Guinea-Bissau, Kenya, Lesotho, Liberia, Libyan Arab Jamahiriya, Madagascar, Malawi, Mali, Mauritania, Mauritius, Morocco, Mozambique, Namibia, Niger, Nigeria, Rwanda, Sao Tome & Principe, Senegal, Seychelles, Sierra Leone, Somalia, South Africa, Sudan, Swaziland, Togo, Tunisia, Uganda, United Republic of Tanzania, Zaire, Zambia, Zimbabwe.

Eastern Europe

Albania, Armenia, Azerbaijan, Belarus, Bosnia and Herzegovina, Bulgaria, Croatia, Czech Republic, Estonia, Georgia, Hungary, Latvia, Lithuania, Poland, Republic of Moldova, Romania, Russian Federation, Slovakia, Slovenia, The former Yugoslav Republic of Macedonia, Ukraine, Yugoslavia.

Latin America and the Caribbean

Antigua and Barbuda, Argentina, Bahamas, Barbados, Belize, Bolivia, Brazil, Chile, Colombia, Costa Rica, Cuba, Dominica, Dominican Republic, Ecuador, El Salvador, Grenada, Guatemala, Guyana, Haiti, Honduras, Jamaica, Mexico, Nicaragua, Panama, Paraguay, Peru, Saint Kitts and Nevis, Saint Lucia, Saint Vincent and the Grenadines, Suriname, Trinidad and Tobago, Uruguay, Venezuela.

Middle East and South Asia

Afghanistan, Bahrain, Bangladesh, Bhutan, India, Iran (Islamic Republic of), Iraq, Israel, Jordan, Kazakstan, Kuwait, Kyrgyzstan, Lebanon, Maldives, Oman, Nepal, Pakistan, Qatar, Saudi Arabia, Sri Lanka, Syrian Arab Republic, Tajikistan, Turkmenistan, United Arab Emirates, Uzbekistan, Yemen.

North America and Western Europe

Andorra, Austria, Belgium, Canada, Cyprus, Denmark, Finland, France, Germany, Greece, Holy See, Iceland, Ireland, Italy, Liechtenstein, Luxembourg, Malta, Monaco, Netherlands, Norway, Portugal, San Marino, Spain, Sweden, Switzerland, Turkey, United Kingdom of Great Britain and Northern Ireland, United States of America.

South East Asia, the Pacific and the Far East

Australia, Brunei Darussalam, Cambodia, China, Cook Islands, Democratic People's Republic of Korea, Fiji, Indonesia, Japan, Kiribati, Lao People's Democratic Republic, Malaysia, Marshall Islands, Micronesia (Federated States of), Mongolia, Myanmar, Nauru, New Zealand, Niue, Palau, Papua New Guinea, Philippines, Republic of Korea, Samoa, Singapore, Solomon Islands, Thailand, Tonga, Tuvalu, Vanuatu, Viet Nam.

ANNEX 2 TO THE TREATY
LIST OF STATES PURSUANT TO ARTICLE XIV

List of States members of the Conference on Disarmament as at 18 June 1996 which formally participated in the work of the 1996 session of the Conference and which appear in Table 1 of the International Atomic Energy Agency's April 1996 edition of "Nuclear Power Reactors in the World", and of States members of the Conference on Disarmament as at 18 June 1996 which formally participated in the work of the 1996 session of the Conference and which appear in Table 1 of the International Atomic Energy Agency's December 1995 edition of "Nuclear Research Reactors in the World": Algeria, Argentina, Australia, Austria, Bangladesh, Belgium, Brazil, Bulgaria, Canada, Chile, China, Colombia, Democratic People's Republic of Korea, Egypt, Finland, France, Germany, Hungary, India, Indonesia, Iran (Islamic Republic of), Israel, Italy, Japan, Mexico, Netherlands, Norway, Pakistan, Peru, Poland, Romania, Republic of Korea, Russian Federation, Slovakia, South Africa, Spain, Sweden, Switzerland, Turkey, Ukraine, United Kingdom of Great Britain and Northern Ireland, United States of America, Viet Nam, Zaire.

TREATY ON PRINCIPLES GOVERNING THE ACTIVITIES OF STATES IN THE EXPLORATION AND USE OF OUTER SPACE, INCLUDING THE MOON AND OTHER CELESTIAL BODIES

(London Moscow, Washington, 27 January 1967)

The conclusion of this Treaty follows various "resolutions" adopted unanimously by the United Nations General Assembly in 1947 and 1963, to the effect of preventing any threat to the peace and the placing in orbit around the earth or on celestial bodies of nuclear weapons and any other kinds of weapons of mass destruction.

Similarly to the Antarctic Treaty (see previous pages) the 1967 Treaty governs the peaceful use of outer space and co-operation among States in this connection, and contains certain provisions prohibiting also nuclear activities other than peaceful ones.

Here are recalled the preamble, articles IV, IX, XI (where reference is made also to nuclear items) and article XVII (final provisions).

The present number of contracting Parties is 91, the Treaty having entered into force since October 1967.

The States Parties to this Treaty,

Inspired by the great prospects opening up before mankind as a result of man's entry into outer space,
Recognizing the common interest of all mankind in the progress of the exploration and use of outer space for peaceful purposes,
Believing that the exploration and use of outer space should be carried on for the benefit of all peoples irrespective of the degree of their economic or scientific development,
Desiring to contribute to broad international co-operation in the scientific as well as the legal aspects of the exploration and use of outer space for peaceful purposes,
Believing that such co-operation will contribute to the development of mutual understanding and to the strengthening of friendly relations between States and peoples,
Recalling resolution 1962 (XVIII), entitled "Declaration of Legal Principles Governing the Activities of States in the Exploration and Use of Outer Space", which was adopted unanimously by the United Nations General Assembly on 13 December 1963,

Recalling resolution 1884 (XVIII), calling upon States to refrain from placing in orbit around the earth any objects carrying nuclear weapons or any other kinds of weapons of mass destruction or from installing such weapons on celestial bodies, which was adopted unanimously by the United Nations General Assembly on 17 October 1963,
Taking account of United Nations General Assembly resolution 110 (II) of 3 November 1947, which condemned propaganda designed or likely to provoke or encourage any threat to the peace, breach of the peace or act of aggression, and considering that the aforementioned resolution is applicable to outer space,
Convinced that a Treaty on Principles Governing the Activities of States in the Exploration and Use of Outer Space, including the Moon and Other Celestial Bodies, will further the purposes and principles of the Charter of the United Nations,

Have agreed on the following:

Article IV

States Parties to the Treaty undertake not to place in orbit around the earth any objects carrying nuclear weapons or any other kinds of weapons of mass destruction, install such weapons on celestial bodies, or station such weapons in outer space in any other manner.
The moon and other celestial bodies shall be used by all States Parties to the Treaty exclusively for peaceful purposes. The establishment of military bases, installations and fortifications, the testing of any type of weapons and the conduct of military manoeuvres on celestial bodies shall be forbidden. The use of military personnel for scientific research or for any other peaceful purposes shall not be prohibited. The use of any equipment or facility necessary for peaceful exploration of the moon and other celestial bodies shall also not be prohibited.

Article IX

In the exploration and use of outer space, including the moon and other celestial bodies, States Parties to the Treaty shall be guided by the principle of co-operation and mutual assistance and shall conduct all their activities in outer space, including the moon and other celestial bodies, with due regard to the corresponding interests of all other States Parties to the Treaty. States Parties to the Treaty shall pursue studies of outer space, including the moon and other celestial bodies, and conduct exploration of them so as to avoid their harmful contamination and also adverse changes in the environment of the Earth resulting from the introduction of extraterrestrial matter and, where necessary, shall adopt appropriate measures for this purpose. If a State Party to the Treaty has reason to believe that an activity or experiment planned by it or its nationals in outer space, including the moon and other celestial bodies, would cause potentially harmful interference with activities of other States Parties in the peaceful exploration and use of outer space, including the moon and other celestial bodies, it shall undertake appropriate international consultations before proceeding with any such activity or experiment. A State Party to the Treaty which has reason to believe that an activity or experiment planned by another State Party in outer space, including the moon and other celestial bodies, would cause potentially harmful interference with activities in the peaceful exploration and use of outer space, including the moon and other celestial bodies, may request consultation concerning the activity or experiment.

Article XI

In order to promote international co-operation in the peaceful exploration and use of outer space, States Parties to the Treaty conducting activities in outer space, including the moon and other celestial bodies, agree to inform the Secretary-General of the United Nations as well as the public and the international scientific community, to the greatest extent feasible and practicable, of the nature, conduct, locations and results of such activities. On receiving the said information, the Secretary-General of the United Nations should be prepared to disseminate it immediately and effectively.

Article XVII

This Treaty, of which the English, Russian, French, Spanish and Chinese texts are equally authentic, shall be deposited in the archives of the Depositary Governments. Duly certified copies of this Treaty shall be transmitted by the Depositary Governments to the Governments of the signatory and acceding States.

TREATY ON THE PROHIBITION OF NUCLEAR WEAPONS IN LATIN AMERICA

(Mexico City, 14 February 1967)

Similarly to the Treaty on the use of outer space, also this Treaty (known as the Tlatelolco Treaty, after the locality where it was signed) follows some "resolutions" adopted by the General Assembly of the United Nations. In particular, Resolution 1911(XVIII) stated that the measures to be adopted with a view to "de-nuclearising" Latin America should be taken in the light of the principles contained in the Charter of the United Nations and of regional agreements; moreover, Resolution 2028 (XX) stated the principle of an acceptable balance of responsibilities and mutual obligations for nuclear and non-nuclear States. The Treaty is the first international instrument prohibiting the total use of nuclear weapons in a vast inhabited geographical area.

As stated in the preamble, the Treaty aims to ensure nuclear safety for Latin America in the framework of the prevention of proliferation of nuclear weapons; indirectly, the Treaty is intended to contribute to the reduction of nuclear armaments and to the general and complete disarmament pursued by the other (broader in scope) international instruments addressed in this Section. Reference is made (article 13) to the IAEA safeguards and special inspections (article 16). The Treaty is of unlimited duration and open to the signature by all the Latin-American republics, as well as by all sovereign States of the western hemisphere below the 35th parallel of north latitude. The Treaty, which has 33 contracting Parties, entered into force (article 29) on April 25, 1969. The entry into force is based on ratification also by nuclear-weapon countries bound to Additional Protocol II annexed to the Treaty.

PREAMBLE

In the name of their peoples and faithfully interpreting their desires and aspirations, the Governments of the States which have signed the Treaty for the Prohibition of Nuclear Weapons in Latin America,

Desiring to contribute, so far as lies in their power, towards ending the armaments race, especially in the field of nuclear weapons, and towards strengthening a world at peace, based on the sovereign equality of States, mutual respect and good neighbourliness,
Recalling that the United Nations General Assembly, in its resolution 808 (IX), adopted unanimously as one of the three points of a co-ordinated programme of disarmament

"the total prohibition of the use and manufacture of nuclear weapons and weapons of mass destruction of every type";

Recalling that militarily denuclearized zones are not an end in themselves but rather a means for achieving general and complete disarmament at a later stage,

Recalling United Nations General Assembly resolution 1911 (XVIII), which established that the measures that should be agreed upon for the denuclearization of Latin America should be taken "in the light of the principles of the Charter of the United Nations and of regional agreements",

Recalling United Nations General Assembly Resolution 2028 (XX) which established the principle of an acceptable balance of mutual responsibilities and duties for the nuclear and non-nuclear powers, and

Recalling that the Charter of the Organization of American States proclaims that it is an essential purpose of the organization to strengthen the peace and security of the hemisphere,

Convinced:

That the incalculable destructive power of nuclear weapons has made it imperative that the legal prohibition of war should be strictly observed in practice if the survival civilization and the survival of mankind itself is to be assured,

That nuclear weapons, whose terrible effects are suffered, indiscriminately and inexorably, by military forces and civilian population alike, constitute, through the persistence of the radioactivity they release, an attack on the integrity of the human species and ultimately, may even render the whole earth uninhabitable,

That general and complete disarmament under effective international control is a vital matter which all the peoples of the world equally demand,

That the proliferation of nuclear weapons, which seems inevitable unless States, in the exercise of their sovereign rights, impose restrictions on themselves in order to prevent it, would make any agreement on disarmament enormously difficult and would increase the danger of the outbreak of a nuclear conflagration,

That the establishment of militarily denuclearized zones is closely linked with the maintenance of peace and security in the respective regions,

That the military denuclearization of vast geographical zones, adopted by the sovereign decision of the States comprised therein, will exercise a beneficial influence on other regions there similar conditions exist,

That the privileged situation of the signatory States, whose territories are wholly free from nuclear weapons, imposes upon their the inescapable duty of preserving that situation both in their own interests and for the good of mankind,

That the existence of nuclear weapons in any country of Latin America would make it a target for possible nuclear attacks and would inevitably set off, throughout the region a ruinous race in nuclear weapons which would involve the unjustifiable diversion, for warlike purposes, of the resources required for economic and social development,

That the foregoing reasons, together with the traditional peace-loving outlook of Latin America, give rise to an inescapable necessity that nuclear energy should be used in that region exclusively for peaceful purposes, and that the Latin American countries should use their right to the greatest and most equitable possible access to this new source of energy in order to expedite the economic and social development of their peoples,

Convinced finally:

That the military denuclearization of Latin America – being understood to mean the undertaking entered into internationally in this Treaty to keep their territories forever free from nuclear weapons – will constitute a measure which will spare their peoples from the squandering of their limited resources on nuclear armaments and will protect them against possible nuclear attacks on their territories, and will also constitute a significant contribution towards preventing the proliferation of nuclear weapons and a powerful factor for general and complete disarmament, and

That Latin America, faithful to its tradition of universality, must not only endeavour to banish from its homelands the scourge of a nuclear war, but must also strive to promote the well-being and advancement of its peoples, at the same time co-operating in the fulfillment of the ideals of mankind, that is to say, in the consolidation of a permanent peace based on equal rights, economic fairness and social justice for all, in accordance with the principles and purposes set forth in the Charter of the United Nations and in the Charter of the Organization of American States,

Have agreed as follows:

Obligations
Article 1

1. The Contracting Parties hereby undertake to use exclusively for peaceful purposes the nuclear material and facilities which are under their jurisdiction, and to prohibit and prevent in their respective territories:

a. The testing, use, manufacture, production or acquisition by any means whatsoever of any nuclear weapons, by the Parties themselves, directly or indirectly, on behalf of anyone else or in any other way; and

b. The receipt, storage, installation, deployment and any form of possession of any nuclear weapon, directly or indirectly, by the Parties themselves, by anyone on their behalf or in any other way.

2. The Contracting Parties also undertake to refrain from engaging in, encouraging or authorizing, directly or indirectly, or in any way participating in the testing, use, manufacture, production, possession or control of any nuclear weapon.

Definition of the Contracting Parties
Article 2

For the purposes of this Treaty, the Contracting Parties are those for whom the Treaty is in force.

Definition of territory
Article 3

For the purposes of this Treaty, the term "territory" shall include the territorial sea, air space and any other space over which the State exercises sovereignty in accordance with its own legislation.

Zone of application
Article 4

1. The zone of application of the Treaty is the whole of the territories for which the Treaty is in force.
2. Upon fulfillment of the requirements of Article 28, paragraph 1, the zone of application of the Treaty shall also be that which is situated in the western hemisphere with the following limits (except the continental part of the territory of the United States of America and its territorial waters): starting at a point located 35° north latitude, 75° west longitude; from this point directly southward to a point at 30° north latitude, 75° west longitude; from there, directly eastward to a point at 30° north latitude, 50° west longitude; from there along a loxodromic line to a point at 5° north latitude, 20° west longitude; from there directly southward to a point at 60° south latitude, 20° west longitude; from there directly westward to a point at 60° south latitude, 115° west longitude; from there directly northward to a point at 0° latitude, 115° west longitude; from there, along a loxodromic line to a point at 35° north latitude, 150° west longitude; from there, directly eastward to a point at 35° north latitude, 75° west longitude.

Definition of nuclear weapons
Article 5

For the purposes of this Treaty, a nuclear weapon is any device which is capable of releasing nuclear energy in an uncontrolled manner and which has a group of characteristics that are appropriate for use for warlike purposes. An instrument that may be used for the transport or propulsion of the device is not included in this definition if it is separable from the device and not an indivisible part thereof.

Meeting of signatories
Article 6

At the request of any of the signatories or if the Agency established by article 7, should so decide, a meeting of all the signatories may be convoked to consider in common questions which may affect the very essence of this instrument, including possible amendments to it. In either case, the meeting will be convoked by the General Secretary.

Organization
Article 7

1. In order to ensure compliance with the obligations of this Treaty, the Contracting Parties hereby establish an international organization to be known as the "Agency for the Prohibition of Nuclear Weapons in Latin America", hereinafter referred to as "the Agency". Only the Contracting Parties shall be affected by its decisions.
2. The Agency shall be responsible for the holding of periodic or extraordinary consultations among member States on matters relating to the purposes, measures and procedures set forth in this Treaty and the supervision of compliance with the obligations arising therefrom.
3. The Contracting Parties agree to extend to the Agency full and prompt co-operation in accordance with the provisions of this Treaty, of any agreements they may conclude with the Agency and of agreements the Agency may conclude with any other international organization or body.
4. The headquarters of the Agency shall be in Mexico City.

Organs
Article 8

1. There are hereby established as principal organs of the Agency a General Conference, a Council and a Secretariat.
2. Such subsidiary organs are considered necessary by the General Conference may be established within the purview of this Treaty.

The General Conference
Article 9

1. The General Conference, the supreme organ of the Agency, shall be composed of all the Contracting Parties; it shall hold regular sessions every two years and my also hold special sessions whenever this Treaty provides, or, in the opinion of the Council, the circumstances so require.

2. The General Conference:
a. May consider and decide on matters or questions covered by the Treaty; within the limits thereof, including those referring to powers and functions of any organ provided for in this Treaty.
b. Shall establish procedures for the control system to ensure observance of this Treaty in accordance with its provisions.
c. Shall elect the members of the Council and the General Secretary.
d. May remove the General Secretary from office if the proper functioning of the Agency requires.
e. Shall receive and consider the biennial and special reports submitted by the Council and the General Secretary.
f. Shall initiate and consider studies designed to facilitate the optimum fulfillment of the aims of this Treaty, without prejudice to the powers of the General Secretary independently to cry out similar studies for submission to and consideration by the Conference.
g. Shall be the organ competent to authorize the conclusion of agreements with Governments and other international organizations and bodies.

3. The General Conference shall adopt the Agency's budget and fix the scale of financial contributions to be paid by member States, taking into account the systems and criteria used for the same purpose by the United Nations.
4. The General Conference shall elect its officers for each session and may establish such subsidiary organs as it deems necessary for the performance of its functions.
5. Each member of the Agency shall have one vote. The decisions of the General Conference shall be taken by a two-thirds majority of the members present and voting in the case of matters relating to the control system and measures referred to in article 20, the decision of new members, the election or removal of the General Secretary, adoption of the budget and matters related thereto. Decisions on other matters as well as procedural questions, and also determination of which questions must be decided by a two-thirds majority, shall be taken by a simple majority of the members present and voting.
6. The General Conference shall adopt its own rules of procedure.

The Council
Article 10

1. The Council shall be composed of five members of the Agency elected by the General Conference from among the Contracting Parties, due account being taken of equitable geographical distribution.
2. The members of the Council shall be elected for a term of four years. However, in the first election three will be elected for two years. Outgoing members may not

be re-elected for the following period unless the limited number of States for which the Treaty is in force so requires.
3. Each member of the Council shall have one representative.
4. The Council shall be so organized as to be able to function contiguously.
5. In addition to the functions conferred upon it by this Treaty and to those which may be assigned to it by the General Conference, the Council shall, through the General Secretary ensure the proper operation of the control system in accordance with the provisions of this Treaty and with the decisions adopted by the General Conference.
6. The Council shall submit an annual report on its work to the General Conference as well as such special report as it deems necessary or which the General Conference requests of it.
7. The Council shall elect its officers for each session.
8. The decisions of the Council shall be taken by a simple majority of its members present and voting.
9. The Council shall adopt its own rules of procedure.

The Secretariat
Article 11

1. The Secretariat shall consist of a General Secretary, who shall be the chief administrative officer of the Agency, and of such staff as the Agency may require. The term of office of the General Secretary shall be four years and he may be re-elected for a single additional term. The General Secretary may not be a national of the country in which the Agency has its headquarters. In case the office of General Secretary becomes vacant, a new election shall be held to fill the office for the remainder of the term.
2. The staff of the Secretariat shall be appointed by the General Secretary, in accordance with rules laid down by the General Conference.
3. In addition to the functions conferred upon him by this Treaty and to those which may be assigned to him by the General Conference, the General Secretary shall ensure, as provided by article 10, paragraph 5, the proper operation of the control system established by this Treaty, in accordance with the provisions of the Treaty and the decisions taken by the General Conference.
4. The General Secretary shall act in that capacity in all meetings of the General Conference and of the Council and shall make an annual report to both bodies on the work of the Agency and any special reports requested by the General Conference or the Council or which the General Secretary may deem desirable.
5. The General Secretary shall establish the procedures for distributing to all Contracting Parties information received by the Agency from governmental sources,

and such information from non-governmental sources as may be of interest to the Agency.

6. In the performance of their duties the General Secretary and the staff shall not seek or receive instructions from any Government or from any other authority external to the Agency and shall refrain from any action which might reflect on their position as international officials responsible only to the Agency; subject to their responsibility to the Agency, they shall not disclose any industrial secrets or other confidential information coming to their knowledge by reason of their official duties in the Agency.

7. Each of the Contracting Parties undertakes to respect the exclusively international character of the responsibilities of the General Secretary and the staff and not to seek to influence them in the discharge of their responsibilities.

Control system
Article 12

1. For the purpose of verifying compliance with the obligations entered into by the Contracting Parties in accordance with article 1, a control system shall be established which shall be put into effect in accordance with the provisions of articles 13 – 18 of this Treaty.

2. The control system shall be used in particular for the purpose of verifying:

a. That devices, services and facilities intended for peaceful uses of nuclear energy are not used in the testing or manufacture of nuclear weapons;

b. That none of the activities prohibited in article 1 of this Treaty are carried out in the territory of the Contracting Parties with nuclear materials or weapons introduced from abroad, and

c. That explosions for peaceful purposes are compatible with article 18 of this Treaty.

IAEA Safeguards
Article 13

Each Contracting Party shall negotiate multilateral or bilateral agreements with the International Atomic Energy Agency for the application of its safeguards to its nuclear activities. Each Contracting Party shall initiate negotiations within a period of 180 days after the date of the deposit of its instrument of ratification of this Treaty. These agreements shall enter into force, for each Party, not later than eighteen months after the date of the initiation of such negotiations except in case of unforeseen circumstances or force majeure.

Reports of the Parties
Article 14

1. The Contracting Parties shall submit to the Agency and to the International Atomic Energy Agency, for their information, semi-annual reports stating that no activity prohibited under this Treaty has occurred in their respective territories.
2. The Contracting Parties shall simultaneously transmit to the Agency a copy of any report they may submit to the International Atomic Energy Agency which relates to matters that are the subject of this Treaty and to the application of safeguards.
3. The Contracting Parties shall also transmit to the Organization of American States, for its information, any reports that may be of interest to it, in accordance with the obligations established by the Inter-American System.

Special report requested by the General Secretary
Article 15

1. With the authorization of the Council, the General Secretary may request any of the Contracting Parties to provide the Agency with complementary or supplementary information regarding any event or circumstance connected with compliance with this Treaty, explaining his reasons. The Contracting Parties undertake to co-operate promptly and fully with the General Secretary.
2. The General Secretary shall inform the Council and the Contracting Parties forthwith of such requests and of the respective replies.

Special inspections
Article 16

1. The International Atomic Energy Agency and the Council established by this Treaty have the power of carrying out special inspections in the following cases:
a. In the case of the International Atomic Energy Agency, in accordance with the agreements referred to in article 13 of the Treaty;
b. In the ease of the Council:
i. When so requested, the reasons for the request being stated, by any Party which suspects that some activity prohibited by this Treaty has been carried out or is about to be carried out, either in the territory of any other Party or in any other place on such latter Party's behalf, the Council shall immediately arrange for such an inspection in accordance with article 10, paragraph 5.
ii. When requested by any Party which has been suspected of or charged with having violated the Treaty, the Council shall immediately arrange for the special inspection requested, in accordance with article 10, paragraph 5.

The above requests will be made to the Council through the General Secretary.
2.
3. The costs and expenses of any special inspection carried out under paragraph 1, sub-paragraph (b), sections (i) and (ii) of this article shall be borne by the requesting Party or Parties, except where the Council concludes on the basis of the report on the special inspection that, in view of the circumstances existing in the case, such costs and expenses should be borne by the Agency.
4. The General Conference shall formulate the procedures for the organization and execution of the special inspections carried out in accordance with paragraph 1, sub-paragraph (b), sections (i) and (ii) of this article.
5. The Contracting Parties undertake to grant the inspectors carrying out such special inspections full and free access to all places and all information which may be necessary for the performance of their duties and which are directly and intimately connected with the suspicion of violation of this Treaty. If so requested by the Contracting Party in whose territory the inspection is carried out, the inspectors designated by the General Conference shall be accompanied by representatives of the authorities of that Contracting Party, provided that this does not in any way delay or hinder the work of the inspectors.
6. The Council shall immediately transmit to all the Parties through the General Secretary, a copy of any report resulting from special inspections.
7. Similarly, the Council shall send through the General Secretary to the Secretary-General of United Nations for transmission to the United Nations Security Council and General Assembly, and to the Council of the Organization of American States, for its information, a copy of any report resulting from any special inspection carried out in accordance with paragraph 1, sub-paragraph (b), sections (i) and (ii) of this article.
8. The Council may decide, or any Contracting Party may request, the convening of a special session of the General Conference for the purpose of considering the reports resulting from any special inspection. In such a case, the General Secretary shall take immediate steps to convene the special session requested.
9. The General Conference convened in special session under this article, may make recommendations to the Contracting Parties and submit reports to the Secretary-General of the United Nations to be transmitted to the Security Council and the General Assembly.

Use of nuclear energy for peaceful purposes
Article 17

Nothing in the provisions of this Treaty shall prejudice the rights of the Contracting Parties, in conformity with this Treaty, to use nuclear energy for peaceful purposes, in particular for their economic development and social progress.

Explosions for peaceful purposes
Article 18

1. The Contracting Parties may carry out explosions of nuclear devices for peaceful purposes – including explosions which involve devices similar to those used in nuclear weapons – or collaborate with third parties for the same purpose, provided that they do so in accordance with the provisions of this article and the other articles of the Treaty, particularly articles 1 and 5.
2. Contracting Parties intending to carry out, or co-operate in the carrying out of such, an explosion shall notify the Agency and the International Atomic Energy Agency, as far in advance as the circumstances require, of the date of the explosion and shall at the same time provide the following information:
a. The nature of the nuclear device and the source from which it was obtained,
b. The place and purpose of the nuclear explosion,
c. The procedures which will be followed in order to comply with paragraph 3 of this article,
d. The expected force of the device,
e. The earliest possible information on any possible radioactive fall-out that may result from the explosion or explosions and the measures which will be taken to avoid danger to the population, flora & fauna, and territories of any other Party or Parties.

3. The General Secretary and the technical personnel designated by the Council and the International Atomic Energy Agency may observe all the preparations, including the explosion of the device, and shall have unrestricted access to all areas in the vicinity of the site of the explosion in order to ascertain whether the device and the procedures followed during the explosion are in conformity with the information supplied under paragraph 2 of the present article and the other provisions of this Treaty.
4. The Contracting Parties may accept the collaboration of third parties for the purpose set forth in paragraph 1 of the present article, in accordance with paragraphs 2 and 3 thereof.

Relations with other international organizations
Article 19

1. The Agency may conclude such agreements with the International Atomic Energy Agency as are authorized by the General Conference and as it considers likely to facilitate the efficient operation of the control system established by this Treaty.
2. The Agency may also enter into relations with any international organization or body, especially any which may be established in the future to supervise disarmament or measures for the control of armaments in any part of the world.

3. The Contracting Parties may, if they see fit, request the advice of the Inter-American Nuclear Energy Commission on all technical matters connected with the application of the Treaty with which the Commission is competent to deal under its Statute.

Measures in the event of violation of the Treaty
Article 20

1. The General Conference shall take note of all cases in which, in its opinion, any Contracting Party is not complying fully with its obligations under this Treaty and shall draw the matter to the attention of the Party concerned, making such recommendations as it deems appropriate.
2. If, in its opinion, such non-compliance constitutes a violation of this Treaty which might endanger peace and security, the General Conference shall report thereon simultaneously to the Security Council and the General Assembly through the Secretary-General of the United Nations and to the Council of the Organization of American States. The General Conference shall likewise report to the International Atomic Energy Agency for such purposes as are relevant in accordance with its Statute.

United Nations and Organization of Member States
Article 21

None of the provisions of this Treaty shall be construed as impairing the rights and obligations of the Parties under the Charter of the United Nations or, in the case of States members of the Organization of American States, under existing regional treaties.

Privileges and Immunities
Article 22

1. The Agency shall enjoy all the territory of each of the Contracting Parties such legal capacity and such privileges and immunities as may be necessary for the exercise of its functions and the fulfillment of its purposes.
2. Representatives of the Contracting Parties accredited to the Agency and officials of the Agency shall similarily enjoy such privileges and immunities as are necessary for the performance of their functions.
3. The Agency may conclude agreements with the Contracting Parties with a view to determining the details of the application of paragraphs 1 and 2 of this article.

Notification of other agreements
Article 23

Once this Treaty has entered into force, the Secretariat shall be notified immediately of any international agreement concluded by any of the Contracting Parties on matters with which this Treaty is concerned; the Secretariat shall register it and notify the other Contracting Parties.

Settlement of disputes
Article 24

Unless the Parties concerned agree on another mode of peaceful settlement, any question or dispute concerning the interpretation or application of this treaty which is not settled shall be referred to the International Court of Justice with the prior consent of the parties to the controversy.

Signature
Article 25

1. This Treaty shall be open indefinitely for signature by:
a. All the Latin American Republics;
b. All other sovereign States situated in their entirety south of latitude 35° north in the western hemisphere; and, except as provided in paragraph 2 of this article, all such States which become sovereign, when they have been admitted by the General Conference.

2. The General Conference shall not take any decision regarding the admission of a political entity part of all of whose territory is still subject, prior to the date when this Treaty is opened for signature, of a dispute or claim between an extra-continental country and one or more Latin American States, so long as the dispute has not been settled by peaceful means.

Ratification and deposit
Article 26

1. This Treaty shall be subject to ratification by signatory States in accordance with their respective constitutional procedures.
2. This Treaty and the instruments of ratification shall be deposited with the Government of the United States of Mexico, which is hereby designated the Depositary Government.

3. The Depositary Government shall send certified copies of this Treaty to the Governments of signatory States and shall notify them of the deposit of each instrument of ratification.

Reservations
Article 27

This Treaty shall not be subject to reservations.

Entry into Force
Article 28

1. Subject to the provisions of paragraphs 2 and 3 of this article, this Treaty shall enter into force among the States that have ratified it as soon as the following requirements have been met:
a. Deposit of the instruments of ratification of this Treaty with the Depositary Government by the Governments of the States mentioned in article 25 which are in existence on the date when this Treaty is opened for signature and which are not affected by the provisions of article 25, paragraph 2;
b. Signature and ratification of Additional Protocol I annexed to this Treaty by all extracontinental and continental States having de jure or de facto international responsibility for territories situated in the zone of application of the Treaty;
c. Signature and ratification of the Additional Protocol II annexed to this Treaty by all powers possessing nuclear weapons;
d. Conclusion of bilateral agreements on the application of the Safeguards System of the International Atomic Energy Agency in accordance with article 13 of this Treaty.

2. All signatory States shall have the imprescriptible right to waive, wholly or in part, the requirements laid down in the preceding paragraph. They may do so by means of a declaration which shall be annexed to their respective instruments of ratification and which may be formulated at the time of deposit of the instrument or subsequently. For those States which exercise this right, this Treaty shall enter into force upon deposit of the declaration, or as soon as those requirements have been met which have not been expressly waived.
3. As soon as this Treaty has entered into force in accordance with the provisions of paragraph 2 for eleven States, the Depositary Government shall convene a preliminary meeting of those States in order that the Agency may be set up and commence its work.
4. After the entry into force of the Treaty for all the countries of the zone, the rise of a new power possessing nuclear weapons shall have the effect of suspending the execution of this Treaty for those countries which have ratified it without waiving the requirements of paragraph 1, sub-paragraph (c) of this article, and which request such

suspension; the Treaty shall remain suspended until the new power, on its own initiative or upon request by the General Conference, ratifies the annexed Additional Protocol.

Amendments
Article 29

1. Any Contracting Party may propose amendments to this Treaty and shall submit their proposals to the Council through the General Secretary, who shall transmit them to all the other Contracting Parties and, in addition, to signatories in accordance with Article 6. The Council, through the General Secretary, shall, immediately following the meeting of signatories, convene a special session of the General Conference to examine the proposals made, for the adoption of which a two-thirds majority of the Contracting Parties present and voting shall be required.
2. Amendments adopted shall enter into force as soon as the requirements set forth in article 28 of this Treaty have been complied with.

Duration and denunciation
Article 30

1. This Treaty shall be of a permanent nature and shall remain in force indefinitely, but any Party may denounce it by notifying the General Secretary of the Agency if, in the opinion of the denouncing State, there have arisen or may arise circumstances connected with the content of the Treaty or of the annexed Additional Protocols I and II which affect its supreme interests and the peace and security of one or more Contracting Parties.
2. The denunciation shall take effect three months after the delivery to the General Secretary of the Agency of the notification by the Government of the signatory State concerned. The General Secretary shall immediately communicate such notification to the other Contracting Parties and to the Secretary-General of the United Nations for the information of the Security Council and the General Assembly of the United Nations. He shall also communicate it to the Secretary General of the Organization of American States.

Authentic texts and Registration
Article 31

This Treaty, of which the Spanish, Chinese, English, French, Portuguese and Russian texts are equally authentic, shall be registered by the Depositary Government in accordance with Article 102 of the United Nations Charter. The Depositary Government shall notify the Secretary-General of the United Nations of the signatures, ratifications and amendments relating to this Treaty and shall communicate them to the Secretary General of the Organization of American States for his information.

Transitional article

Denunciation of the declaration referred to in Article 28, paragraph 2, shall be subject to the same procedures as the denunciation of the Treaty, except that it shall take effect on the date of delivery of the respective notification.

In witness whereof the undersigned Plenipotentiaries, having deposited their full powers, found in good and due form, sign this Treaty on behalf of their respective Governments. Done at Mexico, Distrito Federal, on the Fourteenth day of February, one thousand nine hundred and sixty-seven.

ADDITIONAL PROTOCOL I

The undersigned Plenipotentiaries, furnished with full powers by their respective Governments,

Convinced that the Treaty for the Prohibition of Nuclear Weapons in Latin America, negotiated and signed in accordance with the recommendations of the General Assembly of the United Nations in resolution 1911 (XVIIl) of 27 November 1963, represents an important step towards ensuring the non-prolifertion of nuclear weapons,

Aware that the non-proliferation of nuclear weapons is not an end in itself but rather a means of achieving general and complete disarmament at a later stage,

Desiring to contribute, so far as lies in their power, toward ending the armaments race, especially in the field of nuclear weapons, and towards strengthening a world at peace, based on mutual respect and sovereign equality of States,

Have agreed as follows:

Article 1. To undertake to apply the status of denuclearization in respect of warlike purposes as defined in Articles 1, 3, 5 and 13 of the Treaty for the Prohibition of Nuclear Weapons in Latin America in territories for which, de jure or de facto, they are internationally responsible and which lie within the limits of the geographical zone established in that Treaty.

Article 2. The duration of this Protocol shall be the same as that of the Treaty for the Prohibition of Nuclear Weapons in Latin America of which this Protocol is an annex, and the provisions regarding ratification and denunciation contained in the Treaty shall be applicable to it.

Article 3. This Protocol shall enter into force, for the States which have ratified it, on the date of the deposit of their respective instruments of ratification.

In witness whereof the undersigned Plenipotentiaries, having deposited their full powers, found in good and due form, sign this Treaty on behalf of their respective Governments.

ADDITIONAL PROTOCOL II

The undersigned Plenipotentiaries, furnished with full powers by their respective Governments,

Convinced that the Treaty for the Prohibition of Nuclear Weapons in Latin America, negotiated and signed in accordance with the recommendations of the General Assembly of the United Nations in resolution 1911 (XVIII) of 27 November 1963, is an important step towards ensuring the non-proliferation of nuclear weapons,

Aware that the non-proliferation of nuclear weapons is not an end in itself achieving general and complete disarmament at a later stage,

Desiring to contribute, so far as lies in their power, towards ending the armaments race, especially in the field of nuclear weapons, and toward promoting and strengthening a world at peace based on mutual respect ad sovereign equality of States,

Have agreed as follows:

Article 1. The status of denuclearization of Latin America in respect of warlike purposes, as defined, delimited and set forth in the Treaty for the Prohibition of Nuclear Weapons in Latin America of which this instrument is an annex, shall be fully respected by the Parties to this Protocol in all its express aims and provisions.

Article 2. The Governments represented by the undersigned Plenipotentiaries undertake, therefore, not to contribute in any way to the performance of acts involving a violation of the obligations of article 1 of the Treaty in the territories to which the Treaty applies in accordance with article 4 thereof.

Article 3. The Governments represented by the undersigned Plenipotentiaries also undertake not to use or threaten to use nuclear weapons against the Contracting Parties of the Treaty for the Prohibition of Nuclear Weapons in Latin America.

Article 4. The duration of this Protocol shall be the same as that of the Treaty for the Prohibition of Nuclear Weapons in Latin America of which this Protocol is an annex, and the definitions of territory and nuclear weapons set forth in articles 3 and 5 of the Treaty shall be applicable to the Protocol, as well as the provisions regarding ratification, reservations, denunciation, authentic texts and registration contained in articles 26, 27, 30 an 31 of the Treaty.

Article 5. This Protocol shall enter into force, for the States which have ratified it, on the date of the deposit of their respective instruments of ratification. In witness whereof the undersigned Plenipotentiaries, having deposited their of powers, found in good and due form, sign this Treaty on behalf of their respective Governments.

TREATY ON THE PROHIBITION OF THE EMPLACEMENT OF NUCLEAR WEAPONS AND OTHER WEAPONS OF MASS DESTRUCTION ON THE SEA-BED AND ON THE OCEAN-BED AND ON THE OCEAN FLOOR AND IN THE SUBSOIL THEREOF

(London, Moscow, Washington, 11 February 1971)

After the1963 Treaty banning nuclear weapon tests (CTBT, see previous pages) this Treaty is a further step towards the limitation of and "control" over military nuclear activities worldwide. In fact, the contracting parties commit themselves, under strict international control, to not placing any nuclear weapon or other weapon of mass destruction, or any construction or installation to be used for such weapons.

In order to promote the objectives of the Treaty as well as compliance with it, each State party has the right to observe the activities carried out by another State and having an impact on the areas considered by the Treaty. States may consult with each other in case of doubts concerning the compliance of such activities with the Treaty provisions, they may also carry out enquiries and inspections and, if necessary, seize the Security Council of the United Nations.

Under article VII conferences are held (in Geneva, Switzerland) every five years, where an assessment is made on the application of the Treaty and the respect of its provisions. The Treaty (in force since March 18, 1972) is open to signature by all States and the conditions for its entry into force are laid down in article X, that is ratification by 22 governments, including the depositary governments which are in fact those of the USA, the United Kingdom and the Soviet Union: it is recalled that these countries are the same as the "original parties" to the CTBT. The Treaty has now some 80 contracting Parties.

THE STATES PARTIES TO THIS TREATY,

RECOGNIZING the common interest of mankind in the progress of the exploration and use of the sea-bed and the ocean floor for peaceful purposes,
CONSIDERING that the prevention of a nuclear arms race on the sea-bed and the ocean floor serves the interests of maintaining world peace, reduces international tensions and strengthens friendly relations among States,

CONVINCED that this Treaty constitutes a step towards the exclusion of the sea-bed, the ocean floor and the subsoil thereof from the arms race,
CONVINCED that this Treaty constitutes a step towards a treaty on general and complete disarmament under strict and effective international control, and determined to continue negotiations to this end,
CONVINCED that this Treaty will further the purposes and principles of the Charter of the United Nations, in a manner consistent with the principles of international law and without infringing the freedoms of the high seas,

HAVE AGREED as follows:

Article I

1. The States Parties to this Treaty undertake not to implant or emplace on the sea-bed and the ocean floor and in the subsoil thereof beyond the outer limit of a sea-bed zone, as defined in Article II, any nuclear weapons or any other types of weapons of mass destruction as well as structures, launching installations or any other facilities specifically designed for storing, testing or using such weapons.
2. The undertakings of paragraph 1 of this Article shall also apply to the sea-bed zone referred to in the same paragraph, except that within such sea-bed zone, they shall not apply either to the coastal State or to the sea-bed beneath its territorial waters.
3. The States Parties to this Treaty undertake not to assist, encourage or induce any State to carry out activities referred to in paragraph 1 of this Article and not to participate in any other way in such actions.

Article II

For the purpose of this Treaty, the outer limit of the sea-bed zone referred to in Article I shall be coterminous with the twelve-mile outer limit of the zone referred to in Part II of the Convention on the Territorial Sea and the Contiguous Zone, signed at Geneva on 29 April 1958, and shall be measured in accordance with the provisions of Part I, Section II, of that Convention and in accordance with international law.

Article III

1. In order to promote the objectives of and ensure compliance with the provisions of this Treaty, each State Party to the Treaty shall have the right to verify through observation the activities of other States Parties to the Treaty on the sea-bed and the ocean floor and in the subsoil thereof beyond the zone referred to in Article I, provided that observation does not interfere with such activities.

2. If after such observation reasonable doubts remain concerning the fulfilment of the obligations assumed under the Treaty, the State Party having such doubts and the State Party that is responsible for the activities giving rise to the doubts shall consult with a view to removing the doubts. If the doubts persist, the State Party having such doubts shall notify the other States Parties, and the Parties concerned shall co-operate on such further procedures for verification as may be agreed, including appropriate inspection of objects, structures, installations or other facilities that reasonably may be expected to be of a kind described in Article I. The Parties in the region of the activities, including any coastal State, and any other Party so requesting, shall be entitled to participate in such consultation and co-operation. After completion of the further procedures for verification, an appropriate report shall be circulated to other Parties by the Party that initiated such procedures.
3. If the State responsible for the activities giving rise to the reasonable doubts is not identifiable by observation of the object, structure, installation or other facility, the State Party having such doubts shall notify and make appropriate inquiries of States Parties in the region of the activities and of any other State Party. If it is ascertained through these inquiries that a particular State Party is responsible for the activities, that State Party shall consult and co-operate with other Parties as provided in paragraph 2 of this Article. If the identity of the State responsible for the activities cannot be ascertained through these inquiries, then further verification procedures, including inspection, may be undertaken by the inquiring State Party, which shall invite the participation of the Parties in the region of the activities, including any coastal State, and of any other Party desiring to co-operate.
4. If consultation and co-operation pursuant to paragraphs 2 and 3 of this Article have not removed the doubts concerning the activities and there remains a serious question concerning fulfilment of the obligations assumed under this Treaty, a State Party may, in accordance with the provisions of the Charter of the United Nations, refer the matter to the Security Council, which may take action in accordance with the Charter.
5. Verification pursuant to this Article may be undertaken by any State Party using its own means, or with the full or partial assistance of any other State Party, or through appropriate international procedures within the framework of the United Nations and in accordance with its Charter.
6. Verification activities pursuant to this Treaty shall not interfere with activities of other States Parties and shall be conducted with due regard for rights recognized under international law, including the freedoms of the high seas and the rights of coastal States with respect to the exploration and exploitation of their continental shelves.

Article IV

Nothing in this Treaty shall be interpreted as supporting or prejudicing the position of any State Party with respect to existing international conventions, including the 1958

Convention on the Territorial Sea and the Contiguous Zone, or with respect to rights or claims which such State Party may assert, or with respect to recognition or non-recognition of rights or claims asserted by any other State, related to waters off its coasts, including, *inter alia*, territorial seas and contiguous zones, or to the sea-bed and the ocean floor, including continental shelves.

Article V

The Parties to this Treaty undertake to continue negotiations in good faith concerning further measures in the field of disarmament for the prevention of an arms race on the sea-bed, the ocean floor and the subsoil thereof.

Article VI

Any State Party may propose amendments to this Treaty. Amendments shall enter into force for each State Party accepting the amendments upon their acceptance by a majority of the States Parties to the Treaty and, thereafter, for each remaining State Party on the date of acceptance by it.

Article VII

Five years after the entry into force of this Treaty, a conference of Parties to the Treaty shall be held at Geneva, Switzerland, in order to review the operation of this Treaty with a view to assuring that the purposes of the preamble and the provisions of the Treaty are being realised. Such review shall take into account any relevant technological developments. The review conference shall determine, in accordance with the views of a majority of those Parties attending, whether and when an additional review conference shall be convened.

Article VIII

Each State Party to this Treaty shall in exercising its national sovereignty have the right to withdraw from this Treaty if it decides that extraordinary events related to the subject-matter of this Treaty have jeopardised the supreme interests of its country. It shall give notice of such withdrawal to all other States Parties to the Treaty and to the United Nations Security Council three months in advance. Such notice shall include a statement of the extraordinary events it considers to have jeopardised its supreme interests.

Article IX

The provisions of this Treaty shall in no way affect the obligations assumed by States Parties to the Treaty under international instruments establishing zones free from nuclear weapons.

Article X

1. This Treaty shall be open for signature to all States. Any State which does not sign the Treaty before its entry into force in accordance with paragraph 3 of this Article may accede to it at any time.
2. This Treaty shall be subject to ratification by signatory States. Instruments of ratification and of accession shall be deposited with the Governments of the United Kingdom of Great Britain and Northern Ireland, the Union of Soviet Socialist Republics and the United States of America, which are hereby designated the Depositary Governments.
3. This Treaty shall enter into force after the deposit of instruments of ratification by twenty-two Governments, including the Governments designated as Depositary Governments of this Treaty.
4. For States whose instruments of ratification or accession are deposited after the entry into force of this Treaty, it shall enter into force on the date of the deposit of their instruments of ratification or accession.
5. The Depositary Governments shall promptly inform the Governments of all signatory and acceding States of the date of each signature, of the date of deposit of each instrument of ratification or of accession, of the date of the entry into force of this Treaty, and of the receipt of other notices.
6. This Treaty shall be registered by the Depositary Governments pursuant to Article 102 of the Charter of the United Nations.

Article XI

This Treaty, the English, Russian, French, Spanish and Chinese texts of which are equally authentic, shall be deposited in the archives of the Depositary Governments. Duly certified copies of this Treaty shall be transmitted by the Depositary Governments to the Governments of the States signatory any acceding thereto.

IN WITNESS WHEREOF the undersigned, being duly authorised thereto, have signed this Treaty.

DONE in triplicate, at the cities of London, Moscow and Washington, this eleventh day of February, one thousand nine hundred and seventy-one.

[Signatures not reproduced here.]

SOUTH PACIFIC NUCLEAR FREE ZONE TREATY

(Rarotonga, 6 August 1985)

This Treaty provides for the establishment of a nuclear weapon free zone in the South Pacific, covering an area which extends from Australia and New Guinea to the region covered by the Tlatelolco Treaty (see in this Section), to Equator and to the South of Antarctica (also de-nuclearised, see again in this Section).

The Treaty was adopted during the 16th South Pacific Forum held in Rarotonga (Cook Islands), committing the signatories States to not making any use of nuclear weapons and to complying with the IAEA safeguards system (see Section One). Three Protocols (adopted in 1986) supplement the Treaty, being addressed to five nuclear weapon States (China, France, the Soviet Union, the United Kingdom and the USA), inviting them to apply the prohibitions stipulated by the Treaty to the territories for which they have international responsibilities, and to refrain from using nuclear weapons and from nuclear tests in the nuclear free zone.

The Treaty entered into force on 11 December 1986 and it has now 14 contracting Parties.

It is recalled that a Protocol (not published here) for the protection of the South-East Pacific against radioactive pollution was adopted on 21 September 1989 (and entered into force on 22 August 1990) under the aegis of a Permanent Commission for the South-East Pacific. The Parties to the Protocol agreed to prohibit any burial or dumping or radioactive waste in the area considered, in line with the relevant IAEA recommendations.

PREAMBLE

The Parties to this Treaty,

United in their commitment to a world at peace;
Gravely concerned that the continuing nuclear arms race presents the risk of nuclear war which would have devastating consequences for all people;
Convinced that all countries have an obligation to make every effort to achieve the goal of eliminating nuclear weapons, the terror which they hold for humankind and the threat which they pose to life on earth;
Believing that regional arms control measures can contribute to global efforts to reverse the nuclear arms race and promote the national security of each country in the region and the common security of all;

Determined to ensure, so far as lies within their power, that the bounty and beauty of the land and sea in their region shall remain the heritage of their peoples and their descendants in perpetuity to be enjoyed by all in peace;
Reaffirming the importance of the Treaty on the Non-Proliferation of Nuclear Weapons (NPT) in preventing the proliferation of nuclear weapons and in contributing to world security;
Noting, in particular, that Article VII of the NPT recognizes the right of any group of States to conclude regional treaties in order to assure the total absence of nuclear weapons in their respective territories;
Noting that the prohibitions of implantation and emplacement of nuclear weapons on the seabed and the ocean floor and in the subsoil thereof contained in the Treaty on the Prohibition of the Emplacement of Nuclear Weapons and Other Weapons of Mass Destruction on the Seabed and the Ocean Floor and in the Subsoil Thereof apply in the South Pacific;
Noting also that the prohibition of testing of nuclear weapons in the atmosphere or under water, including territorial waters or high seas, contained in the Treaty Banning Nuclear Weapon Tests in the Atmosphere, in Outer Space and Under Water applies in the South Pacific;
Determined to keep the region free of environmental pollution by radioactive wastes and other radioactive matter;
Guided by the decision of the Fifteenth South Pacific Forum at Tuvalu that a nuclear free zone should be established in the region at the earliest possible opportunity in accordance with the principles set out in the communiqué of that meeting;

Have agreed as follows:

Article 1
Usage of terms

For the purposes of this Treaty and its Protocols:

a. "South Pacific Nuclear Free Zone" means the areas described in Annex 1 as illustrated by the map attached to that Annex; *(Note: the map is not included in this electronic version.)*
b. "territory" means internal waters, territorial sea and archipelagic waters, the seabed and subsoil beneath, the land territory and the airspace above them:
c. "nuclear explosive device" means any nuclear weapon or other explosive device capable of releasing nuclear energy, irrespective of the purpose for which it could be used. The term includes such a weapon or device in unassembled and partly assembled forms, but does not include the means of transport or delivery of such a weapon or device if separable from and not an indivisible part of it;

d. "stationing" means implantation, emplacement, transportation on land or inland waters, stockpiling, storage, installation and deployment.

Article 2
Application of the Treaty

1. Except where otherwise specified, this Treaty and its Protocols shall apply to territory within the South Pacific Nuclear Free Zone.
2. Nothing in this Treaty shall prejudice or in any way affect the rights, or the exercise of the rights, of any State under international law with regard to freedom of the seas.

Article 3
Renunciation of nuclear explosive devices

Each Party undertakes:
a. not to manufacture or otherwise acquire, possess or have control over any nuclear explosive device by any means anywhere inside or outside the South Pacific Nuclear Free Zone;
b. not to seek or receive any assistance in the manufacture or acquisition of any nuclear explosive device;
c. not to take any action to assist or encourage the manufacture or acquisition of any nuclear explosive device by any State.

Article 4
Peaceful nuclear activities

Each Party undertakes:
a. not to provide source or special fissionable material, or equipment or material especially designed or prepared for the processing, use or production of special fissionable material for peaceful purposes to:
   i. any non-nuclear-weapon State unless subject to the safeguards required by Article III.l of the NPT, or
   ii. any nuclear-weapon State unless subject to applicable safeguards agreements with the International Atomic Energy Agency (IAEA).

   Any such provisions shall be in accordance with strict non-proliferation measures to provide assurance of exclusively peaceful non-explosive use;
b. to support the continued effectiveness of the international non-proliferation system based on the NPT and the IAEA safeguards system.

Article 5
Prevention of stationing of nuclear explosive devices

1. Each Party undertakes to prevent in its territory the stationing of any nuclear explosive device.
2. Each Party in the exercise of its sovereign rights remains free to decide for itself whether to allow visits by foreign ships and aircraft to its ports and airfields, transit of its airspace by foreign aircraft, and navigation by foreign ships in its territorial sea or archipelagic waters in a manner not covered by the rights of innocent passage, archipelagic sea lane passage or transit passage of straits.

Article 6
Prevention of testing of nuclear explosive devices

Each Party undertakes:
a. to prevent in its territory the testing of any nuclear explosive device;
b. not to take any action to assist or encourage the testing of any nuclear explosive device by any State.

Article 7
Prevention of dumping

1. Each Party undertakes:
a. not to dump radioactive wastes and other radioactive matter at sea anywhere within the South Pacific Nuclear Free Zone;
b. to prevent the dumping of radioactive wastes and other radioactive matter by anyone in its territorial sea;
c. not to take any action to assist or encourage the dumping by anyone of radioactive wastes and other radioactive matter at sea anywhere within the South Pacific Nuclear Free Zone;
d. to support the conclusion as soon as possible of the proposed Convention relating to the protection of the natural resources and environment of the South Pacific region and its Protocol for the prevention of pollution of the South Pacific region by dumping, with the aim of precluding dumping at sea of radioactive wastes and other radioactive matter by anyone anywhere in the region.

2. Paragraphs l(a) and l(b) of this Article shall not apply to areas of the South Pacific Nuclear Free Zone in respect of which such a Convention and Protocol have entered into force.

Article 8
Control system

1. The Parties hereby establish a control system for the purpose of verifying compliance with their obligations under this Treaty.
2. The control system shall comprise:
a. reports and exchange of information as provided for in Article 9;
b. consultations as provided for in Article 10 and Annex 4 (1);
c. the application to peaceful nuclear activities of safeguards by the IAEA as provided for in Annex 2;
d. a complaints procedure as provided for in Annex 4.

Article 9
Reports and exchanges of information

1. Each Party shall report to the Director of the South Pacific Bureau for Economic Co-operation (the Director) as soon as possible any significant event within its jurisdiction affecting the implementation of this Treaty. The Director shall circulate such reports promptly to all Parties.
2. The Parties shall endeavour to keep each other informed on matters arising under or in relation to this Treaty. They may exchange information by communicating it to the Director, who shall circulate it to all Parties.
3. The Director shall report annually to the South Pacific Forum on the status of this Treaty and matters arising under or in relation to it, incorporating reports and communications made under paragraphs 1 and 2 of this Article and matters arising under Articles 8(2)(d) and 10 and Annex 2(4).

Article 10
Consultations and review

Without prejudice to the conduct of consultations among Parties by other means, the Director, at the request of any Party, shall convene a meeting of the Consultative Committee established by Annex for consultation and co-operation on any matter arising in relation to this Treaty or for reviewing its operation.

Article 11
Amendment

The Consultative Committee shall consider proposals for amendment of the provisions of this Treaty proposed by any Party and circulated by the Director to all Parties not less than three months prior to the convening of the Consultative Committee for this purpose. Any proposal agreed upon by consensus by the Consultative Committee shall be communicated to the Director who shall circulate it for acceptance to all Parties. An amendment shall enter into force thirty days after receipt by the depositary of acceptances from all Parties.

Article 12
Nature and ratification

1. This Treaty shall be open for signature by any Member of the South Pacific Forum.
2. This Treaty shall be subject to ratification. Instruments of ratification shall be deposited with the Director who is hereby designated depositary of this Treaty and its Protocols.
3. If a Member of the South Pacific Forum whose territory is outside the South Pacific Nuclear Free Zone becomes a Party to this Treaty, Annex 1 shall be deemed to be amended 80 far as is required to enclose at least the territory of that Party within the boundaries of the South Pacific Nuclear Free Zone. The delineation of any area added pursuant to this paragraph shall be approved by the South Pacific Forum.

Article 13
Withdrawal

1. This Treaty is of a permanent nature and shall remain in force indefinitely, provided that in the event of a violation by any Party of a provision of this Treaty essential to the achievement of the objectives of the Treaty or of the spirit of the Treaty, every other Party shall have the right to withdraw from the Treaty.
2. Withdrawal shall be effected by giving notice twelve months in advance to the Director who shall circulate such notice to all other Parties.

Article 14
Reservations

This Treaty shall not be subject to reservations.

Article 15
Entry into force

1. This Treaty shall enter into force on the date of deposit of the eighth instrument Or ratification.
2. For a signatory which ratifies this Treaty after the date of deposit of the eighth instrument of ratification, the Treaty shall enter into force on the date of deposit of its instrument of ratification.

Article 16
Depositary functions

The depositary shall register this Treaty and its Protocol pursuant to Article 102 of the Charter of the United Nations and shall transmit certified copies of the Treaty and its Protocols to all Members of the South Pacific Forum and all States eligible to become Party to the Protocols to the Treaty and shall notify them of signatures and ratifications of the Treaty and its Protocols.

IN WITNESS WHEREOF the undersigned, being duly authorized by their Governments, have signed this Treaty.

DONE at Rarotonga, this sixth day of August, One thousand nine hundred and eighty-five, in a single original in the English language.

ANNEX 1
SOUTH PACIFIC NUCLEAR FREE ZONE

A. The area bounded by a line:

1. commencing at the point of intersection of the Equator by the maritime boundary between Indonesia and Papua New Guinea;
2. running thence northerly along that maritime boundary to its intersection by the outer limit of the exclusive economic zone of Papua New Guinea;
3. thence generally north-easterly, easterly and south-easterly along that outer limit to its intersection by the Equator;
4. thence east along the Equator to its intersection by the meridian of Longitude 163 degrees East;
5. thence north along that meridian to its intersection by the parallel of Latitude 3 degrees North;
6. thence east along that parallel to its intersection by the meridian of Longitude 171 degrees East;
7. thence north along that meridian to its intersection by the parallel of Latitude 4 degrees North;
8. thence east along that parallel to its intersection by the meridian of Longitude 180 degrees East;
9. thence south along that meridian to its intersection by the Equator;
10. thence east along the Equator to its intersection by the meridian of Longitude 165 degrees West;
11. thence north along that meridian to its intersection by the Parallel of Latitude 5 degrees 30 minutes North;

12. thence east along that parallel to its intersection by the meridian of Longitude 154 degrees West;
13. thence south along that meridian to its intersection by the Equator;
14. thence east along the Equator to its intersection by the meridian of Longitude 115 degrees West;
15. thence south along that meridian to its intersection by the parallel of Latitude 60 degrees South;
16. thence west along that parallel to its intersection by the meridian of Longitude 115 degrees East;
17. thence north along that meridian to its southernmost intersection by the outer limit of the territorial sea of Australia;
18. thence generally northerly and easterly along the outer limit of the territorial sea of Australia to its intersection by the meridian of Longitude 136 degrees 45 minutes East;
19. thence north-easterly along the geodesic to the point of Latitude 10 degrees 50 minutes South, Longitude 139 degrees 12 minutes East;
20. thence north-easterly along the maritime boundary between Indonesia and Papua New Guinea to where it joins the land border between those two countries;
21. thence generally northerly along that land border to where it joins the maritime boundary between Indonesia and Papua New Guinea, on the northern coastline of Papua New Guinea; and
22. thence generally northerly along that boundary to the point of commencement.

B. The areas within the outer limits of the territorial seas of all Australian islands lying westward of the area described in paragraph A and north of Latitude 60 degrees South, provided that any such areas shall cease to be part of the South Pacific Nuclear Free Zone upon receipt by the depositary of written notice from the Government of Australia stating that the areas have become subject to another treaty having an object and purpose substantially the same as that of this Treaty.

ANNEX 2
IAEA SAFEGUARDS

1. The safeguards referred to in Article 8 shall in respect of each Party be applied by the IAEA as set forth in an agreement negotiated and concluded with the IAEA on all source or special fissionable material in all peaceful nuclear activities within the territory of the Party, under its jurisdiction or carried out under its control anywhere.
2. The agreement referred to in paragraph 1 shall be, or shall be equivalent in its scope and effect to, an agreement required in connection with the NPT on the basis of

the material reproduced in document INFCIRC/153 (Corrected) of the IAEA. Each Party shall take all appropriate steps to ensure that such an agreement is in force for it not later than 18 months after the date of entry into force for that Party of this Treaty.

3. For the purposes of this Treaty, the safeguards referred to in paragraph 1 shall have as their purpose the verification of the non-diversion of nuclear material from peaceful nuclear activities to nuclear explosive devices.
4. Each Party agrees upon the request of any other Party to transmit to that Party and to the Director for the information of all Parties a copy of the overall conclusions of the most recent report by the IAEA on its inspection activities in the territory of the Party concerned, and to advise the Director promptly of any subsequent findings of the Board of Governors of the IAEA in relation to those conclusions for the information of all Parties.

ANNEX 3
CONSULTATIVE COMMITTEE

1. There is hereby established a Consultative Committee which shall be convened by the Director from time to time pursuant to Articles 10 and 11 and Annex 4 (2). The Consultative Committee shall be constituted of representatives of the Parties, each Party being entitled to appoint one representative who may be accompanied by advisers. Unless otherwise agreed, the Consultative Committee shall be chaired at any given meeting by the representative of the Party which last hosted the meeting of Heads of Government of Members of the South Pacific Forum. A quorum shall be constituted by representatives of half the Parties. Subject to the provisions of Article 11, decisions of the Consultative Committee shall be taken by consensus or, failing consensus, by a two-thirds majority of those present and voting. The Consultative Committee shall adopt such other rules of Procedure as it sees fit.
2. The costs of the Consultative Committee, including the costs of special inspections pursuant to Annex 4, shall be borne by the South Pacific Bureau for Economic Co-operation. It may seek special funding should this be required.

ANNEX 4
COMPLAINTS PROCEDURE

1. A Party which considers that there are grounds for a complaint that another Party is in breach of its obligations under this Treaty shall, before bringing such a complaint to the Director, bring the subject matter of the complaint to the attention of the Party complained of and shall allow the latter reasonable opportunity to provide it with an explanation and to resolve the matter.

2. If the matter is not so resolved, the complainant Party may bring the complaint to the Director with a request that the Consultative Committee be convened to consider it. Complaints shall be supported by an account of evidence of breach of obligations known to the complainant Party. Upon receipt of a complaint the Director shall convene the Consultative Committee as quickly as possible to consider it.
3. The Consultative Committee, taking account of efforts made under paragraph 1 shall afford the Party complained of a reasonable opportunity to provide it with an explanation of the matter.
4. If, after considering any explanation given to it by the representatives of the Party complained of, the Consultative Committee decides that there is sufficient substance in the complaint to warrant a special inspection in the territory of that Party or elsewhere, the Consultative Committee shall direct that such special inspection be made as quickly as possible by a special inspection team of three suitably qualified special inspectors appointed by the Consultative Committee in consultation with the complained of and complainant Parties, provided that no national of either Party shall serve on the special inspection team. If so requested by the Party complained of, the special inspection team shall be accompanied by representatives of that Party. Neither the right of consultation on the appointment of special inspectors, nor the right to accompany special inspectors, shall delay the work of the special inspection team.
5. In making a special inspection, special inspectors shall be subject to the direction only of the Consultative Committee and shall comply with such directives concerning tasks, objectives, confidentiality and procedures as may be decided upon by it. Directives shall take account of the legitimate interests of the Party complained of in complying with its other international obligations and commitments and shall not duplicate safeguards procedures to be undertaken by the IAEA pursuant to agreements referred to in Annex 2 (1). The special inspectors shall discharge their duties with due respect for the laws of the Party complained of.
6. Each Party shall give to special inspectors full and free access to all information and places within its territory which may be relevant to enable the special inspectors to implement the directives given to them by the Consultative Committee.
7. The Party complained of shall take all appropriate steps to facilitate the special inspection and shall grant to special inspectors privileges and immunities necessary for the performance of their functions, including inviolability for all papers and documents and immunity from arrest, detention and legal process for acts done and words spoken and written, for the purpose of the special inspection.
8. The special inspectors shall report in writing as quickly as possible to the Consultative Committee, outlining their activities, setting out relevant facts and information as ascertained by them, with supporting evidence and documentation

as appropriate, and stating their conclusions. The Consultative Committee shall report fully to all Members of the South Pacific Forum, giving its decision as to whether the Party complained of is in breach of its obligations under this Treaty.

9. If the Consultative Committee has decided that the Party complained of is in breach of its obligations under this Treaty, or that the above provisions have not been complied with, or at any time at the request of either the complainant or complained of Party, the Parties shall meet promptly at a meeting of the South Pacific Forum.

TREATY DECLARING AFRICA A NUCLEAR WEAPON-FREE ZONE

(Pelindaba, 23 June 1995)

This Treaty, to remain in force indefinitely, was adopted by the Council of Ministers of the OAU (Organization of African Unity) to define the territory to be kept nuclear weapon-free. Such territory includes Africa, island States members of the OAU and all islands considered by the Unity to be part of Africa in a 1996 Resolution adopted by the United Nations General Assembly.

Under the Treaty (opened to signature on April 11,1996 in Cairo, Egypt) the Parties commit themselves to refraining from a number of activities relating to nuclear explosive devices, from receiving or providing assistance in that respect, to interdicting any stationing or testing of the above devices on their territory, to discontinuing any activity which they might have been involved in nationally before entering into force of the Treaty, to allowing for checks (by the IAEA and the Africa Commission on Nuclear Energy) on these activities, and to implementing the measures provided for by the Bamako Convention (1991) as far as the dumping of radioactive waste is concerned. The Bamako Convention is a regional agreement on the ban of the import into Africa and the control of trans-boundary movement and the management of hazardous waste (explicitly including radioactive waste) within Africa.

Other Treaty provisions address promotion of nuclear science for peaceful use, non-proliferation and safeguards and physical protection of nuclear materials and facilities. There are three Protocols (not published here) to the Treaty, addressing the use and testing of nuclear explosive devices, and the application of safeguards in the parts of the "zone" for which the signatory is responsible internationally. Under article 18, the Treaty enters into force on the deposit of the 28th ratification instrument.

The Parties to this Treaty,

Guided by the Declaration on the Denuclearization of Africa, adopted by the Assembly of Heads of State and Government of the Organization of African Unity (hereinafter referred to as OAU) at its first ordinary session, held at Cairo from 17 to 21 July 1964 (AHG/Res. 11 (1)), in which they solemnly declared their readiness to undertake, through an international agreement to be concluded under United Nations auspices, not to manufacture or acquire control of nuclear weapons,

Guided also, by the resolutions of the fifty-fourth and fifty-sixth ordinary sessions of the Council of Ministers of OAU, held at Abuja from 27 May to 1 June 1991 and at Dakar from 22 to 28 June 1992 respectively (CM/Res. 1342 (LIV) and CM/ Res. 1395 (LVI)), which affirmed that the evolution of the international situation was conducive to the implementation of the Cairo Declaration, as well as the relevant provisions of the 1986 OAU Declaration on Security, Disarmament and Development,

Recalling United Nations General Assembly resolution 3472 B (XXX) of 11 December 1975, in which it considered nuclear-weapon-free zones one of the most effective means for preventing the proliferation, both horizontal and vertical, of nuclear weapons,

Convinced of the need to take all steps in achieving the ultimate goal of a world entirely free of nuclear weapons, as well as of the obligations of all States to contribute to this end,

Convinced also that the African nuclear-weapon-free zone will constitute an important step towards strengthening the non-proliferation regime, promoting cooperation in the peaceful uses of nuclear energy, promoting general and complete disarmament and enhancing regional and international peace and security.

Aware that regional disarmament measures contribute to global disarmament efforts,

Believing that the African Nuclear-Weapon-Free Zone will protect African States against possible nuclear attacks on their territories,

Noting with satisfaction existing NWFZs and recognizing that the establishment of other NWFZs, especially in the Middle East, would enhance the security of States Parties to the African NWFZ,

Reaffirming the importance of the Treaty on the Non-Proliferation of Nuclear Weapons (hereinafter referred to as the NPT) and the need for the implementation of all its provisions,

Desirous of taking advantage of article IV of the NPT, which recognizes the inalienable right of all States Parties to develop research on, production and use of nuclear energy for peaceful purposes without discrimination and to facilitate the fullest possible exchange of equipment, materials and scientific and technological information for such purposes,

Determined to promote regional cooperation for the development and practical application of nuclear energy for peaceful purposes in the interest of sustainable social and economic development of the African continent,

Determined to keep Africa free of environmental pollution by radioactive wastes and other radioactive matter,

Welcoming the cooperation of all States and governmental and non-governmental organizations for the attainment of these objectives,

Have decided by this treaty to establish the African NWFZ and hereby agree as follows:

Article 1:
Definition & Usage of Terms

For the purpose of this Treaty and its Protocols:

(a) "African Nuclear-Weapon-Free Zone" means the territory of the continent of Africa, islands States members of OAU and all islands considered by the Organization of African Unity in its resolutions to be part of Africa;

(b) "Territory" means the land territory, internal waters, territorial seas and archipelagic waters and the airspace above them as well as the sea bed and subsoil beneath;

(c) "Nuclear explosive device" means any nuclear weapon or other explosive device capable of releasing nuclear energy, irrespective of the purpose for which it could be used. The term includes such a weapon or device in unassembled and partly assembled forms, but does not include the means of transport or delivery of such a weapon or device if separable from and not an indivisible part of it;

(d) "Stationing" means implantation, emplacement, transport on land or inland waters, stockpiling, storage, installation and deployment;

(e) "Nuclear installation" means a nuclear-power reactor, a nuclear research reactor, a critical facility, a conversion plant, a fabrication plant, a reprocessing plant, an isotope separation plant, a separate storage installation and any other installation or location in or at which fresh or irradiated nuclear material or significant quantities of radioactive materials are present.

(f) "Nuclear material" means any source material or special fissionable material as defined in Article XX of the Statute of the International Atomic Energy Agency (IAEA) and as amended from time to time by the IAEA.

Article 2:
Application of the Treaty

1. Except where otherwise specified, this Treaty and its Protocols shall apply to the territory within the African Nuclear-Weapon-Free Zone, as illustrated in the map in annex I,

2. Nothing in this Treaty shall prejudice or in any way affect the rights, or the exercise of the rights, of any State under international law with regard to freedom of the seas.

Article 3:
Renunciation of Nuclear Explosive Devices

Each Party undertakes:
(a) Not to conduct research on, develop, manufacture, stockpile or otherwise acquire, possess or have control over any nuclear explosive device by any means anywhere;
(b) Not to seek or receive any assistance in the research on, development, manufacture, stockpiling or acquisition, or possession of any nuclear explosive device;
(c) Not to take any action to assist or encourage the research on, development, manufacture, stockpiling or acquisition, or possession of any nuclear explosive device.

Article 4:
Prevention of Stationing Of Nuclear Explosive Devices

1. Each Party undertakes to prohibit, in its territory, the stationing of any nuclear explosive device.

2. Without prejudice to the purposes and objectives of the treaty, each party in the exercise of its sovereign rights remains free to decide for itself whether to allow visits by foreign ships and aircraft to its ports and airfields, transit of its airspace by foreign aircraft, and navigation by foreign ships in its territorial seas or archipelagic waters in a manner not covered by the rights of innocent passage, archipelagic sea lane passage or transit passage of straits.

Article 5:
Prohibition of Testing of Nuclear Explosive Devices

Each Party undertakes:
(a) Not to test any nuclear explosive device;
(b) To prohibit in its territory the testing of any nuclear explosive device;
(c) Not to assist or encourage the testing of any nuclear explosive device by any State anywhere.

Article 6:
Declaration, Dismantling, Destruction or Conversion of Nuclear Explosive Devices and the Facilities for Their Manufacture

Each Party undertakes:
(a) To declare any capability for the manufacture of nuclear explosive devices;

(b) To dismantle and destroy any nuclear explosive device that it has manufactured prior to the coming into force of this Treaty;
(c) To destroy facilities for the manufacture of nuclear explosive devices or, where possible, to convert them to peaceful uses;
(d) To permit the International Atomic Energy Agency (hereinafter referred to as IAEA) and the Commission established in article 12 to verify the processes of dismantling and destruction of the nuclear explosive devices, as well as the destruction or conversion of the facilities for their production.

Article 7:
Prohibition of Dumping of Radioactive Wastes

Each Party undertakes:
(a) To effectively implement or to use as guidelines the measures contained in the Bamako Convention on the Ban of the Import into Africa and Control of Trans-boundary Movement and Management of Hazardous Wastes within Africa in so far as it is relevant to radioactive waste;
(b) Not to take any action to assist or encourage the dumping of radioactive wastes and other radioactive matter anywhere within the African Nuclear-Weapon-Free Zone.

Article 8:
Peaceful Nuclear Activities

1. Nothing in this Treaty shall be interpreted as to prevent the use of nuclear science and technology for peaceful purposes.

2. As part of their efforts to strengthen their security, stability and development, the Parties undertake to promote individually and collectively the use of nuclear science and technology for economic and social development. To this end they undertake to establish and strengthen mechanisms for cooperation at the bilateral, sub-regional and regional levels.

3. Parties are encouraged to make use of the programme of assistance available in IAEA and, in this connection, to strengthen cooperation under the African Regional Cooperation Agreement for Research, Training and Development Related to Nuclear Science and Technology (hereinafter referred to as AFRA).

Article 9: Verification of Peaceful Uses

Each Party undertakes:

(a) To conduct all activities for the peaceful use of nuclear energy under strict non-proliferation measures to provide assurance of exclusively peaceful uses;

(b) To conclude a comprehensive safeguards agreement with IAEA for the purpose of verifying compliance with the undertakings in subparagraph (a) of this article;

(c) Not to provide source or special fissionable material, or equipment or material especially designed or prepared for the processing, use or production of special fissionable material for peaceful purposes to any non-nuclear-weapon State unless subject to a comprehensive safeguards agreement concluded with IAEA.

Article 10: Physical Protection of Nuclear Materials And Facilities

Each Party undertakes to maintain the highest standards of security and effective physical protection of nuclear materials, facilities and equipment to prevent theft or unauthorized use and handling. To that end each Party, inter alia, undertakes to apply measures of physical protection equivalent to those provided for in the Convention on Physical Protection of Nuclear Material and in recommendations and guidelines developed by IAEA for that purpose.

Article 11: Prohibition of Armed Attack On Nuclear Installations

Each Party undertakes not to take, or assist, or encourage any action aimed at an armed attack by conventional or other means against nuclear installations in the African Nuclear-Weapon-Free Zone.

Article 12: Mechanism for Compliance

1. For the purpose of ensuring compliance with their undertakings under this Treaty, the Parties agree to establish the African Commission on Nuclear Energy (hereafter referred to as the Commission) as set out in annex III.

2. The Commission shall be responsible inter alia, for:

(a) Collating the reports and the exchange of information as provided for in article 13;

(b) Arranging consultations as provided for in annex IV, as well as convening conferences of Parties on the concurrence of simple majority of State Parties on any matter arising from the implementation the Treaty;
(c) Reviewing the application to peaceful nuclear activities of safeguards by IAEA as elaborated in annex II;
(d) Bringing into effect the complaints procedure elaborated in. annex IV;
(e) Encouraging regional and sub-regional programmes for cooperation in the peaceful uses of nuclear science and technology;
(f) Promoting international cooperation with extra-zonal States for the peaceful uses of nuclear science and technology.

3. The Commission shall meet in ordinary session once a year, and may meet in extraordinary session as may be required by the complaints and settlement of disputes procedure in annex IV.

Article 13:
Report and Exchanges of Information

1. Each Party shall submit an annual report to the Commission on its nuclear activities as well as other matters relating to the Treaty, in accordance with the format for reporting to be developed by the Commission.

2. Each Party shall promptly report to the Commission any significant event affecting the implementation of the Treaty.

3. The Commission shall request the IAEA to provide it with an annual report on the activities of AFRA.

Article 14:
Conference of Parties

1. A Conference of all Parties to the Treaty shall be convened by the Depositary as soon as possible after the entry into force of the Treaty to, inter alia, elect members of the Commission and determine its headquarters. Further conferences of State Parties shall be held as necessary and at least every two years, and convened in accordance with paragraph 2 (b) of article 12.

2. The Conference of all Parties to the Treaty shall adopt the Commission's budget and a scale of assessment to be paid by the State Parties.

Article 15
Interpretation of the Treaty

Any dispute arising out of the interpretation of the Treaty shall be settled by negotiation, by recourse to the Commission or another procedure agreed to by the Parties, which may include recourse to an arbitral panel or to the International Court of Justice.

Article 16:
Reservations

This Treaty shall not be subject to reservations.

Article 17:
Duration

This Treaty shall be of unlimited duration and shall remain in force indefinitely.

Article 18:
Signature, Ratification and Entry Into Force

1. This Treaty shall be open for signature by any State in the African nuclear-weapon-free zone. It shall be subject to ratification.

2. It shall enter into force on the date of deposit of the twenty-eighth instrument of ratification.

3. For a signatory that ratifies this Treaty after the date of the deposit of the twenty-eighth instrument of ratification, it shall enter into force for that signatory on the date of deposit of its instrument of ratification.

Article 19:
Amendments

1. Any amendments to the Treaty proposed by a Party shall be submitted to the Commission, which shall circulate it to all Parties.

2. Decision on the adoption of such an amendment shall be taken by a two-thirds majority of the Parties either through written communication to the Commission or through a conference of Parties convened upon the concurrence of a simple majority.

3. An amendment so adopted shall enter into force for all Parties after receipt by the Depositary of the instrument of ratification by the majority of Parties.

Article 20:
Withdrawal

1. Each Party shall, in exercising its national sovereignty, have the right to withdraw from this Treaty if it decides that extraordinary events, related to the subject-matter of this Treaty, have jeopardized its supreme interests.

2. Withdrawal shall be effected by a Party giving notice, which includes a statement of extraordinary events it regards as having jeopardized its supreme interest, twelve months in advance to the Depositary. The Depositary shall circulate such notice to all other Parties.

Article 21:
Depositary Functions

1. This Treaty, of which the Arabic, English, French and Portuguese texts are equally authentic, shall be deposited with the Secretary General of OAU, who is hereby designated as Depositary of the Treaty.

2. The Depositary shall:
(a) Receive instruments of ratification;
(b) Register this Treaty and its Protocols pursuant to Article 102 of the Charter of the United Nations;
(c) Transmit certified copies of the Treaty and its Protocols to all States in the African nuclear-weapon-free zone and to all States eligible to become Party to the Protocols to the Treaty, and shall notify them of signatures and ratifications of the Treaty and its Protocols.

Article 22:
Status of the Annexes

The annexes form an integral part of this Treaty. Any reference to this Treaty includes the annexes.

In witness whereof the undersigned, being duly authorized by their Governments, have signed this Treaty.

Done at Cairo, EGYPT, on the 11th day of April 1996

ANNEX I
MAP OF THE AFRICAN NUCLEAR-WEAPON-FREE ZONE

ANNEX II
SAFEGUARDS OF THE INTERNATIONAL ATOMIC ENERGY AGENCY

1. The safeguards referred to in subparagraph (b) of the article 9 shall in respect of each Party be applied by the International Atomic Energy Agency as set forth in an agreement negotiated and concluded with the Agency on all source or special fissionable material in all nuclear activities within the territory of the Party, under its jurisdiction or carried out under its control anywhere.

2. The Agreement referred to in paragraph 1 above shall be, or shall be equivalent in its scope and effect to, the agreement required in connection with the Treaty on the Non-Proliferation of Nuclear Weapons (INFCIRC/153 corrected). A Party that has already entered into a safeguards agreement with the IAEA is deemed to have already complied with the requirement. Each Party shall take all appropriate steps to ensure that the Agreement referred to in paragraph I is in force for it not later than eighteen months after the date of entry into force for that Party of this Treaty.

3. For the purpose of this Treaty, the safeguards referred to in paragraph 1 above shall have as their purpose the verification of the non-diversion of nuclear material from peaceful nuclear activities to nuclear explosive devices or for purposes unknown.

4. Each Party shall include in its annual report to the Commission, in conformity with article 13 , for its information and review, a copy of the overall conclusions of the most recent report by the International Atomic Energy Agency on its inspection activities in the territory of the Party concerned, and advise the Commission promptly of any change in those conclusions. The information furnished by a Party shall not be, totally or partially, disclosed or transmitted to third parties, by the addressees of the reports, except when that Party gives its express consent.

ANNEX III
AFRICAN COMMISSION ON NUCLEAR ENERGY

1. The Commission established in article 12 shall be composed of twelve Members elected by Parties to the Treaty for a three-year period, bearing in mind the need for equitable geographical distribution as well as to include Members with advanced nuclear programmes. Each Member shall have one representative nominated with particular regard for his/her expertise in the subject of the Treaty.

2. The Commission shall have a Bureau consisting of the chairman, the Vice-Chairman and the Executive Secretary. It shall elect its Chairman and Vice-Chairman. The Secretary-General of the Organization of African Unity, at the request of Parties to the Treaty and in consultation with the Chairman, shall designate the Executive Secretary of the Commission. For the first meeting a quorum shall be constituted by representatives of two thirds of the Members of the Commission. For that meeting decisions of the Commission shall be taken as far as possible by consensus or otherwise by a two-thirds majority of the Members of the Commission. The Commission shall adopt its rules of procedure at that meeting.

3. The Commission shall develop a format for reporting by States as required under articles 12 and 13.

4.
(a) The budget of the Commission, including the costs of inspections pursuant to annex IV to this Treaty, shall be borne by the Parties to the Treaty in accordance with a scale of assessment to be determined by the Parties;
(b) The Commission may also accept additional funds from other sources provided such donations are consistent with the purposes and objectives of the Treaty.

ANNEX IV
COMPLAINTS PROCEDURE AND SETTLEMENT OF DISPUTES

1. A Party which considers that there are grounds for a complaint that another Party or a Party to Protocol III is in breach of its obligations under this Treaty shall bring the subject-matter of the complaint to the attention of the Party complained of and shall allow the latter thirty days to provide it with an explanation and to resolve the matter. This may include technical visits agreed upon between the Parties.

2. If the matter is so not resolved, the complainant Party may bring this complaint to the Commission.

3. The Commission, taking account of efforts made under paragraph 1 above, shall afford the Party complained of forty-five days to provide it with an explanation of the matter.

4. If, after considering any explanation given to it by the representatives of the Party complained of, the Commission considers that there is sufficient substance in the complaint to warrant an inspection in the territory of that Party or territory of a Party to Protocol III, the Commission may request the International Atomic Energy Agency

to conduct such inspection as soon as possible. The Commission may also designate its representatives to accompany the Agency's inspection team.

(a) The request shall indicate the tasks and objectives of such inspection, as well as any confidentiality requirements;

(b) If the Party complained of so requests, the inspection team shall be accompanied by representatives of that Party provided that the inspectors shall not be thereby delayed or otherwise impeded in the exercise of their functions;

(c) Each Party shall give the inspection team full and free access to all information and places within each territory that may be deemed relevant by the inspectors to the implementation of the inspection;

(d) The Party complained of shall take all appropriate steps to facilitate the work of the inspection team, and shall accord them the same privileges and immunities as those set forth in the relevant provisions of the Agreement on the Privileges and Immunities of the International Atomic Energy Agency;

(e) The International Atomic Energy Agency shall report its findings in writing as quickly as possible to the Commission, outlining its activities, setting out relevant facts and information as ascertained by it, with supporting evidence and documentation as appropriate, and stating its conclusions. The Commission shall report fully to all States Parties to the Treaty giving its decision as to whether the Party complained of is in breach of its obligations under this Treaty;

(f) If the Commission considers that the Party complained of is in breach of its obligations under this Treaty, or that the above provisions have not been complied with, States Parties to the Treaty shall meet in extraordinary session to discuss the matter;

(g) The States Parties convened in extraordinary session may as necessary, make recommendations to the Party held to be in breach of its obligations and to the Organization of African Unity. The Organization of African Unity may, if necessary, refer the matter to the United Nations Security Council;

(h) The costs involved in the procedure outlined above shall be borne by the Commission. In the case of abuse, the Commission shall decide whether the requesting State Party should bear any of the financial implications.

5. The Commission may also establish its own inspection mechanisms.

TREATY ON THE SOUTHEAST ASIA NUCLEAR WEAPON-FREE ZONE

(Bangkok, 15 December 1995)

This Treaty was adopted by ASEAN (Association of South East Asian Nations) with a view to strengthening security, as well as preserving peace and stability in that area of the globe (Thailand, Indonesia, the Philippines, Vietnam etc.). In addition, the Treaty pursues also protection from pollution and from hazards due to radioactive waste (and other material).

Under Article 3, contracting Parties (so far 10) to the Treaty are mainly committed to refraining from any nuclear weapons-related activity in the above area and outside it, to preventing any other State from carrying out such activities in a State Party, from releasing any radioactive material into the sea or the atmosphere of the area, and from asking for or receiving assistance contrary to these commitments. Certain other provisions are concerned with safeguards for non-proliferation.

The Treaty, entered into force on March 27, 1997, will remain such indefinitely and it is open to signature also by countries such as China, the Russian Federation, the USA, etc.

The States Parties to this Treaty:

DESIRING to contribute to the realization of the purposes and principles of the Charter of the United Nations;
DETERMINED to take concrete action which will contribute to the progress towards general and complete disarmament of nuclear weapons, and to the promotion of international peace and security;
REAFFIRMING the desire of the Southeast Asian States to maintain peace and stability in the region in the spirit of peaceful coexistence and mutual understanding and cooperation as enunciated in various communiqués, declarations and other legal instruments;
RECALLING the Declaration on the Zone of Peace, Freedom and Neutrality (ZOPFAN) signed in Kuala Lumpur on 27 November 1971 and the Programme of Action on ZOPFAN adopted at the 26th ASEAN Ministerial Meeting in Singapore in July 1993;

CONVINCED that the establishment of a Southeast Asia Nuclear Weapon-Free Zone, as an essential component of the ZOPPAN, will contribute towards strengthening the security of States within the Zone and towards enhancing international peace and security as a whole;
REAFFIRMING the importance of the Treaty on the Non-Proliferation of Nuclear Weapons (NPT) in preventing the proliferation of nuclear weapons and in contributing towards international peace and security;
RECALLING Article VII of the NPT which recognizes the right of any group of States to conclude regional treaties in order to assume the total absence of nuclear weapons in their respective territories;
RECALLING the Final Document of the Tenth Special Session of the United Nations General Assembly which encourages the establishment of nuclear weapon-free zones;
RECALLING the Principles and Objectives for Nuclear Non-Proliferation and Disarmament, adopted at the 1995 Review and Extension Conference of the Parties to the NPT, that the cooperation of all the nuclear-weapon States and their respect and support for the relevant protocols is important for the maximum effectiveness of this nuclear weapon-free zone treaty and its relevant protocols.
DETERMINED to protect the region from environmental pollution and the hazards posed by radioactive wastes and other radioactive material;

HAVE AGREED as follows:

Article I
Use of terms

For the purposes of this Treaty and its Protocol:
(a) "Southeast Asia Nuclear Weapon-Free Zone", hereinafter referred to as the "Zone", means the area comprising the territories of all States in Southeast Asia, namely, Brunei Darussalam, Cambodia, Indonesia, Laos, Malaysia, Myanmar, Philippines, Singapore, Thailand and Vietnam, and their respective continental shelves and Exclusive Economic Zones (EEZ);
(b) "territory" means the land territory, internal waters, territorial sea, archipelagic waters, the seabed and the sub-soil thereof and the airspace above them;
(c) "nuclear weapon" means any explosive device capable of releasing nuclear energy in an uncontrolled manner but does not include the means of transport or delivery of such device if separable from and not an indivisible part thereof;
(d) "station" means to deploy, emplace, implant, install, stockpile or store;
(e) "radioactive material" means material that contains radio-nuclides above clearance or exemption levels recommended by the International Atomic Energy Agency (IAEA);

(f) "radioactive wastes" means material that contains or is contaminated with radio-nuclides at concentrations or activities greater than clearance levels recommended by the IAEA and for which no use is foreseen; and
(g) "dumping" means
(i) any deliberate disposal at sea, including seabed and subsoil insertion, of radio-active wastes or other matter from vessels, aircraft, platforms or other man-made structures at sea, and
(ii) any deliberate disposal at sea, including seabed and subsoil insertion, of vessels, aircraft, platforms or other man-made structures at sea, containing radioactive material, but does not include the disposal of wastes or other matter incidental to, or derived from the normal operations of vessels, aircraft, platforms or other man-made structures at sea and their equipment, other than wastes or other matter transported by or to vessels, aircraft, platforms or other man-made structures at sea, operating for the purpose of disposal of such matter or derived from the treatment of such wastes or other matter on such vessels, aircraft, platforms or structures.

Article 2
Application of the Treaty

1. This Treaty and its Protocol shall apply to the territories, continental selves, and EEZ of the States Parties within the Zone in which the Treaty is in force.

2. Nothing in this Treaty shall prejudice the rights or the exercise of these rights by any State under the provisions of the United Nations Convention on the Law of the Sea of 1982, in particular with regard to freedom of the high seas, rights of innocent passage, archipelagic sea lanes passage or transit passage of ships and aircraft, and consistent with the Charter of the United Nations.

Article 3
Basic undertakings

1. Each State Party undertakes not to, anywhere inside or outside the Zone:
(a) develop, manufacture or otherwise acquire, possess or have control over nuclear weapons;
(b) station or transport nuclear weapons by any means; or
(c) test or use nuclear weapons.

2. Each State Party also undertakes not to allow, in its territory, any other State to:
(a) develop, manufacture or otherwise acquire, possess or have control over nuclear weapons;

(b) station nuclear weapons; or
(c) test or use nuclear weapons.

3. Each State Party also undertake not to:
(a) dump at sea or discharge into the atmosphere anywhere within the Zone any radioactive material or wastes;
(b) dispose radioactive material or wastes on land in the territory of or under the jurisdiction of other States except as stipulated in Paragraph 2 (e) of Article 4; or
(c) allow, within its territory, any other State to dump at sea or discharge into the atmosphere any radioactive material or wastes.

4. Each State Party undertakes not to:
(a) seek or receive any assistance in the Commission of any act in violation of the provisions of Paragraphs 1, 2 and 3 of this Article; or
(b) take any action to assist or encourage the Commission of any act in violation of the provisions of Paragraphs 1, 2 and 3 of this Article.

Article 4
Use of nuclear energy for peaceful purposes

1. Nothing in this Treaty shall prejudice the right of the States Parties to use nuclear energy, in particular for their economic development and social progress.

2. Each State Party therefore undertakes:
(a) to use exclusively for peaceful purposes nuclear material and facilities which are within its territory and areas under its jurisdiction and control;
(b) prior to embarking on its peaceful nuclear energy programme, to subject its programme to rigorous nuclear safety assessment conforming to guidelines and standards recommended by the IAEA for the protection of health and minimization of danger to life and property in accordance with Paragraph 6 of Article III of the Statute of the IAEA;
(c) upon request, to make available to another State Party the assessment except information relating to personal data, information protected by intellectual property rights or by industrial or commercial confidentiality, and information relating to national security;
(d) to support the continued effectiveness of the international non-proliferation system based on the Treaty on the Non-Proliferation of Nuclear Weapons (NPT) and the IAEA safeguard system; and
(e) to dispose radioactive wastes and other radioactive material in accordance with IAEA standards and procedures on land within its territory or on land within the territory of another State which has consented to such disposal.

3. Each State Party further undertakes not to provide source or special fissionable material, or equipment or material especially designed or prepared for the processing, use or production of special fissionable material to:
(a) any non-nuclear-weapon State except under conditions subject to the safeguards required by Paragraph 1 of Article III of the NPT; or
(b) any nuclear-weapon State except in conformity with applicable safeguards agreements with the IAEA.

Article 5
IAEA Safeguards

Each State Party which has not done so shall conclude an agreement with the IAEA for the application of full scope safeguards to its peaceful nuclear activities not later than eighteen months after the entry into force for that State Party of the Treaty.

Article 6
Early notification of a nuclear accident

Each State Party which has not acceded to the Convention on Early Notification of a Nuclear Accident shall endeavour to do so.

Article 7
Foreign ships and aircraft

Each State Party, on being notified, may decide for itself whether to allow visits by foreign ships and aircraft to its ports and airfields, transit of its airspace by foreign aircraft, and navigation by foreign ships through its territorial sea or archipelagic waters and overflight of foreign aircraft above those waters in a manner not governed by the rights of innocent passage, archipelagic sea lanes passage or transit passage.

Article 8
Establishment of the commission for the Southeast Asia Nuclear Weapon-Free Zone

1. There is hereby established a Commission for the Southeast Asia Nuclear Weapon-Free Zone, hereinafter referred to as the "Commission".

2. All States Parties are ipso facto members or the Commission. Each State Party shall be represented by its Foreign Minister or his representative accompanied by alternates and advisers.

3. The function of the Commission shall be to oversee the implementation of this Treaty and ensure compliance with its provisions.

4. The Commission shall meet as and when necessary in accordance with the provisions of this Treaty including upon the request of any State Party. As far as possible, the Commission shall meet in conjunction with the ASEAN Ministerial Meeting.

5. At the beginning of each meeting, the Commission shall elect its Chairman and such other officers as may be required. They shall hold office until a new Chairman and other officers are elected at the next meeting.

6. Unless otherwise provided for in this Treaty, two-thirds of the members of the Commission shall be present to constitute a quorum.

7. Each member of the Commission shall have one vote.

8. Except as provided for in this Treaty, decisions of the Commission shall be taken by consensus or, failing consensus, by a two-thirds majority of the members present and voting.

9. The Commission shall, by consensus, agree upon and adopt rules of procedure for itself as well as financial rules governing its funding and that of its subsidiary organs.

Article 9
The Executive Committee

1. There is hereby established, as a subsidiary organ of the Commission, the Executive Committee.

2. The Executive Committee shall be composed of all States Parties to this Treaty. Each State Party shall be represented by one senior official as its representative, who may be accompanied by alternates and advisers.

3. The functions of the Executive Committee shall be to:
(a) ensure the proper operation of verification measures in accordance with the provisions on the control system as stipulated in Article 10;
(b) consider and decide on requests for clarification and for a fact-finding mission;
(c) set up a fact-finding mission in accordance with the Annex of this Treaty;
(d) consider and decide on the findings of a fact-finding mission and report to the Commission;
(e) request the Commission to convene a meeting when appropriate and necessary;

(f) conclude such agreements with the IAEA or other international organizations as referred to in Article 18 on behalf of the Commission after being duly authorized to do so by the Commission; and
(g) carry out such other tasks as may, from time to time, be assigned by the Commission.

4. The Executive Committee shall meet as and when necessary for the efficient exercise of its functions. As far as possible, the Executive Committee shall meet in conjunction with the ASEAN Senior Officials Meeting.

5. The Chairman of the Executive Committee shall be the representative of the Chairman of the Commission. Any submission or communication made by a State Party to the Chairman of the Executive Committee shall be disseminated to the other members of the Executive Committee.

6. Two-thirds of the members of the Executive Committee shall be present to constitute a quorum.

7. Each member of the Executive Committee shall have one vote.

8. Decisions of the Executive Committee shall be taken by consensus or, failing consensus, by a two-thirds majority of the members present and voting.

Article 10
Control system

1. There is hereby established a control system for the purpose of verifying compliance with the obligations of the States Parties under this Treaty.

2. The Control System shall comprise:
(a) the IAEA safeguards system as provided for in Article 5;
(b) report and exchange of information as provided for in Article 11;
(c) request for clarification as provided for in Article 12; and
(d) request and procedures for a fact-finding mission as provided for in Article 13.

Article 11
Report and exchange of information

1. Each State Party shall submit reports to the Executive Committee on any significant event within its territory and areas under its jurisdiction and control affecting the implementation of this Treaty.

2. The States Parties may exchange information on matters arising under or in relation to this Treaty.

Article 12
Request for clarification

1. Each State Party shall have the right to request another State Party for clarification concerning any situation which may be considered ambiguous or which may give rise to doubts about the compliance of that State Party with this Treaty. It shall inform the Executive Committee of such a request. The requested State Party shall duly respond by providing without delay the necessary information and inform the Executive Committee of its reply to the requesting State Party.

2. Each State Party shall have the right to request the Executive Committee to seek clarification for another State Party concerning any situation which may be considered ambiguous or which may give rise to doubts about compliance of that State Party with this Treaty. Upon receipt of such a request, the Executive Committee shall consult the State Party from which clarification is sought for the purpose of obtaining the clarification requested.

Article 13
Request for a fact-finding mission

A State Party shall have the right to request the Executive Committee to send a fact-finding mission to another State Party in order to clarify and resolve a situation which may be considered ambiguous or which may give rise to doubts about compliance with the provisions of this Treaty, in accordance with the procedure contained in the Annex to this Treaty.

Article 14
Remedial measures

1. In case the Executive Committee decide in accordance with the Annex that there is a breach of this Treaty by a State Party, that State Party shall, within a reasonable time, take all steps necessary to bring itself in full compliance with this Treaty and shall promptly inform the Executive Committee of the action taken or proposed to be taken by it.

2. Where a State Party fails or refuses to comply with the provisions of Paragraph 1 of this Article, the Executive Committee shall request the Commission to convene a meeting in accordance with the provisions of Paragraph 3(e) of Article 9.

3. At the meeting convened pursuant to Paragraph 2 of this Article, the Commission shall consider the emergent situation and shall decide on any measure it deems appropriate to cope with the situation, including the submission of the matter to the IAEA and, where the situation might endanger international peace and security, the Security Council and the General Assembly of the United Nations.

4. In the event of breach of the Protocol attached to this Treaty by a State Party to the Protocol, the Executive Committee shall convene a special meeting of the Commission to decide on appropriate measures to be taken.

Article 15
Signature, ratification, accession, deposit and registration

1. This Treaty shall be open for signature by all States in Southeast Asia, namely, Brunei Darussalam, Cambodia, Indonesia, Laos, Malaysia, Myanmar, Philippines, Singapore, Thailand and Vietnam.

2. This Treaty shall be subject to ratification in accordance with the constitutional procedure of the signatory states. The instruments of ratification shall be deposited with the Government of the Kingdom of Thailand which is hereby designated as the Depositary State.

3. This Treaty shall be open for accession. The instruments of accession shall be deposited with the Depositary State.

4. The Depositary State shall inform the other States Parties to this Treaty on the deposit of instruments of ratification or accession.

5. The Depositary State shall register this Treaty and its Protocol pursuant to Article 102 of the Charter of the United Nations.

Article 16
Entry into force

1. This Treaty shall enter into force on the date of the deposit of the seventh instrument of ratification and/or accession.

2. For States which ratify or accede to this Treaty after the date of the seventh instrument of ratification or accession, the Treaty shall enter into force on the date of deposit of its instrument of ratification or accession.

Article 17
Reservations

This Treaty shall not be subject to reservations.

Article 18
Relations with other international organizations

The Commission may conclude such agreements with the IAEA or other international organizations as it considers likely to facilitate the efficient operation of the control system established by this Treaty.

Article 19
Amendments

1. Any State Party may propose amendments to this Treaty and its Protocol and shall submit its proposals to the Executive Committee, which shall transmit them to all the other States Parties. The Executive Committee shall immediately request the Commission to convene a meeting to examine the proposed amendments. The quorum required for such a meeting shall be all the members of the Commission. Any amendment shall be adopted by a consensus decision of the Commission.

2. Amendments adopted shall enter into force 30 days after the receipt by the Depositary State of the seventh instrument of acceptance from the States Parties.

Article 20
Review

Ten years after this Treaty enters into force, a meeting of the Commission shall be convened for the purpose of reviewing the operation of the Treaty. A meeting of the Commission for the same purpose may also be convened at anytime thereafter if there is consensus among all its members.

Article 21
Settlement of disputes

Any dispute arising from the interpretation of the provisions of this Treaty shall be settled by peaceful means as may be agreed upon by the States Parties to the dispute. If within one month, the parties to the dispute are unable to achieve a peaceful settlement of the dispute by negotiation, mediation, enquiry or conciliation, any of the parties concerned shall, with the prior consent of the other parties concerned, refer the dispute to arbitration or to the International Court of Justice.

Article 22
Duration and withdrawal

1. This Treaty shall remain in force indefinitely.

2. In the event of a breach by any State Party of this Treaty essential to the achievement of the objectives of the Treaty, every other State Party shall have the right to withdraw from the Treaty.

3. Withdrawal under Paragraph 2 of Article 22, shall be effected by giving notice twelve months in advance to the members of the Commission.

IN WITNESS WHEREOF, the undersigned have signed this Treaty.

DONE at Bangkok, this fifteenth day of December, one thousand nine hundred and ninety-five, in one original in the English language.

SECTION THREE
INTERNATIONAL CONVENTIONS ON PROTECTION OF THE ENVIRONMENT AND POLLUTION PREVENTION

CONVENTION ON THE HIGH SEAS

(Geneva, 29 April 1958)

This Convention was adopted by the General Assembly of the United Nations at the end of a Conference on the law of the sea held in Geneva from 24 February to 27 April 1958. It is the first international instrument which addresses, although in general and incidental terms, the problem of pollution caused by disposal of radioactive substances into the sea. It came into force on September 30, 1962.

Given the historical importance of the Convention also for the matter under consideration, article 25 is drawn attention to. It is also to be noted that this Convention, similarly to other international instruments not exclusively geared to nuclear energy, refers to specific standards and regulations formulated by the competent international organisations.

CONVENTION ON THE PREVENTION OF MARINE POLLUTION BY DUMPING OF WASTES AND OTHER MATTER

(Mexico City, London, Moscow, Washington, 29 December 1972)

By this Convention the "regional" formula adopted in the 1972 Oslo Convention (see further on Introductory Material to the OSPAR Convention) was resumed and applied on a worldwide scale as regards the dumping of waste in general. The contracting Parties were committed to adopting any possible measure to prevent marine pollution, to harmonizing the respective actions taken in this connection and to submitting to certain conditions the dumping of the wastes considered by the Convention. Among such wastes where those highly radioactive (as under the categorisation adopted by the IAEA) the dumping of which is prohibited, and other radioactive waste subject to the conditions referred to above. The Convention entered into force on August 30, 1975.

It is noted that in the past years, on the occasion of consultative meetings of contracting Parties as provided for by the Convention, various Resolutions were adopted addressing the sea dumping of waste. In particular, the February 1983 Resolution called for a moratorium in this field, given the opposition by a number of contracting Parties to sea dumping of radioactive waste; a September 1985 Resolution extended such suspension, pending further consideration of whether a total prohibition of that dumping should be achieved; in 1994, another Resolution extended the suspension further, to be maintained until a series of additional studies and assessments are completed in connection with the dumping scientific and technical implications. In 1993 the Convention was amended, to the effect of banning the dumping into the sea of low level radioactive waste. On November 7, 1996, a Protocol was adopted, intended to replace the Convention. One of the main innovations consists in the introduction of the so called "precautionary approach". This entails that preventative measures should be taken even in the absence of evidence about a causal link between the input of waste and its harmful effects.

It must be added that the Convention may be considered as the basis for two new conventions (Baltic and Black Sea) adopted in 1992 (see following pages): in fact its article VIII stipulates that contracting parties to such Convention sharing common interests in the protection of the marine environment of a given area, must do their best to conclude "regional" agreements consistent with the Convention.

At present there are 80 contracting Parties to the Convention and 20 to the 1996 Protocol.

SOLAS CONVENTION

(London, 1 November 1974)

This Convention replaced the analogous instrument of 1960, bearing the same acronym meaning Safeguard Of Life At Sea. Like the previous Convention, it was adopted on the initiative of IMCO (International Maritime Consultative Organisation, now IMO, based in London) and does neither address directly the protection of marine environment, nor nuclear matters exclusively. In general, its provisions do not differ significantly from those of the 1960 Convention. As regards in particular nuclear matters, it stipulates conditions for the transport of dangerous goods including radioactive materials (Chapter VII, Part D), and addresses the safety of nuclear ships (Chapter VIII, which refers to the IMO Code of Safety for nuclear merchant ships adopted in 1981).

The Convention underwent very many amendments between 1981 and 2003, some of them touching upon the nuclear sphere: some amendments to Chapter VII (of May 1999, come into force in January 2001, and of June 2001, come into force in January 2003) made the international Code for the safe carriage of packaged irradiated fuel (INF) mandatory.

The SOLAS Convention entered into force on May 25, 1980 and it has 107 contracting Parties.

CONVENTION FOR THE PROTECTION OF THE MEDITERRANEAN SEA AGAINST POLLUTION

(Barcelona, 16 February 1976)

By this Convention, clearly "regional" in scope, the contracting Parties belonging to the Mediterranean area intended to lay down provisions addressing the protection of the Mediterranean Sea. This instrument was supplemented by a first Protocol on the dumping by ships and aircrafts, and by a second Protocol, adopted on 17 May 1980 in Athens (and entered into force on 17 June 1983). The latter refers, among other substances, to certain radioactive materials and waste the dumping of which is not allowed, unless it complies with the radiation protection principles established by the competent international organisations, with a view to protecting the marine environment.

The Convention (which has now 21 contracting Parties) covers not only the pollution from land-based sources and from the dumping referred to above, but also the exploration and exploitation of the continental shelf and of the sea-bed (including its subsoil).

CONVENTION FOR THE PROTECTION OF NATURAL RESOURCES AND THE ENVIRONMENT OF THE SOUTH PACIFIC REGION

(Noumea, 24 November 1986)

This Convention, together with two Protocols addressing respectively co-operation in combating pollution emergencies and prevention of pollution by dumping in the region considered, were adopted on 24 November 1986, all three instruments having entered into force on 22 August 1990. The current contracting Parties to the Convention are 12.

As far as radioactive materials and waste are concerned, under the Convention their dumping or storage in that area as well as the disposal of waste into the sea-bed is prohibited. The Convention refers also to the principles and recommendations issued by IAEA.

CONVENTION ON ENVIRONMENTAL IMPACT ASSESSMENT IN A TRANSBOUNDARY CONTEXT

(Espoo, Finland, 26 February 1991)

This Convention was laid down and open to signature under the aegis of the Economic and Social Council of the United Nations. It is of universal application and provides for a set of measures intended to prevent, minimize and keep under control any significant impact on the environment from human activities. Basically, it requires an exchange of information between the State where the proposed activity is taking place and other States whose environment is likely to be affected by it. This is achieved by means of a prior notification together with a proposal to involve such States in the studies on the assessment of the environmental impact.

As far as nuclear activities are concerned, the Convention assimilates them to industrial hazardous activities likely to entail trans-boundary consequences, thus linking the former to international environmental law. Appendix I of the Convention includes nuclear power stations and other reactors, as well as installations for the production and enrichment of nuclear fuel, for the treatment of irradiated nuclear fuel, and for the storage, treatment and disposal of radioactive waste; Appendix II is concerned with the documentation to be submitted, Appendix IV with the inquiry procedure to be followed, and Appendix VI with bilateral and multilateral co-operation.

The Convention entered into force on September 10, 1997 and has so far 40 contracting Parties. Following entry into force, a standardised procedure is set up for a regular exchange of information also on nuclear installations (prior to their putting into operation) likely to have a trans-boundary impact.

CONVENTION ON THE PROTECTION OF THE MARINE ENVIRONMENT OF THE BALTIC SEA AREA

(Helsinki, 9 April 1992)

This Convention (which after its entry into force on January 17, 2000 has replaced the 1974 Helsinki Convention on the same issue) was adopted by a Diplomatic Conference convened for the specific purpose and is aimed at promoting ecological restoration and preserving the ecological balance of the area addressed. As recalled in the previous pages regarding the 1972 Convention (dumping of waste and other matter), the new convention on the Baltic Sea stems from this as a "regional" agreement.

The contracting Parties (by now 10) are committed, both individually and jointly, to prohibiting or regulating the disposal of harmful substances into the Baltic Sea as under Annex I to the Convention, which includes radioactive substances and waste. A Commission is also set up by the Convention, whose task is to monitor and foster its implementation. In the other annexes indication is given, among other things, also of the actions to undertake in case of pollution.

CONVENTION ON THE PROTECTION OF THE BLACK SEA AGAINST POLLUTION

(Bucharest, 21-22 April 1992)

The elements concerning origin (1972 Convention on dumping of waste and other matter) and nature (regional) of this Convention are quite similar to those recalled in the previous pages for the Convention on the Baltic Sea. The Bucharest Convention adopted at the 1992 Diplomatic Conference covers the whole area of the Black Sea (i.e. also territorial waters and exclusive economic zones).

The Convention is considerably broad in scope, covering any hazardous substances and matter from any sources, to the sole exclusion of State-owned/operated warships or vessels or aircraft which are used by governments for non-commercial purposes. Radioactive substances and waste are included in the annexes to the Convention. In general the Convention provisions apply if the concentration of the substances discharged exceeds the limits internationally accepted or established jointly by the contracting Parties. Spent nuclear fuel is also included in the list considered by the Convention.

The contracting Parties (the six Black Sea countries) are committed to preventing, minimizing, monitoring, eliminating and combating marine pollution by adopting legal, regulatory and any other measures (including a compensation system where necessary), also in mutual co-operation. This co-operation extends to research geared to identifying clean and low waste disposal methodologies.

Similarly to the Baltic Sea Convention, a Commission is set up to monitor the implementation of the Convention, to identify and recommend additional measures, to disseminate information and to co-operate with the competent international organisations in order to ensure pursuance to the purposes of the Convention, which entered into force on January 15, 1994.

CONVENTION FOR THE PROTECTION OF THE MARINE ENVIRONMENT OF THE NORTH EAST ATLANTIC (OSPAR CONVENTION)

(Paris, 22 September 1992)

In the field of pollution prevention of the marine environment, two conventions had been adopted in Oslo (15 February 1972, on prevention of marine pollution by dumping from ships and aircraft) and in Paris (4 June 1974, on prevention of marine pollution from land-based sources). The former contained two lists of materials which, respectively, may not be dumped or may be dumped with a special permission by national authorities. The latter referred to measures to be adopted to prevent or eliminate pollution also from radioactive substances and waste. However, neither convention made it clear whether nuclear materials and radioactive substances were actually and fully within their scope.

On the other hand, the reason for replacing both conventions with a new one "merging" the two under the obvious name OSPAR was a more general one, which may be found in the preamble to this Convention, where it is stressed that the previous conventions did not address effectively the main sources of pollution. The new instrument is in fact conceived so as to address "all sources of pollution of the marine environment". Since the Baltic Sea and the Mediterranean Sea are covered by other international (similarly "regional") instruments, the OSPAR Convention does not apply to those areas (but includes the Artic Ocean).

In order to ensure realisation of the purposes of the Convention, the contracting Parties (at present 16) are required to adopt scientific programmes, to harmonize their policies in the domain of the environment, to make use of the best available technique and practice and to apply the "polluter pays" principle. In this connection, it is worth noting that the Convention is among those international instruments envisaging the application of the relative new "precautionary principle" (flanked by the polluter pays principle), which is taken into account under the last "whereas" of the Convention. Besides, according to its article 2(2)a, contracting Parties are required to apply this new principle by adopting preventive measures whenever "there are reasonable grounds for concerns" that human health and the marine environment are endangered, independently of any conclusive evidence of a link between causes and effects. More specifically, as to radioactivity, radioactive substances and waste (annex II to the Convention) reference is made to several criteria to be followed in setting priorities and assessing the nature and content of actions aiming to prevent and eliminate pollution from dumping and off-shore sources.

Similarly to other conventions addressed in the previous pages, article 10 of the OSPAR Convention sets up a Commission whose task is to evaluate and improve its implementation. In 1998 this Commission met at Sintra (Portugal) and considered a new strategy, with particular regard to radioactive substances, based on a gradual, substantive reduction of relevant discharges, emissions and losses, the ultimate aim (in compliance with the precautionary principle, as per paragraph 53 of the Sintra final document) being to bring concentration of naturally occurring radioactive substances down to negligible values.

Finally, it is recalled that, although the Convention (entered into force on March 25, 1998) prohibits the dumping of low and intermediate level radioactive waste, France and the United Kingdom reserved the right to depart from this rule as of January 1993 for a period of fifteen years.

CONVENTION TO BAN IMPORTATION INTO FORUM ISLAND COUNTRIES OF HAZARDOUS AND RADIOACTIVE WASTES

(Waigani, 16 September 1995)

Adopted in Papua (New Guinea) and signed by nearly all the countries belonging to the South Pacific Forum members (Australia, Cook Islands, Fiji, New Zealand, Solomon Islands, Western Samoa, Tonga etc.), this Convention addresses also the control of the trans-boundary movement and management of hazardous waste in the Region concerned.

The prohibition is directed at the waste coming from outside the area covered by the Convention, hence appropriate measures must be taken by each State Party (article 4) to this effect, and similarly as regards the export to contracting States or areas covered by the Convention, while the trans-boundary movement is allowed under the procedure laid down by article 6 (any movement contrary to it being considered a crime).

The Parties are also committed to prohibiting any dumping of hazardous and radioactive waste into the sea and to implementing the 1990 IAEA Code of practice on the international trans-boundary movement of radioactive waste. The Convention entered into force in 2001 and has 7 contracting Parties.

PREAMBLE

The Parties to this Convention:

Conscious of their responsibility to protect, preserve and improve the environment of the South Pacific for the good health, benefit and enjoyment of present and future generations of the people of the South Pacific;
Concerned about the growing threat to human health and the environment posed by the increasing generation of hazardous wastes and the disposal of such wastes by environmentally unsound methods;
Concerned also about the dangers posed by radioactive wastes to the people and environment of the South Pacific;
Aware that their responsibilities to protect, preserve and improve the environment of the South Pacific can be met only by cooperative effort among all peoples of the South Pacific based on an understanding of the needs and capacities of all Parties;

Taking full account of the Programme of Action for the Sustainable Development of Small Island Developing States adopted in Barbados on 6 May 1994;

Noting with concern that a number of approaches have been made to certain Island Countries of the South Pacific by unscrupulous foreign waste dealers for the importation into and the disposal within the South Pacific of hazardous wastes generated in other countries;

Concerned by the slowness of progress towards a satisfactory resolution of the issues surrounding international trade in goods which have been banned, cancelled or refused registration in the country of manufacture for human health or environmental reasons;

Recalling their commitments under existing regional treaties and arrangements for the protection and preservation of the environment of the South Pacific, including the Convention for the Protection of the Natural Resources and Environment of the South Pacific Region, signed in Noumea on 24 November 1986, the Protocol concerning Cooperation in Combating Pollution Emergencies in the South Pacific Region, adopted by Parties on 25 November 1986, and the South Pacific Nuclear Free Zone Treaty, signed in Rarotonga on 6 August 1985;

Further Recalling the Basel Convention on the Control of Trans-boundary Movements of Hazardous Wastes and their Disposal adopted by the Conference of the Plenipotentiaries on 22 March 1989, and noting decisions of its Conference of the Parties including Decision II 12 of 25 March 1994;

Desiring to conclude an agreement under Article 11 of the Basel Convention;

Mindful of the International Atomic Energy Agency (IAEA) Code of Practice on the International Trans-boundary Movement of Radioactive Waste and recognising the need for its strict observance in the South Pacific Region;

Noting as well the preliminary negotiations on a Convention on the Safe Management of Nuclear Waste;

Further Recalling the Declaration of the United Nations Conference on the Human Environment (Stockholm, 1972), the Cairo Guidelines and Principles for the Environmentally Sound Management of Hazardous Wastes adopted by the Governing Council of the United Nations Environment Programme (UNEP) by Decision 14/30 of 17 June 1987 and the Recommendations of the United Nations Committee of Experts on the Transport of Dangerous Goods (formulated in 1957 and updated biennially);

Recalling also Agenda 21 adopted by the United Nations Conference on Environment and Development in Rio de Janeiro on 14 June 1992, which reaffirms that effective control of the generation, storage, treatment, recycling and reuse, transport, recovery, and disposal of hazardous wastes is of paramount importance for proper health, environmental protection and natural resources management and sustainable development;

Resolving to prohibit the importation of hazardous wastes into Pacific Island Developing Parties, and to regulate and facilitate the environmentally sound management of such wastes generated within the Convention Area; and
Resolving also to prohibit the importation of all radioactive wastes into Pacific Island Developing Parties while at the same time recognising that the standards, procedures and the authorities responsible for the environmentally sound management of radioactive wastes will differ from those in respect of hazardous wastes.

Have agreed as follows:

Article 1
Definitions

For the purposes of this Convention:

"**Approved site or facility**" means a site or facility for the disposal of hazardous wastes which is authorised or permitted to operate for this purpose by a relevant authority of the Party where the site or facility is located;

"**Area under the jurisdiction of a Party**" means any land, marine area or airspace within which a Party exercises administrative and regulatory responsibility in accordance with international law in regard to the protection of human health or the environment;

"**Authorised trans-boundary movement**" means a trans-boundary movement of hazardous wastes to which the consent of the Parties concerned has been given in accordance with the provisions of this Convention;

"**Basel Convention**" means the Convention on the Control of Trans boundary Movements of Hazardous Wastes and their Disposal, 1989;

"**Carrier**" means any person who carries out the transport of hazardous wastes;

"**Cleaner production**" means the conceptual and procedural approach to production that demands that all phases of the life-cycle of a product or process should be addressed, with the objective of prevention or minimisation of short and long-term risks to humans and to the environment;

"**Competent authority**" means any one governmental authority designated by a Party to be responsible within such geographical areas as the Party may think fit for receiving the notification of a trans-boundary movement of hazardous wastes and any information related to it, and for responding to such a notification, as provided in Article 6 of this Convention;

"**Convention Area**" shall comprise:

(i) the land territory, internal waters, territorial sea, continental shelf, archipelagic waters and exclusive economic zones established in accordance with international law of:
American Samoa, Australia, Cook Islands, Federated States of Micronesia, Fiji, French Polynesia, Guam Kiribati, Republic of Marshall Islands, Nauru, New Caledonia and Dependencies, New Zealand, Niue, The Commonwealth of Northern Mariana Islands, Republic of Palau, Papua New Guinea, Pitcairn Islands, Solomon Islands, Tokelau, Tonga, Tuvalu, Vanuatu, Wallis and Futuna, Western Samoa;
(ii) those areas of high seas which are enclosed from all sides by the exclusive economic zones referred to in sub-paragraph (i);
(iii) areas of the Pacific Ocean which have been included in the Convention Area pursuant to Article 2.6;

"**Countries concerned**" means countries of export, import or transit whether or not Parties to this Convention;

"**Days**" means calendar days unless otherwise specified;

"**Disposal**" means any operation specified in Annex V to this Convention;

"**Disposer**" means any person for whom hazardous wastes are destined and who carries out the actual disposal of such wastes;

"**Domestically prohibited goods**" means substances or products which have been banned, cancelled or refused registration by government regulatory action, or voluntarily withdrawn from registration in the country of manufacture, for human health or environmental reasons;

"**Environmentally sound management of hazardous wastes**" means taking all practicable steps to ensure that hazardous wastes are managed in a manner which will protect human health and the environment against the adverse effects which may result from such wastes;

"**Exporter**" means any person under the jurisdiction of the exporting Party who arranges for hazardous wastes to be exported;

"**Exporting Party**" means a Party from which a trans-boundary movement of hazardous wastes is planned to be initiated or is initiated;

"**Focal point**" means the entity of a Party referred to in Article 5 of this Convention responsible for receiving and submitting information as provided for in Articles 7 and 14;

"**Forum Island Countries**" means all Members of the South Pacific Forum with the exception of Australia and New Zealand;

"**Generator**" means any person whose activity produces hazardous wastes or, if that person is not known, the person who is in possession and/or control of those wastes;

"**Hazardous wastes**" means wastes as specified in Article 2 of this Convention;

"**IAEA**" means the International Atomic Energy Agency;

"**Illegal traffic**" means any trans-boundary movement of hazardous wastes as specified in Article 9 of this Convention;

"**Importer**" means any person under the jurisdiction of the importing Party who arranges for hazardous wastes to be imported;

"**Importing Party**" means a Party to which trans-boundary movement of hazardous wastes is planned or takes place for the purpose of disposal therein or for the purpose of loading prior to disposal in an area not under the national jurisdiction of any State;

"**London Convention**" means the Convention on the Prevention of Marine Pollution by Dumping of Wastes and Other Matter, 1972;

"**Management**" means the prevention and reduction of hazardous wastes and the collection, transport, storage, and treatment or disposal, of hazardous wastes including after-care of disposal sites;

"**Other Party**" means a Party listed in Annex IV or any Party which is accepted by the Conference of the Parties to be an Other Party in accordance with the procedures established pursuant to Article 13.4(g);

"**Pacific Island Developing Party**" means a Party listed in Annex III or any Party which is accepted by the Conference of the Parties to be a Pacific Island Developing Party in accordance with the procedures established pursuant to Article 13.4(g);

"**Party**" means a Party to this Convention;

"**Person**" means any natural or legal person;

"**Precautionary principle**" means the principle that in order to protect the environment, the precautionary approach shall be widely applied by Parties according to their capabilities. Where there are threats of serious or irreversible damage, lack of full scientific certainty shall not be used as a reason for postponing cost-effective measures to prevent environmental degradation;

"**Radioactive wastes**" means wastes which, as a result of being radioactive, are subject to other international control systems, including international instruments, applying specifically to radioactive materials;

"**Secretariat**" means the Secretariat established pursuant to Article 14 of this Convention;
"**SPREP**" means the South Pacific Regional Environment Programme;

"**Trans-boundary movement**" means any movement of hazardous wastes from an area under the jurisdiction of any Party, to or through an area under the jurisdiction of another Party, or to or through an area not under the jurisdiction of another Party, provided at least two Parties are involved in the movement;

"**Transit Party**" means any Party, other than the exporting Party or importing Party, through which a movement of hazardous wastes is planned or takes place;

"**Vessels**" and "**Aircraft**" mean waterborne or airborne craft of any type whatsoever. This expression includes air cushioned craft and floating craft, whether self-propelled or not;

"**Wastes**" means substances or materials which are disposed of, or are intended to be disposed of, or are required to be disposed of, by provisions of national legislation.

Article 2
Scope of the Convention and Area of Coverage

Scope of the Convention

1. The following substances shall be "hazardous wastes" for the purposes of this Convention:

(a) Wastes that belong to any category contained in Annex I of this Convention, unless they do not possess any of the characteristics contained in Annex II of this Convention; and

(b) Wastes that are not covered under sub-paragraph (a) above, but which are defined as, or are considered to be, hazardous wastes by the national legislation of the exporting, importing or transit Party to, from or through which such wastes are to be sent.

2. Radioactive wastes are excluded from the scope of this Convention except as specifically provided for in Articles 4.1, 4.2, 4.3, and 4.5 of this Convention.

3. Wastes which derive from the normal operations of a vessel, the discharge of which is covered by another international instrument, shall not fall within the scope of this Convention.

4. Nothing in this Convention shall affect in any way the sovereignty of States over their territorial sea, the sovereign rights and jurisdiction that States have in their exclusive economic zones and continental shelves, and the exercise by vessels and aircraft of all States of navigational rights and freedoms, as provided for in international law and as reflected in the 1982 United Nations Convention on the Law of the Sea and other relevant international instruments.

5. Nothing in this Convention shall affect in any way the rights and obligations of any Party under international law including under other international agreements in force. Such agreements include the London Convention as amended; the 1982 United Nations Convention on the Law of the Sea, including in particular Articles 31, 210 and 236 thereof; the South Pacific Nuclear Free Zone Treaty, 1985, including in particular Article 7 thereof; and the International Convention for the Prevention of Pollution from Ships, 1973.

Area of Coverage

6. A Party may add areas under its jurisdiction within the Pacific Ocean between the Tropic of Cancer and 60 degrees South latitude and between 130 degrees East longitude and 120 degrees West longitude to the Convention Area. Such addition shall be notified to the Depositary who shall promptly notify the other Parties and the Secretariat. Such areas shall be incorporated within the Convention Area ninety days after notification to the Parties by the Depositary, provided there has been no objection to the proposal to add new areas by any Party. If there is any such objection the Parties concerned will consult with a view to resolving the matter.

Article 3
National Definitions of Hazardous Wastes

1. Each Party shall, within six months of becoming a Party to this Convention, inform the Secretariat of the wastes, other than those listed in Annex I of this Convention, considered or defined as hazardous under its national legislation and of any requirements concerning trans-boundary movement procedures applicable to such wastes.
2. Each Party shall subsequently inform the Secretariat of any significant changes to the information it has provided pursuant to paragraph 1 of this Article.
3. The Secretariat shall forthwith inform all Parties of the information it has received pursuant to paragraphs 1 and 2 of this Article.
4. Parties shall be responsible for making the information transmitted to them by the Secretariat under paragraph 3 of this Article available to their exporters, importers and other appropriate bodies.

Article 4
General Obligations

1. Hazardous Wastes and Radioactive Wastes Import and Export Ban

(a) Each Pacific Island Developing Party shall take appropriate legal, administrative and other measures within the area under its jurisdiction to ban the import of all hazardous wastes and radioactive wastes from outside the Convention Area. Such import shall be deemed an illegal and criminal act; and
(b) Each Other Party shall take appropriate legal, administrative and other measures within the area under its jurisdiction to ban the export of all hazardous wastes and radioactive wastes to all Forum Island Countries, or to territories located in the Convention Area with the exception of those that have the status of Other Parties in accordance with Annex IV. Such export shall be deemed an illegal and criminal act.

2. To facilitate compliance with paragraph 1 of this Article, all Parties:

(a) Shall forward in a timely manner all information relating to illegal hazardous wastes and radioactive wastes import activity within the area under its jurisdiction to the Secretariat who shall distribute the information as soon as possible to all Parties; and
(b) Shall cooperate to ensure that no illegal import of hazardous wastes and radioactive wastes from a non-Party enters areas under the jurisdiction of a Party to this Convention.

3. Ban on Dumping of Hazardous Wastes and Radioactive Wastes at Sea

(a) Each Party which is a Party to the London Convention, the South Pacific Nuclear Free Zone Treaty, 1985, the 1982 United Nations Convention on the Law of the Sea or the Protocol for the Prevention of Pollution of the South Pacific Region by Dumping, 1986, reaffirms the commitments under those instruments which require it to prohibit dumping of hazardous wastes and radioactive wastes at sea; and
(b) Each Party which is not a Party either to the London Convention or the Protocol for the Prevention of Pollution of the South Pacific Region by Dumping, 1986, should consider becoming a Party to both of those instruments.

4. Wastes Located in the Convention Area

Each Party shall:
(a) Ensure that within the area under its jurisdiction, the generation of hazardous wastes is reduced at its source to a minimum taking into account social, technological and economic needs;
(b) Take appropriate legal, administrative and other measures to ensure that within the area under its jurisdiction, all trans-boundary movements of hazardous wastes generated within the Convention Area are carried out in accordance with the provisions of this Convention;
(c) Ensure the availability of adequate treatment and disposal facilities for the environmentally sound management of hazardous wastes, which shall be located, to the extent practicable, within areas under its jurisdiction, taking into account social, technological and economic considerations. However, where Parties are for geographic, social or economic reasons unable to dispose safely of hazardous wastes within those areas, cooperation should take place as provided for under Article 10 of this Convention;
(d) In cooperation with SPREP, participate in the development of programmes to manage and simplify the trans-boundary movement of hazardous wastes which cannot be disposed of in an environmentally sound manner in the countries in which they are located. Provided that such programmes do not derogate from the environmentally sound management of hazardous wastes as required by this Convention, they may be registered as arrangements under Article 11 of this Convention;
(e) Develop a national hazardous wastes management strategy which is compatible with the SPREP South Pacific Regional Pollution Prevention, Waste Minimization and Management Programme;

(f) Submit to the Secretariat such reports as the Conference of the Parties may require regarding the hazardous wastes generated in the area under its jurisdiction in order to enable the Secretariat to produce a regular hazardous wastes report;
(g) Subject to Article 11 of this Convention, prohibit within the area under its jurisdiction hazardous wastes from being exported to or imported from non-Parties within the Convention Area; and
(h) Take appropriate legal, administrative and other measures to prohibit vessels flying its flag or aircraft registered in its territory from carrying out activities in contravention of this Convention.

5. Radioactive Wastes

(a) Parties shall give active consideration to the implementation of the IAEA Code of Practice on the International Trans-boundary Movement of Radioactive Wastes and such other international and national standards which are at least as stringent; and
(b) Subject to available resources, Parties shall actively participate in the development of the Convention on the Safe Management of Nuclear Waste.

6. Domestically Prohibited Goods:

(a) Subject to available resources, Parties shall endeavour to participate in relevant international fora to find an appropriate global solution to the problems associated with the international trade of domestically prohibited goods; and
(b) Nothing in this Convention shall be interpreted as limiting the sovereign right of Parties to act individually or collectively, consistent with their international obligations, to ban the importation of domestically prohibited goods into areas under their jurisdiction.

Article 5
Competent Authorities and Focal Points

1. To facilitate the implementation of this Convention, each Party shall designate or establish one competent authority and one focal point. A Party need not designate or establish new or separate authorities to perform the functions of the competent authority and the focal point.
2. The competent authority shall be responsible for the implementation of notification procedures for trans-boundary movement of hazardous wastes in accordance with the provisions of Article 6 of this Convention.
3. The focal point shall be responsible for transmitting and receiving information in accordance with the provisions of Article 7 of this Convention.

4. The Parties shall inform the Secretariat, within three months of the date of the entry into force of this Convention for them, which authorities they have designated or established as the competent authority and the focal point.

Article 6
Notification Procedures for Trans-boundary Movements of Hazardous Wastes between Parties

1. The exporting Party shall notify, or shall require the generator or exporter to notify, in writing, through its competent authority, the competent authority of the countries concerned of any proposed trans-boundary movement of hazardous wastes. Such notification shall contain the declarations and information specified in Annex VI A of this Convention, written in a language acceptable to the importing Party. Only one notification needs to be sent to each country concerned.
2. The importing Party shall acknowledge within reasonable time, which in the case of Other Parties shall not exceed fourteen working days, the receipt of the notification referred to in paragraph 1 of this Article. The importing Party shall have sixty days after issuing the acknowledgement to inform the notifier that it is consenting to the movement, with or without conditions, denying permission for the movement or requesting additional information. In the event that additional information has been sought, a new period of twenty one days recommences from the time of receipt of the additional information.
3. The exporting Party shall not allow the trans-boundary movement until it has received:
   (a) Written consent of the importing Party;
   (b) Written consent from every transit Party;
   (c) Written consent of every non-Party country of transit;
   (d) Written confirmation from the importing Party of the existence of a contract between the exporter and the disposer specifying the environmentally sound management of the wastes in question; and
   (e) Written confirmation from the exporter of the existence of adequate insurance, bond or other guarantee satisfactory to the exporting Party.

4. Each transit Party shall acknowledge within reasonable time, which in the case of Other Parties shall not exceed fourteen working days, the receipt of the notification referred to in paragraph 1 of this Article. Each transit Party shall have sixty days after issuing the acknowledgement to inform the notifier that it is consenting to the movement, with or without conditions, denying permission for the movement or requesting additional information. In the event that additional information has been sought, a new period of twenty one days recommences from the time of receipt of the additional information.

5. In the case of a trans-boundary movement of hazardous wastes, where the wastes are legally defined as or are considered to be hazardous wastes only:

(a) By the exporting Party, the requirement at paragraph 10 of this Article, that any trans-boundary movement shall be covered by insurance, bond or other guarantee shall be as required by the exporting Party; or

(b) By the importing Party, or the transit Party, the requirements of paragraphs 1, 3, 4, and 6 of this Article that apply to the exporter and exporting Party, shall apply mutatis mutandis to the importer or disposer and importing Party, respectively; or

(c) By any transit Party, the provisions of paragraph 4 of this Article shall apply to such Party.

6. The exporting Party may, subject to the written consent of the countries concerned, allow the generator or the exporter to use a general notification where hazardous wastes having the same physical and chemical characteristics are shipped regularly to the same disposer via the same customs office of exit of the exporting Party, via the same customs office of entry of the importing Party, and, in the case of transit, via the same customs office of entry and exit of the Party or Parties of transit.

7. The countries concerned may make their written consent to the use of the general notification referred to in paragraph 6 of this Article subject to the supply of certain information, such as the exact quantities or periodical lists of hazardous wastes to be shipped.

8. The general notification and written consent referred to in paragraphs 6 and 7 of this Article may cover multiple shipments of hazardous wastes during a maximum period of twelve months.

9. Each trans-boundary movement of hazardous wastes shall be accompanied by a movement document which includes the information listed in Annex VI B. The Parties to this Convention shall require that each person who takes charge of a trans-boundary movement of hazardous wastes sign the movement document either upon delivery or receipt of the wastes in question. They shall also require the disposer to inform both the exporter and the competent authority of the exporting Party of receipt by the disposer of the wastes in question and, in due course, of the completion of disposal as specified in the notification. If no such information is received by the exporting Party, the competent authority of the exporting Party or the exporter shall so notify the importing Party.

10. Any trans-boundary movement of hazardous wastes shall be covered by insurance, bond or other guarantee as may be required or agreed to by the importing Party or any transit Party.

Article 7
Transmission of Information

1. The Parties shall ensure that in the case of an accident occurring during the trans-boundary movement of hazardous wastes or their disposal which is likely to present risks to human health and the environment in other States and Parties, those States and Parties and the Secretariat are immediately informed.
2. The Parties shall inform one another, through the Secretariat, of:
   (a) Changes regarding the designation of competent authorities and/or focal points, pursuant to Article 5 of this Convention; and
   (b) Changes in their national definition of hazardous wastes, pursuant to Article 3 of this Convention.

3. The Parties, consistent with national laws and regulations, shall set up information collection and dissemination mechanisms on hazardous wastes to enable the Secretariat to fulfil the functions listed in Article 14.

Article 8
Duty to Re-import

1. The exporting Party shall adopt appropriate administrative and legal measures to ensure that when an authorised trans-boundary movement of hazardous wastes cannot be completed in accordance with the terms of the contract or of this Convention, the wastes in question are returned to it by the exporter. To this end, the importing Party and the transit Party or Parties shall not oppose, hinder or prevent the return of those wastes to the exporting Party.
2. Notwithstanding the provisions of paragraph 1 of this Article, where an authorised trans-boundary movement of hazardous wastes cannot be completed within the terms of the contract or the terms of this Convention, the exporting Party need not re-import those wastes provided that alternative arrangements are made for the disposal of the wastes in a manner which is compatible with the environmentally sound management of hazardous wastes as required by this Convention and other international legal obligations. Such disposal shall take place within ninety days from the time that the importing Party informed the exporting Party and the Secretariat, or such other period of time as the Parties concerned agree.

Article 9
Illegal Traffic

1. For the purpose of this Convention, any trans-boundary movement of hazardous wastes shall be deemed to be illegal traffic if:

(a) Carried out without notification, pursuant to the provisions of this Convention, to all countries concerned;
(b) Carried out without the consent, pursuant to the provisions of this Convention, of a country concerned;
(c) Consent is obtained from countries concerned through falsification, misrepresentation or fraud;
(d) The contents do not conform in a material way with the supporting documentation;
(e) It results in deliberate disposal of hazardous wastes in contravention of this Convention, other relevant international instruments and of general principles of international law; or
(f) It is in contravention of the import or export bans established by Article 4.1.

2. Each Party shall introduce or adopt appropriate national legislation to prevent and punish illegal traffic. The Parties shall cooperate with a view to achieving the objects of this Article.
3. (a) In the case of a trans-boundary movement of hazardous wastes deemed to be illegal traffic as the result of conduct on the part of the exporter or generator, the exporting Party shall ensure that, within thirty days from the time the exporting Party has been informed about the illegal traffic or such other period of time the countries concerned may agree, the wastes in question are either:
(i) taken back by the exporter or generator or if necessary by itself into the exporting Party; or, if impracticable,
(ii) otherwise disposed of in accordance with the provisions of this Convention;
(b) In the case of paragraph 3(a)(i) of this Article, the Parties concerned shall not oppose, hinder or prevent the return of those wastes to the exporting Party.
4. In the case of a trans-boundary movement of hazardous wastes deemed to be illegal traffic as a result of conduct on the part of the importer or disposer, the importing Party shall ensure that the wastes in question are disposed of in an environmentally sound manner by the importer or disposer or, if necessary, by itself within thirty days from the time the illegal traffic has come to the attention of the importing Party or such time as the countries concerned may agree. To this end, the importing Party and the exporting Party shall cooperate, as necessary, in the disposal of the wastes in an environmentally sound manner.
5. In cases where the responsibility for the illegal traffic cannot be assigned either to the exporter or generator or to the importer or disposer, the Parties concerned or any other Parties, as appropriate, shall ensure through cooperation that the wastes in question are disposed of as soon as possible in an environmentally sound manner either in the exporting Party or the importing Party or elsewhere as appropriate.

6. The Secretariat shall undertake the necessary coordination with the Secretariat of the Basel Convention in relation to the effective prevention and monitoring of illegal traffic in hazardous wastes. Such coordination shall include:

(a) Exchanging information on incidents or alleged incidents of illegal traffic in the Convention Area and on the appropriate steps to remedy such incidents; and

(b) Providing assistance in the field of capacity building including development of national legislation and of appropriate infrastructure in the Pacific Island Developing Parties with a view to the prevention and penalization of illegal traffic of hazardous wastes.

Article 10
Cooperation Among Parties and International Cooperation

1. The Parties to this Convention shall cooperate with one another, non-Parties and relevant regional and international organisations, to facilitate the availability of adequate treatment and disposal facilities and to improve and achieve the environmentally sound management of hazardous wastes. Such facilities shall be located within the Convention Area to the extent practicable taking into account social, technological and economic considerations.

2. To this end, the Parties shall:

(a) Upon request, make information available, whether on a bilateral or regional basis, with a view to promoting the environmentally sound management of hazardous wastes, including harmonisation of relevant technical standards and practices;

(b) Cooperate in monitoring the effects of hazardous wastes and their management on human health and the environment;

(c) Cooperate, subject to their national laws and policies, in the development and implementation of new environmentally sound and cleaner production technologies and the improvement of existing technologies. Such cooperation shall be with a view to eliminating, as far as practicable, the generation of hazardous wastes and achieving more effective and efficient methods of ensuring their management in an environmentally sound manner, including the study of the economic, social and environmental impacts of the adoption of such new and improved technologies;

(d) Cooperate, subject to their national laws and policies, actively in the transfer of technology and management systems related to the environmentally sound management of hazardous wastes. They shall also cooperate in developing the technical capacity and infrastructure of Parties, especially those which may need and request technical assistance in this field; and

(e) Cooperate in developing appropriate technical guidelines and/or codes of practice.

3. The Secretariat shall encourage Other Parties and other concerned developed countries to take all practicable steps to promote, facilitate and finance, as appropriate, the transfer of, or access to, environmentally sound technologies and know-how to Pacific Island Developing Parties, to enable them to implement the provisions of this Convention. Other Parties undertake to cooperate with the Secretariat in this regard.
4. Taking into account the needs of developing countries, Parties shall encourage cooperation with international organisations in order to promote, among other things, public awareness, the development of rational management of hazardous wastes, and the adoption of new technologies which are environmentally sound, including cleaner production technologies.

Article 11
Bilateral, Regional or Multilateral Agreements or Arrangements

1. Notwithstanding the provisions of Article 4.4(g), Parties to this Convention may enter into bilateral, regional or multilateral agreements or arrangements with non-Parties regarding the trans-boundary movement and management of hazardous wastes provided that such agreements or arrangements do not derogate from the provisions of Article 4.1 or from the environmentally sound management of such wastes as required by this Convention.
2. The Parties shall notify the Secretariat of any bilateral, regional or multilateral agreements or arrangements referred to in paragraph 1 of this Article and those which they have entered into prior to the entry into force of this Convention for them, for the purpose of controlling trans-boundary movements of hazardous wastes which take place entirely among the parties to such agreements or arrangements.
3. The provisions of this Convention shall not affect trans-boundary movements of hazardous wastes which take place pursuant to such agreements or arrangements provided that such agreements or arrangements are compatible with the environmentally sound management of hazardous wastes as required by this Convention.

Article 12
Liabilities and Compensation

The Conference of the Parties shall consider the preparation and adoption of appropriate arrangements in the field of liability and compensation arising from trans-boundary movements of hazardous wastes in the Convention Area without prejudice to the application and further development of relevant rules of international law.

Article 13
Conference of the Parties

1. A Conference of the Parties to this Convention is hereby established. The first meeting of the Conference of the Parties shall be convened not later than one year after the entry into force of this Convention. Thereafter, ordinary meetings of the Conference of the Parties shall be held at regular intervals to be determined by the Conference at its first meeting. The quorum for meetings of the Conference of the Parties shall be two-thirds of the Parties.
2. The Conference of the Parties shall adopt by consensus at its first ordinary meeting, or as soon as practicable thereafter, Rules of Procedure. It shall also adopt by consensus financial rules, including the scale of contributions of the Parties to this Convention to the regular budget.
3. The first meeting of the Conference of the Parties shall consider the adoption of any additional measures in accordance with the Precautionary principle relating to the implementation of this Convention.
4. The Conference of the Parties shall keep under continuous review and evaluation the effective implementation of this Convention, and in particular, shall:
   (a) Promote the harmonisation, at high levels of protection, of appropriate legislation, policies, strategies and measures for minimising harm to human health and the environment;
   (b) Consider and adopt, where necessary, amendments to this Convention, and its annexes, taking into consideration, inter alia, available scientific, technical, economic and environmental information;
   (c) Examine and approve the regular budget prepared by the Secretariat in accordance with Article 14;
   (d) Consider and undertake any additional action that may be necessary for the achievement of the purposes of this Convention in the light of experience gained in the operation of the Convention and developments elsewhere;
   (e) Consider and adopt protocols as necessary;
   (f) Establish and/or designate such subsidiary bodies or agencies as are deemed necessary for the implementation of this Convention; and
   (g) Determine and adopt appropriate rules and procedures for the acceptance of new Parties to this Convention in accordance with Article 23 and Annexes III and IV.

5. Any State which is eligible to become a Party to this Convention may be represented as an observer at meetings of the Conference of the Parties. Any other State or any body or agency, whether national, regional or international, governmental or non-governmental, with an interest in the subject matter of this Convention which has informed the Secretariat of its wish to be represented as an observer at a meeting of

the Conference of the Parties, may be admitted unless at least one-third of the Parties present object. The admission and participation of observers shall be subject to the rules of procedure adopted by the Conference of the Parties.

Article 14
Secretariat

1. A Secretariat for this Convention is hereby established. The functions of the Secretariat shall be to:

(a) Arrange and service meetings of the Parties to this Convention;

(b) Prepare the regular budget of the Conference of the Parties, as required by this Convention;

(c) Prepare and transmit reports based upon information received in accordance with Articles 3, 4, 7, and 11 of this Convention;

(d) Prepare and transmit information derived from meetings of subsidiary bodies and agencies established under Article 13 of this Convention or provided by relevant inter-governmental and non-governmental entities;

(e) Ensure coordination with the Secretariat of the Basel Convention and other relevant international and regional bodies, and in particular to enter into such administrative arrangements as may be required for the effective discharge of its functions;

(f) Communicate with the competent authorities and focal points established by the Parties in accordance with Article 5 of this Convention as well as appropriate inter-governmental and non-governmental organisations which may provide financial and/or technical assistance in the implementation of this Convention;

(g) Compile information concerning approved sites and facilities available for the disposal of hazardous wastes and means of transport to these sites and facilities and to circulate this information;

(h) Receive and convey on request to Parties information on available sources of technical and scientific expertise;

(i) Receive and convey on request to Parties information on consultants or consulting firms having the necessary technical competence in the field which can assist them with examining a notification for a trans-boundary movement of hazardous wastes, the concurrence of a shipment of hazardous wastes with the relevant notification, and/or whether the proposed disposal facilities for hazardous wastes are environmentally sound, when they have reason to believe that the wastes in question will not be managed in an environmentally sound manner;

(j) Assist Parties to this Convention in their identification of cases of illegal traffic and to circulate immediately to the Parties concerned any information it has received regarding illegal traffic, and to undertake the necessary coordination with the Secretariat of the Basel Convention as provided for in Article 9.6;

(k) To cooperate with countries concerned and with relevant and competent international organisations and agencies in the provision of experts and equipment for the purpose of rapid assistance in the event of an emergency situation in the Convention Area;

(l) To report the information prescribed in paragraph 2 of this Article, to the Parties to this Convention, before the end of each calendar year; and

(m) To perform such other functions relevant to the purposes of this Convention as may be determined by the Conference of the Parties.

2. The Secretariat shall transmit to the Parties, before the end of each calendar year, a report taking into account material provided by Parties under Articles 4.4(f) and 7.3 on the previous calendar year, containing the following:

(a) Information regarding trans-boundary movement of hazardous wastes in which Parties have been involved, including:

(i) the quantity of hazardous wastes exported, their category, characteristics, destination, any transit country and disposal method as stated in the notification;

(ii) the amount of hazardous wastes imported, their category, characteristics, origin, and disposal methods;

(iii) disposals which did not proceed as intended; and

(iv) efforts to achieve a reduction of the amount of hazardous wastes subject to trans-boundary movement.

(b) Information on measures adopted by Parties in the implementation of this Convention;

(c) Information where it is available on the effects on human health and the environment from the generation, transportation and disposal of hazardous wastes in the Convention Area. The information may take the form of statistical data;

(d) Information on accidents occurring during trans-boundary movements, treatment and disposal of hazardous wastes and on measures undertaken to deal with them;

(e) Information on environmentally sound treatment and disposal options operated by Parties; and

(f) Information on measures undertaken by Parties for the development of cleaner production technologies for the reduction and/or elimination of the production of hazardous wastes.

3. The Secretariat's functions shall be carried out by SPREP.

Article 15
Revolving Fund

The Conference of the Parties shall consider the establishment of a revolving fund to assist on an interim basis in case of emergency situations to minimise damage from disasters or accidents arising from trans-boundary movement or disposal of hazardous wastes within the Convention Area.

Article 16
Amendments to this Convention

1. Any Party may propose amendments to this Convention.
2. Amendments to this Convention may be adopted only at a meeting of the Conference of the Parties at which at least two-thirds of the Parties are represented. The text of any proposed amendment to this Convention shall be communicated to the Parties by the Secretariat at least six months before the meeting at which it is proposed for adoption. The Secretariat shall also communicate proposed amendments to the Signatories to this Convention and to the Depositary for their information.
3. The Parties shall make every effort to reach agreement on any proposed amendment to this Convention by consensus. If all efforts at consensus have been exhausted, and no agreement reached, the amendment shall, as a last resort, be adopted by a two-thirds majority vote of Parties present and voting, each Party having one vote, and shall be submitted by the Depositary to all Parties for ratification, approval or acceptance.
4. Instruments of ratification, acceptance or approval of amendments shall be deposited with the Depositary. Amendments shall enter into force between Parties having accepted such amendments on the ninetieth day following the date of receipt by the Depositary of the instruments of at least three-fourths of the Parties to this Convention. Thereafter the amendments shall enter into force for any other Party on the ninetieth day after the date on which that Party deposits its instrument.
5. For the purpose of this Article, "Parties present and voting" means Parties present and casting an affirmative or negative vote.

Article 17
Protocols to this Convention

1. The Conference of the Parties may, at any ordinary meeting, adopt protocols to this Convention.
2. The text of any proposed protocol shall be communicated to the Parties by the Secretariat at least six months before the meeting at which it is proposed for adoption.
3. The procedure specified in Article 16.3 shall apply to the adoption of, and any amendments to, any protocol.

4. The requirements for the entry into force of any protocol or subsequent amendments to such protocol shall be established by that protocol.
5. Decisions under any protocol shall be taken only by the Parties to that protocol.

Article 18
Adoption and Amendment of Annexes

1. The annexes to this Convention shall form an integral part of this Convention and, unless expressly provided otherwise, a reference to this Convention constitutes, at the same time a reference to any annexes thereto. Such annexes shall be restricted to scientific, technical and administrative matters.
2. The following procedures shall apply to the proposal, adoption and entry into force of additional annexes, or amendments to annexes, to this Convention:

(a) Such additional annexes or amendments to annexes shall be proposed and adopted according to the procedure laid down in Articles 16.1, 16.2 and 16.3 of this Convention;

(b) Any Party that is unable to accept such additional annexes or amendments to annexes, shall so notify the Depositary, in writing, within six months from the date of the communication of the adoption by the Depositary. The Depositary shall without delay notify all Parties of any such notification received. A Party may at any time substitute an acceptance for a previous declaration of objection and the annexes or amendments to annexes shall thereupon enter into force for that Party; and

(c) Upon the expiration of six months from the date of the circulation of the communication by the Depositary, the annexes or amendments to annexes shall enter into force for all Parties to this Convention, which have not submitted a notification in accordance with the provisions of sub-paragraph (b) above.

3. If an additional annex or an amendment to an annex involves an amendment to this Convention or to any protocol, the additional annex or amended annex shall not enter into force until such time as the amendment to this Convention or to the protocol enters into force.

Article 19
Verification

1. Any Party which has reason to believe that another Party is acting or has acted in breach of its obligations under this Convention may inform the Secretariat thereof, and in such an event, shall simultaneously and immediately inform, directly or through the Secretariat, the Party against whom the allegations are made. All relevant information should be submitted by the Secretariat to the Parties.

2. The Conference of the Parties shall consider the adoption of a protocol dealing with detailed procedures and arrangements for the verification of alleged breaches of obligations under this Convention.

Article 20
Settlement of Disputes

1. In case of a dispute between Parties as to the interpretation or application of, or compliance with, this Convention or any protocol thereto, the Parties concerned shall seek a settlement of the dispute through negotiation, mediation or any other peaceful means of their own choice.
2. If the Parties concerned cannot settle their dispute through the means mentioned in paragraph 1 of this Article, the dispute, if the Parties to the dispute agree, shall be submitted to arbitration under the conditions set out in Annex VII of this Convention or to the International Court of Justice. However, failure to reach common agreement on submission of the dispute to arbitration or to the International Court of Justice shall not absolve the Parties from the responsibility of continuing to seek to resolve it by the means referred to in paragraph 1.
3. When ratifying, accepting, approving or acceding to this Convention, or at any time thereafter, a Party may declare that it recognises as compulsory ipso facto and without special agreement, in relation to any Party accepting the same obligation:
   (a) Arbitration in accordance with the procedures set out in Annex VII; and/or
   (b) Submission of the dispute to the International Court of Justice.
   Such declaration shall be notified in writing to the Secretariat which shall communicate it to the Parties.

Article 21
Signature

1. This Convention shall be open for signature by the Members of the South Pacific Forum at Waigani, Papua New Guinea, on 16 September 1995.
2. This Convention shall remain open for signature by the Members of the South Pacific Forum from 22 September 1995 until 21 March 1996 at the South Pacific Forum Secretariat, Suva.

Article 22
Ratification, Acceptance or Approval

This Convention shall be subject to ratification, acceptance or approval by Members of the South Pacific Forum. Instruments of ratification, acceptance or approval shall be deposited with the Depositary.

Article 23
Accession

1. This Convention shall be open for accession by Members of the South Pacific Forum from the day after the date on which the Convention is closed for signature. The instruments of accession shall be deposited with the Depositary.
2. Other States not members of the South Pacific Forum which have territories in the Convention Area may accede to the Convention. In addition, other States which do not have territories in the Convention Area may also accede to the Convention pursuant to a decision of the Conference of the Parties under Article 13.4(g).

Article 24
Entry into Force

This Convention shall enter into force thirty days from the date of deposit of the tenth instrument of ratification, acceptance, approval or accession and thereafter for each State thirty days after the deposit of its instrument of ratification, acceptance, approval or accession.

Article 25
Reservations and Declarations

1. No reservations or exceptions shall be made to this Convention.
2. Paragraph 1 of this Article does not preclude a signatory or Party when signing, ratifying or acceding to this Convention, from making declarations or statements, however phrased or named, with a view, inter alia, to the harmonisation of its laws and regulations with the provisions of this Convention, provided that such declarations or statements do not purport to exclude or to modify the legal effect of the provisions of this Convention in their application to that Party.

Article 26
Withdrawal

1. At any time after three years from the date on which this Convention has entered into force for a Party, that Party may withdraw by giving written notification to the Depositary.
2. Withdrawal shall be effective one year after receipt of notification by the Depositary, or on such later date as may be specified in the notification.
3. Withdrawal shall not exempt any withdrawing Party from fulfilling any obligations it might have incurred under this Convention, whilst a Party to this Convention.

Article 27
Depositary

The Secretary General of the South Pacific Forum Secretariat shall be the Depositary of this Convention and of any protocols thereto.

Article 28
Registration

This Convention, as soon as it enters into force, shall be registered by the Depositary with the Secretary-General of the United Nations in conformity with Article 102 of the Charter of the United Nations.

IN WITNESS WHEREOF the undersigned, being duly authorised to that effect, have signed this Convention:

DONE at Waigani, Papua New Guinea, on the sixteenth day of September in the year one thousand nine hundred and ninety five, in a single original in the English language.

APPENDIX
EXAMPLES OF CASE LAW IN THE EUROPEAN UNION

Before addressing these examples, certain aspects are worth recalling for a better understanding of the subject matter.

Firstly, it should be pointed out that internationally the case law in point is not so very copious, but obviously quite significant as to its implications for relevant international legislation as well as its impact on national legislation. Secondly, case law dealt with here pertains to European Union (former Community) legislation in relation to which the European Court of Justice has ruled on certain issues so far. It is recalled that the Court was set up by the treaties creating the Coal and Steel (1951), the Economic (1957) and (same date) the Atomic Energy European Communities. It is based in Luxembourg, and it is called upon to judge on cases submitted by a member State or by another institution of the Communities (European Parliament, Commission, Council). The Court pronounces itself on the correct application of the Treaties. The provisions of the Euratom Treaty (largely similar to the corresponding ones in the other two treaties) concerned with the Court of Justice are articles 136 to 160. In third place, it should be stressed that case law discussed here relates, on one hand, mostly to radiation protection issues, where the Court has ruled quite importantly not only on account of the case submitted, but also considering a certain impact of such ruling on the revision of European Community radiation protection legislation under way at the time; on the other hand, given their general bearing, it was considered worthwhile addressing also two cases, the first dating back to the late seventies, the second to very recent times, concerning respectively physical protection and nuclear safety. The relevant references may be summarized as follows:

- European Community competences in the matter of physical protection under the Euratom Treaty;
- Compliance with certain provisions of the Euratom Treaty on the disposal of radioactive waste (known as the "Cattenom Case", after the name of the installation involved);
- Euratom Regulation of 1989 setting up a permanent system of maximum permissible levels of radioactive contamination of foodstuffs and feeding-stuffs following a nuclear accident;

- Radiation dose limits for apprentices and students under the Euratom Basic Standards on radiation protection;
- European Community competences in the matter of nuclear safety under the Euratom Treaty.

1. Community competences in the matter of physical protection (C-619/78)

This case was triggered by an application lodged under article 103 of the Euratom Treaty (E.T.) by the Belgian government in June 1978. The Court was requested to rule on a number of questions with regard to the Convention on Physical Protection, which at the time was being negotiated at the IAEA (see Part Two, Section One of this volume). It is recalled that article 103 is concerned with a supervisory procedure empowering the Community to examine preliminarily the compatibility of agreements, concluded by member States with third parties, with the requirements of the Treaty.

The Belgian government's request was intended to clarify doubts as to the necessity for the Community to participate in the above-mentioned Convention. The points raised touched essentially upon the in principle possibility for States to participate in the draft Convention without the Community, its right to participate in the draft Convention and the practical implications of its participation in the actual Convention. The ruling is an extremely detailed one, thus here we focus on those aspects which we feel are more relevant for the essence of the case. The Court identified two basic issues: whether one or more member States may participate in the negotiations under way for the Convention, compatibly with the E.T. provisions governing the division of powers between Community and such States, and whether the former is actually empowered to implement the provisions stipulated by the Convention to which it may become a party. The Court also pointed out that in connection with the Belgian application and the expected adjudication, several E.T. chapters were involved, addressing the supplies of nuclear materials, the nuclear common market, safeguards and property ownership. In its analysis, the Court goes through the various Convention provisions, in order to identify clearly its scope, but also the existing links with the subject matter of the Treaty.

The Court recalls preliminarily that article 195 of the E.T. (one of the "general provisions" in Title V) is neither intended to limit the Community's right and obligation to take measures ensuring the security of materials and installations falling under its responsibility, nor to limit its ability to enter international commitments to this end. Article 195 in fact stipulates that "the institutions of the Community shall, in applying the Treaty, comply with the conditions of access to ores, source materials and special fissile materials in national rules and regulations" governing public policy or health. On the other hand, in connection with the subject matter of the various chapters involved in the analysis (from which we single out only a part for the sake of brevity), the Court states that the E.T. provisions concerned with the safeguards "relate to all diversions of nuclear materials entailing a security risk" regarded as a potential interference with "vital interests of the public and the States". The consequence of this is, according to the Court, that the overall concept of safeguards includes also the measures required to ensure physical protection of materials and facilities.

The Court's ruling goes on assessing that such materials and facilities to be covered by physical protection measures are in substance the same under both the Convention and the E.T, as it may be argued when looking to the relevant definitions in the respective instruments. Accordingly, the provisions contained in the latter are fully applicable "within their own ambit" and despite "the differing intensity of Community control as regards those materials and facilities". In addition, other E.T provisions (such as article 2 e) addressing non-diversion of nuclear materials to purposes other than those which they are intended for) lead to conclude that the Convention concerns "matters within the purview" of the E.T.

As to the problem of powers, again according to the Court's ruling, if member States decided to adopt without the Community's participation measures relating to safeguards of materials subject to the authority of the latter, the exercise of its powers and the relevant responsibility in this connection would be "set at naught". With a view to the Community's participation in the Convention on physical protection and its being bound to comply with it, the former must be in a position to exercise quite freely jurisdiction and powers conferred on it by the E.T., since member States, either individually or collectively, may not impose obligations (in terms of conditions affecting Community's prerogatives) which are outside the field of national sovereignty.

Concerning the implementation of the Convention, the Court states that the principles to be applied are the same as those governing the division of powers (between Council, Commission and member States, as provided for by the E.T., articles 115, 124 and 192) in respect of the negotiation and conclusion of the Convention.

The Court's analysis takes therefore into account not only questions of substance but also of jurisdiction and procedure. Its ruling seems to be based on convincing however complex and detailed arguments, whereby the Community competence in the matter of physical protection is assessed and has never been questioned since. It is worth stressing that from a substantive point of view, the adjudication acquires an even higher importance in the present reality, considering that the IAEA Convention has been revised (see again Part Two, Chapter One of this volume) and that a system of physical protection relying also on Community rules can only contribute to reassuring the operators, the workers and the public about the existence of adequate physical protection measures worldwide.

2. The Cattenom Case (C-187/87)

1. Article 37 of the Euratom Treaty puts on each Member State the obligation to notify the Commission of the "general data relating to any plan for the disposal of radioactive waste in whatever form", thus allowing the Commission to determine whether the implementation of such plan could result in radioactive contamination of the environment of another member State. The Commission is called upon to give a non-binding opinion within six months.

Article 37 does not explain what it is meant by "general data", nor does it specify the moment when a disposal plan is to be submitted to the Commission for its opinion. As regards the first point, the Commission has in fact adopted several recommendations (the first one in 1960, then 1982, latest amendment of 1999, see Part One, Chapter Two of the volume) intended to clarify the notion of "general data" for the purposes of article 37, thus assisting member States in complying correctly with this provision; the second point remained questionable until the Court of Justice's ruling which is discussed here.

2. The case involved France, whose nuclear power station named Cattenom is situated near the Moselle river and the German and Luxembourg borders. The disposal plan for the effluents from that power station was submitted by France to the Commission, under article 37, only after the disposal of such effluents had been authorized by the national competent authorities. This was opposed by the government of the Sarre region (Germany) together with the Municipality of Luxembourg, various German local communities, as well as French and Luxembourg associations for the protection of the Moselle valley and of the environment. The administrative court in Strasbourg, before which the case had been put, asked the Court of Justice (1987) to provide an interpretation of article 37 as a preliminary point of law. The arguments brought up by the Sarre government may be summarized as follows.

Since the 1982 Recommendation (amending the 1960 text) had been adopted following a position expressed by the European Parliament on the earlier Recommendation, to the effect that the six months stipulated by article 37 were insufficient for the Commission to give its own opinion, the later Recommendation should be interpreted as implying the need for the Commission to be consulted prior to the granting of national authorization of the disposal. In addition, that Recommendation referred to the possibility of a further Commission's opinion in case of changes to the disposal plans, which only confirmed the interpretation of above. Last but not least, it was stressed that the very notion of "plan" implies a stage where no final decision has been made, and the envisaged analysis of the disposal plans prior to any authorization is aimed at ensuring a uniform application of article 37 throughout member States, hence to protect the interests of all those States, which can only be pursued on the strength of an opinion given before any authorization is granted.

3. The French government (which, incidentally, had notified the Commission of the plan after the Sarre government had filed the case before the Strasbourg court), maintained that such notification should occur before the effluents had been disposed of, whereas the Sarre government argued that the notification to the Commission must precede the granting of national disposal authorization. Pending the case, the Commission had on the other hand given a favourable opinion on the disposal plan notified by France, which seems to imply a "restrictive" interpretation by the Commission of its own powers under article 37. The French position was mainly based on the consideration that, as a matter of fact, the 1982 Recommendation did refer, inter alia, to member States being invited to indicate the stage of national procedure for the waste disposal envisaged or authorized, and that such procedure being at national level, it was to be regarded as independent of the Community procedure under article 37.

4. The Court's decision (September 22, 1988) is focused on the consolidated interpretation principle in Community law indicated as the "effectiveness" of the provision under consideration, as the case may be. According to the Court, article 37 is among the many provisions of the Euratom Treaty the one eminently aimed at preventing radioactive contamination, in that it is in the Commission's powers to evaluate the interests of other member States before national authorities have granted the authorizations required. This is the only way by which the Commission can play a significant role in connection with such authorizations, and therefore it must be enabled to give a timely (however non-binding) opinion. Consequently, the State concerned must become aware of it before any authorization is granted, if the Commission's opinion is to preserve its full effectiveness. Following the Court's decision, the previous French authorities' authorizations had to be withdrawn and granted a second time taking into account the Commission's opinion.

As a consequence of this decision, the 1999 Recommendation was in fact structured in the parts concerned so as to take into account such developments in case law, which are obviously decisive for the interpretation of article 37. More in general, in may be said that after many years of relative "neglect", the Euratom Treaty does benefit from the Court's decision, to the effect of definitely ensuring European Community's larger powers as to the general control over nuclear installations throughout that area.

3. The legal basis for the 1989 Euratom Regulation on the "permanent system" (C-70/88)

1. It should be preliminarily recalled (see Part One, Chapter Two of the volume) that the Chernobyl accident triggered various regulatory actions also at the European Community level, consisting in a series of Regulations on radioactive contamination of foodstuffs and feeding-stuffs. Here we confine ourselves to stressing again the difference between the set of (EC) regulations adopted immediately after Chernobyl and directly associated with that accident, and the (Euratom) regulation adopted in 1987 laying down maximum permitted levels of radioactive contamination of foodstuffs and of feeding-stuffs following a nuclear accident or any other radiological emergency. This instrument (no. 3954/87) was therefore adopted in order to set up a "permanent system" of levels for the eventuality of any future accident and is not linked to the contamination caused by Chernobyl. All these regulations have been amended several times, but the case discussed here concerns Regulation 3954.

2. The Regulation in point had been adopted by the Council based on article 31 of the Euratom Treaty, which lays down the procedure for the adoption of basic standards for the health protection of workers and the public against ionising radiation (including also other standards strictly relating to such protection).

It should be recalled that according to article 100A of the 1986 Single European Act (SEA, see Introductory Material to Part One, Chapter One), the European Parliament (EP) is called upon to actually participate in laying down Community legislation, whereas article 31 of the Euratom Treaty provides for a mere consultative role (hence a non-binding opinion) of the EP as far as the Euratom Basic Standards are concerned.

The case was triggered by the EP seising the Court of Justice as to the legal basis of Regulation 3954, on the grounds that such basis should have been article 100A of the SEA instead, and pleading for the annulment of the Regulation. In doing so, the EP also referred to previous recent CofJ case law, by which the choice of the legal basis of an act must take into account objective elements susceptible of jurisdictional control, and it is not therefore a mere formality. Apart from the obvious preference for the procedure under article 100A which involved it far more significantly, the EP maintained that health protection against radioactive contamination was only one of the two facets of the Regulation discussed, the other one, more important and in fact predominant, being the impossibility of marketing the contaminated items, which would more appropriately be the subject matter for the EEC Treaty (as amended by the SEA).

The Council, on the other hand, objected to the "acceptability" of the Parliament's action, by arguing that no such action was possible which would involve the annulment of an act adopted by any other Community institution. Indeed, the Council pointed out the reasons why the EP was not (under the EEC and Euratom Treaties) entitled to seise the Court for the annulment of the Regulation (as of any act of Community legislation), also on the strength of previous CofJ case law, whereas the EP could certainly assess its views in the framework of the "political" powers conferred on it by the relevant treaties.

3. The Court, however, while reserving its own position as to the merit of the case, did accept (decision of May 22, 1990) the EP's request, to the extent that the issue should be regarded as impinging directly on the EP's prerogatives in connection with the laying down of the instrument under dispute.

This Court's decision was clearly very important, without any prejudice of its decision on the merit, to the effect that was intended to ensure the "institutional balance" implied by the treaties, where they assign competences to the various institutions for the realization of the respective missions. The Court, while recognizing that the treaties do not actually provide for the EP's right to act for the annulment of Community legislation, also pointed out that this "lacuna" in the procedure should not be an obstacle on the way to protect the institutional balance of above. Consequently, the EP was entitled to act with a view to pursuing the annulment of an act adopted by the Council or the Commission, as long as its action aimed at safeguarding its own prerogatives and was based on the "tools" provided to this end (such as, in the case in point, article 100A of the SEA and not article 31 of the Euratom Treaty). It appeared also clear that the Court's decision set a very significant precedent applicable to any future case, where the EP may similarly invoke a "fault" in the procedure adopted for Community legislation likely to impinge on the EP's role under article 100A of the SEA.

4. The decision on the merit (October 4, 1991) taken by the Court confirmed article 31 of the Euratom Treaty as the correct basis for the Regulation discussed. It should be recalled that the Court did not feel it should examine the aspects relating to the form by which the Regulation had been adopted and which had been indicated by the EP as incorrect. The reason for this is that the Court did not identify in the EP's submission any element suitable to prove an actual violation of its prerogatives (although this principle had been acknowledged in the previous Court's decision).

In the judicial debate on the merit the Council was supported by the Commission and by the United Kingdom. The Council stressed again the clear health protection aims of the Regulation, which had led it to adopt article 31 as the legal basis. Indeed, the

Council pointed out, articles 30 to 39 of the Euratom Treaty create a true system eminently concerned with health protection against ionising radiation. Moreover, this Treaty should be regarded as a lex specialis as it may be argued on the strength of article 232 of the EEC Treaty, which stipulates that its provisions shall not derogate from those of the Euratom Treaty.

The points which qualify the Court's decision may thus be summarised as follows. It is a constant feature of the Court's case law that the choice of the legal basis of an act may not be dependent exclusively on an institution's conviction as to the aims pursued by that act, but it should be grounded on objective elements susceptible of jurisdictional control. And in fact, in the case in point, article 31 does fully address health protection of the public against radiation, covering also the contaminated foodstuffs and feeding-stuffs concerned in the specific case.

The Court therefore firmly rejected the EP's interpretation aiming at limiting the bearing of article 31. Such limitation does not find any support in the legal texts under consideration which, on the contrary, are intended to ensure the health protection of the public consistently and effectively, independently of the risk source or the categories of people involved.
A further aspect of the decision is related to the EP's submission, in second place, that the Regulation should have been based in any case on article 100A of the SEA, since such Regulation had an impact on the creation and the establishment of the European internal market (under article 8A of the EEC Treaty, as amended by the SEA). In this respect the Court pronounced itself indirectly also on article 100A, by stating that the prohibition to the marketing of items contaminated above the levels laid down by the Regulation was but one of the conditions for an effective application of such levels. According to the Court, this means that the aim of harmonising conditions for the free movement of the contaminated items (ie avoiding that the exchange of such items be subject to unilateral measures) is only an ancillary one, whereas health protection is far more predominant among the purposes of the Regulation.

The relevance of the Court's decision is self-evident as to the extension of the Community powers under the Euratom Treaty and especially its articles 30 to 39, which are laid down to ensure radiation protection **as a whole** (although this principle seems to be taken into consideration by the Court less strictly, when ruling on case C-376/90 discussed in the following pages).

4. The dose limits for apprentices and students (C-376/90)

1. The Court of Justice's ruling on this case marks a very significant turning point in the Commission's legislative policy in the domain of radiation protection of workers

and the public. In fact, since the first Directive (1959 Basic Standards) governing such domain, the relevant dose limits (together with certain other standards) had traditionally been regarded as absolute standards, which implied that member States, on implementing the Directives, had no leeway to laying down stricter values than those thereby established. The reference to "maximum permissible doses compatible with adequate safety" in article 31 of the Basic Standards was thus intended as a binding element on member States in the sense pointed out above.

The impact of the Court's ruling (November 25, 1992) on Community legislation resulted in a different approach by the Commission when laying down the latest Basic Standards (1996), which is reflected in article 54 (see Part One, Chapter Two of the volume). The terms and the implications of the case under consideration are as follows.

2. Certain provisions of the 1980 Basic Standards addressed the radiation dose limits for apprentices and students (16 to 18 years old) who, in connection with their future profession or in the course of their studies respectively, use radiation sources. These dose limits must not exceed, according to the Basic Standards (article 10, p. 2) 3/10 of those established for exposed workers (i.e. 6 mSv/year instead of 20 mSv).

The Belgian legislation implementing the above standards provided for stricter dose limits (up to 1/10), which led the Commission to seise the Court of Justice, on the grounds that the Belgian government had infringed that part of Community law. Once again, it should be recalled that the Commission is the "watchdog of the treaties", which in the particular case brings along article 2 of the Euratom Treaty, whereby one of the Community's tasks is to "establish **uniform safety standards**" to protect the health of workers and of the general public and ensure that they are applied". This reference to "uniformity" is relevant in connection with the interpretation given by the Court in its ruling.

The arguments put forward by the Belgian government in support to its own legislative policy were basically two: a) the dose limits under the Basic Standards are only values within which operators and users are called upon to keep exposure to radiation as low as possible, but this does not make it impossible for the (national) competent authorities to provide for lower limits, wherever they believe that certain limits might lead to undue exposure; b) the 3/10 dose limit as under the Basic Standards is in conflict with other provisions therein, which stipulate that workers below 18 years may not be exposed to higher dose limits than 1/10.

The Commission based its own position above all on the "uniformity" principle recalled above. This principle, the Commission maintained, is more stringent than that of "harmonization" found in article 33 of the Treaty, and is aimed at avoiding the laying down of different standards, hence at ensuring the same level of protection throughout the Community. In second place, the Commission pointed out that, while the ICRP recommendations (see Chapter Two of the volume) are no doubt the technical-scientific basis for the Euratom Basic Standards, the Commission however avails itself of its own group of experts set up under article 31 of the Euratom Treaty for the purpose of adopting such Standards. This group gives its advice also on the level of "adequate safety" as to the dose limits under discussion and, consequently, such level being an intrinsic feature of the limits laid down by the Basic Standards, member States have no need to provide for stricter ones. If the Belgian government's aim was to protect apprentices and students further, this could have been achieved by applying the "optimisation principle" explicitly laid down by the Basic Standards in harmony with the same principle recommended by the ICRP. Lastly, the Commission drew attention to the absolutely exceptional nature of the provisions invoked by the Belgian government as under b) in the previous paragraph, vis-à-vis the interdiction to expose workers under 18 years. This exception was justified by the need to train nuclear specialists properly, which would not be possible by adopting lower doses than 3/10.

3. It must be stressed that the Court's decision, in favour of the Belgian position, was (and still is) regarded with a certain disappointment and criticism, not only by the Commission for obvious reasons, but also by a number of member States, on account of its serious implications within the Community. More specifically, the qualifying points of the decision may be summarized as follows.

The Court acknowledged (in line with the Belgian position) that the dose limits set out by the Basic Standards are but a minimum protection level and therefore a members State may lay down stricter ones. Besides, the Court rejected the binding effect of the "uniformity" principle, by simply affirming that it does not prevent (nor do the Basic Standards provide for any interdiction to this effect) the establishment of stricter levels nationally (thus ignoring the difference in respect of the "harmonization" principle incorporated in article 33 of the Treaty). Moreover, the Court established a direct link between the ICRP Recommendations (which however are not part of the international legal system) and national legislation. This seems to ignore that such recommendations need to be implemented in that legislation in order to become binding (provided a State so wishes), and that the Euratom Standards are **the** basis , via the relevant directives in which they are incorporated, for national legislation; it must be added that, in any case, the ICRP Recommendations themselves indicate the "optimisation" principle as the most adequate tool to apply dose limits in the practice: these limits therefore are not the only protection tool, nor must they be applied in lieu of the optimisation principle.

4. The decision sets a precedent which might entail practical consequences difficult to manage in the framework of the European Union, in that it "overturns" the previous Community policy as to the safety standards, of which dose limits have always been considered a mainstay (as pointed out in p. 1 above). Secondly, the decision seems to question the very bearing of the Euratom Treaty, which however is not affected by the legal developments in the other treaties (especially the EEC Treaty) intended to ensure the realization of the Single Market and the European Union. It is recalled again that article 232 of the EEC Treaty stipulates that its provisions shall not derogate from those of the Euratom Treaty (see p. 4 of the previous case). This means that the latter has priority (in the particular case, as to the radiation protection regime it lays down) e. g. in respect of article 36 of the former, which leaves some scope for national prohibitions or restrictions in order to protect, inter alia, public health.

Another issue relating to the Court's decision and regarded not without surprise, is the assessment implied when it comes to the relevance of the radiation protection regime **as a whole** established by the Euratom Treaty. It is recalled that, when ruling on case C-70/88 (see previous pages) and in fact barely a year earlier, the Court, in reaction to the European Parliament, had stressed the adequacy and consistency of such regime in connection with any radiation source and **any category of persons** exposed to them, an approach which appears to be in contradiction with the later one. By affirming that the dose limits set out by the Basic Standards for apprentices and students are only a minimum level of protection, and hence member States are free to lay down lower ones, the decision implies potential differences in the protection levels among States. In the framework of the Single Market, this is likely to entail obstacles to the free movement of the persons concerned within the European Union, which is hardly in line with one of the pillars supporting the Single Market. One might add that the need to take into consideration (when establishing protection standards) also "economic and social factors" (as recommended by the ICRP and stipulated by the Euratom Basic Standards themselves) should be met by weighing such factors as prevailing at Community level rather than at the level of individual member States.

5. Being confronted with this Court's decision (however debatable it might be) the European Commission had to cope rather reluctantly with an unexpected development, after decades during which Community legislation in the domain discussed had been applied without giving rise to problems. The Commission felt that the precedent set by the Court would potentially lead to a lack of uniformity in the safety standards, and it started to think about ways and means to minimize this consequence. This resulted in a new provision (article 54) in the latest Basic Standards (Directive no. 96/29) which, while confirming that such Standards aim at ensuring their uniform implementation by member States, puts on any State intending to adopt stricter dose limits the obligation to inform the Commission and the other member States

accordingly. Such information, as indicated in the 1998 Communication from the Commission concerning the implementation of Directive no. 96/29 (see again Part One, Chapter Two of the volume), is normally provided according to article 33 of the Euratom Treaty. Obviously, article 54 can hardly be regarded as a formidable tool, since it merely lays down an information obligation, although prior to the actual adoption of national legislation, as indeed stated by said article 33. However, the reference to that article in the 1998 Commission Communication is seemingly focused on the procedure rather than on the Commission's power to express its opinion concerning the conformity of national legislation to the Basic Standards. On the other hand, even in the case where an opinion were expressed, given the Court's decision clearly the Commission would find it extremely difficult to object to national provisions on stricter dose limits. It may be finally added that in recent years the Commission has indeed been notified of national draft legislation to that effect by certain countries (e.g. Germany, Luxembourg).

5. European Community competences in the matter of nuclear safety under the Euratom Treaty (C-29/99)

The instruments involved in this case are the IAEA Convention on Nuclear safety and the Council Decision approving the accession by the European Atomic Energy Community (Euratom) to such Convention (see Part One, Chapter Two of the volume). The latter is adopted having regard to article 101 of the Euratom Treaty, enabling the European Community to conclude agreements with third States and international organizations. In the particular case, the need to accede stems from the important tasks assigned to the Community by Title II, Chapter 3 of the Treaty in the domain of radiation protection.

The original Commission's proposal for accession to the Convention referred to Community competences in the areas covered by articles 1 to 5, 7 and 14 to 19 of the Convention. These provisions address objectives, definitions, scope; obligations (implementing measures, reporting) for contracting Parties; legislative and regulatory framework for such Parties to establish and maintain; assessment and verification of safety, radiation protection, emergency preparedness; siting, design, construction and operation of installations.

It should be recalled that the domain of nuclear safety (namely safety of nuclear installations) has been traditionally regarded (or, rather, claimed) by States as their own individual and exclusive prerogative, therefore falling under their own responsibility. This feature may be indeed sensed in the very text of the Convention in point, which is basically of an "incentive" nature and does not address nuclear safety standards to any detail. For the same reasons, no binding such standards exist at the international level. There exists an extensive range of technical standards adopted by the IAEA (see again Part One, Chapter Two of the volume), which however have essentially the status of "recommendations" (though their technical and scientific authority is universally acknowledged), while in the Euratom Treaty a specific chapter addresses radiological protection.

From a "political" point of view, all these considerations must have guided the Council when wording its 1998 Decision (and the statement attached to it) in careful terms as to Community competences in the matter of nuclear safety. This Decision, however, departed from the Commission's original proposal, which led the latter to seize the Court of Justice in 1999, on the grounds that the statement attached (in particular the third paragraph, for the annulment of which the Court was called upon) contravened Chapter 3 of the Euratom Treaty. According to the Commission, in the light of these provisions the Community competences in the areas covered by the Convention should not be limited to articles 15 and 16(2) of the Convention, as the Council Decision stated.

The Council, on its part, asked preliminarily the Court to reject the Commission's submission (i. e. to declare it "inadmissible") which in its view was: a) lacking an object, b) addressing a statement which may not be regarded as separate from the Decision itself (a point, in any case, not questioned by the Commission), and c) attempting to obtain an opinion on the extent of the Community competences. These three arguments were dismissed by the Court, who declared on these points in the order that: a) the object of the Commission's submission lied in the absence of a reference, in the statement, to competences other than those thereby mentioned, b) the partial annulment of a Decision was possible insofar as the elements concerned were detachable from the rest of such Decision, and in the particular case the annulment did not affect in the least its essence, c) there was no indication to the effect maintained by the Council. Besides, as pointed out in the ruling, on the strength of article 146 (under which the action was brought) of the Euratom Treaty, the Court is competent to review the legality of an act (other than recommendations or opinions) by which the Community is acceding to an international agreement such as the Convention in point.

As to the substance, the Court took its decision on the basis of the following main arguments.

The Commission, while acknowledging that the Euratom Treaty does not give the Community competences to adopt provisions on the construction and operation of nuclear installations, pointed out that the risk resulting from such operation does fall within the Community's competence.

The Council argued that the limitations pertaining to the Community's accession to the Convention did not entail a violation of the Euratom Treaty, nor did they affect the common rules adopted under the Treaty; besides, the Community competences concerned only the protection of the public which, in connection with the relevant Convention provisions, was adequately reflected in the statement.

In its ruling the Court stressed essentially the following points.

It is of basic importance to bear in mind that the solution of the dispute depends on the interpretation of the Euratom Treaty provisions (Title II, Chapter 3) addressing health protection, which should take into account the objectives indicated in the Treaty preamble ("...to create the conditions of safety necessary to eliminate hazards to the life and health of the public") as well as article 2 b), by which the Community "shall establish uniform safety standards to protect the health of workers and of the general public and ensure that they are applied".

It is recalled that indeed the Court, also on previous occasions, had given Chapter 3 a broad interpretation in order to ensure its practical application (see case C-70/88 in this Appendix). In the case in point, the Court found that when defining the Community competences "it is not appropriate to draw an artificial distinction between protection of the health of the general public and safety of sources of ionising radiation". This criterion, according to the Court, should be the basis for determining whether the Commission is competent also as far as provisions other than articles 15 and 16(2) of the Convention are concerned. Although national nuclear safety authorities preserve their competences to authorize the construction or the operation of nuclear installations, this does not prevent the Community from adopting legislation in the matter: in particular, the Court stresses that even though the Euratom Treaty does not accord the Community the aforementioned competences, on the strength of articles 30 to 32 of the Treaty the latter does have a competence to lay down legislation aiming at ensuring health protection, by an authorization system which member States must apply. Such system is in fact to be regarded within the framework of the "basic standards" under article 30 of the Treaty.

As to provisions other than articles 15 and 16(2) where the Commission according to the Court is also competent, they are articles 7, 14, 16(1) and (3), and 17 to 19 of the Convention. These provisions needed to be referred to in the second paragraph of the statement attached to the Council Decision, as a consequence of the amendment to the third paragraph.

The Court's ruling is clearly of the utmost importance, in that the recognized Commission competences in nuclear safety entail an expansion of its powers to an area traditionally kept out of its sphere of action. Besides, the traditional twofold notion of nuclear safety and radiation protection seems to be brought into a single approach to "safety" as a whole.

The legal follow-up of the Court's ruling consists in an amendment (of 2003, addressed in Part One, Chapter Two of the volume) to the 1998 Council Decision accordingly. The ruling also resulted in a decisive encouragement for the Commission to go ahead with its proposal for two directives (submitted to the Council in November 2002) addressing safety standards for nuclear installations and safe management of radio-active waste. During the finalization of this volume, the debate on those proposals was still in progress.

THE LEGAL REGIME OF NUCLEAR ENERGY: A COMPREHENSIVE GUIDE TO INTERNATIONAL AND EUROPEAN UNION LAW